Montessori

Montessori

THE SCIENCE BEHIND THE GENIUS

THIRD EDITION

Angeline Stoll Lillard

OXFORD
UNIVERSITY PRESS

Oxford University Press is a department of the University of Oxford. It furthers
the University's objective of excellence in research, scholarship, and education
by publishing worldwide. Oxford is a registered trade mark of Oxford University
Press in the UK and certain other countries.

Published in the United States of America by Oxford University Press
198 Madison Avenue, New York, NY 10016, United States of America.

Library of Congress Cataloging-in-Publication Data
Names: Lillard, Angeline Stoll.
Title: Montessori : the science behind the genius / Angeline Stoll Lillard;
photographs by An Vu.
Description: Third Edition. | New York : Oxford University Press, [2017] |
"Translated from the Italian by Claude A. Claremont"—T.p. verso. | Includes index.
Identifiers: LCCN 2016012465 | ISBN 9780199981526 (hardcover : alk. paper) |
ISBN 9780199981533 (UPDF) | ISBN 9780199981540 (EPUB)
Subjects: LCSH: Montessori method of education—United States. |
Montessori, Maria, 1870–1952.
Classification: LCC LB1029.M75 L53 2016 | DDC 371.39/2—dc23
LC record available at http://lccn.loc.gov/2016012465

9 8 7 6 5 4 3 2 1
Printed by R.R. Donnelley, United States of America

Excerpts from THE ABSORBENT MIND by Maria Montessori.
Translated from the Italian by Claude A. Claremont.
First published in the United States in 1967.
Reprinted by permission of Henry Holt and Company, LLC.
Frontispiece image of Maria Montessori: Courtesy of the Archives
of the Association Montessori
Internationale, Amsterdam, Netherlands.

For Bill, Chaney, and Jessica

CONTENTS

First and Second Edition Preface   ix
Third Edition Preface   xi
Acknowledgments   xiii
Notes on the Book   xv

1. An Answer to the Crisis in Education   1

2. The Impact of Movement on Learning and Cognition   37

3. Choice and Perceived Control   81

4. Executive Function   105

5. Interest in Human Learning   137

6. Extrinsic Rewards and Motivation   177

7. Learning From Peers   219

8. Meaningful Contexts for Learning   251

9. Adult Interaction Styles and Child Outcomes   283

10. Order in Environment and Mind   315

11. Recent Research on Montessori Education   351

12. Education *for* Children   377

Works Cited   399
Author Index   447
Subject Index   461

FIRST AND SECOND EDITION PREFACE

Twenty years ago, I was a Montessori skeptic. I had taken a Montessori teacher training course and was frustrated at not being able to discriminate scientifically supported ideas from mere opinion. I had met Montessori teachers who sometimes came across as more devoted to upholding their heroine than to learning about children. And I was convinced that while Montessori surely had its strengths, traditional and other forms of education surely had theirs too, and the best educational system would combine the strengths of each system.

When I embarked on graduate study in developmental psychology, I occasionally came across a study that happened to reiterate a major principle of Montessori, and I had seen enough of such studies by the time I had children to want them to be in a strong Montessori school if I could find one. (Not all Montessori schools would qualify, for reasons that will become clear in this book.) Having my children in a Montessori school led me to study Montessori practices more deeply, and I saw more convergences with research over time. The education director at my children's school, Trisha Thompson Willingham, asked me to write a column about these convergences for the school newsletter, and from that column this book was launched.

The delegates at Oxford University Press asked that I write a balanced assessment of Montessori, pointing out where the evidence is not supportive as well as where it is. I have done my best to do this, but there is a real problem. Their assumption, like my original one, was that Montessori must have aspects that are supported by research, and aspects that are not. Yet her major ideas—that there is a close relationship between movement and cognition, that the best learning is active, that order is beneficial for children, and so on—are supported by a strong body of evidence in developmental psychology. Some of her main developmental ideas that did not take hold until later and are rarely attributed to her are now mainstream, such as that children go through sensitive periods in development, and that language is (in a sense) innate. None of the Montessori ideas that I would consider central have been "disproven." Others are not researched. The most major idea that is not supported by the evidence is her negative view of pretend play, which I discuss at the end of chapter 5.[1] Like Piaget and others of her time, Dr. Montessori saw adaptation to reality as the goal of development, and pretending as a frivolous expression of immature minds that were not adapting to reality.

---

[1] In this third edition I retract this; see end of Chapter 6.

But there is another important point here: Dr. Montessori took her cue from children, observing them in her classrooms. She observed that when the children were offered toys alongside Montessori work, they chose the work and ignored the toys. They did not appear to be interested in pretending in the classroom. The reasons pretend play helps cognitive development may well be satisfied in other ways in Montessori classrooms.

For example, in play and in Montessori, children get to choose what to do, when, and with whom.

It is this practical approach that explains why Dr. Montessori is less "debunkable" today than Piaget. Like Dr. Montessori, Jean Piaget made many brilliant observations of children, based on their interactions with stimuli he developed. Piaget's aim through these observations was to explain the ontogenesis of intelligence, but for him theory came early, leaving him vulnerable to making observations that fit his theory. Dr. Montessori's aim was instead practical: She sought to develop a system of education that worked with children, rather than against them. Dr. Montessori was not particularly interested in theory; she was a physician, concerned with treatments to aid health and well-being. Surely her personal views did sometimes get in the way of objective observation, but her major ideas about treatments that bring about more optimal learning and development, based on her empirical observations, are largely upheld by research today. If schooling were evidence-based, I think all schools would look a lot more like Montessori schools. Yet Montessori schooling can often feel uncomfortable to parents, and even to the teachers who employ the methods, because it is different from what we had as children. For psychology researchers, attitudes toward Montessori are mixed: Some know enough to appreciate it, others misunderstood a small aspect and dismiss the entire approach. Very few know more than a smidgen about it.

In this book I try to make Montessori accessible to researchers, and I try to make psychology research accessible to parents and teachers. I hope the book will help readers better understand how people learn generally, as well as what happens in a Montessori classroom and why. I try to also point out Montessori ideas and issues that are unresolved in modern science and in need of more study. Empirical study should always be the deciding factor for how to best educate children, as it was for Dr. Montessori. Dr. Montessori described herself as an empiricist, but her research methods, although acceptable during her time, are no longer the standard.

I write about Montessori education because that is the alternative system that I know. Others who know Steiner (Waldorf), Reggio Emilio, and other alternative systems of schooling will surely see points of similarity to and differences from Montessori education. Those with knowledge of other systems can evaluate how they fare in relation to research on human learning and development.

THIRD EDITION PREFACE

In the 12 years since the initial publication of this volume, much new and relevant research has been conducted, and this has been incorporated. One change is a full chapter on executive function, a topic that was discussed briefly in the prior editions' chapter 3. Dr. Montessori put much emphasis on concentrated attention. In another case of the science following along behind Dr. Montessori's genius, executive function has become a very important research topic in developmental psychology and has been recently shown to be a very important predictor of life outcomes. Another new chapter covers research on how children in Montessori fare on academic and nonacademic outcomes; it focuses on research that has appeared from 2005 on. This research shows very strong outcomes for Montessori, particularly when it is implemented according to the plans and principles presented in Dr. Montessori's books.

Another noteworthy development, discussed in chapter 5, concerns pretend play. When I wrote the first edition, like many developmental psychologists I believed there was strong support for pretend play being an aid to development, and I mentioned it as one point on which Dr. Montessori was wrong. A group of graduate students and I subsequently conducted a careful review of that literature (Lillard et al., 2013) and concluded that the evidence that pretend play helps development is deficient. However, some conditions of pretend play—for example, it is freely chosen and reflects the child's interest, it often involves peers and movement, and its rewards are intrinsic—are known to be positive for development, and Montessori education shares these features with pretend play.

Another point is worth raising here. Anthropologists note that in cultures that resemble the standard conditions of human history, young children are not excluded from the daily routines of adults; they are active participants. Under such conditions, one sees less pretend play; and indeed, pretend play often involves children recreating adult routines in which they would like to participate (Lancy, 2009; Lillard, 2015). Dr. Montessori studied anthropology, and she developed Practical Life routines that allow children to engage in meaningful adult activities. She observed that in the classrooms she developed, children were more interested in doing real activities than in pretending.

Readers familiar with the first editions will notice other updates, such as research on organized classrooms, sensory discrimination and intelligence, epigenetics, and the Goldilocks effect, and on many other issues.

The 10 years of studying this vast and complex educational system and revisiting Dr. Montessori's books, as well as reading some anew, has deepened my understanding of and respect for this radically different approach to education. In essence, Montessori places a child in a special environment created to respond to human needs. In that environment, a child will become interested in something, often one of the specially created activities, and will begin to concentrate on that activity. Once concentration on a meaningful task begins, an array of changes takes place in the child. In concert with these changes, the child is given the keys to the universe: the Sensorial Materials that abstract the qualities of all things—weight, color, texture, temperature, and so on. The child learns to judge and discriminate those qualities, sharpening his or her perception. The world becomes more accessible, interesting, and understood, and the child moves on to other materials for learning; a life's journey has begun. What the Montessori system aims to do is so different from the aims of the conventional system, it is no wonder that Montessori gets sidelined in discussions of education. Our typical system of teaching children to take tests is so utterly impoverished by comparison.

I hope my deeper understanding of Montessori comes across in this volume, helps more readers to investigate well-functioning Montessori in practice, and leads to their understanding the possibilities Montessori could provide for children's development and a healthier human world.

ACKNOWLEDGMENTS

I am indebted to many people for their role in this work. Trisha Thompson Willingham got me going, and my sisters Paula Lillard Preschlak and Lynn Lillard Jessen, and my parents Paula Polk Lillard and John Lillard gave tremendous encouragement and help throughout the project. All made important comments on previous drafts. Heather Donaldson and Alice Woodard Catlin, my children's teachers during the project, read early drafts, willingly showed me Montessori materials, and taught my children many lessons, descriptions of which became part of the book. Chaney and Jessica have always provided a wonderful window into Montessori life. My colleagues at the University of Virginia, especially Judy DeLoache and Michael Kubovy, kept me focused on tone and purpose, and students in my Advanced Cognitive Development seminar in the spring of 2003 revealed what people new to Montessori needed to know. My graduate students have been patient with my absences as I got the book finished and have indulged me with their interest in the research issues raised. Marcia Descantis and Laura Einbinder gave very helpful parent reviews, and Montessori teacher trainers Phyllis Pottish-Lewis and Virginia McHugh Goodwin provided invaluable comments and advice throughout. Virginia also helped me find An Vu. An worked many late nights to get the photographs in this book done, and he illustrates better than words could ever do the gift of concentration children acquire in good Montessori classrooms. I also thank Peace Montessori School in Portland, Oregon, and the families who allowed these photographs to appear. In addition to An contributing many new wonderful photos for this 3rd edition, Laura Joyce-Hubbard provided several from the Forest Bluff School. I thank her and the school parents for permitting use of these photos. My sister Lynn Lillard Jessen gets heartfelt thanks for doing the yeoman's work in arranging for these photos; she worked tirelessly and willingly, as she does for so many things related to the mission of helping children's development. Carol Dweck provided a review as well, and Susan Goldin-Meadow contributed useful comments for chapter 2. My mentor at Stanford University, John Flavell, gave thoughtful comments on the manuscript on top of many wonderful years of mentorship for which I am forever grateful. The University of Virginia library, one of the best libraries an academic could ever hope for, delivered hundreds of articles and books to my computer desktop or mailbox within hours of my requesting them. All of these people and dozens more provided encouragement throughout. For the first two editions, my editor at Oxford, Catharine Carlin, helped see the manuscript through to the end, Steve Holt cleaned up the prose on the last draft considerably, and Christine Dahlin carried it through production. For this third edition, Joan Bossert was a terrific editor, and Lynn Luecken and Emily Perry fabulously carried it through production. My husband Bill Detmer came up with the title and was unremitting in his support. Like Montessori, he is ingenious, respectful of evidence, and full of love, and he inspired me at every step of the way. I am grateful to all these people for their enthusiasm and their help in making this manuscript a much better one than I ever might have on my own, and I take full responsibility for any mistakes that remain.

NOTES ON THE BOOK

It is difficult to write about a system that is named after a person. To differentiate the two, the person is always referred to as Dr. Montessori in this text, and the system simply as Montessori. Sometimes this leads to awkward contrasts (Dr. Montessori versus Piaget), but it clarifies references to the person versus the system.

I repeatedly refer to certain Montessori materials and lessons in this book, but these are only a tiny representative fraction of the entire set.

For convenience, I use the word "method" on occasion to refer to Montessori. Some will object, on the grounds that Montessori is much more than a method: It is grounded in a philosophy for life. Also, for convenience of expression, I sometimes use the word "curriculum" to refer to the entire set of Montessori lessons, although it is not technically like a traditional school curriculum.

Montessori

1}

An Answer to the Crisis in Education

The conceptions of the old schools, where teaching continues in the same
way as in times profoundly different from ours, are clearly inadequate
      —Maria Montessori (*1949/1979, p. 14*)

Two fundamental cornerstones of American schooling today were placed at
the turn of the 20th century: the school as a factory and the child as a blank
slate. Students of child development know that these ideas are obsolete, but
they continue to have a profound effect on how schooling is done. The persistence of these outmoded ideas explains why so few children really flourish
in school, and why so many strongly prefer snow days to school days. Yet for
most of us, envisioning how to eliminate two such entrenched ideas is difficult.
    Early in the 20th century, Dr. Maria Montessori did envision a radically
different approach to education, an approach grounded in close and insightful
observations of children rather than in adult convenience and misconception.
Modern research in psychology suggests the Montessori system is much more
suited to how children learn and develop than is the conventional system. In
the chapters to come, I describe nine of Dr. Montessori's basic insights, recent
psychological research concerning those insights, their incorporation into
Montessori classrooms, and why they are often incompatible with conventional
schooling. In this chapter I discuss the need for reform, and I trace the roots
of the two misguided ideas that form the basis of typical American schooling.
I close this chapter with an introductory view of Montessori education.

Dissatisfaction With Schooling

Children and adults alike often proclaim dissatisfaction with conventional
schooling. William Blake (1794/1984) expressed the child's disenchantment in
his poem *The Schoolboy*:[1]

> But to go to school in a summer morn,
> O, it drives all joy away!

1

---

[1] I am grateful to Mark Lepper for pointing out this poem and the Einstein example that follows.

Under a cruel eye outworn,
The little ones spend the day
In sighing and dismay.

Albert Einstein hired a scribe to take notes so he could skip classes to escape boredom (Schlip, 1949). Negative feelings toward school remain prevalent today: Children applaud the days when they are out of school, and adults frequently comment to children that they are lucky and must be happy when school is canceled. Children, of course, do not always know what is good for them, but education would be more successful were it not so frequently disliked. Indeed, a positive emotional climate within a classroom has been shown to be the most powerful predictor of students' motivation to learn (Stipek et al., 1998), and happier students are more engaged in learning in school (King, McInerney, Ganotice, & Villarosa, 2015); indeed, more happiness *leads to* better life outcomes (Lyubomirsky, King, & Diener, 2005). Positive moods are associated with more expansive and integrated thinking and learning and with detecting global patterns (Fiedler, 2001; Fredrickson, 2001; Gasper & Clore, 2002; Isen, 2000). A possible reason for this is that affective states provide information (Huntsinger, Isbell, & Clore, 2014). In this account, feeling good in school would inform students that they like school and like learning, resulting in fuller engagement, which then would lead to better performance. Infants have an intense drive to learn, and school-aged children maintain this drive for learning *outside* school (Bransford, Brown, & Cocking, 1999). Yet from the early years of schooling, children's motivation to learn *in school* steadily declines (Anderman & Maehr, 1994; Harter, 1981; Wang & Eccles, 2012).

Survey research reveals that adults are also discouraged with our schools. The 2014 Phi Delta Kappa/Gallup poll showed that 48% of people would give their local public schools a grade of C to F, and only 12% would give them an A—numbers virtually unchanged since 2003. To the nation's public schools, conversely, 80% of Americans assigned a C to F, and virtually none gave them an A. City schools are often of very poor quality, so families who can afford private schools choose them, and others ask for vouchers to expand their options. Millions of children sit on wait lists for public charter schools. Education seems to be in a state of constant crisis in this country.

The Pendulum Response

The U.S. response to this constant crisis has been to swing from conservative and traditional test-oriented programs to progressive and permissive ones, then back to test-oriented programs again, which is where we stand today.

A key feature of the U.S. Elementary and Secondary Education Act of 2001 ("No Child Left Behind")—the major multimillion dollar school reform act of this era—is its requirement that from 2006 on, all children in Grades 3 through 8 take standardized reading and mathematics tests annually, and schools are sanctioned if overall student performance does not improve. "Race to the Top," instituted in 2009 under President Barack Obama, adds Common Core standards as the basis for testing and teacher evaluation based in part on student test results. The current test-oriented program is driven largely by politicians, who must not be aware of research on the outcomes of such testing. When tests become the focus, teachers teach to and children learn to the tests (Jennings & Bearak, 2014). As is discussed in chapter 6, research has shown that when people learn with the goal of doing well on a test, their learning is superficial and quickly forgotten. This is to say nothing of the sad, widely publicized cases of school administrators and teachers cheating by altering student answers on such tests in Atlanta, Chicago, and Texas. The 2013 Phi Delta Kappa/Gallup polls show that American parents have very unfavorable views of standardized testing (http://pdkpoll2015.pdkintl.org/236).

The opposite swing of the pendulum, to more permissive, child-centered, discovery learning programs is also problematic, because in many instances, children in such programs fail to get a good grounding in the basics (Egan, 2002; Loveless, 2001; Mayer, 2004). Discovery learning occurs when key target information is not provided, and learners must discover it on their own. In some cases, extensive guidance is provided (more structured learning) and in others, there is no guidance (pure discovery learning). A recent meta-analysis clearly showed that pure discovery learning is a failure; children need structure to learn, and in fact learn better in guided discovery learning than conventional didactic programs (Alfieri, Brooks, Aldrich, & Tenenbaum, 2011). Yet progressive school programs have often lacked sufficient structure, and children's learning suffers. When this is noticed after a period in which innovative programs are tried, the pendulum swings back to traditional test-oriented programs.

Neither extreme addresses the basic problems with schooling. In fact, the record of distally instigated reforms for schools, such as No Child Left Behind, is not good: State and federal government–led changes in schools have not appeared to make any difference to learning (Wang, Haertel, & Walberg, 1993). Under No Child Left Behind, children occasionally appear to do better on the state-sponsored tests, sometimes because the tests are dumbed down to be easier; but their performance on some other standard measures has remained the same or has declined (e.g., see the recent Program for International Student Assessment [PISA] test results, available at www.oecd.org. One recent analysis using the National Assessment of Educational Progress (NAEP) tests as the standard showed a positive effect on mathematics performance in fourth grade, but no influence on reading and no general improvement for eighth grade (Dee & Jacob, 2011); the 2012 PISA results also showed little to no improvement since 2009 (see http://nces.ed.gov/surveys/pisa/pisa2012/pisa2012highlights_6.asp; see also NAEP, 2012). It is an absolute travesty that politician-instigated school reforms are rarely based on sound research showing how children learn, but instead are usually based on people's personal intuitions.

Beyond this, however, is an even deeper problem. When anyone—be it an education professor, a school administrator, or a politician—considers school reform, the changes one tends to consider are rather superficial: this math curriculum or that one? Longer school day or longer school year? How many children per class—15 or 24? Education discourse in our country does not penetrate the roots of the problem, which are the underlying models on which our education system is founded. To really effect change, reformers must address the fundamental models on which our school system is built, as those models create a host of impediments to children's learning.

Two Poor Models

Conventional schooling is forever in turmoil because of its poor ideological foundation. First, conventional schools are modeled on factories, because the birth of mass public schooling coincided with the age of efficiency. Efficiency is a laudable goal, but it led to the creation of a school system that treats children as if they were all pretty much the same. In some ways they are, but in many ways they are not, and the factory model has a host of consequences that result in suboptimal learning conditions. We might also question its relevance to today's social and economic conditions, in which individual initiative, rather than blind obedience to the bells of a factory, is the key to progress. To wit, the earliest schooling of the founders of some of the most innovative and important technology interfaces today—Larry Paige and Sergey Brin of Google, Jeff Bezos of Amazon, Jimmy Wales of Wikipedia, and Will Wright of SimCity—was not in a factory system: all are Montessori school graduates. In Will Wright's (2007) TED talk, he speaks glowingly of Montessori school, which he attended through sixth grade; Montessori was "the high point of my education; from that point on everything else was pretty much downhill." The second poor model inherent in conventional schooling is an outmoded model of the child-learner inherited from behaviorism, in which the child is an empty vessel filled and shaped by deposited information, rewards, and punishments. The factory model and the behaviorist model work together in a mutually supportive fashion creating the conventional model we still typically use today.

THE SCHOOL AS FACTORY

Prior to 1850, the one-room schoolhouse was the dominant form of schooling in America. In such environments, education could be individualized, a wide age span of children occupied a single classroom, and teachers had significant independence in carrying out their didactic duties, responding only to a local board of directors. From the mid-19th century on, a change gradually took place as mass public schooling swept across the United States (and Europe). This coincided with the age of efficiency, in which a great deal of public discourse was focused on how to streamline business operations for maximum efficiency. Simultaneously, waves of immigrants were arriving on U.S. shores, intensifying the pressure for mass schooling. And by that point the Industrial Revolution had made factories a prominent organizational unit.

Because of this temporal synchrony, modern schools were consciously modeled on factories, with their priority of efficient operation (Bennett & LeCompte, 1990). Like factories, schools were expected to operate under then-popular "scientific management principles." In the public discourse, which Raymond E. Callahan documented in his classic opus *Education and the Cult of Efficiency*, schools were referred to as "plants," children as "raw materials," and teachers as "mid-level managers" (Callahan, 1962). Elwood Cubberly (1916/1929), then dean of Stanford University's School of Education, put it bluntly: Schools are "factories in which the raw products (children) are to be shaped and fashioned into products to meet the various demands of life" (p. 512).

One historic moment in this new approach to schools was the 1909 publication by a former school superintendent of Puerto Rico, Leonard Ayers. As secretary of the Russell Sage Foundation's Backward Children Investigation, Ayers ranked 58 school systems in various U.S. cities by their level of efficiency, meaning how many children moved up a grade each year (Ayers, 1909). Ayers was "one of the first educators to picture the school as a factory and to apply the business and industrial values and practices in a systematic way" (Callahan, 1962, pp. 15–16). His analysis was very influential, and low efficiency rankings had school boards across the country up in arms against their administrators. The notion of school as factory, efficiently using taxpayer money to produce educated final products, took firm hold in the wake of this publication.

At around the same time, Taylor management principles were being applied to many aspects of American life, beginning with efficient operation of factories but quickly extending to other businesses, the army and navy, the home, and schools. The aim of Taylor's principles was to increase production via scientific application of conservation practices. Ayers had popularized the goal of efficiency in education; Taylor showed the means. His principles specified that to maximize efficiency, worker tasks had to be analyzed, planned, and controlled in detail by the factory manager. In the case of schools, the factory manager was the administrator. The workers, in this case the teachers, were to do as they were told.[2] Taylor management "was given national recognition at the 1913 convention of the Department of Superintendence when the main topic for discussion was 'Improving School Systems by Scientific Management'. There were scores of articles, books, and reports during the next decade on economy in education, efficiency in education, standardization in education, and the like" (Callahan, 1962, p. 23).

John Franklin Bobbitt, a University of Chicago education professor, prescribed steps for the training of teachers in the model of school as factory. School administrators were to tell the teacher training colleges what sort of teachers they needed, and expect those training programs to deliver. School administrators, he wrote, "have the same right to say to colleges what product shall be sent to them as a transportation system has to say to a steel plant what kind of rails shall be sent to it" (Bobbit, as quoted in Callahan, 1962, p. 88). Once the trained teachers arrived on the job, administrators were to tell teachers exactly how and what to teach. "The worker must be kept supplied with detailed instructions as to the work to be done, the standards to be reached, the methods to be employed, and the appliances to be used" (Bobbit, 1913, as cited in Callahan, 1962, pp. 89–90). Responsibility for teaching was switched from teacher to administrator during this era, which must have profoundly changed the teaching profession and hence schools. Administrators were urged to run the school as a business, teachers were dehumanized (likened to steel rails!), and the child was lost in this early 1900s discourse on how schools should be run.

Several practices that appear to prioritize adult convenience over children's welfare stemmed from these reforms. The practice of having single-age classrooms began early, apparently in 1847 in Quincy, Massachusetts (Nelson, 2002). Whole-class teaching is convenient for teachers and sensible if one has a particular model of children as learners (discussed later), but it also has high costs for children. Children of the same age are often at different levels within a topic. They can have different interests, which makes them benefit from somewhat different teaching. They can learn at different speeds and can be helped tremendously by interacting with other children who are older and younger than themselves. Whole-class teaching fits the factory model well, but not the child.

Another common practice instituted at this time was the "Gary" or "platoon" practice of shifting children from room to room every 50 minutes at the ring of a bell. This was instigated in the early 1900s (Bennett &

---

[2] In some discussions of the factory model, the children appear to be the workers, and the teachers, the mid-level managers.

LeCompte, 1990) as part of an effort to make schools more efficient in their use of space, but it eventually became integral to teachers' daily lesson plans. Conventional classrooms today still shift topics not when the teacher and children are at a good transition point, but when the bell rings. The teacher is responsible for timing the lesson to match the bells. Every classroom of children is different, but preestablished schedules restrict the possibility of children's needs guiding the lessons and their timing. Another drawback is that children can rarely pursue individual interests and activities, but instead have to follow the program that all the children follow, which is predetermined by the teacher or administrator. When it is math time, everyone must do math, no matter how engrossed some might be in a writing project. The world we are preparing children to work in today is not like this: Educated people often determine for themselves when to move from one piece of work to another. Yet the conventional school system still operates like a factory (Bennett & LeCompte, 1990).

The factory model and its consequences emerged from a need by school administrators to justify their use of tax dollars to produce educated citizens for a factory-based economy (Callahan, 1962). The school was yet another factory, producing workers for the factories into which they would graduate. What was best for the child was clearly not in view. It is interesting that schools have become more and more inefficient as laws have increasingly required schools to educate every child regardless of individual variation. Schools with diverse groups of immigrant children must accommodate several languages, schools that enroll many children with learning disabilities must provide special classes, and so on. The per-pupil cost of education in public schools averaged $11,014 in 2011-12 (National Center for Education Statistics, 2016). School spending has increased enormously over the past 30 years (Camera, 2016), with no difference in education outcomes.

Despite these problems, the factory model prevails today, and Taylor management principles are alive and well (Au, 2011). Children in conventional schools are still marched lockstep through an educational system, and even daily schedules and physical structures reflect the factory model. Indeed, these models are being driven downward (Hamre & Pianta, 2007; Zigler & Bishop-Josef, 2004), as shown by a comparison of kindergarten classroom time allocated to play versus academic subjects in 1998 and 2010 (Bassok, Latham, & Rorem, 2016). In our current information age, when we deal in more of a commerce of ideas and entrepreneurship than in factory production, use of such a model in education should be particularly suspect. The school system in a sense trains children to be alike, whereas the economy thrives on variations in individual initiative, at least at the levels to which most parents aspire for their children. The factory model makes poor sense both from the standpoint of how children learn and from the standpoint of what society seeks.

THE LOCKEAN CHILD

The second suboptimal model on which our schools are based is the child as empty vessel or blank slate, a view typically associated with the 17th-century philosopher John Locke. The early 1900s instantiation of this view was behaviorism, which is the view that one could elicit a number of different behavioral profiles in an organism by varying the consequences of its behaviors. The continued prominence of behaviorism in schooling is clear:

> We have inherited an education system designed in the early part of this century.... [This system's] espoused curriculum and teaching norms were based on prevailing scientific assumptions concerning the nature of knowledge, the learning process, and differential aptitude or learning. Although they have been profoundly challenged by the past three decades of research in cognitive science and related disciplines, the assumptions of the 1920s are firmly ensconced in the standard operating procedures of today's schools. (Resnick & Hall, 1998, pp. 90–91)

The Lockean or empty-vessel model of the child was adopted in schools of the early 1900s in part because it was embedded in school practices prior to that time. For example, in schoolrooms prior to 1900, rewards for good performance and punishments for poor learning were commonplace. These prior practices paved the way for behaviorism to become the prominent learning model during the period of transition from one-room schools to large public schools. Another important reason the model gained such prominence was the work of one of the great figures in behaviorism, Edward Lee Thorndike.

An eminent professor of psychology at Columbia University's Teachers College for 40 years, Thorndike vastly influenced teacher education. Still prominent today, Teachers College was then, when the field was still new, the foremost teacher-education institution. Its early PhDs became the establishing professors at other new schools of education across the nation. Thorndike was a man of such force, according to his dean, James Earl Russell, that he shaped not only the character of Columbia Teachers College, but also the entire field of teacher education in its infancy (Russell, 1926, as cited in Jonich, 1962). "Coming to the field of educational psychology in its early, formative days, Thorndike was able to dominate its course to an extent hardly possible to one man today" (Jonich, 1962, p. 2). Spreading his influence through writing as well, he published more than 500 articles and books, including a series of popular elementary school textbooks (Jonich, 1962).

Thorndike viewed the teacher as the major force in educating the child, and the teacher's task as being to change the child. To do so, he said, the teacher must "give certain information" (Thorndike, 1906/1962, p. 59) and "control human nature" (p. 60). The only means the teacher possessed to do this were speech, gestures, expressions (p. 60), and a behaviorist curriculum based on associations between items learned and rewards administered.

To cement such associations, Thorndike argued that every topic should be broken down into discrete learning items on which students would then be drilled to form mental bonds. Well-formed bonds were to be rewarded with "kind looks, candy, and approval" (Thorndike, 1906/1962, p. 79), and poorly formed ones were to be met with punishment. Repetition was the key to well-formed bonds. Against any notion of discovery learning, Thorndike argued that bonds should be created for the information necessary, and no more.

An illustrative example of how Thorndike thought about necessary information concerns vocabulary. He believed that children should focus only on the most common words in the language, and he, therefore, published *The Teacher's Word Book*, listing the 10,000 most commonly used words in the English language (Thorndike, 1921b). Children's textbooks were considered useful to the degree to which they used these words, and few other "useless" (to Thorndike) ones (Hilgard, 1987). Evidently the age of efficiency and behaviorism were mutually reinforcing.

The Teacher's Word Book was but one of Thorndike's widely acclaimed books. His many textbooks supplied teachers with information already broken down into discrete learning items, and via these learning programs he wielded tremendous influence. His textbooks were adopted by the state school systems of California and Indiana. The income generated from sales of his textbooks across the United States was said to be five times his teaching salary in 1924 (Jonich, 1968, p. 400, as cited in Hilgard, 1987).

Thorndike's textbooks are classic illustrations of the decontextualized material common in U.S. textbooks today. For example, one Thorndike textbook problem is: "Tom had six cents in his bank and put in three cents more. How many cents were in the bank then?" (Thorndike, 1917, p. 18). The reader knows nothing about Tom or his bank, and so must process disembodied information. In contrast, the problems one regularly encounters outside school tend to have a meaningful context.

Thorndike believed that children could not transfer learning from one context to another unless elements of the situations were identical, so supplying context was useless. This belief was based on his 1898 dissertation, one of the most frequently cited studies in American psychology (Hilgard, 1987). In his study, adults were asked to estimate the area of different polygons (including rectangles), were then given feedback (training) as they estimated the area of rectangles, and, in a final test phase, were asked again to estimate the area of various polygons. Thorndike found that training on rectangles did not lead to improved performance on all of the polygons, but only on the rectangles. From this, he inferred a general principle that human learning does not transfer to different situations, and he concluded that one could and should therefore educate children merely by strengthening bonds for the very information they needed to know, stripped of context. Thus, children were instructed in Thorndike's texts as follows: "Learn this: 1 dime = 10 cents. 1 nickel = 5 cents" (1917, p. 59). And so on. Thorndike's view that knowledge can and should be presented in textbooks, as a set of disembodied, unconnected written facts that children have to commit to memory to become educated beings, still dominates.

Psychological research since has quite clearly demonstrated that children are capable of transferring learning from one context to another, and that a more apt view of learning is that the child can construct knowledge, rather than simply form associations (Bransford et al., 1999; Kuhn, 2001; Peterson, Fenneman, Carpenter, & Loef, 1989). We also know today that learning with a meaningful context can be far superior to learning that is unconnected to its use. For example, street children who sell things show mathematical understanding that they cannot even apply to the decontextualized problems in schoolbooks (as discussed in chapter 8). Sometimes people have knowledge that they can use in everyday situations but cannot transfer to the more removed contexts of school. We also know that rewards can have detrimental effects on children's engagement in learning activities, and yet we continue to reward and punish children with grades. Schools today commonly use programs in which elementary school children "read for pizza" or other rewards (including money). Despite advances in our understanding of how children learn, the legacy of behaviorism is still quite clear in the textbooks, curricula, and methods of schooling in place today.

WHY POOR MODELS STICK

Over the years, several alternatives to the behaviorist view have been provided by educational theorists such as Dewey, Piaget, Bruner, and Montessori. These theorists are referred to as *constructivists*, because they view children as constructing knowledge, rather than simply taking it in like an empty vessel. When one takes a constructivist stance, meaningful settings become important for learning, because one uses tools and materials from the environment for that construction. Because constructivism aligns with results from recent research on children's learning, it is taught in schools of education. One might say that constructivism has won out over behaviorism in the halls of academe. However, although constructivism is taught in education courses today, research suggests that teachers have difficulty implementing the constructivist approach in U.S. schools. As a result, the approach has had waves of popularity followed by retreat (Zilversmit, 1993). John Dewey, America's most famous progressive educator, lamented near the end of his life that he had not made any real effect on schooling (Dworkin, 1959). Given that constructivism is a better model for learning, there must be strong reasons for its failure to penetrate schooling.

One reason, proposed by the historian Arthur Zilversmit (1993), is response to social and economic circumstances. He noted that retreats from constructivism have come at times of economic and social upheaval, such as the Great Depression and McCarthyism. At such times experimentation falls away in many domains as people opt for the comfort of familiarity. Conventional schooling, for all its faults, always offers the benefit of familiarity to adults who themselves were educated in conventional ways.

Another reason is that education students rarely fully understand constructivism and thus fail to implement it well (Renninger, 1998). When they begin teaching, the superficiality of their understanding becomes apparent, and they take up the conventional methods used by their own elementary and high school teachers. Conventional teaching fits both a teacher's memory and the culturally dominant view of what school is, and teachers who have less understanding of alternatives will naturally fall back on it.

Another reason, I believe, is that the very structure of schools, from physical arrangements to schedules to the ubiquitous use of textbooks and tests, supports behaviorist techniques and thereby leads teachers to take a fundamentally behaviorist approach. If the teacher has a desk in front of a blackboard at the front of the classroom and students are seated in rows facing the teacher, small group or individual work is unnatural. The physical format is designed for lecturing. Although elementary teachers in particular increasingly allow children to sit in clusters instead of rows, other physical learning structures still gear them toward the model of an empty vessel. Learning in conventional schools comes largely from books, even during years when children in conventional schools are not yet particularly good readers. Because of this, teachers must tell children the information that is in the books in order for children to learn. This can only be reasonably accomplished through whole-class teaching.

The 50-minute hour requires that all information be delivered in a set period, rather than allowing for fluid and flexible learning depending on the children's interests and needs. Standardized tests on factual knowledge require that a certain body of information be transmitted by a certain date. Standardized tests also embody a view of knowledge as a fixed set of formulas and facts that can be applied and circled on tests. The materials used in conventional schools are geared toward this inert view of knowledge (D. K. Cohen, Raudenbush, & Ball, 2002). Teachers have to work very hard to use unconventional methods in the face of all the structural support schools provide for the conventional method.

Another important reason we continually retreat from constructivist approaches is that with the exception of Maria Montessori, constructivists, in contrast to Thorndike, have not provided teachers with a broad, detailed curriculum. Dewey had many ideas that have stood the test of time, but he did not leave the legacy of a full curriculum. In the absence of a curriculum, teachers who want to teach from a constructivist model of learning are on their own in figuring out how to implement the ideas. Because not enough teachers have succeeded in doing so well, the approach has repeatedly been branded as inadequate.

Few schools today have truly constructivist programs, and although teachers might leave schools of education versed in constructivist theories, their classrooms are run largely according to conventional schemes. Cook and colleagues demonstrated this in a case study of a star elementary education student as she moved from university coursework to practicum to classroom (Cook, Smagorinsky, Fry, Konopak, & Moore, 2002): At each step, the student endorsed a more behaviorist approach to teaching. Penelope Peterson and colleagues demonstrated the endorsement of behaviorist principles on a larger scale with a study of first-grade teachers (Peterson et al., 1989). However, they also noted that after about 15 years of experience, teachers returned to endorsing more constructivist views.

Although constructivists have had the greater influence in the academic world, behaviorists were "more influential on the practices in the conventional schools, which were always more numerous than the innovative ones" (Hilgard, 1987, p. 678). Despite research and teaching experience leading to a constructivist model of the child, elements of educational institutions—textbooks, the basic structure of the classroom, and so on—reinforce the Lockean model so much that it continues to dominate. Beyond the physical artifacts reinforcing the Lockean model are the collective memories of teachers and parents. When considering children and how to treat them, there is a strong tendency to revert to one's own childhood.

The same situation plays out today regarding a more recent rebirth of a Montessori idea in the context of traditional schooling: "differentiated instruction" (Tomlinson, 2014), which refers to individualized teaching based on students' needs and experience rather than the one-size-fits-all factory approach. Teachers fail to differentiate, even when they have been explicitly instructed and have learned how to do so, as indicated by paper tests, in part because the conventional school culture thwarts their efforts (Santangelo & Tomlinson, 2012). Finally, behaviorist methods appear to work in the short run. As will be discussed in chapter 6, once children are trained to study for rewards, removing the rewards negatively impacts learning. All these factors work in concert to impede school change.

Implications

The empty-vessel and factory models have many implications for schooling, which are discussed in the chapters to come. To preview, when the child is seen as an empty vessel into which one pours knowledge and then creates bonds, there is no need to involve the child actively in the learning process: Empty vessels are passive by nature. Yet people learn best when they are actively engaged. Good teachers try to keep children active by asking lots of questions during lectures, but the physical structure of the classroom is designed for passivity: The child sits and listens to the teacher, who stands at the blackboard and delivers knowledge. There is no need to consider the child's interests in the prevailing model because empty vessels have nothing in them from which interests could stem. When interests do arise, because all vessels have been filled with the same stuff, all vessels should share interests. Empty vessels certainly cannot make choices, and so teachers or school administrators choose what should be learned, down to the micro-details tested on statewide examinations.

The factory model also has certain implications for schooling. Factories at the turn of the century were efficient because all raw materials were treated alike. Factory workers operated on material, and material was passive. The material was moved from one place to another, assembled on a set schedule. Based on the factory model, all children in a class are given the same information simultaneously and are often moved from one place to another at the ring of a bell. It is a significant strike against the factory model that even true factories are changing practices to improve long-term productivity by allowing teams of workers to develop products from start to finish rather than having the product moved from place to place (Wompack, 1996). Yet schools still operate like the factories of yore.

Innovations *are* happening in conventional schooling. Some people will read the chapters to come and respond that their own children's schools are incorporating evidence-based changes, making them more like Montessori schools—eliminating grades, combining ages, using a lot of group work, and so on. One could take the view that over the years, conventional schooling has gradually been discovering and incorporating many of the principles that Dr. Montessori discovered in the first half of the 20th century. However, although schooling is changing, those changes are often relatively superficial. A professor of education might develop a new reading or math program that is then adopted with great fanfare by a few school systems, but the curricular change is minute relative to the entire curriculum, and the Lockean model of the child and the factory structure of the school environment still underlie most of the child's school day and year. "Adding new 'techniques' to the classroom does not lead to the developmental of a coherent philosophy. For example, adding the technique of having children work in 'co-operative learning' teams is quite different than a system in which collaboration is inherent in the structure" (Rogoff, Turkanis, & Bartlett, 2001, p. 13). Although small changes are made reflecting newer research on how children learn, particularly in good neighborhood elementary schools, most of the time, in most U.S. schools, conventional structures predominate (Hiebert, 1999; McCaslin et al., 2006; NICHD, 2005; Stigler, Gallimore, & Hiebert, 2000), and observers rate most classes to be low in quality (Weiss, Pasley, Smith, Banilower, & Heck, 2003). Superficial insertions of research-supported methods do not penetrate the underlying models on which are schools are based. Deeper change, implementing more realistic models of the child and the school, is necessary to improve schooling. How can we know what those new models should be?

As in medicine, where there have been increasing calls for using research results to inform patient treatments, education reform must more thoroughly and deeply implement what the evidence indicates will work best. This has been advocated repeatedly over the years, even by Thorndike. Certainly more and more researchers, educators, and policy makers are heeding the call to take an evidence-based stance on education. Yet the changes made thus far in response to these calls have not managed to address to the fundamental problems of the poor models. The time has come for rethinking education, making it evidence based from the ground up, beginning with the child and the conditions under which children thrive. Considered en masse, the evidence from psychological research suggests truly radical change is needed to provide children with a form of schooling that will optimize their social and cognitive development. A better form of schooling will change the Lockean model of the child and the factory structure on which our schools are built into something radically different and much better suited to how children actually learn.

Montessori Education

In the first half of the 20th century, Dr. Maria Montessori, a highly intelligent, scientifically minded woman who herself had been bored in school, decided to address the problem of education with a fresh outlook. In effect, she redesigned education from the ground up.

HISTORICAL OVERVIEW

How Dr. Montessori went about developing her program is an interesting story (Kramer, 1976; O'Donnell, 2007; Povell, 2009; Standing, 1957). She lived for much of her childhood in Rome and had unusual pluck and drive, aiming for a degree first in engineering and later in medicine, both unheard-of courses of study for a young Italian woman at the time. After her medical training, she worked in psychiatric clinics, where she became interested in helping mentally retarded children. At the beginning of the 20th century, mentally retarded people were often institutionalized in bare rooms, their food thrown at them. Dr. Montessori saw in their grasping at crumbs of food on the floor as starvation not for food, but for stimulation. She studied the methods of Jean-Marc Itard, who had worked with the Wild Boy of Aveyron, and his student Eduard Seguin seeking methods of providing such stimulation. Seguin had developed a set of sensory stimuli for the education of retarded children, and Dr. Montessori adopted these in her work, creating what in Montessori terminology are called the Sensorial Materials.

In 1901, the mentally retarded children with whom Dr. Montessori had worked passed state educational tests designed for normal children, an event that aroused international attention. Newspaper articles the world over marveled at the amazing Italian physician who had brought "defectives" (as they were then called) to this feat. Dr. Montessori had a different reaction. Rather than marveling at what the mentally retarded children had done, she instead marveled that normal children were not doing better on such tests, given their obvious advantages. Then, as the famous Swiss psychologist Jean Piaget (1970) described it, "generalizing her discoveries with unparalleled mastery, Mme Montessori ... immediately applied to normal children what she had learned from backward ones: during its earliest stages the child learns more by action than through thought [, leading her to develop] a general method whose repercussions throughout the entire world have been incalculable" (pp. 147–48). Dr. Montessori turned her studies to the process of normal development in order to discover how human beings could reach their potential more fully than they did in conventional schools.

The process of application was not actually as immediate as Piaget described. First, following her success with retarded children, Montessori returned to school herself, this time to study education. She observed children in conventional classrooms to try to decipher why they were not advancing more in that environment. As she developed new ideas, Montessori requested permission to apply them in public elementary schools, but the governing bodies in Rome at the time would not give her access to those children. In retrospect, this limitation was probably providential, because the system she eventually developed for older, Elementary school children was based on children who had been in her Primary programs from ages 3 to 6. These children had at the outset a different set of skills and knowledge relative to other 6-year-olds, and the Elementary program could thus be built for children who were already reading and writing, who knew how to follow procedures and to make their own decisions about what to do next, and who understood some basic principles about how to get along as individuals in a large group.

Because she could not initially work in elementary schools, Dr. Montessori took an opportunity that arose to work with younger children. A housing project was undergoing renovation in a poor section of Rome, and children who were old enough to run about unsupervised but were not yet of the age for school were causing problems in the renovated buildings. The project developers decided to intervene. Knowing Dr. Montessori was interested in working with normally developing children, they offered her a space in one of the projects and the care of 50 or 60 children, aged 3 to 6. A young woman served as teacher, and Dr. Montessori began her "experiment" in January 1907. She viewed her schools as laboratories in which to study how children learn best (Montessori, 1917/1965, p. 125).

Because legally the classroom could not be called a school, Dr. Montessori was not allowed to order typical school furniture or items, another limitation that ended up being advantageous. She furnished the classroom instead with small furniture she had specially designed for children. This furniture was typical of what one might find in a home, like small tables and armchairs. She put in various materials, gave the young teacher instructions on what to do, and then retreated to her other roles as a professor at the University of Rome, a researcher, a practicing physician, a renowned speaker on women's rights, and a student taking classes in education (Kramer, 1976). But she found time to observe the classroom, and the teacher also reported to her in the evenings about what had transpired. Dr. Montessori is said to have worked late into the nights making new materials for the teacher to try. By testing new approaches and materials and noting children's reactions, over the next 45 years, Dr. Montessori and her collaborators developed a radically different system of education.

Dr. Montessori developed materials for education in concert with ideas about it, and the materials were field-tested until she believed she had found reasonably optimum ones for teaching a given concept. She also tested materials across ages and frequently found a material appealed to children much younger than those for whom she had designed it. "We watched the younger children go among the older ones, and . . . we saw them become interested in things which we had thought previously too remote from their understanding" (Montessori, 1989, p. 68). Young children, she found, are much more capable than conventional curricula hold them to be, a finding that put her at odds with the educational trends of her time to lighten the curriculum for young children (Egan, 2002; Hall, 1911).

In contrast to other constructivists, Dr. Montessori left the legacy of a broad, field-tested curriculum covering all the major subject areas—math, music, art, grammar, science, history, and so on—for children ages 3 to 12. This system was developed by trial and error over her lifetime, with children in places as diverse as Rome, India, Spain, the Netherlands, and the United States. Dr. Montessori gave many lectures and wrote several books about her system, and she founded the Association Montessori Internationale (AMI) to carry on her work, including the training of Montessori teachers. A *Casa dei Bambini* operates today at the original location, at 58 Via dei Marsi near the University of Rome (Figure 1.1).

FIGURE 1.1 The *Casa dei Bambini* today at the original location, at 58 Via dei Marsi near the University of Rome. Photograph by the author.

A PORTRAIT OF A MONTESSORI CLASSROOM

For the next half century, Dr. Montessori adjusted and adapted her educational system to better serve children's needs, and well-functioning Montessori classrooms typically share many features reflecting those adjustments. The importance of several features is emphasized here; later chapters discuss psychology research pertinent to many of these features and more.

A Montessori classroom is usually a large, open-feeling space, with low shelves, different sizes of tables that comfortably seat one to four children, and chairs that are appropriately sized for the children in the classroom (Figure 1.2). Although not unusual today, making furniture that was appropriately sized for the children who would use it was one of Dr. Montessori's innovations (Elkind, 1976). Conventional Montessori classrooms always have at least three-year age groupings; at smaller schools all 6 years of Elementary might be combined.

The Montessori classroom is arranged into areas, usually divided by low shelving. Each area has "materials," the Montessori term designating educational objects, for working in a particular subject area (art, music, mathematics, language, science, and so on). This contrasts sharply with conventional education, in which learning is derived largely from texts. Books become more important as tools for learning at the Montessori Elementary level, but even there, hands-on materials abound. Dr. Montessori believed that deep concentration was essential for helping children develop their best selves, and that deep concentration in children comes about through working with their hands, hence, materials. Concentration is discussed at length in chapter 4.

FIGURE 1.2 A Montessori classroom. Photograph by An Vu.

Montessori classrooms also contrast with many conventional ones in having a pristine appearance. Extra materials are kept out of sight in a closet and rotated in and out of the classroom as children seem ready for or no longer in need of them. Every material has its place on the shelves, and children are expected to put each material neatly back in its place after use, ready for another child. Attention to the community and respect for the needs of others are highly valued. Such attention is also reflected in how teachers arrange the classroom. Materials both within and across subject areas are placed thoughtfully, so the arrangements make logical sense.

Children are not assigned seats but are free to work at whatever tables they choose, moving about during the day. They can also work on the floor atop small rugs. Children can choose to work alone or in self-formed groups, except when the teacher is giving a lesson. With very few exceptions, all lessons are given to individuals (more often in Primary, the 3- to 6-year-old level) or small groups (more often in Elementary, the 6- to 12-year-old level). Lessons are given as the children are ready for them; the teacher might write on the board or announce the day's planned lessons early in the day, so that children will know what to expect. Care is taken so that the effect is not to impose control on the children, but simply to alert them so they can plan their day accordingly.

Montessori education is organized to the core. At the preschool level, this sometimes puts people off. They enter a Montessori classroom, and unlike preschools they normally see, it is very quiet. Children are calmly working alone or in groups. And their work is organized. They are concentrating, carrying out activities in a series of steps that have been shown to them by the teacher or other children. As will be discussed in chapter 10, research suggests that orderly environments are associated with the best child outcomes, but the degree of order can make parents feel uncomfortable.

The materials on the shelves are designed to attract children's interest and to teach concepts via repeated use. Most of the materials are made of wood and are either natural or painted in bright colors selected because those colors were found to attract children. Each material has a primary reason for its being in the classroom; most also have several secondary purposes as well. Rather than giving tests to assess competence, Montessori teachers observe children at work, noting whether children use the materials correctly. Correct use is believed to engender understanding. Teachers repeat lessons when children appear to be using a material improperly and thus will not draw from it the learning it is intended to impart; new lessons are given when children appear to have mastered a material and to be ready for the next material in a sequence.

In keeping with each material's having a primary purpose, there are particular ways to use the materials, which the children are shown in the lessons. Children are not supposed to make music with Metal Insets (a material shown in Figure 1.3, consisting of standard geometric shapes made of metal,

FIGURE 1.3 The Metal Insets. Photograph by An Vu.

each inside a square metal frame); the Metal Insets serve other purposes, and different materials are provided that are more suited to making music. In addition to the use of each material being highly structured, the overarching Montessori curriculum is also tightly structured. Materials within a curriculum area are presented in a hierarchical sequence, and there is a complex web of interrelationships with materials in different areas of the curriculum. As far as I know, no other single educational curriculum comes close to the Montessori curriculum in terms of its levels of depth, breadth, and interrelationship across time and topic.

The materials break important activities into a series of organized steps that children learn separately before bringing them together to do the main activity. These steps often constitute indirect preparation; children are not aware of what the steps can lead to, but the teacher is aware and presents the materials methodically. A good example of how instruction in Montessori proceeds is in the teaching of writing and reading.

LEARNING IN MONTESSORI: WRITING AND READING

In Montessori programs, children learn to write before they learn to read, and reading follows spontaneously several months after writing has begun. Several steps lead to the onset of writing in the Montessori Primary classroom. Three-year-olds first engage in activities through which they practice the thumb–index finger (pincer) grip needed for holding a pencil. One exercise that uses this grip involves lifting solid Wooden Cylinders by their small round knobs out of an oblong wooden case (Figure 1.4). There are four sets of these Wooden Cylinders. The cylinders in one set vary systematically in

FIGURE 1.4 The Wooden Cylinders. Photograph by An Vu.

width while height remains the same, those in another vary in height while the width remains the same, and those in a third change by both height and width together. The fourth decreases in width and increases in height. The exercise of lifting the cylinders out, mixing them up, and then returning them to their appropriate holes was designed primarily to educate the child's intelligence by engaging the child in an activity requiring that he or she observe, compare, reason, and decide (Montessori, 1914/1965). Focusing on dimension with this exercise also prepares the child for math, and the work enhances the child's powers of observation and concentration. But the addition of the knobs allows the material to confer two additional benefits geared toward writing: strengthening the finger and thumb muscles and developing the coordination needed for holding a pencil.

The child goes on to develop the wrist action associated with writing by tracing shapes from the Geometry Cabinet, a wooden cabinet containing several trays, each holding six blue two-dimensional wooden shapes set in natural wood frames (Figure 1.5). One tray holds rectangles of gradually increasing widths; another has different triangles (equilateral, right angle, isosceles, and others); another has a set of irregular geometric shapes, such as an ellipsoid and a parallelogram, and so on. Children learn the names of the shapes as they trace along their edges, first with their fingers, developing lightness of touch and the wrist action needed for writing. Later they trace the outlines of leaf shapes in the Botany cabinet, but use a delicate orange stick that allows them to get into the corners (Figure 1.6). This delicate orange wooden stick allows children to practice holding something pencil-like, but without the added concern of making marks that would damage the material. Children learn the names of various shapes of leaves while also (without knowing it)

FIGURE 1.5 Triangle Tray from the Geometry Cabinet. Photograph by An Vu.

FIGURE 1.6 The Botany Cabinet. Photograph by An Vu.

learning the wrist action and pencil grip for writing. Even prior to using the orange wooden stick, "The little hand which touches, feels, and knows how to follow a determined outline is preparing itself, without knowing it, for writing" (Montessori, 1914/1965, p. 96). Clear writing is exact, and such exercises prepare children by engaging them in precise movements.

Later, children learn to hold and use pencils with the 10 Metal Insets (see Figure 1.3), which have the same geometric shapes as the items from the Geometry Cabinet, but are made of metal, with the outer frame painted red and the inset geometric shapes painted blue. Metal is an unusual choice for a Montessori material because metal is cold to the touch; wood is the norm because it feels warmer, and Dr. Montessori perceived this as inviting use. However, metal has the advantage of not being as easily marked by straying pencils, and thus it is the material of the first objects with which children use actual pencils. The child initially sits down with all 10 Metal Insets at once, as Dr. Montessori noticed this inspired children to do all of them, whereas having just one did not (Montessori, 1914/1965, p. 144).

Each of the Geometry, Botany, and Metal Inset items has a small knob like those the children first encountered with the Wooden Cylinders, so working with these materials continues to exercise the pincer grip in preparation for holding the pencil. Dr. Montessori intended that exercising such muscles would prevent fatigue when children first begin writing. When 4-year-olds start writing in Montessori, as teachers describe it, they want to do so nonstop. If these exercises really do strengthen the pincer grip, they might support an early enthusiasm for writing. In addition, Montessori teachers pay close attention to whether children are correctly holding the pencil, another step thought to reduce the muscle fatigue that can come from a great deal of writing.

With the Metal Insets, children use 10 colored pencils to trace inside the red frame or along the outside of the inset shape. Later they work on filling in the inset drawings with lines, to work on pencil control (Figure 1.7). The repeated use of 10 objects (pencils, Metal Inset shapes, and so on) is intentional in Montessori, to reinforce the decimal system. Markers were, of course, not available when Dr. Montessori developed this system, but many Montessori schools today eschew the use of markers because pencils provide the children with more finely tuned feedback. The intensity with which the child presses a pencil onto paper has immediate and visible consequences: A pencil tip will break if pressed too hard and will not make a mark if not pressed hard enough. In addition, pencils allow shading, and one exercise with the Metal Insets is to shade the inside of a shape from darkest to lightest. Markers do not educate the child as carefully, because no immediate touch-dependent feedback results.

Colored pencils and Metal Insets are later employed to make a wonderful variety of creative illustrations in art, an area many people mistakenly

FIGURE 1.7 Metal Inset designs. Photograph by An Vu.

think is not part of the Montessori curriculum (e.g., Stodolsky & Karlson, 1972). The same misconception is often found regarding music, although Montessori also has a full music curriculum. Not all Montessori teachers implement the full curriculum, sometimes because their training courses are of insufficient duration to cover it (e.g., the Tone Bars, used for musical composition, in Figure 1.8, are sometimes absent from Elementary classrooms for this reason). Indeed, Dr. Montessori used 2 years to teach the Elementary curriculum to teachers, whereas the longest-running Elementary training courses today teach it in a year.

After learning to trace the Metal Insets, children learn to draw a series of connected parallel straight lines inside of the frame, which teaches children to control the hand and pencil in the natural flowing motion of writing. Dr. Montessori saw this flowing motion to be easier for children than stopping and lifting the pencil frequently, so she had children learn cursive writing before learning to print.

During the same period when children are using the Metal Insets in these ways, they are also learning to trace cursive Sandpaper Letters with their fingers, following the same paths of motion one uses to write. As they trace the letters (shown in Figure 1.9), children learn to say the phonetic sound (not the name) associated with each letter. Later, the Metal Inset and Sandpaper

FIGURE 1.8 Montessori music: composing on the Tone Bars. © Laura Joyce-Hubbard, 2014. All rights reserved.

Letter activities come together. Children hold pencil to paper while making the same hand motions they made with the Sandpaper Letters, saying the sounds of the letters, and eventually stringing letters together to write words in cursive. This process is also assisted by the provision of the Movable

FIGURE 1.9 The Sandpaper Letters. Photograph by An Vu.

Alphabet, a wooden box of cardboard letters that children use to make words (shown in Figure 5.5).

There are more materials and also forms of these materials that lead to writing, but this description gives a flavor for the carefully organized curricula a child is given in a Montessori classroom. The outcome of using the materials in this carefully orchestrated sequence, for most children who enroll in Montessori as older 2- or young 3-year-olds, is to be easily writing in cursive during the year when they are 4. Reading emerges spontaneously during the months after writing begins.

Research suggests many long-term advantages for early reading (Mol & Bus, 2011). Eleventh-graders' vocabulary, reading comprehension, and general knowledge were all strongly predicted by their reading ability 10 years earlier, when they were in first grade, even when cognitive ability was controlled for (Cunningham & Stanovich, 1997). There is also support for Montessori's phonemic approach to early reading over the less successful whole-language approach (Rayner, Foorman, Perfetti, Pesetsky, & Seidenberg, 2001). Preschoolers who were trained in phonemic awareness scored significantly higher on tests of reading comprehension 3 years later, relative to children in a matched control condition (Byrne & Fielding-Barnsley, 1995). Montessori's haptic approach to learning to read, by first tracing letters while making their sounds, has also gained support in recent research. French preschoolers who were taught to either just look at letters, or look and trace the letters, while making the associated sounds were later given letter–sound and pseudo-word recognition tests (Bara, Gentaz, & Cole, 2007). The haptic group performed significantly better on the latter, and showed a trend to being better at the former. In another study, among children who were twice read alphabet picture books, those who traced block capital letters made of sandpaper learned to recognize letters at a level significantly greater than chance, whereas children who did not trace the letters or traced plain paper letters were at chance (Chiong & DeLoache, 2013). Research has also shown (not surprisingly) that the more one reads, the more one knows, controlling for intelligence and for years of education (Stanovich & Cunningham, 1993). Long-range reading skills are best predicted by a young child's degree of interest in reading (Whitehurst & Lonigan, 1998). Obviously, making reading unpleasant early on by putting children through a difficult and laborious process would not instill enjoyment of reading, and enjoyment of reading is characteristic of those who read a lot.

Unlike the laborious process most first-graders go through, learning to read and write in Montessori appears to be a painless process for children. The organized approach Dr. Montessori took to the learning process would seem to be part of why it seems easy. She performed task analyses of different areas, and the Montessori curriculum presents the child with a series of manageable steps in each area, aimed at mastering each task. The steps, derived from observations of children, are carefully organized, focus on important skills and information, and culminate in the child's mastery. Moving to a larger scale, these observations led to a method of schooling with a different model of the child and the school than those that prevailed in conventional schooling.

Montessori Models of Child and School

Underlying Montessori education is a model of the child as a motivated doer, rather than an empty vessel. The active child is a view often credited to Jean Piaget, who may have been influenced by Dr. Montessori. He was 26 years her junior and early in his career had conducted observations for his book *The Language and Thought of the Child* in a Montessori school. He apparently attended at least one Montessori conference, in Rome in 1934, and was president of the Swiss Montessori Society. Letterhead from the early days of the AMI lists Piaget as one of its sponsors (Kramer, 1976). Thus it is not surprising that Piaget and Montessori's theories share some crucial ideas, such as the notion of children as active learners (Elkind, 1967). Children in Montessori classrooms work as motivated doers, learning through self-instigated actions on the environment.

The model of the school in Montessori education is also different. Rather than being modeled on the factory, a Montessori school seems more like a miniature and eclectic university research laboratory. Montessori children pursue their own projects, just as do researchers in their laboratories. Like university researchers, children choose what they want to learn about, based on what interests them. They get lessons across the curriculum, which bears some similarity to researchers going to colloquia or conferences to learn about new areas or techniques. The children talk with and collaborate with colleagues of their choosing. They pass on the fruits of their labors to others by giving talks to the class or other classes in their school and writing up papers. Thus, in Montessori, the child can be seen as a motivated doer in a research university, versus the conventional school model of the child as an empty vessel in a factory.

This book describes nine insights Dr. Montessori derived through her observations of children that undergird her approach to schooling. These insights are supported today by a good deal of research in psychology and education. Some of the principles can also be implemented in conventional classrooms; in fact, some of the research showing the validity of the principles was conducted in conventional school contexts. However, to develop a system from a principle is very different than to insert a principle into a system that was designed with something else in mind. The nine principles I discuss emerged in the early days of Montessori education, through Dr. Montessori's observations of children's behavior in classrooms that were unusual to begin with. The principles coexist and are deeply engrained in the Montessori system.

Nine Principles of Montessori Education

The nine principles of Montessori education discussed in the following sections are:

1. Movement and cognition are closely entwined, and movement can enhance thinking and learning.
2. Learning and well-being are improved when people have a sense of control over their lives.
3. The ability to direct one's attention in a sustained and concentrated way fosters an array of positive developments and is itself trainable.
4. People learn better when they are interested in what they are learning.
5. Tying extrinsic rewards to an activity, such as money for reading or high grades for tests, negatively impacts motivation to engage in that activity when the reward is withdrawn.
6. Collaborative arrangements can be very conducive to learning.
7. Learning situated in meaningful contexts is often deeper and richer than learning in abstract contexts.
8. Particular forms of adult interaction are associated with more optimal child outcomes.
9. Order in the environment is beneficial to children.

MOVEMENT AND COGNITION

The first principle is that movement and cognition are closely entwined. This observation makes sense: Our brains evolved in a world in which we move and do, not a world in which we sit at desks and consider abstractions. Dr. Montessori noted that thinking seems to be expressed by the hands before it can be put into words, an idea with which Piaget apparently concurred (Ginsburg & Oper, 1979). In small children, she said, thinking and moving are the same process. Piaget restricted this identity claim to the sensorimotor period, but, consistent with recent work in psychology, Dr. Montessori saw at least a close relationship between the two processes continuing past age 2. Based on this insight, she developed a method of education in which a great deal of object manipulation occurs. In recent years, there has been an explosion of fascinating research on the connection between movement and cognition that speaks to Dr. Montessori's ideas about movement's importance to thought. The findings imply that education should involve movement to enhance learning.

CHOICE

A second principle is free choice. Dr. Montessori noted that children seemed to thrive on having choice and control in their environment, and she envisioned development as a process of the child's being increasingly able to be independent in his or her environment. Although good Montessori programs impose definite limits on this freedom, Montessori children are free to make many more decisions than are children in conventional classrooms: what to work on, how long to work on it, with whom to work on it, and so on. Research in psychology suggests that more freedom and choice (within a carefully designed, ordered structure; see the "Order in Environment and Mind" section) are linked to better psychological and learning outcomes, as shown in chapter 3.

EXECUTIVE FUNCTION

A third principle is that the development of executive control, especially the ability to focus and sustain attention, is key to other important developments. Dr. Montessori noticed this early in the school in San Lorenzo, when a child became so engrossed with a set of Wooden Cylinders that she was able to lift the armchair in which the child was working and not disturb the child's concentration. Dr. Montessori realized that developing this ability to concentrate was associated with changes in personality that she called "normalization." This principle is new to this edition, because only in the last 10 years has research on this burgeoned both in developmental psychology and in research on the positive effects of meditative practices. These are reviewed in chapter 4.

INTEREST

A fourth principle is that the best learning occurs in contexts of interest. Interest can be more personal, as when an individual has an abiding interest in ladybugs or dogs that seems to come from within, or it can be situational, an interest that would be engendered in many people exposed to such events and activities. Dr. Montessori created situational interest in part by designing materials with which children seemed to want to interact. She also trained Montessori teachers to give lessons in a manner that would inspire children, for example by presenting just enough information to pique curiosity and by using drama in their presentations (particularly with Elementary-aged children). Montessori education also capitalizes on interests that appear regularly at particular times in development, such as the intense interest children have in learning language in the preschool years. Dr. Montessori noted that young children seem to be driven to acquire word labels for the objects in their environment, so in the Primary classrooms, children are given a great deal of vocabulary. Montessori education also capitalizes on unique individual interest. Children pursue learning that is of personal interest to them—not in a manner that excludes large swaths of curriculum, but in a manner consistent with how we know the very best learning takes place. Rather than memorize facts chosen by a faraway state legislative body, children in Montessori Elementary schools write and present reports on what fascinates them, tying it into the foundational curriculum. The Montessori materials and basic lessons ensure a core of learning across curriculum areas, but each child's imagination is invested in the particular avenues of learning that the child pursues beyond that core. These topics are discussed in chapter 5.

EXTRINSIC REWARDS ARE AVOIDED

Dr. Montessori saw extrinsic rewards, such as gold stars and grades, to be disruptive to a child's concentration. Sustained, intense periods of concentration are central to Montessori education. Dr. Montessori recounts children repeating problems (such as getting the Wooden Cylinders into their proper holes) dozens of times in succession, displaying a level of concentration that she herself had previously thought young children were incapable of. At the Primary level, children might concentrate intensely for 30 minutes at a time. By the Elementary level, they might work on the creation of a single chart for much of the day or even several days in succession. The rewards in Montessori education are internal ones. A good deal of research suggests that interest in an already-loved activity, such as learning seems to be for most children, is best sustained when extrinsic rewards are not part of the framework, as discussed in chapter 6.

LEARNING WITH AND FROM PEERS

In conventional schooling, the teacher gives the children information, and children rarely learn from each other or directly from materials (except texts, which often tell children rather than helping them discover). Although on the increase, working together is still rare in (conventional) elementary classrooms, where tests, problem sets, and papers are usually if not always done alone. In conventional preschool classrooms, in contrast, children usually play in groups. Montessori education is opposite in these arrangements, and is actually more in line with what developmentalists know about children: Younger children are more apt to play side by side but not necessarily together, whereas elementary-age children are intensely social.

In Montessori Primary classrooms, children may often work alone by choice, but in Elementary classrooms children are rarely seen working alone. They pursue knowledge in self-formed groups, creating products ranging from reports to dioramas, charts to plays, and timelines to musical scores. They leave the classroom together in small self-created groups to interview people outside the school or to visit museums or businesses that are relevant to a current project stemming from their own interests. Asked what happens in these small learning groups when one child understands better than the others—a concern that arises out of the individualistic conventional model in which one child might do most of the work—I recently heard a 9-year-old Montessori child respond, "We help each other." Chapter 7 discusses research on what happens when students work together to learn, rather than working as individual units striving for the highest grades.

LEARNING IN CONTEXT

In conventional schooling, children sometimes learn without understanding how their learning applies to anything besides school tests. Dr. Montessori reacted to this by creating a set of materials and a system of learning in which the application and meaning of what one was learning should come across to every child. Rather than learning largely from what teachers and texts say to them, children in Montessori programs learn largely by doing. Because they are doing things, rather than merely hearing and writing, their learning is situated in the context of actions and objects. For example, as described earlier, children go out of the Elementary classroom and into the world to research their interests. A small group of children who have become interested in bridges, for example, may choose to locate a local engineer who will meet with them to explain how bridges are designed. This approach, sometimes referred to as "situated cognition," reflects a movement in education that goes alongside current interests in cultural psychology, apprenticeship, and how people learn through participating in their culture. Evidence concerning the validity of this approach is reviewed in chapter 8.

TEACHER WAYS AND CHILD WAYS

Dr. Montessori's recommendations on how teachers should interact with children anticipated later research on parenting and teaching. When adults provide clear limits but set children free within those boundaries, and sensitively respond to children's needs while maintaining high expectations, children show high levels of maturity, achievement, empathy, and other desirable characteristics. Conventional schools have sometimes erred by being too authoritarian, conveying a "do it because we said so" attitude that is not associated with positive child outcomes. When progressive schools fail, it may sometimes be because they trade the authoritarian teacher-centered features of many conventional schools for their opposite: permissive, overly child-centered ones. Dr. Montessori prescribed a third style, one consistent with what is called authoritative parenting and known to be associated with the most optimal child outcomes. Her advice to teachers is reminiscent of the adult styles associated with positive child outcomes in other domains as well. This research is reviewed in chapter 9, "Adult Interaction Styles and Child Outcomes."

ORDER IN ENVIRONMENT AND MIND

Montessori classrooms are very organized, both physically (i.e., layout) and conceptually (i.e., how the use of materials progresses). This organization sometimes turns people off: It seems finicky, even obsessive-compulsive. Yet research in psychology suggests that order is very helpful to learning and development, and that Dr. Montessori was right on target in creating very ordered environments in schools. Children do not fare as well in less ordered environments. Chapter 10 reviews research on order and its effect on children. It also speculates on the potential neurological impact of presenting orderly sequences of materials intended to tune the senses.

Further Montessori Insights

Dr. Montessori also forecast other current ideas in developmental psychology not reviewed here. For example, she drew extensively on the idea of sensitive periods, which she credited to Hugo de Vries, the Dutch horticulturist best known for rediscovering Mendelian inheritance. Developmental scientists consider sensitive periods to be times when an organism is particularly primed to develop in certain ways, given certain environmental stimulations (Bornstein, 1989). It was many years later that Konrad Lorenz popularized this notion with strong evidence of such periods in goslings, and ethological theory began to be incorporated into theories of human development. Among other sensitive periods, Dr. Montessori identified the first 5 years as a sensitive period for language in children. She went so far as to claim the innateness of human language (Montessori, 1967a/1995) years before Noam Chomsky (1959) rocked the world of psycholinguistics with that same claim. She talked repeatedly of how important early experience is to development (Montessori, 1967a/1995), well before research in neuroscience backed that idea (Bransford et al., 1999). She also considered development to continue all the way to age 24, about the age when gray matter volume stops increasing in the human brain (although white matter—the myelinated connections between neurons—continues to increase thereafter) (Lebel & Beaulieu, 2011;

see also Gogtay et al., 2004; Lillard & Erisir, 2011). In these and other ways, Dr. Montessori was clearly well ahead of her time. A natural question at this point is whether the educational system she developed, which incorporated such insights, has outcomes that are superior to those of conventional schools. In the following section I will review research that had been conducted prior to the first edition of this volume in 2005. Chapter 11 covers research done since that time, including my own studies that were inspired by what I had learned in writing this book.

RESEARCH ON MONTESSORI OUTCOMES

Most published work on Montessori shows positive outcomes; however, like most fieldwork on education outcomes, the findings must be taken with a grain of salt because of methodological shortcomings. Good research on the effectiveness of different school programs is actually very difficult to do (Mervis, 2004). One common shortcoming is lack of random assignment: Parents elect to send their children to Montessori programs. Features of parenting tend to swamp features of schools when it comes to education outcomes. Parents who happen to like Montessori programs might be, by and large, excellent parents: They like order, they like children to be able to make choices, and so on. Such parents would incorporate those features into the child's home life, and the additive benefit of having those features in school might be nil. A research study comparing such children with children not in Montessori would thus show differences, but the cause of the differences would actually be the parents, not the school program. In the absence of random assignment, one can always argue that parenting or some other variable was the source of difference.

Some of the first research on Montessori outcomes was done in Head Start programs in the 1960s (Karnes, Shewedel, & Williams, 1983; Miller & Bizzell, 1983, 1984; Miller & Dyer, 1975). Two Great Society-era studies addressed the self-selection problem by randomly assigning children into different Head Start programs and looked at long-term outcomes. Montessori was one of several programs compared. The Miller study, in Louisville, followed children through 10th grade, and the Barnes study, in Urbana, Illinois, followed children through high school. Results are described in some detail in the following paragraphs, but the main thrust was that initial results did not favor Montessori, yet longitudinal results did.

It is important to note, however, that regarding fidelity, these Montessori Head Start programs left much to be desired. In the Louisville study, there were just two Montessori classrooms, with a total of 33 children, so roughly 16 per group; Montessori classrooms are expect to have 30 to 35 children and in Dr. Montessori's descriptions, they often had 50 or more. Each Head Start classroom included only 4-year-olds, not the full 3-year age grouping. Each was in its first year of existence. Each also had teachers with minimal training of just 8 weeks; in contrast, the AMI training course for primary teachers lasts 9 months. In the Miller study, a consultant rated programs for fidelity, and the Montessori classrooms scored 6.5 on a 10-point scale (with 10 being very high). The Karnes Montessori program study was subject to the same problems regarding limited ages and teacher training, and children worked for just 30 minutes per day with the Montessori materials rather than the expected 3 hours for 3- and 4-year-olds, and 6 hours for 5-year-olds. In sum, both Head Start Montessori studies involved lower fidelity programs and did not show immediate effects. Still, both showed some Montessori program advantage over time (Karnes et al. 1983; Miller & Bizzell, 1983, 1984; Miller & Dyer, 1975).

In both studies, children had less than a year of mediocre-quality Montessori at age 4, yet some positive outcomes were obtained for Montessori children relative to children in other types of preschool Head Start programs and these advantages lasted as far out as high school, when the studies terminated. For example, in the study by Karnes and colleagues (1983; Illinois), fewer Montessori children dropped out of school or were retained a grade. In the Miller (Kentucky) study, the Montessori boys (in particular) had higher standardized test scores than the children from the comparison Head Start programs (such as conventional preschool and Bereiter-Engleman and Darcy, school programs that were in vogue at the time). Although the results were reasonably positive across these two studies conducted in different states, caution must be exercised because of several shortcomings in the studies.

One problem with these two Great Society program studies is that very few classrooms were involved. Because of this, one cannot tease apart individual teacher effects from program effects. Perhaps the one or two Montessori teachers whose classrooms were sampled in one study were superb teachers, and in another study the Montessori teachers were poor ones. Respectively positive and negative findings would result, with an effect of teacher quality misattributed to an effect of program. In conventional education, quality of teacher interaction is the main predictor of child outcomes (Early et al., 2007; Pianta, Hamre, & Allen, 2012). Teachers' ability to sensitively respond to students' needs is also vital for Montessori education, and variation in teacher quality could have a meaningful impact when few classrooms were sampled.

Another issue that is true of these studies and many others is that the quality of implementation of the Montessori philosophy and materials was poor. There is no litmus test for calling a school a Montessori school. Even if one uses an accredited school, the different Montessori organizations have very different accreditation criteria, with some adhering more closely to Dr. Montessori's methods than others. Researchers often have not known how to determine whether a program adheres sufficiently to the principles and curriculum to be considered a good example of Montessori, and instead they tend to trust that if a school calls itself Montessori, then it is a good place to test whether Montessori education matters for outcomes. In this book, I describe Montessori education as conveyed in Dr. Montessori's writings and in the training courses of the AMI. Although most Montessori schools surely support many of these principles, implementations vary widely. (Variation in Montessori schools is discussed in chapters 11 and 12.)

Another problem in these and many other Montessori outcome studies is that the numbers of children involved was small. Because of these problems and others, conclusions about the impact of Montessori from existing research usually must be very tentative. The right study, using randomly assigned children, a large sample size, many teachers, an excellent Montessori implementation, a long time span, and a variety of outcome measures is yet to be done, although some headway has occurred since the first edition (described in chapter 11). A different approach, taken in the next nine chapters, is to evaluate evidence for component aspects of Montessori education and their support in research.

Chapter Summary

Conventional schools have not fared well owing to the fact that the models of the child and school on which they are built—the empty vessel in the factory—fit poorly with how humans learn. The solutions Americans have devised to fix the problems in our schools repeatedly fail because they do not change these fundamental models. The educational system should instead draw on scientific study of how children learn. Taking such an approach clearly points to the value of revising these fundamental models.

Dr. Maria Montessori took just such an approach in the early 20th century, and the importance of her insights is reflected in their similarity to educational principles generated by modern psychological research. This book discusses nine of Dr. Montessori's major insights on how people learn and develop more optimally. Other authors might have arrived at a different nine: It is clearly not an exhaustive list of Dr. Montessori's insights. The insights discussed here are well supported by modern psychological research and have clear implications for more optimal ways of educating children.

2 }

The Impact of Movement on Learning and Cognition

One of the greatest mistakes of our day is to think of movement by itself, as something apart from the higher functions. . . . Mental development must be connected with movement and be dependent on it. It is vital that educational theory and practice should become informed by this idea.

—Maria Montessori *(1967a/1995, pp. 141–42)*

Movement and learning are perpetually entwined in Montessori education. Beginning in the home or day care, infants sleep on floor beds instead of cribs, so they can move around an entire room to explore and get objects. In Primary classrooms, children move to wash tables and trace Sandpaper Letters, to put large wooden map pieces in place as they learn their names, and to play scales and then compose music on Musical Bells. Older children carry out verbal commands written on cards, both to develop semantic precision and to experience what a verb is. They place colored symbol cards next to words to designate parts of speech. Countable squares and cubes illustrate mathematical concepts: A child can see, feel, and manually experience why 3^3 equals 27. Other mathematics materials work through the child's hand to show how the same formula for area can apply to a regular and an irregular shape. The possible examples are endless: In Montessori classrooms, learning is accomplished through movement.

In contrast, in conventional classrooms most learning is accomplished through listening and reading, reciting and writing. Children spend much of the day seated at desks, taking in lecture information, practicing written exercises, or transitioning between class topics. Except for the symbolic translation involved in writing, their learning is rarely connected to their body movement. For example, children tend to learn what a verb is by reading sentences and finding the verb, not by enacting the verb. They usually learn how to cube numbers by watching the teacher write a cubing problem on the board, then writing out problems themselves, rather than by making cubes and taking them apart. In conventional schooling, bodily movement is limited and consists largely of writing numbers and letters that abstractly represent the concepts being learned. Today, some teachers in conventional schools incorporate hands-on exercises, which is positive. Yet the exercises are add-ons to an essentially lecture-and-recite-based system and are rarely integrated with other work across subject areas.

The conventional classroom's lack of movement fits the Lockean model of the child, in which learning occurs because the child takes in new information and commits it to memory. Behaviorists believed that the child does this because he or she is rewarded (with stars or good grades) for doing so and/or or punished (with demerits or low grades) for not doing so. Behaviorists were not concerned with what goes on inside of the child's mind, only with the outcome: proper recitation on an exam. Movement is not important to learning in this view. In fact, it is easier to pour things into empty vessels or to write on blank slates if they are still.

Conventional education's absence of movement is also convenient for a factory model, because all children do a single lesson in concert. If factory-based education relied on hands-on materials through which children move to learn, it would require one set of such materials for each child. This would be prohibitively expensive and impractical for storage of the materials. Providing children with several textbooks, into each of which many concepts can be packed and then read about in unison, is far more convenient. The factory and empty-vessel models seem to preclude any sizable portion of school learning occurring through movement.

Dr. Montessori saw the stationary child as problematic, because she believed movement and thought were very closely tied. Movement is integral to the educational program she developed. Recent psychological research and theorizing support Dr. Montessori's idea, with many theorists now claiming that cognition is profitably viewed as embodied (Barsalou, 2002; Lakoff & Johnson, 1999; Shapiro, 2011). "Embodied cognition" covers many bases, from the idea that we think in metaphors reflecting how our bodies are constructed and function (Lakoff & Johnson, 1999) to the view that organisms are dynamic systems that develop largely in response to—in adaptation to—their environment (Thelen, 2001).

In this chapter, I describe research supporting the close interconnection of bodily movement with development, thinking, and learning, and how movement is involved in Montessori education. I begin with basic developmental processes and research that shows how development and movement are closely entwined.

Movement and Basic Developmental Processes

Until now, almost all educators have thought of movement and
the muscular system as aids to respiration, or to circulation, or as
a means for building up physical strength. But in our new conception

the view is taken that movement has great importance in mental development itself, provided that the action which occurs *is connected with the mental activity going on.* . . . Watching a child makes it obvious that the development of his mind comes about through his movements. . . . Mind and movement are parts of the same entity.

    — Maria Montessori *(1967a/1995, p. 142, italics in original)*

In this section I discuss research suggesting the importance of movement to very basic developmental processes in infancy, ending with a discussion of Dr. Montessori's ideas about infant movement and about the Practical Life activities in Infant-Toddler and Primary classrooms.

In a classic work published in 1963, Richard Held and Alan Hein tested the effect of self-directed movement on a very basic developmental process: vision. They studied this with kittens because for kittens, as for humans, crucial visual development occurs in the months after birth. Ten pairs of kittens, one a leader and one a follower, were reared in the dark except for 3 hours each day, when they were placed in a normally lit room. While in this room, the leader kitten had attached to its body a harness and cart that pulled the follower kitten around. This set-up allowed the leader to actively explore the environment, guided by vision, while the follower kitten was passively pulled through the same environment. Although the follower had the same visual experience of moving through the environment, it was not actively engaged in the exploration. After three months, the kittens' vision was tested, and the findings suggested that active movement guided by one's vision was crucial to normal visual development. Whereas the leader kittens responded to such events as looming objects and apparent drop-offs, the follower kittens did not show evidence of understanding the possible impact of these environmental features. This classic study set the stage for a wealth of research on the effect of movement on the development of human babies. Learning to move is increasingly recognized as a key development. Children must learn to plan each movement, and successive motor accomplishments accompany cascades of psychological developments (Adolph & Robinson, 2015). That the brain and movement are so closely entwined should perhaps not be surprising. Doidge (2015), in pointing out that plants lack brains because they lack movement, refers to Ascidiacea (the simple sea squirt), an organism that has a brain until it plants itself in a set spot where it will spend the rest of its days—whereupon, no longer needing a brain, it eats it (Llinas, 2001, p. 15). The basic insight regarding the connection between the brain or mind and movement is fundamental to Montessori education and has been entirely lacking in conventional education systems. In this chapter, I first consider an earlier developmental movement, grasping, before moving to the topic of crawling in human babies.

THE IMPACT OF GRASPING OBJECTS

Learning to grasp objects has an important effect on an infant's interest in and knowledge about the physical world. First, infants who more actively explore the environment with their hands are also advanced in their ability to perceive object boundaries, noting where one object ends and another begins (Needham, 2000). We know this because infants at 3 and 4 months who were more actively engaged with teething toys during a pretest phase were more likely to show surprise when two objects moved together than when they moved separately, whereas less-active object explorers showed the opposite pattern. This suggests that interacting with objects may confer important knowledge of the physical world and how objects should behave. Several researchers have noted that once infants begin to reach for objects, they show increased interest in the world of objects (Fogel, Dedo, & McEwen, 1992), and such interest could be the basis of the later knowledge (see chapter 5).

The finding that babies become more interested in objects once they are able to reach for and grasp them is fascinating in light of recent research with monkeys and adult humans. Specific neurons in monkeys fire in response to objects in reachable space. When the monkeys are given a tool (a rake) that enlarges reachable space, those same neurons fire to objects farther away (Iriki, Tanaka, & Iwamura, 1996). The same process occurs on a cognitive level for the perception of space in human adults: When adults are given a tool that will reach more distant objects, they judge those objects to be objectively closer than when they lack such a tool (Witt, Proffitt, & Epstein, 2004). Objects that are harder to grasp are seen as further away than objects that are easier to grasp (Linkenauger, Witt, Stefanucci, Bakdash, & Proffitt, 2009). We respond to what we can interact with, and once babies begin to reach for objects, they become capable of interacting in an expanded world. Once infants can reach out and grasp objects, they also become more attentive to such objects.

The psychologist Amy Needham and her colleagues were interested in whether artificially induced experience picking up objects could precociously induce a heightened interest in objects. If so, that would suggest that it is the ability to get objects, rather than a developmental coincidence in timing, which leads to increased interest in objects. Infants at just 3.5 months were given early experiences getting objects via Velcro mittens that enabled them to pick up objects before their manual coordination was sufficient to do so. The results were striking. Infants who had had 10 to 12 brief play sessions with Velcro mittens later showed far more visual attention to new objects, a much greater propensity to reach for those objects, and even a greater tendency to mouth new objects than did other infants of the same age (Needham, Barrett, & Peterman, 2002). Interest in and knowledge of the physical world were importantly influenced by the ability to get objects.

The development of manual control also appears to be related to intelligence more generally. In a study of adults ages 18 to 62, finger dexterity was found to be importantly related to general intelligence (Dreary, Bell, Bell, Campbell, & Fazal, 2004). In children, fine motor skills are a strong predictor of later school success (Cameron et al., 2012; Grissmer, Grimm, Aiyer, Murrah, & Steele, 2010) and possibly intelligence as well.

Other work shows that advances in infants' manual movements are related to advances in their social cognition. Even by 5 months, infants appear to attribute goals to others. In some of these experiments, infants watched a human hand repeatedly reach out and grab one of two objects (Woodward, 1998). When the infants seemed to be bored with this scene, as indicated by their looking at it less, the placement of the two objects was switched. The person then either reached for the same object in a new location or a new object in the old location. A tendency to look longer—apparently, to regain interest—when the hand got a new object, suggests the beginning of an insight that people have goals, which is a speculation supported in more recent research using imitation tasks as well (Thoermer, Woodward, Sodian, Perst, & Kristen, 2013). Similar findings were obtained for anticipating the actions of others. Infants who successfully put objects inside of other objects were also more likely to anticipate others' similar actions, as indicated by where the infants looked (Cannon, Woodward, Gredebäck, von Hofsten, & Turek, 2012). Interestingly, infants who have the artificially induced early grasping experience (again, conferred by Velcro mittens) attribute goals to others earlier (Sommerville, Woodward, & Needham, 2005). This insight also extends to using a tool versus watching someone else use a tool. Ten-month-olds who had previously manipulated a tool themselves later attributed goals to another person using that tool, whereas 10-month-olds who had previously only observed someone else manipulating the tool did not (Sommerville, Hildebrand, & Crane 2008).

This work extends to manual movements besides grasping. Using a similar paradigm, the psychologist Amanda Woodward and her colleagues found that infants who have themselves reached the important developmental milestone of pointing are more likely to understand the function of pointing in others (Woodward & Guajardo, 2002). In addition, infants who are better at carrying out means-ends activities (such as using a cloth to pull a toy toward themselves) earlier are better at interpreting the means-ends actions of others (Sommerville & Woodward, 2005). Six-month-olds given practice making sounds with a drum later perceived synchronous drum beats (i.e., ones in which the audio matched what was seen) better than did infants who were merely given practice listening (Gerson, Schiavio, Timmers, & Hunnius, 2015). Advances in the use of the hand are clearly related to advances in cognition about both the physical and the social world.

THE IMPACT OF CRAWLING

Some infants scoot themselves around early in life; most then go through a stage in which they crawl; and then virtually all infants finally walk. Although some skip the crawling phase with no apparent disadvantage (Adolph & Robinson, 2015), in those who do crawl, the onset of crawling has been linked to a broad array of advances in both the physical and social domains. These advances include perception of distance, perception of one's own body motion, representation of spatial layout, ability to refer to objects by point-ing, and other social and emotional developments (Campos et al., 2000).

One example of the developmental advances that come with self-locomotion in humans is seen in a study of infants' ability to find hidden objects. Infants, some of whom were already moving themselves (crawling or cruising along on two legs while holding something) and others of whom were not yet mov-ing on their own watched from a distance as an experimenter hid a toy under one of two colored cups. Infants were then carried to the hiding place. Even though all infants were of the same age (7 to 8 months), those infants who had been moving on their own the longest were significantly more likely to find the hidden object than were infants with less or no locomotor experience (Bai & Bertenthal, 1992). This suggests that the onset of self-locomotion is related to developmental advances in the representation of self and space.

Self-generated locomotion is also linked to human babies avoiding steep drop-offs, echoing the Held and Hind finding with kittens reported earlier. Knowledge about how to move safely in the environment develops with self-generated movement (Adolph & Berger, 2006; Campos et al., 2000). Fascinating research by Karen Adolph (summarized in Adolph & Berger, 2006 and Adolph & Robinson, 2015) has shown that this is modality-specific. That is, infants who know to avoid a steep drop-off when crawling need to learn about steep drop-offs all over again when they first begin to walk.

As with grasping, developments accruing with the onset of self-locomotion extend to the social realm as well. A social advance that appears to be related to self-locomotion is following a person's gaze. Following someone's gaze indicates at least rudimentary sensitivity to others' mental lives, and thus is an important milestone in social cognition. Some studies of self-locomotion and gaze following occurred in China (Tao & Dong, 1997, described in Campos et al., 2000). Urban Chinese infants spend much of their awake time propped in a sitting position on a very soft bed, surrounded by thick pillows to prevent falling. Their parents discourage crawling to prevent dirty hands, and they crawl late relative to suburban Chinese infants, who are more often permit-ted to crawl. When tested in a gaze-following procedure, suburban Chinese infants followed about 75% of gazes, whereas urban ones followed only about 50%. Other studies in both the United States and China have shown that even among crawlers, a child's tendency to follow gaze is significantly related to the length of time the child has been crawling (Campos et al., 2000). Self-produced locomotion thus appears to open the door to sharing others' mental experiences.

Learning to walk leads to tremendous changes in social interaction. As compared to crawlers on the floor and crawlers made upright in a baby walker (to eliminate the possible confound of posture), walkers spend much more time interacting with their mothers, vocalizing, and making socially-directed gestures (Clearfield, 2011).

THE IMPORTANCE OF MOVEMENT WITH GOALS

Developments in the use of one's body, both what one can do with one's hand and being able to move in space, surely also influence one's sense of self as agent. Supporting this is research showing that infants who are given a contingency experience early—kicking their legs causes a mobile to move overhead—engage in a lot more kicking than do other infants (Rovee-Collier & Hayne, 2000). Making the mobile move became a goal that inspired movement. In another example of this, when premature infants are given attainable goal objects to reach for, they reach earlier than do other infants (Heathcock, Lobo, & Galloway, 2008). Research with rats shows the neural underpinnings of one's movements having a more challenging goal, as distinct from movements that are mere exercise. Rats were either trained to traverse an elevated obstacle course or given an exercise wheel. Increased density of neural connections was observed only in the rats who did the obstacle course (e.g., Kleim et al., 1998; see also Lillard & Erisir, 2011).

This is not to say that spontaneous movements serve no developmental purpose. Rat fetuses spontaneously display an alternating limb movement pattern, akin to what they will later use to locomote. When a tether is attached to fetal legs causing them to move together, this new pattern continues after the tether is removed. Fetuses thus appear to learn from their spontaneously generated movement (Robinson, Kleven, & Brumley, 2008). Spontaneous movement, including twitching while sleeping, also drives neural development (Blumberg, Marques, & Iida, 2013). In human infants, what are initially "flails" can later be harnessed for intentional purposes, as when a flailing arm accidentally hits a mobile, and then the infant purposely repeats the action (Adolph & Robinson, 2015).

Purposeful activities are reinforcing for infants, and self-generated movement is clearly tied to even very basic processes of mental development. Even spontaneous movements are important to development. These research findings support Dr. Montessori's contention that, to assist development, children should be encouraged to move their hands and their bodies from an early age.

Movement in the Infant-Toddler and Primary Programs

Movement is deeply implicated in Montessori education. Chapter 1 described a sequence of materials involved in learning how to write, each of which employed carefully prescribed movements: tracing Sandpaper Letters; tracing geometric shapes with one's finger and in the process, creating wrist movements; running a delicate wooden stick around the borders of leaf shapes; picking up cylinders by their small knobs to strengthen the pincer muscles; tracing the insides of Metal Insets to educate the hand in use of the pencil; arranging objects and moving cards that state each object's name near it; moving cardboard letters to form words; and so on. That description shows the variety of movements children engage in for one learning sequence in the Primary curriculum and contrasts sharply with the traditional method of looking at letters to eventually memorize them for reading (which is traditionally learned prior to writing). Yet the importance of movement in Montessori education is apparent well before the Primary curriculum.

ENCOURAGING GRASPING IN MONTESSORI

First, Dr. Montessori advised that infants be given objects to explore manually. This seems banal today, but Dr. Montessori's idea that infants should have objects, such as mobiles, rattles, and bells, to inspire reaching and grasping was apparently revolutionary for her time. Rattles had been provided earlier, but expressly for medical reasons: They included coral, which people thought protected children from illness (Calvert, 1992; McClary, 1997). Surely people must have also seen the entertainment value of such toys, but concern with their use in guiding development was not common at the time. The field of child study, in fact, was in its infancy in the early 1900s. More recently, discoveries concerning the effect of "enriched" environments on the brains of laboratory rats has led to Americans filling cribs with all kinds of objects for exploration, but Dr. Montessori advised giving young children only a limited choice of carefully selected objects (see chapter 3).

Her purpose in providing objects was to assist children's manual—and thus their mental—development. "In order to develop his mind a child must have objects in his environment which he can hear and see. Since he must develop himself through his movements, through the work of his hands, he has need of objects with which he can work that provide motivation for his activity" (Montessori, 1966, p. 82). The benefits of objects continue beyond infancy, as suggested by findings that across seven countries, provision of a greater variety of manipulable objects in preschools was associated with better cognitive development (Montie, Xiang, & Schweinhart, 2006); stressing their importance beginning in infancy was prescient.

Montessori infant courses present a sequence of objects to be presented to babies as they become more able to move (see P. Lillard & Jessen, 2003). These are intended to encourage babies to move their hands and their whole bodies. For example, as babies become old enough to wave their arms above them, Montessorians hang a graspable ring on an elastic band above babies' heads, close enough so it can be grasped, mouthed, and allowed to pop back in place for an interesting result. Caregivers are encouraged to place attractive objects, such as bright wooden rattles, just outside of infants' reach, giving an incentive for movement.

ENCOURAGING SELF-LOCOMOTION IN MONTESSORI

Whereas rattles have become commonplace, a still-radical Montessori recommendation for infants is that they sleep on a low mattress on the floor, to give them a larger space in which to move.[1] This of course requires that parents childproof the entire bedroom. Theoretically, being able to move to interesting places in the environment (such as a low shelf with books or toys) could assist infants' development in learning to move with a purpose. In addition, being able to crawl to objects makes them reachable, and (consistent with the research just described) the environment to which the child attends thus probably expands as well. As stated, Dr. Montessori recommended that a baby's toys be placed at a slight distance away at first, in order to encourage the baby to move a short distance to them. As the baby becomes more competent at moving (even prior to crawling), the toys are moved farther away, again to encourage movement. An interesting issue for further research is the Montessori claim that even prior to crawling, babies who sleep on floor beds push themselves about with their legs much more so than do crib babies, and that, once crawling, they crawl more because they are inspired to get objects they can see at a distance. Given the findings just reviewed, such experiences would be expected to have associated developments in understanding the social and physical world.

Montessorians also recommend that babies be given sufficient time on their stomachs to develop upper arm strength, to encourage crawling. Recent research showing a reduced incidence of sudden infant death syndrome in back sleepers precludes advocating putting babies on their stomachs to sleep, but research has shown that children who sleep on their stomachs reach many gross motor milestones, including crawling, somewhat earlier than do children who sleep on their backs; side sleepers are intermediate between the two (Davis, Moon, Sachs, & Ottolini,

---

[1] Floor beds are mentioned as a positive childrearing innovation by G. Stanley Hall (1911), suggesting the idea was in vogue in Europe at that time.

1998), perhaps because they sometimes roll to their stomachs and get some experience pushing up their heads. In another study, at 6 months, stomach sleepers were more advanced in their social development and communication relative to back sleepers. In absolute terms, these differences were still apparent at 18 months, but statistically they were no longer significant (Dewey, Fleming, & Golding, 1998). However, one problem dampening the results of this study was that mothers were asked about sleep position only once, at 4 weeks, and it is likely that sleep position changed later. Because parents tend to relax with time, and (at least anecdotally) many babies sleep better on their stomachs, it is likely that a proportion of babies who were sleeping on their stomachs by 3 or 4 months were still classified in the "back sleepers" group. Another study found that only 44% of infants' sleep positions were consistent from 1 week to 6 months (Davis et al., 1998). Montessorians recommend that babies get sufficient time on their stomachs, and research suggests this would impact the precocity of development.

Dr. Montessori recommended that as soon as children are able to walk, use of strollers and other carriers should become minimal (Montessori, 1967a/1995, p. 157). She believed children would develop best if they were in charge of their own movements and free to explore the environment (with limitations imposed when safety or social regulation would be compromised). She also recommended that young children have a small, stable table and chair at which to eat, from which they can move about themselves, rather than a high chair to which they would have to be lifted—again to encourage their independence with respect to their own movement. She also believed children's furniture should be lightweight, so children could move it if they desired. Such light furniture would also allow them to learn to control their own movements: If one bumps a light table, the table moves. She believed this would teach children to control their movements better than would bumping into heavier objects, which do not move. In sum, Montessori advocated encouraging movement to assist mental development by virtue of the objects available to infants, the physical space they could access, and the implements with which they are reared.

POTENTIAL EFFECTS OF MONTESSORI PRACTICES
ON BASIC DEVELOPMENT

Many current cultural practices with infants inhibit self-directed movement. Infant swings, strollers, cribs, and playpens are all about confining infants and making them move passively, like Held and Hein's follower kittens. Do children who live among lighter pieces of furniture learn to control their body movements better? Do any lasting effects accrue from these different approaches to infant movement? These are interesting topics for further research.

The research presented here suggests that over the short term, there might be psychological impacts, such as advanced social cognition. However, one principle of development is that very little of a given experience is needed to set a normal developmental trajectory in motion, so whether such arrangements would have any effect beyond the first year is questionable and would require careful study. In addition, babies who lack self-locomotor experience owing to developmental problems otherwise appear to function normally, so there are alternative paths that can be taken to "normal development" in broad strokes. Whether there are developmental differences that only more refined tests would reveal is an empirical question.

An example of the subtlety of differences one might examine is suggested by cross-cultural research. Although Asians and Americans on the surface appear to think quite similarly, more refined studies have shown that there are fascinating differences in how we perceive scenes. When asked to describe a scene showing fish swimming in a fishbowl, adult Asians are more likely to mention the background (the rocks and plants) than are Americans, who are apt to focus exclusively on the central element or agent, such as the most prominent fish (Nisbett, 2003). This subtle difference, one might speculate, could *in part* result from such factors as opportunities for movement in infancy. Unlike American babies, who, until recently, usually slept on their stomachs, Asian babies have traditionally slept on their backs, so chances are the Americans in these studies were prone sleepers as infants and the Asians were supine sleepers. The prone position leads to earlier crawling and might be one among many cultural practices that subtly influence a focus on agency and the American tendency to locate agents in scenes. Clearly, normal development occurs in both cultures with both sleep positions, and many different cultural practices, including differences in language (see A. Lillard, 1998), could feed into these different orientations toward agency and the world.

Dr. Montessori's ideas about giving infants objects were revolutionary for her time, and her ideas about providing locomotor experience are against the grain today as strollers are increasingly employed to get children through shopping malls and airports. Research clearly supports the view that grasping and self-locomotion have short-term effects on children's understanding of the physical and social world. Over the long haul, normal development (as viewed in broad strokes) still occurs even in the absence of movement, and whether precocious self-movement has subtle but meaningful psychological influences is an open question. Montessori practices in this case are not necessarily prescribed by the research: At least in the ways that have been tested, and in ways that are readily apparent, children with more and less early locomotor experience still reach the same end points in development. For example, children who crawl earlier show fear of drop-offs earlier, but all children with normal vision and experience do develop this fear at the point in development when it becomes useful (e.g., when they crawl). However, Dr. Montessori's insight that movement and development are closely entwined presaged current psychology research, and knowing earlier that one can move about in the environment and do things may have lasting effects on psychological development that have not yet been noticed or studied.

Beyond Infancy: Montessori's Exercises of Practical Life

Montessori Toddler and Primary programs have exercises designed to inspire movements directed to constructive ends, called the Exercises of Practical Life. These activities take care of such practical life concerns as washing floors, polishing wood, watering plants, and preparing and serving a snack or lunch. Some of the main purposes of including such exercises in the classroom are (1) to educate children's movements to be geared to a purpose; (2) to develop children's ability to concentrate on a task; (3) to help children learn to carry out a series of steps in sequence; and (4) to help children learn to care for the environment. As such, these exercises are foundational to many aspects of Montessori education. Regarding the relationship between movement and cognition, these exercises are particularly important because they employ the body in the service of the mind to fulfill a meaningful goal. Research has not addressed the relationship between development and the longer sequences of actions toward goals that are the Exercises of Practical Life, but the research about the impact of such simpler activities toward goals as grasping objects and crawling to destinations suggests the possibility of a relationship.

Dr. Montessori observed that children are motivated to care for the environment and are capable of doing so if provided with attractive sets of materials geared to that end. She also believed young children to be very attracted to precision in the early years, such that they like to know exactly what sequence of steps to perform in an exercise, or exactly how to place the soap in a soap dish, for example. She considered early childhood to be a sensitive period for attention to precision, a possibility that would be interesting to explore in research. The Exercises of Practical Life are intended to appeal to such motivations in children.

As one example of a Practical Life exercise, Montessori Toddler and Primary classrooms are normally equipped with a set of materials for Table Washing.[2] This set typically includes a large basin to fill with water, a plastic mat to go under the table, soap, a scrub brush, a sponge, and a towel for

---

[2] Table Washing is capitalized because it is a Montessori exercise, taught in Primary Teacher Training courses.

drying. The items are all of a size and weight appropriate to a small child, and are usually of the same color, so that they obviously go together. Like other materials in Montessori classrooms, they are chosen to appeal to children, in order to inspire use. The teacher demonstrates for the child a precise sequence of actions that are carried out in Table Washing (described in more detail in chapter 10): Carry the items to the table, lay out the plastic mat just so, fill the bucket to this line, and so on. The child has probably also observed other children carrying out the sequence of actions, enabling him or her to learn by observation (discussed in chapter 7).

What is important about these movements, from a Montessori perspective, is not so much that the table becomes clean, but that the child is engaged in a purposeful activity, employing the hands in the service of the mind. The motions to be carried out are executed in a particular sequence and manner that suit the purpose. This overarching goal of executing a series of actions to fulfill a goal began with the simple operations of reaching and crawling to objects. For Montessori education, it culminates in the schoolwork to come, for example, in the sequence of steps needed to execute a mathematical proof. Practical Life activities educate the child to perform organized sequences of activity, employing the body in the service of the mind.

A somewhat different Practical Life activity for children at the Toddler and Primary levels is Dressing Frames, square wooden frames with a cloth "shutter" on each side and a series of ties, snaps, or buttons or a zipper down the center (Figure 2.1). These frames assist children in developing the skills needed for fastening their own clothes. This activity is somewhat different from most Montessori Practical Life exercises in that using the Dressing Frames does not accomplish a practical purpose directly: Their purpose is indirect. It is interesting to consider why Dr. Montessori developed special frames for learning these particular skills, rather than having children learn on their own clothing, which is the ultimate goal. Practical Life activities normally have a practical end, filling a real need in the classroom. Tables really do get dirty and need to be washed; carrots need to be cut up for snacks; plants need to be watered; shoes are more aesthetically pleasing when polished; and so on. Movement serves real and apparent goals in a Montessori classroom. As is discussed in chapter 8, finding meaning in one's activities is important at all ages, and educators should be concerned that no activity be "busy work." The Dressing Frames are an exception to the Montessori norm of "real" goals, because unlike buttoning one's own shirt, buttoning a Dressing Frame serves no direct practical purpose. Instead of *directly* serving an important goal, the Dressing Frames indirectly assist in that goal by teaching children to use clothing fasteners. The Montessori rationale for this is that working on one's own clothing can be frustrating to an extent that can hamper learning. Dressing Frames provide an alternative, less frustrating, way to learn those skills than using one's own clothing. Some Montessori

FIGURE 2.1 Dressing Frames. Photograph by An Vu.

activities are preliminary; when children master preliminary steps, they move on to the full activity.

That Practical Life activities serve a practical purpose is theoretically important because Dr. Montessori believed that for action to be useful to mental development, "the action that occurs must be connected with the mental activity going on" (Montessori, 1967a/1995, p. 142). Only real goals truly engage the mind in the movement. Thus in authentic Montessori classrooms, children polish their actual shoes, not a demonstration shoe that lives on a shelf. In addition to providing meaning for actions, Practical Life activities lead children to practice concentration, a hallmark of Montessori education. Through concentration, Dr. Montessori believed children develop an inner calm that they bring to their other activities in the classroom. Dr. Montessori called the peace that she saw to be achieved through concentration "normalization," a term she borrowed from anthropology to indicate that one can participate in society. She observed that most of children's troublesome behaviors disappeared when they experienced concentration on meaningful activities. Young children's concentration often occurs in the context of their motor activities, for example, in learning to walk, or feeding oneself with a spoon. Concentration is discussed further in chapter 4.

The foundations of Practical Life activities in the Primary years are considered vital to the ability to function well in Elementary classrooms; children who lack the Primary Montessori experience might have more difficulty concentrating on Montessori work. They can also lack other skills and knowledge learned in Primary, including such specifically academic skills as reading, writing, and math, foundational vocabulary, and more general skills such as self-motivation, self-direction, and self-discipline. These building blocks for work in Montessori Elementary are expected to be established during the Primary years.

Research on Movement and Cognition

When one moves with a purpose, there is a sense in which one's body is aligned with one's thought. Thought guides action. In the embodied cognition perspective, the purpose of the brain is to guide action, and we think as we do because of the bodies we have (Glenberg, Witt, & Metcalfe, 2013). Indeed, paraplegics are significantly impaired in their ability to perceive a person walking in an impoverished stimulus display (Arrighi, Cartocci, & Burr, 2011). Research concerning three other ways that body and thought are aligned is discussed next, followed by presentation of two sequences of Montessori materials to illustrate how Montessori education capitalizes on body–mind connections. The first area of research concerns the representation of space, objects, and mathematics.

REPRESENTATION OF SPACE, OBJECTS, AND MATHEMATICS

Studies have shown that when people move themselves through space, both real and imagined, they are better able to represent that space than when they are passively moved through it or do not move at all. In one study, 10-month-olds watched as an experimenter hid a toy under one of two cloths. On four such trials, the infants were then allowed to crawl to where they could remove the cloth and get the toy, and on four other trials, they were carried to that place (at crawling speed) by their mothers (Benson & Uzgiris, 1985). On the crawling trials, most the infants found the toy at their first try (by removing the right cloth) on most of their trials. In contrast, only 1 of the 26 infants had this level of success when they were carried to the hiding location. The act of moving themselves in space, rather than being carried, apparently allowed the infants—all of whom were developmentally able to crawl—to better keep track of the spatial layout of the environment.

In another study, school-aged children more accurately imagined a familiar spatial arrangement after walking through the imagined space. To test how well the space was represented, children, who were blindfolded in their bedrooms at the time of testing, were asked to imagine they were in their school classroom, and were then asked to point to various locations in the classroom from the vantage point of the teacher's desk. This exercise was sometimes preceded by walking from their own imagined desk to the teacher's desk. When children had walked across the imagined room to the teacher's desk first, they more rapidly and accurately pointed out locations of objects from the teachers' perspective than they did when they remained at their own imagined desk (Rieser, Garing, & Young, 1994). Walking across one's room, engaging one's body with one's imagination (even while blindfolded), stimulated a more accurate and accessible representation of the imagined school classroom.

This finding naturally extends to walking through the actual space one is representing. In another illustration of movement assisting spatial representation, children learning to read maps did so better when they walked across the territory to be mapped (a new campus) than when they sat in a classroom and merely imagined that territory (Griffin, 1995). This experiment is also particularly relevant to chapter 8, which deals with the importance of meaningful contexts for learning. These three experiments show that infants and children represent space better when moving themselves through the represented space than when remaining still or being moved passively.

In addition to better imagining where objects are in space, people also better imagine how objects and substances move when they perform actions that simulate those movements. One study asked people to judge the angle at which both a wide and a thin glass, each containing imagined water to the same level, would pour. People were often wrong when they simply thought about the problem: They judged that water would pour out of both glasses at the same angle. However, when they were allowed to tilt glasses of imaginary water, even with their eyes closed, they correctly tilted the narrow glass farther than the wide one (Schwartz & Black, 1999). Thus, when cognition aligned with movement, more accurate representation resulted.

Another study showing the positive effect of movement on cognition addressed the incorrect intuition that when a single object moves, all parts of the object move at the same speed (Levin, Siegler, & Druyan, 1990). Sixth-graders were given one of two treatments aimed at correcting this intuition. One was visual training: Children watched as a carousel-like device carried two teddy bears around in a circle. The teddy bears were placed on a single rod, one closer to the center and the other further out on the rod as it rotated around the center of the carousel. The second condition involved the children taking the place of the teddy bears, walking themselves in either the outer or the inner position on the rods of the carousel. After having either the visual or the kinesthetic experience, children judged whether two dogs on a similar device were moving at the same speed. During the pretest, all of the children had incorrectly responded that they were moving at the same speed. After training, the children who moved around the carousel themselves responded correctly on 79% of trials that the outside dog must be moving faster. In contrast, those in the visual training condition were only 46% correct. Bodily movement that was consistent with what was being learned led to better learning than merely observing.

A somewhat different example of the effect of movement on cognition comes from studies of abacus experts (Stigler, 1984). Children who are more expert at using the abacus are more proficient at solving math problems, even when they are not using the abacus. This proficiency apparently stems from the fact that abacus experts imagine the movements they would make were the abacus present. Thus, even in the absence of the actual movement of the abacus beads, rendering the symbolic concrete via routine use of the abacus improved calculation. Another study compared learning on a virtual abacus (instantiated symbolically on a two-dimensional screen, with parts moved by a computer mouse) with learning on a physical abacus. Although the two groups performed similarly on basic problems, third-graders who learned with the physical abacus were significantly more likely to transfer their learning to new problems than were children who learned with the computer application (Flanagan, 2013). Comparison of virtual versus physical materials for learning is an active and exciting area of research (Manches & O'Malley, 2012; Pouw, Van Gog, & Paas, 2014). Many "apps" of Montessori materials are also available, and it is crucial that their efficacy be tested (see the following sections).

In sum, several studies show that representations of space and objects are improved when movement is involved. The entwining of movement and cognition is also shown in tasks concerning evaluation and categorization of verbal material.

MOVEMENT AND JUDGMENT

Many studies also show that when cognitive processing of verbal material and actions are aligned, the processes or actions are faster or more accurate than when they are not so aligned. For example, when asked to shake or nod one's head while listening to messages that are either agreeable or disagreeable, people move their heads faster when the direction of nodding corresponds to the valence of the message (Wells & Petty, 1980). Thus, movement that aligns with what one is thinking is faster than movement that contradicts what one is thinking, even when the relationship between the movement and the thought is fairly abstract, as in nodding and finding something agreeable.

When the central verb of sentences is consistent with their own action, people make quicker judgments as to whether sentences make sense (Glenberg & Kaschak, 2002). Specifically, people are quicker to judge (by pressing a button) the sense of sentences such as "He threw the ball to me" when, to register that judgment, they have to move their hand toward themselves (to press a button that is closer to them than their hand's resting position), consistent with "threw to me." They are slower to judge "He threw the ball away from me" when the button they have to press is closer to them. When the hand and button positions are reversed, the pattern of results reverses, showing that the results stem from the relationship between direction of movement and the concept embodied in the central verb, not some other feature of the experiment. People also categorize objects faster when they simultaneously perform the prototypical action for those objects (Barsalou, 2008; Tucker & Ellis, 2001).

Another kind of movement is gesture, which occurs frequently when people engage in conversation. Some have suggested that people might gesture to assist their own cognitive processing of abstract ideas in conversation. A naturalistic study by the anthropologist Elinor Ochs and her colleagues showed that people tend to gesture more when the thoughts they need to convey are more complex. High-energy physicists gestured in ways that simulated what they were thinking, particularly when struggling to understand a new hypothesis (Ochs, Gonzales, & Jacoby, 1996). The physicists seemed to have been capitalizing on the possibility that gesturing can assist cognition (McNeill, 1992). Whereas some believe that gestures can assist the thinking of listeners as well as speakers and that gestures serve a communicative function, others believe that gestures serve to assist lexical retrieval: Meaning is often reflected in one's gestures right before the words that denote that meaning are uttered (Krauss & Hadar, 1999). Both of these theories agree that gesture facilitates thought, a supposition confirmed by a recent meta-analysis of 63 studies (Hostetter, 2011). This analysis revealed a moderate effect of gesture on comprehension that is stronger (1) for children than adults, (2) for concepts related to movement than for abstract concepts, and (3) when speech and gesture partially but do not completely overlap. Later in the chapter, I will return to the issue of gestures and symbolic developments such as language.

MEMORY

Many studies have shown that memory improves when one's movements align with what is to be remembered. For example, when students enact the content of action-describing sentences at encoding, they remember those sentences better than when they learn the sentences without enacting them (R. L. Cohen, 1989; Engelkamp, Zimmer, Mohr, & Sellen, 1994). One might be concerned that this is only because when one has to move while memorizing something, one has to put more effort into the memorizing, thus one processes the stimuli more deeply. Other work, however, suggests it is not caused by deeper processing. Discussion and writing also involve deep processing, and yet student actors recalled a play character's monologue better when they actively improvised what the character was like than when they wrote about or discussed the character (Scott, Harris, & Rothe, 2001).

In another illustration of the effect of movement on memory, actors have been shown to better recall, 5 months after the final performance of a play, the dialogue they issued while moving on the stage than the dialogue they issued while standing in one place (Noice, Noice, & Kennedy, 2000; see also Noice & Noice, 2006). Stage movements tend to reflect in some manner the content of what is being uttered, again suggesting that when movement is in concert with thinking, memory is improved.

Even facial movements are associated with improved memory. People remember humorous information better when they smile (accomplished by making them hold a pencil between their teeth) and anger-provoking information better when they are frowning (the pencil is between their lips) (Laird, Wagener, Halal, & Szegda, 1982; Niedenthal, 2007). These findings might stem from making facial expressions affecting one's mood, which then affects memory, rather the expression affecting memory directly, because people who reported no mood alteration in this paradigm did not show the memory effect. But when facial movement corresponds with the valence of what one is thinking about, one remembers it better, illustrating the close connection between the body and the mind.

Mimicking others' faces also appears to lead to improved recall of those faces. When asked to memorize high school yearbook photographs, people remembered the faces better to the degree that they mimicked those others' facial expressions while viewing them. Interfering with that imitation interfered with the ability to memorize: When participants were asked to chew gum while viewing the faces, thereby eliminating their ability to mimic the expression during encoding, memory performance dropped significantly (Zajonc, Pietromonaco, & Bargh, 1982). Chewing gum did not interfere with other cognitive tasks, so the face-memorizing result was probably not caused by the mental diversion imposed by gum chewing.

Finally, research done by Sierra Eisen in my laboratory shows that children learn geography much more efficiently from a hands-on Montessori geography puzzle than from a Montessori "app" intended to mimic that puzzle. After limited exposure in the laboratory, children who took out, traced around, and moved physical puzzle pieces remembered significantly more Australian states than children who used an app; when children took the puzzle or app home for a week, children learned far more per minute of usage from the puzzle than the app.

SOCIAL COGNITIVE PROCESSING

Another illustration of the effect of movement on cognition concerning faces and emotion is that to the degree that people mimic a facial expression while judging the content of that expression (smile, frown, and so on), they discriminate the expression more quickly (Wallbott, 1991). This relation exists even for reading about emotions (Niedenthal, Winkielman, Mondillon, & Vermeulen, 2009). People are also faster at reading sentences when they can express an emotion that is congruent with the sentence (Havas, Glenberg, & Rinck, 2007). Botox, which people inject in their faces to remove wrinkles, actually slows emotion processing, with profound implications for social relationships (Havas, Glenberg, Gutowski, Lucarelli, & Davidson, 2010). When we are engaged in conversation with others, we move our faces to mimic theirs (Bavelas, Black, Lemery, & Mullett, 1987; Bavelas, Black, Chovil, Lemery, & Mullett, 1988). That married couples really do come to look more alike over time (which they do; Zajonc, Alderman, Murphy, & Niedenthal, 1987) may be a consequence of this, presumably because habitually mimicking facial expressions in empathic communication leads to the same wrinkle lines (Bargh, 2001). Supporting this, the degree of similarity in married couples' faces is highly related to their level of marital satisfaction (Zajonc et al., 1987). In other words, those who imitate the other's facial expression, perhaps thereby more quickly discriminating and empathizing with their underlying mental state, have better marriages than those who do not!

Research Summary

Abundant research shows that movement and cognition are closely intertwined. People represent spaces and objects more accurately, make judgments faster and more accurately, remember information better, and show superior social cognition when their movements are aligned with what they are thinking about or learning. Conventional classrooms are not set up to capitalize on the relationship between movement and cognition. In contrast, Montessori has movement at its core.

Movement in Montessori Primary and Elementary Classrooms

The study of a child's psychological development must be
bound up with the study of his hand's activities. . . . Those
children who have been able to work with their hands make
headway in their development.
    — Maria Montessori *(1967a/1995, p. 152)*

In this section, I show how specific Montessori materials capitalize on movement. First I present some Sensorial Materials, followed by an early sequence of mathematics materials.

SENSORIAL MATERIALS IN THE MONTESSORI
PRIMARY CLASSROOM

In addition to assisting the development of concentration, the ability to make judgments, and the ability to move with purpose, the Montessori Sensorial Materials educate the senses. In sharp contrast to conventional schooling, sensory education is foundational in Montessori. Primary children shake and listen to the various sounds made by the Sound Cylinders. Two are filled with the same type of material and therefore make the same sound, and the child's task is to listen carefully and pair them up. In another Sensorial exercise, children line up Color Tablets from darkest to lightest, or match Color Tablets by color first, and later (as color perception becomes more finely tuned) by increasingly more similar hues. In another exercise, the Rough and Smooth Boards, children feel different degrees of roughness and smoothness on sandpaper tablets, and pair them or arrange them from smoothest to roughest.

Sensorial Materials are discussed further in chapter 10, which focuses on order, because the methodical approach Montessori takes to educating the senses has interesting implications for the organization of the developing brain. They are also discussed in chapter 4, which focuses on executive function, because of the relation between sensory awareness and mindfulness. The important point for this chapter is that the senses are educated not in the context of passively perceiving, but in the context of making perceptual judgments while acting on the environment. In contrast to conventional education, in which the body is merely a house for the mind, which takes in information, in Montessori education the body is an active entity that moves in the service of the mind. In using the Sensorial Materials, the child has to perceive, make judgments, reason, and decide by his or her actions on materials.

Some of the Sensorial Materials also form the basis for mathematics, by educating the child to attend (via movement) to dimension. There are three materials, introduced after the Wooden Cylinders described in chapter 1, to teach three basic concepts: size (the Pink Tower), thickness (the Brown Stair), and length (the Red Rods). These materials are described in some detail to give a flavor of how Montessori materials have been integrally designed to gradually introduce children to increasingly complex concepts. These concepts are conveyed to children not so much through the eyes and ears (the teacher's verbal introduction is minimal), but through the child's hands with repeated use of the material. Cognition is born from manual movement.

The Pink Tower (shown in Figure 2.2) is a series of 10 graduated cubes, the dimensions of which increase by one unit (1 cm) on all sides as one moves from the smallest cube to the largest. The cubes are all the same color, which Dr. Montessori claimed helped keep the child's focus on the dimension of interest, the gradually increasing size. Research shows that Dr. Montessori was correct about this. The "pop-out" effect occurs when just one feature

FIGURE 2.2 The Pink Tower. Photograph by An Vu.

of an object is different from other objects it is among. In such cases, people are much faster to pick out that object, relative to when several features vary among the background objects in a display (Treisman & Gelade, 1980). In contrast, many toys designed for young children vary several dimensions simultaneously (such as differently colored stacking cups). Whether this delays children's ability to stack the cups, relative to when they are the same color, is an empirical question. The research with adults suggests that it would.

The smallest Pink Tower cube is 1 cm long on each side, the second is 2 cm, and so on, up to the largest, which is 10 cm per side. The decimal system is thus inherent in this material, which the 3-year-old uses by building a tower of the cubes, placing the largest one on the bottom, the next largest one next, and so on, up to the smallest.

The Pink Tower is normally found in its stacked tower form on the floor in the Sensorial area of a Primary Classroom. To use the Pink Tower, a child takes a small (2-foot × 3-foot) rug rolled up in a rug container and finds an open area on the floor on which to roll out the rug. The child then goes and gets the pieces of the Pink Tower, one by one, and carries them to the rug. Having to learn to walk through the maze of tables, shelves, and other children's rugs is considered to be important for educating children in control of the body: If you bump into something, it has consequences. The act of carrying the cubes singly from their usual place to the rug is also considered important, because it provides an opportunity for the child to feel the difference in weight and size in the cubes, something the child will notice again when he or she creates the tower. When the child has placed all the pieces in a random arrangement on the rug, he or she finds the largest one and begins the tower, placing each successively smaller cube on top of the previous one.

An important aspect of this and many Montessori materials is that they are self-correcting. If children go wrong, and miss one of the cubes in the series, they will later be faced with a larger cube needing to go on top of a smaller one. In this way, Montessori materials incorporate what is called the Control of Error, a topic discussed more in chapter 6.

Using the Pink Tower material is intended to bring many concepts to the child's mind via the hand, such as the concept of natural numbers from 1 to 10, the decimal system, and the notion of cubing. Eight cubes the size of the first would be needed to make the second, and so on. It might appear to be odd that a complicated notion such as cubing is indirectly introduced at such an early stage, yet Dr. Montessori was not loathe to implicitly introduce complex concepts early, and she believed a three-dimensional difference is easier for children to perceive than a one- or two-dimensional difference, which is an interesting question for research.

It is worth noting here the brilliance of Montessori education in introducing mathematics through spatial concepts. Mathematics is fundamentally about measuring the world. Conventional education begins with numeracy, but spatial understanding is conceptually more foundational to math (Mix & Cheng, 2012). In keeping with this, preschool children's performance on spatial tasks, including learning geometric figures, predicts their later performance on numeracy-related tasks (Verdine, Golinkoff, Hirsh-Pasek, & Newcombe, in press). First introducing the child to spatial dimension and then to its measurement it is a fundamentally different approach to math education, as radical as Dr. Montessori's idea of introducing reading through writing.

Working with objects such as the Pink Tower also is intended to train the child's powers of observation, judgment, and decision making, in that the child must carefully observe features of objects, discriminate differences, and decide which cube to place upon the tower next. Dr. Montessori maintained that by handling these cubes and creating the tower, the child is both coming into contact with basic mathematical concepts and developing important life skills. Whether such work actually does assist the child in these ways remains a topic for empirical investigation. Clearly the intent is that the child's developing cognition is embodied: The child moves in the service of thought, perceiving and then acting on differences in size.

The Pink Tower, like all of the Montessori materials, is used in many more ways, in a series of lessons called *extensions*. For example, a child will place a second rug across the classroom from the first and will build the Pink Tower on the second rug from a collection of blocks randomly arranged on the first one. This requires that children keep in mind what they need as they traverse the room, so the extension exercise challenges skills of attention and concentration. Another extension has the teacher, or another child, bring some of the cubes to the second rug and ask the child to "Get me the one that is just larger than this one" or "Get me the one that is just smaller." Again, the child has to traverse the obstacle course of rugs and tables in the classroom, all the while bearing in mind the size of the cube that is needed. The Montessori materials have a wealth of extension exercises, leading children to engage with the materials in new ways over many repetitions to further understanding.

The next Sensorial Material to be introduced in the curriculum is the Brown Stair, shown in Figure 2.3, which consists of 10 solid oblong wooden blocks ("prisms") of the same length, but of gradually increasing height and width, which can be arranged like a staircase. The height and width of the smallest Brown Stair prism are one-tenth the height and width of the largest one; the ones in between are successively 1 cm different along both dimensions. The children's task is to arrange the prisms from smallest to largest, creating a stair. The mathematical concept of squares is inherent in the materials, as it would take four of the first prism to make the second, nine of the first to make the third, and so on. In building the stair, the child is introduced to the rudiments of such concepts and is given a reason to attend to relative height and width (to arrange them in sequence). Again, there are many extensions on the use of this material; this basic introduction gives a flavor of how dimensional concepts are introduced via the child's actions on objects.

The next material is the Red Rods. These rods are all of the same thickness, 2.5 cm on each side. This size was intentionally chosen to be thick enough to support the length of the rods, yet be easily grasped by a small child's hand. The rods vary only in length. The shortest one is 10 cm long, and each successive one is 10 cm longer than the previous one, so the longest rod is 100 cm. One Montessori teacher observed to me that some children do not appear even to see the difference in these lengths at first, but must learn to perceive the difference. The teacher assists the child's learning by showing the child how widely one has to stretch one's arms to hold the longest one

FIGURE 2.3 The Brown Stair. Photograph by An Vu.

versus a shorter one, how the rods differ in weight, and so on. With the help of their bodies, children learn to perceive the differences in the Red Rods and to line them up from shortest to longest. In addition to helping children perceive dimension (which leads into math, as described in the following section), these materials assist children in learning to reason and decide, to concentrate on an activity, to work toward a goal, and so on.

EARLY MATH MATERIALS

The Sensorial Materials in Montessori are designed to introduce mathematical concepts. The transition from Sensorial to Math Materials is a simple step: A new set of rods is introduced, just like the Red Rods, except on the Number Rods each 10 cm unit is painted alternately red and blue (Figure 2.4). The child carries these rods to his or her rug and arranges them from shortest to longest. The teacher shows the child how to count the units on each rod, arriving at the cardinal number with which it is identified, and to name the rods, "One," "Two," "Three," and so on, while touching each rod. The teacher begins with the shortest few rods, gradually adding more as the child appears to be ready for them. The child touches each unit as he or she

FIGURE 2.4 The Number Rods. Photograph by An Vu.

counts, so the hand is bringing the information to the mind. The child also learns to play a game with the rods: One person says, "Give me One, give me Two," and so on, at which the other person hands over the appropriate rod. Later the other party (a teacher or perhaps another child) will say, "What is this?" while holding up each rod, and they will count the parts together, touching each unit with their hands as they name it. The sequence of (1) the teacher showing the child, then (2) asking the child for a particular item, then (3) asking the child to name a particular item is called the "Three Period Lesson." Discussed in chapter 6 as a means of evaluation, the Three Period Lesson is essentially first teaching the child a new concept, then asking the child to recognize the concept, and then finally asking the child to recall the concept.

The Sensorial Materials and the Number Rods introduce abstract concepts via concrete objects. The next step in this sequence of materials is to give children abstract symbols standing for numbers, enabling the possibility of eventually working with larger numbers. To take the child from a concrete understanding of number, based on the length of the rods, into this abstract realm, the teacher shows the child how to place Sandpaper Number cards beside each rod. These are similar to the Sandpaper Letters shown in Figure 1.9.

Montessori introduces numbers not as individual units summed, but as wholes: the length of a rod. This carries over to learning to add numbers. The concept of adding 1 and 3, for example, is introduced by placing the 1 rod at the end of the 3 rod, placing the 4 rod adjacent to that sum, and seeing that the combination of the 1 and 3 rods is equivalent to the 4 rod. Dr. Montessori believed that to learn in individual units, for example by counting out single chips as might be done in conventional schools, the child learns $1 + 1 + 1 + 1$, but not $3 + 1$ (Montessori, 1914/1965). The question of whether children learn to sum numbers more easily from materials such as the Number Rods rather than individual items is ripe for empirical research. Children have been shown to partition amounts better when using simple blocks than when using paper and pencil or no materials (Manches, O'Malley, & Benford, 2010).

Individual units are introduced next, with a material called the Spindle Box. Shown in Figure 2.5, the Spindle Box is a wooden box with 10 equal compartments labeled 0 to 9. There are 45 wooden spindles ($1 + 2 + 3 + \ldots + 9 = 45$), and the child learns to count them out, placing the appropriate number in each compartment in the box. As with other materials, the child should

FIGURE 2.5 The Spindle Box. Photograph by An Vu.

notice if he or she makes an error, because the child will not have the correct number available for another compartment.

With the Spindles, quantity is introduced in a new way, with "9" being nine individual objects grouped together. This way of thinking about numbers was gradually introduced, from the Red Rods, to the Number Rods (alternating blue and red units), to the Spindles. After the child has mastered the Spindle Box, different kinds of counters, such as small cubes or sticks, are placed in appropriate groupings beside numbers. Importantly, these objects are perceptually simple (a feature discussed later in the chapter) and do not have some other function; toys, for example, are not used to count in Montessori. Research by Judy DeLoache suggests that Montessori programs are on the right track in not mixing toys with symbolic materials. When an object is both a symbol and something to play with, children have trouble seeing it as a symbol (DeLoache, 2000). For example, if young children are allowed to play with a dollhouse that is also a model for a larger space, they have more trouble using the dollhouse as a symbol for the larger space than they do when they do not play with it. People are sometimes disturbed that children are not permitted to play with Montessori materials, for example to build a house from the Brown Stair. DeLoache's research suggests that in fact such play might inhibit children's recognition of the underlying concepts intended to be conveyed by these materials.

From the Spindle Boxes, children move on to use Golden Beads that come in units, 10 bars, 100 squares, and 1,000 cubes, and later, Bead Bars of two to nine differently colored glass beads, and then Bead Chains that are made by chaining together the Bead Bars (Figure 2.6). The 10-bead bar holds 10 golden-orange beads, the 9-bead bar holds 9 dark blue ones, the 8-bead bar holds 8 lavender beads, and so on. In essence, these bars of beads are like miniature versions of the number rods without alternating colors. Figure 2.7 shows a girl laying out a long chain of these beads, placing numeral labels at points along the chain. For example, a child will use a chain of 5-bead bars to count 0, 5, 10, 15, and so on.

In chapter 1, I mentioned that Montessori education is based on empirical observation of children, and that Dr. Montessori adjusted what she presented to children based on how children responded to the materials. The beads are an example of this. Dr. Montessori initially intended the glass bead material only for Elementary children, but she noticed 4-year-olds watching with great interest when older children used it. She presented the material to younger children, and seeing that it effectively presented mathematical concepts to younger children and that younger children were interested, she placed the bead material in the Primary classroom as well. With these materials, children in Montessori Primary classrooms perform mathematical operations that many would think too advanced for them, such as adding and subtracting four-digit numbers. Because the children seemed interested, Dr. Montessori saw no harm in this, and indeed believed other school systems hold children

FIGURE 2.6 The Bead Chains. Photograph by An Vu.

FIGURE 2.7 Skip Counting with Bead Chains. Photograph by An Vu.

back. However, some (including Piaget and other of her important contemporaries) believed Montessori presents concepts too early and have dismissed Montessori on that basis. Research on child outcomes (see chapter 11) suggests that the system is effective.

In all these exercises, movement of the body is closely entwined with cognition, because every learning exercise involves materials that children touch and move, bringing concrete embodiment to abstract concepts. Abstract concepts are embedded in the Montessori math materials, and even in the Sensorial Materials that lead to them. The extent to which the underlying abstractions are conveyed through using the Montessori materials is a topic in need of empirical study. Some research does suggest that hand movements are a privileged means for understanding symbols.

Research on Gesture and Symbolic Understanding

Gesture appears to aid symbolic understanding even in infancy. First, children who gesture more when they are 14 months have larger vocabularies at 42 months, even controlling for a host of other important factors such as family income, parent speech, and even child speech at 14 months (Rowe & Goldin-Meadow, 2009). Importantly, parents' own gesturing at 14 months does not predict child speech at 42 months—but does predict child gesture at 14 months. Indeed, children who were trained to gesture (asked to point at a picture in a book, while the experimenter labeled the picture) later used more spoken words than children who only watched the experimenter point at pictures while labeling them (LeBarton, Goldin-Meadow, & Raudenbush, 2015).

Children also produce their earliest grammatical constructions by combining gesture with speech, rather than in speech alone (Goldin-Meadow & Alibali, 2013).

Some have questioned whether infants can learn gestural signs earlier than words. Children appear to reach language milestones at the same time in the spoken and gestural modalities (Petitto et al., 2001). Still, Linda Acredolo and her colleagues have developed a set of very iconic signs and have found that infants learn these signs earlier than words, even when both types of symbols are presented to children at the same rate (Acredolo, Goodwyn, Abrams, & Hanson, 2002). For example, if a parent consistently uses both a flapping gesture and the word "bird" to name birds, her child will use a flapping gesture to name a bird about a month earlier, on average, than the child will use the word "bird" (Goodwyn & Acredolo, 1993).

Another study showed that parents' frequent use of gestures in communication with their children even hastened their spoken language development (Goodwyn, Acredolo, & Brown, 2000). One group of parents was trained to use gestural communication with their 11-month-olds, a second was trained to make special efforts at using verbal labels, and a third group was left to behave as usual. The children's language abilities were tested several times from 15 to 36 months. The gestural training group was found to excel on most of the measures of language acquisition that were administered during the 2 years of the study. However, by 36 months, the differences were less pronounced. A possible explanation for this is that children are exposed to fewer semantic gestures than words. Another explanation is that the underlying motor system—control of the hands and arms—develops earlier than the fine motor control needed for speech production.

There is another way that parents enhance children's language via gesture: When children use a gesture (often because they lack the word), parents actually say back the word to the child, teaching spoken language in response to child gesture (Goldin-Meadow, Goodrich, Sauer, & Iverson, 2007). Children whose mothers do this more frequently have accelerated language development; the very words that mothers translate are also incorporated into the children's spoken vocabularies more quickly than the words for other gestures that mothers do not translate.

Goldin-Meadow and her colleagues also observed a close relationship between children's use of gesture and the transition from one- to two-word speech (Goldin-Meadow & Butcher, 2003). Two-word speech often expresses two different ideas, such as "want" and "apple." During the transition to two-word speech, children sometimes make gestures that are redundant with speech, thus expressing a single idea, for example, flapping their hands while saying "bird." At other times during this transitional period, children make gestures that convey a different meaning from their speech, for example, pointing at an apple while saying "eat." For the children studied, use of gesture-speech combinations conveying two distinct ideas always preceded their first two-word utterance by an average of 2.3 months. Furthermore, the age at which children produced their first distinct gesture-speech combination correlated very highly with the age at which they produced their first two-word utterance ($r = 0.90$). Importantly, gesture-speech combinations that conveyed a single idea were not related to two-word utterances. The gestural modality may have allowed thoughts to be conveyed earlier than they could be conveyed in speech, and using such combinations in gesture may have even facilitated their use in spoken language.

Another example of gesture possibly aiding symbolic cognition in young children is that children can interpret symbols designated by actions earlier than they understand symbols designated by models (Tomasello, Striano, & Rochat, 1999). In this research, children were taught to select an object and then put it down a chute. Which object to select was designated in one of two ways: via an adult pointing out a small model of the object, or via an adult carrying out the action typically performed with that object. For example, a hammer could be designated by a miniature hammer or by a hammering gesture. Even the youngest children tested (18 months) performed better in response to gestures that conveyed how an object would be used than to miniature models of those objects. That is, they were more apt to put the full-sized hammer down the chute after the experimenter pretended to hammer via hammering gestures with an imaginary hammer than after the experimenter pointed to a miniature hammer.

In sum, symbolic understanding can be effectively communicated both by and to children through gesture even before it can be communicated verbally or even by physical models. Hand movements that convey meaning might be privileged for children relative to spoken words that convey meaning.

Rendering the Symbolic Concrete: More Montessori Math

Many Montessori materials are designed to expose the child's hand to abstract concepts, which are then gradually revealed to the mind. The sequence presented earlier from the Pink Tower to the Beads (which continues further) is one example of this. Another example is the Binomial and Trinomial Cubes (Figures 2.8 and 2.9). These materials are wooden boxes with two hinged sides that open to expose a set of blocks inside. The blocks fit perfectly inside the wooden box. Embodied in those pieces is the algebraic formula for finding the volume of a cube. For example, for the Trinomial Cube, the sides are of length $a + b + c$: $(a + b + c)^3 = (a^3 + 3a^2b + 3a^2c + b^3 + 3ab^2 + 3b^2c + c^3 + 3ac^2 + 3bc^2 + 6abc)$. This is because the small blocks that fit inside the cubes have sides of lengths a, b, and c. The red cube is a^3, the blue cube is b^3, and the yellow cube is c^3. There are 3 cubes that embody a^2b, which are red on some

FIGURE 2.8 The Binomial Cube. Photograph by An Vu.

sides and black on others. And so on. The Binomial Cube works in the same way, but presents the simpler eight-part binomial formula.

In the Primary classroom, the Binomial Cube is a Sensorial Material and is like a puzzle in that one fits the pieces together. When children are reintroduced to the Binomial Cube in Elementary, they are specifically shown how it embodies the binomial formula. The Montessori material is a hands-on instantiation of what the formula represents. These materials can seem like small miracles to those of us who went through conventional courses, plugging numbers into formulas often without understanding what the formulas represent. Montessori children sometimes get so excited by the possibilities they realize from using the Binomial and Trinomial Cubes, that on their own, they decide to go on to more complex renditions, for example, creating Septanomial cubes $(a + b + c + d + e + f + g)$ out of cardboard and working out the formula needed to measure a cube's volume when broken down in this way.

Conventional schools are discovering and using similar materials on occasion. Manipulatives can vary in their usefulness, however, with some studies showing that children sometimes make interpretations very different from what adults intended (DeLoache, Uttal, & Pierroutsakos, 1998; Uttal,

FIGURE 2.9 The Trinomial Cube. Photograph by An Vu.

O'Doherty, Newland, Hand, & Deloache, 2009). A different problem arises when the manipulatives are themselves "perceptually rich" (McNeil, Uttal, Jarvin, & Sternberg, 2009); in such cases, the materials can distract rather than help children, although the exact circumstances when they distract (versus help) is unclear (for a recent meta-analysis and discussion of math manipulatives, see Carbonneau, Marley, & Selig, 2013). The relative plainness of Montessori materials is good; using butterflies or other rich materials to teach mathematics would not be. As much of the research presented here suggests, manipulatives can be used successfully when they are well-chosen and well-presented (e.g., Carbonneau et al., 2013; Sayeki, Ueno, & Nagasaka, 1991; also see Pouw, van Gog, & Paas, 2014 for a good recent review). Research should also be done on Montessori math materials specifically, to determine whether the underlying mathematical purpose of the materials is conveyed. The materials clearly involve movement that is aligned with cognition, which research suggests would be associated with better learning.

Movement in Other Domains in Montessori Education

Movement is also incorporated into other areas of the Montessori curriculum, such as botany and geography. For example, while learning the parts of a plant, children draw the plant parts; when learning the countries of Europe, children first learn simply to put the countries in place like pieces of a puzzle. They trace the outlines of the wood pieces representing countries with their finger and then later make a paper map, tracing the outlines onto paper with a pencil. They then color in the pencil outlines, label the countries with labels that they write, and place the appropriate national flags on the countries. A great deal of their learning geography, then, involves movement that is consistent with thought: Move the puzzle pieces, trace the country, draw the country, color the country in, and so on. Although fundamentally based on textbooks and lectures, conventional schooling can incorporate such activities; Montessori education is infused with them, and textbooks and lectures are virtually absent until middle school.

In Montessori Elementary classrooms, children continue to physically move about as they perform much of their work. By the later years, as children perform independent research projects, they do spend increasing amounts of time at tables reading and writing. Still, Elementary children have hands-on materials for most topics, including math, science, music, art, grammar, and learning about other cultures. For example, Elementary school children investigate how people over the ages and in different climates have solved the basic problems of getting food, shelter, and clothing. In doing so, they create charts and make models (see Figure 5.1), for example of houses around the world. Their work continues to involve the hand and connects back to the more basic work done much earlier. Through their earlier work with maps in Primary, Elementary school children have a sense of where the countries whose houses they are researching are located. In other work they study biomes (again by drawing maps), so they have a sense of the varying climates of those regions.

In conventional schooling, children might occasionally have projects where they work with their hands (and these projects are usually well regarded by children), but much of their learning is from listening to the teacher, taking notes, and memorizing for tests. In contrast, in Montessori, the Elementary teacher presents stories about how people live that inspire the children to go find out more, as discussed in chapter 5. Children are not assigned to make models of houses from around the world; they decide to, as is discussed in chapter 3. They do not make those models because they will be tested on them and graded; they make them because they are motivated to learn, as discussed in chapter 6. Thus in Montessori the hands-on activities are rooted in a fundamentally different soil than are similar projects that one sometimes sees enacted in conventional schools.

Montessori involves movement even in reading and vocabulary building, generally thought of as tasks for which one sits still. As they learn the vocabulary for new objects, children move cards from a storage box and place them by the objects they name. Dr. Montessori noted that through this process, children were inherently learning what a noun is, and she reasoned that other parts of speech could also be learned via such exercises. The Command Cards allow this. These are cards with commands written on them, such as "walk," "sing," and "jump." Children read the commands and execute the action, so the overarching concept of "verb" is conveyed. Adverbs are embodied in commands to "Tiptoe rapidly to the door, then tiptoe slowly back to your seat." Children practice tiptoeing rapidly, then tiptoeing slowly, thus moving as they commit to mind what an adverb is. They learn about the importance of conjunctions by carrying out commands in which conjunctions are present and missing.

Acting out what one reads sharpens one's attention to words and their precise meaning, which is another goal of the Command Cards. Phrases such as "Close the blinds; open the front door; wait a moment; then rearrange everything as before" or "Very politely ask eight of your companions to leave their chairs, form double file in the center of the room, and march back and forth on tiptoe, making no noise" convey precise meanings. Although it is ultimately an empirical question, it fits with the research presented earlier and seems logical that one would be more apt to notice exactly what a word means when one has to do what it says than when one simply reads it. As a teacher of writing, I know the problem in many a student's writing is not paying close attention to what words mean, and exercises that get students to pay attention to meaning (because they have to perform actions based on them) might serve that end.

GOING OUT

In addition to moving about in the classroom as they learn, an integral part of children's Montessori education involves moving out of the classroom. For example, children learn about trees or birds or flowers in the classroom (from cards, charts, books, and models), and these provide an objective for their walks. Children can go out to find that which they have seen in the classroom. The objects can be brought back into the classroom for classification and further study. Walking outside with an educational purpose, to find objects in the world, is incorporated into the program.

Montessori children not only go for walks to learn about nearby surroundings, but also to venture farther afield to learn about the world. Going out of the classroom takes on a new character in Elementary, driven by the children's personal interests and goals because they are becoming more independent. A child (or more likely a small group of children; by Elementary, children are usually very socially inclined) who is interested in learning more about birds might visit a bird sanctuary, an ornithologist, and a natural history museum as part of the research for a report on birds that the child (or they) will later give to the class. Unless the school is situated in a safe place, an adult, usually a parent volunteer or class assistant, accompanies children on these trips. Any given child might leave the classroom twice a month, for a half or whole day, on such a venture, called a "Going Out" trip. Elementary children thus move on a grand scale, out of the classroom, as part of their learning.

Recess and Physical Education

In what might strike people as a bizarre twist, Dr. Montessori argued against having recess as part of the Montessori school day. Her reasons for this are quite clear in her books: It interrupts concentration, and it is unnecessary in the Montessori program. The concentration issue is considered first.

Recess time could be detrimental in Montessori because for any given child on a given day a clock-imposed recess time might well come at a moment of intense concentration on work. Of course such concentration must be broken at some times, such as the end of the school day, but Dr. Montessori's goal was to minimize these interruptions:

> Montessori schools have proved that the child needs a cycle of work for which he has been mentally prepared; such intelligent work with interest is not fatiguing, and he should not be arbitrarily cut off from it by a call to play. Interest is not immediately born, and if when it has been created the work is withdrawn [for recess or any other adult-imposed break], it is like depriving a whetted appetite of the food that will satisfy it. (1948b/1967, p. 118)

Any scheduled events, from recess to extracurricular activities, could easily break children's concentration. Montessori teachers who have experienced classrooms deep in concentration have expressed that on days when the children know they will be interrupted (for a field trip or even a regularly scheduled art class which some Montessori schools add), they do not settle into their work as deeply as they do on mornings when nothing is scheduled.

A second reason Dr. Montessori did not include recess in her programs is that she saw it as unnecessary. In conventional schools, recess serves physical, mental, and social functions. Physically, it may well be necessary in a conventional program, because children are asked to sit and listen much of the time and sitting still can be tiring, even sometimes for adults. Like a stretch break in the middle of a 1-hour lecture, recess can give the child a chance to recuperate attention by allowing the body to move from a sedentary position (Pellegrini & Bohn, 2005). In Montessori classrooms, children are constantly on the move. Even when they sit for lessons, the lessons keep the child active. Because children are constantly moving their bodies to do work in

Montessori classrooms, Dr. Montessori saw recess as physically unnecessary. "The mental life shown by our children brings the whole of their musculature into constant use" (Montessori, 1967a/1995, p. 145). Indeed, preschool children in Montessori classrooms move significantly more than children in conventional classrooms controlling for child sex, ethnicity, and body mass index, and parent education; interestingly, this difference extended to outside school as well, as if being more active during school causes children to be more active outside school too (Pate et al., 2014).

The mental recreation function of recess in conventional schools might also be unnecessary in Montessori because children freely choose their work and hence are likely to be interested in it (see chapter 5 on interest). In addition, when a child needs a break from work in Montessori, the child can take it. Children can stop and daydream for a time, pick up a recreational book, engage in free drawing, perhaps go outside and play, and so on. Of course, children are not free to abandon their education, and the teacher is responsible for noticing if a child is not using time wisely and intervening if needed. But children are free to make such choices as long as they behave responsibly, and thus the mental-break function of recess may be unnecessary in Montessori.

Regarding the social function of recess, in Montessori classrooms children can be as social as they like. As long as they are learning, they are allowed to chat with friends while they are working, and they are allowed to work with friends. Social interactions in Montessori occur within a structured classroom environment rather than on playgrounds, which might also help children establish positive social relationships. Bullying and teasing tend to be problems of the school playground, where adult supervision is more difficult. These are all interesting issues for further research.

In sum, Dr. Montessori saw recess both as an impediment to concentration and as unnecessary, as the functions it serves in conventional schools (exercise, a mental and physical break from the status quo, and social time) are already served within the Montessori classroom. Montessori schools that closely follow Dr. Montessori's program therefore do not always have recess; those that do may well have it in only in response to parent pressures, or as a routine that is hard to eliminate once instituted.

How might one allow for more gross motor outdoor activity without recess? This is a particularly important issue in light of rising obesity rates among children in the United States. Ideally, a Montessori school has an outdoor area and some sports equipment, and a child might choose to play soccer or baseball for up to 20 or 30 minutes of the school day. To get a group sport going, the child has to gather together a group of willing others to go play, which is itself a learning opportunity. Children who have not been good social partners get feedback, if other children do not choose to go with them. Physical education or recess time is a choice children can make, rather than something imposed by the clock and adults' schedules. After-school sports programs can of course also serve this function, as they often do in Europe. Ultimately, the responsibility that children get adequate exercise and have a healthy diet lies with the parents and the children themselves. Perhaps that is where it best resides regardless: Although conventional schools today typically provide physical education, childhood obesity is perceived to be a major national health problem.

The final topic discussed in this chapter is the potential effect of movement on how teachers teach.

Creating a Learning Environment Through Gesture

Additional work by Susan Goldin-Meadow and her colleagues suggests that children's gestures can also be subconsciously interpreted by teachers, causing them to teach differently. An educational system that capitalizes on this by bringing gestures out might be beneficial. Montessori teachers watch children move as they learn, and it is possible that those movements convey important information to teachers.

GESTURE LEADS COGNITION: GESTURE–SPEECH MISMATCH

Goldin-Meadow and her colleagues have shown that in several domains, movement not only assists cognition, but leads it as well. That is, children reveal understandings in gesture that they cannot yet reveal in speech. Studies in the domains of conservation and mathematical understanding will be used to illustrate this.

Piaget's classic conservation tasks test children's understanding that superficial changes do not create deep ones. For example, in a Piagetian number conservation task, an experimenter lays out two rows of five checkers each. At first, the checkers are evenly spaced, and the experimenter asks the child which row has more. A child of 4 or 5 years can normally tell you the rows are the same. The experimenter then spreads one of the rows out, so it still contains five checkers, but now is perceptually longer than the other row. The experimenter again asks which row has more (or whether they are both the same). Children younger than 6 years often make a conservation error, claiming that the spread-out row has more. This happens even if the items involved are money and the child gets to take them home, and even if the perceptually shorter row actually has more. Children will claim they would rather take home five pennies than six, if the row of five pennies is perceptually longer than the row of six.

Goldin-Meadow and her colleagues (Church & Goldin-Meadow, 1986) noticed an interesting aberration when some children solve these tasks. At the same time as the child verbally gives the wrong answer, claiming the spread-out row has more,

> the child moves his pointing finger between the first and second checker in the spread-out row and the first checker in the unspread-out row, and then continues pairing the checkers in the two rows. In his speech, the child focuses on the fact that the experimenter spread the checkers out. In his gesture, however, the child demonstrates some understanding of the fact that the checkers in the two rows can be paired with one another, thus demonstrating an incipient understanding. (Goldin-Meadow, 2002, p. 137)

The hand thus leads the mind; the child tells it in gesture before he or she can tell it in words. In addition, a child who gives the wrong verbal answer but the right one in gesture today will, in the coming days, begin to give the right verbal answer as well. Movement thus leads cognition.

The same sequence has been noticed in conservation of liquid tasks (Church & Goldin-Meadow, 1986) and reasoning about arithmetic problems (Perry, Church, & Goldin-Meadow, 1988). For example, in one study asking children to solve number equivalence problems, such as $4 + 7 + 5 = 4 +$ —, some children's gestures matched their speech and others' did not (Alibali & Goldin-Meadow, 1993). An example of a gesture that matched speech would be "if a child [who incorrectly answered '16'] said 'I added the 4, the 7, and the 5' . . . while pointing to the left 4, the 7, and the 5" (p. 485). This child is incorrect but consistent across speech and gesture. If tested at a later time, this same child might still say "16" but indicate the correct solution with gestures, for example, point to the left 4, 7, and 5 (totaling 16), and then produce a flick-away movement near the right 4, which needs to be subtracted from 16 to arrive at the correct solution. In fact, 44% of the problem-solving strategies children expressed in this study were expressed in gestures that did not match their speech and that were in fact more advanced than their speech.

Children's emergent knowledge is thus sometimes expressed with the hands even before it is expressed with speech. Other research has shown that this pattern is not limited to children. Adults also use gestures conveying how they are going to solve a problem, even when they do not express those strategies in speech (Goldin-Meadow, 2002). Interestingly, children who are told to gesture before or during a math lesson learn more from the lesson (Goldin-Meadow, Cook, & Mitchell, 2009); gesture seems to carry some of the cognitive load, and also appears to make learning last (Cook, Mitchell, & Goldin-Meadow, 2008).

GESTURE–SPEECH MISMATCHES AND INSTRUCTION

Children whose gestures do not match their speech are particularly apt to benefit from instruction (Perry et al., 1988; Perry & Elder, 1997). In the experiment already mentioned (Alibali & Goldin-Meadow, 1993), fourth-graders who had failed a pretest of 10 mathematical equivalence problems and naturally gestured while trying to solve them were randomly assigned either to a group that received instruction or to a control group that did not. They were then given 12 addition equivalence problems to solve, like the one shown earlier. For each problem, children in the instruction group were given feedback emphasizing equivalence:

> That's a good try, but it's not the right answer because it doesn't make both sides equal. . . . It seems to me that you were thinking of the equal sign as an instruction to add up all the numbers in the problem, but that isn't really what the equal sign means. Really the equal sign means "is the same as." It tells you to make both sides of the problem the same. (p. 482)

A test of understanding mathematical equivalence was given after the training. Not surprisingly, only children who received instruction did better at the post-test than they had at pretest. But among those who received instruction, those whose gestures and speech did not match during the pretest were especially likely to perform better on the post-tests. It appeared that these mismatching children were in some sense entertaining the correct method, as indicated by their gesture, and that instruction served to bring the method to the fore (Perry et al., 1988).

TEACHERS APPEAR TO UNCONSCIOUSLY NOTICE GESTURE

Do teachers naturally capitalize on gesture-speech mismatches in giving instruction? To address this question, eight teachers were recruited to teach math-equivalence problems to third- and fourth-grade children who had previously failed on such problems (Goldin-Meadow & Singer, 2003). Whereas in the prior study all children were given the same instruction by an experimenter, in this study the teachers' instructions were unscripted. At issue was whether teachers teach differently to students whose gestures and speech do not match. Teachers were told to put the first problem on the board, ask the child to solve it, and explain the solution. Each teaching session was videotaped. Children's gestures were coded as matching or not matching their speech, as were the number of different instructional strategies employed by the teacher.

The teachers showed twice as many different types of problem-solving strategies, on average, to the children whose gestures and speech did not match as to the children whose gestures and speech matched. Because children in both groups expressed a similar set of strategies overall, the change in teaching apparently stemmed from the teachers' noticing the gesture-speech mismatch. Children appear to create their own instructional environment by their gesturing.

Other research has shown that what the teachers were doing with the mismatch children—presenting an array of different strategies rather than just one—facilitates the understanding of new concepts (Perry & Elder, 1997; Siegler, 1994). In keeping with this conclusion, the children who were shown the greatest variety of strategies (the gesture-speech mismatch group) performed the best on the post-test. Of course, we cannot know for sure in this case that the teaching was responsible, because we know that the children who produce mismatches are more likely to advance regardless. Still, it appears that teachers are sensitive to speech-gesture mismatches in natural situations, and that they do vary their teaching accordingly.

As Goldin-Meadow has noted, gesture may be one of the best ways for teachers to see where the upper edge of the child's competence lies. Seeing how children use their hands may allow teachers to direct their teaching strategies to the top of what the famous developmental theorist Lev Vygotsky (1978) termed the child's "zone of proximal development"—the set of competencies the child does not show when working alone, but does show when working with the assistance of a more competent other. Apparently children's gesture-speech mismatches did indicate to teachers that children were ready to learn, teachers responded by providing more varied learning strategies to such children, and those children profited from the instruction and showed the greatest gains in learning. Teaching methods that capitalize on this by engaging children's hands in the learning process would be expected to enable better learning.

Chapter Summary

Even scientists and educators have failed to notice the great importance of movement in human development.

— Maria Montessori *(1966, p. 100)*

[The child needs] activity concentrated on some task that requires movement of the hands guided by the intellect.

— Maria Montessori *(1966, p. 138)*

Dr. Montessori was deeply concerned with the relationship between movement and cognition and advised that from birth infants be given opportunities and incentives to move their bodies in purposeful ways. Children in Montessori classrooms freely move about, working at tables and at small rugs on the floor, allowing for far more movement than in conventional classrooms, where children are often seated at their desks until recess. In addition, most Montessori work involves manipulating objects with one's hands and even moving one's whole body as part of the particular task. Children carry large maps to rugs, remove and trace the countries, carry and set flags on those countries, and color in small pictures of the flags. Children handle the math materials and come across the basic concepts of arithmetic. Cognition is embedded in action, by virtue of learning through these materials. Hand gestures also help us to understand others' thought processes, and with Montessori materials, hands are constantly in motion, which might allow for better communication at that level. Children see the hands of the teachers as they present those materials, and the teachers see the hands of the children as they enact the exercises.

The integration of movement and cognition in Montessori classrooms contrasts sharply with conventional education, in which children sit at desks and do much of their learning in workbooks. Because there is little for the hand to do besides write letters and numbers, conventional education cannot easily capitalize on the findings that movement and gesture both reveal and lead cognition.

Dr. Montessori's respect for movement was profound, as she saw society as founded upon movement and civilization as founded on the particular movements of human hands: "The skill of the hand is bound up with the development of [the] mind, and in the light of history we see it connected with the development of civilization ... all the changes in [our] environment are brought about by hands" (1967a/1995, pp. 150–51).

Because humans have free will, we decide how we will move our hands and our bodies. Another very important educational insight of Montessori, and the topic of the next chapter, is the importance of free choice to learning and well-being.

3 }

Choice and Perceived Control

These children have free choice all day long. Life is based on
choice, so they learn to make their own decisions. They must
decide and choose for themselves all the time. . . . They cannot
learn through obedience to the commands of another.
— Maria Montessori *(1989, p. 26)*

Children in Montessori classrooms freely choose their work. They arrive in
the morning, look around the classroom, and decide what to do. They work
on it for as long as they are inspired to, then they put it away and select something else. This cycle continues all day. Occasionally children, particularly
young ones, might need some guidance in their choices. A teacher might present a 3-year-old with the option of doing Table Washing or Sound Cylinders,
or a child who has not followed up on a grammar lesson might be asked to
choose a time when he or she will do the work. But for the most part, children's choices are limited only by the set of materials they have been shown
how to use, by the availability of a material (because with few exceptions,
there is only one set of each), and by what is constructive both for the self and
society. Home time is also relatively free. Practically speaking, this is because
the learning materials stay in the classroom. In addition, probably because
of differences in structure, Montessori children appear to achieve enough
during the school day to obviate the need for homework (in the traditional
sense of worksheets and the like; that said, evidence suggests that homework
is not particularly helpful to achievement in conventional schools anyway;
see Cooper, Robinson, & Patall, 2006; Kohn, 2007). As one child who moved
from a Montessori to a conventional school put it, "In Montessori we did our
work at school. In my new school, we do our work at home."

   In a conventional school classroom, the teacher, the school administrator, or even the state legislature chooses what the children study and when.
Children arrive in the morning, then are ushered hour by hour through a
preset curriculum, with nary a choice over what topic they study at each
hour, with whom they will study it, when they will take breaks, and by
when work should be completed. Thus, conventional schooling is tightly

controlled. The exception to this is recess. Although the time of recess is scheduled, during that period, children are usually free to choose their activity and social partners. Because recess is the only established free choice time in conventional schooling, it may be an important part of why it is so popular. For conventional schoolchildren, even time at home is restricted by homework (and, increasingly, other scheduled and adult-controlled activities).

The high level of externally imposed control in conventional classrooms may be a natural sequela of the factory model. For a factory to operate efficiently, raw materials must be ushered down the assembly line without regard to individual differences among materials of the same type—and certainly materials can make no choices. Factory workers are treated similarly as well, with no allowance for personal choices about what a worker would like to work on at any given moment. The assembly line might break down if everyone arrived in the morning and chose the job they most wanted to do.

The factory model is reinforced by the Lockean model of the child. If learning occurs when a teacher pours knowledge into children and reinforces children's correct answers, then whole-class learning is the most practical format. First, the teacher can only pour out one stream of knowledge at a time, and second, the teacher cannot attend simultaneously to 25 or so children's different choices of activities and reward each child appropriately. Even the possibility of children making choices is philosophically juxtaposed to this model. Behaviorists do not attend to inner impulses that might lead to choices; instead, an organism should do what it has previously been rewarded for doing.

Yet psychological research clearly shows that restriction of choice and control are not optimal for human learning and well-being. People have a basic need for autonomy (Deci & Ryan, 2011; Ryan & Deci, 2000), which American culture particularly nourishes (Iyengar & Lepper, 1999; Kitayama & Uskul, 2011; Markus & Kitayama, 1991). Feeling one can make choices fulfills this need and allows people to flourish. Too much choice can be debilitating and serve to undermine one's sense of control (Schwartz, 2004), but some choice is clearly good. In fact, when choice is restricted, people are vulnerable to illusory pattern perception—thinking they see patterns where none actually exist (Whitson & Galinsky, 2008). In this chapter I first discuss research on the benefits of choice for task performance and well-being, both in experiments and in conventional classroom situations. I then discuss choice in Montessori classrooms before moving on to the issue of how limited choice is optimally beneficial.

Research on the Benefits of Choice

When people are able to make choices, they tend to feel better and perform better. In the following sections, I first consider studies of performance, then studies of well-being. The last section concerns studies that focus on both performance and well-being in conventional classroom situations.

THE EFFECT OF CHOICE ON TASK PERFORMANCE

Having a sense of control over one's environment and over what one does has been shown to benefit the performance of both adults and children. A few studies with adults will be considered first to show the broad applicability of this principle; results with children are even stronger (Patall, Cooper, & Robinson, 2008) and will be presented after the adult findings.

In one study adults performed two tasks: tangram puzzles (in which several smaller shapes must be combined to make a larger one; the puzzles used in this study were actually unsolvable) and proofreading a paper, both in a room where a buzzer repeatedly made a loud noise (Glass & Singer, 1972). Half of the subjects were told they could terminate the noise at any time with a switch, but they were discouraged from doing so and few people actually used the switch, whereas others were simply subjected to the loud noise, with no suggestion that they could control it. Even though they had not opted to control the noise, those who believed themselves able to control it noticed significantly more errors on the proofreading task and were significantly more persistent in their attempts to solve the tangram puzzles. Although both groups were trying to work under the same noisy conditions, the group that believed it had control over those conditions performed better on tasks requiring careful attention and persistence.

Another study reported similar effects in adults for solving anagrams, in which letters are unscrambled to make words. In this case the anagrams were patterned, so the rearrangement of letters was the same (by placement) for each anagram (Hiroto & Seligman, 1975). One might learn to detect this arrangement in the first few anagrams and thus solve later ones very quickly. The manipulation of interest was a pretreatment of uncontrollable noise, as opposed to controllable noise. After a period in which participants heard noise from which they believed they could escape, participants were subsequently significantly more likely to discover the pattern in the anagrams. When participants thought the noise was inescapable, they were much less likely to subsequently discover the pattern. Later learning of a real pattern was thus influenced by a prior provision of choice.

Choice has also been shown to affect memory in adults. In a paired-associate task, people are given pairs of words to memorize; later they are asked to recall the second word of each pair when presented the first. In one study, half of the participants were allowed to choose which words were paired, whereas the other half was assigned pairs (Perlmuter & Monty, 1977). To ensure that the chosen pairs were not easier than the assigned ones, participants were "yoked" so the groups were in fact memorizing the same pairs. Even though they were assigned the same word pairs, the participants who chose their word pairs remembered significantly more than did yoked participants.

One could of course argue that even though both groups had the same pairs, personal connections between words for the choice participants could be responsible for this result. In a second study checking for this, choice participants first chose a set of associate pairs, but subsequently learned a list of pairs that were preselected. Although these participants had been able to make choices only about the first set of pairs, they still learned the second, assigned set better than did a control group that had not been allowed to choose associate pairs initially. Again, believing one has control over one's situation was associated with improved task performance (see also Patall, 2013, which shows that although choice interacts with interest to affect motivation, choice reliably affects task performance regardless of interest; the interaction of interest with choice is discussed in chapter 5).

The positive effects of choice on learning and performance are also seen even more strongly in children. In one experiment, 7- to 9-year-olds were asked to solve anagrams, and one group was allowed to choose from among six categories of anagrams, such as animals, foods, or parties (Iyengar & Lepper, 1999). A second group was told the experimenter had chosen their categories, and a third was told their mothers had made the choice. Categories were in fact yoked, so all the children had the free-choice group's anagrams.

There were two significant findings of interest here. First, among Anglo-American children, those who had chosen their own category solved more than twice as many anagrams as did those who thought their mothers or the experimenter had chosen their category. Second, during an optional free-play period after the initial anagram task, those who had chosen their own category spent much more time freely choosing to solve anagrams than did those whose category had been chosen for them. Free choice was thus associated with both initial level of performance and with task persistence, which undoubtedly would lead to additional performance gains over time.[1]

One might argue that children who chose their own category chose categories they knew more about, and that the findings all derived from this knowledge. Alternatively, they might have been more interested in their categories, which would also influence learning, as discussed in chapter 5. A second experiment addressed this problem by replicating these results with a very superficial choice manipulation that was not in any way related to what was being learned. Children used a computer math game designed to teach mathematical operations. Some of the children were given two trivial

---

[1] The findings given here are for Anglo-American children. For Asian Americans, maternal choice was associated with somewhat better learning.

choices: what kind of spaceship (of a set of four) they traveled in during the game, and the name of the spaceship (from among four choices). Other children were told that their spaceship and its name were designated by their agemates. During the game, all children could opt for more and less challenging problems and could ask for hints. Pre- and post-tests of children's proficiency with mathematical operations were given, along with several other measures such as ratings of how well children liked the game.

The children who had chosen and named their own spaceship liked the computer game better and played it more than children who did not choose and name their spaceship. They also chose more challenging games and asked for fewer hints. They even rated themselves as generally liking math more. Finally, the choice children showed greater improvement from pretest to post-test and performed better on the problems while playing the game (even though they chose more challenging problems). Clearly, having a sense of control over one's environment is associated with better learning and performance in children. A wide range of positive outcomes stemmed from a very simple choice manipulation.

Another study focused only on the motivational aspects of choice, which surely lead to performance gains. First- to third-graders were presented a drawing game, either as a choice or as an assignment (Swann & Pittman, 1977). Children were brought individually into a room where several activities, including the drawing game, were available. Children in the choice group were told they could do whatever they liked, but it was strongly suggested that they start with the drawing game. Children in the no-choice group were told that the experimenter used to let children choose, but not anymore, and that they should start with the drawing game. Following a few minutes of drawing and other activities, the experimenter told the children they had a few minutes left and could do whatever they wanted. The experimenter noted what activity the child chose first and how long children engaged in the drawing activity during this free choice period.

Whereas 80% of the children in the choice condition chose the drawing activity first, only 20% of the children in the control group did so. Furthermore, children in the choice group drew for an average of five minutes, whereas children in the no-choice group drew for an average of one and a half minutes. Thus, the provision of choice surrounding an activity—even when the choice children made was strongly suggested by an adult—dramatically increased the likelihood that children willingly engaged in it. This would surely impact learning as well.

Another study showed that a child's general sense of control in his or her life, as opposed to control of a particular task, was related to performance on a spatial task. Fifty elementary school children were given drawings with embedded figures to find and a "locus of control" measure (Crandall & Lacey, 1972). Locus of control refers to the extent to which one sees oneself or external forces as being in control of one's life. Children who saw themselves as more in control of their lives identified more hidden figures, and found those figures faster, than did other children. Interestingly, when age and IQ were controlled for, this finding held for girls but not for boys. For boys, performance on the hidden-figures task and IQ were synonymous, perhaps reflecting that boys' IQ performance was particularly swayed by spatial skills. Studies of the relationship between perceived control and performance do not typically report a gender difference.

Extending these findings further, children's locus of control has also been related generally to academic performance, both for school grades and for achievement tests (McGhee & Crandall, 1968). The longer children spend in conventional school environments, the more external their locus of control in those environments becomes (Harter, 1981), but children who buck that trend and manage to retain an intrinsic locus of control do better. This is supported by the work of Carol Dweck (1999) on mastery versus performance orientations, which will be discussed particularly in chapters 6 and 9.

In addition to improving task performance, interest, and persistence, the provision of choice has also been shown to positively impact children's creativity. Preschoolers were grouped into choice and no-choice groups and asked to make collages (Amabile & Gitomer, 1984). Those in the choice group were given a choice of collage materials, and those in the no-choice group were yoked, so each no-choice child was given the same collage materials as a choice child had freely chosen. A group of artists blind to the children's condition then judged each collage for its creativity. They rated the collages of children who had been given a choice of materials as more creative than the collages of children given no choice but using the very same materials.

Even 2-month-olds appear to take positively to experiences of control. In one study, a group of infants learned that turning their heads to the right (or left) would result in a mobile above their heads moving (Watson & Ramey, 1972). For a second group of infants, the mobile moved on its own every three or four seconds. These mobiles were set up above the infants' cribs at home for just 10 minutes per day for 2 weeks. Over the 2 weeks, the infants with control increased their head turns to nearly double the rate of the noncontrolling infants. Even more interestingly, the infants with control over their mobile were reported by their mothers as being much more engaged with it, smiling and cooing while interacting with it. Later, in the laboratory, the infants were shown a new mobile they could control (Watson, 1971). Only infants with a prior experience of control figured out that they could control the new mobile; ones who were exposed to a randomly moving mobile did not figure out that they could control this one. Six weeks later the infants returned to the laboratory and were exposed to yet another mobile that they could control, and the results were the same. Thus, even in infants, control over one situation transferred to control over another and was associated with more positive emotion.

In sum, both in adults and children, the provision of choice is associated with several positive consequences. People learn and remember better, solve tasks better, and opt to engage in tasks more and longer when they think they have more control.

STUDIES OF CHOICE AND WELL-BEING

Other studies focus on how a sense of control relates to well-being more generally, both in the elderly and in infants. Well-being is apparently enhanced even in very young infants when they feel a sense of control. In a more recent study using a paradigm similar to the one just described, 2-month-olds who learned to kick their legs to make a mobile move above their heads not only increased their kicking frequency but also engaged in a great deal of smiling and laughing at the mobile (Rovee-Collier & Hayne, 2000).

A second study combined the positive effects of contingency experience with the negative effects of removing the contingency with infants. Infants aged 2 to 8 months were placed in an infant seat in a small theater, where they received several 3-second presentations of a pleasant audiovisual stimulus: a picture of a smiling infant, with the Sesame Street theme song piped in (Lewis, Alessandri, & Sullivan, 1990). During a learning phase, for half of the infants, the stimulus presentation occurred whenever the infant moved an arm, activating a switch to which the arm was tied. For the other half, the display came on at random times. During a later extinction phase, arm movements were not tied to stimulus presentation for either group. During the learning phase, the contingent group expressed greater joy than the non-contingent group, consistent with the prior work; this experiment also rated interest and found increased interest in the display for the contingent group. Infants who had more control over their environments were apparently more interested in their environments, which undoubtedly would lead to more learning. During extinction, when infants lost stimulus control they previously had had, those in the contingent group expressed more anger, and during a third relearning phase, these infants expressed more interest and joy.

Perceived control continues to impact well-being across the life span, as demonstrated in a classic investigation by the psychologists Ellen Langer and Judith Rodin (1976). This study is notable for the subtlety with which control was communicated and for the extended time course over which the control communication had influence. Nursing home residents were given a short talk about decision making in their nursing home. The administrator opened by stating that the nursing home had a good deal available to the residents. Then, for residents receiving a passivity-inducing message, it was emphasized that the nursing home was making good decisions for them, and that if they had complaints, the staff would do its best to provide each of them with time and attention. The residents were given a plant as a gift and told that the nursing staff would care for the plants for them. Finally, they were told there would be a movie shown on the following Thursday and Friday, and that the staff would let them know to which night they had been assigned.

For the other, active-control group, it was emphasized that the residents were responsible for making their needs known, and that they should be thinking about and deciding what should be changed and what they liked in the nursing home. They were also given a plant, but were allowed to choose that plant and were told it was their responsibility to care for it as they would like. Finally, they were told about the new movies, and that they could decide whether and on which night to go.

Residents were interviewed and the nursing staff was given a questionnaire to fill out both 1 week prior to and 3 weeks following these communications. The questions addressed the well-being of the residents, such as how active, happy, and sociable they were, how much control they felt they had, and their visiting patterns. Following the interview, the experimenter, who was blind to the residents' condition and to the purpose of the study, rated each resident on level of alertness. Also measured were the attendance at the movies and participation in a contest.

The pretest questionnaire ratings revealed no significant differences between the residents receiving each type of treatment, indicating that the two groups were similar at the start of the experiment. The changes from pretest to post-test, however, revealed significant improvements in the active communication group: They reported themselves to be happier and more active after the communication than they had reported themselves to be before it. The interviewer rated them as more alert. The nurses rated them as generally more improved, as visiting others more, and as talking with others more. Among the passive group, in contrast, there was little change across the two rating times. In addition, a significantly greater number of residents in the active communication group attended the movies and participated in the contest than did patients in the passive group. This study dovetails with a host of studies of nonhuman animals showing that having little or no control over one's environment ("learned helplessness") is not good for well-being; having a sense of power and choice is (Seligman, 1975).

Thus, from infancy to old age, a sense of control over one's environment has positive effects on well-being, whereas loss of such control is negative. Both the performance and the well-being findings have also been observed in the setting of most interest for this book: schools.

Natural School Settings

In a famous study of natural school settings and motivation, Richard De Charms (1976) defined what he called "origin" and "pawn" orientations in classrooms. In a classroom with an origin orientation, the students appear to have some say in the classroom; in contrast, in pawn classrooms, children are treated like pawns, controlled by the teacher. Teachers in origin classrooms are like "authoritative" parents: They are warm and accepting, but provide clear and consistent rules, and insist children go by them (see chapter 9). In contrast, teachers in pawn classrooms are controlling and directive, employing a style called "authoritarian." De Charms's research showed that children tend to be internally motivated and have a greater sense of personal responsibility in origin classrooms, and that they are more externally motivated in pawn classrooms (De Charms, 1976). One might wonder if the children were driving the teacher styles to begin with. However, when teachers in pawn classrooms were instructed on how to change the classroom orientation, changes in the children ensued. This suggests that teachers can at least sometimes create their classrooms' orientation, irrespective of the students.

Other studies have also shown that the degree of control children perceive themselves to have in the classroom affects learning and well-being. For example, in one study, when teachers of fourth- through sixth-graders were more autonomy-oriented, children were more intrinsically motivated to learn, saw themselves as more competent, and expressed a greater sense of self-worth (Deci, Schwartz, Sheinman, & Ryan, 1981). In addition, teacher's self-ratings of how autonomy-oriented they were in the classroom were highly correlated with the perceptions of their students, indicating that, in such studies, one can go either to the teacher or to the students to determine to what degree children have a sense of control in the classroom.

A more extensive study examined how fourth- through sixth-graders' perceptions of their classrooms related to their sense of competence, self-worth, and motivation (Ryan & Grolnick, 1986). The results again indicated that when children perceived themselves to be more in control of their classroom environment, they were also more likely to see themselves as academically competent, as more worthy (in a global sense), and as motivated more by learning (mastery motivation). However, in this study, because the questionnaires assessing classroom environment and well-being measures were administered together, it is possible that children filled them out with the same valence: "I am more powerful, I am better and more motivated." It was therefore advisable to confirm the findings using different instruments and allowing a time lapse between assessments. To do this, the researchers returned to the school two months later and gave a common psychology test called a Thematic Apperception Task. For this task, the children were shown a picture of a child in a conventional classroom situation and were asked to write a story about the picture. Independent coders rated the stories on the degree to which the author expressed an origin orientation for the protagonist in the story, the degree to which the teacher in the story was portrayed as controlling, the level of aggression in the story, its creativity, its technical merit, and the effort expended.

Relating the stories back to the questionnaire ratings taken two months earlier, students tended to create protagonists whose origin versus pawn perceptions mirrored what they had expressed on the prior questionnaire. Thus, the students' own origin orientation in their classroom was reflected two months later in their stories about a fictional classroom, suggesting that the prior result was not only caused by having filled out similar questionnaires in the same way. Not surprisingly, then, the children's own origin orientations and the degree of autonomy allowed by the teacher they created in their stories were significantly related. What is new in this study is the finding that origin orientation and degree of autonomy were also significantly related to the technical merit ratings of the essays and the degree of effort the judges believed had gone into the essays. That is, students who saw their classrooms as more child-controlled also wrote better stories and appeared to have worked harder on the stories, replicating the laboratory findings described earlier in a classroom setting.

In addition, the degree of origin orientation was in inverse proportion to the degree of aggression in the stories, raising the possibility that more student-controlled classrooms may have a lower degree of aggression. This makes sense in light of findings discussed in chapter 6: When adults become more involved in children's relationships, children become more aggressive toward one another. (Obviously there are times when intervention is nonetheless warranted.)

Finally, students who two months earlier had described their classroom environment as more child controlled were rated as more creative in their stories. Children's perceptions of the degree to which they control the classroom environment and are free to make choices were therefore related to several variables pertinent both to well-being and to school performance: technical skill, effort, lack of aggression, and creativity.

Again, one might question the degree to which these findings are all child-driven to begin with: Teachers can allow certain kinds of children more freedoms, and those kinds of children also tend to be more intrinsically motivated, perform better in school, and so on. To some degree, that is undoubtedly true. However, there are good grounds for suspecting that the teacher can lead children to these positive outcomes. In De Charms's study, when teachers were trained to give students more of a sense of personal autonomy in the classroom, students subsequently achieved more, showed more adaptive risk taking, and were absent and tardy for school less often than in classrooms in which the teachers received no autonomy training. Second, recall that in the experimental studies described in earlier sections of this chapter, participants were randomly assigned to choice and no-choice conditions, and the results aligned with those from natural classroom situations. People assigned to more internally controlled situations performed better and felt more positively than those who were assigned to the more externally controlled situations. However, the best test would be to apply the experimental techniques that have shown choice's effects in the laboratory in a natural classroom situation.

Patall and colleagues (Patall, Cooper, & Wynn, 2010) randomly assigned 207 high school students in 14 urban high school classrooms to a choice (two options) or no-choice homework condition for a first assignment across an array of subjects (history, math, and so on). For a second assignment, students were in the other condition, providing a lovely within-subject control. In addition, each "no-choice" case was yoked to a free choice. They found that students were more intrinsically motivated, felt more competent, and performed better on a unit test when they had made a choice; students also were somewhat more likely to complete homework that they had chosen. Thus, even in a real-life context with a high-quality experimental design, having a greater sense of choice and control over one's education resulted in superior learning and well-being.

In sum, research on having choice and control over one's environment and life reveals positive consequences for both cognitive and emotional functioning. Participants ranging from infants to senior citizens show higher degrees of emotional well-being and higher levels of performance when they have a sense of being able to control their environment and tasks. Conventional schools are not designed to give children a lot of choice over what they do: Schedules, books, and topics are set. Even within these limitations, conventional teachers who give children more of a sense of control have classrooms that are more apt to flourish. In Montessori classrooms, choice is built into the day-to-day program.

Choice and Control in Montessori Education

Dr. Montessori's description of how she came to see the possibility of free choice in school is illustrative of her talent for making valid yet quite sweeping inductions from single events. The text also illustrates how allowing children more control over their activities enabled her to see the children's natural tendencies, and in turn to select more useful materials for the classroom. As she described it, in the first Montessori classroom in the housing projects in Rome,

> One day the teacher came a bit late to school after having forgotten to lock the cupboard. She found that the children had opened its door. Many of them were standing about it, while others were removing objects and carrying them away.... I interpreted the incident as a sign

that the children now knew the objects so well that they could make their own choice, and this proved to be the case.

This began a new and interesting activity for the children. They could now choose their own occupations according to their own particular preferences. From this time on we made use of low cupboards so that the children could take from them the material that corresponded to their own inner needs. The principle of *free choice* was thus added. . . .

The free choices made by the children enabled us to observe their psychic needs and tendencies. One of the first interesting discoveries was that the children did not choose all the various objects provided for them but only certain ones. They almost always went to choose the same things, and some with an obvious preference. Other objects were neglected and became covered with dust.

I would show them all to the children and had the teacher distribute them and explain their use, but the children would not take some of them up again of their own accord.

I then came to realize that everything about a child should not only be in order, but that it should be *proportioned to the child's use*, and that interest and concentration arise specifically from the elimination of what is confusing and superfluous. (1966, p. 121, italics in original)

From this simple observation, Dr. Montessori developed a school system in which children choose what they want to do. Children arrive in the morning and decide whether first to continue with a report they might have already started, work with a math material, do a science experiment, play music with the Musical Bells (Figure 3.1), and so on. Children decide when they are done with each activity and will go on to the next one. They decide with whom to

FIGURE 3.1 The Musical Bells. Photograph by An Vu.

sit and with whom to collaborate. They choose what field trips ("Going Out" trips) they will arrange, and how they will be arranged. In Montessori classrooms, within reasonable limits that will be discussed, children have choice and control over their lives.

People often wonder how a school program in which children make their own choices all day long could work. Indeed, this feature is very unusual. Other major progressive programs today, such as Reggio Emilia and Steiner, lean more heavily on teacher direction (although children can be the source of the teacher's plan) and whole-class exercises. Montessori programs can operate on individual choice in part because of the carefully prepared environment.

THE PREPARED ENVIRONMENT OF A
MONTESSORI CLASSROOM

Dr. Montessori believed that for a child to make productive choices, the environment had to be prepared—specially designed to stimulate constructive activity in children. Free choice in an environment that did not have an appropriate quantity of materials designed for organized activity, and that was not populated with concentrating, constructively engaged classmates might lead to chaos.

One way in which Montessori environments are prepared to facilitate child choice and control is through order. Common sense suggests it is easier to make choices when the alternatives are arranged in an orderly fashion. Stores arrange aisles by item type, and clothing stores continually fold and reshelve items after customers have tried them on, always returning to order. The orderliness of Montessori environments, as compared with the average conventional school classroom, is striking (although individual conventional teachers vary). Order is the topic of chapter 10. Here I discuss other ways in which the prepared environment's materials, layout, and furniture facilitate the child's constructive choices and sense of control.

Montessori materials facilitate children's making choices because the materials are exposed on shelves in the classroom, or on tables and rugs when other children are using them. Because Montessori work is done with hands-on materials spread out on tables or rugs, children can walk around the classroom and see what will be available to use when the child currently using a material puts it away. Another feature facilitating choice is that the materials are within a child's reach. The shelves in a Montessori classroom are all low and normally, only as deep as a child's arm could easily reach. It is easy for a child to take a material off a shelf, use it for a time, and then put it away. In contrast, in conventional classrooms hands-on materials are often stored in a cupboard where they cannot be seen or easily taken out to use. The teacher controls when the materials are used.

Another feature facilitating the child's sense of choice and control is that the furniture is movable and appropriately sized for children, so a child can even choose to rearrange furniture to suit his or her needs and desires. At the time when Dr. Montessori opened her first school, children's school furniture was not typically appropriately sized. In conventional schools of the day, small children sat on benches that were too high, so their legs dangled. Furthermore, the furniture was usually bolted to the ground. Making movable furniture the proper size for children, rather than having children sit in adult-sized furniture, was apparently a Montessori innovation (Elkind, 1976). As Dr. Montessori described it:

> The principal modification in the matter of school furnishings is the abolition of desks, and benches or stationary chairs. I have had tables made with wide, solid, octagonal legs, spreading in such a way that the tables are at the same time solidly firm and very light, so light, indeed, that two 4-year-old children can easily carry them about. I also designed and had manufactured little chairs.... We permit the child to *select* the position which he finds most comfortable. He can *make himself comfortable* as well as seat himself in his own place. And this freedom is not only an external sign of liberty, but a means of education. [Through such furnishings, the] *child has learned to command his movements.* (Montessori, 1912/1964, pp. 81–84, italics in original)

According to her biographer, E. M. Standing (1957), Dr. Montessori designed such furnishings as a matter of necessity:

> It was not in her power to furnish it with desks like an ordinary schoolroom, because her expenses, being borne by a building society, had to be put down as an indirect item in the general upkeep of the building. For this reason the only expenditure permitted was such as would have been required by an office for furniture and equipment. That is why she had tables made for these small children, with chairs to match, instead of school desks which were universally in use at that time. This turned out, as it happened, to be a fortunate limitation. She also had a number of little armchairs made, presumably under the excuse that, even in an office, people have to rest sometimes. (p. 37)

The child-sized furniture was apparently an opportune reaction to an administrative requirement, and it allowed both for education of movement and for choice regarding where and how one sits to do work. Via the layout, materials, and furnishings, the Montessori-prepared environment facilitates children's sense of control and their ability to make good choices. But although the child sees many materials on the shelves, in fact for very few children are all those choices available, which leads to the next topic: the limitation of choice.

Not Taking It Too Far: The Benefits of Limited Choice

Given the positive benefits of having choice and a sense of control, it is important to bear in mind that an abundance of options is not associated with well-being; indeed, there are circumstances under which choice can be problematic (for discussion, see Patall et al., 2008). Sometimes, too many options demotivates us—extensive restaurant menus are a case in point. One study demonstrated this in a fancy grocery store setting in which a display was set up offering special jams. When a very large selection (24 or more) of sample jams was available to try, people were less likely to purchase a jam than when only six sample jams were available. When they did purchase jam, people selecting from fewer options were more satisfied with their choices (Iyengar & Lepper, 2000). A replication showed this same phenomenon with gourmet chocolates. In fact, people who had to choose one among many chocolates later preferred to take money rather than additional chocolates as a reward; people choosing from among six types opted for more chocolate. A third experiment offered students the opportunity to write essays for extra credit in a college course, which allowed the experimenters to examine the effect of limited choice on performance as well. Students who were given six possible essay topics not only were more likely to write an extra credit essay than were students who were given 24 topic choices, but they also wrote better essays. Hence, there is a point at which having too many choices becomes negative and works against people's sense of control (for more discussion, see Schwartz, 2004).

Limiting Choice in Montessori Classrooms

Although children freely choose what to do in Montessori classrooms, there are several limits on their choices. Choices are limited by the amount of material, by what children know how to use, and by the requirement that they be constructive and responsible. Before considering how choice is limited, however, it is pertinent to discuss the number of choices available in light of the research just discussed. Montessori classrooms have vastly more than six options available to children, and even given the limits, one might wonder if there is too much choice.

THE NUMBER OF CHOICES IN MONTESSORI CLASSROOMS

Montessori classrooms have many materials—far more than six—for the child to choose among. The experiments just mentioned suggest that Montessori classrooms might proffer more choice than is optimal. After all, the experiments showing that having choice is better than not having choice had few choice options—one could choose to turn off noise or not, or one could choose one of four spaceships or six categories of anagrams. When the number of choices rose to 24, the experience of choosing became negative. A Montessori classroom has more different kinds of work options than can easily be quantified, so a question arises as to whether the options are too many.

First, it is important to remember that no child has a choice of all the materials, except perhaps a few children who are about to move on to the next level of classroom, and they are not likely to be interested in much of the first-level work (e.g., Sandpaper Letters). Every classroom has an amount of material that children gradually master in about three years. Every child's choices are limited to the materials that he or she has been shown how to use. Further, a child's choices might be helped because there are only six or eight basic subject areas to choose among; in Elementary, for example, the subject areas are mathematics, geometry, science, language, music, art, history, and geography. Still, within each area, a child does have the choice of doing any work she or he has been shown how to do, and the amount of choice might be perceived as too great.

Learning to make good choices for oneself is considered part of one's education in Montessori. As the epigraph for this chapter put it, "Life is based on choice, so they learn to make their own decisions." Thus, even if choices might be difficult to make, learning to make them is seen as part of Montessori education. Yet there are also reasons to think that the choices children face in Montessori are less difficult than those faced in experiments showing that having more than 20 choices is detrimental.

Dr. Montessori (1917/1965, p. 79) claimed to have "experimentally determine[d] the quantity of material necessary for development" in her classrooms by watching children with varying amounts of material. Every material that should be in a classroom, its underlying logic, and exactly how it should be shown to children are presented in the training courses Dr. Montessori developed. Although there are many materials, the total amount was chosen intentionally, through trial and error. In the following paragraphs, I will discuss three considerations relevant to whether there is too much choice in Montessori classrooms.

First, perhaps larger numbers of choices work for children in Montessori classrooms because children are not choosing among the same types of categories. Rather than needing to choose one among 30 jams to eat, children are choosing whether to prepare carrots to eat, wash tables, work with Sandpaper Letters, and so on. These are rather different types of activities, more akin to the choices an adult faces when spending a day at home. There are more than 20 options on what to do, but the choices are among different sorts of activities. Indeed, the grocery store is typically not overwhelming to us because we purchase in categories within each of which there are not necessarily too many choices: There might just be six types of soap or four types of olive oil.

The other two considerations can be derived from a major theory of why abundant choice can be problematic (Schwartz, 2000). The theory maintains that abundant choice is problematic because people are not equipped to process the information they need to make choices among many new, fairly similar alternatives. Hence the second consideration is that for children in Montessori classrooms, the information about each choice is presented gradually over the course of the 3 years. At no point are they suddenly given a lot of information about many new kinds of work and expected to process it all, which is the case for adults in limited-choice experiments. To return to the grocery store example, even when there are many choices, some familiarity with some products might help us.

As to the third consideration, Schwartz's theory claims an abundance of choice is problematic because it leads to more "buyer's regret." Buyer's regret refers to situations in which one makes a choice and then cannot undo the decision. A child in Montessori can take out a material, work with it for a while, and then decide to do something else, at no cost. For this reason as well, having many options for work in a Montessori classroom may not be problematic for children.

Dr. Montessori saw that "over-abundance debilitates and retards progress" (Montessori, 1917/1965, p. 79). Although there are more than six choices for most Montessori children most of the time, choices are still limited. Next I consider some of the ways that choice is limited in Montessori classrooms.

LIMITING CHOICE VIA THE MATERIALS

Although there are many dozens of materials out in a classroom at once, very few children really have the choice of using all of the materials. For young children, in fact, Dr. Montessori advised giving only a very limited choice. For example, a parent of a 2-year-old might just keep two or three shirts in a drawer that the child can access to choose his or her outfit, keeping the rest of the child's clothes on a high shelf out of view. A Primary teacher might greet a 3-year-old who seems to need help with choices by asking, "Would you like to build the Pink Tower or use the Metal Insets now?" As children get older and are able to handle more choices, they are given more.

Occasionally a child might avoid doing a particular kind of work. In such cases, the Montessori teacher might very subtly limit the child's choice. The teacher would not usually ask the child to do the work, because that would take away the child's sense of control. Instead, a Montessori technique for handling such a situation is to ask children to choose a day or time by which they will complete an activity. Children have a sense of control—they will choose the time—even as the teacher is making sure the work gets done. This technique is consistent with the research on constructive deadlines, discussed later in the chapter.

Another way choice is limited in Montessori is that with very few exceptions, there is only one of each material in the classroom. If another child or group of children is using a material, then for that moment, it is not an option. Dr. Montessori claimed that in general, it is important to have only one of each type of material in the classroom (1989, p. 64). There are two reasons for this. First, children need to learn to work together as a society, and learning to share limited resources is part of that learning (Montessori, 1917/ 1965, p. 174). Second, because one of the ways Montessori children purportedly learn is by observing others doing different work (as discussed in chapter 7), and watching others use a material is supposed to inspire them to do work with that material, having only one material of each set is intended to increase learning in the entire class.

In sum, the materials themselves create limitations on choice in Montessori. There is only one of each material, so children learn to share resources and see a greater variety of work out at any given time. Children are also limited to the materials they have been shown how to use. Besides limits on choice posed by materials, there are also limits posed by society.

LIMITATIONS IMPOSED BY SOCIETY

The liberty of the child should have as its limit the collective
interest; as its form, what we universally consider good [behavior].
We must, therefore, check in the child whatever offends or
annoys others, or whatever tends towards rough or ill-bred acts.
    — Maria Montessori (*1912/1964, p. 87*)

Dr. Montessori is sometimes misrepresented as claiming that every child should always be allowed to do whatever he or she chooses. Clearly Dr. Montessori meant children should have the freedom to make *constructive* choices. Choice has to be limited to what works for the classroom and society. Freedom is issued hand in hand with responsibility in Montessori; children who do not handle the responsibility of freedom are not granted it. Although once children are concentrating on work, it is imperative that adults not disturb them, when children are misbehaving, their freedom must be curbed:

> Do not apply the rule of non-interference when the children are still the prey of all their different naughtinesses. Don't let them climb on the windows, the furniture, etc. You must interfere at this stage. At this stage the teacher must be a policeman. The policeman has to defend the honest citizens against the disturbers. (Montessori, 1989, p. 16)

One might wonder how Montessori teachers handle children who typically misbehave. The simple answer is that their freedom is restricted: They might be asked to stay right by the teacher, perhaps for the entire morning or day. In this way, the teacher can, by his or her presence, help children control themselves. Research suggests that fewer children would misbehave in Montessori classrooms than in conventional ones, however. First, as described earlier, children in origin classrooms see others as less aggressive, which could translate to their own behavior. Second, as will be discussed in chapter 4, training in attention appears to reduce aggressive behavior. Because they can make their own choices among interesting work, and because of the prevalence of concentration, children may be less apt to misbehave in Montessori classrooms than in conventional ones. This would be an interesting topic for research.

LIMITING CHOICE TO WHAT IS USEFUL
FOR SELF-DEVELOPMENT

Choice in Montessori classrooms is also limited to what is useful for the child.

> When we speak of the freedom of a small child, we do not mean to countenance the external disorderly actions which children left to themselves engage in as a relief from their aimless activity, but we understand by this the freeing of his life from the obstacles which can impede normal development.... This goal leads to the creation of a suitable environment where a child can pursue a series of interesting objectives and thus channel his random energies into orderly and well-executed actions. (Montessori, 1967b, p. 62)

Children are free to choose among activities that can provide for themselves at their current stage of development. Typically, a child who is beginning Primary is not allowed to choose the Movable Alphabet. The child is not mentally ready for this material, so it would not be a useful choice. Once a child has developed enough self-control (generally considered to be age 3 in Montessori classrooms), the child is not allowed to take every item off the shelf, but can use only those items she or he has been shown how to use.

One effect of this limitation might be to assist younger children with choices because such children might benefit from having only a few options. Another effect might be to inspire excitement about lessons because they expand one's choices. A child can see himself or herself growing up as more choices become available. Montessori teachers report children asking to be able to work with new materials that they see another child using, or see newly put out on the shelves, suggesting the children want to expand their choices.

Choice is also limited in terms of what a child can do with each object, again for self-development. For example, a child can make words with the Movable Alphabet but not use the letters as dolls. Each material has its carefully designed purpose, and the Movable Alphabet is for making words, not using as dolls or bending and breaking. Some are concerned that this limitation on what one can choose and how objects are used stifles creativity in Montessori classrooms. Studies of Montessori children's creativity have yielded mixed results, perhaps reflecting the type of creativity tests and comparison groups used. This is discussed more in chapter 11.

In sum, in Montessori classrooms, choices are limited both by materials and by the dictate that choices be constructive for the child and for the larger group.

The Effects of Deadlines on Performance and Motivation

In terms of self-development, sometimes children do not make the best choices. A child who needs to do more science work in order to complete that part of the curriculum might simply not make the choice, day after day. As noted earlier, Montessori teachers have a technique for handling such situations, which is consistent with the research on deadlines.

Deadlines clearly take away one's sense of choice: There is a set date on which one must finish something, or one "drops dead." Yet people occasionally need deadlines; conventional schooling functions by them. The practice of imposing deadlines on students is widespread, and at times is necessary. Children must learn to handle deadlines, just as U.S. adults must comply with the Internal Revenue Service filing deadlines. But research shows that deadlines can be demotivating and suggests that their widespread use in school should be curbed.

In one study illustrating the negative effect of deadlines on task interest, Stanford University undergraduates were given a crossword puzzle–creating game called AdLib (Amabile, DeJong, & Lepper, 1976). Some students were told, either directly or implicitly, that there was a deadline for completing the games, after which their data would be of no use. In fact this deadline could be easily met. Others were told only to work as fast as they could, and yet others were not given any information about working fast or completing by a certain time. All participants actually completed the games in the allotted time, confirming that the deadline was a comfortable one.

Interest in the game was measured both by how much time participants spent on it during a later free period and by their answers on a questionnaire about their interest. Students who had been told to work fast and students with no deadline spent more than half of their free time in the subsequent period continuing to play AdLib, whereas students in both deadline conditions spent less than a third of their time playing it. Given free choice, then, those with deadlines were simply not as interested in the game later as those who had played it earlier without deadlines. Responses on the questionnaire also reflected varying degrees of interest, with the deadline group reporting less interest in and enjoyment of AdLib. Merely being led to believe one had a deadline decreased motivation for the task.

A later study replicated this result with a different task. College students were asked to play a game of Labyrinth, a motor skill task requiring one to move a metal ball through a maze suspended on a wooden frame (Reader & Dollinger, 1982). All of the students were asked to get the ball through the maze as quickly and accurately as possible, and half of the students were also asked to set a timer for 10 minutes, in effect giving them a deadline. After 10 minutes, the experimenter returned (for all participants), engaged them in another task, and then left them alone in the room with Labyrinth and some magazines for 8 minutes during which they were instructed to do as they please. More than half of the participants who had played without a deadline spontaneously played the game during these 8 minutes, whereas fewer than a third of those who played with the timer did so.

Although deadlines set by others have a negative effect on task interest and motivation, self-imposed deadlines do not. Indeed, studies suggest that students even work faster when they impose their own deadlines. In one study comparing self- to instructor-imposed deadlines, students who set their own deadlines for coursework complied with their self-imposed schedules better and completed work faster than students on an instructor-imposed schedule (Roberts, Fulton, & Semb, 1988). This fits with what is known as self-determination theory (Deci & Ryan, 2011): Deadlines imposed by others are demotivating because they reduce one's sense of control. When deadlines are self-administered, control is maintained, so deadlines are not demotivating.

Taken together, this research indicates that the regular administration of deadlines for schoolwork has negative consequences that could be avoided by changing the source of the deadline for completion from teacher to student. However, it might be the case that deadlines are less necessary in Montessori because of the presence of other factors known to positively impact motivation: a sense of choice, interest in what is being learned, and removal of expected extrinsic rewards. These are the topics of this and the next two chapters. Because all three factors are at work in a Montessori classroom, motivation might generally be less of an issue than it is in conventional schools. Interestingly, Montessori education is also well aligned with the research regarding when and how deadlines are imposed.

Specification of Completion Times in a Montessori Classroom

As will be described more fully in chapter 5, Montessori Elementary teachers keep track of children's progress in work via each child's Work Journal.

The child and teacher meet, usually weekly, to go over the Journal, in which the child records the week's activities, including the time when each unit of work was done and how much was accomplished. If a child is not choosing to follow up on a lesson, the teacher can bring it up at this meeting as they examine the Work Journal together. The teacher might say, "I see you have not followed up on the Grammar Box lesson I gave you on Tuesday. When do you plan to do that?" The child makes a time commitment, but it comes from himself or herself. The child has a sense of control.

This aligns with the research showing that externally imposed deadlines reduce subsequent interest in an activity. The commitment is made by the child, with some help from the teacher. If children do not adhere to the time frame they have set up, the teacher gradually might consider ways to enhance the child's interest in the activity, or if necessary might gradually remove freedoms (e.g., asking the child to always do that work first thing in the morning). The research suggests that there are motivational costs to this approach, but if a child was not motivated to begin with, it might become necessary.

What is important is that these externally imposed structures remain minimal for what a particular child requires, so the child's personal control is maximal for what that child can handle. The Montessori teacher watches each child carefully and uses a level of structure—a degree of freedom—that fits what that child is ready for and adjusts it as the child changes. In this way, the factory model of having all children do the same activities at the same times is replaced with individual allowances. The Montessori system can adjust to the individual child's ability to take responsibility for doing his or her work.

Concern about children not choosing to work across the curriculum has led to the development of work checklists in some Montessori implementations. With such checklists, children may choose from a very limited selection of work. This might include one type of language work, one type of math work, one type of geography work, and so on. Every day, once a child has checked off a work of each type, then the child is free to choose any work he or she likes. Although such an implementation might sound good on the surface, research reported in chapter 6 on rewards shows a serious problem with implementations involving checking off work in order to get to other work: When one activity is posed as a means to an end, that activity is devalued relative to when it is simply presented on its own (Lepper, Sagotsky, Dafoe, & Greene, 1982). The result of such systems can be devaluation of the very work that was considered most important. There might well also be attention and concentration costs, discussed later in this chapter. Children who are told they must check off some work in order to get to other work might engage in initial work superficially, without deep concentration. With the Work Journals, in which Elementary children simply record what they have done each minute of the day, the child has a greater sense of choice and freedom. Teachers still ensure that children do not leave large areas of the curriculum untouched, but this is done in a way that gives the child a sense of control. Research suggests this is a better way to enhance learning than imposing deadlines and using checklists.

In sum, Elementary Montessori teachers employ a method consistent with research on deadlines: They ask children who are not making the choices needed for a full education to set their own deadlines. In this way, the child retains a sense of control, and the teacher ensures that the child's progress is not retarded. The degree of control imposed by the teacher is kept at the minimum level for what that child needs.

Can Montessori Children Adapt to Conventional School Settings?

A question people often have after learning how much choice children have in Montessori classrooms is whether such children can possibly adapt to settings where they are told what to do and are ushered through a preset curriculum. Anecdotally, parents whose children have experienced the change repeatedly say it was not a problem and that their Montessori children continued to thrive in conventional schools. The best scientific evidence is from studies presented in chapter 11. Montessori Head Start children who went on to conventional schools were by second grade showing academic outcomes superior to those of children in conventional no-choice, whole-class learning programs. Other evidence is from a Milwaukee study in which children were in Montessori through fifth grade. When tested in high school, with the comparison sample matched at test and thus a very high standard of comparison, the Montessori children fared as well as (in English and Social Studies) or better than (in Math and Science) children who had been in other pre- and elementary school situations. Clearly, the average Montessori child adjusts quickly to conventional school programs.

Chapter Summary

By leaving the children in our schools at liberty we have been able with great clearness to follow them in their natural method of spontaneous self-development.
— Maria Montessori *(1912/1964, p. 357)*

Freedom in intellectual work is found to be the basis of internal discipline.
— Maria Montessori (1917/1965, p. 108)

In conventional school environments, children have little choice, yet research shows that the greater their sense of control in the classroom, the better they fare. Montessori classrooms are based on personal choice and freedom within the limits imposed by being constructive for oneself and society.

Children make choices in part by being in touch with postulated inner guides that direct them toward what they need, an interesting speculation ripe for empirical research. Thus far, we have considered what the environment and the teacher do to assist the child in making good choices. A third source of good choices is the child's own self. A certain degree of self-regulation is required if one is to make good choices. In Montessori classrooms, children are thought to make good choices in part because their personalities have been "normalized" through concentration. Concentration stems from a larger array of abilities termed the "executive functions," which is the topic of the next chapter.

4 }

Executive Function

The task of education is to fix the wandering mind of the child
upon an object. When we succeed in our aim, it is as though the
child saw the object for the first time. [The child] concentrates
upon the object with such enthusiasm, as though it was something
[the child] had been seeking for a long time . . . as though . . . to
form the unity of [the] personality"

— Maria Montessori *(1994a, p. 159)*

In teacher training for conventional education, "behavioral management" of
children is strongly emphasized. A major reason for this emphasis is that in a
conventional system, control comes from the outside—from the teacher and
rules he or she establishes. Many readers will remember their own experiences in conventional elementary school classrooms when the teacher left the
room: Mayhem broke out. The teacher keeps children under control in conventional classrooms.

By contrast, in Montessori education the emphasis is on helping children
to build self-control, so each child independently becomes responsible for his
or her own behavior. As Dr. Montessori expressed it:

> In the old school, one goes from the outside and then evidently it is
> the teacher who has the greatest role: the teacher must first work to
> achieve order and then she must put in the child's mind those things
> which she wishes him to learn. Here, on the other hand, progress comes
> from within the child. It is the child who begins to exercise himself; he
> constructs his own conduct, so that this order becomes a phenomenon
> of development. (1997, p. 154)

Self-control arises in an extraordinary way—by setting children free in an
environment that has been specially prepared to correspond to their needs
at their current stage of development. Discovering those needs and inventing
those environments was the genius of Dr. Montessori and her collaborators.
As was quoted in the previous chapter, and bears repeating, "Freedom in

intellectual work is found to be the basis of internal discipline" (Montessori, 1917/1965, p. 108).

Dr. Montessori's books have several anecdotes reporting children going about their business as usual in the classroom even with the teacher absent (see Montessori, 1946/1963, pp. 62-63). It happened at the first school at San Lorenzo, when the children asked the janitor to let them into the classroom when the teacher was late, and on another occasion when a visitor showed up on a holiday. It also happened at the World's Fair exhibit in San Francisco in 1915. And it still happens today. For example, the head of a Dallas school told me that a few months earlier, she'd needed to speak with the Lower Elementary teacher and had dropped in the classroom to do so. The children were busy working, but the teacher was out, which the head assumed was only for a few minutes, so she left. This happened twice more in the course of the morning, and finally she asked the children, "Have you seen Ms. X?" "No," the children replied, "She has not come in today." The children's behavior was unchanged, although the force that would in a conventional setting cause children to work was absent. Control, in Montessori, comes from within children; it is self-control.

Self-control is part of a family of constructs that include self-regulation, emotion regulation, and what psychologists call "executive function" (Blair & Raver, 2012; Müller & Kerns, 2015). Executive function specifically refers to processes that enable goal-directed behaviors. The executive processes allow us to create plans and execute them, controlling our impulses to engage in other behaviors that might be fun for the moment, but are not aligned with a longer-term or more important goal. The study of executive function has a long history in psychology and has lately become prominent in child development as we have discovered that executive function (or self-control or self-regulation) is an extremely important predictor of life outcomes—more important than intelligence, and above and beyond other key influences such as parent income and education.

Executive function is also sometimes referred to as "prefrontal processes," because damage to the prefrontal cortex is associated with its decline. A famous case of this is occurred in 1848, when an American railroad worker named Phineas Gage was struck through the head with an iron pole, creating a hole clear through the left side of his forehead, through his prefrontal cortex. Amazingly, he survived, but as a changed man (at least initially; see MacMillan, 2000). Previously subdued and polite, he became boisterous, rude, and subject to sudden violent attacks. He seemed unable to inhibit or control these impulses. As Gage's case exemplifies, the prefrontal cortex plays an important role in executive function. It is also the latest-maturing area of the brain, evolving into one's mid-20s (Casey, 2015; Kawakubo et al., 2011; Sowell, Thompson, Holmes, Jernigan, & Toga, 1999). Interestingly, Dr. Montessori's four developmental stages culminate at age 24 (Grazzini, 2004).

Dr. Montessori saw her form of schooling not as the passing on of information, but as an "aid to life," which is why in Montessori, the development of executive skills is paramount. For the first and second editions of this book, however, there was not a sufficiently large body of research on the development of these functions to warrant a chapter. In the years since, this area of research has exploded. In this chapter I will first address the global concept of executive function, what it predicts, and what it is predicted by, including the negative effects of television. Next I will explain Montessori theory regarding deep concentration, including discussion of Montessori's human tendencies, and then how concentration is facilitated in a Montessori environment. In the last section, I will discuss recent research on mindfulness, both in adults and children, and point out how Montessori classrooms embody mindfulness principles. Research showing that authentic Montessori education improves children's executive function, relative to other types of schooling, is described in chapter 11.

Executive Function in Psychology and Education Research

WHAT IS EXECUTIVE FUNCTION?

Formally, the term "executive function" refers to "cognitive processes that are required for the conscious, top-down control of action, thought, and emotions, and that are associated with neural systems involving the prefrontal cortex" (Müller & Kerns, 2015, p. 571). There are many processes involved in this; psychologists often focus on three in particular (Miyake, Friedman, Emerson, Witzki, & Howerter, 2000): inhibition (of a thought or behavior), working memory (which can range from simply holding information in mind to manipulating that held information), and shifting (e.g., following one set of rules and then a different set of rules). There are certainly other executive functions; sometimes people also include planning, and I would also include attention (see also Garon, Bryson, & Smith, 2008; Petersen & Posner, 2012). In fact, I think willed inhibition (or excitation) is the heart of all executive function: We choose what to attend to and do, initiating some thoughts or behaviors while inhibiting others in order to carry out a plan and reach a goal (see Logan, Van Zandt, Verbruggen, & Wagenmakers, 2014; Miyake & Friedman, 2012). When information is kept active and transformed in working memory, we are willing ourselves to attend to it, keep it activated, and transform it; when we inhibit a thought or behavior, we willingly inhibit neural firing. The reason it is so difficult not to think about a white bear (Wegner, 1989) is presumably because we are exciting our white bear-related neurons to keep the rule in mind while simultaneously trying to inhibit our white bear-related neurons to comply with the rule.

Development of Executive Function

Executive processes have a protracted course of development. We see very early vestiges in infants' emotional self-regulation, for example, when an upset 1-year-old changes focus of attention, or finds a blanket and sucks his or her thumb, and subsequently relaxes. The disappearance of the Piagetian A-not-B error, in which children who have repeatedly found an object under cloth "A" continue to search for the object under "A" even when it was—in plain sight and while the child watched—placed under "B," is another milestone in the development of executive function. This error usually goes away around age 12 months, and Diamond provided convincing evidence that prefrontal development is an important factor (see Diamond & Doar, 1989). The development of executive function continues through the preschool years (Carlson, Zelazo, & Faja, 2012; Müller, & Kerns, 2015), when children learn to control their temper tantrums when they are upset, and stay hidden while playing hide-and-go-seek. It continues as well through the teenage years. Teens take risks, emblematic of insufficient executive function. Adolescent risk-taking is speculated to be caused by the reward centers in the brain (deep structures, such as the amygdala) maturing earlier than the prefrontal structures. When the prefrontal structures mature in one's mid-20s, one ceases to engage in as much risky (but potentially rewarding) behavior (Casey, 2015; Luna, Paulsen, Padmanabhan, & Geier, 2013).

Executive function can be an elusive concept, and one way to understand it is to consider the many ways it is measured. There are both experimental and survey measures. In adults, one classic experimental measure is the Stroop task, in which words that refer to colors are printed in colors that differ from their semantic referent—for example, the word "blue" is printed in red letters. People are asked to say the color of the letters, inhibiting the prepotent response of reading the word. Another kind of executive function test is backwards working memory, in which people must repeat in backward order letters, words, and/or numbers from a list they were just read. A specific child task is "bear/dragon" for which children must always do what a bear says and inhibit doing what a dragon says (Murray & Kochanska, 2002); this and some other tasks are like "Simon Says" games. Another quite famous task is the "marshmallow task," in which children are given a choice of two plates of marshmallows: one with several that they could have if they waited for the experimenter to return in his or her own time, and one with just a few that they could have if they rang the bell for the experimenter to return early (Mischel, 2014). Survey measures might ask people (or their parents and teachers, in the case of young children) how well certain phrases describe them. For example, one questionnaire (Goodman, 1997) uses, "Sees tasks through to the end. Good attention span" and "Easily distracted, concentration wanders" (the latter is reverse scored) among its executive-function-related items.

The study of these processes has exploded in recent years, largely because executive function is highly predictive of many measures of "life success." This research is considered next.

WHAT EXECUTIVE FUNCTION PREDICTS

Executive function predicts measures of life success as well as specific cognitive and social outcomes. For example, in the marshmallow task, children's ability to wait for a plate of marshmallows, rather than eat a lesser amount immediately, when they were age 4 predicted social competence 10 years later (Mischel, Shoda, & Peake, 1988), and SAT scores and other measures of executive function at the end of high school (Mischel, Shoda, & Rodriguez, 1989; Shoda, Mischel, & Peake, 1990), and even body mass in their 30s (Schlam, Wilson, Shoda, Mischel, & Ayduk, 2013).

Many other studies looked specifically at school and cognitive outcomes. Children's performance on a wide variety of executive function measures predicts cognitive functioning (Blair & Razza, 2007) and success in school (e.g., Bull, Espy, & Wiebe, 2008; Cameron et al., 2012; Duncan et al., 2007; Kim, Nordling, Yoon, Boldt, & Kochanska, 2013; Röthlisberger, Neuenschwander, Cimeli, & Roebers, 2013). Self-regulation in early childhood explains a fair portion of the achievement gap between low- and middle-income students (Fitzpatrick, McKinnon, Blair, & Willoughby, 2014). Regarding the famous Perry Preschool Project of the 1960s, there has been much hand-wringing over the fact that IQ gains for low-income children were not sustained after the program ended. However, other long-term benefits suggest that the project had lasting effects on self-regulation. For example, there were fewer school dropouts and teen pregnancies in the intervention group than in the control (see Heckman & Kautz, 2012). Self-regulation also appears to be an important contributor to the positive academic effects of a successful intervention for low-income preschoolers (Raver, Jones, Li-Grining, Zhai, Bub, & Pressler, 2011).

One particularly large study of the predictive power of early childhood executive function for life success more generally followed over 1,000 children born in Dunedin, New Zealand, in the early 1970s (Moffitt et al., 2011). Childhood self-control was measured in three ways. First, their parents and their teachers were asked to rate the children's impulsivity, hyperactivity, lack of persistence, inattention, and impulsive aggression when they were ages 5, 7, 9, and 11. Second, at the older ages, children were asked to rate these factors for themselves; and third, while children were being given measures for the study at ages 3 and 5, their behavior was observed and rated by experimenters on its degree of self-control. All these measures were highly consistent, and they were statistically combined into one variable reflecting childhood self-control. The researchers then looked at the relationship between this measure and a range of outcomes at age 32. Because self-control differed by gender in childhood (girls had more), socioeconomic status, and childhood IQ, all these variables were controlled for in the prediction models.

First, childhood self-control predicted later health, assessed by a physical examination and laboratory tests assessing cardiovascular, respiratory, and mental health, specifically depression. For example, those participants with poor self-control as children were more likely to have suffered from depression by age 32. Second, childhood self-control predicted financial status at age 32. Specifically, it predicted whether participants had saved money, owned their own homes, had investment plans, and had credit problems. For the subset of participants who at age 32 had one or more children, childhood self-control predicted whether they were raising the children alone (negatively) or with a partner (positively). Childhood self-control predicted these factors even more strongly than social class origins or IQ. Third, those who had poor childhood self-control were also more likely to have been convicted for a criminal offense by age 32. In addition, all these findings showed a gradient of self-control; even removing from the sample those diagnosed with attention deficit hyperactivity disorder (ADHD, which is associated with low executive function) and remaining participants who were very low as well as very high in childhood self-control, every step of increase in self-control predicted a higher level of functioning across the domains studied. These results were reiterated by a large study of twins in the United Kingdom: In twin pairs, the twin with lower executive function at an earlier age fared worse over time (Moffitt et al., 2011). In sum, executive function is unquestionably important to later life outcomes.

Children who are better at self-regulating also show more positive social behavior on a variety of measures (Eisenberg, Smith, & Spinrad, 2011). For example, one study obtained teacher ratings of 82 preschool children on four dimensions of self-regulation, each consisting of multiple items: focused attention (items such as "When drawing or coloring in a book, shows strong concentration"), attention shifting ("Can move on to a new task when asked"), inhibitory control ("Can lower his/her voice when asked to do so"), and the reverse of impulsivity ("Sometimes interrupts others when they are speaking"; Cumberland-Li, Eisenberg, & Rieser, 2004). Parents' ratings were also obtained on these measures for about half of the sample. In addition, children nominated three classmates who were nice, three who were cooperative, and so on, and these nominations were summed to give each child an agreeableness rating. Teachers also gave agreeableness ratings of children, using a 20-item scale, including descriptions such as "cooperative," "warm," and "generous."

Strong correlations were found for teacher-rated agreeableness and all four of the teacher's self-regulation ratings. Children who were more able to regulate their attention and behavior were seen by their teachers as more generous, warm, cooperative, and so on. Of course, one could argue that the regulation measures are simply qualities teachers like and thus a "halo effect" governed all these results. The parent and classmate ratings can address this. Teacher ratings of children's abilities to control their attention were fairly well related to classmate ratings of the children's agreeableness, and classmate ratings were even more strongly related to parent ratings of the children's ability to focus attention and control impulses. These interconnections are not easily explained as halo effects. Thus, although some halo effects might have been operating, the results present a consistent picture whereby preschoolers who are higher in self-regulation are also seen by others as being warmer, more cooperative, and so on.

The findings with preschoolers are consistent with a larger body of research showing similar findings for children in elementary school and even for adults. Emotion regulation is positively related to psychological adjustment, competent social functioning, empathy, sympathy, and prosocial behavior in elementary school (Eisenberg et al., 1995, 1996, 1997, 2001, 2004, 2011; Riggs, Jahromi, Razza, Dillworth-Bart, & Müeller, 2006; Rothbart, Ahadi, & Hershey, 1994). On the reverse side, low executive function is linked to conduct disorder, bullying, and delinquency (Riggs, Jahromi, et al., 2006).

According to the psychologist Mary Rothbart, the relation between executive function and positive personality characteristics may exist in part because effortful control is needed to subjugate one's own feelings and perspective to consider those of another. For this same reason perhaps, inhibitory control is significantly related to tasks assessing an understanding of another's beliefs (Carlson, Moses, & Hix, 1998; Devine & Hughes, 2014); in this case one must inhibit one's knowledge of reality. Indeed, many studies have shown a solid relationship between executive function and social cognition (Müller & Kerns, 2015) or the ability to predict and explain mental states, and theory of mind in turn predicts social competence (Wellman, 2014). In addition, more related to Rothbart's view, social competence often involves inhibiting what one would want to say or do, in the interest of the relationship. I might really want my dining partner's chocolate cake, but I don't just take it.

Another possible reason for the relationship between self-regulation and positive social behavior is specific to the attention aspect of executive function. Attention is a key aspect of self-regulation (Ruff & Rothbart, 1996) because to pay attention is to regulate one's thoughts.

Research shows that when people's attention is focused, they are happier. Perhaps this positive mood leads to better social behavior. Killingsworth and Gilbert (2010) queried more than 2,000 people from 83 countries using an iPhone app, which asked them what they were feeling and doing at random points during the day, including specifically asking if they were thinking about something other than what they were currently doing. They found that *not* being focused on one's current activity significantly predicted unhappiness, and time-lag analyses suggested that the mind wandering led to the unhappiness, rather than the reverse. In the workplace as well, the mood state most commonly reported during focused attention states is happiness (Mark, Iqbal, Czerwinski, & Johns, 2014). People are happy when their attention is engaged in what they are presently doing, and this happiness might lead to better social functioning.

This is consistent with Dr. Montessori's descriptions. "When the children begin to be interested in the work and to develop themselves . . . lively joy . . . mutual respect and affection" become manifest (Montessori, 1917/1965, pp. 93–94). In sum, the literature suggests that self-regulation predicts many positive characteristics, including better cognitive, social, and life skills, increased happiness, and reduced aggression.

What Predicts Executive Function

First, executive function appears to have a strong underlying genetic substrate, even in childhood (Engelhardt, Briley, Mann, Harden, & Tucker-Drob, 2015) when genetic effects on psychological characteristics are generally weakest. Yet experiences do influence executive function, both positively and negatively (Diamond & Lee, 2011; Rueda, Rothbart, McCandliss, Saccomanno, & Posner, 2005; Thorell, Lindqvist, Nutley, Bohlin, & Klingberg, 2009). One set of techniques that have been shown to improve executive functions falls under the umbrella term "mindfulness," which means paying attention to what is happening in the present moment; these are discussed at the end of the chapter, as they tie in interesting ways to several Montessori practices. Other training models exist as well.

Even in monkeys, attention training (specifically, training monkeys to use a joystick in preparation for space flight) appears to reduce aggression and improve self-regulation even outside the training contexts.[1] Nonhuman primates raised in captivity can be notoriously difficult and are described as natural models for ADHD. Training them on tasks requiring sustained attention results not only in better attention, but also in general improvements in their behavior (Rumbaugh & Washburn, 1996).

Similar kinds of exercises have been used with children. For example, in one set of studies 4- and 6-year-olds participated in nine training exercises over 5 days (Rueda et al., 2005). One exercise involved using a joystick to move a cat from muddy to grassy areas on the screen; the grassy area gradually shrank. Another task involved moving the cat through a maze to get

---

[1] David Washburn, personal communication, April 20, 2004.

food, and another involved catching an umbrella to keep it over the cat's head. A conflict task required that children press a button indicating whether a fish was facing right or left; the fish sometimes was "flanked" by fish facing the opposite direction (conflict) and other times by fish facing the same direction (congruent trials). (Such tasks are referred to a "Flanker" tasks.) After just 5 days of this training, 4-year-olds performed markedly better on a new conflict task. Overall, computerized training studies are effective, although the training does not always transfer to tasks other than those on which one was trained (Diamond & Lee, 2011). I would also ask whether, all things being equal, one would rather a child develop his or her attention skills on artificial tasks, such as the ones just described, or useful tasks, such as washing a table.

School curricula have sometimes improved executive function. A well-known example is the PATHS (which stands for Promoting Alternative Thinking Strategies) curriculum, in which children are taught strategies such as to take a deep breath and consider alternative responses in emotional situations (Kusché & Greenberg, 1994). Children aged 7 to 9 who were exposed to one year of this curriculum showed significantly better executive function than control children (Riggs, Greenberg, Kusché, & Pentz, 2006). Another school curriculum that has received some attention is Tools of the Mind, which requires children to spell out pretend play plans ahead of time and engage in exercises such as holding an ear or a mouth while "buddy reading," with the symbol indicating their role (Bodrova & Leong, 2007). Although some initial results were promising, several large follow-up attempts failed (see discussion in Lillard, 2015); just one, with a no-intervention control group, has shown positive results (Blair & Raver, 2014) and the reasons for the nonreplications are unclear. Montessori schooling has also been shown to improve executive function, as discussed in chapter 11, and these results have been replicated.

Further research has shown that genotype interacts with training to lead to improvements on executive function tasks (Söderqvist, Matsson, Peyrard-Janvid, Kere, & Klingberg, 2014). Unsurprisingly, practice at paying attention, or concentrating, is evidenced in the neurological changes that undergird that practice as well as in behavior (Klingberg, 2014; Rueda et al., 2005).

In addition to certain kinds of activities improving executive function, other experiences appear to be detrimental. One detrimental experience is television.

TELEVISION AND CHILDREN'S EXECUTIVE FUNCTION

A growing body of research links television watching to attention problems, even ADHD (which also clearly has a genetic component; Li, Sham, Owen, & He, 2006). American children watch an average of about 4 hours of television a day (including DVDs, streaming, and other forms of "moving pictures"; Tandon, Zhou, Lozano, & Christakis, 2011). Although not every study has found an association between watching more television and having lower executive function, most published studies do (e.g., Jolin & Weller, 2011; Nathanson, Alade, Sharp, Rasmussen, & Christy, 2014; Pagani, Fitzpatrick, & Barnett, 2013; Swing, Gentile, Anderson, & Walsh, 2010; Zimmerman & Christakis, 2007), as evidenced by a recent meta-analysis (Nikkelen, Valkenburg, Huizinga, & Bushman, 2014). Specific types of content are apparently responsible for this association; for example, entertainment and violent television, but not educational television, were associated in one study (Zimmerman & Christakis, 2007). In another, adult-directed but not child-directed television at ages 1 and 4 predicted lower executive function at age 4 (Barr, Lauricella, Zack, & Calvert, 2010). Correlational associations cannot tell us about causes (there might be a "third variable" that studies did not control for, which is associated both with television and executive function), and it would be unethical to do a true experiment and assign some children to watch violent, entertainment and adult-directed television in their early years. In such cases, animal models can be useful, and a study using a "mouse model" is consistent with a causal relationship (Christakis, Ramirez, & Ramirez, 2012). Young mice were subjected to Cartoon Channel audio piped into their cages for 6 hours a day. To simulate the visual effects of television, a strobe light apparatus was rigged to change color in concert with the audio. A series of cognitive tasks was given to the mice after 42 days of this experience followed by 10 days of normal cage life. Compared with control mice, the mice with the simulated television experience showed ADHD-like symptoms: They were hyperactive and overly bold in an open field, had poor short-term memory, and were impaired in their learning.

Research in my laboratory suggests a possible explanation for the association between television and executive function. We were looking for a television program that might make children behave more or less nicely, to see whether children who watch bratty shows become bratty themselves. For this, we wanted to find episodes of the same show in which characters were sometimes nice and sometimes impudent, but we were having trouble finding shows where characters were nice—snarkiness was much more common. We finally settled on *SpongeBob SquarePants* for showing a full spectrum of behaviors.

The next step was to find particular episodes to use as experiment stimuli, which meant we had to watch many hours of *SpongeBob* in the laboratory. After these sessions, I found myself unable to concentrate, and I began to wonder what happens to the young children who watch the show. A University of Virginia student, Jennifer Peterson, was also interested in this, and we conducted a study in which for 9 minutes, 60 four-year-olds either watched *SpongeBob SquarePants*, watched *Caillou* (a slow, realistic show about a little boy), or drew. Afterwards, we gave the children four standard tests of executive function. The results showed that after watching *SpongeBob*, children had significantly lower executive function than after drawing or watching *Caillou* (Lillard & Peterson, 2011).

What about *SpongeBob* might be responsible? One possibility is pacing. Things happen very quickly in the show, and it might exhaust prefrontal resources just to track that activity. Another possibility is fantasy events. In *SpongeBob* and many other cartoons, a lot of things happen that cannot happen in the real world—they are physically impossible. People go through walls, far more cat food emerges from a box than could have fit inside it, and a talking sponge drives a car at the bottom of the sea. In another experiment, we pitted pacing and fantasy elements against each other, using a fast and realistic show, a slow and realistic show, a slow and fantastical show, and *SpongeBob* (fast and fantastical). To our surprise, even a slow fantastical show was associated with diminished executive function (Lillard, Drell, Richey, Boguszewski, & Smith, 2015, Experiment 3); a fast and realistic one was not. This is just one of many studies suggesting that fantasy information may not be helpful to young children; others will be reviewed in chapter 6.

In sum, executive function and its many forms, from attention control to self-regulation, are important to children's outcomes, are trainable with the right sorts of environment and input, and also are susceptible to impairment. Although Montessori education might conceivably influence many aspects of executive function (e.g., the extension exercises with the Red Rods, described in chapter 2, tax working memory), its particular focus is on concentrated attention.

Concentration in Montessori Education

One outstanding feature of Montessori classrooms, relative to other types of classrooms, is that children concentrate deeply and for long periods on their work, and regardless of teacher oversight. Dr. Montessori was initially surprised by this concentration. She wrote that one day, in her first school in San Lorenzo,

> I happened to notice a little girl of about three years old deeply absorbed in a set of solid insets, removing the wooden cylinders from their respective holds and replacing them. The expression on the child's face was one of such concentrated attention that it seemed to me an extraordinary manifestation; up to this time none of the children had ever shown such fixity of interest in an object. (Montessori, 1917/1965, p. 68)

This level of concentration later appeared in another child, and then another. It led to one of the most important and unique aspects of Montessori theory, which put the development of concentration at its core. In this section I first discuss this theory, then explain its practical application in the classroom.

MONTESSORI THEORY

According to Dr. Montessori, being free to make constructive choices in a specially prepared environment develops positive personality characteristics. Following on the preceding description, she wrote, "And each time that such a polarization of attention took place, the child began to be completely transformed, to become calmer, more intelligent, and more expansive" (1917/1965, p. 68). This reminds one of the association seen in conventional settings between concentration and self-regulation and positive character outcomes. Dr. Montessori adopted a term from anthropology, "normalization," to describe this change; normalization essentially means "being a contributing member of society" (Shaefer Zemer, 2006; see also the Wikipedia entry on the term in sociology).

Normalization

Dr. Montessori believed that her method of education returns children to their true nature, or their normal state, free of perturbations. She described the normal state of a child as "precociously intelligent, one who has learned to overcome himself and to live in peace, and who prefers a disciplined task to futile idleness" (1966, p. 148). In Montessori theory, normalization of the personality occurs naturally when children are able to make their own choices in a prepared environment; in such a situation, they begin to concentrate their attention.

> Normalization comes about through "concentration" on a piece of work. For this we must provide "motives for activity" so well adapted to the child's interests that they provoke his deep attention [...] *The essential thing is for the task to arouse such an interest that it engages the child's whole personality.* (Montessori, 1967a/1995, p. 206; italics in original)

It is important that children are free to make choices, rather than forced to do (except when truly necessary) what the teacher directs them to do, as in conventional schooling or when a Montessori school has children do "Specials," addressed later in this chapter. Rather, children need to be able to follow inner guides that will lead them to make choices that correspond to their evolving developmental needs. Concentration assists children in being normalized, and when normalized, they make good choices because they "know" what they need.

> All we have to do is set [the child's developmental] energy free. It is as simple as that. This is not giving freedom to children in the common

sense. What is the use of freedom to children, if it is freedom to develop their deviations? When we speak of freedom in education we mean freedom for the creative energy which is the urge of life towards the development of the individual. This is not casual energy like the energy of a bomb that explodes. It has a guiding principle, a very fine, but unconscious directive, the aim of which is to develop a normal person. When we speak of free children we are thinking of this energy which must be free in order to construct these children well. (Montessori, 1989, p. 12)

Although children having "inner guides" sounds mystical, developmental psychology research does show that young children, when free to choose, make good choices among certain sets of alternatives. For one, they choose material that optimizes their development, by selectively attending to material that is just above their current level of competence. Formerly called the *moderate discrepancy hypothesis*, this was recently renamed the Goldilocks effect, and Kidd, Piantadosi, and Aslin (2014) explain it as follows:

Imagine, for example, attempting to complete an open-book examination on an unfamiliar subject in a vast library by drawing books from the shelves at random. An alternative strategy would be to make attention dependent upon relevant properties of the stimulus itself, perhaps actively allocating attention to auditory material that is most useful for learning. (p. 1796)

Over a series of studies, Kidd and colleagues have revealed that infant attention has an upside-down U-shaped function: When infants are left to their own devices, material that is both too simple (in this case, highly predictable) and too complex (such that to a developing system it would likely seem random) gets ignored; infants attend instead to information that is "just right," meaning at an intermediate level of challenge (moderately probable). This can be seen both across populations and within individual infants (Piantadosi, Kidd, & Aslin, 2014). Thus when free to choose, infants conserve their processing resources by engaging their attention with stimuli that will assist their development to a higher level—not stimuli that are already known or unknowable. "Infants implicitly seek to maintain intermediate rates of information absorption and avoid wasting cognitive resources on overly simple or overly complex events—in both visual and auditory modalities" (Kidd et al., 2014, p. 1802; see also Gerken, Balcomb, & Minton, 2011; Kidd et al., 2012). Children make these choices because they are interested in information at a certain level; this points to biologically driven interests that will be discussed in chapter 5.

Children (and adults; Kang at al., 2009) actually learn the most when new material is pitched just above but not too far above their current level of understanding (Kuhn, 1972; Turiel & Rothman, 1972). That children are apt to imitate other people who are just older rather than much older than themselves (Hanna & Meltzoff, 1993; Ryalls, Gul, & Ryalls, 2000; see chapter 7), and that children choose more challenging tasks when no external rewards are offered (see chapter 6), both also suggest that inner guides direct children to what is most optimal for their current stage of learning.

Another situation where psychologists have seen healthy choices under free-choice conditions concerns nutrition. People with mineral deficiencies are sometimes driven to consume clay, and chicks who are permitted to select their own diet select ones that yield maximum growth, normal body temperature, and high activity levels (Rovee-Collier, Hayne, Collier, Grieser, & Rovee, 1996). Likewise, young children also appear to regulate their caloric intake naturally, consuming fewer calories following high-calorie snacks than low-calorie ones (Johnson, McPhee, & Birch, 1991). When parents interfere with these natural tendencies, admonishing children to clear their plates and offering poor food choices, healthy food intake is disrupted (Frankel, Hughes, O'Connor, Power, Fisher, & Hazen, 2012).

Dr. Montessori believed that the same principles apply when children are given choices regarding their psychological development, such that all children in a prepared environment with only good choices available will spontaneously engage with that which they need to further their development. "The pivot, the medium of this construction of the personality, is working in freedom" (Montessori, 1917/1965, p. 108). In a properly prepared environment, meaning one that provides positive choices, children who are normalized (through concentration) will take what they need from among those choices.

Psychology research has not addressed how concentration affects choice, such as whether people make better choices after a bout of deeply concentrated work. We do know that sustained attention on a *dull and boring* task can lead to poorer choices (Xiao, Ma, Lv, Cai, Teng, Xu, & Chen, 2015), but Dr. Montessori saw children being energized by their focus on real (not boring) work, more akin to a flow experience:

> To ensure the continuance of this [intelligent] attitude and of the development of personality it is essential that *some real task* should be performed each day; for it is from the completed cycle of an activity, from methodical concentration, that the child develops equilibrium, elasticity, adaptability, and the resulting power to perform the higher actions, such as those which are termed acts of obedience. (Montessori, 1917/ 1965, p. 105).

A child who is set free in the prepared environment of a Montessori classroom manifests a set of reactions, to which Dr. Montessori referred throughout her writings; her son Mario Montessori compiled and wrote about these "human tendencies" in a pamphlet published in 1956, and they are considered an important part of Montessori teaching training courses (see also Sackett, 2012; Stephenson, 2000).

The Human Tendencies

Concentration, Dr. Montessori claimed, brings out healthy psychological characteristics that she saw as the natural state of human beings. The *human tendencies* are manifestations of human nature that evolved to satisfy the physical needs of food, shelter, clothing, and transportation. Dr. Montessori saw these human tendencies when children were set free in the prepared environment, where and when they begin to concentrate. In the Primary classroom, the first activities available to children are the Exercises of Practical Life and the Sensorial exercises; these activities often instigate initial bouts of deep attention that bring out these tendencies. In a cyclical fashion, expressing the human tendencies then further serves to bring about the control of attention and behavior that manifest in strong executive function. How the human tendencies are grouped leads to some variation in their number; I express them as 11 human tendencies here:

1. Humans, like other organisms, are interested in *exploring* their environments, learning what is where and how things work. This tendency stems from the very basic need of finding food and shelter. We use our senses to move around in the environment, exploring it. Babies crawl about the house; children explore the classroom and the materials within it, for example, trying different ways to pour water. We are curious, and seek to become familiar with the environment through exploration.

2. Coupled with this tendency to explore is a tendency to be active, to *move and to work,* including *work with the hands.* People move in order to better their situations, to respond to their needs and wants. In all cultures, people move to create homes, means of transport, fabrics, tools, and art, and they do so with their hands. We could not fashion clothing and houses and gather our food without moving and without working with our hands. The connection between movement and cognition, discussed in chapter 2, is fundamental.

3. We *orient* to the environment, so we have an internal map that corresponds to the external space. This allows us to explore and return home. Babies learn where the stairs are, where to find their beds, and where food is given; likewise children learn the map of the classroom and where to find different types of work. Orientation, exploration, and activity are all related.

4. We tend to prefer and to put things in *order*, finding delight in the predictability of the environment. Order is necessary for orienting,

and for exploring to lead to orientation. If the environment were different every time we encountered it, we could not orient. Any sort of journey has a beginning, a middle, and an end. When a child engages in a Montessori activity, the beginning involves removing it from the shelf, the middle is carrying out the activity, and the end is returning it to the shelf. Every Montessori activity has an ordered pattern of execution; young children are drawn to follow that order, which has been carefully presented by an adult or learned by observing another child. A child "has the tendency to organize a set of movements around an idea, which constitutes a definite aim" (Montessori, 1994a, p. 60; see also chapter 10).

5. Humans have a tendency to *imagine*, to create and to invent with the intellect. For example, an act of imagination allowed humans to use animal fur and plant fibers to construct clothing. A child in the classroom imagines a new constructive way to use a material or how the globe represents the earth.

6. Closely related to imagining is the human tendency toward *abstraction*, toward taking ideas, perhaps recombining them, and sometimes materializing those ideas in the world. The Sensorial Materials support abstraction, giving the child volume, weight, warmth, color, dimension, texture, sound, and so on—all the abstract qualities of which every object in the universe is composed. The Sensorial Materials thus provide the keys to the world, abstracting for children every physical dimension of every object in the world.

7. Another human tendency is *precision*. "It is necessary to arouse the child's interest with something exact" (Montessori, 1994a, p. 107). This is a principle that applies both to lining up the Sensorial Materials (like the Pink Tower) very precisely and carrying out a Practical Life activity as an exact series of steps; it is manifested also as a preference for using just the right word to denote a concept, and laying bricks in a precise line to build a house, and executing mathematical equations. "If we offer the child an exact technique, it draws forth an immense inner power which helps the construction of the self" (Montessori, 1994a, p. 107). Dr. Montessori described a child cleaning "a table with a care absolutely out of proportion to the amount of dust that the table carried. Not only did he clean the top of the table, but also the edges, below the edges, the corners and the legs" (1994a, p. 54). The child was manifesting this tendency toward precision. Note that self-discipline is inherent in this tendency: One inhibits all the alternate ways one might accomplish something by attending to a particular goal and working precisely toward it.

8. Another tendency is *repetition* leading to *perfection* or virtuosity (Kubovy, 1999). Moving on from the preceding table cleaning example, when the child had finished, he started the work all over again. "The child carries out these actions not with the same aim that adults have, which is to clean, but with . . . an inner aim . . . to exercise himself. It is as if the child has an instinct to form his own co-ordination by carrying out actions on objects . . . because it is a means of concentrating the attention on a series of movements" (Montessori, 1994a, p. 55). From a child repeatedly falling and rising again while working at walking without support, to an Olympic gymnast working at perfecting a move on the parallel bars, we see humans strive for perfection through repetition.

9. Relatedly, in repetition lies a human tendency to note and *control error*; this is necessary to doing things better, moving us toward the ideal. Dr. Montessori gave the example of a child pouring rice into a cup—a common type of Practical Life activity, which a teacher presents to a child very slowly, showing the precise coordinated movements needed to carry it out. Initially children typically spill, but they continue to repeat the exercise. "Gradually the movements become so perfect that no rice is spilt . . . the purpose of the exercise is to help perfect the movement of the child . . . the child is his own critic, and strives to carry out work perfectly controlling his error" (pp. 57–58). Dr. Montessori noted that this is part of why Montessori classrooms have breakable objects: They are the best teachers, and help inspire children to perfect their movements, because there are important consequences when they do not. The objects provide feedback that helps users to control their behavior, resulting in fewer errors.

10. In every society, humans *communicate*; this communication unfolds from early infancy, as children use different cries to communicate different internal states, and then gradually learn the languages used around them. Communication is not synonymous with language: We communicate nonverbally as well, with facial and other bodily expressions.

11. Finally, there is a human tendency for *self-preservation*, and even to better one's situation. At its core, self-preservation involves the lowest levels of Maslow's hierarchy of needs—our needs for food, shelter, and safety. Humans tend not only to preserve the good things they have, but also to seek nicer places to live, better foods, and so on.

When a children are set free in an environment that responds to their needs, these human tendencies manifest, and children flourish. Concentration is inherent and seen particularly in repetition, control of error, and the drive to perfect one's actions. These tendencies do not manifest immediately when a child enters a Montessori environment. "When a child who is disorderly in movement, who jumps about and breaks everything, who is very noisy, and speaks in a very loud voice, comes to our school we just wait until the child's attention becomes fixed upon an external object" (Montessori, 1994a, p. 177). This fixed attention involves purposeful movement, typically either carrying out a Practical Life activity with the hands toward some practical end or arranging a Sensorial Material with the hands. "Through the exercises of practical life, which have a useful aim, and the sensorial activities, [a child] becomes master of his [or her] own movements, his [or her] own intellect, and his [or her] own senses" (Montessori, 1994b, p. 11). Independence, or doing each activity oneself, is important. "Anger, impatience, rebellion—which are connected with the incapacity of doing ... disappear when an action chosen by our own will is carried out joyfully and calmly ... through the exercises, the child becomes capable of planning and carrying out his own actions" (Montessori, 1994b, pp. 4–5). Dr. Montessori called deep concentration on a difficult task, one that holds the child's "entire attention ... [and involves the child's] entire being ... *the great work*" (Montessori, 1956, p. 83, italics added).

As stated, through concentration, children's personalities normalize, meaning their deviations and misbehaviors go by the wayside, and they become kinder and more interested in work (see, e.g., Montessori, 1994b, p. 2). According to her observations, children who can concentrate treat others kindly and work constructively with materials, rather than choosing to distract classmates or abuse materials. Research suggests her observations have merit and are particularly relevant in today's world of attention-controlling television and computer programs.

The level of concentration children appear to attain in Montessori classrooms is reminiscent of what Csikszentmihalyi (1997) terms "flow." Primary classrooms can have a "hushed" quality when children are busy with their work; other times they buzz, with the children seeming like a lot of busy bees going about their tasks. Elementary classrooms are more likely to include children chatting as they work, displaying an ability to multitask and a greater need for social engagement. Dr. Montessori saw concentration as crucial to children making constructive choices.

IN PRACTICE: HOW MONTESSORI ENVIRONMENTS FACILITATE CONCENTRATION

Montessori environments facilitate concentration in at least three ways: the prepared environment, including engaging materials (initially those of Practical Life and Sensorial education); 3-hour work cycles (Figure 4.1); and minimizing forces that might disrupt concentration.

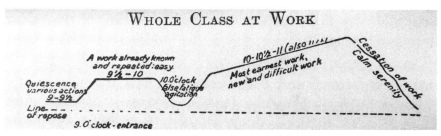

FIGURE 4.1 Activity cycle in a Montessori classroom. Reprinted from M. Montessori, 1917/1965, *Spontaneous Activity in Education: The Advanced Montessori Method* (F. Simmonds, Trans.), New York: Schocken, p. 98.

The Prepared Environment of a Montessori Classroom

Dr. Montessori inferred that her provision of an orderly environment of specific types of self-correcting, hands-on materials enabled normalization.

> Whereas the ancient pedagogy in all it various interpretations started from the conception of a 'receptive personality'—one, that is to say, which was to receive instructions and to be passively formed, this scientific departure starts from the conception of an active personality developing itself by a series of reactions induced by systematic stimuli which have been determined by experiment. (1917/1965, p. 73)

What are these systematic stimuli? All Montessori materials are designed to deeply engage childrens' hands and minds. The hands-on aspects of the materials were discussed in chapter 2, and their inspiring interest is the topic of chapter 5. In a Primary classroom, the initial materials that capture the child's attention are the Exercises of Practical Life and the Sensorial Materials: "An interesting object, a series of movements revolving around this object, and the fixing of attention by the action being done, is the most effective manner of calling the wandering mind of the child" (Montessori, 1994a, p. 59).

PRACTICAL LIFE

In the first stage of a newly established Montessori classroom, a teacher uses collective activity to arouse the children's interest—together carrying a bowl of water without spilling, or carrying a chair with great care (Montessori, 1994a, p. 182). Once interest is engaged (often in a few days), Practical Life activities are shown to individual children. Alternatively, a new child entering an established classroom will be individually presented with the Exercises of Practical Life. Chapter 2 introduced the Practical Life activities and alluded to their particular characteristic of often leading children to concentrate. A child might, for example, work very hard to clean a table, and when the child is finished, might start all over again. Although the activity has an immediate practical purpose (getting the table clean), its deeper purpose is to engage the hand in the service of the mind's goal and to engage the attention completely in that service. Other aspects and goals of Practical Life activities are discussed in chapters 2 and 10; here I focus on the goals of concentration and precision that are germane to executive function.

Dr. Montessori noted that children want to perform the activities they see adults carrying out. Left free to play, children reproduce the activities of adults in their culture (Lancy, 1996; Lillard, 2015). Children also like to care for their environments, and to do so independently. However, adults' tools are typically not useful for children; for example, they are too large or heavy. Hence Dr. Montessori developed materials that were appropriate for children. In addition, adults' exact techniques are not always suitable for children, so Dr. Montessori revised the techniques. She also made those techniques precise, because she saw that children liked exactly reproducing a specific sequence of activities. She also noted that children like having a purpose in their activities, and like to use objects that "call out" for their use—in part because the objects are very attractive and also because they reveal themselves; for example, light-colored tables reveal when they are dirty and need cleaning.

These principles all come together in the Practical Life activities. Children are shown an exact series of steps. For example, for polishing a set of small brass objects, a tray containing all the necessary implements is carried to the table; a matt is laid out; the objects—a polish bowl, a polish applicator, and a polishing cloth—are placed in specific formation; a specific quantity of polish is squeezed into the bowl; and so on (Figure 4.2). To some adults, the exactness seems obsessive-compulsive, but Dr. Montessori noted young children liked such precision and worked hard to repeat the steps exactly—an observation recently made by psychologists, resulting in a wave of research on "overimitation" (e.g., Keupp, Behne, & Rakoczy, 2013).

> It is as if the child has an instinct to form his [or her] own coordination by carrying out actions on objects ... because it is a means of concentrating the attention on a series of movements. For the child, the purpose of the activity is the activity itself ... which evidently develops something inside [the child]. (Montessori, 1994a, p. 55)

Because of how children repeat an activity over and over—a child who just polished all the brass objects will immediately begin again—Dr. Montessori decided the child's purpose was the activity and not the goal. That said, Dr. Montessori still claimed that having a goal is key to Practical Life activities. What fixes the attention is precise movement focused on a goal to which the child can relate, a goal that corresponds to children's need to care for the environment and engage in activities they see adults do. "Movement is the secret for holding the attention of the child" (Montessori, 1994a, p. 59).

FIGURE 4.2 Concentration while Polishing. Photograph by An Vu.

THE SENSORIAL MATERIALS

Once a child has begun to concentrate on the Exercises of Practical Life, the child (still of age 2.5–3 years) is ready for the Sensorial Materials. (It is interesting that the first child Dr. Montessori saw concentrating was concentrating on a Sensorial Material, not a Practical Life activity.) Chapter 2 also discussed the Sensorial Materials, particularly the group of materials that leads into mathematics; these materials are also discussed concerning Interest (see chapter 5) and Order (see chapter 10, where recent research linking skill at sensory discrimination with intelligence is also presented). Here again I focus on the aspect of these materials that concerns concentrated attention and precision.

The Sensorial Materials abstract the qualities of the world, isolating them to provide children keys to the world. And because we encounter every object through our senses, the Sensorial objects give children an organized framework for accessing the world. Yet rather than the child simply observing, the child moves; access to the properties of the world is provided through movement, because movement results in self-development.

There is again a precise way to perform actions on the materials. For example, the blocks of the Brown Stair are grasped in the center, whereas the Red Rods are grasped at the ends, because these particular modes of grasping highlight for children the quality that each material is intended to impart (Montessori, 1994a, p. 106). The materials also are lined up in a manner that draws attention to their key qualities. Dr. Montessori and her collaborators designed the materials carefully in response to children's reactions so as to create interest and provide just enough difference to evoke appreciation of these qualities. The Sensorial Materials are "instruments prepared exactly and carefully, which cause our intelligence to move, giving us a part of something in the exterior world [...] enabling our minds to concentrate, giving us ideas" (Montessori, 1994a, p. 198).

These exercises, then, capture a child's attention, leading one to concentrate on movements that unlock features of all the objects of the universe. What is most important is that the child is set free to do this in a carefully prepared environment. Self-development occurs spontaneously as children focus their concentration on these two types of exercises (Practical Life and Sensorial) in an environment carefully prepared to correspond to children's developmental needs (Montessori, 1917/1965, p. 81).

The 3-Hour Work Cycle

Regular interruptions, by definition, disrupt concentration. Concentration, according to Dr. Montessori, is necessary for children to tune into the postulated inner guides that help them to make good choices (recall research on the Goldilocks effect). Every adult-imposed interruption at which children are removed from their freely chosen work during 3-hour morning and afternoon work periods diminishes the quality of concentration children can achieve.

Research on adults' reactions to interruptions in the workplace is interesting in this regard. Studies of these reactions show that after an interruption, such as an arriving email, adults often follow with a chain of further, self-imposed distractions (Iqbal & Horvitz, 2007) and take 23 minutes on average to get back to work on the task that was interrupted (Mark, Gonzalez, & Harris, 2005). After 40% of interruptions, adults do not return to the original task at all (O'Conaill & Frohlich, 1995).

Dr. Montessori believed that children need sufficient time to delve into work, concentrate, and develop their inner guides. This period is 3 hours in the morning for all levels of the classroom. The oldest children in the Primary classes and children in Elementary classrooms stay for an additional 2- to 3-hour work period after lunch (Montessori, 1917/1965).

Dr. Montessori made activity graphs of children's work cycles (Montessori, 1917/1965, pp. 97–108; see Figure 4.1). A line in the middle represented the child at rest; above the line represented ordered activity; and below the line, disordered activity (such as disturbing others). The higher or lower the line (the y-axis), the more intense the activity. The x-axis represents time.

Dr. Montessori described a normal cycle as beginning with about 30 minutes of preparatory work; in a well-normalized child, even this work is not easy work, for example, it might involve using the Moveable Alphabet. Hence it is well above the rest line. After a half-hour period of this activity, a normalized child will do something really difficult, such as writing and then reading command cards for a couple of hours. This will be followed by easy work, such as looking at picture books.

Earlier in the stages of normalization, however, things look different. A half hour of preparatory work might be followed by a few brief moments of rest (perhaps walking around the classroom looking at others' work, perhaps even disturbing them, hence descending into disorder), then a 1- to 2-hour period of intensely challenging work, followed by a serene period during which the child disengages from work. Earlier still, Dr. Montessori described a child who was probably fairly new to Montessori:

> He enters, is quiet for a moment, then goes to work. The curve [on his activity chart] is drawn upward into the space representing order. The child tires and, as a result, his activity is disorganized. The curve is then drawn through the line representing rest downward into the space representing disorder. After this, the child begins a new task. If, for example, he at first works with the cylinders, then takes up some crayons, works assiduously for some time, but then disturbs his neighbor, the curve must again be drawn downward. After this, he teases his companions, and the curve remains in the space designating disorder. Tiring of this, he takes up the bells, begins to work out the scale and becomes very absorbed; the curve again ascends into the space representing order. But as soon as he is finished, he is at a loss to occupy himself any further and goes to the teacher. (Montessori, 1956, p. 81)

The teacher, she advised, must have faith and patience through this period, waiting for the environment (including the materials) to do its job of attracting the child's interest and helping the child to order his or her activities. The period the boy just described spent working with the Musical Bells (see Figure 3.1.) was a beginning. After some time in the classroom, children begin to adopt constructive work cycles independently.

Another warning Dr. Montessori gave to teachers was that they not be swayed by a false fatigue that sometimes appears after early work. Teachers might be tempted to take children outside because they appear tired, but in fact the great work has not yet begun. Really deep concentration, she saw, leaves children feeling refreshed, not tired.

It bears repeating that interruption during the 3-hour work cycles is detrimental. A "negative action is the interruption of work at fixed times in the daily program. They say to the child, 'Don't apply yourself for too long at any one thing. It may tire you'" (Montessori, 1967a/1995, p. 241). Dr. Montessori believed that children need to be free to complete their work, without unnecessary interruption. "There is a vital urge to completeness of action, and if the cycle of this urge is broken, it shows in deviations from normality and lack of purpose" (Montessori, 1948b/1967, p. 57). Montessori teachers who adhere to 3-hour work periods without interruption claim that a difference can be seen in the quality of children's concentration on days when children know they will be leaving the classroom in an hour for a field trip or doctor's appointment or special music class. Formal comparison of concentration of children in Montessori classrooms with and without interruptions, such as mid-morning recess and Specials, would be very interesting.

In sum, during 3-hour work cycles, children are not removed from work for extracurricular activities or recess. Visitors to the classroom are another extrinsic element that can be disruptive to concentration and accessing inner directives.

Possible Effect of Classroom Visitors on Concentration and Choice

Dr. Montessori's belief in inner forces that guide children to what they need is responsible for one practice that sometimes concerns people regarding the Montessori school program: Classroom visits are often kept to a minimum. Many American parents want to be part of their children's day, and indeed conventional schools encourage a close parent–school partnership, because in conventional schools it is associated with better student outcomes. Montessori schools do not, as a whole, *discourage* close contact with parents. They may, however, discourage parents from entering the classroom during concentrated 3-hour work periods.

Some reasons for this are related to concentration and the sequelae discussed in this chapter. First, visitors (including parents) often interrupt children's concentration by asking children what they are doing, commenting on their work, or even just by being there. Visitors might not notice that children are concentrating, because it is unusual for children in our culture to concentrate deeply. Or they might not realize that the concentration is crucially important in Montessori programs. To minimize disruption, if parents and other visitors are allowed in a Montessori classroom, they may be asked to sit quietly and not speak unless spoken to. This can leave visitors who do not understand the reasons feeling unwelcome.

Second, parents may, consciously or unconsciously, directly or even by their mere presence, sway their children's choices in work. For example, they might directly or indirectly influence their child to choose a particular work, causing the child to do that work not from the child's own inner impulse, but in order to please the parents. As discussed earlier, many American children are less motivated toward work chosen by their parents, and they do their work less well when their parents choose it for them (Iyengar & Lepper, 1999).

In the same vein, some Montessori schools do not regularly send children's work home, out of concern that parental praise might lead children to value work that they can show their parents more than work that they cannot. For example, children in Primary may come to prefer Metal Inset drawing to working with the Brown Stair because their parents praise the former but not the latter (because there is no product that comes home), yet both activities are important to the child's development in Montessori.

Another concern about parents influencing a child's work is that parents might focus on errors when what may be important for their child at that time is not that the work be error-free, but that it have some other feature, such as that the child is independently choosing it and concentrating on it. For example, a child who had been resisting writing an original research report on early language but finally has freely chosen to do it might make some spelling errors. The teacher knows the child will work on the spelling, but for the time being, the advance is that the child did the work. The teacher sees the child's work in the context of everything the child is doing in the classroom. The parent, however, sees only the tiny slice of the child's school day represented by the work he or she brings home. In addition, parents have conventional schooling attitudes about errors. Because Montessori education is about the development of the personality, errors are not of central concern; there is faith that errors will work themselves out, and a view that what is foundational to other developments is the child becoming a confident human being who can make good choices.

> So long as the child has used the material well, does it matter if he commits an error? ... The important thing to develop in the child is courage.... What is important is not to take a second step, but the effort that is made to walk! ... If this courage is given to the child, he [or she] will repeat the exercise again and again, becoming more and more perfect, eliminating all the errors that he [or she] committed in the beginning. This is why the material is so exact! This is why the technique is so exact! This is also why the material has the control of error! (Montessori, 1994b, pp. 306–307)

Parents, failing to understand this, often become concerned about errors. The negative effects of extrinsic interferences are considered further in chapter 6. In Montessori theory, such input from parents could distract children from the inner guides helping them make choices about what work to do.

To summarize, Montessori classrooms facilitate concentration by provision of interesting, hands-on materials, by incorporating 3-hour work periods without interruption, and by minimizing the presence of parents and visitors in the classroom. By allowing concentration on work, the classroom environment brings about normalization in the child. Such normalization also comes from the child's being able to freely choose activities in the prepared environment; these specially prepared activities facilitate concentration in time, and in response, the child becomes increasingly normalized and makes more and more constructive choices for his or her development.

Mindfulness and Human Psychology

Another area of research pertinent to Dr. Montessori's theory regarding concentration and normalization concerns mindfulness, which means attending fully to the here and now. Meditation practice facilitates mindfulness (Kabat-Zinn, 1994). There are many forms of meditation, but they can be boiled down to three:

1. Paying full and concentrated attention on a single stimulus, such as the breath
2. Allowing ideas to flow through the mind, considering them in a nonjudgmental fashion, and acknowledging that they are temporary, just thoughts, and not the same as oneself
3. Mind-body practices, such as yoga and tai chi, which involve making specific movements while remaining calm and nonjudgmental, and paying close attention to the body and mind

Although research is still in early phases, and the level of methodological rigor is variable (Sedlmeier, Eberth, Schwarz, Zimmermann, Haarig, Jaeger, & Kunze, 2012), there is growing consensus that mindfulness practices have positive effects on people's attention and emotion regulation (Tang, Hölzel, & Posner, 2015). Both aspects of executive function are pertinent to Montessori education and the concept of normalization. Interestingly, Dr. Montessori saw this connection when she was interned in India for 7 years during World War II. French doctors had noticed a co-occurrence of irregular heartbeats and "psychological deviations" in French patients, that when patients' lives became very orderly, both problems disappeared. They also noticed that Indian yogis were free of both problems. Dr. Montessori saw an analogy to normalization in her classrooms and wrote, "We have seen this phenomenon in children. It is just this upon which everything is based" (Montessori, 1994b, p. 299).

Several studies have shown that mindfulness practices affect attention and emotion regulation. Researchers have also looked at neural changes associated with these effects. These are examined in turn.

TRAINING ATTENTION

Mindfulness meditation has been shown to improve executive function, including attention (e.g., Hölzel, Lazar, Gard, Schuman-Olivier, Vago, & Ott, 2011; Jha, Krompinger, & Baime, 2007; Moore, Gruber, Derose, & Malinowski, 2012; Tang et al., 2015). For example, in one study 80 undergraduates who signed up for a meditation course were randomly assigned to either "integrative mind-body training" (IBMT) or a relaxation control.

For 20 minutes a day for 5 days, an IBMT trainer helped participants achieve a relaxed alert state in which their attention focused on the environment, their body, and their own mental states (Tang et al., 2007). Before and after the intervention, participants were tested for attention, intelligence, and emotion regulation. One particular type of attention, namely conflict monitoring (using a Flanker task, described earlier) was especially improved by the short meditation training, relative both to the pretest and to the relaxation training control. Interestingly, the meditation group also improved on the Raven's Progressive Matrices intelligence test. This is just one of many studies showing that mindfulness training leads to improved attention.

EMOTION REGULATION AND EMPATHY

Many studies have also shown positive effects of meditation on emotion regulation (e.g., Jain et al., 2007) and empathy (Winning & Boag, 2015). For example, in the study just described, emotion regulation was also improved in the meditation group. First, on a Profile of Mood States pencil-and-paper measure, the meditation group experienced significant improvement in measures of anger-hostility, depression-dejection, fatigue-inertia, tension-anxiety, and vigor-activity, whereas the relaxation group showed no improvements. Second, following a brief stressful event, physiological stress indicators (e.g., cortisol) were better regulated in response to a meditation than a relaxation session. Many other studies have similar findings (e.g., Teper, Segal, & Inzlicht, 2013) and a meta-analysis suggested that meditation's strongest effects are for emotionality and relationship quality; these effects are medium to large in size (Sedlmeier et al., 2012).

NEURAL CHANGES

Some studies of meditation directly examine whether the practice alters brain structure or function (e.g., Lazar et al., 2005; Moore et al., 2012; see Fox et al., 2014 for a recent review). In one study using electroencephalography (EEG) to examine patterns of neural activity, people who had applied for a course in mindfulness meditation were divided into two groups, one of which was given the course, and the other of which was told the course was full (Davidson et al., 2003). This is a choice control group, because it eliminates the possibility that the meditators had differed to begin with. Whereas other studies have shown differences in the patterns of neural activation of meditators during meditation courses, this study was unusual in looking at people several months after the meditation course was completed. Meditators (who were still engaged in regular meditation sessions) at that point had more activation in the left hemisphere than the right hemisphere of their brains. This pattern is typical of people during meditation courses and is generally considered a "happy pattern." People with stronger left than right hemisphere activation at rest report higher levels of well-being, presumably because they have a stronger "approach" than avoidance tendencies (Urry et al., 2004). Interestingly, even several months after the course, the meditators also had a stronger immune response to a flu vaccine, suggesting they might be less likely to become ill as well.

Other studies have looked for structural changes in brain areas. These show changes with meditation to specific brain regions, including the anterior cingulate cortex (a region that is involved in the attention network, especially when people are monitoring conflicting inputs), and the dorsolateral prefrontal region (also implicated in executive function) (see Cahn & Polich, 2006; Fox et al., 2014). These two brain areas are also active when empathy is aroused (Shamay-Tsoory, 2011), supporting the behavioral findings.

In sum, mindfulness meditation leads to improvements in attention and in emotion regulation, and neuroimaging shows contingent changes to brain function and structure in response to meditation. Research on mindfulness in adults has been extended to children as well, leading to child-oriented mindfulness exercises (Zelazo & Lyons, 2012). Interestingly, Montessori education germanely incorporates mindfulness (Lillard, 2011b).

Montessori and Mindfulness

There are several ways in which Montessori education is aligned with mindfulness. The first way was discussed earlier in the chapter, that is, concentration. Mindfulness also involves and privileges deep concentration; meditation is after all a form of concentrated attention.

Second, both mindfulness and Montessori privilege mind-body awareness. In mindfulness meditation, one often focuses closely on the breath, monitoring the sensory experience of breathing. Another mindfulness exercise is to focus carefully and intently on what one is eating, for example, "the raisin exercise" in mindfulness-based stress reduction courses (Kabat-Zinn, 1990), or Thich Nacht Hanh's (2001/2009) prescription to focus completely on the act and sensory experience of eating an orange. Some researchers suggest that the benefits of mindfulness are rooted in this somatosensory attention (Kerr, Sacchet, Lazar, Moore, & Jones, 2013). As has been discussed elsewhere in this chapter and volume, Montessori offers the Sensorial exercises to bring children in touch with their sensory experiences, so children learn to detect fine gradations between different colors, textures, weights, sounds, temperatures, and so on. It would be interesting to know how the Sensorial exercises influence brain structure and function (see chapter 10) and degree to which such changes might be responsible for normalization.

A third intersection of mindfulness and Montessori concerns the Exercises of Practical Life, discussed earlier in the chapter as well as in chapters 2 and 10. Dr. Montessori (1956) claimed, "There is a strict relationship between manual labor and deep concentration of the spirit" (p. 71). The Exercises of Practical Life always are to have a practical end, so children can see a reason to engage in them. Children are taught to perform all steps of the exercises with great care, not unlike the steps of a Japanese tea ceremony. Likewise, Kabat-Zinn (1990) recommends that we "attempt to bring moment-to-moment attention to the tasks, experience, and encounters of ordinary living such as setting the table, eating, washing the dishes, doing the laundry" (p. 134). Buddhists are urged to "chop wood" and "carry water" as part of their mindfulness training. The hands-on physical work is intense in Montessori adolescent programs, with children doing farm work, building structures, going on strenuous hikes, and so on.

Two additional elements of Montessori education that resemble mindfulness practices are the Silence and Walking on the Line.

THE SILENCE

Montessori education includes a "game" called the Silence, in which all the children in a classroom are asked to be absolutely still for a short period and to listen very carefully. Dr. Montessori described the origins of the game of Silence (1966, 1994a): One day she held a small baby up to the 40 children in a Primary classroom and pointed out how still the baby was. She suggested that the children could not possibly be as still as the baby, and in response the children became very, very still. She next pointed out the baby's very quiet breathing and that the children could not possibly breathe as quietly as the little baby, and the children became aware of their breathing noises and quieted them. Dr. Montessori noted that children became increasingly calm over the course of this encounter and seemed to display a heightened sensitivity to sound.

The Silence is presented in Dr. Montessori's early books as an exercise that the teacher initiates by writing "Silence" on the chalkboard. One or more children would notice the word and become silent, and others would follow suit, until the entire room would be quiet save for the ticking of a clock, natural noises, and some noises from children who could not maintain perfect silence. After some time, the teacher, perhaps from behind the children or in the next room, would begin to very quietly call each child by name, until the last child was called, and the Silence was over.

In some training courses today, the Silence is presented as an organized activity done when all the children are seated on a circle and the room is darkened; at the teacher's direction, either everyone simply sits as still as they can and listens, or the children listen for their names to be very quietly called.

Dr. Montessori noted that the Silence served several purposes. One is a higher-order appreciation of and sensitivity to sound than children usually have. She claimed the game makes children more aware of the sounds they make and helps them to attend to sound. Second, the exercise is about willpower and developing the ability to inhibit one's impulses and control one's movements—getting oneself in order, so to speak. Awareness and self-control are among the cornerstones of Montessori education, and both are key in mindfulness practices as well. The Silence also serves a social purpose, in that the children work together as a collective to achieve silence. One child making noise spoils the silence for everyone. Children learn to work together in concert to achieve a collective goal—something Dr. Montessori saw as important to know how to do, although she did not see it as requiring that children do everything together all the school day. Dr. Montessori also spoke of the Silence having a spiritual purpose, which led to its being adopted in conventional schools too. "[Conventional educators] saw that the children were calmer when the silence lesson was taught" (1994a, p. 80).

The silence led to children trying to be quiet in all their classroom activities, to move more carefully around the classroom, and to be kinder (Montessori, 1994a, p. 81). The effects of this exercise are similar, then, to the effects reported for meditation practice, in which one also sits quietly and notices the sounds around one. In this way, Montessori's silence is similar to a sitting meditation practice.

WALKING ON THE LINE

Another Montessori exercise used in Primary classes is Walking on the Line (Figure 4.3), which bears resemblance to a walking meditation practice. Dr. Montessori described it thus:

> We must draw a line on the floor, and ask the children to walk laying their feet on the line so that no part of [a foot] falls outside the line. It is a very simple method of making the child go straight. The attention of the child is centered, concentrated, upon this line. By trying to keep on the line, and maintain equilibrium at the same time, the mode of walking becomes more perfect. [...] The muscular sense is an inner sense which guides the personality. The exercise also shapes the personality, as a perfected technique can be achieved only through [challenging] muscular exercise. The fact that the child interests himself in this exercise shows that the child longs to achieve higher perfection, and that [the child] is always happy to acquire something which is difficult to acquire. (1994a, pp. 65–66)

To increase the difficulty, children can be shown to place their feet heel to toe, and then to carry objects, and finally to carry a full glass of water or

FIGURE 4.3 Walking on the Line. Photograph by An Vu.

balance something on the head while walking on the line. Children might also be taught to walk to different rhythms (Montessori, 1997, p. 217). The underlying idea is that children come to pay very close attention to all their movements.

The venerable monk Thich Nacht Hanh (2001/2009) describes learning to attend carefully to his movements. As a novice monk he was very excited when his teacher sent him on an errand, and he ran through the door, slamming it behind him. His teacher called him back, and he wrote, "Since that day, I know how to close the door behind me ... with 100% of my being" (p. 79). This sort of precision, with fully engaged attention, is at the heart of Montessori education.

Montessori education, then, incorporates several features that resemble features of mindfulness. In both, there is strong emphasis on concentration, sensory experience, and mind-body awareness. In addition, two discrete practices are similar. The Silence is similar in some ways to sitting meditation, and Walking on the Line is similar to walking meditation. Perhaps some of the benefits that researchers show stem from mindfulness practices are congruent with the normalization that Dr. Montessori described for children in Montessori classrooms.

Chapter Summary

When the child develops his attention, he changes completely . . . solidifies and strengthens his inner self . . . [and] passes from disorderliness in his acts to orderliness.

— Maria Montessori *(1997, p. 152)*

Dr. Montessori anticipated modern science in seeing the importance of deep concentration and the development of the executive functions. Setting children free in a specially prepared environment that allows for constructive activity aids their development. That special environment includes Exercises of Practical Life, including the group Silence and Walking on the Line, and many individual exercises in which movements are carried out in precise detail, the mind guiding the hand and body to an intelligent end. It also includes the Sensorial exercises, which ask the child to attend carefully to their senses, making judgments, reasoning, and deciding matches and gradations of stimuli. Such exercises inspire concentration in young children, and their personalities develop in ways that are consistent with reports concerning the effects of concentrated attention in mindfulness meditation. This deep attention is inspired in part because using the Montessori materials in precise ways evokes deep interest, which is the topic of the next chapter.

5 }

Interest in Human Learning

The secret of success [in education] is found to lie in the right use
of imagination in awakening interest, and the stimulation of
seeds of interest already sown.
    — Maria Montessori *(1948b/1967, pp. 1–2)*

Montessori education is designed to awaken interest and allow children to
pursue learning about issues that already personally interest them. This is a
natural corollary to a system of education based on choice: One chooses to do
what one is interested in doing. Interest naturally leads to sustained intrinsically guided engagement, which develops attention and concentration. It is
also necessary to a system that is based on intrinsic motivation, rather than
on extrinsic motivators such as grades, as discussed in chapter 6.

Interest researchers discriminate two types of interest. Personal interests,
such as hobbies, are subjective and not universal. In contrast, topic interests have broad appeal and therefore are shared by most people. Both types
of interest naturally facilitate engagement (Renninger & Bachrach, 2015)—
a subject of recent concern in secondary education particularly, because
American adolescents are often disengaged in school (Allen & Allen, 2009;
Wang & Eccles, 2013). Montessori education addresses both forms of interest;
it encourages topic interest, and it capitalizes on individual interest.

Regarding topic interests, Montessori materials and activities have been
very carefully developed over many decades to appeal to children's interests.
Dr. Montessori would create a material and then test it, observing how children interacted with it. Materials that did not capture their interest and serve
their learning were rejected, and she revised each material until she got good
results. This same care was put into the development of the lessons. In thorough Montessori teacher training courses, future teachers are taught every
lesson for the level at which they will work. The teachers write each lesson
down like the script of a play, replete with illustrations, creating albums of
the entire curriculum. While practicing these lessons with each other and the
teacher trainers, Montessori teachers-in-training work at having a captivating delivery style. Lesson scripts are not always followed to the letter, just as

actors might vary their lines from the script of a play, but the intention, spirit, and interest-provoking properties of the lessons are preserved. The education committee at the Association Montessori Internationale reviews lessons and materials regularly and changes them when change is warranted. Topic interest is thus embedded in the Montessori materials and lessons, freeing the teacher to focus on individual children and their personal interests.

Regarding specific personal interests, Montessori education encourages children to pursue issues that fascinate them, allowing more general learning to accrue through pursuit of those individual interests. For example, a child who is obsessed with frogs can obviously learn about biology through frogs. More generally, though, the child can also learn how to find information for—and write—a report, can practice penmanship, spelling, and punctuation, and can develop skill at realistic drawing. The child might also use frogs as a springboard to study sound (beginning with croaking) or adaptation (how different species of frogs have adapted to different biomes). One role of the teacher is to connect the child to various areas of the curriculum through the child's personal interests. Thus the teacher ensures that the child's education is broad despite personal interest being an important engine. Common concerns about educational breadth and how they are dealt with in Montessori education are discussed at the end of this chapter.

In conventional schooling, in contrast, personal interests are rarely allowed to direct children's learning. The teacher usually gives the entire class the same assignment, be it to read and write a paper on *The Adventures of Huckleberry Finn* or to do problems 10 to 20 on page 98 of the math text. Interest researchers often lament the impossibility of incorporating their findings in conventional schools. For example, the psychologist Suzanne Hidi wrote, "identifying and using individual interests to promote subject-matter learning could prove to be a time and effort consuming task for teachers … few teachers have the time needed to individualize efficiently enough to profoundly affect learning" (1990, p. 554).

The factory model bears part of the responsibility for this difficulty. With all children ushered through the system in lockstep, personal interests cannot drive learning: They would take the class in too many different directions, and it must go one place, all together. The factory-like daily schedule in conventional schools also precludes interest driving learning. A child cannot arrive in the morning and decide whether to work on a report on butterflies or to work on a math problem encountered at home, whichever seems more interesting at the moment. The child must do what is on the schedule. Some might argue that it is good for children to learn to follow someone else's schedule. However, children in Montessori learn the important skill of scheduling their own time. As was discussed in chapter 4, the ability to plan is an important predictor of many life outcomes. Research confirms the anecdotal observation that Montessori children adapt well to conventional school schedules when they need to (Dohrmann, Nishida, Gartner, Lipsky, & Grimm, 2007).

The model of the child as an empty vessel also bears responsibility for the difficulty, since the model presumes the child has no internal matter from which interests might spring. The child is empty, waiting to be filled. The reward structure imposed by behaviorism also precludes interest's directing education. All children must complete the same assignments, so they can be judged and rewarded by the same metric. Fair assignment of grades in mathematics would be difficult if all the children were working on different problems. Indeed, in the mass-testing climate in schools today, it is impossible to incorporate a meaningful degree of learning based on personal interest: Students must learn the material that will be on the state examinations, and studying material of personal interest would take time away from it.

Although pursuing personal interests is particularly problematic, conventional education can facilitate topic interest, and whether it does so is largely up to the individual teacher. This facilitation is referred to as "triggering" in the interest literature (see Ainley, 2012, for discussion). Good teachers who have time, energy, and a sense of what captivates an audience can create lessons that trigger topic interest. How to do so is often left up to individual teachers. In contrast, in Montessori education, the materials and lessons alike are provided to teachers and were experimentally created to stimulate children's interest, so teachers can focus on individual children instead of spending time making up their own personal set of lessons. Montessori teachers do not have to create their own way to explain the trinomial formula, for example; its explanation is inherent in the material and the lesson that presents it. Montessori also easily capitalizes on one of the important triggers of interest: peers (as discussed in chapter 7). Many studies show that various forms of engagement with one's peers increase topic interest (e.g., Thoman, Sansone, Fraughton, & Pasupathi, 2012).

Dr. Montessori was certainly not the sole person in her era to note the importance of interest. Her contemporary Dewey (1913) also emphasized the importance of interest to education, and Piaget (1981) spoke of the energizing role of affect in learning. Even Thorndike expressed the importance of interest, although topic interest was most likely what he had in mind. Yet conventional schooling methods make it very difficult to follow personal interests, and children's motivation to learn is generally left out of discussions on education (Renninger, Hidi, & Krapp, 1992; Simon, 2001a; Tobias, 1994). This is unfortunate, because the influence of interest on learning has been clearly demonstrated.

Studies on Interest and Learning

Interest has been defined as a psychological state involving "focused attention, increased cognitive functioning, persistence, and affective involvement" (Hidi, 2000, p. 311). Renninger and Hidi (2011) point out five widely accepted characteristics of interest: (1) interest refers to specific person-object/content relations and is indicated by focused attention and engagement; (2) the capacity for interest is a human trait, individuals are particularly apt to have certain interests, and the environment can nourish that trait for particular interests; (3) interest has affective and cognitive aspects; (4) interest is sometimes subconscious; and (5) interest is manifest in the neural circuits that process rewards (Kang et al., 2009). Interest is seen as developing in four stages (Hidi & Renninger, 2006): First, it is triggered by the situation; then it is maintained; next, individual interest emerges; and finally, individual interest becomes sustained and ongoing.

Considering that interest involves focused attention, increased cognitive and affective engagement, and persistence, it makes sense that interest-based learning would be superior, and many studies have confirmed that this is the case (Schiefele, Krapp, & Winteler, 1992). The studies generally proceed by identifying children's interests, asking them to learn material concerning their interests as well as topics of non-interest, and then testing their learning. Although the research tends to concern personal interests, one would expect the findings to extend to topic interest as well, and at least one study supports this. In the following section, I first consider studies involving elementary school through college students, and then turn to studies with preschoolers.

THE INFLUENCE OF INTEREST FROM ELEMENTARY SCHOOL THROUGH COLLEGE

In one early study, elementary school children chose from a list of six topics the ones of most and least interest to them (Estes & Vaughan, 1973). Each child was then given two passages to read, one on the topic the child had ranked of most interest, and the other on the topic the child had ranked as of least interest. The passages were aimed to be one to two years above the children's current reading level. After reading each passage, children were tested on the main idea, facts, inferences, and vocabulary. Scores on the comprehension test averaged 67 (of 100) for passages on which children had indicated low interest, compared with 86 on those for which they had indicated high interest, suggesting students learned better about topics they had indicated they were most interested in. However, children had just noted what they were interested in prior to the reading, and it is possible that this in itself was partially responsible for the effect. In addition, it was not clear if perhaps topics that children were more interested in were also by chance easier passages.

Ann Renninger (1992) remedied these problems. First, she used an open-ended interest questionnaire to discover the particular interests of fifth- and sixth-graders, then over the ensuing weeks developed reading passages as well as math worksheets based on their reported interests. Half of the reading passages and math problems for each child were couched in scenarios that the child had identified as particular interests, whereas half were couched in other children's interests. This addressed the second problem of the prior study: The same reading passages and math problems that were interest stimuli on one student's test were non-interest stimuli on another student's, making a balanced design in which the same stimuli served different categories for different children. For the reading task, students read one passage (of four), turned the paper over and answered two buffer questions, and then were asked to recall as much of the passage as they could before going on to the next passage. For the math component, they were simply asked to solve the problems.

The findings for reading reiterated those of the prior study. For passages embedded in contexts that students had identified as interests, students were "more likely to recall more points, recall information from more paragraphs, recall more topic sentences, write more sentences, provide more detailed information about topics read, have no errors on their written recall, and provide additional topic-relevant information" (Renninger, 1992, p. 381) than for passages embedded in contexts of non-interest. Because the same passages were classified as non-interest for some students and interest for others, these effects must have been entirely caused by students' personal interest in the topics. In addition, because interest was assessed many weeks before, the effects were not caused by having just claimed an interest.

Results were not significant for the math problems in this study, possibly because the math problems were brief and the context through which the interest was connected to them was therefore superficial, a mere add-on. For example, one problem given to children high and low in basketball interest was, "The basketball captain scored 24 points in each game. There were 14 games in the season. How many points did the captain score during the season?" (Renninger, 1992, p. 383). Students might have converted the problems to their numerical components so rapidly that no interest effects accrued.

Another study that went to a greater extent to embed math questions in personal interests did find a significant effect on math performance. Fifth- and sixth-grade students were presented a supplementary set of lessons focused on fractions (Anand & Ross, 1987). Children were randomly assigned to groups and for each group, instruction using the same example problems was couched in contexts designed to have different interest appeal. For the abstract group, all of the instruction examples were presented with general referents ("solid, liquid") without any meaningful background theme. For example, one item read, "There are three objects. Each is cut in one-half. In all, how many pieces would there be?" (p. 73). The concrete group received hypothetical but concrete referents, for example stating that Bill had three candy bars, each of which he cut in half. The third group had examples that were intended to be most interesting, because they were personalized to concern matters of subjective importance, such as one's birthday, teachers and friends, hobbies, and so on. For example, their teacher (mentioned by name) presented them with three Mars bars (their favorite candy) on their birthday, and if they cut each candy bar in half, how many friends could they share with?

As bookends to these lessons, children took pre- and post-tests of their understanding of fractions. The results were clear in supporting that children learn best when the material is of personal interest. On the post-test, the abstract group scored lowest (averaging 2 of 11 problems correct), the concrete next lowest (3.5 of 11), and the personalized group had the highest score (6 of 11). The fact that the learning environment had a personally interesting context apparently made a great deal of difference to learning.

Another study reiterated this finding with nursing students, who of course are personally interested in medical contexts (Ross, 1983, Experiment 2). When learning about statistical probability from examples couched in health-care contexts, nursing students learned better than when examples were either abstract or were couched in educational contexts.

In another study examining math learning and interest, children at risk for poor mathematics performance were asked to make up their own math problems rather than take problems from a book (Resnick, Bill, Lesgold, & Leer, 1991). Stimulating interest even further, they were also asked to discuss those math problems with their classmates (see chapter 7). The results showed that these students advanced dramatically in math, from the 30th to the 70th percentile, during the year of the intervention. The same teacher had used conventional methods (assigning problems from books, and not having students discuss them) the previous year with a similar group, and had seen nothing near the level of gain. Both of these steps (having children make up their own problems and discussing those problems with others) naturally occur in Montessori education.

The studies reviewed thus far have shown that interest influences learning in the realms of math and reading. Other studies have shown that interest affects a host of factors ranging from grades, to self-esteem, to perception of one's own skill, to intrinsic motivation, and does so on a range of school subjects, from history to biology to vocabulary to music (Asher, 1979; Asher, Hymel, & Wigfield, 1978; Asher & Markell, 1974; Schiefele & Csikszentmihalyi, 1994, 1995; Simpson & Randall, 2000). The effects of interest are also evident both over short and long time spans.

A study by Rathunde and Csikszentmihalyi (1993) demonstrates the effects of interest on achievement extending over several years across a range of "talent areas" from math to music. More than 200 Chicago-area high school students identified as having a particular area of talent were given electronic pagers that paged them at random times for 1 week. When paged, they filled out a form specifying their thoughts and activities at that moment. Three years later, the students' progress in their talent areas was assessed. Children's achievement across the 3 years was directly related to the level of interest and excitement they expressed when engaged in the activity at the first time point. Because all the students had previously been identified as talented in the area of concern, and socioeconomic factors were statistically controlled for, their degree of interest in the activity was the likely determinant of their subsequent progress.

As mentioned at the beginning of this section, interest studies have typically concerned personal interests, which according to Hidi and Renninger's (2006) developmental model, occurs with more developed interests. This raises the question of whether topic interest is also associated with better learning. At least one recent study with college students addressed topic interest directly (Rotgans & Schmidt, 2014). In their first experiments, they asked whether being aware of a gap in one's knowledge would promote interest in a new topic, and indeed it did. This is in keeping with several studies showing that topic interest is generated by puzzles—interesting phenomena we cannot easily explain or intriguing questions that we do not know the answer to. A third experiment showed that interest declined as that gap was filled, suggesting that for the group as a whole, individual interest in the topic had not developed.

THE INFLUENCE OF INTEREST ON PRESCHOOLERS

Results thus far have concerned school-age children and college students. Following on the effect of puzzles, recent research on guided learning shows that preschoolers best learn to identify shapes when figuring out shape characteristics that are posed as a puzzle (Fisher, Hirsh-Pasek, Newcombe, & Golinkoff, 2013). Posing puzzles is one way to arouse topic interest. But preschoolers also have personal interests. A survey of 177 parents showed that about a third of young children develop very intense personal interests, for example in dinosaurs, trains, or dress-ups (DeLoache, Simcock, & Macari, 2007). One of my daughters was captivated by large eyes, manifested by a fascination with cats from 6 months, owls from around 14 months (leading her to memorize their distinct faces on cards— ferruginous, barn owl, and so on), and finally horses from 48 months on. We know little about the origins of the particular intense interests many children develop, but studies have demonstrated the effects of interest on learning even in very young children. Because effects with such young children would compound over many years, and because they even appear to influence the organization of children's mental representations of the world, the effects of personal interest for preschoolers might be even more profound than the marked effects already seen for older children. Exemplifying such long-range effects, young children's reported interest in reading has been related not only to their contemporaneous literacy skills (Frijters, Barron, &

Brunello, 2000), but also is the best predictor of their long-range literacy skills (Whitehurst & Lonigan, 1998). Getting children interested in reading is thus even more important to their eventual success as readers than is helping them with early reading skills. Some sensitivity is warranted in how interest is generated, however. Although manipulative (such as pop-up) features inspire preschooler interest in books (Kaderavek, & Justice, 2005), they also interfere with children's learning from those very books, presumably because children get distracted by the features (Tare, Chiong, Ganea, & DeLoache, 2010). The same appears to be true of ebooks (Parish-Morris, Mahajan, Hirsh-Pasek, Golinkoff, & Collins, 2013). Ways of generating interest that help children focus on content are more helpful.

Other studies have examined the contemporaneous effects of interest, but because interest influences such factors as preschool children's memory, activities, and cognitive organization, these studies have clear long-range implications (Anderson, Mason, & Shirey, 1984). In a fascinating study of the effect of interest on memory and attention in preschoolers, researchers videotaped six 40-minute sessions of 16 different children's free play activities at school (Renninger & Wozniak, 1985). Tapes were examined for which toys (of a possible 16) each child played with most frequently and for the longest bouts. All 16 children studied were identified as having two toys that they played with especially often. For example, two children were especially apt to play with a train, five with a doll, and so on.

In an experimental portion of the study, the researchers examined children's attention to and memory for their own particular two interest toys versus other toys from their classroom. Attention was measured by having children focus on a dot in the center of an oval. Six pictures of toys then appeared, evenly spaced around the oval. An observer noted to which toy the child looked first and for how long. Children's gaze shifted to their interest toys significantly more often than to the other toys, showing that shifts in attention are engendered more by personal interests than by characteristics of the toys. If toy characteristics were responsible for attention shifts, then all children would have looked most often to the brightest toys, for example, regardless of interests. Given that children pay the most attention to objects of greatest personal interest, it is likely that they learn the most from those objects as well. In addition, because sustained attention is part of deep concentration, the beneficial effects of concentration (discussed in chapter 3) might be best conferred through objects of interest.

A second task in this study involved recognition memory. The children were asked to recall 12 presents (shown on cards) that another child had supposedly received for his or her birthday. The present cards were mixed with 12 additional cards displaying other toys that were not presents. Some of the present cards showed the test child's high-interest toys, others showed other toys in the classroom, and yet others were distractors. Results on the memory test showed that interest influenced recognition: Children were likely to point out, from the set of 12 cards, their own interest toys first, and overall, they were more likely to recognize their own interest toys as being part of the set of presents than they were to recognize the non-interest toys and the distractors. Clearly, children's recognition memory was very much affected by their level of interest in each object. Even when all they had to do was recognize whether a toy had been in the set of presents, they did so most often if they were particularly interested in that toy at the outset. A third task involved recall memory. The experimenter showed children a set of nine toys, which were placed one by one into a box. The child's interest toy was always placed in the box fifth in the series. Normally an item in the middle position would be remembered less well, as people are known to best recall the first and last items in a list. However, there was a whopping effect of interest, with children recalling the item in the fifth position significantly more often than the items in any other position.

This study suggests that interest drives young children's acquisition of knowledge. They are more apt to notice and to remember items of particular interest, which is bound to lead to further accumulation of knowledge about those interests. Interest thereby influences the early organization of children's mental representations of the world. They pay attention to, recognize, and recall the world in terms of what most interests them.

In another study (Renninger, 1992), children's temperament and persistence were evaluated as they played with interest and non-interest toys. When children were engaged with toys of interest, their temperaments were more positive and their persistence in play was greater, possibly developing concentration. Research with adults suggests that when people feel more positively, they expand their intellectual, social, and psychological resources (Fredrickson, 2001). The increase in both the positive feelings and temporal engagement with interest toys should lead to children learning more through objects of interest than through other objects.

A further study expanded on the influence of interest on young children's learning (Renninger, 1990). This study found that children played with interest toys for longer, repeated action scripts more, engaged in more types of play, and used more variations in those action scripts with their interest toys. Preschoolers' increased use of scripts with interest toys would serve to deepen their understanding of what usually happens in the world. Because play with interest toys was more generative and creative, this study also suggests that children are trying out new, nonscripted events more with interest toys.

In sum, even in preschool, interest appears to organize cognition and influence motivation, so that children can learn the most when able to engage with articles and issues of greater personal interest. Conventional preschools tend to allow children to work with what interests them for at least part of the day, although those toys are not designed to confer specific concepts (play with clay, blocks, and so on, in contrast to the Pink Tower, Sandpaper Letters, and so on). Usually there is also time devoted to whole-class learning, which is not focused on topics of individual interests. Unfortunately this tendency is increasing in the current testing environment, inspiring researchers to ask, "Is kindergarten the new first grade?" (Bassok et al., 2016). By elementary school, children in conventional programs only rarely pursue topics of particular interest, perhaps most often in reports or art projects. In contrast, because children are free to choose their work in Montessori classrooms all day long, they can gravitate to their interests, deriving the benefits that interest has been shown to confer.

Personal Interests in Montessori Education

The choices children make daily about what they do in a Montessori classroom naturally stem from their interests. A Primary child might be driven to work with the Wooden Cylinders or the Button Frame. An Elementary child might be inspired to study the origins of life on earth and spend hours pondering the Timeline of Life (Figure 5.1), or might want to better understand river ecosystems and arrange a "Going Out" trip to visit a river.

Dr. Montessori held that some personal interests come from within, are part of biological development, and answer a specific need the child has at that moment. These needs seem to have a developmental course, meaning they arrive at particular ages for all children and are worked through. She called the times during which children are working through such needs "sensitive periods," and they bear consideration with respect to the use of the same term by developmental psychologists today.

BIOLOGICALLY GUIDED PERSONAL INTERESTS: SENSITIVE PERIODS

As noted in chapter 1, Dr. Montessori believed that there are sensitive periods when an organism is attracted to a feature of the environment that confers advantages to the organism at that time in its development. Dr. Montessori used the example of caterpillars moving toward light at a particular time of life, when going to light aids their development by bringing them to the soft young leaves at the ends of the tree branches. Caterpillars have no way of knowing that going to light will provide good food; they are biologically programmed to do so. As they become more mature, coincident with no longer needing the tender leaves, they no longer have such a drive. Dr. Montessori believed this same principle governed the psychological development of the human child. "Psychic development does not come about by hazard, and does not originate in stimuli from the outer world; it is guided by transient sensibilities, temporary instincts connected with the acquisition of certain characteristics" (Montessori, 1939, p. 44).

The use of "sensitive period" in developmental psychology today is slightly different from Dr. Montessori's use, in that it emphasizes environmental input (Bornstein, 1989), whereas she emphasized inner impulse. Today's psychologists emphasize that if proper input is not provided during a sensitive period, the learning will not be acquired, at least not as easily or as well, as it would have during that period. For example, if a child is not given normal visual input during a certain period of postnatal development, the child's vision will never be normal. In both the biological and psychological literatures, sensitive periods are not necessarily mentioned with respect to interest (although the Goldilocks effect described in chapter 4, previously referred to as the moderate discrepancy hypothesis, can be viewed that way). For Dr. Montessori, sensitive periods are periods of intense interest in particular stimuli that aid psychological development. In discussing these periods, Dr. Montessori suggested modularity, the idea that the human mind is composed of modules that perform specific psychological functions (Fodor, 1983). She called these modules "mental organs."[1]

> Just as there is no complete man already formed in the original germinative cell, so there seems to be no kind of mental personality already formed in the newborn child. . . . [The child's development is organized around] *points of sensitivity*, which appear in turn. These are of such intense activity that the adult can never recapture them, or recollect what they were like. We have already hinted at this in the child's conquest of language. For it is not the mind itself that these sensitivities create, but its organs. And here, too, each organ develops independently of the others. For example, while language is developing on the one hand, the judgment of distances and of finding one's way about, is developing quite separately; so is the power to balance on two feet, and other forms of co-ordination.
>
> Each of these powers has its own special interest and this form of sensitivity is so lively that it leads its possessor to perform a certain series of actions. None of these sensitivities occupies the whole period of development. Each of them lasts long enough for the construction of a psychic organ. Once that organ is formed, the sensitivity disappears, but, while it lasts, there is an outpouring of energy. (Montessori, 1967a/1995, p. 51, italics in original)

A Sensitive Period for Language

One early sensitive period Dr. Montessori discussed is the period of learning language. Foreshadowing the thinking of the most influential

---

[1] The concept of mental organs was invoked by G. Stanley Hall (1911) as well.

linguistic theorist, Noam Chomsky, Dr. Montessori believed that an area of the human brain is specially predisposed for learning language during a sensitive period early in life. She expands on this at length in *The Absorbent Mind*:

> A special mechanism exists for language. Not the possession of language in itself, but the possession of this mechanism which enables men to make languages of their own, is what distinguishes the human species. Words, therefore, are a kind of fabrication which the child produces, thanks to the machinery which he finds at his disposal. (1967a/1995, p. 119)

Dr. Montessori noted that infants around age 4 months have a special interest in adults speaking, as suggested to her by their carefully observing and attempting to imitate adults' lip movements during speech. Sophisticated eye-tracking technologies have recently shown that 4-month-olds look at the mouth of a speaking face about 15% of the time (versus 36% of time to the eyes); selective attention shifts from 4 months to 8 months to favor the mouth; and by 12 months, the preponderance of their attention reverts to the eyes when the native language (but not a nonnative language) is spoken (Lewkowicz & Hansen-Tift, 2012). Infants' sensitivity to the mouth region as they are learning language is speculated to help them see how to produce the sounds they need for language; note that this sensitivity is strongest when babbling proper begins around 8 months.

Dr. Montessori believed the preschool years to be sensitive periods for grammar as well as for vocabulary:

> Experience has shown us that little children take the liveliest interest in grammar, and that this is the right time to put them in touch with it. In the first period (from 0 to 3) the acquisition of grammatical form was unconscious; now it can be perfected consciously. And we notice something else: that the child of this age learns many new words. He has a special sensitiveness for words; they attract his interest, and he spontaneously accumulates a very great number. (1967a/1995, p. 174)

To capitalize on this sensitive period for language development, lessons on the Function of Words (early grammar lessons) begin in Primary, along with the provision of many vocabulary terms. In-depth discussion of Dr. Montessori's ideas on language development can be found in her book *The Absorbent Mind*.

Other Sensitive Periods

Dr. Montessori noted several other sensitive periods. One was a sensitive period for walking, when at around 12 months (subject to much individual variation), children become consumed with learning to walk. In Montessori infancy courses, adults are advised to facilitate children's efforts during this sensitive period by providing a ballet bar that the child can pull up and cruise along, supportive but soft shoes, and a "walker wagon" that the child can walk behind. Most especially, Dr. Montessori advised that children be allowed to walk, rather than be carried or placed in strollers, to allow them to pursue their interest in developing this important new skill. Once walking is conquered, children turn to new interests.

Developmental theorists today do talk of a sensitive period for language and would not be surprised at the notion of a sensitive period for learning to walk. Dr. Montessori's other sensitive periods are not generally noted in the psychology literature and might prove interesting topics of study. Dr. Montessori believed that in the first two years of life, children are in a sensitive period for order and are especially attentive to things being put in their proper places and done in their proper ways (Montessori, 1956, pp. 24–25; 1966, pp. 49–59). She noted that during this period, children get upset if someone who usually wears a hat is not wearing one, or if a chair that is always in one place gets moved to a different place. The temper tantrums of the 2-year-old, she claimed, are often caused by adults being insensitive to the child's particularly strong need for order and sameness during that time:

> The child makes himself out of the elements of his environment, and this self-making is not accomplished by some vague formula, but following a precise and definite guidance. . . . For the tiny child order is like the plane on which terrestrial beings must rest if they are to go forward. (1939, pp. 61–62)

Order in Montessori education is discussed further in chapter 10.

Dr. Montessori saw children as being in a sensitive period for the perception of tiny objects beginning in the second year of life. One-year-olds become captivated by very little things, stopping for example to watch ants on a sidewalk or to gather little pebbles. "Children are no longer drawn . . . to showy objects or bright colors, but rather to tiny things that we should not notice. It is as though what now interests them is the invisible, or that which lies on the edge of consciousness" (Montessori, 1939, p. 76). During this period, she noted that children are attracted to tiny elements of pictures, background aspects that adults usually fail to notice. She claimed that the sorts of objects typically aimed at children (often oversized, in very bright colors, and so on) are a distraction from these inner-guided sensibilities which are a critical source of mental development.

Another sensitive period, in Montessori theory, is for precision or exactness, described further in chapter 10. This sensitivity is part of what led Montessori to introduce mathematics around age 4 (Montessori, 1946/1963). Many considered this too young for children to engage in equations with four-digit numbers, and Dr. Montessori herself was at first surprised. But the children's interests were her guide, and the children's attraction to such exercises, she decided, stemmed in part from their passion for precision. During this time, they are also meticulous about following specific steps in specific ways, perhaps as an outgrowth of the need for order. Older children are less concerned, she noted, with following steps precisely. Montessori education plays to this observed early sensitivity by providing very specific steps for Primary children's activities, as is described for the Practical Life activities. Yet another sensitive period that may be capitalizing on order and precision is that for counting (M. M. Montessori, 1976). Dr. Montessori observed that children go through a phase when they seem driven to count objects, over and over.

In sum, Dr. Montessori believed there are sensitive periods in which particular activities or environmental stimuli are especially interesting to children, and that educators should capitalize on such periods by providing a great deal of high-interest input at the right time. The child is in a period of self-construction and biologically tuned to be interested in what will best provide for that construction. She believed that by watching children closely, noticing what interests them, and providing environmental support for them to pursue those biologically guided interests, adults can assist children's development. In Montessori classrooms, materials are provided that correspond to the interests Dr. Montessori observed were common to children at corresponding ages. Dr. Montessori's sensitive periods suggest interesting possibilities for future research.

INTERESTS AS BIOLOGICALLY MOTIVATED AND ADAPTIVE: THE RESEARCH

Next I consider a prominent idea in developmental psychology today that bears on Dr. Montessori's ideas: Namely, that interests or preferences are adaptive. This idea was discussed in chapter 4 with reference to the Goldilocks effect, indicating that when children are free to choose, they choose stimuli that are at just the right level to further their development. Such choices go along with interest, hence the idea is also relevant in this chapter, where I provide more historical context.

Like Dr. Montessori, developmental psychologists today theorize that what children freely choose—what they are interested in—is sometimes internally guided by what they need at the moment for optimal development. Cognitive systems might be tuned to seek out what they need to advance to further stages of development. This is not, of course, because of any conscious knowledge on the child's part about optimal development, but because neural systems have evolved such that optimal choices are the ones that usually win out. As mentioned in chapter 4, this claim was previously called the moderate discrepancy hypothesis (McCall, Kennedy, & Appelbaum, 1977). The idea is that children seek out stimuli that are moderately discrepant from what they already have understood. Early experimental evidence for this showed that with children, adults, and even rats, attention is sustained longest if stimuli are at an intermediate level of novelty for the perceiver, neither too simple nor too complex (Berlyne, 1960). In vision research, developmental psychologists claim that children are drawn to look at patterns that are at the right level of complexity for their visual development. Here is how this principle is explained in one developmental psychology textbook:

> Whereas 3-week-olds look longer at a 6-by-6 checkerboard than at a 12-by-12 or a 24-by-24 checkerboard, 6-week-olds are more likely to look longest at the intermediately complex display and 3-month-olds at the most complex display (Karmel & Maisel, 1975).
>
> ... Most investigators now believe that babies are attracted to the displays that offer the most edge contrasts that they can see at a particular age (Banks & Ginsburg, 1985). Why? Perhaps these findings suggest what babies are trying to accomplish with their visual behavior.
>
> When babies move their eyes over edges, they activate cells of the visual areas of the brain. The strongest brain activity occurs when the baby adjusts the eye so that images of the edges fall near the center of the eye—that is, when the baby looks straight at the edges. Also, the more detail the baby can see, the stronger the activation. Haith (1980) has suggested that the baby's visual activity in early infancy reflects a biological "agenda" for the baby to keep brain-cell firing at a high level. This agenda makes sense because, as we have seen, cells in the brain compete to establish connections to other cells. Activity tends to stabilize the required connections, while inactive pathways deteriorate (Greenough, Black, & Wallace, 1987). (Vasta, Haith, & Miller, 1999, pp. 211–12)

Underlying the moderate discrepancy hypothesis is the idea that young children are interested in particular stimuli because those stimuli evoke patterns of neural activity that further development in optimal ways. As shown in chapter 4, this idea now has even stronger research support in the areas of vision and language development.

Young children also show some predictable interests that have nothing to do with discrepancy. Very young babies have strong interest in stimuli related to people. This is adaptive, because people are key to infant survival. Given the choice of looking at human faces or other stimuli, infants look the most at faces (Fantz, 1961). Given the choice of listening to sounds that fall within or outside the range of the human voice, even 1-month-olds prefer to listen to sounds in the range of the voice (Aslin, Jusczyk, & Pisoni, 1998). Infants also prefer voices talking "baby talk" to those talking in adult-to-adult mode

(Fernald, 1984), and even at birth they prefer the voice of their own mother to the voices of other women (DeCasper & Fifer, 1980). These preferences may be adaptive because they help to establish attachment relationships. In sum, some of children's interests may be biologically driven because they assist optimal development, and over the course of human evolution, babies with such preferences were more likely to survive.

INDIVIDUAL PERSONAL INTERESTS IN MONTESSORI EDUCATION

Interests invoked in sensitive periods are shared because they are biologically programmed and thus appear in many children. Other interests are more individual. Such individual passions can also guide children's learning in Montessori classrooms, because children are free to choose what to study. An example regarding frogs was provided earlier in the chapter. As another example, a child who had been to the beach might become interested in shells and bring a few to the classroom. This might inspire a long-term exploration of shells, leading to presentations on geographical forms to show the different places mollusks live, the layers of the earth containing shells from different ages, and so on. It might also lead to work in biology on what different organisms eat and how their digestive systems operate. Likewise, a child who is particularly interested in horses can make charts on special breeds of horses and thereby master the principles of genetics, write reports on the history of domestication of horses and thereby learn about human history, write stories concerning horses and thereby develop creative writing, study the horses of Leonardo da Vinci and thus stimulate study of art history, and so on. Such interests can be infectious: A group of several children or even the entire class sometimes adopts an interest that drives learning for a portion of the year.

Dr. Montessori described the development of an interest in one 7-year-old child, which was inspired by a standard teacher presentation.

> The teacher had prepared a map of the Rhine River and its tributaries, but a child was not satisfied with it. He wanted to know the relative length of each of the tributaries. (Here we see the idea of mathematics awakened.) He used graph paper to draw a better map. It was in this way that the sense of proportional size and the interest in study were born in him at the same time. He remained at the same task, by his own choosing, for more than two months. He was not satisfied until he had meticulously completed it. His satisfaction came with his being able to express these concepts in mathematical terms. (1948a/1976, p. 38)

A teacher might not anticipate what particular aspect of a lesson will capture the imagination of a particular child, leading the child to further explorations that link to new parts of the curriculum. The Montessori system is open enough to allow the evolution of interests and learning to happen organically.

A Montessori teacher is not supposed to give questions directly to children, but only to stimulate their imaginations, such that children develop their own questions. The research presented earlier suggests that learning based on such interests is superior to learning that has its roots in the interests of others.

Topic Interest in Montessori Education

The role of education is to interest the child profoundly in an external
activity to which he will give all his potential.
    — Maria Montessori *(1948a/1976, p. 24, italics in original)*

In Montessori education, topic interest is not really up to the individual teacher: It is institutionalized. I will explain this first regarding lessons, then regarding the environment and materials, and finally regarding how the teacher is involved in creating interest.

INSPIRING INTEREST THROUGH MONTESSORI LESSONS

When giving lessons in Primary, teachers use very few words, focusing children on the relevant aspects of the activities they will carry out with materials. The Elementary child, however, is introduced to new lessons in a different way, because Dr. Montessori believed that abstract thought and the imagination come to figure prominently in learning around age 6. As is enabled by these new forms of thought, the entire Elementary curriculum is rooted in a central set of five stories called the Great Lessons.

    This structural foundation of the Montessori Elementary curriculum is perhaps its most extraordinary aspect. First, consider conventional Elementary school education. In conventional classrooms, each topic is taught separately, with its own book and time slot. This makes sense given its heritage. According to Thorndike, "Improvement in any single mental function rarely brings about equal improvement in any other function, no matter how similar, for the working of every mental function-group is conditioned by the nature of the data in each particular case" (Thorndike & Woodworth, 1906/1962, p. 51). If learning in one topic area is believed to have no bearing on learning in another, then it follows that there would be no profit from integration of topics during education. In conventional schooling, therefore, as children get older, each topic even has its own teacher and is taught in its own classroom. At the beginning of each school year, children review what they learned in the prior grade, then proceed to the information they are supposed to learn in the current grade. Interest is clearly not driving the curriculum, and there is very little integration across topic areas. In fact, a survey of mathematics teachers in the United States showed that only about 23% think teachers should integrate across subjects even within mathematics, such as algebra and probability (Weiss, 1995).

In contrast, Dr. Montessori understood that interest comes in part through integration and interconnection, and the Elementary curriculum was taught with an eye to making connections across disciplines in what she called Cosmic Education. As the Montessori trainer Phyllis Pottish-Lewis described,[2]

> Cosmic Education is a way to show the child how everything in the universe is interrelated and interdependent, no matter whether it is the tiniest molecule or the largest organism ever created. Every single thing has a part to play, a contribution to make to the maintenance of harmony in the whole. In understanding this network of relationships, the child finds that he or she also is a part of the whole, and has a part to play, a contribution to make.

This interrelationship is one reason that Dr. Montessori advocated having one person and only one person teach children all subjects: It enables topic connection. In conventional schooling, when different teachers teach different subjects, at each hour a new teacher will "talk about something completely different, which has no logical connection with the preceding topic" (1989, p. 88). This is at odds with developing topic interest as it is stimulated by seeing the interrelationships among things.

Dr. Montessori saw the world of humans as based in five critically important developments: the creation of the universe, the beginning of life, the coming of human beings, and two stellar achievements of human civilization—the development of language and the development of numbers. These five developments are described in the five Great Lessons, given early in the fall every year in Elementary classrooms. (In schools that have some children change classrooms mid-year, as they are ready, the stories are also told mid-year.) The stories are delivered with drama and are often accompanied by demonstrations such as pouring sulfur into ammonium dichromate to show how volcanoes spewed forth in the formation of the earth. (The effect is similar to, but more dramatic than, the effect obtained when pouring vinegar into baking soda.) The information given in these stories is built on throughout the year, in an ever-expanding spiral. In addition, each story is told with reference to the stories that came before it, facilitating integration across the curriculum.[3]

The stories are grand and impressionistic, designed to give children a framework for many of the lessons children will engage in over the year. This framework approach is consistent with psychology research. For example,

---

[2] P. Pottish-Lewis, personal communication, 2005.
[3] P. P. Lillard's *Montessori Today* (1996) has a chapter describing these stories, and Dr. Montessori's *From Childhood to Adolescence* also discusses how lessons are presented at the Elementary age.

people who look over outlines prior to reading material understand material better than people who dive right in (Anderson, 1990). Having a framework assists the assimilation of information.

The stories are intended to leave the children with more questions than answers, inspiring them to go learn more. There are no follow-up assignments; if the child's interest has been sparked, he or she will have questions and will follow up on his or her own. The information transmission aspect of the stories is also not the point; the points of telling these stories are to give the child a framework and to inspire interest. Dr. Montessori wrote that the child "needs an impression, an idea which above all awakens interest. If he acquires the interest he will later be able to study and understand these subjects rapidly" (1948a/1976, p. 63). Indeed, Dr. Montessori specified that the teacher should feel awe and marvel at the stories and should also be very curious to learn more about the world. In this way, the teacher models interest and the urge for discovery.

The first story is of the Birth of the Universe and is often titled "God with No Hands," to reflect the mysterious power that seems to underlie this event rather than to convey a particularly religious belief. One day shortly after the arrival of new children in the classroom, the Elementary teacher gathers the new children and any children already in the class who are interested (they usually are) in a circle, sits down before them, and begins his or her story, which might go something like this (the exact wording is flexible; teachers make the story their own):

> There was a time, long ago, when there was nothing here—no classroom, no town, no America, no oceans, no earth, no planets, no stars, no sun, no solar system—nothing. Can you imagine that? A time of nothing, nothing but darkness and cold. How did all this change, so that all these things just mentioned came to be? What could have made all the nothing turn into all of these things we know? There is a tremendous power in nature, a power that could turn nothing into all these planets and stars and even our Earth.

After the first part of the story, in which the teacher inspires awe in the children, he or she goes on to explain that the universe exists in stable form because natural elements follow laws, like the law of gravity. The teacher does not tell about the laws but demonstrates them so the children can see and discover them for themselves. For example, the teacher might stop the story and sprinkle tiny squares of paper on the surface of water, pointing out how some pieces move and attach to each other, a simplified demonstration of the law of attraction. Later, after the story, the children might wonder about what they saw, set up similar experiments (usually with prepared experiment cards that guide their investigations), conduct studies, and draw conclusions.

Within the story, the teacher only raises questions and gives children the grand framework that because of these laws, there is harmony in the universe. Teachers say this appears to comfort children and inspire them to learn about the laws. Next in the story of the birth of the universe, the teacher delves into the narrative describing the main event: the Big Bang. He or she talks about the chaos that reigned, and the darkness, and the cold, helping the children to imagine a possible world before the universe was formed. "Then there appeared a fiery cloud, and everything that later became the universe was in this cloud—its ingredients would become every planet and moon and star." With the aid of four charts and six experiments, the teacher helps the children imagine the explosion and the result. Children learn how the Big Bang resulted in gases, liquids, and solids, such as the planets, including Earth, which were very hot and then cooled. Children leave the lesson with a sense of awe. Montessori teachers say they do not "see" the children then for days, as they become deeply absorbed in investigations of aspects of the story. The lesson could bring on exploration of geology, tectonic plates, volcanoes, different kinds of mountains and how they are formed, crystallization, and so on. The underlying idea is that the teacher should inspire the children to ask their own questions, which they then are motivated to pursue answers to through books, through materials provided in the classroom, and through "Going Out" trips.

The second lesson, the Coming of Life on Earth, tells how life emerged. The story is followed by presentation of the Timeline of Life, which is about 20 feet long and 3 feet wide and depicts the development of life forms from the earliest single-cell organisms to mammals (see Figure 5.1). At the very end of the Timeline, the human being is shown, and children marvel at what an extremely short amount of time we have been here, compared to other life forms. Some children are inspired to pursue explorations of plants, while others might focus on particular types of animals. The classroom might feature trilobites, crinoids, ferns, or other early life forms to explore. There is a blank timeline and movable pieces showing different animals that children use to reconstruct the original, reminiscent of the blank maps used with the Wooden Maps for geography. This blank timeline allows children to work manually on a part of the story that interests them. When sufficiently intrigued, children might be moved to create their own timelines with other creatures whose existence they discover through their independent investigations. Rather than simply memorizing what life forms emerged when, as children might do in conventional schools, children in Montessori classrooms learn actively, guided by their own interests.

The third story is that of the Coming of Humans. The story points out special qualities of humans: our unusual minds, our capacity to love, and the human hand, which can fashion and make things. As a result of these

FIGURE 5.1 The Timeline of Life. © Laura Joyce-Hubbard, 2014. All rights reserved.

attributes, humans were able to make a life for themselves that allowed them to meet their basic needs for clothing, shelter, and food. Children can explore how these three basic needs have been met by various civilizations. Later lessons discuss two other basic physical needs: defense and transportation. Children might be inspired to study any aspect of human civilizations, such as food and how different civilizations have obtained it. Because of such an interest, children might begin work on a garden or visit a farm. Children might focus on the three major revolutions of agriculture, urbanization, and industrialization, and how technology has changed people's relationship to the earth, especially how they get food. The story about people thus connects to biology as well as history and culture.

The fourth story is the story of Communicating in Signs. It begins with a discussion of the ancient Egyptians and a consideration of how people began to draw pictures to communicate. However, pictures could be confusing; for example, a leg might depict legs or running. The Egyptians addressed this by coming up with a second system, which represented sounds instead of ideas. Meanwhile their contemporaries, the Phoenicians, were busy traders, in possession of a very special dye. To assist all the trading for that popular dye, they found written symbols very useful. From the Egyptians they borrowed the sound pictures, but not the idea pictures. Their Phoenician alphabet became the basis of our own. This story is accompanied by a set of pictures, including illustrations of the signs. Children hearing this story might develop an interest in other sign systems, such as Egyptian hieroglyphs or Chinese characters. They might even develop their own systems of signs. Investigations of papermaking and early writing instruments might also follow, as might explorations of early written languages, such as Latin, and early written stories.

The fifth Great Lesson is the Story of Numerals. The teacher first talks about ancient peoples' need to count, and then about various systems by which this was done, including the systems of the Mayans, Sumerians, and Babylonians. Interesting facts are always included in these stories, such as the root of our division of hours and minutes into 60 originating with the Babylonian 60-based number system. Chinese, Greek, and Roman number systems are also presented. Through such lessons, Dr. Montessori repeatedly grounded children in history, showing how our civilization rests on the shoulders of those that have gone before.

The five Great Lessons form a core of impressionistic knowledge that is intended to leave the child inspired to learn more. The stories involve charts and diagrams, are linked to other work in the classroom, and are followed by further lessons.

One such follow-up lesson, given early in the study of geometry, is called How Geometry Got Its Name. This Elementary lesson provides another example of how Montessori lessons stimulate topic interest, and how Montessori integrates knowledge across different areas of the curriculum. After children have been given a few lessons on angles, using sets of manipulatives to create angles of different sizes, the teacher tells a small group of children who are at the same level in learning about angles a story about how the Nile River often flooded early in the year, washing away people's property lines. There were people called the Rope Stretchers whose job was to create the property lines again, work so important it was supervised by the pharaoh himself. Children are told that the word "geometry" comes from Gaia (or earth) and metric (or measure), because these people were measuring the earth. Besides assisting children with vocabulary, reviewing the word's roots helps children to see that geometry has practical origins. Although Elementary children can think abstractly, tying the abstract to the concrete might assist understanding, and thereby interest, for students of any age.

Also linking to the concrete, the teacher gives the children a long string with a series of evenly spaced small and large knots. Each child holds a different part of the string, and the children become, in effect, the Rope Stretchers: They see how the string can be stretched to make different angles. The sides of the ropes, when stretched into a scalene (right-angle) triangle, are 3×, 4×, and 5×. As the story goes, Pythagoras was visiting Egypt and saw the Rope Stretchers at work and learned there the principles of the famous theorem that bears his name (discussed further in chapter 8). The idea of angles is thus tied to a piece of history and geography, and it is a hands-on activity involving one's classmates and imaginary tracts of land that must be divided up, all of which appears to stimulate interest and inspire them to learn not only about geometry, but also the Egyptians, the Nile, Egyptian numerals and their derivation, history, and so on. Older children might go on to do research on Pythagoras, Plato, Euclid and his *Thirteen Books of the Elements*, and so on. Montessori teachers say they are often surprised at children's ambitions and what they are able to accomplish in their work.

One can also get a general flavor for how Montessori elicits topic interest in Elementary through her description of the presentation of water in *From Childhood to Adolescence* (1948a/1976, pp. 43ff.). This passage is apparently a description for future teachers regarding how they might present an aspect of the world that could then launch children into the study of different sciences.

Dr. Montessori advised beginning with the immense quantity of water, because this will impress children and captivate their imaginations. She also urged that they mention animals early in the lesson, because animals tend to evoke interest for many children. She urged that they also connect the lesson to mathematics, explicitly stating that they should tell children that fish deposit 70×10^4 eggs per year, that other very small animals exist in similarly great numbers, and that the largest number a child is capable of writing would not be sufficient to depict the number of eggs those fish deposit each year. Dr. Montessori suggested teachers go on to show children the tiny aquatic organisms through a microscope, and explain that a group of those tiny organisms can cause a spot in the sea so large it would take a ship 6 days to circumnavigate it. They might also describe how the Mississippi River discharges 70 million kilograms of limestone into the sea each day, and how in fact all the rivers discharge minerals into the ocean. The teacher asks, "Where could all this go without changing the composition of the sea?" This leads to discussion of shells and coral reefs. Elementary lessons are thus made interesting via connections to other aspects of the world and curriculum, hands-on activities, and personal involvement (telling the child he or she could not write a number big enough, and so on). Through lessons like these, the Elementary child's imagination is stimulated to learn about the world.

In sum, Montessori education elicits topic interest in part through carefully crafted lessons designed to be captivating to children by connecting students to history, biology, and all the curriculum, and by bringing alive concepts that might otherwise not spark interest.

MONTESSORI ACTIVITIES

Montessori education also elicits interest by engaging children in very interesting activities. Chapter 2 was replete with examples of activities in Montessori education; here I consider activities with particular regard to interest. Dr. Montessori observed children closely and built on those things in the classroom that seemed to excite their interest. Her aim was that the learning should captivate children, leading to the concentration she believed would result in normalization and self-development. Every activity is thus designed with interest in mind.

For example, very young children tend to be particularly interested in doing the activities they often see adults doing—cleaning up the home, caring for plants, and so on. In every culture, when children are unable to do these things for real, they pretend to do them (Lancy, 1996; Lillard, 2015). Montessori education capitalizes on children's interest in doing the activities that they see adults do by providing many Practical Life activities. From these activities, children learn a range of important lessons: to carry out steps in sequence, to do work thoroughly, that they can do important activities on their own, that they can get a sense of satisfaction from carrying out an activity and observing the results, and so on.

Activities for older children are of course also intended to be very interesting. Grammar exercises can serve as an example. As an important part of their learning grammar, Elementary Montessori children act out interesting sentences, an exercise that Dr. Montessori incorporated after noticing that children spontaneously imitated the actors after watching a play. For learning adverbs, for example, one sentence (of scores of examples in *The Advanced Montessori Method—II* [1916]) children act out is, "Walk lightly into the other room; return to your place, walking sedately as though you were a very important person; walk across the room and back again resting heavily on each step as though it were hurting you to walk" (p. 90). Many elementary school children love drama, and therefore carrying out such actions conveys the concept of the adverb through an interesting activity.

Montessori children also make up their own sentences for grammar. An Italian child devised: "Pretend you were two old men; speak softly as if you were very sad, and one of you say this: 'Too bad poor Pancrazio is dead!' And the other say: 'Shall we have to wear our black clothes tomorrow?' Then walk along silently" (Montessori, 1916, p. 96). "Compare the aridity and uniformity of the commands we [adults] invented . . . with the variety and richness of ideas appearing in the children's commands!" (p. 95). Clearly such work would be fun and interesting for most elementary school children, and as the math research reported earlier suggests, children might learn particularly well from examples they make up themselves. Children also frequently make up their own problems for math, for example regularly deciding which two numbers to multiply, or what large number to symbolize with beads and in writing. Such involvement is known to improve learning, presumably through interest.

THE MONTESSORI ENVIRONMENT AND MATERIALS

Interest researchers point out several different triggers for interest (Ainley, 2012); one is peers (Thoman et al., 2012), as mentioned earlier; another is having a puzzle to solve (Kang et al., 2009). Peers are the topic of chapter 7, but here I will discuss the use of puzzles in Montessori materials, and then point out another trigger for interest that is not discussed in the literature: aesthetic beauty.

Many studies have shown that puzzling things trigger interest. Rotgans and Schmidt (2014), in a study described earlier, showed this regarding students' knowledge levels: Students were more interested when presented a problem to which they did not know the answer. A different study of college students showed that being more curious about something leads to better retention of the answer, once it is received (Kang et al., 2009). In this same study, increased curiosity led to increased activation in memory areas of the brain after giving a wrong answer (presumably because participants were searching their knowledge stores for the right answer), and willingness to give away more resources to get the correct answer. Another example given earlier concerned preschoolers learning the properties of geometric shapes (Parish-Morris et al., 2013). Many of the Montessori materials appear to evoke curiosity and make clear the gaps in one's knowledge. For example, a child who has been putting cylinders into the base of the Wooden Cylinder set, and finds that the final one does not fit, must figure out what has happened—the child knows all the cylinders fit previously. This applies to many of the materials: They are self-correcting, a fact that likely also stimulates interest.

A second way in which a Montessori classroom and its materials inspire interest is beauty; because beauty inspires interest, Montessori classrooms are supposed to be beautiful. The classroom walls are kept relatively uncluttered (as compared to many conventional classrooms), with only a few works of art on the walls. As will be discussed in chapter 10, such simplicity has been shown to enhance children's learning. The furniture (usually shelves, tables, and chairs) is generally made of smooth wood. Teachers often play soothing classical music. The purpose of this was to create an environment that Dr. Montessori believed would most interest children in work, and thus be most conducive to learning: "We have repeatedly emphasized that both in the environment at school and in the materials used everything should be carefully considered in its artistic bearings, to provide ample room for development for all the phenomena of attention and persistence in work which are the secret keys of self-education" (1917/1965, p. 197). In agreement with Dr. Montessori, some theorists today believe beauty and interest are both closely related emotions (Armstrong & Detweiler-Bedell, 2008).

Dr. Montessori prescribed that the materials be in mint shape: "The apparatus is to be kept meticulously in order, beautiful and shining, in perfect condition" (1967a/1995, p. 277). Wood and glass are the materials of choice for most of the Montessori apparatus. Of course plastic was not available when Dr. Montessori designed the materials, but Montessorians today often shun plastic as less aesthetically pleasing than natural materials. The fact that the wooden materials feel good to touch is intended to make the materials more interesting, to inspire activity. Even the colors of the materials were selected through trial and error based on what seemed to evoke children's interest.

Books were created for children to read in the classroom, and these books were revised until they provoked a high level of interest. One feature is their simplicity, creating uncrowded, open-seeming texts.

> The simplicity of these texts occasions surprise when one observes how completely and enthusiastically absorbed in them children become.... [Each] little book was composed very carefully on the basis of rigid experimentation. As the book is opened only one page of print appears, the verso of the right hand page being always blank. Never does the text ... cover the entire page. The spaces above and below the print are decorated with designs. (Montessori, 1916, p. 180)

The Geometric Solids (Figure 5.2) are another particularly good example of a simple yet engrossing material. The Solids are slightly heavy (made of a dense wood), painted a shiny cobalt blue, and smooth to the touch. Standing about 4 inches tall, the shapes include a cylinder, a sphere, a cone, a cube, a rectangular prism, a rectangular pyramid, a triangular-based pyramid, an ovoid, and an ellipsoid. The Solids are lovely to hold and feel and look at,

FIGURE 5.2 The Geometric Solids. Photograph by An Vu.

and adults and children alike seem to enjoy handling them. Perhaps because the objects have such a pleasant feel, preschoolers spend a long time investigating these objects, repeating their names and feeling their shapes, and through that exercise, they learn which shape is which. But more importantly, preschoolers learn via such exercises to focus their attention on something of interest. A teacher once told me of a child who was using the Geometric Solids one morning, but was spending a good deal of time apparently spacing out, laying on his back on the rug, and looking about at the contours of the room. The teacher was concerned that he was off task, and she was looking for a break in her other activities to offer him a lesson, when he came to her and announced, "This room is a rectangular prism."

Every object, from a Golden Bead Thousand Cube to a lowly dish towel, is chosen in part for its aesthetic qualities, because Dr. Montessori noted that children engaged more with materials that are beautiful. "Attractive objects invite the child to touch them and then to learn to use them" (1956, p. 67).

The degree to which aesthetic features actually impact children's choices and the persistence of their activity, as well as the degree to which children's aesthetics coincide with those of adults, would be interesting topics for empirical research. We do know that babies and adults prefer to look at human faces that adults consider good-looking (Langlois et al., 1987; Rhodes, Geddes, Jeffery, Dziurawiec, & Clark, 2002), and that both babies and adults prefer to look at pure colors, such as red and blue, over mixed ones (Bornstein, 1975) although these color preferences have lately been argued to not be universal (Taylor, Clifford, & Franklin, 2013). Conversely, parents' and children's aesthetics do not always agree, nor do their perceptions of what is *interesting*. Child and adult ratings of the interest of certain topics are only moderately correlated (Hidi & McLaren, 1990). Adults cannot assume that what is interesting or beautiful to them will have that same appeal for children, which is one reason to allow children to make their own choices, when conceivable, about what they work on. Seeing what a child freely chooses tells adults what is interesting to the child. Only when children are free to choose can one experimentally determine what is interesting to the child. Dr. Montessori's making children the final arbiter in features of the material is thus crucially important.

In contrast, the manipulatives one might see in conventional schools often appear to have passed only the test of adult convenience. One school I observed used cut-up pieces of drinking straws for manipulatives for counting. The pieces were very light and rolled across the table, but also seemed to distract rather than enhance interest: Children were inspired to blow through them. This would presumably interfere with children's using them for their intended purpose. The visual materials used in conventional schools also often do not seem to have been designed with the child in mind. Conventional elementary school classrooms often feature an alphabet strip with pictures illustrating each letter of the alphabet. In one school I observed every first- to fourth-grade classroom used a cartoon of a chest X-ray to symbolize "X," which surely few if any young children would recognize. Likewise, a cartoon of a windmill, certainly not a common feature in today's American landscape, was used to represent "W." Although children in conventional schools learn to call the letter "C" "see," what was used to illustrate it was a cat. Perhaps such visual materials are interesting to children, but they also might be confusing. Dr. Montessori's observations of children guided her choices of materials that achieved the effects she sought. Experimental research could examine whether the Montessori materials inspire in today's children more interest in the task at hand, and better learning, than do manipulatives and visuals commonly used in conventional schools.

Computers are increasingly a "material" in conventional school environments, and clearly they are very engrossing—although young children do not always choose to use computers or other electronic devices. For example, Sierra Eisen and I (Eisen & Lillard, unpublished-a) found that when children were asked what object they would prefer to learn about dogs, their preferred object was a book. In another study, we found that children spent much more time at home with a tablet-based geography app than a hands-on map, but their learning was no better—hence in terms of efficiency, the real map was much better (Eisen & Lillard, unpublished-b).

One issue that arises is whether the type of engagement children have with computers (and television) is of the right sort for helping development. If learning to regulate one's attention is important to development, and the research in chapter 4 implies it very much is, then materials that use bells and whistles above and beyond what one normally encounters in life might do them a disservice. Television and computer programs frequently regulate children's attention for them because they are multisensory, fast paced, and present sequences of images that are not possible in the real world. As mentioned earlier, research in my laboratory has shown that children's executive function scores are lower after watching television shows with a great deal of fantastical (physically impossible) content (Lillard, et al., 2015; Lillard & Peterson, 2011). Successful attention-training programs are frequently done with computer programs, but these programs are often simpler than the programs used to attract children's attention (e.g., Klingberg, Forssberg, & Westerberg, 2002). Whether the interest-grabbing features of television and computer programs are ultimately positive or negative for development is yet another interesting topic for empirical research.

The Montessori materials are designed not only to be interesting in and of themselves, but also to make children be more interested in the world. The Sensorial Materials of the Primary classroom, for example, isolate various sense perceptions. The Color Tablets are paired by colors (Figure 5.3) initially, and then later arranged by shades of the same color, from lightest to

FIGURE 5.3 The Color Tablets. Photograph by An Vu.

darkest. They bring on observations by the child of variations in color and then in shades of color in the world. The Sound Cylinders (Figure 5.4) isolate various sounds and thus sensitize children to sounds in the world. Other Sensorial Materials work on other senses to isolate qualities for children. (These are described further in chapter 10.) Such materials are not only interesting in and of themselves, they also are intended to make the world more interesting by allowing children to see it in a more differentiated way. Again, this assertion is ripe for empirical research. It would stand to reason that children who work with materials that call on them to notice slight gradations in color would notice such gradations in the world, but do they? Furthermore, what benefits are conferred by noticing such gradations? Is there an influence on child affect or attention, for example, or is it merely that the child's senses are more finely tuned (see chapter 10)?

THE MONTESSORI TEACHER

Dr. Montessori also specifically noted that teachers must be interesting to children: "The teacher also must be attractive, pleasing in appearance, tidy and clean, calm and dignified. These are ideals that each can realize in her own way. . . . The teacher should study her own movements, to make them as gentle and graceful as possible" (Montessori, 1967a/1995, p. 277). In so doing, the teacher, Dr. Montessori believed, could serve to further arouse the children's topic interest.

FIGURE 5.4 The Sound Cylinders. Photograph by An Vu.

In addition to stimulating interest via the manner in which he or she presents lessons, the Montessori teacher is supposed to influence the child's interest by correctly timing the child's lessons. To achieve maximum interest, Dr. Montessori noted that a lesson must be given at the opportune moment in a child's development. If given too early, the children will find it too difficult, and if given too late, the child will be bored by it. In either case, the child will not be interested. Therefore, the teacher is responsible for watching the children very closely, aiming to present each material to each child at a time in the child's development when that lesson will be particularly interesting. "The teacher will note whether or not the child is interested in the object, how he shows his interest, how long he is interested in it, and so on, and she will take care not to force a child's interest in what she is offering" (Montessori, 1967b, p. 107). When the teacher realizes the timing is wrong, the teacher puts the material away and tries again later. Assisting with this task, many of the materials have a predetermined sequence that Dr. Montessori empirically tested and found worked well across children, with each material building on what came before. But not all materials work this way, and even those that do still need to be timed well. Montessori teachers are meant to observe the children carefully and to be sensitive to the timing of each lesson so as to elicit maximal interest. In contrast, in conventional schools, teachers have a syllabus set at the beginning of the year, and this guides the timing of lessons.

Several ideas concerning interest discussed so far are apparent in this one passage by Dr. Montessori:

> Many people must have noticed the intense attention given by children to the conversation of grown-ups when they cannot possibly be understanding a word of what they hear. They are trying to get hold of words, and they often demonstrate this fact by repeating joyously some word which they have been able to grasp. We should second this tendency in the child by giving him an abundant material and by organizing for him such exercises as his reactions clearly show us are suitable for him.
>
> The material used in our system not only is very abundant, but it has been dictated to us by rigid experimentation on every detail. However, the same successive choices of material do not appear among the children as a whole. Indeed their individual differences begin to assert themselves progressively at this point in their education. The exercises are easy for some children and very hard for others, nor is the order of selection the same among all the children. The teacher should know this material thoroughly. She should be able to recognize the favorable moment for presenting the material to the child. (1916, pp. 12–13)

INTEREST BUILT ON PRIOR KNOWLEDGE: CONNECTIONS ACROSS THE CURRICULUM

In addition to stimulating topic interest via engaging lessons, materials, environment, and teacher, Montessori education also uses prior knowledge to create interest. Expounding on the importance of prior knowledge for interest:

> It is necessary that "interest" should be awakened and should persist in all instruction.... It is well-known that ... [one must link] all new knowledge to the old, "going from the known to the unknown," because what is absolutely new can awake no interest. (Montessori, 1917/1965, p. 45)

Psychology research supports the idea that interest stems from having some knowledge, but not too much, about something already (Berlyne, 1960; Tobias, 1994). Prior knowledge has clear effects on learning, which might result in part from interest. For example, activating prior knowledge structures can assist in storage and retrieval of new knowledge (Anderson, 1983). One classic example of this is presented in chapter 8: If one reads an ambiguous passage with no idea of what it is about, one will not remember the passage nearly as well as someone who reads the ambiguous passage with some prior knowledge of what it was about (Bransford & Johnson, 1972). Although interest was not assessed in this experiment, I would guess that the people who knew the passage topic were also more interested in what they were reading. This also bears on the issue of using advance organizers in learning text materials. Students who review tables of contents, giving themselves some "prior knowledge" on which to hook the new incoming information, learn better than do those who simply take off on an uncharted journey through the chapter. Having some knowledge of a topic also stimulates learning, and it is quite possible that this is partly because prior knowledge stimulates interest. Taking a college course on China might lead to a lifelong interest in China, which could easily have been an interest in Africa if a course on Africa had been taken instead.

To build on prior knowledge, the Montessori curriculum frequently introduces information or a material at one stage, then builds on it later. The Great Lessons are an example of this in that throughout their Elementary school years, children can return to the skeletal knowledge from those stories and take off from it in new directions.

The extent to which prior knowledge is built on in Montessori, both within a curriculum area and across areas and in truly specific ways, may be unique. The fact that a single person with a vast grasp of academic disciplines—Dr. Montessori—had a hand in developing the materials across the entire curriculum from ages 0 to 12, enabled this interconnection. Dr. Montessori knew intimately what had come before, what was to come later, and what was to be presented across topic areas, for children at each age level, and she specialized in interconnections. Learning in Montessori takes the form of a vast web, connected across topic areas and years. Using a single classroom teacher rather than different teachers for different topics echoes this arrangement.

Reflecting connections to prior knowledge across the years, for example, in Primary classrooms, 2- to 6-year-old children learn nomenclature for different parts of plants. Later, in Elementary, as 6- to 9-year-olds, children go back to those parts and learn the functions they serve. An appreciation of diversity is fostered through this study. For example, the function of the leaf is to make food for the plant, and to do so it requires water and light. Different plants have evolved to capture light in myriad ways, resulting in a vast diversity of leaves. The awareness of diversity that comes from this lesson then extends to all forms of life.

As another example of interconnections, in Primary, children learn about different geological formations, such as capes and bays, and in Elementary, they study particular capes and bays around the world. These lessons are in turn connected to people and diversity, as the children confront how people live differently if they live near a bay, in a valley, or in a mountainous area. Children learn how food, shelter, and clothing also differ depending on how people live.

New knowledge thus is built on the old, and all learning is interconnected: It is a Cosmic (comprehensive, interconnected) Education. Conventional school curricula might strive to make interconnections, but for many reasons, parts of the curricula are usually not well integrated. For example, different teachers make up their own lessons for different areas; different texts from different publishers convey different topics; school systems change textbook series frequently; and so on. Conventional school systems also normally begin with and build from age 6, not age 3. If the years up to age 6 are sensitive periods for rapid acquisition of vocabulary, which Dr. Montessori claimed and which is consistent with language research (Carey & Bartlett, 1978; Dollaghan, 1985), age 6 may be too late to have children easily and enthusiastically learn the foundational vocabulary on which much of the additional knowledge is built (see Markson & Bloom, 1997 for evidence that this rapid learning is not unique to new words).

Children in Montessori also use the same material in new and more expansive ways as they learn. The Binomial Cube was presented earlier. This (and the Trinomial Cube) is considered a Sensorial Material in Primary, but reappears as a Math Material in Elementary, with its associated mathematical formula. A series of further cubes are also presented in Elementary, building on the old knowledge with very similar materials. Thus, new concepts are introduced with old materials across classrooms, creating interest by linking new information to the old.

Within classrooms as well, younger children observe the activities of older children, familiarizing them with activities they will later learn. For example, 3-year-olds observe 4-year-olds making words with the Movable Alphabet (Figure 5.5): The older child takes each letter out of the box, utters the phonetic sound, and places it on a rug until he or she has made a whole word. By watching, the 3-year-old can learn the process and even some of the content of the activity he or she will later do. Learning a little about an activity by watching lends familiarity to that activity, which should then engender more interest in learning it. In addition, of course, there is a motivating element in that older children do that activity. When the teacher shows a child how to do the Movable Alphabet, the child has the sense that he or she has advanced to doing what the older children do, and that is likely to make it all the more interesting. Research presented in chapter 7 shows that children's observational learning is enhanced when they see slightly older peers engaged in an activity. Conventional schooling cannot capitalize on this, because there is only one age level per class. Even were more than one grade level included in a conventional classroom (as one sometimes sees), learning occurs mostly in books, unavailable for observation by other children.

In all these ways, then, Montessori education works to stimulate topic interest in children. The lessons, the environment and materials, the teacher, and the constant integration of new knowledge with old are intentionally designed to captivate children.

FIGURE 5.5 The Movable Alphabet. © Laura Joyce-Hubbard, 2014. All rights reserved.

Balancing Expertise and Integration in Education

Integration is an interesting issue to consider in light of specialist versus generalist teachers. As children move through conventional schools, they are increasingly given specialist teachers, and recommendations from the National Research Council have been for even greater use of specialist teachers in schools (Bransford et al., 1999; although this stance has apparently softened, see Quinn, Schweingruber, & Keller, 2012). In contrast, Dr. Montessori believed that there should be one teacher in each classroom and no more (although there might be a non-teaching assistant to the teacher, particularly in Primary). Clearly a single teacher cannot be an expert in every subject; instead, the Montessori teacher's principal job is to connect children to the environment. "The teacher's principal duty [is to] explain the use of the material. [The teacher] is the main connecting link between the material ... and the child" (Montessori, 1967b, p. 151). Because he or she serves as this link, the Montessori teacher has to thoroughly understand the material. This is one reason excellent, deep training is necessary to become an effective Montessori teacher. Yet Dr. Montessori believed that the teacher should be a generalist, rather than an expert in a single area of the curriculum.

EXPERTISE AND TEACHING

Dr. Montessori's apparent preference for generalist teachers is interesting in light of research on expertise. A difference between the knowledge of experts and that of novices in a domain lies in how their knowledge is organized. For example, when asked to reason about a physics problem, experts refer first to general physical principles and why they are applicable to the problem, whereas novices jump immediately to equations they would use and how they would use them (Larkin, McDermott, Simon, & Simon, 1980). Novices' knowledge is stored as lists of facts that are not well integrated. Experts' knowledge is organized around core concepts, sets of important ideas that guide thinking in a domain (Chi, Feltovich, & Glaser, 1981), much as the five Great Lessons provide a central structure for the Elementary curriculum.

This is why the National Research Council has recommended specialist teachers. Conventional schooling often provides children with discrete sets of facts that are not usually presented as interrelated, perhaps in part because different teachers are often responsible for different parts of the curriculum. Even facts within a discipline are often not related to other facts within that discipline, perhaps because teachers are often not experts in what they teach. As Bransford and colleagues noted in the 1999 National Research Council report on learning,

> Many approaches to curriculum design make it difficult for students to organize knowledge meaningfully. Often there is only superficial coverage of facts before moving on to the next topic; there is little time to develop important, organizing ideas. History texts sometimes emphasize facts without providing support for understanding [e.g., Beck, McKeown, & Gromoll, 1989; Beck, McKeown, Sinatra, & Loxterman, 1991]. Many ways of teaching science also overemphasize facts (American Association for the Advancement of Science, 1989; National Research Council, 1996). (p. 42)

Expert teachers could help children adopt the integrated knowledge structures that experts are known to have. Actually, there is not a good body of research on the degree to which teacher expertise is related to student teaching; even "pedagogical content knowledge" or teachers' understanding of how to best teach their topic is not clearly related to student learning (Van Driel & Berry, 2012). Teacher expertise could facilitate student learning. Learning is known to be better when rooted in orderly structures, as discussed in chapter 10, and experts are more likely to deliver knowledge in orderly fashion. The question arises as to whether the single Montessori Elementary teacher should be replaced by a set of teachers with expertise in different parts of the curriculum.

GENERALIST VERSUS SPECIALIST TEACHERS
IN MONTESSORI EDUCATION

When psychological research recommends a practice that is not followed in Montessori, it deserves careful consideration. Because Montessori is so different from conventional education, different practices might be warranted. Here I consider whether children in Montessori classrooms might be better served by a cadre of expert teachers. One consideration is that a generalist provides interconnections that might inspire fuller learning than having each area taught as a discrete topic would, and another is that children might become more resourceful and independent with a single, generalist teacher because they go outside for expertise.

Another consideration is that Montessori learning is based on student interest, and it would be impossible for a teacher to be an expert in every child's individual interests. Only in a school system with a preset curriculum and/or whole-class learning could a teacher be reasonably expected to have more expertise in every topic studied, and the findings reviewed thus far suggest learning under such conditions is compromised by the inability of such systems to incorporate much choice or personal interest.

Another consideration regarding replacing the generalist teacher with experts arises when one considers the Montessori materials. The concern here is with basic knowledge imparted in the classroom, on a par with the basic knowledge the National Research Council suggested experts impart in conventional schools.

In Montessori education, the materials and lessons, rather than the teacher, are intended to operate for the child as organizing structures. Rather than an expert teacher providing core principles around which the child can organize his or her knowledge, the materials provide those principles. The Montessori materials embody basic principles, and they structure knowledge in each area of the curriculum. By connecting the child to the material at the right moment in the child's development, the generalist Montessori teacher has done his or her job; the material does the rest. This is clear, for example, in Dr. Montessori's description of working with a math material to learn decimals.

> In fact, to make the idea of decimal relations apparent to a child, it is sufficient to direct his attention to the material he is handling. The teacher experienced in this method knows how to wait; she realizes that the child needs to exercise his mind constantly and slowly; and if the inner maturation takes place naturally, "intuitive explosions" are bound to follow as a matter of course. The more we allow the children to follow the interests which have claimed their fixed attention, the greater will be the value of the results. (1917/1965, p. 210)

The materials provide the organizing structures. The teacher knows those structures from training, but does not impart them him or herself, and does not need to be a mathematician by training.

The materials concern the organization of knowledge within parts of the curriculum. In Elementary, Montessori education is unique in that the Great Lessons provide children a central organizing structure that extends across the entire curriculum. Whether the approach taken in Montessori helps organize children's knowledge into structures resembling those held by experts is an issue worthy of experimental examination. Future research should test whether the structure of children's knowledge about topics that are covered in both Montessori and conventional school differ. (Many examples of such tests are provided in chapter 2 of Bransford et al., 1999.)

Common Concerns With Letting Interest Drive Learning

As was mentioned in the previous chapter concerning choice, one might be concerned that if children are allowed to learn only what they are interested in, large swaths of the curriculum could go unknown. Children could avoid what they do not perform well at.

In light of this concern, it is interesting to consider research on mastery versus performance goals in learning (Dweck, 1999, 2006), discussed more in chapter 6. People with mastery orientations, in brief, are people who are interested in learning in order to master a topic. They tend to like challenges, and they persist at them. People with performance goals, in contrast, tend to like to do easy jobs that make them look good. They want to be judged positively. Although these two different orientations appear to characterize different people, the same person can adopt different orientations under different environmental conditions. And it ends up that the particular conditions under which people are more apt to adopt mastery goals bear striking similarities to Montessori environments (Ames, 1992; see chapter 6). For example, Montessori has no tests or grades. As will be discussed in chapter 6, when children are given tests and graded or otherwise rewarded for their performance on those tests, they tend to adopt performance orientations, and therefore choose tests that are of a lower level. If they are not offered extrinsic rewards, they tend to adopt mastery goals, and thus choose challenging tasks. In a Montessori classroom, all rewards are intrinsic. Children learn because the work is interesting, not because they have to bring home a report card. This in itself might go some way toward eliminating the problem of children doing only what they are already good at. When one's primary goal is to learn, rather than to do well on a test, one is less likely to avoid what one does poorly at and more likely to gravitate toward what is challenging.

Still, children might avoid an area, and one task of the Montessori teacher is to ensure that children engage in all areas. To do this, teachers need to keep track of what children do in order to see if they are avoiding certain activities. Many people wonder how teachers can manage this in the absence of the factory model of whole-class learning. In a Primary Montessori class, a teacher may be able to keep track of where children are in the sequence of different work in his or her head and will notice if a child is not progressing in an area at the rate that would be expected. Children should get through the 3-year sequence of activities for a level in the 3 years they are in that classroom. For Elementary, few teachers can keep track of it all in their heads because there is a much larger number of lessons and materials. In Elementary, the teacher might keep track of where each child is in the sequence with a chart in a teacher's closet or another system she or he has developed. In addition, in Elementary, children keep track of their own work in a Work Journal, the notebook mentioned in chapter 3 in which a child records all his or her activities, from arrival in the morning to departure in the afternoon, with times. For example, an entry for one day might begin, "8:10–9:25: Horse report. Three books investigated for information. 9:38–10:14: Soccer. 10:19–11:06: Bank Game. Three problems with a three-digit multiplier." The child and teacher together, usually once weekly, go over the work the child has recorded in his or her Journal. (More independent children might meet to go over the Journal less often, and less independent ones might have meetings more often.) The teacher checks to ensure that the child is following up on lessons and getting to all areas of the curriculum.

When a child is not working in a certain area, optimally the teacher can inspire the child by connecting the area to the children's personal interests. For example, if a child is not interested in techniques of writing, such as capitalization and punctuation, the topics might be made more palatable through a paper on a topic of great interest, such as frogs or dogs. Humor is also used liberally in the Elementary years, because Dr. Montessori noted it can assist interest. The teacher might point out, for example, the difference between describing her pet as "ginger" versus "Ginger" as an inspiration to follow up on a lesson on capitalization. Personal interests are thus used to inspire learning across the curriculum. In some cases, this might not work, and the teacher might need to ask children to commit to a time, as was discussed in chapter 3. The teachers are responsible for ensuring that an education based on interest does not end up being a narrow one.

Chapter Summary

In sum, Montessori programs are designed to stimulate topic interest through the environment, the presentation of lessons, and the linking of old knowledge to new. Montessori education also capitalizes on children's personal interests. A single teacher who is aware of all the materials, of what lessons each child has had, and of what else has particularly inspired each child can be aware of how to make interconnections and inspire further interest for an individual child.

Psychology research suggests that being interested in a topic has a nontrivial influence on one's proficiency in learning about the topic. The Nobel laureate Herbert Simon had a prescription for learning environments based on his many years of research in cognitive psychology. His prescription refers repeatedly to interest, and it sounds remarkably like a Montessori classroom:

> Children left to themselves in a rich environment find, and attend to, stimuli that are at the right level of complexity for them—in which they can find interesting pattern. With experience, they learn to discover and enjoy more and more complex patterns. We say that they have curiosity, and we are concerned that this curiosity seems often to be burned out of them in the process of growing up and being schooled.
>
> Although I know of only a little research that supports (and none that refutes) my conjecture, I would guess that curiosity—the habit of examining the environment for interesting pattern—can be learned. Extrapolating from Berlyne's research, I would venture further that a reasonably rich environment, but one that does not continually force new stimuli on children instead of leaving the initiative to them in seeking pattern, is most conducive to encouraging active curiosity. I would venture a third guess that the environments that are best for this purpose respond to the child's exploration of them by revealing progressively clearer and more interesting patterns with each modest investment of new effort (Qin & Simon, 1990). (Simon, 2001b, p. 7)

I would guess that Simon would have very much liked Montessori education. Interest researchers, who are also concerned about curiosity being burned out of children in conventional schools, have expressed how difficult it would be to base conventional school classrooms on individual interest. Estes and Vaughan (1973), who conducted the first study described in this chapter, on the effect of interest on reading comprehension, wrote:

> Why have the implications of such results had such an insignificant impact on testing and teaching strategies? Several answers may be hypothesized. First, these past studies have not drawn the attention they warrant. Second, the implications of these studies have not been explicitly emphasized—that is, the results may have been accepted as interesting without consideration for their implications. Third, the implications for readjustments in philosophy and strategies are so wide-sweeping that they are difficult to accept or implement. (p. 150)

Montessori school children learn not because they have to memorize for tests—typically there are no tests—but because they are interested in what they are learning. Montessori education is set up to create interest in topics and to capitalize on the interests children already have, thereby optimizing learning.

Being interested can be viewed as being internally motivated to learn about something. Whereas most chapters in this book present elements that are part of Montessori education but are often lacking in conventional schools, the next chapter deals with something that is not present in Montessori but is present in conventional schooling: extrinsic rewards, such as gold stars and grades. Such factors unfortunately can negatively influence children's motivation to learn.

6 }

Extrinsic Rewards and Motivation

The prize and the punishment are incentives towards unnatural or forced effort, and therefore we certainly cannot speak of the natural development of the child in connection with them.

— Maria Montessori *(1912/1964, p. 21)*

In Montessori schools, there are no grades, gold stars, demerits, honor rolls, pizza for reading programs, and so on. Teacher evaluation is invisible to children, with comments limited to matter-of-fact notes ("Need comma here"). Montessori children do schoolwork and behave positively apparently because they are internally motivated. In contrast, conventional schools are steeped in extrinsic incentives to get children to learn and to behave well. Many schools issue demerits or take away recess to punish bad behavior and give smiley-face stickers, extra recess, less homework, or even money to reward good behavior. At one of my childhood schools, students who had done well during the week could go to a room called "The Learning Center" on Friday afternoons and play games like Master Mind and chess in exchange for candy. The most ubiquitous extrinsic incentive to learn in conventional schools is grades. Although on the one hand, grades might be simply a measurement device, on the other hand, they can be perceived as a reward for doing well or a punishment for doing poorly. Some people back this perception by tying privileges to grades.

The use of extrinsic rewards, particularly grades, in conventional schools may stem from a cultural assumption that children do not like school and cannot be motivated in school any other way. This assumption is often true for children after they have been in school for a time, and may stem from such factors as that schoolwork is not interesting and that children have little choice in the classrooms. If one really is not motivated to do something, extrinsic rewards can get one to do it.

The use of rewards and punishments to induce learning fits with both the factory and the empty-vessel models, but it has been in place since well before either were applied to schools. The factory model contributes to their continued use because whole-class learning requires a certain degree of paying attention on the part of all students, and when students are not sufficiently interested (owing to lack of personal interest or topic interest) the threat of a poor external evaluation can help to motivate them to pay attention.

The empty-vessel model clearly upholds the use of rewards and punishments, because behaviorism is based on the idea that organisms act to receive rewards and avoid punishments. In a classic behaviorist paradigm, food pellet rewards cause hungry rats in Skinner boxes to learn to press levers in particular patterns. Thorndike urged teachers to reward correct associations with candy and pats on the head and to punish incorrect ones with stern looks (Jonich, 1962).

Reward systems are frequently used outside school contexts as well. Some toddlers are given candy every time they use the toilet. Businesses give raises and bonuses for work well done. Many states reward and punish schools monetarily for having a certain percentage of students pass the state's proficiency exams. The use of extrinsic rewards is ubiquitous both inside and outside schools. However, as Alfie Kohn (1993) has repeatedly argued, in the end, rewards do a disservice. We use them because the immediate results are compelling (Allan & Fryer, 2011[1]), and we fail to notice the long-term results.

Dr. Montessori came to see rewards and evaluation as a great interference with children's learning, and the research suggests that her perception is correct. Although extrinsic incentives work (in some ways) over the short term, over the long haul, under the circumstances of most children in school, they disrupt the very behaviors they aim to promote. Intrinsic motivation to engage in activities further, cognitive functioning, creativity, and prosocial behaviors are all negatively impacted by extrinsic rewards and evaluations. Once children lose motivation to learn in school, rewards might be necessary; conventional schools cannot simply pull grades from schools with older children and still expect them to learn. But even in conventional contexts, studies show that school environments that emphasize mastery over performance goals are more positive environments for learning and development.

In this chapter I consider research on the negative effect of rewards on intrinsic motivation, cognitive function, creativity, and prosocial behavior. Next I discuss research on how theories about the self and learning are tied to evaluation and how different conventional school environments appear to impact this. Then I turn to the issue of how Montessori education proceeds in the absence of extrinsic rewards and obvious adult evaluation. The chapter ends with a discussion of Dr. Montessori's views on pretend play, since, as will be evident later in this chapter, she initially used play with attractive toys as a reward in her classrooms; children's responses indicated this was unnecessary: They chose real activities instead.

---

[1] Students were administered measures of intrinsic motivation in this study, but when is not indicated; other findings would suggest that motivation fell after the incentive program was removed.

As compared with other chapters in this book, which discuss positive outcomes from practices that characterize Montessori education but are not ingrained in conventional education, this chapter discusses the negative outcomes of a conventional practice (using extrinsic rewards) that is not part of Montessori. Because the point to be made here is so counter to people's everyday sense, several studies are presented to make a clear case. I turn to Montessori halfway through the chapter.

Research on Motivation and Rewards

Research shows that if a person was already motivated to do an activity, expected rewards actually interfere with their subsequent interest in that activity. This result often surprises people, but the research supporting it is very strong. Learning is something young children are interested in and are intrinsically motivated to do.

> Few of us have ever seen or even heard of a three- or four-year-old with a "motivational deficit." Instead, young children seem eager and excited about learning of all sorts, and the more typical parental complaints concern their children's apparently insatiable curiosity and boundless energy. Yet, by the time these same children have entered school, a sizable fraction are quickly labeled as having motivational difficulties of one sort or another in learning. (Lepper, Sethi, Dialdin, & Drake, 1997, p. 23)

Indeed, children's intrinsic motivation in school has been shown to decline every year over the course of conventional schooling (Eccles, Wigfield, et al., 1993; Harter, 1981; Lepper, Corpus, & Iyengar, 2005). This is at odds with conventional school goals. A 2005 study showed intrinsic motivation was positively related to both grades and standardized test scores for a sample of 797 children in third through eighth grade, whereas extrinsic motivation was negatively related to those outcomes (Lepper et al., 2005; see also Corpus & Wormington, 2014). Although there are undoubtedly many reasons for children's diminishing intrinsic interest in learning in school (the lack of choice in schools, learning not being made interesting, and so on), research strongly suggests that heavy reliance on grades and other superfluous extrinsic motivators is one factor. In the following sections, I first describe the three classic studies that brought the problems of extrinsic motivators to light at the end of the behaviorist era in psychology. Next I discuss the breadth of application of this finding, revealing the kinds of activities influenced by extrinsic motivators and the types of rewards that disrupt motivation.

Before going on to the research, a personal anecdote might help readers connect the findings to their own lives. As a child, I engaged in a competitive sport that I initially did for pleasure. As I improved and began to win prizes, I came to do it for the prizes. Then one year, due to being unable to practice for a long time, I ceased to win the prizes, and at that point I lost all interest in the sport. This loss of motivation when extrinsic rewards are removed is a phenomenon that many people have experienced, and that studies have shown again and again.

THREE CLASSIC STUDIES

In the early 1970s, as psychology changed course away from behaviorism, three studies surprised people by showing that expected extrinsic rewards—the currency of behaviorism—subsequently reduced motivation to engage in behaviors that people had formerly engaged in at will. Several other negative effects were observed in addition to reduced motivation, but the motivation finding was common to all three studies. In one study involving preschool children, Mark Lepper and his colleagues placed new sets of markers in classrooms of 3- to 5-year-olds and watched to see which children used them a lot (Lepper, Greene, & Nisbett, 1973). Heavy marker users were then brought, one at a time, to a testing room, and a third of them were immediately shown a "Good Player Award"—a fancy note card with a big gold star and a red ribbon. They were asked if they would like to receive a Good Player Award, and all the children assented. They were told that all they had to do to win the award was draw with the markers. After each child had drawn for six minutes, a Good Player Award was placed with great fanfare on an "Honor Roll Board." For the other two conditions, children were simply allowed to draw with the markers for 6 minutes and then were unexpectedly given a Good Player Award, or they drew for 6 minutes and no award was ever mentioned. A panel of judges who were blind to what condition the children had been in rated the drawings' creativity.

There were two important findings. First, drawings done by children who expected rewards were judged as significantly lower in quality than drawings done in the other two conditions. Second, a few weeks later, when the classroom was observed for marker use, children who had expected a reward used the markers much less than they had previously, and half as much as the other children. Engaging in a well-liked activity with the expectation of a reward led to reduced creativity during that activity and to decreased voluntary participation in that activity later.

Two other studies conducted at about the same time also suggested that extrinsic rewards undermine motivation once the rewards are removed. In one experiment, undergraduates solved 3-dimensional puzzles, in which one creates a specific shape from a set of smaller shapes, across three puzzle-solving sessions (Deci, 1971). Participants had leeway as to how long they worked on each puzzle and whether they actually solved them. During the middle session, some participants were offered $1 for each puzzle they correctly solved. The experimenters tracked how long the students engaged in the activity in the third session as compared with the first. Participants who were rewarded in the middle session decreased the amount of time spent on the puzzles in the last session, whereas participants in the control group showed no change (see also later work by Deci & Porac, 1978).

To investigate whether such effects hold only in the laboratory, Deci (1971) went on to do a field experiment. This time the concern was not how long people freely chose to engage in a task, but rather, how long a creative task, writing newspaper headlines, took them to complete. Eight undergraduates who wrote headlines for a college newspaper participated, and their average time for writing a headline was measured. For the reward condition, four of the headline writers were offered 50 cents per headline written over a 3-week period. The average time each participant took to write headlines during the 3 weeks before the reward period was compared with their time during the 3 weeks after the reward period. The findings suggested that people who had not been rewarded were better off: Whereas members of the control group were writing headlines significantly faster during the last period, those in the experimental group were writing them at the same pace. The provision of an external reward had blocked the acceleration that normally occurs with practice.

In the third classic study showing the negative effect of extrinsic rewards, high school students were offered a tour of a Tel Aviv University laboratory as an extrinsic reward for doing puzzles (Kruglanski, Friedman, & Zeevi, 1971). As compared with students who participated without a reward, those who were rewarded subsequently were less interested in the activities, had lower incidental recall of the activities, and were less creative. The findings were replicated with elementary and other high school children (Kruglanski, 1978), and across all ages studied, the provision of extrinsic rewards reduced motivation, quality of performance, and even enjoyment relative to when rewards were not involved.

WHEN REWARDS HARM

These initial studies, conducted with students ranging in age from preschool to university, all indicated that receiving a reward for engaging in an activity negatively impacts (among other things) motivation for that activity once the reward is removed. Rewards are not always harmful. Rewards have negative effects mainly when they are clearly contingent on doing another activity, when they are expected, and when they are tangible, such as money or prizes or grades (Lepper & Henderlong, 2000, p. 261). Results of verbal feedback are more complicated, but appear to vary both by the age of recipient (younger children are more adversely affected) and the type of feedback (evaluation of person or performance, or specifying how to improve), as will be seen later in the chapter.

In addition to these features, rewards seem to interfere particularly when tasks are open ended, lacking explicit and precisely stated steps one must follow to be successful. The best school tasks are open ended: They do not specify exactly how to draw a picture or exactly how to write a report in order to get a good grade. Part of the task is coming up with one's own way, using one's own judgment about how to do well, because in life one will be faced with unique conditions in which set instructions would not apply. Rewards might particularly interfere with tasks that have open-ended solutions, because rewards encourage surface-level strategies (Ryan & Laguardia, 1999) that do not work as well with open-ended tasks.

The conditions under which rewards are demotivating are particularly applicable to school. Children know in advance that they will be graded or rewarded, those rewards are contingent on their performance, the rewards are tangible, and the assignments (at least the best of them) are open ended. Thus these findings have profound implications for how schools usually operate, with gold stars and grades reinforcing learning behaviors.

WHEN REWARDS ARE OKAY

There are circumstances in which rewards have been shown to be helpful. A tradition of research in behavior modification shows that rewards can enhance performance when there is a set, algorithmic solution to a problem. This is perhaps related to the fact that rewards appear to enhance performance on low-interest tasks (Alvarez & Booth, 2014; Cameron, Banko, & Pierce, 2001). This might apply to older children in school, as their intrinsic motivation to learn in school has diminished (Eccles, Wigfield, et al., 1993; Harter, 1981). Yet if their interest has diminished in part because of grades, then the practice creates a vicious cycle. Second, rewards are often effective at the moment of their offering, so if there are no long-term goals, rewards are fine. Third, some studies, discussed in chapter 7, also suggest that peer learning programs work well when rewards are given to a group for the group's performance. These studies were conducted with older children, who are well-accustomed to receiving extrinsic rewards for school learning.

Despite the wealth of evidence showing negative impacts of rewards, there are still those who claim rewards are generally positive. Some of these detractors are spurred by an inadequate meta-analysis (an analysis of the results of many experiments put together) that came to a different conclusion (Eisenberger & Cameron, 1996) (see commentaries in the 1998 *American Psychologist, 53*, no. 6, and Deci, Koestner, & Ryan, 1999). Yet a large number of studies, some of which are reviewed in this chapter, and more recent meta-analyses (Cerasoli, Nicklin, & Ford, 2014; Deci et al., 1999), provide convincing evidence that the reward structure that exists for much of school learning has serious negative consequences for subsequent motivation (see Sansone & Harackiewicz, 2000) as well as for performance, creativity, proso-cial behavior, self theories, and classroom environments. In the next section, I briefly discuss a few of the many later studies as well as two more recent, better meta-analysis regarding rewards before moving on to discuss research showing a host of other negative consequences of rewards.

FURTHER STUDIES ON MOTIVATION

The negative effects of extrinsic rewards on motivation to engage in previ-ously appreciated activities have been seen in dozens of studies since these three original ones (e.g., Deci et al., 1999; McGraw & Fiala, 1982). Notably, the negative effects tend to occur only when the reward is expected and the activity was already of interest. But they hold across many types of activi-ties and types of rewards, and even hold for evaluation. One example of a different sort of activity is the game of pinball, which many undergraduates are intrinsically motivated to play (Harackiewicz, Manderlink, & Sansone, 1984). Undergraduates who were either expecting to receive a reward (movie tickets) or expected to be comparatively evaluated on their pinball skills after playing showed less interest in playing pinball later than those who received nothing or received the reward or evaluation unexpectedly.

One way to view the problems of expected rewards is that the first activ-ity (pinball or schoolwork) is cast as the means to an end (movie tickets or a good grade). The net result of an activity's being cast as a means to an end (the reward) is that people come to devalue the first activity and overvalue the second (Lepper, Sagotsky, Dafoe, & Greene, 1982). In another study, two activities of equal and high inherent initial interest were presented to pre-schoolers. One group of children was told to engage in one of the activities so that they could later engage in the second one. Other children were simply told to engage in one activity, and then the other one, without it seeming as though the second were contingent on the first. About 3 weeks later, observ-ers noted that during free time, children who had participated in the contin-gent activity condition showed decreased interest in whichever activity they had first, and increased interest in the second activity. The other children showed no such difference. This is a reward structure that is often used in schools: Students are told that once they complete Activity A, then they can do Activity B (finish your geometry, then you can do art).

The expectation of a reward also has been shown to influence the level of difficulty students prefer in a task. In everyday settings, we see this when stu-dents opt to take easier courses so they can get a better grade. In one study, students were allowed to choose which of seven puzzles they would most like to solve, with the puzzles ranked in order of difficulty (Shapira, 1976). Some of the students were told before choosing that they would receive a small reward if they solved the puzzle. Those who were solving for a reward chose significantly less difficult puzzles.

Psychology professor Susan Harter (1978) obtained similar findings with grade-school children. Sixth-graders who were told they would be receiving a grade for performance on a set of anagram problems chose less challenging anagrams than did children who were told the task was a game. In addition, children in the graded group showed less pleasure and more anxiety than children in the games group.

These studies have nontrivial implications for schooling. Students in school work all too much for grades. In the face of grades, these studies show, students opt for less challenge, and therefore learn less. The negative affect and anxiety they experience (discussed later) when they expect grades, even as they engage in less challenging tasks, is also suggestive of less optimal engagement and therefore less optimal learning in school.

A final mention regarding motivation concerns meta-analyses of this research area. One meta-analysis showed no negative impact of rewards (Eisenberger & Cameron, 1996), but several researchers in commentaries on that article and other places since have pointed out numerous errors and problems with how that analysis was conducted, about which studies it included, how it classified rewards, and so on. In an attempt to resolve the controversy, results from 128 experiments were combined in a later meta-analysis (Deci et al., 1999). Across these experiments, tangible and expected rewards were found to reliably interfere with subsequent motivation when participants later chose whether to engage in the task. Verbal rewards (such as praise) that were not given in a controlling style increased intrinsic motivation, but only for college students, not for children; the authors cautioned that this may have been because verbal rewards were generally unexpected and the negative impact of rewards is most reliably seen when the rewards are expected. As shown by this meta-analysis, the most detrimental rewards resembled the grade structure of schools: performance-contingent rewards in which not all participants received the maximum.

An even more recent meta-analysis (Cerasoli et al., 2014) of 154 studies, many of them field (rather than laboratory) studies, aligns well with Deci and colleagues (1999) and the analysis given here. This analysis examined how extrinsic incentives and intrinsic motivation interact to predict different types of performance. Intrinsic motivation was the strongest predictor of performance. Its effects were particularly strong for what they termed "qualitative" performance, as opposed to rote, closed-ended tasks—although even "quantitative" performance was sensitive to the level of intrinsic motivation. Also in keeping with results presented here, the more directly an extrinsic incentive was tied to performance (such as a grade for getting a certain percentage of problems right), the more negative its impact; the suggested reason for this is that such incentives are interpreted as controlling.

Obviously, motivation to pursue an activity or solve a problem will be related to how well one does at that activity or problem, so clearly the impact of rewards does not stop at motivation. Other studies indeed show the effect of rewards on various aspects of cognitive functioning, artistic creativity, and prosocial behavior.

The Effect of Rewards on Cognitive Functioning, Creativity, and Prosocial Behavior

Expecting and receiving rewards and evaluations not only influences interest and motivation, but also influences how well one does at the activity. In the following paragraphs, I consider studies that are particularly concerned with cognitive functioning before moving on to artistic creativity and then pro-social behavior. These are all desired human developments. As we shall see, they appear to develop better in the absence of the sorts of reward structures typically used in schools. Conventional schools set up a reward structure that seems to bring the best out in people, because students who succeed often work hard to make the honor roll. Yet the studies suggest that their performance would be even better had that reward structure never existed.

COGNITIVE FUNCTIONING

One study already reviewed showed that cognitive functioning was below par when a reward was expected: Participants were able to think of fewer titles for a literary paragraph and showed less incidental recall of tasks than under no-reward conditions (Kruglanski et al., 1971). Several other studies reiterate that point.

One particularly interesting study involved fifth-graders from three elementary schools (Grolnick & Ryan, 1987). All children read a passage, then were asked how much they enjoyed the passage, how difficult it was, and how pressured they felt. Then they were told they would read a second passage, with directions that varied by condition. Some children were told, "After you are finished, I'm going to test you on it. I want to see how much you can remember. You should work as hard as you can, because I'll be grading you on the test to see if you're learning well enough." Another group of children was told, "After you are finished, I'll be asking you some questions similar to the ones I just asked about the other passage." Recall that these questions were about their personal reactions to the passages. After answering the questions about interest, pressure, and difficulty for the second reading, the children were asked to recall as much of the second passage as they could.

To test for conceptual learning, they were also asked to write an essay on the main point of the passage. To test long-term retention, a week later, children were asked to once again recall the second passage by rote and to write an essay describing the passage's main point.

The results suggest what expectations about getting a grade do for learning. Students who thought they would be graded rendered the passage by rote best at the first test, but had also forgotten the most a week later, making their long-term retention equal to that of the children who thought they would be questioned only about their personal reactions. At second testing, the "personal-reaction" children retained almost all of the rote information reported at the first session.

Conceptual learning—drawing the main point from what was read—was also tested. The essays of the students who did not expect a test or a grade showed significantly greater conceptual learning than did the essays of the children who did expect one. The upshot is that students who expect to be tested initially learn the facts better, by rote, but as soon as the test is over, they forget much of what they learned. Results from tests taken under such conditions are therefore probably not indicative of long-term knowledge gains. Students who are just reading for reading's sake, attending to their own interest and the difficulty of the passage, apparently develop deeper conceptual understanding, and later retain most of the factual information gleaned during their initial reading. Their long-range factual retention is equal to that of students who were specifically trying to memorize for a test, but they also have conceptual knowledge.

Another study involving fifth- and sixth-graders also showed that expectation of evaluation negatively impacts deep processing. The children were asked to respond to 120 questions such as, "Is the word part of the human body? Spine," which had to be processed at a conceptual (meaning) level, and "Does the word rhyme with line?" which could be solved with surface-level processing (Graham & Golan, 1991, p. 189). One group of children was told that their performance would indicate to the experimenter how good they were at such tasks, a second group was told that the problems were ones people get better on as they go, and a third group was only given the task directions without preamble. All of the questions were easy to answer correctly; the measure of interest was performance on an unexpected recall test on which children were asked to remember as many of the questions as they could. The beauty of this design is that it separates out deeper conceptual learning from surface-level learning. Children in all conditions recalled the surface-level questions equally well. However, for the questions requiring deeper processing, children in the second and third groups recalled significantly more than did children in the first. Once again, the evidence suggests that focusing on performance and evaluation interferes with deeper conceptual learning.

The expectation of rewards and evaluation also interferes with problem solving (McGraw & McCullers, 1979). Students were given 10 Luchins water jug problems, such as "A mother sends her son to the well to get 3 quarts of water. She gives him a 4-quart can, a 5-quart can, and a 12-quart can. How can the boy get exactly 3 quarts of water using only these containers and not guessing at the amount?" (p. 287). Half were told that they would receive a nickel for each correct solution, and a $1 bonus if all 10 solutions were correct. Correct solutions to the first nine problems all involved a particular pattern of use of three jugs, but a correct solution to the 10th one involved just two jugs, so the 10th problem was a set breaker: It required that the participant break a response set to consider a problem in a new way. What was of interest was not whether problems were solved correctly, since that was expected, but instead how long it took to solve them, particularly the set breaker. Whereas participants in both groups took equally long on the initial nine items, the set-breaking 10th problem took participants in the reward condition twice as long to solve as the participants who were doing without the problems without expecting a reward. Hence, on a task requiring one to find a new type of solution, the expectation of a reward negatively impacted performance.

Discrimination learning is also negatively impacted by rewards. Fourth-graders were asked to distinguish between 100 drawings of "Bill" and his twin brother, whose appearance differed only in the height and spacing of the eyebrows (Miller & Estes, 1961). Those who were not rewarded at all performed better than children rewarded with 1 cent per correct identification, and they performed better than those rewarded with 50 cents per correct identification. The latter two groups showed no difference in performance, indicating that small rewards have as much negative impact as larger ones.

Other studies have shown people are more insightful in no-reward than reward conditions (see review in McGraw, 1978). For example, on the Duncker's candle problem, in which one is asked to figure out how to attach a candle to the wall using a box of thumbtacks and a matchbook, participants who were told they would receive a reward for quickly coming up with a correct solution took 3.5 minutes *longer* to solve it than did subjects who were not promised a reward (Glucksberg, 1962).

Rewards appear to narrow attention to that for which one will be rewarded, reducing the possibility for other learning (see also Bahrick, Fitts, & Rankin, 1952). Under reward conditions, what is learned is only what students are told to learn, no more. Rewards thus support an empty-vessel model of the child, because they in fact create a learner who takes in just those nuggets of information that he or she expects to be rewarded for. Induction, inference, and other acts of creative thinking are diminished.

To summarize, across several kinds of cognitive tasks, from problem solving to discrimination, from concept formation to incidental learning, extrinsic rewards appear to interfere with learning. Other tasks on which rewards have been shown to interfere involve artistic competence and creativity.

ARTISTIC COMPETENCE AND CREATIVITY

Several of the studies reviewed thus far could be viewed as involving creativity—making up titles for newspaper articles, solving the Luchins water jug problems, and so on. Broadly speaking, tasks involving creativity are often open ended in solution, with no single obvious way to solve them. They involve the use of novel approaches appropriate to the task at hand (Hennessey, 2000). Several studies of the influence of rewards focus specifically on artistic creativity.

One of the initial reward studies described earlier showed that children who were drawing for a Good Player Award did not draw as well as children who were drawing for drawing's sake. In another study, the creativity of elementary school children's stories was examined by asking them to produce one line about each picture in a series (Amabile, Hennessey, & Grossman, 1986). Before beginning the task, some children were given an advance reward: They were allowed to take two pictures with an instant camera if they promised to later participate in other activities. To cement this promise, they signed an elaborate vow to later write the story. Other children also took two pictures before writing their story, but it was not construed as an advance reward. A second manipulation was that for half of the children in each group, the activities were labeled play, and for half they were labeled work. The researchers expected that the play label would be associated with higher creativity. The results indicated no significant effect of the work or play label on creativity, but a significant effect of how the picture taking was construed. Children who believed they had used the camera as an advance reward for what they later did in the experiment produced significantly less creative stories.

Other research has shown that when people know they will be evaluated based on originality, their creative endeavors are less original than when they do not expect to be evaluated. Stanford University undergraduates were directed to spend 15 minutes making collages that would convey a feeling of silliness (Amabile, 1979). Some students were told that the researchers were interested in the quality of their collages, whereas others were told that the researchers were only interested in the mood that resulted from working on the collage. Of those who were told the quality of collage was important, some were told the specific criteria by which collage quality would be judged. A team of 15 judges with extensive studio art experience evaluated the collages for those criteria, such as novelty of material use, novelty of idea, evident effort, shape variation, detail, and complexity.

The judges' ratings showed that participants who did not expect to be evaluated produced more original and creative designs than did people who expected to be evaluated but did not know by what criteria. However, when participants were given exact criteria upon which their designs would be evaluated, they produced designs that satisfied the criteria (e.g., by using a variety of shapes). This raises again the point that when a task is not open ended—when one knows exactly how to get a good score—the expectation of evaluation is not necessarily associated with degraded performance. Yet, as a teacher, telling children exactly what to do to get a good grade on an open-ended assignment, such as writing a paper or making a collage, seems counter to part of what one is after in giving it: the development of creativity and ingenuity.

In another study of the effects of evaluation, this time on artistic competence, children in kindergarten through fifth grade were asked to copy a flower as well as they could under either competitive or noncompetitive conditions (Butler, 1990). Children in the competitive condition were told that the experimenter would collect all the copies to see who had made the best one. Judges rated the quality of the drawings of the noncompetitive group more highly. Motivation and interest in the task were also affected, such that children in the competing group were less likely to want to engage in the activity again (see also White & Owen, 1970).

There is not universal agreement regarding the effects of rewards on creativity (Eisenberger & Shanock, 2003). A meta-analysis of 60 studies attempted to provide a more nuanced view of when rewards have a positive versus negative influence on creativity; it concluded that rewards positively relate to creativity when it is clear that creativity is being rewarded, as opposed to task completion (Byron & Khazanchi, 2012). However, when rewards are offered for completing a creative task, and/or presented in a way that can be construed as controlling, creativity declines. In sum, the expectations of rewards or evaluation in the manner typically used in school settings results in products that are less creative than are products produced without those expectations.

PROSOCIAL BEHAVIOR

Another outcome that is adversely affected by the provision of rewards is prosocial behavior, or being kind to others. Prosocial behavior is desirable both in school and out and is one aim of the character education often noted to be lacking in schools (Bennett, Rosenzweig, & Diamond, 1969). In this section, I consider both rewards for positive behavior, which are more often given at younger ages, and the effect of rewards on the prosocial atmosphere of classrooms, which is particularly pertinent at older ages.

In one study, some second- through fifth-graders were told they would receive a small toy if they helped some hospitalized children by sorting colored paper into piles while they waited for an experimenter to finish another task; others were simply offered the opportunity to help the children during that time (Fabes, Fultz, Eisenberg, May-Plumlee, & Christopher, 1989). A second opportunity to sort papers arose later, while waiting for the experimenter to find a tape recorder. During this time, other activities, such as reading comic books, were also available. Children's mothers also contributed to the data by describing how they used rewards for their children's behaviors at home and how prosocial their children were.

Children in the reward condition spent significantly less time sorting paper during the second, free-choice period than did children who did not receive a reward. Thus motivation to subsequently engage in prosocial acts was negatively impacted by a prior expected reward. A particularly interesting finding is the relationship between mothers' habitual use of rewards and children's responses. Children whose mothers reported that they liked and used extrinsic rewards at home were most affected by the reward manipulation. They sorted significantly less paper, on average, and fewer than half of them sorted any paper at all at the second opportunity. Children whose mothers did not use rewards at home were much less impacted by rewards; 85% of them helped by sorting paper. In addition, children whose mothers felt positively about the use of extrinsic incentives for prosocial behavior engaged in less prosocial behavior at home than did the children of the other mothers.

Another study tested 20-month-olds (Warneken & Tomasello, 2008). An experimenter dropped objects (such as a pen, while writing) and pretended to be unable to reach the objects. Previous studies have shown that toddlers' natural tendency is to help out in such situations, for example, to pick up the pen and give it back. In this study, during a "training" phase, one group of children was rewarded for doing so: After they returned the pen, the experimenter said, "For this, you get a cube" and showed the child an interesting display in which a cube went down a chute. Other children were praised instead: The experimenter said, "Thank you, [child's name]; that's really nice!" A third group of children got no response; the experimenter simply kept on with the task, dropping objects. The training phase continued until children had helped five times. Following this were nine test trials, which were exactly the same but always lacked feedback. On these test trials, children in the third, neutral condition helped on 89%, children in the praise condition helped on 81%, and children in the reward condition helped on 53%. Having been rewarded for their prosocial behavior clearly diminished prosocial behavior once the reward went away.

A naturalistic study of the relationship between extrinsic rewards and older children's prosocial behavior had similar results (Grusec, 1991). Mothers of 4-year-olds recorded their responses to their children's prosocial acts over a

1-month period. The children who were most likely to engage spontaneously in prosocial acts were those whose mothers were least likely to respond after such acts. Children whose mothers did not respond at all to their prosocial acts engaged in the most such acts, those who received acknowledgment (such as a simple "Thanks") engaged in them less frequently, and children who received approval or praise ("What a good boy you are!") were least likely of all to engage in prosocial acts.

Yet another study showed that mothers who were less involved with their children's interactions and were less likely to respond to children's bids for attention and help, had children who were more likely to help, comfort, and share with each other, and to engage in more enjoyable social interactions with others (Crockenberg & Bryant, 1978). The rewards of attention are more subtle in this case, but withholding even such subtle rewards is associated with more prosocial behavior.

Being rewarded also affects how one views one's own prosocial tendencies: Children who were rewarded for charitable behavior considered themselves less altruistic than did children who were not rewarded (Smith, Gelfand, Hartmann, & Partlow, 1979). Assuming people tend to behave in ways that conform to their self theories, changing people's perceptions of the roots of their own altruism would be expected to change their altruistic behavior over time.

The naturalistic findings need to be regarded cautiously, as it is possible that children who are by nature less inclined to be prosocial cause their parents to use more rewards, rather than the other way around. But taken in concert with the laboratory studies, the results strongly suggest that habitual use of verbal and tangible rewards when young children do nice things for others actually leads children to do fewer nice things.

Other work on prosocial behavior and rewards concerns the classroom environments that reward systems such as grades appear to produce. Research has shown that among cooperative, competitive, and individualized learning environments for 8- to 10-year-olds, cooperative environments are associated with the most prosocial behavior (Crockenberg & Bryant, 1978; Nadler, Romek, & Shapira-Friedman, 1979). Grades are linked to competitive environments. In school environments with grades, children check each other's work competitively, to evaluate where they are in relation to others (Butler & Ruzany, 1993). Grades and evaluation therefore seem to reduce prosocial behavior in the classroom by fostering a competitive atmosphere. This could be partly responsible for people often perceiving Montessori classrooms as places where children are particularly kind (a perception confirmed by research described in chapter 11): Competition is minimized by the lack of grades. Elementary school children are notorious for comparing themselves to others even without grades, but the provision of grades appears to exacerbate the tendency.

This raises a more general issue of how grades affect students' self theories and behavior. This is addressed next, followed by a discussion of the atmosphere that the provision of grades appears to produce in school classrooms.

Grades, Goals, and Self Theories

The use of grades in schools is perhaps most insidious for its influence on how students view themselves and their work, particularly their theories of intelligence. Carol Dweck and her colleagues have shown that about 43% of Americans tend to be entity theorists, who think of their intelligence as a fixed quantity, and about 43% tend to be incremental theorists, who think of their intelligence as something that can be increased with effort (this work is summarized in Dweck, 1999, 2006). Everyone to some extent entertains both of these ways of thinking, and the situation one is in at any given moment has a temporary impact, yet most people will adopt one or the other theory more routinely. Importantly, no differences in analytic ability or other measures of intelligence characterize those habitually holding each type of theory.

A variable or "incremental" view is the far healthier one. People who think of their intelligence as malleable adopt mastery goals and try to learn in the face of challenges, whereas fixed entity theorists adopt performance goals and seek to show how bright or good they are. Incremental theorists strive for improvement, and entity theorists strive for adulation. When entity theorists succeed, all is well. However, they break down miserably when they fail. Failure, for entity theorists, results in not wanting to engage in the activity further and wanting to avoid the situation in which they failed (by dropping a class, changing their major, etc.) (Dweck, 1999, 2006). Second, they respond to negative feedback in the same way as depressed people respond, casting themselves as dumb, worthless, and total failures. In contrast, incremental theorists seem to tie failure experiences to the one event, not taking the failure as a judgment on their entire being. They tend to regard failures as indicating areas in which they should work harder.

These theories are malleable, and a change in theories predicts a change in outcome. In one study, an intervention designed to increase incremental beliefs about intelligence in seventh-graders led to improvements in math motivation and performance in the months following the intervention, whereas performance of the control intervention group declined (Blackwell, Trzesniewski, & Dweck, 2007).

Dweck's work is important to the issue of rewards and grades in school because research shows that receipt of grades leads children to adopt performance instead of mastery goals. In fact, as will be discussed in chapter 9, even praise that insinuates an entity theory ("You are really smart!") brings on an unhealthy response to subsequent failures.

One interesting study examined the effect of grades on self theories, goals, and performance in sixth-graders using tasks with both fixed and open-ended solutions (Butler & Nisan, 1986). Some of the fixed-solution tests were word games, such as making as many words as possible from the letters of a long word and constructing new words using the first and last letters of a prior word. The open-ended tasks included a "creative uses" task in which one comes up with as many uses as possible for an object, and a "circles" task, in which one is given a page of nickel-sized circles to draw on, and the creativity of one's drawings is rated.

All children performed similarly on a pretest composed of these tasks. Two days later, some of the children were surprised by the return of their test booklets with either verbal feedback specifying how they could have performed better ("You wrote many short words, but not many long ones") or a score. All of the children then engaged in slightly different versions of the same tasks. A third session 2 hours later repeated the original tasks, and children answered questions regarding their motivation on the tasks and the sources of their performance.

An important factor to remember for the results of these experiments is that they were conducted in the children's school classroom, in a manner reminiscent of school assignments. By sixth grade, students have learned that what one does in school is important only when there is evaluative feedback. Unfortunately, university students often appear to feel the same way, visibly going on vacation when told something will not be on the examination. In keeping with this, students who had not gotten their test booklets back before the second session (no feedback) did not perform as well as the others on the later tests. They probably did not see the assignment as important and did not put in effort.

Consistent with other studies, the two different kinds of feedback led to differences in performance on the open-ended tasks (not on the fixed-solution ones). For example, students who received verbal feedback about how to do better thought of more uses for objects later than did students who had received grades. In addition, students who received comments reported higher levels of motivation on and more liking for the tasks than did those who received grades.

What was new about this study was that grades and comments also had different effects on what the students felt contributed to their performance: their theories of intelligence. Students who received comments attributed their performance to effort, interest, and skill, whereas students who received grades were more apt to attribute their performance to the reader's mood, which is an external, uncontrollable variable. If one has an incremental theory, effort—something one can choose to increase—matters. The reader's mood, conversely, is outside one's control. The literature on learned helplessness and issues discussed in chapter 3 arise. As was discussed there, entity theorists tend to feel helpless in the face of failure.

Attributions of effort aligned with these different perceptions of what underlay their performance. Students in the grades group attributed their effort to a desire to avoid failure, whereas those who received comments attributed their effort to their interest in the task. The entity theorists' performance goals are thus apparent in the group who received grades.

Grades and other evaluations, then, undermine motivation perhaps in part because they tend to lead to performance goals instead of mastery ones. Grades appear to lead children to view their level of performance as reflecting their being smart or dumb, not as indicative of having studied hard or not.

Classroom Environments and Learning Goals

The environments of many conventional school classrooms appear to push children to adopt performance goals. First, research has shown that two types of classroom activity that are very prevalent in conventional American classrooms, individual seat work and teacher-led group presentations (Stigler et al., 2000), tend to lead children to adopt ability-oriented self theories (Ames, 1992), which go along with performance goals. In contrast, project-based work, both collaborative and individual, tends to result in the mastery-oriented approaches that go along with incremental theories. Second, the current test-oriented system of American schools surely leads many teachers to emphasize performance: Schools need students to pass the state exams or the schools' funding suffers.

Exemplifying the relationship between learning environment and learning goals, one study queried the learning orientations of 4- to 8-year-old Israeli children in kibbutz versus urban schools (Butler & Ruzany, 1993). Kibbutz schools tend to use project-based, small-group, collectivistic approaches, whereas urban Israeli schools tend to use teacher-led, whole-class approaches with individual evaluation. When the children at these different schools were asked why they looked at other children's work, children on the kibbutz tended to supply a learning goal ("My ground came out crooked, so I wanted to see how to do it straight," p. 36). In contrast, children in the urban schools gave evaluative reasons ("I wanted to see if my flower was good," "I wanted to see if I did the best flower," p. 36). Different approaches to schooling were therefore associated with different goals among students, goals aligned with mastery rather than performance theories. Of course, life on a kibbutz is in general less competitive than life in the city, so the children's replies might reflect more than their experience in the classroom, but the responses fit with other research showing that the different teaching styles are associated with different learning orientations.

In some of this other research, American junior high and high school students who perceived their classes as emphasizing mastery of material over performance also reported using more effective learning strategies, expressed a preference for challenging tasks, saw their effort as more tied to success, and liked their classes better than did students who saw their classes as dominated by performance goals (Ames & Archer, 1988). Students who saw their classes as dominated by performance goals focused on their ability, which they tended to evaluate negatively. This is also the case for middle (Anderman, Maehr, & Midgley, 1999) and elementary (Corpus, McClintic-Gilbert, & Hayenga, 2009) school students; when mastery rather than performance is emphasized, intrinsic motivation remains (see also Yeager & Dweck, 2012).

A possible criticism of this sort of research is that the classrooms or schools differed because the students differed a priori. Thus, the classroom environments were not *causing* differences in the students, but in fact were the *result* of those differences. One study addressed this by randomly assigning fourth-graders to conditions in which mastery or performance goals were emphasized for a unit on learning fractions (Schunk, 1996). Even under conditions of random assignment, students in the group that emphasized learning goals had higher motivation, task orientation, and achievement outcomes than did children in the group that emphasized performance goals.

All these studies suggest that at younger ages, performance goals are detrimental to most children. Competitive classroom goals, which grades tend to foster, negatively impact learning (Covington, 2000). The age delimiter is important here, because the natural allocation of children's mastery and performance goals in school settings tends to change with age. As children go through school, they increasingly adopt performance goals. This might be caused by developmental factors, or it might be caused by the impact of the conventional school system itself. Most likely it is caused by the school system, as the Cerasoli et al. (2014) meta-analysis discussed earlier found that in general intrinsic motivation increases with age. Research in nonconventional school settings would help determine the degree to which any school, versus conventional schools in particular, are responsible (see Rathunde & Csikszentmihalyi, 2005a, discussed in chapter 11).

Although most young children begin school with a mastery orientation, by high school most children have a performance orientation. For elementary school children, learning or mastery goals have been shown to be related to self-regulation and academic achievement (Bouffard & Vezeau, 1998). For older students, however, performance goals are related to self-regulation and achievement (Bouffard, Vezeau, & Bordeleau, 1998). Putting this together, it appears that as children go through school, they increasingly replace learning goals with performance ones. This may be because of the structure of schools, including the emphasis on evaluation, and because of coming to see how achievement is often tied to grades in school. Whereas mastery goals are associated with better learning at younger ages, this ceases to be the case for students in high school and college. Why would this be the case? Because of attrition from school, many of the performance-oriented children in the high school sample may have been higher-achieving students to begin with, whereas low-performing entity theorists would be more likely to have found the reward system discouraging, perhaps leading them to have dropped out of school by then. Some of the initially mastery-oriented children will have adopted performance goals by this time, replacing the dropouts in the sample. However, as is indicated by many studies reviewed here, it is likely that under the influence of grades, these performance-oriented high school and college students do not retain their learning after testing, nor achieve deeper conceptual learning, nor develop continuing interest in what they study. A host of ill consequences stems from having performance orientations, including test anxiety (Atkinson & Litwin, 1960; Deci & Ryan, 1985; Wigfield & Eccles, 1989), which has been on the increase in recent years (McDonald, 2001). Students who are highly test-anxious perform as well as non-anxious students under non-evaluative conditions, but when evaluation is involved, their performance declines (Kurosawa & Harackiewicz, 1995; McDonald, 2001). Conventional school practices, such as whole-class instruction and ability grouping, tend to increase concerns about evaluation, social comparison, and competitiveness (Eccles, Midgley, et al., 1993), and thus would be expected to bring about poorer learning outcomes.

Teachers can clearly influence the extent to which grades have negative impact by the classroom environments they establish. One review of the research on classroom environments found that when teachers focus on meaningful aspects of activities, emphasize learning goals rather than grades and test scores, and provide students with opportunities to develop responsibility and independence (among other factors), children are more likely to have mastery goals (Ames, 1992). Yet to do these things in conventional classrooms, teachers have to work against the grain: Conventional schools were designed to function with extrinsic rewards and controls.

Summary: Research on the Impact of Rewards and Evaluation

Mark Lepper has noted that when he describes the body of work on rewards to teachers, he gets two sorts of reactions.

> When the results of this literature were described to audiences of educators who worked primarily with young children, the typical response was unadulterated approbation. These teachers clearly understood the phenomenon under discussion and thought that research documenting such effects was long overdue. By contrast,

when these same findings were presented to educators who themselves worked more with older students, a second prototypic response began to appear. Although these teachers would often grant the importance of the phenomenon, they were quick to point out its lack of relevance to their own classroom situations. After all, they routinely indicated, students in their classes rarely displayed any intrinsic motivation whatsoever. There was simply nothing to be undermined. (Lepper et al., 1997, p. 28)

This sad state of affairs reflects the reality of our nation's schools. Children who were initially excited to go to first grade all too soon lose their motivation to learn in school, and their best days are days out of school. There are certainly many reasons for this reduction in motivation, but the results presented in this chapter suggest the use of grades and other extrinsic incentives might be an important contributor.

Conventional school practices, such as giving grades, gold stars, and other incentives, undermine intrinsic interest, cognitive performance, creativity, prosocial behavior, and a host of other good outcomes in children. The use of extrinsic awards may well contribute to children's coming to dislike school *and* to poorer performance than many children would otherwise achieve.

Could grades be good for children in our competitive culture, despite undermining children's intrinsic motivation and leading them to entity theories of intelligence? Given that children will be in a reward-based system someday, some believe it is important that they get acclimatized to rewards early. Do children who are in schools that do not give grades fail to thrive when they enter systems where grades and other types of rewards are used? Perhaps the best evidence on this point is the Milwaukee study described in chapter 1, and elaborated on in chapter 11. The children had been in public Montessori school classrooms from ages 3 to 11. They were tested 4 and more years after their move to non-Montessori public schools and compared to other children at those same schools (several of which were magnet schools for high-achieving children), matched for socioeconomic status (SES), ethnicity, and gender. As a group, the Montessori children fared as well as or better than the non-Montessori children on every measure taken. This suggests that adjustment to a competitive, grade-based system was not an issue. Many anecdotal reports support this, including that the founders of Google and Amazon are among many Montessori graduates who have had no trouble succeeding in a competitive business climate. Conversely, it might be difficult for children who are used to learning for grades to rediscover their love of learning in school once such a system is withdrawn, as this is essentially what the extrinsic rewards literature shows us.

How Dr. Montessori Came to Perceive Rewards as Negative

Initially Dr. Montessori was not against extrinsic rewards.

> Like others I had believed that it was necessary to encourage a child by means of some exterior reward that would flatter his baser sentiments ... in order to foster in him a spirit of work and of peace. And I was astonished when I learned that a child who is permitted to educate himself really gives up these lower instincts. (1967b, p. 59)

Dr. Montessori saw very early on in her schools that rewards, even verbal praise, were unnecessary, and indeed could interfere with children's concentration: "A child does not need praise; praise breaks the enchantment" (1989, p. 16). She was led to a different view of rewards by the children, who on numerous occasions rejected adults' well-intended rewards. Apparently the first such rejection was a reward she herself offered, in her first school in Rome. As described in chapter 1, children who worked with Sandpaper Letters spontaneously began to write, and Dr. Montessori was interested in seeing if they could then read.

To examine the transfer to reading, she made cards with the names of different toys on them, and brought a basket of the toys to the children, to use as rewards. If children could read the name on a card, she promised, they could play with the toy as a reward. Like many adults, she assumed rewards were positive and even necessary to get children to engage in difficult tasks.

The children, however, showed her otherwise. They eagerly read the words, but had no interest in the toys, asking instead for another word to read. This suggested to her that a challenging activity, reading (for new readers), could be motivating in and of itself. The extrinsic reward of playing with a toy was not valued, and in fact seemed an undesired distraction from reading. Using new, important abilities was apparently more inspiring than was playing even with these very attractive toys. Dr. Montessori was very interested by this reaction and followed it up on other occasions.

In one such effort, she tried to give children candy as a reward for being quiet during the Silence Game, described in chapter 4. The Silence Game is an important Montessori exercise, done particularly in Primary, when the teacher asks all the children to be utterly silent and as still as possible for a few moments, and to listen. Near the end of such a Silence, Dr. Montessori quietly whispered each child's name, and asked that they come to her (an initial reason for this was to test the sharpness of their hearing; psychophysics and the limits of human perception were dominant concerns in these early days of psychology). When the children responded, Dr. Montessori offered them candy as a reward, but the children refused to take it. "It was almost as if they were saying, 'Do not spoil this beautiful experience. Our minds are still elated. Do not distract us'" (1966, p. 124).

In a third anecdote, Dr. Montessori described how one of her teachers gave a large silver cross to a child who had been good, and sat a child who had misbehaved in a chair with nothing to do. The child wearing the cross was carrying objects back and forth near the seated child when the cross fell to the ground, and the seated child tried to give it back. The rewarded child was not interested and consented to the seated child's wearing it himself.

In a fourth anecdote showing rejection of an adult's reward system, Dr. Montessori described how a visitor had brought a box of little bronze medals to the classroom, and announced, "'The teacher will attach these to the breasts of the brightest and cleverest children.'" One of the brightest and cleverest 4-year-old boys "wrinkled his brow in protest and cried out several times, 'But not to the boys! But not to the boys!'" (1967b, p. 60).

These four anecdotes reveal that children in early Montessori environments were not just uninterested in rewards—they outright rejected rewards. Dr. Montessori believed that this rejection was in part because the children had achieved a sense of dignity in the classroom. These children lived in slums, and she described them as being quite dirty and in tattered clothing when they first started going to school. In her classrooms, they had been shown how to clean themselves up, to care for themselves in simple acts such as blowing their noses, and even to write and read— activities their own parents could not do. She believed their rejection of rewards was in part an expression of inner dignity that was awakened through participation in the classroom. These inferences led to her establishing classrooms in which rewards and evaluation reside in the activity, not in the teacher.

How Montessori Classrooms Function
Without Rewards and Evaluation

The remainder of this chapter concerns how Montessori classrooms function in the absence of grades and other rewards. First I discuss control of error in the Montessori materials, the role of repetition, and how teachers evaluate children both with the three-period lesson and with ongoing observations. The issue of standardized testing is raised as well, followed by discussion of how peers also contribute to evaluation. Finally, play is discussed because play with toys is often considered a reward, and Dr. Montessori, who had initially tried to use toys as rewards, came to have controversial ideas about their use.

THE CONTROL OF ERROR

Montessori schools do not grade children, and teachers' comments on children's work tend to be fairly matter-of-fact, perhaps recording the date. This can raise the concern of how children ever know what is right, and how teachers can know that children have learned. The first way is via incorporation in the Montessori materials of a factor known as the *control of error*.

Control of error is a very important Montessori concept that goes hand in hand with not using extrinsic rewards. In a conventional school, children receive grades corresponding to the level of correctness of their work. These marks on the students' papers provide important information to students: whether they produced correct responses. If teachers did not provide such marks, children might never know they had made an error.

It is certainly important in any educational system that learners be given some way of knowing when they have been correct or not, but Dr. Montessori believed that vesting that authority in the adult was problematic. She also saw marks of right and wrong on written work to be demotivating. "All the crosses made by the teacher on the child's written work ... only have a lowering effect on his energies and interests" (1967a/1995, p. 245). Instead, she incorporated feedback in the Montessori materials themselves.

> To make the process one of self-education, it is not enough that the stimulus [the material] should call forth activity, it must also direct it. The child should not only persist for a long time in an exercise; he must persist without making mistakes. All the physical or intrinsic qualities of the objects should be determined, not only by the immediate reaction of attention they provoke in the child, but also by their possession of this fundamental characteristic, the control of error, that is to say the power of evoking the effective collaboration of the highest activities (comparison, judgment). (1917/1965, p. 75)

Montessori materials incorporate control of error. For example, the Wooden Cylinders, the set of graduated wooden cylinders described in chapter 1, control error because if a child puts a cylinder into a hole that is too large, there will be a leftover cylinder at the end. All of the sets of matching Sensorial Materials, such as Sound Cylinders and Color Tablets (see chapter 5), also result in a leftover item if the child errs. For the Spindle Box (see chapter 2), if a child counts incorrectly for one slot, the error should become apparent when the numbers fail to work out for subsequent slots. Likewise, when the child builds the Pink Tower, described in chapter 2, if the child skips a block in the sequence, later the child will be confronted with a block that is larger than the one under it. A child can easily spot such an error. For many Montessori materials, then, corrective feedback from the teacher is unnecessary; a child can clearly see if he or she made an error due to incorporation of control of error in the Montessori materials.

CONTROL MAPS AND OTHER STANDARD MATERIALS

Another way error is controlled by the materials is through the use of a standard material against which children can compare their own work, again allowing them to find their own errors. When children are doing geography, for example, they use large (about 18" × 30") wooden Puzzle Maps (see the cover photograph). The countries are painted different colors, and each has a knob allowing it to be easily lifted out. As mentioned in chapter 2, after initial work simply putting the "puzzle" together (which in itself is self-correcting), the child traces each country onto another sheet of paper, recreating the map. The countries are then colored in on the new map. Finally, the child writes a label for each country. Rather than turning these maps in to the teacher, who in a conventional system would then correct errors, and likely give the child a grade, Montessori children get a "Control Map" to which they refer: a labeled map against which to check their work. Because there are no grades, and the learning goal is kept paramount, there is no sense in which children would be cheating if they were to refer to the control map too early. Apparently what engages children is the challenge of memorizing the names of the countries. People sometimes find this hard to believe, but the research reviewed earlier fits with it perfectly: When grades are not present, children adopt mastery goals.

Likewise, when children use the Grammar Boxes to label parts of speech, there are control cards they can get out that show whether they labeled the parts of speech correctly (Figure 6.1). Children can find their own errors, rather than needing the teacher to point the errors out. Again, because there are no grades, there is no incentive to cheat.

The sequence of work arriving at the multiplication table provides another example of the use of control materials. One material early in the sequence is the Multiplication Board, a square board with 100 indentures (10 × 10), into each of which a bead can be placed, and a small wooden box containing 100 such beads (Figure 6.2). The numbers 1 through 10 are printed across the top of the board, and along the left side is a slot for a number card. To carry out an operation, such as the multiples of 4, a child places a "4" card in the slot on the left, and a red marker by the "1" on the top (to mark the place), then puts four beads under the number 1. The child then takes a printed piece of paper with the header "4, Multiplication Table, Combination of FOUR with the numbers 1 to 10" (Montessori, 1916, p. 218). Below the title are printed the basic operations: $4 \times 1 = \underline{\hspace{1cm}}$, $4 \times 2 = \underline{\hspace{1cm}}$, and so on. The child fills in the first space on the paper (4×1) with the number 4. Then the red marker is moved to the "2" on the board, and four more beads are added. The child continues through the whole exercise, filling in the sheet with the multiples of 4.

FIGURE 6.1 Diagraming Sentences. © Laura Joyce-Hubbard, 2014. All rights reserved.

The control or test card for this material contains the entire multiplication table from 1 to 10. After completing the work, children go to this test card for verification and can thereby check their work on their own.

Further controlling error with the multiplication tables is the next step, in which children get another sheet of paper and write their verified results.

FIGURE 6.2 The Multiplication Board. Photograph by An Vu.

This sheet contains a 10 × 10 table, with the numbers 1 through 10 across the top row and down the left column. Children fill in this blank table (for the child just mentioned, multiples of 4, to be followed later by multiples of other numbers) and compare it with a control card as well.

Finally, today, with many of the math materials, Montessori children are also taught to use a more modern control device: the calculator. Children first do math work with the materials, then they might get a calculator in the classroom to check their work.

Children do exercises such as the multiplication table many times over, and the urge to do the work comes from within the child. The materials are said to inspire children to do the work, because they were field tested on children until they evoked interest, concentration, and repetition. As the research presented earlier suggests, one feature of the Montessori materials that probably helps inspire children to repeated use is probably that the correction of errors resides not in an adult evaluator, but in the materials themselves.

REPETITION

The multiplication tables work raises another way in which Montessori classrooms can function without teachers marking children's work: repetition. Dr. Montessori highlighted repetition as leading children to perform exercises correctly without teacher feedback (Montessori, 1989, p. 15). For Dr. Montessori, repetition was key to many aspects of development, but it also raises one's level of performance. By assembling the Pink Tower over and over again, the children come to do it correctly. By doing the Multiplication Board over and over, children come to memorize the multiplication tables. If children sometimes make errors along on the way, they will see their error through the control materials, and through repetition, they come to do it right. According to Montessori theory, we have a human tendency toward perfection. As mentioned earlier, this postulated tendency is reminiscent of what the psychologist Michael Kubovy (1999) calls "virtuosity": Humans the world over take pleasure in doing things well. Dr. Montessori observed that children do repeat the exercises over and over. When the environment provides feedback so that children do not keep repeating the same errors, and children are driven to repeat exercises until they can do them perfectly, then they eventually master the exercises. There is no need for teachers to correct children's errors, because children eventually see and correct their errors themselves.

THE THREE-PERIOD LESSON

Teachers do of course evaluate children in Montessori; it is simply not obvious to the children that they are being evaluated. One way in which Montessori teachers evaluate children is by the manner in which they give lessons.

Following Seguin, Dr. Montessori advised that lessons involving nomenclature be given in three stages, or periods, as was mentioned in chapter 2 for the Red Rods (1912/1964, pp. 177–78). The three periods might be thought of as association, recognition, and recall. These nomenclature lessons figure prominently in Primary, because Dr. Montessori believed children should have precise terminology for describing the world and, as previously noted, she believed the first 5 years are a sensitive period for acquiring vocabulary (Montessori, 1967a/1995). Children in Montessori programs learn sophisticated terminology that many an educated adult does not know, but that children appear to learn easily.

The format of the three-period lesson is as follows. The teacher first shows the child the materials to be named—for example, the Rough and Smooth Boards, which are wooden tablets covered with different grades of rough and smooth sandpaper. As the student runs a finger over each, the teacher gives the child the referring vocabulary, "rough" and "smooth." For the second period, the teacher tests recognition: "Give me the rough one" and "Give me the smooth one." If a child is unable to pick the correct one at this second stage, the teacher does not correct the child, but assumes that the child did not get the concept to begin with. The teacher would then repeat the presentation another day. If the child did correctly choose the rough one, the teacher would go on to the third period, holding up one of the sandpaper tablets and asking the child, "What is this?" A great deal of vocabulary is taught in the Primary classrooms through such "three-period" lessons, and they give the teacher an opportunity to evaluate whether a child has mastered key concepts.

THE TEACHER'S ONGOING EVALUATION

Montessori teachers also evaluate children by constantly observing their work. Making the teacher's task easier, children's work is normally spread out and easily visible, so observations can be made without the teacher's appearing to look closely at the work. Dr. Montessori admonished teachers not to interfere with the child's ongoing work for correction. "If you interfere, a child's interest [evaporates, and] the enchantment of correcting himself is broken. It is as though he says, 'I was with myself inside. You called me, and so it is finished. Now this work has no more importance for me'" (1989, p. 16).

Surveillance, Dr. Montessori noted, can interfere with concentration, and thus teachers have to be careful not to appear to be peering at children's work.

> Praise, help, or even a look, may be enough to interrupt him, or destroy the activity. It seems a strange thing to say, but this can happen even if the child merely becomes aware of being watched.... The great principle which brings success to the teacher is this: *as soon as concentration*

has begun, act as if the child does not exist. (1967a/1995, p. 280, italics in original)

Research supports Dr. Montessori's observation. Summarizing work done on audience effects with animals and adults in the first half of the 20th century, Robert Zajonc (1965) concluded that when one is being watched, activities that one is just learning become undermined. Surveillance apparently influences motivation as well. Using a paradigm similar to that described earlier, children were asked to draw with markers, and some of those children knew that a camera was directing their image to a television screen outside the room (Lepper & Greene, 1975). Two weeks later, children in the surveillance condition were significantly less likely to use the markers than were children who had not been observed while drawing. Hence knowing one is being watched apparently decreases subsequent motivation and also appears to interfere with learning new tasks.

In addition to subtle observation of children's work as it occurs, Montessori teachers also can evaluate children's finished products, usually stored in the classroom in children's folders or cubbies, at the end of the school day. Elementary teachers can also go over recent work in each student's Work Journal at a weekly meeting with each student, as described in chapters 3 and 5. This allows the teacher to see that children have been working in all areas of the curriculum.

Montessori teachers evaluate children's progress when giving lessons, through ongoing observations in the classroom, by examining the products of their work, and by going over the Work Journal. It is not often obvious to children that they are being evaluated, since they are not given grades, praise, or other tokens of evaluation.

PEERS AS SOURCES OF FEEDBACK AND INSPIRATION

Another way in which Montessori education provides children feedback on their work is via other students. As is discussed more fully in chapter 7, much Montessori work, particularly in the Elementary, is done in collaboration with other children. When children work together, executing math problems, writing reports, or producing charts, for example, they can notice and point out errors in each other's work. Perhaps because there are no grades (recall that grades create a competitive atmosphere), this kind of feedback is said to be usually supportive and collegial, truly in the interest of getting things right.

When discussing control materials, I said there was no incentive to cheat. Peers also contribute to this, since children often use materials together. For example, two children might work with a map together, with one child lifting out pieces and asking the other child to state the country. Such games are common in Montessori.

Montessori children also get feedback indirectly from peers via peer teaching (described in chapter 7). In explaining how to do a certain kind of work to a peer, a child can see whether his or her explanation was effective. If a child does not really understand how to do a certain kind of work, he or she cannot explain it well to another child. "There is nothing which makes you learn more than teaching someone else, especially when you don't know the subject very well. The struggles of the other act like a control of error for yourself and urge you to acquire more knowledge in order to give him what he needs" (Montessori, 1989, p. 69).

Yet another way that peers contribute to evaluation in Montessori is by going over each other's work. Particularly by the final years of Elementary, a major focus of the child's work is writing reports. A Montessori teacher might have children find three peers to read their reports and offer suggestions prior to the teacher reading them, just as colleagues do in the workplace. If a child questions another child's "correction," they can check in a book, or check with other children, or ask the teacher. Peers in this way serve to help with evaluation.

Thus, working with peers provides feedback as well, both directly and via peer teaching. Peers also serve as a source of inspiration. Because there are three age levels in each classroom, children can see where they have been and where they are going to go in the sequence of materials. This might provide an incentive to work in the absence of an extrinsic reward system, as will be discussed in more depth in the next chapter.

MONTESSORI AND STANDARDIZED TESTS

Many Montessori schools, particularly less established ones, choose to give an occasional standardized test to let parents and themselves know how their children are faring relative to children in conventional schools. To do so, they might dedicate some time toward the end of the school year taking practice tests and preparing children for the methods of standardized testing. Although distracting from the Montessori work, and limited in what they assess (social behavior, for example, is not tested, but is an important part of the Montessori curriculum), such tests can be seen as a useful occasional evaluative tool. More established schools might rely instead on the records of past graduates to assure parents of the preparation of graduating children. Some research using such tests is reported in chapter 11.

WHEN CHILDREN MISBEHAVE

People often wonder how, without the help of extrinsic incentives, Montessori teachers can handle children when they do not conform and settle down to work. First, it is important to bear in mind the discussion of concentration and attention in chapter 4. According to Dr. Montessori, misbehaviors cease when children begin to concentrate. Psychology research today shows that children who are better able to regulate their own attention, or concentrate, are more agreeable, more empathetic, and so on. If Montessori education enhances children's self-regulation skills, perhaps children are less apt to misbehave in Montessori classrooms. This would be an interesting topic for investigation.

But, of course, some children do misbehave, particularly when they are first introduced to the classroom and sometimes later as well. Although more helpful to development, it seems, than conventional classrooms, Montessori classrooms do not magically transform all children into perfect angels. Misbehaviors, Dr. Montessori said, have to be checked. Children are not well served by being allowed to climb on tables, handle materials roughly, and poke their classmates. Dr. Montessori advocated treating children who are misbehaving as if they were ill and needed special care. Children who misbehave are often asked to stay near the teacher or in a particular spot, thereby removing their freedom, because they have indicated that they are not yet responsible enough to have freedom. While in that spot, though, they are not punished; instead, they are given their favorite activities to do. Their punishment is the loss of freedom. Occasionally the teacher will turn to the problem child with great sympathy and give her or him sympathetic attention. As Dr. Montessori described it, "Little by little [a child treated in this way] came to realize the advantages of being with the others and to desire to act as they did. In this way we imparted discipline to all the children who at first had seemed to us to be rebels" (1967b, pp. 60–61). Empirical work on the success of such methods in the prepared environment of Montessori would be an interesting issue for research.

SUMMARY: HOW MONTESSORI FUNCTIONS WITHOUT EXTRINSIC REWARDS

In sum, evaluation does happen in Montessori classrooms, as it must in any educational system. Children evaluate their own work with direct feedback from materials, the use of control materials, and their level of success in peer teaching. Teachers evaluate children through three-period lessons, observation, the products of their work, and reviewing their Work Journals. All these evaluations are in the background, however, in the sense that children are not being told they are being evaluated. The intrinsic value of learning is kept paramount.

Play and Fantasy

This chapter is an apt place to discuss fantasy, play, and toys in the Montessori context, because Dr. Montessori abandoned toys as a reward when she saw that the children chose to do Montessori work rather than engage in play. Dr. Montessori initially included baskets of toys among the choices of materials in the classroom, but she reported that children showed little interest in them.

> Although the children in our first school could play with some really splendid toys, none cared to do so. This surprised me so much that I decided to help them play with their toys, showing them how to handle the tiny dishes, lighting the fire in the doll's kitchen, and placing near it a pretty doll. The children were momentarily interested but then went off on their own. Since they never freely chose these toys, I realized that in the life of a child play is perhaps something of little importance which he undertakes for the lack of something better to do. A child feels that he has something of greater [importance] to do than to be engaged in such trivial occupations. He regards play as we would regard a game of chess or bridge. These are pleasant occupations for hours of leisure, but they would become painful if we were obliged to pursue them at great length. (1966, p. 122)

In this passage, Dr. Montessori divided our hours into those for leisure (after school) and those spent at school. She implied that children may well choose to play with toys in their leisure time, just as we may choose to play chess, but that in the schools she structured, children chose work over play. She described the home, however, as a place for children to work *and play* (Montessori, 1956).

Here I discuss Dr. Montessori's views on play and fantasy, and look at how they stand up to current research. It is useful to consider two periods of development separately: before and after age 6. Children in these two periods are in what Montessorians call two different planes of development. In Montessori theory there are four such planes: 0–6, 6–12, 12–18, and 18–24, and each is divided into two 3-year periods. Discussion of these planes can be found elsewhere (P. P. Lillard, 1996).

MONTESSORI'S VIEWS ON PLAY AND FANTASY IN YOUNG CHILDREN

For children younger than age 6, Dr. Montessori came to believe adult-issued fantasy had no place. This stemmed primarily from her observations of certain behaviors, for example, young children leaving when a teacher told a fairy tale (Montessori, 1989, pp. 45–46). Two of Dr. Montessori's theoretical views align with such observations. First, like Piaget (and perhaps his views derived from hers, or both their views might have derived from some other, common source), she believed that pretend is "not a proof of imagination, rather it is a proof of unsatisfied desire" (Montessori, 1997, p. 41).

Pretending was thus primarily assimilation of reality to the ego, rather than the self adapting to reality. The child's developmental task is to adapt to reality, so for adults to encourage fantasy was (to Dr. Montessori) to encourage the child toward something that deviates from the developmental path he or she is on. In this view, when children play house, they are expressing a desire to really keep house. Hence Dr. Montessori gave them a real house, the Casa dei Bambini, with child-sized housekeeping objects to really work with. Her claim was that when the environment responds to children's needs, giving them motives for purposeful activity, the desire to engage in pretend play goes away (Montessori, 1966, pp. 155–56).

The second (related) theoretical view aligning with Dr. Montessori's observations regarding young children and play is that Dr. Montessori saw a major goal of childhood as authentic perception of the real world. Giving the child fantasies, or even encouraging fantasies, as she saw it, thwarted the perception of reality. Regarding Christmas myths, she said, "How is it possible for the child's imagination to be developed by that which is in truth the fruit of the adult's imagination? We alone imagine, not they; they merely believe. . . . Credulity is indeed a characteristic of an immature mind which is lacking in experience" (1997, p. 43). Children younger than age 6 tend to really be duped by the fantasies adults tell them, such as those involving Santa Claus and the Sandman. For example, Jacqui Woolley and her colleagues made up a new pretend creature, the Candy Witch, who visits children in the night after Halloween and trades all their candy for a toy (Boerger, Tullos, & Woolley, 2009; Woolley, Boerger, & Markman, 2004). Beliefs were strongest and most persistent when parents participated in creating the fantasy (see also Goldstein & Woolley, 2016). Dr. Montessori believed that adults abuse children's trust by telling them such tales. This is an interesting point to consider regarding the state of current research on play and fantasy in young children. But the main point here is that she believed putting children in touch with reality was most essential for the development of the child's imagination. "As we study great works of art, we see that [great and wonderful] things created by imagination are always in close touch with the real. . . . If we give children the possibility of observing things and being sensitive to these things, we are giving children a help to the possibility of being creative" (Montessori, 1997, pp. 56–57).

RESEARCH ON PLAY AND FANTASY IN YOUNG CHILDREN

In the first two editions of this book, I wrote that a great deal of psychology research suggests that play is helpful for development. This is a view one sees expressed repeatedly, and it corresponds to many people's intuitions. But play encompasses many activities; it is in fact very difficult to define. When it comes to preschool-aged children, "play" often designates a particular type of play: pretend play, in which children project one reality onto another, in a spirit of fun (Lillard, Pinkham, & Smith, 2011). Over the years since the second edition, I became less certain of this claim, leading to me to closely examine the issue. My graduate students and I wrote a review paper (Lillard et al., 2013) examining every peer-reviewed article we could find concerning whether pretend play helps development. The developments examined fell into domains: cognitive development, including intelligence, creativity, and problem solving; social cognition or "theory of mind"; social skills; language; narrative skills; executive function; and emotion regulation. Our conclusion was that the existing evidence did not support strong causal claims of pretend play helping any area of development. The best evidence existed for narrative, perhaps because developed pretend play often involves acting out stories. But for the most part, the research on this question has problems that preclude strong conclusions. Many studies are correlational, and there are other variables besides pretend play to which one might attribute effects. Training studies usually use trainers who know what skills are being looked for, and/or testers who know what condition children are in (the pretend play condition or a control condition); without these problems, positive results have disappeared. Thus, the idea that children in Montessori environments might be unable to meet their developmental needs because the environments are not centered on pretend play seems misguided. In fact, studies of school programs (Chien et al., 2010), including a meta-analysis (Alfieri, Brooks, Aldrich, & Tenenbaum, 2011), suggest that more structured school programs are better for children—although not structured in the way that elementary schools are conventionally structured. Rather, the types of structures that seem to work best are scaffolds (Bruner, 1975) or what has recently been called "guided play," which is in many ways very much like Montessori (Diamond & Lee, 2011; Elkind, 2007; Hirsh-Pasek, Golinkoff, Berk, & Singer, 2009).

One "guided play" school curriculum that has attracted a lot of attention is Tools of the Mind (Bodrova & Leong, 2007), a Vygotsky-inspired program emphasizing pretend play. It was shown, in two randomized controlled trials, to lead to better executive function (Diamond, Barnett, Thomas, & Munro, 2007) although not better math or literacy (Barnett et al., 2008). The executive function boost is usually attributed to its pretend play component, yet Tools also has a strong planning component: In a Tools classroom, one's pretend play must be planned in advance, and the script must be adhered to. To take the finding that Tools assists executive function as evidence that pretend play assists executive function is wrong. One would need to systematically study different aspects of Tools to learn which aspect helped children. Furthermore, three more recent large randomized controlled trials with the Tools program have not replicated the original results (Clements, Sarama, Unlu, & Layzer, 2012; Farran, Wilson, Lipsey,

& Turner, 2012; Lonigan & Phillips, 2012). More recently, Blair and Raver (2014) did report a strong replication of results, both for executive function and for early academic skills, as well as for physiological measures of stress regulation, in children whose classrooms were randomly assigned to Tools versus business as usual. My concern with this study is that the Tools teachers received intensive coaching, self-reflection exercises, and development opportunities not given to the control teachers, and it is possible that these experiences were the causes of changes in the Tools children. Regardless, the authors of this study emphasize that Tools is about training in self-regulation and uses very scripted sorts of play (in some ways anathema to the definition of play) in its execution.

Beyond pretend play, one might consider the issue of fantasy in a more general way. Is it positive for development, and do children generally prefer it? First, consider cartoon-illustrated children's books. One study showed that children learn new words from such books significantly less well than from books showing photographs of the same objects, and in fact also less well than simple line drawings. Several studies from Paul Bloom's laboratory at Yale show that young children actually prefer realistic stories to fantasy ones. In one study, children and adults were given the choice of five story pairs; each pair included a realistic ("a true story about X. It really happened") or a fictional story ("this is a make-believe story about Y. It's make-believe"). Across participants the content of the stories was counterbalanced so sometimes it was presented as a make-believe story and sometimes as a real one. Of five story pairs, young children (ages 4–5) preferred the make-believe story for just 1.31 of the five pairs, on average, suggesting a strong preference (3.69 choices) for realistic stories; older children (ages 6–7) chose fantasy for 1.87 of the five (3.13 realistic choices), and adults, for 2.19 of the five (2.81 realistic choices; Barnes, Bernstein, & Bloom, 2015). In another study, young children were given a choice of how to complete realistic stories and fantasy stories, and they actually preferred to give both kinds of stories a realistic ending (Weisberg, Sobel, Goodstein, & Bloom, 2013). These results suggest that the frequent supposition that young children prefer fantasy might be misguided.

A second issue to consider is whether children learn well from fantasy. Children often are duped by the kinds of stimuli we give them. Li, Boguszewski, and Lillard (submitted) showed children a book or a video of an anthropomorphized train or a real train, and after, asked them questions about whether trains have feelings and other human characteristics. Those who had watched or read about the fantasy train video were confused, and tended to anthropomorphize the trains. Several studies suggest that children learn about what is real versus fantastical though their perception of what is real, hence they are "grounded in reality (Lillard & Woolley, 2015). For example, young children are duped by exaggerated fake-acting displays, thinking that people who pretend to cry really are sad (Goldstein & Bloom, 2015). Another study showed that children are less likely to see the analogy from a story to a real-life situation when the story characters are fantastical (Richert & Smith, 2011). However, in some cases, a small number of fantastical events increased learning such analogies, apparently because they increased children's attention to the story (Hopkins & Lillard, submitted). As described in chapter 4, presenting children with a plethora of fantastical events in animated cartoons depleted executive function (Lillard et al., 2015).

In sum, although some believe that inclusion of pretend play would improve Montessori education (e.g., Soundy, 2009), it is not clear that this is the case. Evidence that pretend play is key to development, such that the more there is of it the better, is weak (Lillard et al., 2013), and children are often confused by what is fantastical. Children also might not be as drawn to fantasy as we think; perhaps it is often imposed on them because adults like it. Dr. Montessori believed fantasy was not positive for young children. One reason is the same one Piaget professed: Pretending is largely assimilation of reality to one's own thoughts, rather than adjustment of one's own ideas to fit reality. A second reason is that fantasies often really dupe children. Particularly in Dr. Montessori's era, such fantasy figures as Santa Claus and the Sandman were often used in a manipulative fashion, to get children to behave well. This legacy is apparent in a popular Christmas song: "He knows if you've been bad or good, so be good for goodness' sake"—or you might end up with coal in your stocking! She believed that for adults to tell children lies was an abuse of children's credulity and trust in them.

Dr. Montessori objected to adults' imposing their fantasies on children, and she was concerned about children whose pretend play seemed to represent a "fugue." She was not against young children playing: "Let [children construct with blocks and sand] in relation to what they have in their minds, give them something new which is in line with their natural psychology" (1989, p. 47). However, as noted in the following sections, Montessori materials were not to be the objects of play, because these materials have other purposes.

The Elementary Child

Some think that because Montessori classrooms do not have toys and orient children to reality, Montessori does not value imagination. Yet Dr. Montessori clearly held human imagination as one of our highest powers. Children in Montessori initially work with concrete materials, but in Elementary begin to move back and forth from the materials to an abstract plane. "The imagination elevates and goes above that which is simply positive; first, to the abstract, then to the creative" (Montessori, 1997, p. 51).

With the Great Stories as well, Montessori Elementary education is based on the stimulation of children's imaginations. New information is presented as stories to stimulate the imagination and arouse curiosity so children will go learn more about the world. Dr. Montessori also noted that the greatest acts of imagination have their roots in reality. "Truth," she said, "is the basis of every great artistic production of the imagination" (1997, p. 47). If fantasy became part of children's lives before they had a reasonable basis in reality, she believed the result would be a confused mind, rather than a mind from which great creativity could emerge. Correct use of Montessori materials guides children's minds from the concrete to the abstract, whence children's creative imaginations can take over.

Observations of Children

As presented in the anecdotes in this chapter, Dr. Montessori observed children rejecting toys in favor of work. They preferred reading new words to playing, and cleaning the classroom with child-sized brooms and mops to setting up dolls in a doll house. Dr. Montessori was an empiricist, and she based her ideas on what children did. "If I were against fairy tales, it was not because of a capricious idea but because of certain facts, facts observed many times. These facts come from the children themselves and not from my own reasoning" (1989, p. 45). Once children had been working in her classroom with the materials, they became very interested in the real world, and "the great love of fairy tales disappear[ed]" (p. 45). Had those children chosen instead to play with toys, a very different educational system would have been developed. Montessori classrooms lack toys because the children did not use them, and all items that were superfluous were removed from the classrooms because Dr. Montessori saw superfluous items as detracting from children's education. Every item in the classroom is meant to serve a purpose.

The Historical Backdrop

At some places in her books, Dr. Montessori sounds rather vehement in her opposition to toys, which might well have been in part a reaction to the Victorian era, as was discussed by her son Mario in his book *Education for Human Development* (1976, pp. 30–33). During this era, adults offered children toys that were not considered with regard to development, but (according to Mario Montessori) "mainly determined by what attracted adults" (p. 30). Fairies, fairy tales, and other fantasies were also big fare for children. As Dr. Montessori describes it, the cultural view was that children were capable only of fantasy and no more. She believed that adults held children back by giving them fantasy instead of reality. "To artificially halt the child's stage of development and to amuse oneself thereby is one of the unnoticed faults of our times" (1997, p. 45). Her writings might in part reflect a desire to change that view. She believed adults impeded children by providing them only with toys and assuming they wanted and needed mainly to play.

Children's Reactions to Montessori

Observations already provided have shown that children rejected toys in Montessori environments. Two additional ones suggest that children liked being in her classrooms even more than playing outside school. Once at the original school in Rome, and again at a classroom set up at the Panama-Pacific International Exposition in San Francisco in 1915, the children were locked out of the classroom without a teacher. In both cases, they found a way to get into the classroom and work even with the teacher not present. They had a clear choice to avoid school, but they instead found a way in.

Also showing children are highly motivated to engage in Montessori schoolwork, a study of children in middle schools (discussed in chapter 11) showed that while they were doing schoolwork, Montessori children were significantly more engaged than were children in conventional middle schools (Rathunde & Csikszentmihalyi, 2005a). They reported greater affect, energy, intrinsic motivation, "flow," and interest than did conventional children, matched for SES and a host of other variables, who reported more feelings of drudgery while engaged in schoolwork. When engaged in other activities (such as socializing at lunch), there were no differences in children at the two kinds of schools. Play is a state of greater affect, energy, and so on. It might simply be the case that in Montessori schools, work is, affectively speaking, more like play.

Anecdotally, I have been told of children at some Montessori schools crying when summer is approaching because they do not want school to end. The idea that children enjoy Montessori education as much as play thus has some support, although further research with children today would be helpful. It would be interesting to know whether Montessori children's enjoyment of school varies depending on the extent to which their Montessori schools align with conventional Montessori practices. For example, against Dr. Montessori's writings, some "Montessori" schools reserve children's free-choice time as a reward for having previously finished a set of required activities.

Similarities between Play and Montessori Work

Why might the structure of Montessori schools have led, in her initial observations, to children's preferring the Montessori work to free play? Children appear to be drawn to play; indeed, pretend play occurs in virtually every culture, regardless of whether it is encouraged by adults (Lillard, 2015). Even when adults actively discourage pretend play, children engage in it (Carlson, Taylor, & Levin, 1998). One possibility is that Montessori education already serves some of the functions that make children choose to play (Lillard, 2013).

First, pretend play is embodied cognition (see chapter 2). When a child acts out a fantasy that she is a mother tending a baby (doll), her mental representations direct her actions. This is what happens in Montessori education. In Montessori classrooms, there are also child-sized tools that allow children to perform many of the domestic themes that are common in young children's play: They can chop vegetables with a small knife and serve them on child-sized dishes, they can mop the floor with a child-scaled mop, and so on. The objects we give children to play with are often miniaturized versions of real objects; Montessori materials are appropriately sized for children's smaller bodies, hence also miniaturized. The child's use of those objects connects the child's mind to the child's body, in play and in Montessori education.

Second, with Montessori work and in play, children are able to direct their own activities: They choose what to do (see chapter 3). In some cultures, playtime might be the only time children's activity is self-directed; at most other times, they do what adults tell them to do. Because Montessori gives children choices about what to do almost all of the time, they might have less of a drive to engage in play.

Third, in a similar vein, Ann Renninger (1992; see also Hirsh-Pasek, Golinkoff, Berk, Singer, 2009) stated that free play may assist development because free play involves play with objects or themes of interest to the individual child (see chapter 5). Whereas in a conventional school children are usually required to participate in the group activity of the moment—a class, a given sport, a specific art activity, and so on—at recess they are usually free to play as they like. Children's high valuation of play, and its contribution to development, might stem in part from children being able to play about and with whatever is interesting to them.

Fourth, play, like Montessori work, has intrinsic rewards (as discussed in this chapter). Adults do not give children grades or gold stars for the quality or quantity of fantasies they enact in free play. This might make play activities more attractive to children than schoolwork. This is also a feature already inherent in Montessori schoolwork.

Finally, pretend play often involves a social aspect, and children enjoy interacting with peers (see chapter 7). In conventional classrooms, particularly after age 6, children typically are required to work alone and are not allowed to interact with other children except at recess and other select times when they are outside of the classroom. Montessori education does not restrict children's social engagement in the classroom, and this aspect of play, which might be part of what makes play so attractive and helpful to children, is inherent in Montessori work.

In sum, then, many of the usual features of play are incorporated into Montessori, such as using one's body to carry out one's thoughts, doing what one chooses and having control over what one does, doing what is interesting, doing those activities for intrinsic reasons, and doing them with others when one wants to. These features of play might be important factors making play helpful to cognitive development and making it preferable to conventional schoolwork. Montessori education might not need to be supplemented by play because it incorporates these important features already. These suggestions are open to empirical research.

The Problem of Imposed Structures

People are sometimes put off in Montessori schools when they learn that children cannot use Montessori materials in ways other than those for which they were intended. That is, they cannot take the Pink Tower and make a small village from it, or animate the Cylinders as if they were people. The reason behind this injunction is that every material in the classroom was designed to serve a specific purpose, and Dr. Montessori believed that children needed to respect those purposes in order to get the intended value from the material. Montessori materials are not toys so much as specific tools to support specific developmental advances, according to Dr. Montessori. Research by Judy DeLoache, discussed in chapter 2, suggests that when children play with objects, they are less likely to access those objects' underlying symbolic features. This suggests that Montessori teachers might have direct didactic reasons for requiring that children use Montessori materials only in the ways in which they were intended to be used. Future research might examine whether this injunction does assist development. Some Montessori teachers are looser than others about how children use materials, and whether that makes a difference to learning is a topic for empirical research.

The Problem of Life without Fantasy

Some adults believe fantasy is important both because it is fun and because it stimulates the imagination. They recall a sense of wonder at Santa Claus and tremendous pleasure and excitement over setting out cookies and milk and waiting for him to deliver their presents. They do not recall being hurt or upset at learning or figuring out that Santa Claus must be mythical, or if they do, they feel the prior fun outweighed the later disappointment. This provides fascinating fodder for empirical research. Do children whose parents work to instill such myths as Santa Claus and the Easter Bunny (American culture's two main myths; Clark, 1995) have more fun childhoods? Are their imaginative capacities helped by these myths? How might holding these myths compare in impact to holding beliefs about real figures from whom they derive, such as Saint Nicholas and Christ? These are questions for further research.

SUMMARY: DR. MONTESSORI'S VIEWS ON FANTASY AND PLAY

Dr. Montessori was not against creative play, but she was against people's viewing children as limited to fantasy, and against adults' imposing their fantasies on children's credulity. She formed these views during the Victorian era, when fairy tales and fantasies for children were perhaps more preponderant than they are today, and she claims to have based them on children's responses to toys and fairy tales. Dr. Montessori proposed that the real world be presented to children with the same liveliness and emotional appeal with which fairy tales were delivered. She also established an educational system that had many of the features of pretend play, features that are known to confer benefits (although pretend play itself has not been clearly shown to confer benefits it is often claimed to confer).

Chapter Summary

Research presented in this chapter shows that although expected rewards may work to increase participation in the short run, they serve to demotivate people when the rewards are removed. Children show a steady decrease in intrinsic motivation to learn in school for each year they are in school (Harter, 1981). Furthermore, people report significantly higher levels of psychological well-being and competence when they are engaged in intrinsically rewarding activities (Graef, Csikszentmihalyi, & Gianinno, 1983), but schoolwork becomes less intrinsically rewarding as children age. Viewed in this light, it is no wonder that so many children come to dislike school when it is enacted in the conventional way. Extrinsic rewards not only decrease interest in an activity, they are also associated with less learning and creativity, with decline in prosocial behaviors, and changes in classroom environment and self theories that leave many children unmotivated to learn in school.

Dr. Montessori saw early in San Lorenzo that extrinsic rewards were not needed to motivate children who were already interested in pursuing school activities, and she saw that adult correction and praise both served to disrupt the self-guiding concentration she considered fundamental to development. She developed a set of materials and a method of learning that could be self-correcting and in which intrinsic motivation to learn would be expected to stay strong.

Although Montessori is often decried as being asocial (e.g., Stallings & Stipek, 1986), it is in fact much more social than conventional schools, especially at the most intensely social period of a child's life: after age 6. The next chapter deals with the collaborative aspect of Montessori classrooms and the large body of research showing the benefits of peer learning.

7 }

Learning From Peers

Our schools show that children of different ages help one
another. The younger ones see what the older ones are doing
and ask for explanations. These are readily given, and the
instruction is really valuable, for the mind of a five year old is so
much nearer than ours to the mind of a child of three. . . . The
older ones are happy to be able to teach what they know. There
are no inferiority complexes, but everyone achieves a healthy
normality through the mutual exchange.

— Maria Montessori *(1967a/1995, pp. 226–28)*

In conventional elementary school classrooms, children learn mainly from
the teacher and texts. The teacher stands before the children, who are seated
at individual desks, and delivers knowledge. Elementary school classrooms are
engaged in this form of instruction (on average) 60–70% of the time, with much of
the rest of the time spent in individual seat work and transitioning; the percentage of time spent in lectures is thought to increase in high school (Greenwood,
Delquadri, & Hall, 1989; Hiebert, 1999; Stigler et al., 2000). Unfortunately, such
structures are increasingly being implemented in prekindergarten and kindergarten classes as well (Hamre & Pianta, 2007; Zigler & Bishop-Josef, 2004).

To the extent that children might interact with other children in conventional schooling arrangements, those others are usually of about the same
age and ability. One might say that children are grouped in narrow bands.
The first band is by age level: Most of the children in the classroom are born
within one year of each other, with a set birth date as the cut-off for being
part of a classroom. Within each classroom, in many schools children are
also grouped by ability level for each subject ("tracked"). By learning in this
manner, children are removed from other children who are at very different
levels. Their learning occurs in a narrow ability band. This is convenient to
a factory model, because factories operate most efficiently if all of the raw
materials are uniform. It suits the Lockean model of the child as well, as
children at the same level are assumed to be alike and thus ready for the same
knowledge to be poured in.

In the sense that children are usually not supposed to confer in class except with the teacher, conventional school learning is usually done alone. Looking at others' work is frowned upon, and grades are given individually for assignments or tests completed alone. Children in conventional American schools operate as self-enclosed, individual units among other such units. This is also in keeping with a behaviorist view: Behaviorists did not study rats (or other organisms) as parts of social communities, but focused on the behavior of individual rats, aggregating their data (although this social isolation profoundly and negatively influences their social and cognitive development [Pellis & Pellis, 2009; see also Zhang & Meaney, 2010]). It also fits the Euro-American heritage of individualism (Nisbett, 2003; 2009), which is interesting to consider in light of differences in American and Asian schooling (Stevenson et al., 1990; Stigler, Lee, & Stevenson, 1987).

In contrast to conventional educators, the developmental theorists Jean Piaget and Lev Vygotsky both assigned peers a prominent role in development. Piaget argued that peers are important because by presenting different ideas, they create a state of disequilibrium in the child. Because mental development occurs when the child has to resolve disequilibrium by changing his or her mind, or "accommodating," to incorporate new ideas, peers can be an important engine of development (De Lisi & Golbeck, 1999; Piaget, 1926). Vygotsky argued that learning occurs in a zone of proximal development, meaning over tasks one cannot yet accomplish alone but can accomplish in the company of a more advanced other. In his view, slightly advanced peers serve as important leaders of development (Hogan & Tudge, 1999; Vygotsky, 1978).

Partly in reaction to these theories and subsequent research, and because they can be integrated fairly easily into the conventional system, social learning arrangements are increasingly being implemented in conventional schools (e.g., Johnson & Johnson, 2009; O'Donnell & King, 1999) and are recommended by the National Association for the Education of Young Children (2009) and many other education organizations. However, in a conventional system, such forms of learning are additions, because the system was not designed for peer interaction.

In contrast, peer learning is embedded in the structure of Montessori education. Children are free to work together and they often do, particularly as they get older and are more socially inclined. Self-formed groups of two or more children might work together on maps or math problems or reports. Yet Dr. Montessori noted that others often criticized her schools as asocial, because of the lack of whole-class, uniform activity.

Teachers who use direct methods cannot understand how social behavior is fostered in a Montessori school. They think it offers scholastic material but not social material. They say, "If the child does everything on his own, what becomes of social life?" But what is social life if not the solving of social problems, behaving properly and pursuing aims acceptable to all? [It is not] sitting side by side and hearing someone else talk. . . .

The only social life that children get in the ordinary schools is during playtime or on excursions. Ours live always in an active community. (1967a/1995, p. 225)

Although each class works in unison in conventional school arrangements, the children are rarely interacting with each other. In contrast, in Montessori schools, only occasionally does the entire class engage in a single activity. At both age levels, children are sometimes in small group lessons with the teacher (Figure 7.1), but most of the time they choose their social arrangements. In Primary, children often choose to work alone, and in Elementary, children often choose to work together in small, self-formed groups. These differences are appropriate to the children's different developmental levels. Children become increasingly interested in peer interaction as they grow older (Hartup, 1983). Younger children are not even particularly good at peer interaction. As psychology professor Robert Siegler put it, "Even 5-year-olds, competent problem solvers in many instances, have difficulty working together to solve any but the simplest and most familiar problems" (1998, p. 277). By elementary school, children are more knowledgeable about how to work together. Whereas conventional schools seem to work against how children are, by having them work more collaboratively before age 6 and independently thereafter, Montessori is structured such that children can choose

FIGURE 7.1 A Language Lesson. Photograph by An Vu.

the social arrangements that are developmentally suited to their abilities and motivations.

In this chapter I discuss three forms of learning from and with peers in terms of research on those forms and their presence in Montessori education. The first, learning from peers by observation and imitation, is rarely implemented in conventional schools, as will be discussed. The second, peer tutoring, is increasingly implemented. In such arrangements, peers help each other in the learning process, rather than working as competing autonomous units (Topping & Ehly, 1998). The third form is collaborative learning, or learning interactively among people of fairly similar ability levels, and it is also being implemented with increasing frequency in conventional classrooms.

Learning Through Observation and Imitation

Clearly all people learn in part by observing and imitating others (Tomasello, Kruger, & Ratner, 1993). Yet the importance of imitative learning was not highlighted in psychology and education during the heyday of behaviorism in the first half of the 20th century. In the early 1960s, the psychologist Albert Bandura provided the classic evidence that learning can occur through observation and imitation (Bandura, Ross, & Ross, 1963). Bandura showed children films of an adult hitting a wobbly blow-up "Bobo" doll and noted that children were later apt to behave toward the doll as the adult had. (Interestingly, we are seeing far less of such behavior in children in my laboratory today, Lillard, Smith, & Richey, 2015, but the point remains: Children can learn from observation.). According to behaviorists, such learning should not have occurred, because children were not rewarded directly for the behaviors they later enacted. The studies confirmed that learning can occur by simply watching what others do, irrespective of personal rewards. Along with other important developments at the time, Bandura's work helped to turn the dominant paradigm of American psychology from behaviorism to cognitive science.

Conventional schooling capitalizes very little on this ubiquitous form of learning. In conventional arrangements, children may learn how to sit still at their desks and answer questions by observing others doing so, and perhaps might gain some insight into the thought processes of others when hearing them answer a question out loud. But because most learning in conventional schools occurs by transmission from teacher or text to student, and then within each student as he or she works out problems alone, very little of the learning process is available for others to absorb through observation and imitation. In Montessori, as will be seen, learning by observation and imitation happens easily and naturally. Other children's work is a concrete analog to their thought processes and is spread out on the floor and tables for all to see.

EXPERIMENTAL FINDINGS: OBSERVATIONAL LEARNING

Whereas the fact that children imitate others, and thus can learn by observation, seems banal today, new and surprising aspects of observational learning are coming to light all the time. One is how early it can occur. Babies who are just a few hours old imitate facial movements such as opening one's mouth and sticking out one's tongue (Meltzoff & Moore, 1983). Babies imitate actions that produce arbitrary events even after long delays, so 9-month-olds imitate pushing a button to hear a sound after intervals of 24 hours, and 14-month-olds do so after a 1-week delay (Bauer, 1995; Meltzoff, 1988a, 1988b).

As children get a bit older, what they can learn from observation becomes more complex. In one study, toddlers were shown how a special stick could be used in a particular way to retrieve an object from a tube (Want & Harris, 2001). Even 2-year-olds could repeat the precise actions necessary to retrieve the object, showing that toddlers can learn to use tools in very particular ways via observation and imitation.

Very young children also know better than to imitate mistakes. If a person says, "There!" as she performs an action, 18-month-olds are much more likely to imitate her than if she said, "Whoops!' while performing the same action (Carpenter, Akhtar, & Tomasello, 1998). Even younger children seem to consider multiple goals when choosing what to imitate. At 14 months, if a child sees a person turn on a light by pressing his or her head against a switch, most children will imitate the behavior exactly. But if the person's hands were occupied (holding a blanket around his or her shoulders) when turning on the light, 14-month-olds instead will turn the light on with their hands (Gergely, Bekkering, & Kiraly, 2002). Imitation is thus selectively attuned to goals from a very young age (Nielsen, 2006).

Another surprising finding regarding observation and imitation is how effective (at any age) even almost subliminal modeling can be. If a person sees someone else engage in such behaviors as yawning, scratching their nose, or shaking their foot, the observing person is quite likely to engage in that same behavior (Chartrand & Bargh, 1999). Further, people imitate the tone of voices they hear, so if they hear a sentence spoken in a happy voice, they repeat the sentence in a happy voice, and likewise if they hear a sad voice, they repeat the sentence in a sad voice (Neumann & Strack, 2000). Even 2-month-olds match the pitch of voices they hear (Snow, 1990).

Just thinking about human attributes leads people to behave in ways that correspond to those attributes. The psychologist John Bargh and his colleagues asked university students to make sentences out of a randomly arranged set of words, supposedly as part of a study of language ability (Bargh, Chen, & Burrows, 1996). For some students, some of those words related to politeness (patient, polite, respect), and for others, to impoliteness (bold, rude, aggressively). When they finished making up sentences, the students were told to go down the hall to meet the experimenter, who was always engaged in a telephone conversation when they arrived and continued talking on the telephone rather than attending to the student. The measure of interest was whether the student would interrupt the experimenter's telephone conversation.

As it turned out, the presence of words pertaining to rudeness or politeness in the earlier exercise had a significant effect on the students' behavior. A full 63% of those who had made sentences with words related to rudeness interrupted the conversation, whereas only 17% of those who used words related to politeness did so. The same result is obtained when participants simply read stories about rude versus polite characters, and it also occurs with other kinds of behaviors: In some studies people walked out of a room faster after thinking about cheetahs, and more slowly after pondering the elderly. Although these sorts of "priming" studies do not always replicate (Cesario, 2014), they are seen often enough that I suspect they have real-world application. Reading about a professor led to college students adopting professor0like traits in the moments afterwards (Galinsky, Wang, & Ku, 2008), a finding we extended to 7-year-olds (Dore, Smith, & Lillard, 2015). The human tendency to behave in particular ways extends from watching what others do to merely entertaining particular concepts. This research suggests that people should carefully consider what children are exposed to, from the words in vocabulary-building books to the types of characters and events populating children's media.

OBSERVATIONAL LEARNING IN MONTESSORI EDUCATION

The hands-on nature of Montessori work enables learning by observation and imitation. With Montessori materials, the abstract is made concrete, and (as the theory goes) by manipulating the concrete objects in particular ways, the abstract concepts are discovered. All that children have to learn via their observations, then, is the steps one takes with the concrete materials, which are easily visible. The abstract learning is intended to follow suit when children take those steps themselves. Whether it in fact does follow so would be a good topic for empirical investigation.

Dr. Montessori described an early case in which it became apparent to her that children's tendency to imitate others can be a useful source of inspiration in school, advancing children to new abilities. This observation, called the "explosion" into writing, recurs annually in well-functioning Montessori Primary classrooms when the first 4-year-old suddenly realizes, after months of working with the preparatory materials, that he or she can write. "The first word to be written by one of them brought a great outburst of joy and laughter. Everyone looked admiringly at 'the writer,' and thus they felt moved to follow his example. 'I can do it too!' they cried. The achievement of one started off the whole group" (Montessori, 1967a/1995, p. 231). Other 4-year-olds, having also been indirectly prepared to write through the use of knobs on Wooden Cylinders and other materials, pencils in Metal Insets, and so on, as was described in chapter 1, spontaneously began writing in reaction to having observed a first child reaching that milestone. Obviously children also see others learn to write in conventional schools; what is unique in Montessori is the series of steps, all visible and imitable, that lead children along the path to writing, so that a community of 4-year-olds can discover they already have the ability to write once they see it done by another child.

Montessori teachers capitalize on observational learning in how they give lessons. Dr. Montessori repeatedly claimed that people learn not by being told, but by watching and by doing—a constructivist perspective endorsed by Piaget and dominant in psychology for years. In a bit of a backlash against this perspective, psychology has recently seen an explosion of research on "testimony," or how children also learn from what they are told (Harris, 2012). Clearly people also learn from what they are merely told, but this does not belie that observation is a very important source of learning, and that learning through activity can cement knowledge better than merely being told it. Thus Montessori teachers show, rather than tell, children how to engage in the work. "The fewer the words, the more perfect will be the lesson. Special care should be taken in preparing the lesson to count and pick out the words to be used" (Montessori, 1967b, p. 106). The teacher places the pieces of the Pink Tower on the rug and shows the child how to build the tower piece by piece. The teacher enacts the steps of Table Washing, being sure the child observes each step so he or she can later recreate it. Whether minimizing verbiage assists learning on these tasks is an empirical question, but Dr. Montessori clearly believed that adults often use too many words with children, when a demonstration with a few carefully chosen words would be better understood. She also believed that adults often used words without clear meaning for children. Children are notoriously poor at requesting clarification (Markman, 1977), so adults who are unclear might not realize it.

LEARNING SOCIAL BEHAVIOR IN MONTESSORI

Another aspect of Montessori education that is learned in part via observation and imitation is social behavior. Montessori education includes explicit instruction on social behavior in a part of the curriculum called the lessons of Grace and Courtesy, which are on a par with lessons in math, music, and language. The goal of Montessori education, in fact, is explicitly stated to be the education of the whole person, not only the intellect.

Unlike other lessons, the lessons of Grace and Courtesy are often shown to the entire class at once, perhaps because gracious social behavior is so clearly a community endeavor. In the lessons of Grace and Courtesy, Primary children are shown how to quietly push in a chair, how to walk alongside someone's rug without knocking over their work, how to make a polite request, how to serve food, and so on. Dr. Montessori even gave children lessons on how to blow their noses, something adults routinely do but rarely stop to teach (1966, p. 126).

At older ages, for the lessons of Grace and Courtesy, children might be asked to act out social scenarios for the class, demonstrating successful and unsuccessful ways to interact with others. Acting out in front of the class specific behaviors and how to respond provides children with practice in the good behaviors, as well as opportunities to observe such behaviors (good and bad) in others. Elementary Montessori teachers say that children of these ages find acting out bad behaviors (either by the teacher pretending to be a child, or by another child) hilariously funny, and that this makes it a particularly effective way to teach. Children can then imitate the good behaviors and should know not to imitate the bad ones. Given the research just described, it would be interesting to know whether this is fully successful or if simply acting out the bad behaviors leads children to be somewhat more apt to be rude. Perhaps watching a rude example that is explicitly designated as rude enables children to inhibit copying it.

Another component of Grace and Courtesy lessons used particularly in Elementary is the telling of stories in which children behave well, even in adverse circumstances. Teachers tell stories of heroes and heroines, with the aim of inspiring children to perform heroic deeds in their turn. This practice better aligns with the research showing that merely entertaining particular concepts leads to behaving analogously. The Montessori curriculum explicitly uses modeling and stories to teach social behavior.

Children also can learn about social behavior in Montessori classrooms by observing how others behave in natural, nonscripted situations. Whereas in conventional classrooms, children learn how to sit still and listen to the teacher, in Montessori, they can learn how to interact with each other. The oldest children in the classroom can serve as examples to the younger ones. "The undisciplined child enters into discipline by working in the company of others, not by being told that he is naughty" (Montessori, 1967a/1995, p. 246).

BEST MODELS FOR IMITATION

Imitation studies have often involved adults as models, although the implication of the studies is clearly that children learn from all models, peer and adult alike. Research has shown that young children can learn from peer as well as adult models. Two recent reviews synthesized basic principles about how children imitate from models. The first made five proposals, based on existing research, about whom children are disposed to imitate (Wood, Kendal,

& Flynn, 2013). First, children are apt to imitate those who intend to teach them. Studies show that people who are more engaging, lean in, establish eye contact, and in other ways seem that they are trying to teach are more apt to be copied (Nielsen, 2006). Second, children are more apt to imitate people who do a better job (Poulin-Dubois, Brooker, & Polonia, 2011). In studies of learning from testimony, this translates to copying (learning) new labels for novel objects spoken by people who earlier had correctly labeled known objects (Koenig, Clément, & Harris, 2004). Children are also more likely to imitate models who belong to a group that is known to be more competent. For example, if children are shown relevant and irrelevant actions leading to a goal, that are modeled by both same-age peers and adults, with the peers, children imitate only the relevant actions, whereas with the adults, they imitate all actions (Wood, Kendal, & Flynn, 2012). This seems to make sense in that adults transmit the established culture, which allows for in-group identification. Fourth, children are more likely to imitate models who are like themselves, for example in language (Shutts, Kinzler, McKee, & Spelke, 2009) or gender (Shutts, Banaji, & Spelke, 2010). Finally, children are sensitive to status and are more apt to imitate high-status individuals, even in preschool (Flynn & Whiten, 2012).

The second review focused on the types of information children are apt to learn from a same-aged versus an adult model (Zmyj & Seehagen, 2013). When a behavior is familiar, for example, like clapping is often for a young child, then peer models are more apt to be imitated. When a behavior is novel, then adults are more likely to be imitated. Finally, children who have more experience with peers, for example children who have been in day care, are more apt to imitate from peers than are children with less peer experience.

Most studies use either a same-age or an adult model. An interesting question when considering multi-aged classrooms is what age of model are children most apt to learn from, same-age, slightly older, or much older (adult)? In one study addressing this, researchers exposed 14- to 18-month-olds to either a female adult or a 3-year-boy performing a variety of actions (Ryalls, Gul, & Ryalls, 2000). While sitting on their mothers' laps, the toddlers observed the model performing action sequences such as inserting a ball into a plastic egg, closing the egg, and shaking it. To see if they imitated the model's actions, children were given the objects immediately and again after a 1-week delay. Regardless of the delay time, children who had seen an older peer model replicated a greater number of complex action sequences than did children exposed to an adult model, suggesting the older peer elicited more imitation. Because only one model was used for each condition, it is possible that some other difference in the models besides their peer or adult status was responsible for the result. We know, for example, that people are particularly apt to imitate those with whom they have better rapport (Bernieri, 1988), and perhaps children felt more rapport with the child for reasons other than age.

More research is needed on this issue, using several different peer and adult models, but the finding is intriguing.

Studies have shown that preschool children benefit from multi-age groupings (Bailey, Burchinal, & McWilliam, 1993). In terms of motor, cognitive, communication, and overall development, children in mixed-age classrooms (ranging from 2 to 6 years) showed quadratic improvements over the year, whereas those in single-age classrooms showed only linear improvements. These differences were less pronounced as children reached the upper age limits of their classrooms, perhaps because of the lack of older models and tutoring opportunities. A similar finding has been observed regarding children's social cognition. A Chinese study involving urban children without siblings found that those in multi-aged preschool classrooms performed better on false belief tasks than did those in single-aged classrooms (Wang & Su, 2009). These findings might be explained by younger children learning by observation and imitation of just-older children.

An important issue that arises from this work is class composition. As noted, conventional schools tend to have one age per class. Montessori schools, in contrast, use 3-year age groupings, which offer a wider spectrum of ability level in peers from which to imitate.

MONTESSORI'S 3-YEAR AGE GROUPING

[After some time in a Montessori classroom] the child . . .
suddenly becomes aware of his companions, and is almost as
deeply interested as we are in their progress and their work.
— Maria Montessori *(1917/1965, p. 335)*

Montessori encourages learning from peers in part by using 3-year age groupings. This ensures that as children move through the classroom they will be exposed to older and younger peers, facilitating both imitative learning and peer tutoring (discussed later). Dr. Montessori was explicit about the need for this mix of ages: "The main thing is that the groups should contain different ages. . . . To have success you must have these different ages. . . . The older children are interested in the younger, and the younger in the older" (Montessori, 1989, pp. 68–69). A child enters the Primary classroom at age 2½ or 3 and remains there until he or she has completed the "cycle of materials," the full set of materials Dr. Montessori determined was optimal for a Primary classroom. For most children, the full set takes about three years to master. Then the child moves on to Lower Elementary for about three years and masters the complement of materials there. The child then moves on to the Upper Elementary.

The multi-age groupings extend the possibility for learning by imitation, because children can learn from others who are just older. By viewing a 9- or even a 7-year-old at work, a 6-year-old can observe how the same material he or she uses to do a simpler mathematical procedure will be employed in progressively more complex ways as he or she gets older. Slightly older children might serve as the best kinds of models for learning to reenact structured sequences of action, from which much Montessori learning stems. Note that this fits the proposal (given earlier) that children are particularly apt to imitate from high-status peers: In a mixed-age classroom, the older children are naturally high-status. By repeating structured sequences of actions during states of deep concentration, children are said to arrive at particular insights.

Earlier I gave the example of children being inspired to write by seeing a peer begin to write. Dr. Montessori noted that mixing ages have motivational benefits. "To understand what the older ones are doing fills the little ones with enthusiasm" (1967a/1995, p. 228). A younger child might watch an older child make a gorgeously creative and intricate design using Metal Insets and later strive to make one herself. This can extend to getting children to work with materials they might not otherwise be inspired to work with. Children might observe older children using the Movable Alphabet, an activity they have not yet been shown how to do, and when they ask to do it, the teacher will decide if they are ready. If the children are not ready, the teacher can show them what they need to do to get there. The children might be told they need to work more with the Sandpaper Letters first. The goals of the work they are currently doing are thus made visible by being able to see others just ahead, doing the work they will soon be doing themselves.

One might wonder how learning by observation in a Montessori classroom is possible for the oldest children, who are working at the highest levels with many of the available materials. Facilitating their learning by observation, Dr. Montessori urged that children be allowed to visit other classrooms. "The classroom for those of three to six is not even rigidly separated from that of the children from seven to nine. Thus, children of six can get ideas from the class above. . . . One can always go for an intellectual walk!" (1967a/1995, p. 227).

Another issue that arises when children learn from peers is class size. How many peers are available to watch and imitate? This is one point on which Montessori education is clearly against the mainstream.

LARGE CLASS SIZE

The provision of an adequate number of models to learn from is a factor in Montessori's advocating classes that are large by today's standards: about 30 to 35 children to one teacher.[1] Dr. Montessori believed that when there are not enough other children in the classroom, there are not enough different kinds of work out for children to learn sufficiently from watching each other

---

[1] The first classroom in San Lorenzo is said to have had more than 50.

work, nor are there enough personalities with whom children can practice their social skills. "When the classes are fairly big, differences of character show themselves more clearly, and wider experience can be gained. With small classes this is less easy" (Montessori, 1967a/1995, p. 225).

In contrast, in conventional schools, people's sense is usually that smaller classes are better for children. Research on this is actually equivocal, at least about achievement (Ehrenberg, Brewer, Gamoran, & Willms, 2001). Even if smaller class sizes were clearly advantageous in conventional settings, it does not mandate their being better in settings where learning occurs largely through interaction with peers and materials. In conventional settings, when one person is teaching the whole class simultaneously, that person would have more attention to devote to each child, and fewer children would conceivably allow for better teaching. When children are learning from materials and each other, having more varied possible tutors and tutees, a greater variety of people to collaborate with, and more different types of work out (inspiring one to do such work oneself) might be more beneficial. Empirical research with smaller and larger Montessori classrooms could address this issue.

Montessori advocated only one teacher in Primary and Elementary classrooms and consistently refers to the teacher in the singular (although she made at least one reference to an assistant, Montessori, 1967a/1995, p. 279, apparently for a Primary room). Theoretically, having fewer adults relative to peers would provide more opportunity for peer teaching, and less possibility of adult control (chapter 3 discussed the benefits of having more child-controlled environments). Anecdotally, Montessorians report that when more than one adult is active in a classroom, children are less apt to work independently and with each other, but turn instead to an adult. This is an interesting question for formal study. Other arguments for a single teacher, such as integration of knowledge, were discussed in chapter 5.

In sum, research clearly shows that children learn by imitation, that they do so quite early, and that they may be particularly apt to imitate just-older peers. Montessori education capitalizes on imitative learning in both the academic and social realms. It does so by using hands-on materials, by how lessons are given, by having 3-year age groupings, and by having large classes with a single teacher.

Peer Tutoring

There is nothing that makes you learn more
than teaching it yourself.
— Maria Montessori *(1989, p. 69)*

People learn more effectively from individualized instruction than from whole-class instruction (Falvey & Grenot-Scheyer, 1995; Galanter, 1968).

Montessori education can capitalize on this because the teacher is free to work individually with children. The teacher can do so because the other children are busy learning from the materials and each other. In conventional schooling, the teacher does not have time to tutor all the children individually, because school is not structured to have the remaining children work independently for most of the day. In addition to individual instruction from teachers, children can effectively tutor each other. Recent meta-analyses confirm that peer tutoring programs have strong academic and social-emotional benefits, across all grades and dosages, income levels, and for typically developing students as well as students with disabilities (Bowman-Perrott et al., 2013; Ginsburg-Block, Rohrbeck, & Fantuzzo, 2006). The next section describes some of these interventions.

PEER TUTORING PROGRAMS IN CONVENTIONAL SCHOOLS

When tasks are appropriately structured, peers can be very effective tutors, and both tutor and tutee benefit academically and socially from the arrangement. Montessori involves such structured tasks. Education researchers have also developed structured peer tutoring tasks and programs that have been successful in conventional schools. In peer tutoring programs, the teacher assigns student pairs (perhaps changing them each week), and children take turns tutoring each other on a particular topic. Using spelling as an example, the tutor reads a word, the tutee spells it, and if the tutee is incorrect, the tutor might suggest trying again, provide cues, or simply spell it correctly. The entire class engages in such a session for limited periods of the day. For example, in a 25-minute session, each member of the pair plays each role for 10 minutes, and 5 minutes are allotted to assessment at the end.

One study of the efficacy of such a system involved first- and second-grade classrooms in low-income schools (Greenwood et al., 1987). Classrooms were randomly assigned to tutoring and control conditions for spelling. In control classrooms, teachers used standard methods of teaching spelling: a workbook with word lists and vocabulary exercises, chalkboard, self-study, and homework assignments. In classrooms that used the tutoring program, the tutoring process described earlier replaced some in-class spelling work. Over the 2 years of the study, children in the peer tutoring classrooms were spelling 87% of the words correctly on average, whereas children in other classrooms were spelling 75% of words correctly. This is not an enormous difference, but it is certainly a meaningful one. Peering tutoring programs also appear to confer many social benefits on the classroom (Fantuzzo, Riggio, Connelly, & Dimeff, 1989; Maheady & Sainato, 1985). In addition, they apparently benefit learning other topics, and over the long term.

In one demonstration of these benefits, a follow-up study expanded the peer tutoring to cover reading, math, and language, and examined children's performance over multiple years. Children in the tutoring program performed significantly better than those in the control group on all three topics both immediately and 2 years later, when they had moved on to middle school and no longer had the program. They also performed better in two nontutored topics: science and social studies. They even performed as well as children in a higher SES group in all these areas (Greenwood et al., 1989). In addition, fewer children from the peer tutoring group were placed in special-education classes (Greenwood, Terry, Utley, Montagna, & Walker, 1993). This study is among many suggesting that peer tutoring programs, appropriately structured, improve learning in conventional schools and that the benefits extend across time and topics (see Topping & Ehly, 1998).

STRUCTURE AND REWARDS IN PEER TUTORING

Peer tutoring programs vary in how structured each tutoring session is, and more structured programs are typically associated with greater success. Reciprocal peer tutoring (RPT) is an example of a more structured tutoring program (Fantuzzo & Ginsburg-Block, 1998), and it has also been used to examine the effect of rewards. RPT begins with training sessions about teamwork and cooperation, and children are told they can win rewards by using teamwork. In the RPT program, teaching aides show the children how to tutor each other. Then RPT sessions are held twice weekly for 45 minutes each. Special flash-card materials are used, with a problem on one side and steps to the solution on the other. Children decide who will be tutor first in each session, and work for 10 minutes on problems before switching roles. After the initial 20 minutes, problem drill sheets are administered, and students attempt the problems, then switch papers with partners for correction. Performance on the drill sheets accrues points, which lead to such rewards as being teacher's helper or working on a special project.

When children were randomly assigned to RPT versus conventional instruction groups, those in the RPT groups consistently showed higher levels of mathematics achievement (Fantuzzo & Ginsburg-Block, 1998). Two alternative groups were also formed, one with the reward but lacking the structure provided by the flash cards, and the other having the structure but no reward. The combination of rewards and structure led to the most gains in both achievement and positive social behavior. Structure alone, without rewards, was associated with better behavior both in the tutoring sessions and in the regular classroom situation. Students also perceived themselves to be more competent when using structured than when using unstructured tutoring, but achievement was not improved in the absence of rewards (Fantuzzo, King, & Heller, 1992). Thus, within a conventional school environment, more structured peer interactions with a reward structure optimized learning and behavior. The issue of rewards is important and is discussed further in the context of collaborative learning.

As this study suggests, peer tutoring can be more successful when tutoring sessions are tightly structured. A criticism people sometimes have of Montessori education is that it is too structured. Montessori materials are meant to be used in a particular way, following a particular sequence of steps, which (among other likely advantages discussed in chapter 10) would be expected to optimize learning from peers in Montessori classrooms.

BEST TUTORS: ADULTS VERSUS PEERS

Although supplementing whole-class teaching with peer tutoring improves achievement, adults are even more effective tutors than peers. The research suggests several reasons for this that shed light on how peer tutoring can be most effective. First, adults structure the task in ways that keep the overarching goal in clear focus, whereas child partners tend to focus on parts of the problem, losing sight of the whole—a difference reminiscent of the differences between same-age experts and novices. For example, if the task is planning a route for doing a set of errands as efficiently as possible, child pairs will get the errands done, but not as efficiently, because they focus on each individual item to be retrieved separately, rather than thinking about how several items can be grouped to make for more efficient routes. Adult tutors get children to think about grouping items. However, when the peer tutor is trained in this task and taught to consider how to group items, tutee performance does improve. Nonetheless, performance even with a trained peer tutor does not improve to the level obtained when the tutor was an adult (Gauvain, 2001).

A second probable reason for the greater success of adult tutors is that adults tend to include children more in the task at hand. Other children can become autocratic, as children are inclined to focus on who gets to do what. Children tend to like to do; adults more easily sit back, watch, and guide. Research has shown that peer learning is also more successful when peers listen to each other and question each other more (reviewed in the following section), skills that many adults have but many children have not yet learned (Gauvain & Rogoff, 1989). Thus, a second problem for peer tutors is that when the task is not structured in a way that relegates roles, and the task involves doing, peer tutors tend to want to do the task and control the interaction, which makes them less effective than adult tutors. For this reason again, structured or scripted peer tutoring programs are more effective.

OPTIMAL LEVEL OF PEER TUTEE

Perhaps in part because peer tutors can become autocratic, some research suggests that, when tutored by a peer, the tutee benefits maximally from a peer who is just a bit more advanced rather than much more advanced. For example, research on both scientific and moral reasoning has shown that children benefit from exposure to thought processes that are just above their current level (Damon & Killen, 1982; Kuhn, 1972; Turiel & Rothman, 1972). This makes sense within both a Piagetian and a Vygotskian framework. If the peer's thought processes are too advanced, the tutee cannot accommodate his or her mental structures to fit the new information. Likewise, if the peer is operating above the tutee's zone of proximal development, the tutee cannot adopt the new reasoning or behavior. The success of slightly older peers in these frameworks would stem from their being able to adapt their own behaviors to more closely match the child's level.

Besides being less able to adapt to a lower level of tutee, much older and more advanced peer tutors sometimes practice social dominance. The problems of autocracy mentioned earlier thus become exacerbated, and the tutee learns less, because he or she is less involved in the decision-making process. This was found in a study in which 5-year-old novices were paired either with 5- or 7-year-olds who were considered experts at planning routes (as in the study just described; Duran & Gauvain, 1993). Children were more involved with the task when paired with an advanced planner of their own age, as opposed to an older planner, and this increased involvement predicted better performance. Whether the particular age gap used in this experiment (5–7) is a particularly problematic one would be an interesting topic for research. The age of 6 is a pivotal one, recognized in many of the world's cultures as an appropriate time to ask more of children, such as by beginning formal schooling (Rogoff, 1981). Six is the age at which Piaget speculated children advance to being able to perform mental operations (e.g., imagining addition and subtraction), and which Dr. Montessori considered transitional between her first and second planes of development. At each plane, she said, children think differently. Examining whether 6- and 8- or 7- and 9-year-olds make more effective tutoring pairs would be of interest. The research suggests that peers who are slightly advanced, but not too advanced, make more optimal tutors, but it might also be the case that tutors who are within particular age spans are best.

THE BENEFITS OF BEING TUTOR

It is not always the case that child tutors and tutees switch roles in peer tutoring programs; sometimes more capable classmates regularly assist less capable ones. One might be concerned that this disadvantages the more capable student, but this does not generally appear to be the case. Others have noted, for example, that, "It is when students are forced to explain and justify their position to others that they come to understand better themselves" (Brown, Collins, & Dugid, 1989, p. 317), a position basically echoing that of Piaget. The psychologist Deanna Kuhn (2001) colorfully recounts "the orangutan test": "If I have some new ideas and I go into a room with an orangutan to explain them, the orangutan will simply sit there and eat its banana. I will come out of the room, however, knowing more than I did before" (p. 239). Several studies support the idea that tutors benefit at least as much as tutees in peer learning situations.

In one study, college students were divided into three groups: one that was simply read a passage and would be tested, one that read the passage and was told they would teach it but did not end up doing so, and a third that read the passage and did go on to teach it (Annis, 1983). Students who both prepared to teach and went on actually to teach showed the highest levels of understanding of the passage, those who prepared to teach but did not performed next best, and those who read to be tested performed worst of all.

Other studies have found that students who expected to teach benefited in more ways than just their learning (Benware & Deci, 1984). Students in a general psychology class read a passage on brain development over vacation, in order either to be examined on it themselves or to teach it to another student. After they returned from vacation, they were tested on the material and asked about their engagement with and enjoyment of the study process. Those who had read the passage in order to teach it rated themselves as more actively engaged in reading, as more interested in the material, and as enjoying the experiment more. In terms of conceptual learning, there was a significant difference between the groups, with the teaching group's score almost double that of the exam group's score. On rote learning, there was a slight but nonsignificant advantage for the teaching group. Recently, a more tightly controlled study showed similar effects: Just expecting to teach resulted in better learning than did expecting to take a test on the same material (Nestojko, Bui, Kornell, & Bjork, 2014).

Even 3-year-olds appear to benefit from teaching. Children were given three pairs of problem stories with conceptually similar solutions (Brown & Kane, 1988). For example, one story involved a man who needed to put tires on a high shelf, and the solution was to stack some tires and use the stack as a step stool. After hearing the first story, children who did not solve it spontaneously (about 80% of them) were shown the solution. The second story was about a man who needed to get hay bales on a high tractor—a problem that could also be solved by stacking items. Some children were simply told the story, whereas others were asked to teach the solution to a Kermit the Frog puppet. Children who taught Kermit the Frog spontaneously came up with the solution to the second story of the pairs twice as frequently as children who were simply read the story.

Many others have also shown that positive academic and social effects accrue to those who teach as well as to those who are tutored (Bargh & Schul, 1980; Greer & Polirstok, 1982; Polirstok & Greer, 1986). Increased motivation appears to be partly responsible for this, because students report being more engaged in learning when they expect to teach. Others have suggested that more organized cognitive structures are employed when learning with the expectation that one will pass information on, and that this is responsible for the cognitive gains accrued by those who are intending to teach (Bargh & Schul, 1980; Zajonc, 1960). The issue of why peer learning situations are advantageous is explored further at the end of the chapter.

SUMMARY: RESEARCH ON PEER TUTORING

In sum, situations in which children learn from their peers via specific, structured tutoring are clearly beneficial. Tutees are particularly apt to benefit when they are more involved in the task, as they tend to be with peers who are closer in age. Moreover, peer tutoring episodes benefit both tutor and tutee. Peer tutoring programs can be incorporated into conventional methods of schooling, and they are being used increasingly to the benefit of children in such programs. In Montessori education, they are integral.

PEER TUTORING IN MONTESSORI

People sometimes fear that if a child of five gives lessons, this will hold him back in his own progress. But, in the first place, he does not teach all the time and his freedom is respected. Second, teaching helps him to understand what he knows even better than before. He has to analyze and rearrange his little store of knowledge before he can pass it on.
— Maria Montessori *(1967a/1995, p. 227)*

Peer tutoring occurs both formally and informally in Montessori classrooms. Informally, younger children can learn from older ones in Montessori by asking them questions while watching them work. More formally, at the teacher's discretion, children in Montessori also sometimes show each other how to use a material. As discussed, both tutors and tutees benefit from peer teaching arrangements, raising levels of both motivation and performance. Children who are teaching learn by doing so, and children who learn from other children often learn very well. Because the use of Montessori materials is very structured, it suits the condition that peer tutoring is most effective when the tutor's teaching steps are spelled out clearly. In addition, because children tend to request help from their friends, and friends are generally less likely to try to dominate each other, the problem of social dominance interfering with learning in some tutoring situations is probably alleviated.

Montessori education also easily involves arrangements that are more analogous to conventional schools' peer tutoring programs. For example, Montessori children might quiz each other on math facts or on spelling words. This can happen spontaneously, at any point in the day, since children work independently. Another natural peer tutoring opportunity in Montessori education occurs when children work together with any material: They are always in a position to watch and help one another. An older child might even simply stop to help after noticing a problem in a younger child's work. The frequency with which such assistance occurs would be interesting to know, but clearly a Montessori setting is conducive to it. Unlike school environments that emphasize grades, and like schools that downplay them (see chapter 6), Montessori schools are structured in a way that is likely to foster cooperation among students, which presumably improves the likelihood of peer tutoring.

In sum, peer tutoring programs are beneficial to children even in conventional educational programs, where they are inserted as a break in the usual whole-class teaching day. In contrast, in Montessori education peer tutoring opportunities are built into the structure of the classroom. Children naturally learn from each other by asking, and teachers might ask children to show each other how to do a new work. Tutees and tutors alike should benefit from such arrangements.

Collaborative Learning

Whereas peer tutoring involves one student teaching another, collaborative (sometimes called cooperative) learning refers to a group of two or more children working together. Many studies show that people learn better when working collaboratively than when working alone (Azmitia & Crowley, 2001; P. A. Cohen, Kulik, & Kulik, 1982; Damon, 1990; Gauvain & Rogoff, 1989; Glachen & Light, 1982; Johnson, Maruyama, Johnson, Nelson, & Skon, 1981; Okada & Simon, 1997; Phelps & Damon, 1989; Qin, Johnson, & Johnson, 1995; Slavin, 1980; Teasley, 1995; Tomasello et al., 1993); a recent meta-analysis focusing on studies done since 1995 confirms these findings (Kyndt et al., 2013). As with peer tutoring, the benefits of collaborative learning arrangements extend beyond academic achievement to improve the social climate of the classroom (social relations, discipline, and so on) and enhance individual well-being (Aronson, 2002; Johnson & Johnson, 1983; Maheady, 1998; Wright & Cowen, 1985). A classic example of collaborative learning is the Jigsaw classroom.

The psychologist Elliot Aronson designed the Jigsaw program initially to address the disturbances that followed the integration of public schools in Austin, Texas, in the 1960s (Aronson & Patnoe, 1997). He reasoned that close student contact, for the purpose of helping others, might alleviate problems, and so created learning arrangements that would lead to such contact. In the Jigsaw model, children are placed in groups of five or six and topics of study are broken into as many segments. For the topic of the Civil War, for example, one person might be assigned to study the history of slavery, another the type of weapons used in the era, another the major battles, and so on. Children research their topic on their own, and then temporarily join a new group composed of the child from every other group in the class who was assigned their same topic. These "homogenous" groups share information and practice presentations of their topics. Finally, children reunite with their original groups, and each child teaches the material. A test on all the material generally follows. The Jigsaw method has repeatedly been found to improve learning as well as classroom social relations (Aronson, 2002; Bridgeman, 1981; Doymus, 2008; Lazarowitz, Hertz-Lazarowitz, & Baird, 1994). In terms of academic achievement, it is particularly successful with minority youths, but in some cases it has improved, and in no cases (to my knowledge) has it negatively affected, the learning of other students (Lucker, Rosenfield, Sikes, & Aronson, 1977; Slavin, 1983).

Several variants on the Jigsaw method have been developed; one of the better-known examples is the Communities of Learners program, initiated by the psychologists Ann Brown and Joseph Campione (1994). Collaborative systems share such characteristics as viewing all children as a potential resource for others' learning, children joining the teacher in providing guidance and direction for class learning, and the learning process being considered as important as its products. Researchers have noted that children participating in such programs engage in higher levels of reasoning and learning than would normally be expected at their ages (Brown & Campione, 1994; Rogoff, Turkanis, et al., 2001).

In one study of collaboration, teams of four students worked together to learn about the particulate theory of matter, presented in benchmark lessons punctuated by specific problem-solving tasks (Palincsar & Herrenkohl, 1999). Students first attempted to solve the problems alone, then had structured meetings in which they were coached about how to identify substances, describe events, apply their learning in their explanations, and interact with their partners. Children who participated in this structured collaborative program scored significantly higher on a post-test of their conceptual understanding of matter than children in a standard control group studying the same topic in the conventional manner.

Even very limited peer collaboration sessions have been linked to improved performance. In one study, peer collaboration took place over only six sessions, each occurring 1 week apart, yet significant gains were still observed in children's learning on tasks that required reasoning (Phelps & Damon, 1989). No gains were seen for rote learning and copying tasks. Again, this is consistent with both Piagetian and Vygotskian theory. Peers would especially assist when learning was pushing the child into new territory.

Even peer collaboration among adults has been linked to positive outcomes. Especially creative individuals, as nominated by their peers, produced their best work via a common pattern of intense study, followed by idle time, discussion with colleagues, and then a final period of hard work to bring the ideas to fruition (Csikszentmihalyi & Sawyer, 1995). A period of discussion, of meeting other minds and sharing ideas, was considered fundamental to the production of highly creative work.

At the other end of the life course, children as young as 14 months are able to collaborate with adults in simple activities, for example by opening doors that adults are clearly having trouble opening (Warneken, Chen, & Tomasello, 2006; Warneken & Tomasello, 2007). By age 2 to 3, children can engage in a simple cooperative task with a same-aged peer. In one study, for example, two handles were pulled simultaneously or sequentially to activate a toy (Brownell, Ramani, & Zerwas, 2006). Although collaboration seems quite positive, it's not clear how collaboration influences young children outside the collaborative context itself.

In a study examining this (Plötner, Over, Carpenter, & Tomasello, 2015), groups of 3.5-year-olds and 5-year-olds were introduced to two puppets; for half of each group, one puppet collaborated with the child while the other puppet ostensibly went to play with someone else under the table. The collaboration involved working a device to get the final two blocks that were needed to complete a puzzle. For the other half, a "minimal group" paradigm was used, in which children were assigned to a group based on a minimal characteristic—in this case color. Children were told that their group membership would be determined by picking one of the experimenter's closed hands, one of which had a green coin and the other a yellow coin. After children picked, they were given clothing to wear to match their new group, and two puppets were brought out; one wore green and the other yellow.

Next, children in both conditions were given five tasks in which they had to choose between the two puppets; their first choice was scored. In one case the puppets were both trying to reach something, and at issue was which one the child helped first. Children also had to divide five stickers between the puppets; the puppet who was given the most was scored. In another, both puppets expressed liking the contents of a different (but identical) closed box; the question was which puppet the child trusted ("Which box do you like most?"). Fourth, children were simply asked which puppet they liked most, and finally, children were given permission to hug the puppets good-bye.

The results showed that for all tasks except sticker sharing, 5-year-olds were significantly more likely to choose (or choose first) the puppet with whom they collaborated or were in a group, whereas 3.5-year-olds showed no preference. Furthermore, results were stronger for collaboration than for minimal groups. This fits with an evolutionary model proposed by Tomasello and his colleagues (Tomasello, Melis, Tennie, Wyman, & Herrmann, 2012). They argue that humans would first have needed to collaborate to hunt, and then because of the culture that developed around such collaborations, would have begun to form groups.

In sum, peer collaboration is clearly helpful to learning by the time one is in school, and by age 5 collaborating with others leads to more trust, liking, and prosocial behavior toward those others even outside the collaborative situation. However, in the context of conventional schooling, collaboration is an insert, rather than integrated at its foundation.

LIMITING CONDITIONS FOR BENEFICIAL COLLABORATIVE LEARNING

There are limiting conditions for the benefits of peer collaboration, such that not all studies of collaboration have shown improvements in learning (Siegler, 1998). For one, although by age 5 collaboration has social benefits, very young children's learning does appear not to benefit much, and even 5-year-olds' learning may benefit mostly from the observational rather than the interactional aspects of collaborative settings (Azmitia, 1988). The learning benefits of collaborative learning begin to accrue particularly in the elementary school years (Azmitia, 1996; Tomasello et al., 1993). This is consistent with Dr. Montessori's observations: Younger children tend not to even pursue a great deal of collaborative work. However, they do engage in some; for example, table-washing often requires a bit of cooperation, as a second child might be needed to help to carry the table to the washing mat.

Perhaps the reason collaborative learning becomes more beneficial for learning with age is that children who benefit the most in collaborative learning situations are those who engage in a particular type of dialogue, termed "transactive dialogue." In such dialogues, children focus on each other's ideas and build on them, a skill that children achieve increasingly with age as they come to take others' perspectives (Flavell, 1999). Children who are less apt to engage in such dialogues benefit less from collaborative engagements.

Children have also been shown to benefit in collaborative learning exchanges to the extent that they use interpretive statements (explanations, inferences, strategies, and so on) as opposed to descriptive ones (Teasley, 1995). Ten- and 11-year-olds were assigned to one of four conditions, crossing "working in pairs/alone" with "encouraged to talk/not," and asked to solve puzzles, such as to determine how a spaceship moved or to decipher the effect of using a particular function key on a computer. Children who worked together and were encouraged to talk were most likely to solve the puzzles and produced the most interpretive talk. Even when children were alone and encouraged to talk to themselves, their use of interpretive talk was positively related to their ability to solve the puzzles. Descriptive talk, which is more characteristic of children in the kindergarten years, was associated with low levels of performance on the problem-solving tasks. The children who performed the worst were ones who worked alongside others but were discouraged from talking at all, which is the typical arrangement in conventional elementary schools. In contrast, children at these ages in Montessori schools tend to work together, and they frequently talk while they work. This study suggests that elementary school children particularly benefit from collaboration because by ages 6 to 12 children are apt to engage in the kind of discussion that advances understanding: interpretive talk. Younger children are less apt to engage in interpretive talk.

Another limitation on collaboration's benefits is a child's particular developmental level relative to the task. There appear to be particular moments in development when children are most apt to benefit from collaborative exchanges on specific tasks, echoing the work by Goldin-Meadow and her colleagues presented in chapter 2. Just as children who exhibited more gesture-speech mismatches were most apt to benefit from instruction, children who are not strong adherents of a single theory tend to benefit most from peer collaboration (Pine & Messer, 1998). For example, on a task in which children have to figure out how to make a balance beam balance, children who were strong proponents of an incorrect theory (such as that distance from the center of the beam does not matter) were least apt to benefit from collaboration. Unfortunately, a factory approach to schooling cannot accommodate individual readiness to learn. Montessori education might accommodate readiness to learn better because teachers give lessons to children as the children appear to be ready for them. Because teachers can tailor instruction to each individual child's level, children might be less likely to end up in a situation where the task at hand and the peer collaborators were not appropriately calibrated.

OPTIMAL COLLABORATORS

Just as the characteristics of a peer model matter for observational learning, characteristics of the collaborator matter for learning with others. One important characteristic is the degree of friendship among collaborators. Several studies suggest that collaborative learning exchanges are enhanced when children are paired with friends. In part this may be because when children choose their own partners (who would often be their friends), they interact more (Berndt, 1989). From a Piagetian perspective in particular, interaction is crucial to learning, and the more of it there is, the more one would be expected to learn.

In one study demonstrating improved reasoning when paired with friends, fifth-graders engaged in a series of problems requiring them to isolate variables, such as figuring out which of several factors made plants fail to prosper, and which of several pizza ingredients were responsible for the demise of some diners (Azmitia & Montgomery, 1993). Pairs of friends engaged in more transactive and interpretive dialogues than nonfriend pairs. They also were more likely to critique each other's ideas, offer explanations, and elaborate on each other's ideas. And they solved more of the most difficult problems better than did nonfriends. On less difficult problems, however, nonfriends did as well as friends.

Perhaps related to this, children have also been shown to learn more in the context of sustained relationships than in new ones. Not only is social interaction more positive and frequent with more familiar peers, but the cognitive level of one's interactions is raised as well (Doyle, Connolly, & Rivest, 1980). In addition, collaborative problem solving is improved when peers are more familiar (Brody, Graziano, & Musser, 1983). Children also learn more from older siblings than they learn from older peers who play frequently with those siblings, perhaps in part because they spend more time with and know the siblings better (Azmitia & Hesser, 1993). Collaborators benefit from knowing each other better.

Putting all this together, it suggests that children learn the most in collaborative exchanges when they collaborate with people with whom they have deeper and more positive relationships. Although I know of no research supporting this, my experience is that when teachers assign children to collaborative teams, they often choose to pair nonfriends. The research suggests that this is not beneficial to learning, and that allowing children the freedom to arrange their own collaborative groups would be more optimal.

That children are particularly apt to learn when grouped with others with whom they are very familiar suggests another advantage to Montessori's 3-year age groupings. Children who are the same age remain together for 3 years, and ones who are a year apart are together for 2 years. In addition, if a school continues through Elementary, children who graduate to a new classroom are reunited with children who graduated 1 and 2 years previously from their last classroom. Such arrangements give time for friendships to develop across ages, expanding the group of children who can serve as good collaborators. Children learn best in groups of friends, and 3-year age groupings, particularly ones that repeat as children move through higher-level classrooms, provide ample opportunity for relationships to form.

COLLABORATION IN MONTESSORI

Many Montessori activities, especially at the Elementary level, can be done in pairs or small groups. Dr. Montessori noted this change in the orientation of the child at the second plane in her levels of development, as the child enters the Elementary classroom: "A third interesting fact to be observed in the child of six is his need to associate himself with others, not merely for the sake of company, but in some sort of organized activity. He likes to mix with others in a group wherein each has a different status" (1948b/1967, p. 6).

In Elementary Montessori a few materials are specifically designed to be used in groups, although most materials easily allow for group activity. In the Primary only a few materials are specifically designed to be used with a group. One of these, the Golden Beads (Figure 7.2), teaches older Primary children about the four basic mathematical operations. Because children of these ages are not particularly adept at group work, the teacher is closely involved in the Golden Bead material, normally with a group of three children. Each child takes a small rug and a set of Arabic number cards, and the teacher takes a big rug and his or her own set of number cards (up to 9,999). Children also each have a tray with a small dish. The tray holds bars of 10, squares of 100, and cubes of 1,000 beads (as needed), and the small dish holds single beads.

The Golden Bead work proceeds with the teacher asking each child to get a particular number, say 2,566, or 3,102. Children select the numbers from their cards, then carry their trays to the open cabinet (sometimes referred to as "the store" or "the bank") that contains the Golden Beads, where they take

FIGURE 7.2 The Golden Beads. © Laura Joyce-Hubbard, 2014. All rights reserved.

out beads corresponding to their number, for example, 2 thousand-cubes, 5 hundred-squares, 6 ten-bars, and 6 units. They bring these to their smaller rugs, where, as a group, they go over each child's number and count what they have brought, and correct any errors. Then the teacher announces what they will do, for example, "Today, we're going to do addition." Children bring all their beads to the large rug, and their beads are combined and grouped. Counting begins with the units. Groups of 10 units are exchanged for ten-bars, then groups of 10 ten-bars are exchanged for hundred squares, and so on.

The manipulatives are matched by the Arabic numeral cards laid out on the large rug. Each child puts his or her small number cards on the rug, and the children select the large number cards that correspond to the sum they arrived at with the beads. The teacher then has the group all read the cards together, showing how "2,566" plus "3,102" and so on arrives at the sum. This same material can be used to show subtraction, multiplication, and division. It is the beginning of a collaborative exercise, a foundation the children have as they enter Elementary and begin to engage in collaborative work without the close engagement of the teacher.

The "Bank Game" is an Elementary material designed specifically for group use, particularly to work on multiplication. The materials for the Bank Game are sets of the same Arabic numeral cards used with many other Montessori math materials, such as the Golden Beads, a second set of gray number cards, which serve as the multiplier, and a third set of cards, which are used to indicate the product. These last cards can indicate numbers up to 9 million.

Three children, usually around 9 years old, take roles: One child plays the "Banker," the second, the "Teller," and the third, the "Customer." The role of the teller is more communicative than substantial, and thus the teller can be a younger child whose mathematical knowledge is less advanced: He or she will learn by watching the customer and the banker. The customer may say to the teller, "I want 8,642 multiplied by 34." The children then decompose the multiplicand into its categorical parts (thousands, hundreds, and so on), and then do the same for the multiplier. They lay out cards showing the problem and begin their series of multiplications category by category. The teller then gives the banker the first transaction: "I would like to have the product of 4×2, please." The banker offers the customer the card for 8 units. The teller continues through each of the subproblems one at a time, collecting the cards, after which the teller sums them to arrive at the final product. The teller carries that number back to the customer, who checks the work. The material is designed to be used collaboratively, and having the social roles of banker, teller, and customer may enhance its interest for children. This work is also notable regarding imagination and fantasy play, which was discussed in chapter 6. Children in the Elementary years appear to like taking roles, and several Montessori exercises involve their doing so.

Although few materials *require* collaborative use, most Montessori Elementary materials can easily accommodate two or more users. The Grammar Box Command Cards are an example of a work that can be done with others or alone. Children pick up a card and read its message, which (for a verb card) might be "Waddle across the room like a duck." To use these cards collaboratively, others guess what command is being enacted. Montessori teachers say that the cards seem to increase inspiration for reading among younger children; for all children, they help make clear the parts of speech. Elementary children seem to particularly like that in enacting these commands, they are temporarily able to break the usual classroom rules, for example, a card might command them to drop a pile of papers onto the floor. As examples of other Montessori math materials that can easily accommodate collaboration, with the Peg Board, used for mathematical operations, one child can move the beads and another can write; and with the division material called the Test Tubes (which are, literally, test tubes into which children count beads representing division problems) up to four children can do a single problem.

Another way children work collaboratively in Montessori Elementary is that they may (and usually do) choose to work together on reports on topics of mutual interest (such as "The History of Weaving" or "Volcanoes"). These topics are often inspired by one of the teacher's lessons. Recall that the Great Lessons and their follow-up lessons are designed to raise more questions than they answer, so that children will research issues on their own. Children usually end up doing so in small groups, because especially at these ages, they like to work together. Unlike the collaborative methods described here for conventional schools (such as Jigsaw), Montessori does not dictate the structure of the collaboration nor who works together.

In sum, many of the kinds of work children do in Montessori classrooms can be done in collaboration with others, from cooking projects (Figure 7.3) to table washing (Figure 7.4) to elaborate reports. Whether working with the scientific material to classify plant specimens, constructing models of molecules, researching colonial America, mastering multiplication facts, or analyzing the grammatical structure of sentences, by Montessori Elementary, children often choose to work collaboratively in small, self-formed groups.

The Use of Rewards in Peer Tutoring and Collaborative Learning Programs

Following the chapter on the negative effects of expected extrinsic rewards, the success of extrinsic rewards in peer tutoring and collaborative learning programs in conventional school settings might be surprising. Although their use is a point of controversy in the literature (Johnson & Johnson, 1983), some

FIGURE 7.3 Collaborative Cooking Project. Photograph by An Vu.

FIGURE 7.4 Collaborative Work. Photograph by An Vu.

studies have found that performance under no-reward collaborative conditions is no better than in whole-class teaching arrangements (Fantuzzo et al., 1989; Slavin, 1996). Whether rewards are necessary to the success of peer tutoring and collaborative learning programs in conventional settings is not clear (Cotton & Cook, 1982; Johnson et al., 1981; Slavin, 1996).

An important consideration is that children in the peer tutoring and collaborative learning studies comparing reward and no-reward situations were generally in older grades. Because they had been operating for several years in graded school systems, any intrinsic motivation they once had to learn in school would be expected to have already been supplanted by the extrinsic motivation to exert effort in school for grades or other rewards. Collaborative arrangements at older grades may require rewards because children by those ages are accustomed to working for tangible, expected rewards in school, and if there are no rewards (intrinsic or extrinsic) for learning and they are with their peers, they would rather socialize than engage in school tasks. As a Montessori Middle School study discussed in chapter 11 shows, children in conventional schools tend to feel relatively disaffected when engaged in schoolwork, and they are more motivated when engaged in nonacademic tasks (Rathunde & Csikszentmihalyi, 2005a). If intrinsic motivation to learn in school had not been previously disrupted, as the research suggests it probably has (Harter, 1981; Lepper et al., 2005), perhaps extrinsic rewards would not be necessary in peer tutoring and collaborative learning studies in conventional schools.

The research presented in chapter 6 showed that extrinsic rewards not only reduced subsequent interest in a task but also disrupted the quality of children's work when criteria for high-quality work were not clearly spelled out. This might also explain the positive results of rewards in peer learning situations, as successful peer tutoring occurred only with highly structured tasks. When the road to success is clearly demarcated, rewards are not harmful. In keeping with this, the education researcher Robert Slavin (1996) proposed that controversial tasks without single answers might not require a group reward structure to achieve successful outcomes. Examples of this would be debates and other kinds of structured controversy where students are exposed to others' thought processes by virtue of engaging in the task. Successful collaborative approaches that lack rewards have involved such tasks (Johnson & Johnson, 1979).

Mechanisms of Learning From Peers

The final section of this chapter addresses the issue of why learning from peers is helpful to children. Four possible mechanisms are considered here: incorporation, distributed cognition, active learning, and motivation.

INCORPORATION

One manner by which peers impact development is via imitation of others' behaviors and thought processes, which in due course may alter one's own cognitive structures. Piagetian and Vygotskian perspectives are compatible with this view. Clearly this sort of process occurs in observational learning. In one illustration of this, pairs of 5-year-olds were asked to recreate a LEGO figure from a sample (Azmitia, 1988). Experts behaved differently toward the model than novices, in that expert LEGO builders looked a lot at the model. Novices benefited from being paired with an expert peer, but this was mediated by the extent to which they watched and imitated the expert. In particular, novices who were paired with experts and later went on to look a lot at the model themselves were more adept at building LEGO forms that matched a sample. This study shows how observing others solve problems can directly impact how a child goes on to solve a problem him- or herself. Observation and imitation, themselves important processes in peer learning, also serve collaborative learning, because children can incorporate a peer's behavior into their own repertoires. It is possible that in some peer tutoring situations such processes might also operate.

DISTRIBUTED COGNITION

Distributed cognition is another explanation for why peer exchanges assist learning (Kuhn, 2001). In collaboration, cognitive work is socially distributed, so the cognitive workload of each party is reduced. Unlike the orangutan described earlier, people can talk back, exchange ideas, and fill in gaps in each other's knowledge, thereby raising the level of discussion. This can be especially important when each party brings skills or knowledge that another may lack, allowing different partners to serve as scaffolds for each other's learning. Peer tutoring exchanges can also allow for this kind of distribution, in that the tutor can scaffold the tutee's understanding.

As psychologist Ann Brown and her colleagues described distributed cognition,

> Within a culture, ideas are exchanged and modified, and belief systems developed and appropriated through conversations and narratives, so these must be promoted, not inhibited. Though they are often anathema to conventional schooling, [conversations] are an essential component of social interaction, and thus, of learning. They provide access to much of the distributed knowledge and elaborate support of the social matrix (Orr, 1987). (Brown et al., 1989, p. 40)

Supporting the idea that distributed cognition underlies the benefits of collaborative learning, studies show that transactive dialogues are essential to successful collaborative learning arrangements (Siegler, 1998). In such dialogues, children clearly build on each other's ideas, each providing a bit of scaffolding for the next idea that comes along. In a study of moral development, children were found to advance more in moral reasoning after discussing moral dilemmas with classmates than with their mothers, and this finding appeared to hinge on the degree to which transactive reasoning was used in discussion of the dilemmas (Kruger, 1992). Building ideas with another person distributes cognition, and this appears to be part of how collaboration and peer learning work. Thinking is shared across a network, easing the processing load on each member of the network.

ACTIVE LEARNING

When cognition is distributed, and transactive dialogues are engaged in, learning is clearly more active. Children sharing information and comparing understandings are engaged; in contrast, those who learn in conventional situations can be passive, simply listening to the teacher or reading texts. Ann Brown described how collaborative learning was active in the Community of Learners program:

> Students seeking an encompassing explanation ... create an active learning environment for themselves that is quite different from the passive reception of assigned knowledge that too often dominates classroom interaction. Involved students brought their own outside material to the classroom—books, newspaper articles, and reports from television news. Students felt a sense of ownership over the knowledge they were acquiring. They formed a culture of learning, where reading, writing and thinking took place in the service of a recognized, reasonable goal—learning and helping others learn about a topic that deeply concerned them. (Brown & Campione, 1990, p. 123)

Providing explanations is an active process and is known to improve learning (Chi & Bassok, 1989). Children are clearly more active when they learn with peers. In one study, tutees asked 240 times more questions when being tutored by a peer than during whole-class learning with an adult teacher (Graesser & Person, 1994). As compared to passively listening to teachers, as typically occurs in whole-class learning environments in the United States, children appear to more actively contribute to their own education in collaborative and peer tutoring situations.

MOTIVATION

When engaged in peer learning, children are involved with each other. This involvement probably motivates learning, as suggested by the studies showing high levels of student satisfaction with peer learning situations.

Throughout elementary school and high school, social life is increasingly important to children (Hartup, 1983). Conventional schools separate children during the learning process, in the sense that children are not supposed to talk to or interact with each other during class. Children try desperately to interact during lecture time in school, passing notes, whispering, and winking, but they usually must wait for recess, lunch, and after school to openly engage in the social interaction that is apparently so desirable. Collaborative learning might achieve its success in part by allowing children to interact socially during these very social years, and through motivating the learning process by having it take place in the context of that highly desired interaction. This hypothesis garners some support from the evidence that collaborations among friends are particularly successful. Children are motivated to interact with each other, especially with friends, and they become motivated about learning when it is an avenue for interaction.

In sum, learning from peers might achieve success in part because it allows incorporation of the behaviors and ideas of more advanced others, or because it involves distributed cognition. Another source of the effect might be the level of activity and attention involved in working with peers. Finally, schoolchildren tend to be motivated to interact, and this could also explain the success of peer learning programs.

When schools use collaborative learning or peer tutoring programs, they are usually instituted as a special program, something children do for an hour each week or perhaps each day. Even such limited exposure has benefits. However, as the psychologist Barbara Rogoff and her colleagues (Rogoff, Bartlett, & Turkanis, 2001) describe (and it bears repeating), "adding the 'technique' of having children work in 'cooperative learning' teams is quite different than a system in which collaboration is inherent in the structure" (p. 13).

Chapter Summary

Children in Montessori classrooms have ample opportunity for learning by imitating models, through peer tutoring, and in collaboration. Montessori education is built on these forms of learning supplementing interaction with the material and teacher lessons. Research in schools and psychology laboratories has shown that learning occurs in these situations. Furthermore, peer tutoring and collaborative arrangements are superior to conventional whole-class teaching for both the learning and the social climate that they support. The next chapter addresses how all these forms of learning are situated in meaningful contexts, both inside and outside the Montessori classroom.

8 }

Meaningful Contexts for Learning

Education, as today conceived, is something separated both from biological and social life. All who enter the educational world tend to be cut off from society. . . . People are prepared for life by exclusion from it.

— Maria Montessori *(1967a/1995, pp. 10–11)*

One of the most crucial and large differences between Montessori and conventional schooling is in the realm of meaning. If conventional education represents a factory for transforming the behaviorist child into a knowledgeable citizen who can pick the right answers on standardized multiple-choice tests, Montessori is more of a secular monastery for the encouragement of the realization of each person's full potential as a connected, aware, intelligent being. Although the best school brochures describe their aims in a more Montessori-like fashion, when I attend academic talks aimed at conventional teachers-in-training and their professors, the former goal (performance on multiple-choice tests) seems most prevalent.

In keeping with this, conventional schooling is sometimes criticized for not being "meaningful," in the sense of not being obviously related to real life. Clearly many of the skills and facts learned in school are intended to serve learners outside the school context, but the manner in which they are taught sometimes obscures those purposes, reducing the extent to which school learning is transferred to contexts outside school. As Conley (2015) puts it, conventional schooling's

> focus on the parts and pieces has had a clear impact on instruction. In order to prepare students to do well on such tests, schools have treated literacy and numeracy as a collection of distinct, discrete components to be mastered independently, with little attention to students' ability to assemble those components into an integrated whole or to apply them in the context of the discipline, or, where appropriate, to other subject areas. The net effect is to reduce the extent

to which [conventional schooling and its content] is experienced as meaningful. (p. 6)

Conley (2015, p. 6) then asks, "What if understanding the parts and pieces is not the same as getting the big picture that tells whether students truly grasp concepts, can apply knowledge, and, perhaps most important, can transfer knowledge and skills from one context to an entirely new one?" The disembodied nature or conventional schooling is problematic.

Conventional schooling is separated from other life contexts in at least two ways. One seems to reflect the factory model of the school and the other seems to reflect the behaviorist model of the child. First, it is physically separated, usually occurring in a special building. This makes good sense for a factory: Special structures best serve the goal of turning out finished goods. Physically separating the learning context from the context of use can be desirable: Clients would normally prefer their accountants learn the tax code in a classroom rather than in an appointment (Anderson, Reder, & Simon, 1996). Some have argued, however, that the divide between school and contexts of use has a negative effect on learning, and that learners are better served when learning is "situated" in the context in which it will be used (e.g., Lave & Wenger, 1991). Internships are a clear case of learning in the context of use. Internships exist because some skills and knowledge seem to be better learned at the point of need, where there is contextual support for learning. In addition, learning is motivated by the context in which it is needed. By physically separating learners from the sites where knowledge will be applied, conventional schooling reduces both contextual support and motivation for learning. As Allen and Allen (2009) noted in their compelling book about the recent struggles of American teens, this problem of disconnection, or lack of clear meaning, becomes particularly acute in adolescence (see also Wang & Eccles, 2013).

Related to this is the second way in which school learning is separated from life: conceptually. Even in a separate setting, learning can be embedded in examples and contexts that have meaning for the learner, and often can be readily applied to real-life settings. But if one's model of the learner is the behaviorist one, namely an empty vessel, context should not matter. One can pour information into the same vessel just as well in a factory as on a farm. In fact, from his finding that knowledge could not transfer across situations, Thorndike seemed to take the message that learning should be stripped of all context. His writings on teaching refer to the stimuli presented by the teacher, not to the context in which those stimuli are presented. Even today, in conventional school classrooms using standard textbooks, the importance of meaningful contexts for engaging minds and enhancing learning is often neglected. Word problems in math textbooks ask about hypothetical people engaged in activities that often have nothing to do with the lives of the children working the problems. History has traditionally been taught as a series of people, places, and dates to memorize, and only in the hands of more gifted teachers can children see how the learning relates to their own lives. Vocabulary is taught in lists taken from workbooks made by someone else, someplace else, rather than stemming organically from what a child currently needs to know to describe something more precisely. School learning is conceptually removed from contexts and issues whose importance is clear to the children. In fact, the grade-based reward structure can be thought of as a substitute motivating device, given the inherent lack of intrinsically motivating contexts in conventional schooling. Taken to extremes, this has even resulted in school personnel promising students they will eat worms or engage in sumo wrestling if the students improve their scores on state exams (Herricks, 2004).

Montessori education, in contrast, is designed to provide meaningful contexts. One means is by actually going out of the classroom and into the world to learn, a process formalized in the Elementary Going Out and adolescent Erdkinder programs. Within the classroom, meaningful contexts are derived from hands-on materials that render the abstract concrete, have clear applications, and are complexly interconnected with other materials.

The issues in this chapter touch on some points discussed in chapters 2 (movement and cognition) and 5 (interest). Additional issues and research bearing on meaningful contexts for learning are addressed here. I first consider research showing that learning is enhanced when meaningful contexts are supplied, explore some possible reasons why, and describe how meaningful contexts are supplied in Montessori education. Next I consider the issue of knowledge transfer from one context (school) to another, dealing first with failures of transfer, and then with conditions of successful transfer. The chapter ends with consideration of how Montessori education facilitates transfer of learning between the classroom and the world outside.

Giving Knowledge Meaning

"Learners, especially in school settings, are often faced with tasks that do not have apparent meaning or logic" (Bransford et al., 1999, p. 58). How does one make a situation meaningful for students? It does not happen when teachers merely emphasize the importance of a topic (Shouse, 2001). Research suggests simple ways to create contexts that assist learning. One way is to provide sufficient background information to allow people to relate new information to their existing knowledge.

ORIENTING LEARNERS WITH OLD KNOWLEDGE

The following paragraph is a classic illustration of the importance of a meaningful background framework for learning:

> The procedure is actually quite simple. First you arrange items into different groups. Of course one pile may be sufficient depending on how much there is to do. If you have to go somewhere else due to lack of facilities that is the next step; otherwise, you are pretty well set. It is important not to overdo things. That is, it is better to do too few things at once than too many. In the short run this may not seem important but complications can easily arise. A mistake can be expensive as well. At first, the whole procedure will seem complicated. Soon, however, it will become just another facet of life. It is difficult to foresee any end to the necessity for this task in the immediate future, but then, one can never tell. After the procedure is completed, one arranges the materials into different groups again. Then they can be put into their appropriate places. Eventually they will be used once more and the whole cycle will have to be repeated. However, that is part of life. (Bransford & Johnson, 1972, p. 720)

After reading such a passage, study participants were asked to recall what they had read verbatim. Not surprisingly, they were not very good at doing so, because the passage simply does not make sense when no context is supplied. However, some participants were given the context of the paragraph, in the simple form of a title: "Washing Clothes." These participants were much better at recalling the passage, showing that having a structural context strongly affected memory. Such findings are in marked contrast to Thorndike's (1917) contextless methods of teaching; as an example, one of his textbooks dictates, "Learn this: Dime = 10 cents" (p. 59).

When new information is taught in conventional schools, it is too often taught in an abstract manner with no obvious connection to one's knowledge of the real world—in a sense, the equivalent of learning the "washing clothes" paragraph without the title. An easy case in which to see this is mathematics, in which abstract rules are often presented with no clear indicator of when one might apply those rules (besides to the next few problems in one's textbook). Several studies have looked specifically at mathematics learning in school situations and have found effects for providing meaningful contexts.

In one study, students were given materials with which to learn about probability, with examples embedded in either an abstract context, an educational context, or a medical context (Ross, 1983). Some of the students learning the material were training to become teachers, whereas others were training to become nurses. Thus, for some students the examples were personally relevant, for others the material was contextualized but not personally relevant, and for still others it was abstract. For the Multiplication Rule regarding probability, students in all three learning conditions were first shown the following paragraph: "Multiplication Rule: The probability that event A, which has a probability P(A) of occurring on any one trial, will occur n times in n independent trials, is as follows: $P(A) \times P(A) \times \ldots \times P(A) = P(A)^n$" (p. 521). The students who were in the abstract condition then read, "A random response is made on each of two trials. The probability of outcome Y occurring on any one trial is 1/3. What is the probability that outcome Y will occur on both trials?" Students in the education condition instead read, "A student makes a completely random guess on each of two multiple-choice items containing three alternatives. The probability of randomly guessing the correct answer is thus 1/3. What is the probability of randomly guessing it on both items?" Students in the medical condition read the first paragraph, followed by a second paragraph about two patients who might get a cataract operation with a success rate of 1/3.

Students were tested on items with problems from all three contexts (abstract, education, and nursing). Students who had trained in the meaningful context conditions—the latter two—performed better on the probability problems than did students in the abstract condition, and the best performance was achieved when the training examples were embedded in personally relevant contexts—those pertaining to the profession for which each student was studying.

Mark Lepper and his students have done several studies with school-aged children that make the same point. In one study, they taught 10-year-olds the basic elements of the LOGO graphics program language (Papert, 1980; Parker & Lepper, 1992). A control group was taught in an abstract form, whereas experimental groups were given a choice of meaningful contexts in which to complete the same task. In the abstract form, a child had to navigate the cursor between and touch five circles. In the meaningful context conditions, the child's task was structurally the same, but the circles were described as islands with treasure that must be collected, or as planets that a spaceship had to land on.

Having a meaningful context influenced many aspects of the children's learning and motivation with LOGO. Immediately after training, children in the contextualized conditions had learned the programming language better, and reported liking the exercise more than children in the control group. Two weeks later, children who had learned the program with a contextual description performed better on a geometry test of the underlying concepts and skills, such as estimation of angles and distances. They also showed better mastery of an important life skill embedded in computer programming: following a series of steps in executing a plan.

A follow-up study combined contextualization with personalization and choice (Cordova & Lepper, 1996). Nine- to 11-year-olds were taught a computer math game, strangely titled (in the real world), "How the West Was One + Three × Four" (Seiler, 1989). This game presents children with a number line from 1 to 50, and for each turn, the child has to combine three numbers using parentheses to maximize a move along the number line. The child plays against the computer, and can request that the computer play its best or just pretty well. The child can also request hints.

Children in the control condition saw the game in an unembellished, rather banal format, with the title of "Math Game." For the other children, the game was presented within a spaceship fantasy context and either had the title "Space Quest" and involved the child imagining she or he was piloting a spaceship to other planets to save Earth from an energy crisis, or else had the title "Treasure Hunt," and involved imagining he or she was the captain of a ship seeking buried treasure. Some children also had personalized games that began with the child's name ("Best of luck in your journey, Commander Christy!") and sent the child off on the journey with his or her own personal favorite foods.

Children played these games three times at school over a 2-week period, for 30 minutes each time. A week later they were tested on their knowledge of the use of parentheses in arithmetic expressions as well as their knowledge of arithmetic operations in a different context. Their enjoyment of the game, their own assessment of their performance, and their desired level of challenge in future games were also assessed.

The results were clear. When interesting contexts had been provided, children showed better knowledge of how parentheses affect arithmetic operations and were better able to transfer that knowledge to non-computer contexts. Personalization augmented these effects. In addition, students' motivation was clearly influenced by the manipulation. Students in the context conditions were much more likely to opt for the computer playing its best game; they liked the game more; they were more willing to stay after school to play the game; they believed themselves to be better at the games; and they indicated they would seek a more challenging game later. Meaningful contexts clearly enhanced their educational experience.

Another example of how embedding school math material in an interesting context enhances learning stems from Vanderbilt University's "Jasper Project" and its forebears (Cognition and Technology Group at Vanderbilt, 2012). "The major idea [behind the Jasper project] has been to situate (anchor) learning in meaningful problem-solving environments that invite sustained inquiry about important academic topics" (p. 35). This was accomplished initially by presenting mathematics problems in popular movies, for example getting children to consider the weight of a gold object in the middle of *Raiders of the Lost Ark*. Later the researchers developed a series of movies about the adventures of a character named Jasper, again with academic problems embedded. In both cases, the movies supplemented the regular curriculum for some classrooms. Results from a nine-state study of the Jasper project indicated that children in the classes that embedded mathematics problems in interesting movies were better at complex problem solving than were children in conventional mathematics classes.

Very young children also benefit from being given meaningful contexts. Three-year-olds were asked to memorize lists of items, and for some children, those lists were presented as shopping lists needed to play store. The children remembered twice as many items on a shopping list when the context was one of playing store, as opposed to when they were simply told to remember a list (Istomina, 1975).

These are just a few among many studies showing that embedding learning in a meaningful context is associated with better learning, more interest, and greater embracing of challenges than embedding learning in the abstract contexts that school materials too often use. That education students even excel when examples are provided in medical terms suggests that having *any* concrete meaningful context raises learning to a level above that achieved in an abstract context, although personally relevant contexts are best of all.

The examples given so far have concerned supplying context by provision of a simple heading for what one is learning, and embedding the examples for what one is learning in contexts that are personally meaningful to the learners. Learning is also improved when the learners are merely familiar with the learning materials because they have seen them in other contexts. An extreme case of familiarity occurs with expertise. The next two sections describe how familiarity and expertise improve cognition more generally.

The Effect of Mere Familiarity on Thinking

When one is already familiar with something, it has meaning. Even mere familiarity with the tasks or objects one is learning about assists performance on cognitive tasks. In one classic demonstration of this, the researcher Helen Borke (1975) gave children Piaget's famous three-mountains task, in which children are asked to indicate what a doll in various locations in a diorama of three mountains would see. Children typically do not do well on this task until around age 8; prior to then, they often indicate that from every vantage point the doll will see whatever they themselves currently see.

Borke wondered if part of the problem was that the materials used—for example, a "policeman" doll and miniaturized mountains—were not familiar to some children. In her twist on Piaget's procedure, children were asked to judge what Grover from Sesame Street would see when he stopped his car along the road. Rather than views of three mountains, the elements in the views were small plastic animals, a lake with a sailboat, and a house. Surprisingly, even 3-year-olds demonstrated correct perspective-taking on about 80% of trials with these familiar objects, compared with about 40% correct on a parallel version she gave of Piaget's original three-mountains task.

Borke's study was done with children in Pittsburgh, Pennsylvania, but the familiarity effect has also been demonstrated with different types of tasks in a very different culture: Papua, New Guinea (Lancy & Strathern, 1981). There, village children were given sets of standard cognitive tests involving memory and classification. When the objects involved in those tests were familiar everyday items, such as shells frequently encountered in their daily life, children were better at solving class-inclusion problems, recalling items, and using optimal memory strategies (such as clustering items in recall) than when novel Western toys were used.

Just as what is interesting to adults is not always the same as what is interesting to children (noted in chapter 5), what adults think is familiar is not always familiar to children (Bjorklund & Thompson, 1983). In a study showing that it is children's, not adults,' familiar concepts that are associated with better learning, researchers had children and adults rate clothing and fruit items for how good an example each was of its category. The items children rated as most typical often did not match those rated as most typical by adults. Children in kindergarten and first and sixth grade were then asked to memorize items off both the adult and the child lists. Children recalled significantly more items from the children's lists of good exemplars than from the adults' lists. Summarizing these studies, the authors stated, "Children often demonstrate enhanced levels of recall when memory is assessed in tasks using materials that are meaningful and well known to *them*, in comparison to when more conventional materials (i.e., items which are more familiar to adults) are used" (p. 341, italics in original). Meaning is derived in part from familiarity. When children are free to choose, it seems likely that they choose what is sufficiently familiar to be meaningful to them.

The Influence of Expertise

Expertise entails deep familiarity, thus research on expertise provides more examples of the impact of prior knowledge for the assimilation of new knowledge (Chi & Ceci, 1987). As discussed in chapter 5, numerous studies have shown that having expertise in a domain is associated with different kinds of thinking about that domain. For example, if chess pieces are arranged in a way that reflects their possible placement in a real game of chess, then chess experts (both child and adult) recall the placement of pieces much better than do novice players. However, if the chess pieces are randomly placed on the board and do not reflect the organization of a real game, then chess experts are no better at recalling their placement than are chess novices (Chase & Simon, 1988). Expertise apparently confers knowledge structures that influence memory, but only when the information supplied conforms to those structures. When learning occurs in a context about which one is more expert, one can learn better. School curricula that clearly build new knowledge on old would result in superior learning, and yet schools change textbook programs frequently. This presents a challenge.

Not surprisingly, expertise in a domain also confers more complex reasoning in that domain. This was demonstrated in a study of low-IQ horse-racing aficionados (Ceci & Liker, 1986). Although all the participants attended races almost daily, indicating high interest, and all had low IQs (in the 80s; the population average is 100), some were judged as being more expert, as determined by their skill at computing odds (based on the amount of money people have bet on each horse). These experts also appeared to reason about racing at a higher level than the nonexperts. When asked to handicap races (to determine how much extra weight a horse should carry to equalize the chances of each horse winning), they used a complex multiplicative model. In contrast, those with less expertise used a simpler additive model. Expertise as determined by one aspect of a domain thus resulted in a different and more complex way of using information in another aspect, even when IQ levels were the same. A context in which one has expertise allows for superior cognitive functioning.

The importance of having a meaningful context for learning has been seen in several domains. In studies of school learning, even when participants were merely familiar with the objects involved in a task, they performed better on the task than when they were unfamiliar with the materials. Expertise is perhaps an extreme example of this. When participants were very familiar with and had achieved expertise in the domain, they used higher levels of reasoning. All this suggests that school material that is meaningfully situated, and in which new concepts are clearly built upon what is already known, results in greater learning. Unfortunately, when schools change curricula and textbooks from year to year, and texts from different areas are not integrated, the ease with which teachers can provide such integration is compromised.

WHY THE PROVISION OF MEANINGFUL CONTEXTS ASSISTS LEARNING

Operating in a meaningful, familiar context appears to improve cognitive functioning. Three possible reasons for the effect of prior knowledge and context on acquiring new knowledge are assimilation, processing, and motivation. Next, I discuss each of these concepts, following which I turn to how meaningful context is created in Montessori education.

Assimilation

Piaget borrowed the term "assimilation" from biology, where it refers to incorporating nutrients into the body, and applied the term to knowledge, referring to how a person absorbs new knowledge into their existing mental structures (Flavell, 1963). For example, a child learning about a new kind of animal will normally assimilate the knowledge to her concept of animals and will assume the new animal also breathes, moves on its own, and so on. The pair process of assimilation is accommodation, in which mental structures are altered in reaction to new information. These processes work in tandem, and all learning entails some of each. At points where the new animal differs from the child's generalized concept of animal, the child might change her animal concept (accommodate) to fit that new information.

The findings just reviewed can be interpreted as exemplifying Piaget's concept of assimilation. When new information can be interpreted in the context of other information, such as one's clothes-washing script, or familiar objects, or how chess boards might look, new information is more easily incorporated. This appears to be largely because the prior knowledge—the meaningful context—provides a structure into which the new information can be assimilated.

The literature on study skills gives prime examples of assimilation of new knowledge being improved when the cognitive structures into which that knowledge fits are set up in advance. Reviewing an outline of a chapter and/or reading chapter summaries prior to reading the chapter enhances learning and retention, as does reading with questions in mind (Anderson, 1990; Thomas & Robinson, 1972). Both reviewing outlines and coming up with questions presumably activate mental structures into which information can be assimilated.

Both techniques provide meaningful contexts for the learning, and thus can enhance learning. Without meaningful underlying structures, learners lack key anchors for new knowledge.

Processing

Having cognitive structures in place and/or activated prior to new information's being input to the system can reduce the processing load involved in incorporating new information. Familiarity effects across all these studies can also be viewed in this way: Such effects stem from the conservation of cognitive resources, because presumably fewer resources are needed to create and maintain a mental representation of objects with which one is already familiar. In neurological terms, one might say that if a set of synapses is already (to use Hebb's [1949] famous phrase) wired to fire together (as it is with familiar items), the energy needed to make those neurons fire as a set again should be less than the energy needed to make a new, previously ungrouped set of neurons fire together (Lillard & Erisir, 2011). With familiar items, more cognitive resources are available for other cognitive processes, such as keeping a memory trace active. Although not entirely distinct from an assimilation explanation, easier processing is another lens through which to view the benefits of meaningful contexts for learning.

Motivation

Another possible reason for why learning is enhanced when it is connected to something one already knows is motivation. In learning new information, one might be more motivated if the information is needed to fill gaps in one's existing knowledge, for example, than if one begins with no knowledge whatsoever.

Some of the studies just mentioned asked about motivation directly and found motivation effects for meaningful contexts. For example, in the "How the West Was One" computer math study, not only had the students in the context conditions learned more math, but they also took on greater levels of challenge, responded more positively to the game, rated their own ability on it more highly, and were even willing to stay after school to play the game. Clearly, having learned the information in an interesting context affected their motivation to engage in a learning activity. Children in the Jasper project also indicated increased motivation, in that they expressed more positive attitudes toward mathematics than did children in control classes. People are more motivated to learn when what they are learning is embedded in a meaningful context, and that motivation might explain the enhanced learning.

SUMMARY: RESEARCH ON CONTEXT EFFECTS

In conventional schools, teachers and textbooks too often fail to use meaningful contexts for imparting new information (Bransford et al., 1999). Meaningful contexts connect new knowledge to old knowledge, and/or make clear its applicability, or simply make the learning environment more rich, interesting, or fun. In the absence of meaningful contexts, children not only lack clear means of assimilating new information, they also might lack the motivation to learn it at all, and/or might expend more cognitive resources on the encoding process, resulting in fewer resources being available for other aspects of learning. Meaningful contexts can provide anchors for assimilation, reduce some of the processing load, and increase motivation for learning.

Montessori's Use of Meaningful Contexts in Learning

Here then is an essential principle of education: to teach details
is to bring confusion; to establish the relationship between
things is to bring knowledge.
— Maria Montessori *(1948a/1976, p. 94)*

Dr. Montessori was deeply concerned with making education meaningful to children, and this concern is reflected throughout the educational program she developed.

Montessori education supplies meaningful contexts for learning in many ways. First, new knowledge is incorporated with old knowledge in a manner that seems far more coherent than is typical of conventional schooling. Second, lessons and exercises are constructed so that students can see the meaning of what they learn. Stories are also used to provide meaningful contexts. Finally, the social context of learning in Montessori, discussed in chapter 7, might increase children's motivation to learn.

FITTING NEW KNOWLEDGE WITH OLD

In conventional school curricula, it is very difficult if not impossible for teachers to do a really good job of integrating new information with children's prior lessons. Different textbooks are used for each topic, and these are likely published by different publishing companies with no cross-consultation. Schools routinely change textbooks and curricular programs as new administrators are elected or appointed, and the new programs are rarely chosen with reference to what the students were taught previously. Teachers typically have children for only 1 year, and may not know what was covered the prior year, for any given child (especially if the child transferred from another school). As children advance through school, they are increasingly likely to have different teachers for different topics, and are often also tracked, placing children at different levels in different topics. Under these circumstances, it would be very difficult for a teacher to develop lessons that integrate information across the curricula for all the children in a class, and given the frequency with which new textbooks and curricula are adopted, a teacher who attempted to do so would be chasing a moving target.

Montessori education is distinguished by involving lessons and materials that were developed with the entire educational program from birth to 12 in mind. Dr. Montessori had a close hand in the development of this entire curriculum. She was a very intelligent person, with a gift for penetrating and communicating meaning and integrating information. That she knew so well all the elements of the curriculum across these ages lends Montessori education a remarkably high degree of rationality, coherence, and human relevance. The fixed set of lessons and materials also lends stability across authentic Montessori schools, so if a child's family moves, a child will find the same materials and lessons at the new school. The new teacher need only know where the child is in the sequences of lessons and materials. Although the pedagogical committee at the Association Montessori Internationale reviews and adjusts those lessons and materials when warranted, it does so from the vast and deep knowledge of the whole Montessori system represented on that committee.

An advantage resulting from having a single person develop the entire curriculum across topics and age span is that knowledge is connected, both

FIGURE 8.1 The Snake Game: Negative Numbers. © Laura Joyce-Hubbard, 2014. All rights reserved.

contemporaneously across the curriculum and historically over years of the child's life. Children can create mental structures from previously learned material into which new, carefully designed material can be assimilated (with timely accommodation of mental structures occurring as well).

For example, children learn the names of different shapes in the Geometry Cabinet in Primary, and go on to learn how to calculate the area of those shapes in Elementary. They learn to count, as well as "skip count" (count by twos, threes, and so on) and work with negative numbers in "the Snake Game" (Figure 8.1) in Primary using the Glass Beads (see also Figures 2.6 and 2.7), and they use those same materials to learn squaring and cubing in Elementary. The Fraction Insets (Figure 8.2) are used in Primary to make designs and to learn about equivalence, and in Elementary are used to learn about carrying out the four mathematical operations on fractions. In Primary, children learn about six major parts of plants, and in Elementary, they learn the varieties of each part and how features of those varieties facilitate adaptation to different environments. Children learn grammar symbols in the Function of the Word exercises in Primary, which are then used to assist their writing style in creating original compositions in Elementary (see Figure 6.1). Research suggests that the assimilation of new concepts is eased by such interconnections, which are possible because of the internal coherence of a curriculum that was developed for a wide range of ages by a single person over the course of 50 years.

FIGURE 8.2 The Fraction Insets. Photograph by An Vu.

There is coherence across the curriculum as well. For example, children consider the import of the part of speech "adjective" in conjunction with science experiments in which they discover which membranes are permeable and impermeable. Grammar and science are deliberately connected, and the child can see the use of a normally abstract set of concepts (grammar) in the hands-on context of understanding the world through science. When children make designs using Metal Insets, they are simultaneously working on artistic creativity and geometry. These connections are explicit and preconceived, not accidental as they would probably be in a conventional classroom situation where the person who developed the art curriculum might never have even spoken to the person who developed the math curriculum. Recall how water was introduced in the lesson described in chapter 5: Montessori lessons are designed to entwine knowledge, to help children see connections across curriculum areas and to the world outside the classroom. The Elementary child, Dr. Montessori noted, "is not satisfied with a mere collection of facts; he tries to discover their causes. It is necessary to make use of this psychological state, which permits the viewing of things in their entirety, and to let [the child] note that everything in the universe is interrelated" (1948a/1976, p. 36). The "psychological state" that Dr. Montessori claimed characterizes the Elementary child, an ability to connect disparate facts into an integrated whole, is not generally noted in discussions of middle childhood, and might be an interesting issue for further research. Existing research suggests that people of all ages learn better when what they are learning is interconnected, and even young children seek out explanations (Wellman, 2011) and find them rewarding (Alvarez & Booth, 2014).

MAKING MEANING CLEAR

A second way that Montessori education provides meaningful content is by the type of exercises children engage in. In Primary, for example, children can easily grasp the meaning of the Practical Life activities. When a child washes a table, the table becomes clean; when a child squeezes oranges, juice appears, and children in the class can drink it. As was described in chapter 2, these activities have many purposes besides engaging the children in meaningful activities, and the activities themselves can serve to impart abstract concepts. For example, Practical Life activities can impart that one's actions have a constructive purpose, that a series of steps should be executed in a specific order, that one can concentrate on tasks to their completion, and so on. Yet children need not see all that to understand the immediate meaning of the activity.

The material for teaching the Pythagorean theorem illustrates how context provided by Montessori materials renders an abstract formula meaningful (and also heightens interest, as was discussed in chapter 5). While most children learn in school that $a^2 + b^2 = c^2$, few have any basis on which to understand what that means. It is simply a formula one executes to get the result. The Montessori material to teach this formula shows children what it means, opening the door for them to ponder why it works (Figure 8.3). The

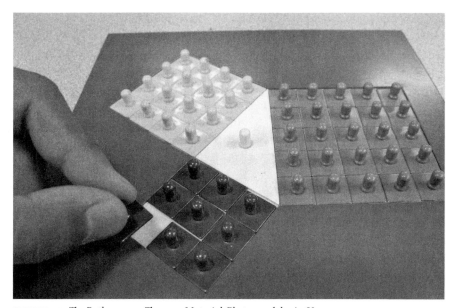

FIGURE 8.3 The Pythagorean Theorem Material. Photograph by An Vu.

material features a scalene triangle with a square extending outward from each side. The square on one side is divided into 9 small squares and thus is made of 3 × 3 units, or 3 squared. The square on the other side fits 16, or 4 × 4 units. The child is shown how by taking the 9 units from one side and the 16 units from the other, one can exactly fill the square that extends off the hypotenuse: 9 + 16 = 25, or 5^2. The child can thus truly see that $a^2 + b^2 = c^2$. The abstract formula is no longer simply an abstraction; it has been given meaning.

Another way to make purpose and meaning clear is to provide information at the point of need. Many have experienced how much steeper one's learning curve for a new language becomes when one enters a new country, and this is in part because suddenly one really needs to know the language. Montessori capitalizes on this by giving children new information at the point of need. Vocabulary learning is one example of this. In conventional schooling, vocabulary is often taught from lists of words, often in commercial workbooks; children need to look up definitions and use the words in sentences they might make up, or that might even be made up by the textbook developers, with the child's task being merely to insert the correct word. The words are disconnected from anything in the child's life except the workbook.

In Montessori, children learn new words in the presence of the real objects (or miniatures of them) they are learning about, grounding new vocabulary in situations the child is in. In learning the parts of plants, for example, Primary children examine a plant and make free drawings of the whole plant, and then, on separate pages, draw each of its parts. The separate parts are colored in to set them off, the name of the highlighted part is written on each page, and the pages are put together into a booklet. Primary children thus learn the words "stamen," pistil," and so on, in the context of a real plant and their own drawings of it. The vocabulary allows children to precisely describe objects in the classroom and the world. In Elementary, much new vocabulary comes across from writing reports, which constitute a large part of Montessori Elementary education (as opposed to an occasional exercise in most grade schools). A child writing about Antarctica might need to apply new terminology to describe different kinds of ice, for example. Children learn the words that they need to use in describing aspects of the world that interest them.

Montessori applies the same approach to teaching spelling. Rather than having a published spelling workbook, from which every child in the class learns the same words (the factory), Montessori children learn words they personally need to know, because they misspelled them in a report or other writing. Indeed, all the information children learn as part of writing reports, not just the spelling and vocabulary, but all the facts and relationships, are learned at the point of need. The purpose of learning a particular word or concept is clear: The word or concept is embedded in other learning experiences.

Stories as Contexts for Learning

The psychologist Jerome Bruner was a strong proponent of the view that "we organize our experience and our memory of human happenings mainly in the form of narrative—stories, excuses, myths, reasons for doing and not doing, and so on" (1991, p. 4). Humans by nature find meaning in narrative. The five Great Lessons in Elementary (introduced in chapter 5) and many of the Key Lessons that follow them are narratives, hence the core of the Elementary curriculum is given in a structure that people inherently find meaningful. Because the stories are told with attention to interconnections, they lend an interconnected organizational structure to the children's representation of the knowledge. When a Montessori teacher engages the child's imagination in stories, he or she connects the new information to the child's prior knowledge and to hands-on materials and demonstrations that go along with the stories. Recall that in the introduction to water, described in chapter 5, Dr. Montessori related water to such other elements as animals and mathematics. As in all good stories, the descriptions were given in concrete terms, for example, equating the mountains under the ocean with mountains above ground that children have seen, and describing the size of a school of fish in terms of how long it would take a boat to get around it. The human imagination resonates to such images. The story of the Rope Stretchers, mentioned in chapter 5, is another example of this: A historical tale is used (along with with presentation of the material shown in Figure 8.3) to get across that $a^2 + b^2 = c^2$. Children come to the geometric formula in the same way Pythagoras did (as the story goes), and the formula may take on added interest as one thinks of it in the real and practical context of people needing to redraw property lines after a flood. Images abound in Montessori lessons. For example, a lesson on the atmosphere's getting thinner at higher altitudes is given in terms of the air being in layers, like a pile of blankets. Closer to the earth's center are more, thicker blankets, and the blankets become fewer and thinner as one goes out. Children become fascinated by such images and are inspired to repeat the lesson on air and atmosphere again and again.

The lessons in Montessori Elementary are thus laden with images, often provided in stories that are connected to other parts of the curriculum and familiar concrete entities. Such contextualization would be expected to facilitate comprehension. The stories are of course intended to inspire children to study aspects of them, for example, to go on to do experiments about the three forms of water (solid, liquid, and gas), and the mathematical composition of water. Relating back to issues raised in chapters 5 and 6, this personally motivating engagement is surely also important. When teachers are trained in Montessori education, the training refers explicitly to creating context for children's learning, connecting ideas to what they know and helping children see the meaning. In conventional teacher training, this could be done in the abstract, but it could never be done with regard to specifics, because the teachers will go on to schools where they use different textbooks and have different information to teach. Montessori teacher training includes the specific lessons the teacher will be teaching, and ways to make the lessons meaningful to children. The Montessori lessons have been described as a gift that frees the teacher to focus on individual children and their needs. In conventional schools, in contrast, teachers spend a good deal of time making up their own lessons, then revising them when the academic program is changed.

THE SOCIAL ELEMENT: SHARING KNOWLEDGE WITH OTHERS

People are social creatures, and Elementary school children are especially so. The collaborative nature of learning in Montessori provides a context that might also facilitate learning by making it more personally meaningful to children. As was seen in chapter 7, when people think they will later be asked to impart information to others (in order to teach), they learn the information better, and this might be in part because the information now has connections beyond oneself. Children in the Jasper project described earlier were so motivated to write books to be shared with others that teachers made a rule (odd as it is): "No leaving recess early to go back to class to work on your book" (Bransford et al., 1999, p. 61). Montessori children know they might teach another child about a material, and that they might share with the class the knowledge they acquire in writing a report. Because Elementary children are usually working on reports with others, sharing also occurs in the context of discovering new knowledge. Children seem to like to share the knowledge they acquire, and knowing they will present material to others gives the learning an additional purpose.

Even within Montessori lessons, children's social nature is used to motivational advantage. One example of this is the lesson on Divergent and Convergent Lines (Figure 8.4). When learning these distinctions, children are given small paper dolls to place on the lines. The child can see that when angles are convergent, the people are walking toward each other, and that when angles are divergent, the people are walking away from each other. Even such small insertions of the social into geometry may make the abstract concept of divergent and convergent lines more meaningful, and more delightful, for children of these ages. Whether it improves learning would be interesting to test.

In sum, Montessori education may facilitate the acquisition of new knowledge in part by building it on old knowledge in a very coherent curriculum, by using materials and lessons with clear underlying purposes and connections to the abstract, and by the use of stories and social contexts. In all these

FIGURE 8.4 Divergent and Convergent Lines. Photograph by An Vu.

ways, new knowledge is connected to old knowledge and to the environment in Montessori education.

Knowledge Transfer

A second important issue regarding meaningful contexts is that of transfer, including transfer within topics in a classroom, across classrooms, and from the classroom to the world outside school. Knowledge acquired in any situation is most useful if it can be used in other situations. Montessori education facilitates transfer in two ways: a high degree of similarity across materials, and having children actually cross from school to external "real-world" contexts and back. In the following sections, I consider circumstances in which transfer fails and succeeds, including a case study of two very different schools in Great Britain, before discussing transfer in Montessori education.

FAILURE TO TRANSFER KNOWLEDGE

Failure to transfer from a particular school context to other contexts has been described as an

> almost universal phenomenon: Students who are capable of performing symbolic operations in a classroom context, demonstrating "mastery" of certain subject matter, often fail to map the results of the

> symbolic operations they have performed to the systems that have been described symbolically. That they fail to connect their formal symbol manipulation procedures with the "real-world" objects represented by the symbols constitutes a dramatic failure of instruction. (Schoenfeld, 1988, p. 150)

Mathematics classes that appear to be very well taught, with teachers carefully going over material and children apparently understanding the material and performing well on tests and homework, can be prime examples of this. Despite the pedagogy, students often fail to apply concepts outside the narrow context in which they were taught. One study of this involved teaching math to shopkeeper apprentices in Nepal. Although the apprentices performed well in class, their knowledge proved inflexible, in that they could not apply it to the real-life store context for which it was being learned (Beach, 1995).

In addition to classroom learning not being applied outside school, lack of transfer occurs even within school contexts. In one study, a teacher explained to students how to find the area of a parallelogram (Wertheimer, 1959). The students applied the formula to several problems, and were assigned 10 more problems for homework. The following day they did well on a quiz, so it appeared that the students had learned the lesson well. A researcher then presented a new parallelogram that was oriented differently than all the ones the teacher had used for examples. The children were at a loss; one said, "Teacher, we haven't had that yet." Although they applied the formula correctly for a set type of problem, they did not understand the formula well enough to flexibly apply it. This exemplifies the problem some have with a drill approach: Children can perform well yet lack understanding. Learning basic facts is important (Willingham, 2006), but learning that lacks understanding is inert, inapplicable to new situations.

One also sees cases of lack of transfer from real-world problems to school problems. In these cases, knowledge revealed in the context of use could not be applied to abstract representations of that same knowledge. American household shoppers are quite able to evaluate best buys in supermarkets, but are often unable to transfer these very skills to mathematically equivalent but abstract paper-and-pencil measures (Lave, 1988). Zinacatecan Mayan children had no trouble reconstructing weaving patterns with colored sticks in a wooden loom, but when the same sorts of problems were given to them using paper, the children appeared confused and were unable to reconstruct the patterns (Greenfield & Childs, 1977). Similarly, Brazilian street children showed mathematical abilities in their work as candy sellers on the streets that were not apparent when the children were asked to demonstrate these same abilities in school contexts (Carraher, Carraher, & Schliemann, 1985). The same has been shown with low-income children in the United States

(Taylor, 2009). School tests lack value when they fail to tap abilities children clearly show in the context of use.

SUCCESSFUL TRANSFER

There certainly are also cases of successful transfer, both from school to other contexts and from abstract to concrete stimuli. Features of stimuli associated with successful transfer are considered next. Following discussion of these features, I describe their implementation in Montessori.

Source and Target Similarity

Transfer is more likely to happen when the similarity between the source and target situation is more apparent (Singley & Anderson, 1987). In Judy DeLoache's studies of symbol understanding, mentioned in chapters 2 and 5, children are shown a full-sized room and a miniature model of that same room, and the similarities are pointed out (DeLoache, Kolstad, & Anderson, 1991). For example, there is a big couch in the big room, and a miniature version of it, in the same relative location and with the same slipcover, in the model room. There is a big table in the big room, and a miniature model of it, again in the same relative place in the model room. After pointing out the similarity across the two spaces, the experimenter shows the child a big Snoopy animal and a miniature model of it. In full view of the child, the little Snoopy is hidden in a place in the model, perhaps under a pillow on the miniature couch. The child is told, "Now I'm going to go hide big Snoopy in the exact same place in his big room. You wait here." The experimenter goes out of sight of the child and hides big Snoopy behind the big pillow on the big couch, returns, and reminds the child that big Snoopy is hidden in the same place in his big room as little Snoopy is in his little room. The child's task is to find the toy in the larger room, given information about the whereabouts of the toy in the model.

Children younger than 2½ tend to fail this problem, searching randomly for big Snoopy, apparently failing to understand the small space as a symbol for the larger one. There is a rapid period of transition at the end of the third year, however; by age 3, most children go immediately to the pillow and find big Snoopy. The relevant point here is that the surface similarity of the model to the target can make a big difference to children's competence. Performance declines, for example, if one changes the slipcovers on the furniture, or the shape of the table, making the similarity between the two spaces less obvious (see also Gentner & Toupin, 1986). Surface similarity assists children's ability to see relations between two spaces and to apply knowledge acquired in one space to another space. Research on familiarity and cognitive processing also suggests that surface similarity assists transfer. One can connect the new to what one already knows because one sees the similarity.

The effects of similarity on learning appear not only when the content is similar, but also when the context in which one learns is similar to the context in which one is tested. The effects of this are not always enormous, but they do appear to be real (Willingham, 2001), suggesting that when we learn information it binds with the context in which we learn it. A classic study showing this had divers learn list of words either underwater or on dry land (Godden & Baddeley, 1975). When later tested on the lists, those who studied in the same place in which they were tested remembered about 40% more words than those who switched contexts. In a more recent study, words were superimposed on videos; when the video was replayed at retrieval, memory for the words was much stronger (Smith & Manzano, 2010). Consistency across contexts improves people's ability to use information from one context in another one. Source and target similarity is therefore an important element in the transfer of knowledge from one situation to another one.

Similarity Across Curricular Materials

These same findings apply across the curriculum. When materials are more obviously similar, people are more likely to transfer learning. In conventional schools, such similarity is rare. Different textbook programs are used from year to year, and programs are changed frequently, so consistency in notations and symbols is not easily achieved. Consistency across disciplines is also not found. "At present, our various research specialties—science researchers, math researchers, literacy researchers, and so forth—reflect the structure of the academy rather than the structure of the school day. Classroom teachers who recognize the problem of fragmentation must either strive to connect subjects on their own or let the pieces fall where they may" (Wineburg & Grossman, 2001, p. 489).

Clear Application

Another condition under which transfer is more likely is when the relationship between the instruction and the application is made very clear. In the study of Nepali apprentice shopkeepers mentioned earlier, the shopkeepers themselves were also among the students. Whereas the apprentices did not transfer knowledge, the shopkeepers did (Beach, 1995). Their understanding of the math presented in the class was more flexible than was that of the apprentices, presumably because of their familiarity with the situations to which they needed to apply the knowledge. In the DeLoache model room studies as well, making clear to children the correspondence between the model and the room is crucial to success for children who do pass: When the relationship is not explicitly pointed out, 3-year-olds fail to use the model as a symbol for the larger room.

Another case of successful transfer when the application of information was made clear is a study involving the sexing of chickens (Biederman & Shiffrar,

1987). Determining the sex of day-old chickens is apparently a very difficult task that normally requires years of experience before one attains a high level of accuracy. However, awareness of a particular perceptual feature—a more concave or convex contour in a specific region of the genitalia—makes correct judgment quite likely. Some study participants unfamiliar with chicks were told about that feature, and others were not. Importantly, for those told about the feature, the context of its application was clear: They knew the feature was relevant to the sexing of chicks. The informed participants went on to sex chickens at the same level of proficiency as expert sexers, whereas those who were not told about the feature performed at chance on difficult-to-classify chickens. In sum, when the application of abstract information is made clear, transfer to the real context of use can occur.

Another classic example in which explicit verbal instruction successfully aided transfer of knowledge from one situation to another is found in studies examining children's accuracy in hitting underwater targets with darts (e.g., Hendrickson & Schroeder, 1941). In these studies, children first threw darts at an underwater target, establishing a baseline level of performance. Then half of the children were given a lesson in light refraction that was clearly applicable to the dart problem they had just encountered. The other half were not given this lesson. Following instruction, the depth of the target in the water was changed, and children's accuracy in hitting the target was again assessed. Those who had been given the light-refraction lesson were much more accurate in throwing the darts at the newly located target, relative to baseline performance, than were those without the information. Again, knowing an abstract rule assisted performance when the rule was given with particular and clear reference to its application.

Another study showing successful transfer when applicability was made clear involved telling college students a story problem and its solution, from which they had to abstract a rule and then apply that rule to a second story problem (Gick & Holyoak, 1980). First participants read about a military problem with its solution:

> A general wishes to capture a fortress located in the center of a country. There are many roads radiating outward from the fortress. All have been mined in such a way that while small groups of men can pass over the roads safely, a large force will detonate the mines. A full-scale direct attack is therefore impossible. The general's solution is to divide his army into small groups, send each group to the head of a different road, and have the groups converge simultaneously on the fortress.

After reading this, participants were asked to solve a medical problem:

> You are a doctor faced with a patient who has a malignant tumor in his stomach. It is impossible to operate on the patient, but unless the tumor

is destroyed, the patient will die. There is a kind of ray that may be used to destroy the tumor. If the rays reach the tumor all at once and with sufficiently high intensity, the tumor will be destroyed, but surrounding tissue may be damaged as well. At lower intensities the rays are harmless to healthy tissue, but they will not affect the tumor either. What type of procedure might be used to destroy the tumor with the rays, and at the same time avoid destroying the healthy tissue?

After reading these passages, very few college students were able to solve the second problem. However, when explicitly told to use the military problem information in solving the medical problem, 90% were able to solve it. Again, then, when the applicability of one situation to another one is made clear, people of all ages are more likely to be able to apply to one setting information gleaned in another setting. Before discussing how transfer is facilitated in Montessori education, I review an interesting case study of contextualized learning. Although case studies are limited with regard to the conclusions that can be drawn, this was a particularly in-depth study, offering food for thought about the conditions when transfer (and deep learning) are more or less likely to happen. As is discussed next, the research is being replicated in schools in the United States, with similar findings thus far.

Boaler's Case Studies of Contextualized Learning

The studies reported here demonstrate the importance of understanding how what one is doing connects to other aspects of one's life beyond the learning situation. The manner in which information is conventionally taught in school requires that teachers make a special effort to establish those connections; lectures and recitation of abstract rules alone do not suffice.

The education professor Jo Boaler's 3-year intensive study of two school programs in the United Kingdom is illustrative of how even apparently excellent conventional schooling can fail on this account (Boaler, 1997; for a more recent application, see Sullivan, Jorgensen, Boaler, & Lerman, 2013). The study also shows how successful nonconventional approaches can be in promoting transfer of new knowledge across contexts. The nonconventional approach described here included several elements that probably assisted learning, but the particular focus in this chapter is on how the manner in which the school operated probably made learning more meaningful and assisted the transfer of learning to new contexts.

Four mathematics classrooms in two schools, one conventional and one using contextualized methods, were the objects of study. The two schools were in similar neighborhoods and served mainly low-income students. Importantly, parents chose the schools because of their proximity to home, rather than because of the methods employed at each (one school was known to have more progressive methods generally, even prior to the new math curriculum). Before the study commenced, both schools had used the same mathematics curriculum, involving individual learning packets in Grades 7 and 8, and the performance of children at each school was equivalent on several different math tests at the start of the study.

Amber Hill, the conventional school, continued with this math program during the 3 years of the study, supplementing it with textbooks. Like their American counterparts (Stigler et al., 2000), the British Amber Hill teachers stood at the chalkboard and provided lecture and examples for the first half of each class, then set the children to work alone on several problems. Children were tested periodically, and grades were assigned. Children at the school were very well disciplined and worked hard, as did the teachers. Lessons were tightly structured and taught as self-contained units. The children believed math to be an important subject and were motivated to do well. Observing 10 lessons, each with about 20 students, Boaler noted that 100% of students were attending at the first 10 minutes, 99% halfway through, and 92% at 10 minutes prior to the end of lesson, which were excellent ratings of student attention. Amber Hill also strongly emphasized preparation for national tests.

In contrast, teaching at the other school, called Phoenix Park, was project based. The teacher set out a problem for the children to solve (or several for them to choose among), and then would step back and let them work at it for the next few weeks. For example, one problem was to consider what a shape could possibly be, given that its volume was 216. Children were then free to come up with ways to make the problem meaningful to themselves. Children could work individually or in groups, as they chose, and were free to work in the main classroom or a small adjoining room. Teachers went around to children and guided their learning on the problems. Although sometimes new techniques were presented when a problem was given, more often the teacher would present new techniques to small groups or individuals, as suited their particular approach to the problem. For example, in response to the volume 216 problem, some students might be fixed on the idea of rectangular solids; the teacher might show them the technique for finding factors of 216, which would lead the children to discover that particular rectangular solids could meet the criteria. Teachers assessed work with comments but not grades, and national tests were not emphasized except in 11th grade, when a conventional curriculum was incorporated specifically to prepare students for those tests. Mass testing encourages factory-style learning, because every child needs to learn the same information. The reduced emphasis on extrinsic reasons for learning prior to 11th grade at Phoenix Park might also have increased children's sense of meaning about the work.

The study lasted for 3 years, during which students were interviewed and assessed at multiple time points and in multiple ways. One important finding, reflecting a common problem with conventional schooling, was that the Amber Hill children performed well only on questions similar to those in their textbooks, and only shortly after studying the unit on which they were tested. They did not seem to know how to apply the learning from the classroom to problems that did not look exactly like the textbook problems, and even this they could do only during a brief period after having studied such problems. This deficiency was revealed in responses to the standardized and custom tests, as well as in interviews.

For example, one of Boaler's custom tests was to have students design a flat (i.e., apartment). Students had to designate the owners of the flat, decide what rooms they would need, and arrange the rooms, with respect to a few restrictions on such matters as the locations of windows and the numbers of doors between the kitchen and the bathroom. They then had to calculate approximately how much carpet they would need for the flat, and state whether an existing street door passed regulation (determined by calculating an angle). The projects were scored for making correct measurements, using scale appropriately, taking account of building regulations, and producing well-proportioned designs.

The Amber Hill children were enthusiastic about the project, but they received low marks. Their designs were rated as sketchy, inaccurate, and mundane. Their estimations of carpet were often inaccurate: Only 43% estimated correctly, despite 96% of the students having correctly calculated structurally similar problems in their mathematics textbooks. The students thus exemplified the transfer problem cited earlier: inability to apply classroom learning to new contexts.

Children from Phoenix Park, in contrast, demonstrated more flexible use of mathematics and were able to apply knowledge to situations they had not previously encountered. On the carpet estimation, 71% of the Phoenix Park students received the highest mark, whereas only 38% of Amber Hill students did. On flat designs, 61% of Phoenix Park students received the highest mark, in contrast to just 31% of Amber Hill students. Interestingly, many Phoenix Park students also gave themselves a more challenging task: 33% included unusual rooms such as bowling alleys in their designs, which only 3% of the Amber Hill students did.

Tests of long-term retention revealed similar positive results for the project-based school versus the conventional one. Following the teaching of a particular concept, a test was given on that concept immediately and again 6 months later. Overall long-term retention among Phoenix Park students was about twice that of the Amber Hill students.

On standardized state examinations, students from Amber Hill (who were supplied with calculators) performed somewhat better on purely procedural problems, but those from Phoenix Park outperformed students from Amber Hill on conceptual problems. Whenever a problem asked for deeper understanding, or for application to a new situation, the Phoenix Park children did well. The Amber Hill students had expressed in interviews a much stronger motivation to do well on the tests than was expressed by the Phoenix Park children, but on the aspects of those tests that involved transfer to new kinds of problems and conceptual understanding, they did not fare as well.

Phoenix Park students also saw math in very different ways. For example, they said that of all their school subjects, math was most similar to English and art, whereas Amber Hill students did not find math similar to anything. In addition, asked to describe the link between mathematics and "life," Phoenix Park students reported a close connection, whereas Amber Hill students felt an enormous disconnect. Amber Hill students reported that in their everyday math outside the classroom they used different mathematical strategies than they used inside the classroom.

Case studies can be interesting, but always should raise the concern that the results apply only to the particular circumstances of the subjects and circumstances involved, and that other aspects of the subjects and circumstances may even be responsible for the findings. Perhaps, for example, it was the move to a new curriculum rather than other aspects of the program at Phoenix Park that led to the differences. Or perhaps it was the manner in which the teachers at each school implemented the approaches, rather than the approaches themselves. To address such issues, Boaler and her colleagues followed up on this study in California high schools (Boaler & Staples, 2008). In this study as well, a reformed mathematics program greatly improved math achievement.

In addition to improved achievement relative to time on task, students in the integrated contextualized programs responded very differently than students in the conventional programs in terms of attitudes and beliefs concerning mathematics: They were significantly more interested in mathematics, saw math as more important to their future careers, saw math as more related to "things that happen in real life," saw math as involving thinking rather than memorization, were more motivated by intrinsic factors than grades, and tended to disagree with the statement, "I like mathematics when I do not have to work hard." The follow-up research therefore appears to demonstrate some of the general trends seen in Great Britain.

Although the Boaler studies are limited in the number of classrooms studied, they are extraordinarily rich in detail and methods of testing, and the results align with those of several laboratory studies. There are many possible reasons for enhanced performance, even as indicated by other chapters in this book. These include lack of emphasis on evaluation, collaborative work, and provision of choice and interest in the nonconventional classrooms studied. The more contextualized learning approach may well be one other reason. Taken together with other research presented in this chapter, the implication is that when connections between learning and application are made clear, learning and transfer are enhanced.

Transfer in Montessori Education

Transfer in Montessori education is facilitated in at least three ways. First, there is a great deal of surface similarity in materials. Second, Elementary children actively cross school and real-world contexts, literally going out of school to apply and gather information. Third, there is clear application of school knowledge to practical contexts, something best exemplified by the Adolescent Erdkinder program.

SURFACE SIMILARITY IN MONTESSORI MATERIALS

Montessori materials have both surface and deep structural similarities both within classrooms and across levels. The same materials are often used in presenting different lessons or concepts, making materials familiar and reducing the encoding demands of the child. Colors used to denote particular properties are also held constant, so for example units, tens, and hundreds are consistently colored green, blue, and red (respectively) across materials that highlight the decimal system. Vowels are consistently red in materials that highlight them, and consonants are blue. In parsing sentences, nouns are always black, articles are tan, adjectives are brown, verbs are red, and so on. As was described earlier, the same materials are used to present different concepts at different levels, so the Binomial Cube is a puzzle to put together in Primary and the conveyer of the binomial theorem in Elementary. More advanced materials also build on less advanced ones, so the Trinomial Cube is very similar to the Binomial one, only more complex. The high degree of similarity across Montessori materials might facilitate children's learning by making old information more easily accessible and transferable when learning new information.

TRANSFER BETWEEN MONTESSORI CLASSROOM
AND THE WORLD OUTSIDE: GOING OUT

Let us take the child out to show him real things instead of
making objects which represent ideas and closing them in cupboards.
      — Maria Montessori *(1948a/1976, p. 34)*

The outing whose aim is neither purely ... [health] nor
[a practical need], but that which makes an experience live,
will make the child conscious of realities.
      — Maria Montessori *(1948a/1976, p. 26)*

Transfer from school to world (and back) is probably facilitated by the frequency with which Montessori children leave the classroom to study in the world, as was described in chapter 2. Primary children might occasionally go for walks to find plant or animal specimens, and venturing into the world becomes very common in Elementary, formalized in the Going Out program. A child or small group of children arranges to leave the classroom to learn more about a topic they have been studying in the classroom. For example, a small group of children studying weather might make arrangements to visit a weather forecasting center, where the application of the knowledge is obvious.

The teacher's task is to help children prepare themselves for the trip: Help them to figure out where to go, help them make the practical arrangements, help them know what they need to bring, help them figure out how to learn from the experience (e.g., by having interview questions prepared), and so on. It is vital that all this be facilitated rather than done for the children, because learning to operate in the real world is an explicit goal of Montessori. "Let the teacher not lose sight of the fact that the goal sought is not the immediate one—not the hike—but rather to make the [child whom] she is educating capable of finding his way by himself" (Montessori, 1948a/1976, p. 26). Like the adage, Montessori teachers are to teach children to fish, not give them fish outright.

Even the mechanics of the Going Out program exemplify meaningful contexts for learning. When children have to calculate how much money they will need for a Going Out trip involving a bus ride, museum tickets, and lunch, the application of mathematics to real-life problems is obvious. When they have to call a parent and politely request the parent take them on a Going Out trip, the importance of Grace and Courtesy becomes clear. Young Elementary children rehearse courteous calling with the teacher.

The Elementary Going Out program removes the usual walls that exist between school and the outside world. Unlike a conventional school field trip, Going Out trips emerge from the children's current personal interests. The children know exactly why they are going out—they even set up the trips—and the application to what they are doing in school is therefore clear. Dr. Montessori saw these trips as crucial to children's development. "A child enclosed within limits however vast [like the walls of the school] remains incapable of realizing his full value and will not succeed in adapting himself to the outer world. For [the child] to progress rapidly, his practical and social lives must be intimately blended with his cultural environment" (Montessori, 1948a/1976, p. 26).

ERDKINDER: "THE LAND CHILDREN"

Transfer of learning from Montessori class to world is also exemplified in the culmination of Montessori schooling, the adolescent program, which Dr. Montessori called the Erdkinder. Presaging the sentiments of many researchers of adolescence today, she wrote that "schools … are adapted neither to the needs of adolescence nor to the times in which we live" (1948a/ 1976, p. 97). Dr. Montessori's ideas for adolescent programs were not as fully specified as her plan for younger children, but the basic idea she was developing near the end of her life was to bring adolescents to a protected yet very real-world context, a farm (Montessori, 1948a/1976). David Kahn, founder of the North American Montessori Teachers' Association and a person with deep and broad understanding of Montessori education, has developed Montessori programs and curricula for children ages 12 to 18. These have been implemented at the Ohio Hershey Montessori Farm School (ages 12–15) and Montessori High School at University Circle in Cleveland, and now at many other places as Adolescent level teachers are trained and proliferate.

Dr. Montessori noted adolescence to be a time of tremendous physical change, and in her framework of four 6-year planes of development, the second two planes parallel the first two. From 0 to 6 the infant is forming into the child, and from 6 to 12 this person consolidates; then from 12 to 18 the child is forming into the adult, and from 18 to 24 this person consolidates. Thus the young teen, in her conceptualization, shares many characteristics with the 2-year-old, and is in a time of great change. Furthermore, having attended Montessori schools until age 12, a child will have already acquired, according to Dr. Montessori, all the knowledge normally acquired in a regular school curriculum working through high school, an assertion presumably made based on the then-typical high school curricula of the countries she lived in (1948b/1967, p. 1). This might not be the case today, and academic learning does continue (alongside practical application of learning) in the adolescent programs.

Adolescence, according to Dr. Montessori, is characterized by difficulty concentrating, "a state of expectation, a tendency toward creative work and a need for the strengthening of self-confidence" (1948a/1976, p. 101). To assist with this confidence, she believed adolescents needed to be in a situation where they could begin to "earn money by their own work" (1948a/1976, p. 103).

Considering that the child has a unique combination of vulnerability and knowledge in adolescence, what Dr. Montessori prescribed was practical application of knowledge in an environment with closer adult supervision than was had in the previous stage. An ideal environment, she proposed, would be a farm in the country, which the children would run, applying the knowledge they had learned in prior years. In the years in which children often seem at a loss trying to see how they might fit into the adult world, Montessori education provides a way to do so. The application of one's knowledge to the problems one faces in running a farm—building barns, growing vegetables, breeding pigs, selling eggs, and so on—is perfectly clear. She also mentioned that the farm school might include a hotel, which the children would run. The school could also establish a store in a nearby town, selling produce from the farm. The children would live together on the farm, establishing a social community. In all these endeavors they would apply their school learning to real-world contexts as part of their continuing education. As mentioned, Dr. Montessori's ideas and variations on them are being implemented in several adolescent programs in the United States, with a particularly close rendition being the Hershey Montessori Farm School near Cleveland, Ohio. The Erdkinder is yet another illustration of how Montessori education attempts to break down the barriers that typically separate school from "real life" contexts. In the years since publication of the first edition of this book, many more Montessori adolescent programs, including public and private Montessori high schools, have been established.

Chapter Summary

We discovered that education is not something which the teacher does, but that it is a natural process which develops spontaneously in the human being. It is not acquired by listening to words, but by virtue of experiences in which the child acts on his environment. The teacher's task is not to talk, but to prepare and arrange a series of motives for cultural activity in a special environment made for the child.

— Maria Montessori *(1967a/1995, p. 8)*

Several theorists have underscored the importance of contextualizing learning by embedding lessons in the real-world situation in which the learning will be used, a concept sometimes referred to as "situated cognition." "If we value students' learning to participate in practices of inquiry and sense-making, we need to arrange learning practices of inquiry and sense-making for them to participate in" (Greeno, 1998, p. 14). One of Mark Lepper and Jennifer Henderlong's (2000, p. 290) three prescriptions for improving motivation in schools is to "promote children's sense of curiosity by placing learning in meaningful and exciting contexts that illustrate its inherent utility and would capitalize on students' prior interests," and an influential paper on situated cognition stated that educational approaches "that embed learning in activity and make deliberate use of the social and physical context are more in line with the understanding of learning and cognition that are emerging from research" (Brown et al., 1989, p. 32). Many reform efforts, perhaps most notably those of the National Council of Teachers of Mathematics (1989), suggest programs aimed at contextualizing learning, and there is evidence suggesting that the implementation of those reforms is associated with increases in student learning (Stipek et al., 1998; but see Shouse, 2001).

Situated cognition is sometimes taken in its extreme form to suggest that all abstract learning is useless and that information is never transferable from school settings. That clearly is not the case. What the evidence does support is that meaningful contexts assist learning by providing frameworks and motivation for the acquisition of new knowledge. Conventional schooling can fail to provide such contexts, although there surely is considerable variability from teacher to teacher. Montessori education embeds meaningful context in its methods such that less variability across teachers may be evident.

In sum, Montessori education was developed with an eye to making what happens in the classroom meaningful and transferable. Future research could examine the extent to which the programs are successful in these aims. Teachers of course are very important in helping children make connections and see how what they are learning is meaningful. The next chapter addresses adult behaviors and their association with different child development outcomes.

9 }

Adult Interaction Styles and Child Outcomes

> It is true that the child develops in his environment through
> activity itself, but he needs material means, guidance and an
> indispensable understanding. It is the adult who provides these
> necessities. . . . If [the adult] does less than is necessary, the child
> cannot act meaningfully, and if he does more than is necessary,
> he imposes himself upon the child, extinguishing [the child's]
> creative impulses.
>
> — Maria Montessori *(1956, p. 154)*

Texts for conventional teachers from the early 1900s are not particularly specific about how teachers should behave toward children. Proponents of the factory model repeatedly refer to the teacher as a worker, on a par with a factory employee, who is expected to mechanically perform the function of running efficient classrooms that will enable children to pass exams at minimal expense to the taxpayers. Efficiency was key, and the instructions as to how to run the classroom were provided by the school administrator.

Behaviorist approaches, notably that of Thorndike, specified that the teacher's role was to establish useful bonds in the child's mind and eliminate useless and negative ones. Being businesslike was important in this approach as well; such concepts as "emotional warmth" are virtually absent from behaviorist discourse (for a rare mention, see Thorndike, 1906/1962, p. 63). Thorndike's recommendation for how a teacher should give instructions, for example, was to say, "Do the work on this page. Do it again, keeping track of how many minutes you spend. Practice again until you can get all the answers right in 12 minutes" (Thorndike, 1921a, p. 17). The recommended communication was simple, direct, and dry. Beyond a few such mentions, the literature reflecting the factory and empty-vessel models is not particularly detailed regarding how teachers should behave toward children.

In contrast, Dr. Montessori was very specific about how teachers should behave with children, and her recommendations align very closely with the behaviors that recent psychology and education research shows are associated with better child outcomes. The research to be considered here concerns secure attachment between children and their caregivers, authoritative parenting, self theories, and classroom management. After each section in this chapter, I discuss Dr. Montessori's convergent recommendations to teachers, and at the end I discuss the role of the teacher in Montessori education and Dr. Montessori's approach to teacher training.

Before proceeding, a caveat about the issue psychologists refer to as "direction of effects" is needed. Up to this point in the book, much of the research has been experimental, involving a group given some sort of treatment and a control group without it. With experiments, one can confidently say that the treatment caused the effect. Research on parenting, however, is rarely experimental, as few parents would acquiesce to having their parenting behaviors determined by random assignment to a control or treatment condition. Therefore the research is more often naturalistic and correlational, examining what adult and child behaviors go together. The problem with this kind of research is that one cannot always tell what the direction of effects is (did the parent create those behaviors in the child, or did the child bring those behaviors out of the parent?), or even whether some third variable (such as genes) is responsible for the association of particular behaviors in a parent and child. Some studies are experimental, and thus do allow such inferences. With other studies, it is often reasonable to suppose the adult behaviors led to the child outcomes, although the alternate possibilities must be borne in mind. This issue pertains to a good deal of the research presented in chapter 10 on order as well. However epigenetic research also points out the complexity of these nature–nurture relationships, as described in the following discussion.

Attachment

One literature on optimal adult interaction with children concerns "attachment": the bond that forms between infants and their primary caregivers. Particular styles of adult interaction are associated with particular types of attachment, and styles of attachment in turn predict a good deal about children's developmental outcomes. Dr. Montessori's recommendations about how teachers should respond to children mirrors the interaction style associated with the most optimal attachment pattern, secure attachment.

The construct of attachment was first discussed by the British ethnologist and psychoanalyst John Bowlby (1969) as an explanation for the failure of many babies to thrive in European orphanages following World War II: They lacked a close relationship with an adult. According to attachment theory, children need a close adult who will function as a secure base from which to explore the world, and who will be a safe haven to which to retreat in times of stress. Children raised in Romanian orphanages under the Ceaușescu regime are a more recent example of the devastating effects that result from the lack of such relationships early in life (Fox et al., 2014). The psychologist Mary Ainsworth (1967), Bowlby's colleague, moved the attachment construct from the theoretical to the empirical realm by establishing a method to assess attachment. Her method has been very important to our understanding of child development because it allows us to make reliable long-term predictions of child outcomes.

THE STRANGE SITUATION

The paradigm Ainsworth devised to measure attachment is called the Strange Situation (Solomon & George, 2015). The infant, usually between ages 12 and 18 months (the test may not be valid outside that age range, but other tests have been developed for older children), is brought into a room full of toys with his or her mother or other attachment figure. (Young children can have more than one attachment relationship.) Over the next 15 or 20 minutes, the mother and a stranger come and go in a series of prearranged episodes. At one point the child is alone with the toys, then the door opens and in walks not the mother but the stranger. This is often very upsetting to the child, who usually already appeared stressed over being left alone. A moment later the mother returns. The behavior of the child during this reunion is particularly diagnostic for attachment classification.

Different patterns of child behavior characterize different attachment styles (Weinfield, Sroufe, Egeland, & Carlson, 2008). The most common pattern in American babies, termed *secure attachment*, is characterized by a child seeming unambiguously glad to see the mother, and seeking and obtaining comfort from her. Approximately 70% of American babies respond in this way at 12 to 18 months, and they tend to develop most positively in the years to come, as will be described next.[1] But some babies appear to avoid the mother. They do not look her in the eye, and they seem determined to try to be independent. Other babies approach the mother, but then push her away. These latter two patterns are characteristic of insecure attachment relationships, and children who display these forms of attachment fare less well over time.

OUTCOMES OF DIFFERENT ATTACHMENT STYLES

As stated, long-term outcome studies favor the secure attachment style. For example, in one study children whose attachment status had been classified when they were infants returned to the laboratory at age 2 to engage in

---

[1] Attachment patterns and associated outcomes are different in some cultures, probably because the Strange Situation itself holds different meaning under different childrearing conditions. The discussion here concerns research with American samples.

some problem-solving tasks with their mothers. Children previously rated as securely attached were more competent problem solvers, were more persistent, showed more enthusiasm, and were also more compliant with their mothers (Matas, Arend, & Sroufe, 1978).

Another study had children return to the laboratory as 3-year-olds to engage in a competitive game with a stranger (Luetkenhaus, Grossmann, & Grossmann, 1985). Children who at 12 months had been classified as securely attached interacted more smoothly with the stranger than children previously classified as insecurely attached. When children were told they were not doing well in the game, securely attached children upped their efforts, whereas insecurely attached children decreased their efforts. After failing, securely attached children displayed sadness more openly, which child psychologists regard positively; "internalizing" or not showing one's feelings is associated with such later problems as childhood depression.

Another study examined children's attachment status in infancy and their behavior in summer camp at ages 9 to 11 (Urban, Carlson, Egeland, & Sroufe, 1991). Children with insecure attachment histories were more likely to be rated as dependent on adults at camp. They formed fewer friendships and were less socially competent as well.

Other studies have shown that even as they enter adulthood, people who were classified as securely attached infants have more friends, engage more actively with their peers, explore more, have higher self-esteem, have more positive romantic relationships, and show more positive emotion than do adults with insecure attachment histories (Roisman, Booth-LaForce, Cauffman, Spieker, & NICHD Early Child Care Research Network, 2009; Thompson, 1999; Weinfield et al., 2008). This is only a small sampling of an abundant literature showing that secure attachment in infancy predicts positive developmental outcomes. The traditional explanation for these effects is cognitive: Young child form internal working models of their most important relationships, which then influences a host of other outcomes (Sherman, Rice, & Cassidy, 2015). Yet a different possibility is that the initial relationships influence biological development in ways that then cascade through different developmental outcomes.

EPIGENETIC MECHANISMS

Fascinating animal studies shed light on a biological mechanism that might underlie how attachment security influences later outcomes. Michael Meaney and his colleagues had noticed that rats who had been handled in the laboratory early in life were calmer than rats that had not been handled, and they wondered why. Through intensive observation and a series of experiments, they discovered that handling of pups induced intensive licking and grooming of pups by rat mothers once the pups were returned to the cage. To insure that this activity caused the effect, they simulated it by brushing some pups with paintbrushes; sure enough, later in life those rats were calmer. The timing for the brushing was very specific: 9 to 18 postnatal days (Zhang & Meaney, 2010).

In further research they discovered the mechanism by which the stroking influences later personality. Rats, like other mammals, release corticosteroids when they are stressed. A healthy stress response is to release the corticosteroids but then return to baseline quickly as the stressor recedes. Less healthy individuals are less effective at returning to baseline levels. Cortisol suppression is controlled by a specific gene, but for genes to express themselves, they must be demethylated: A methyl group on the gene must be removed, uncovering the gene and allowing its transcription. Meaney and his colleagues discovered that the licking and grooming behaviors actually cause this demethylation. Rat pups who are licked and groomed less during a specific developmental period therefore have less apt stress responses throughout their lives, because of the effect on their gene expression. Nurture therefore influences nature. And the influences extend beyond stress responses: Rats who are licked and groomed more during this period also function better cognitively (Bagot et al., 2009). Similar mechanisms could explain the relations between child development, sensitive parenting, and attachment (Meaney, 2010). Research on human epigenetics is in the early stages, but results are promising (for review, see Moore, 2015, chapter 12).

ATTACHMENT BEYOND INFANCY

The secure attachment construct has also been extended beyond its roots in infancy and applied to people's representations of intimate relationships throughout the lifespan. The attachment Q-sort was developed to measure attachment security in the preschool and school years (Waters & Deane, 1985). For this measure, the child's teacher or some other trained observer sorts preselected statements concerning a child's possible profile into piles indicating whether the statements are more or less characteristic of the child. The statements are about such issues as how the child responds to fearful situations, the child's predominant mood, and how often the child seeks proximity and comfort. Sort patterns are used to place children into the different attachment style categories, and these categories correspond closely with attachment classifications from the Strange Situation months or years earlier, and predict a similar range of developmental outcomes.

A measure used to assess attachment in adults is the Adult Attachment Interview, in which people are asked to describe their relationship with their parents (Bakermans-Kranenburg & van Ijzendoorn, 1993; Hesse, 1999). Responses on this interview are related to the interaction style of one's current relationships (Treboux, Crowell, & Waters, 2004), to parenting behaviors

(Adam, Gunnar, & Tanaka, 2004), and to one's attachment classification as an infant. In one study with people who were tested in the Strange Situation as infants and as adults, 72% had the same attachment styles at both time points (Waters, Merrick, Treboux, Crowell, & Albersheim, 2000). Thus, attachment is an enduring construct, applicable even beyond infancy.

ANTECEDENTS OF SECURE ATTACHMENT

Given the importance of the construct to predicting later competence and well-being, a pertinent question is what leads a child to have a particular type of relationship with a caregiver. Bowlby (1969) and Ainsworth (Ainsworth, Blehar, Waters, & Wall, 1978) believed that an important antecedent factor in attachment style was adult sensitivity, and research has borne out that possibility (De Wolff & van Ijzendoorn, 1997). The following discussion refers to *maternal* sensitivity because that was Ainsworth's main concern, but the constructs apply to other close caregivers as well. Of course, important attachment relationships also develop with fathers (Grossmann et al., 2002), and with day-care providers and teachers. Children growing up on Israeli kibbutzim become attached to their caregivers, and the quality of those relationships also predicts children's outcomes (Oppenheim, Sagi, & Lamb, 1988). Although not specifically using attachment constructs, Hamre and Pianta (2001) showed that American children's relationships with their kindergarten teachers are related to their academic and behavioral outcomes through eighth grade. In fact, a positive teacher relationship can even ameliorate negative outcomes of an insecure attachment to the mother (Buyse, Verschueren, & Doumen, 2011). Thus, although the vast majority of the research on attachment concerns attachment to mothers, the same principles appear to apply to young children's other important relationships.

Ainsworth's Sensitivity Concept

Ainsworth (1969) analyzed maternal sensitivity as having four components: *awareness* of the infant's signals, accurate *interpretation* of those signals, delivering an *appropriate* response, and doing so *promptly*. As will be seen, these components correspond closely with Dr. Montessori's ideas about teachers.

Awareness requires that the mother be proximate to the infant so that she can perceive the infant's signals. This aspect of attachment theory led to a concern beginning in the 1970s about whether babies placed in day care could become attached to their mothers. After many years of controversy, the National Study of Early Child Care, involving a representative sample of more than 1,000 American children in a variety of day-care arrangements, showed that day care in infancy in and of itself has no significant effect on child–mother attachment relations (NICHD Early Child

Care Research Network, 1997). The mother's awareness of and response to the child's signals when they are together is what matters. One might revise Ainsworth's criteria for awareness, then, to read that the adult must be proximate to the infant for some reasonable amount of time (full-time employment allows enough other time), and when proximate, must be able to perceive the infant's signals. A second aspect of awareness, besides proximity, is having a low perceiving threshold. The adult must notice the child's signals.

The second major aspect of sensitivity for Ainsworth is accurate interpretation. Adults must interpret the infants' signals for what they are, rather than distorting the signals in some way. Distortions could be caused by adults projecting their own needs on the infant, denying the infant's needs because of their own needs, or any other biasing to accord with the adult's own wishes and needs. Ainsworth noted that to overcome such proclivities, the adult must have self-insight.

A second feature necessary to accurate interpretation, according to Ainsworth, is empathy. Adults who lack empathy, she said, would have detached, intellectual relations with babies instead of warm, sensitive ones. "A mother might be quite aware of and understand accurately the baby's behavior and the circumstances leading to her baby's distress or demands, but because she is unable to empathize with him—unable to see things from the baby's point to view—she may tease him back into good humor, mock him, laugh at him, or just ignore him" (Ainsworth, 1969, p. 2). Lack of empathy thus leads to inappropriate response.

Even correctly interpreted signals can be followed by inappropriate responses. The third main feature of sensitivity for Ainsworth is that the response to the perceived and accurately interpreted signal be an appropriate one. Ainsworth noted that in the first year, the appropriate response to the infant is almost always what the child "asks" for via his or her signals: Pick the child up when the signal indicates a desire to be held, feed the child when the signal indicates hunger, and so on. After the first year, Ainsworth noted that doing exactly as the infant asks is no longer always the best response. As they get older, children increasingly need to adapt to the world, rather than always expecting the world to adapt to them. Conversely, children also need to feel some sense of control or efficacy, as suggested by the research presented in chapter 3. Ainsworth advised that the best response after age 1 is a compromise response that keeps the child's long-range interests at heart.

The final feature of sensitivity concerns timing of the response. Ainsworth noted that responses must be prompt to be effective. Adults who were devoted to a rigid feed or sleep schedule would be insensitive on this point. Responses need to be timed closely after the infant's calls for attention for the infant to experience the efficacy of his or her actions.

Findings on Sensitivity and Attachment

Ainsworth's original study of 23 mother–child pairs found a remarkably strong relationship between maternal sensitivity and child attachment classification (Ainsworth et al., 1978). A recent meta-analysis of this relation shows that (in statistical terms) a child's chances of being securely attached move from 38% if a mother is not sensitive to 62% if the mother is sensitive (De Wolff & van Ijzendoorn, 1997).

The issue of direction of effects naturally arises here. Perhaps the reason some mothers respond sensitively has to do with characteristics of the infant, and those infant characteristics lead to the later positive outcomes. In this view, the mother has no direct bearing on the child's later outcomes. The obvious infant characteristic to consider is the child's personality (or temperament), and studies have been done examining the relationship between child personality and attachment security (Vaughn & Bost, 1999). One conclusion from these studies is that although personality predicts some aspects of behavior in the Strange Situation, it does not predict reunion behaviors, which are the most diagnostic of relationship quality.

One could still argue, however, that some aspect of the child is responsible for attachment classification. Experimental designs can address this, and several intervention studies have been conducted, in which mothers were trained to respond more sensitively to their infants. A recent meta-analysis of 88 intervention studies showed that short, focused interventions on maternal sensitivity were effective both in making parents respond more sensitively to their infants and in changing infant attachment status (Bakermans-Kranenburg, van Ijzendoorn, & Juffer, 2003). Such work strongly suggests that maternal sensitivity causes attachment classification. Web-based teacher training programs also suggest that teachers can be trained to foster better relationships with children in their classrooms (Pianta, Mashburn, Downer, Hamre, & Justice, 2008).

Maternal Sensitivity Beyond Infancy

Ainsworth's rating scales were designed for observation of mothers with their infants. But a mother's interaction style with a child evolves over time. Other research has looked at how parents of securely attached infants behave toward them somewhat later, as toddlers and preschoolers. Mothers whose children were insecurely attached as infants interact more intrusively with them in first and second grades (Egeland, Pianta, & O'Brien, 1993). They are also more directive, meaning more apt to tell their children exactly what to do. In contrast, parents of securely attached children tend to instead make suggestions, helping children to figure things out for themselves (Fagot, Gauvain, & Kavanagh, 1996; Frankel & Bates, 1990; Matas et al., 1978; Moss, 1992). They are closely involved, but nonintrusive. In Bruner's (1975) terms, echoing Vygotsky, parents of securely attached children provide ideal scaffolds for children, structuring the environment such that children can internalize problem-solving strategies (see also Gauvain, 2001), whereas parents of insecurely attached children are more directive. (Readers may recall the discussion of guided play in chapter 6.) Secure attachment styles in infancy are associated with parenting styles that evolve in positive ways as children get older.

SUMMARY: RESEARCH ON ATTACHMENT

The attachment literature suggests that certain adult behaviors lead to secure attachment, which leads to the best child outcomes. Other literature suggests the same findings hold true for teachers as well. The particular behavior that seems most important is sensitivity to the child's signals, including proper interpretation of those signals and prompt contingent responses to them. Conversely, children do not fare well when adults either ignore them or are overly directive and interfering.

Warmth and Sensitivity as Characteristics of Montessori Teachers

A teacher . . . [must be] ready to be there whenever she is called
in order to attest to her love and confidence. To be always
there—that is the point.
       — Maria Montessori *(1956, p. 76)*

Dr. Montessori advised that teachers show a degree of warmth and sensitivity that is reminiscent of the characteristics of parents whose children are securely attached. The focal period for forming attachment relationships (12 to 18 months) is usually prior to the age of entry into a Montessori classroom. Yet there is nothing to indicate that the adult behaviors associated with particular attachment styles cease to matter, and indeed those behaviors are consistent with literature suggesting optimal parenting practices for older children as well. As children get older, they still appear to need a safe haven and a secure base; they simply need it less often and feel comfortable venturing farther away.

   Dr. Montessori saw the task of childhood as becoming independent, and the role of the adult as assisting children toward that independence. As is indicated in the section opening quote, Dr. Montessori maintained the teacher should serve as a safe haven whenever the child needs that. Yet when the child is ready to explore, the Montessori teacher was advised to be sensitive to the child's need for increased independence, heeding the child's call to " 'Help me to do it alone!' " (Montessori, 1948a/1976, p. 103).

   To determine when a child needs a secure base, the Montessori teacher was advised to be very attentive to the children, with the observational acuity of a well-trained scientist. Indeed, Dr. Montessori (1917/1965) said, "The fundamental quality [teachers must possess was] a capacity for observation" (p. 130). Like the sensitive parents described by Ainsworth (1969), teachers' thresholds for perceiving signals should be low. They should be trained to notice and correctly interpret the behavioral manifestations of the child's inner state, in order to know what to do next. As is discussed later in the chapter with regard to teacher training, Dr. Montessori also advised teachers to develop self-understanding, so they do not misinterpret children's signals in ways that align with their own needs.

When children are concentrating on work, Dr. Montessori held that they should be left alone, because during such moments, she believed, they are developing themselves. In chapter 4, I discussed the idea that concentration might be an engine of self-regulation, which is associated with many positive personality variables. Because Dr. Montessori saw concentration as the driver of self-development, she called on teachers to watch for and protect children's concentration. For example, Dr. Montessori described an incident in which a child who had thus far been disorderly in school one day began to rearrange the furniture, with an expression of intense interest. The teacher was inclined to stop him, but Dr. Montessori saw his activity as coordinated toward a useful end and manifesting that child's first moments of concentration on purposeful activity in the classroom.

The Montessori teacher must also be sensitive to when the child is ready for something new, because "the brain always asks for work which becomes more complex" (Montessori, 1989, p. 89). After great concentration a child may need to rest or simply observe others (Montessori, 1989, p. 19), but at a certain point the child will be ready for more complex work, and the teacher must be attuned to such moments and give the child new work. Further, like parents of securely attached children in problem-solving situations, the Montessori teacher must structure the environment in such a way that children can make discoveries on their own. A directive teaching style, in contrast, is associated with insecure attachment relationships.

As noted earlier, parents of insecurely attached children behave in two opposing ways. Parents of insecure-resistantly attached children interfere with the child, failing to give the child sufficient independence; parents of insecure-avoidantly attached children push independence too strongly, failing to provide a secure base when the child needs one. Dr. Montessori appears to have explicitly advised against both of these errors well in advance of the research on attachment: "We must never force our caresses on him, greatly as we may be attracted by his fascinating graces; nor must we ever repel his outbursts of affection, even when we are not disposed to receive them, but must respond with sincere and delicate devotion" (1917/1965, p. 332).

Coincident with the long-range impact of various attachment styles, Dr. Montessori also believed that early experiences with adults are important to later development: "In the first two or three [years], the child may undergo influences that will alter his whole future. If he has been injured, or suffered violence, or met with severe obstacles during this period, deviations of personality may ensue" (Montessori, 1967a/1995, p. 195). Although such statements are consistent with modern notions of the importance of early experience for development (Fox et al., 2014), in the early 1900s such ideas were revolutionary.

Level of Adult Direction: Parenting Styles

Whereas the attachment literature is particularly concerned with parental sensitivity to infants and later child outcomes, the parenting-styles literature is concerned with parents' degree of warmth and control during early and middle childhood and concurrent child outcomes (Maccoby & Martin, 1983). The influential work of the psychologist Diana Baumrind on this issue is discussed next, followed by consideration of Dr. Montessori's prescriptions for teachers.

BAUMRIND'S PARENTING STYLES

From extensive study of American families, Baumrind (1989) has defined four basic styles of parenting, often conceptualized as warmth and control (Maccoby & Martin, 1983) (Figure 9.1). Particular child outcomes are associated with each of these styles (Baumrind, 1991; Lamborn, Mounts, Steinberg, & Dornbusch, 1991; Williams et al., 2009).

One parenting style is termed "authoritarian." Authoritarian parents are high in control but low in warmth. They are demanding and do not often display affection with their children. Authoritarian parents rarely provide reasons for what they ask their children to do, saying instead that children must do as they say because they say so. The children of authoritarian parents tend to be low in motivation. As preschoolers, they are often withdrawn and distrustful. As they get older, the girls of such parents tend to lack independence,

| | | Warmth | |
		High	Low
Control	High	Authoritative	Authoritarian
	Low	Permissive	Neglecting

FIGURE 9.1 Parental warmth and control.

and the boys are often hostile. As adolescents, children of authoritarian parents tend to have low social and academic competence.

Permissive parents are low on control but high on warmth. They let their children set the agenda, going along with whatever their children want to do: stay up until 11, have ice cream for breakfast, and so on. Permissive parents are openly loving, but when it comes to setting any sort of structure for the child, one might characterize them as abandoning. When their children violate social norms or are unkind to others, permissive parents do not confront the children, but simply continue to give warm love. In terms of outcomes, children of permissive parents tend to have little self-control. They are often considered immature, and they show little self-reliance and exploration. As they get older, they tend to be low in achievement orientation, and the girls especially tend to be nonassertive. Older children of permissive parents are prone to drug use and delinquency.

Neglecting parents are low on both warmth and control. Neglecting parents simply do not pay any attention to their children. There is no structure, and there are no signs of affection. Children of neglecting parents tend to be low on social responsibility and social assertiveness. They are more likely to show antisocial tendencies than are other children and are more likely to suffer from psychological problems such as depression.

Finally, there are authoritative parents, who are high on control and warmth. They tend to be very strict about what the rules are, but also willing to discuss them, reason with the child, and when sensible even alter the rules in response to the child's expressed views. Yet within the limits they set, authoritative parents allow children considerable freedom. They are warmly affectionate and communicate openly. They also are demanding and expect maturity. Children of authoritative parents are clearly the best off, high in achievement motivation and in self-control. They tend to be more popular, competent, and self-assured than other children. Children of authoritative parents also show high levels of social responsibility.

Summarizing this research, Baumrind (1989) wrote,

> The optimal parent-child relationship at any stage of development can be recognized by its balance between parents' acknowledgment of the child's immaturity—shown by providing structure, control, and regimen (demandingness)—and the parents' acknowledgement of the child's emergence as a confident, competent person—shown by providing stimulation, warmth, and respect for individuality (responsiveness). (pp. 370–71)

Although the results described so far are well accepted regarding white middle-class Americans, as is the case with attachment constructs, parenting styles can carry different meanings in different cultural settings (Deater-Deckard et al., 2011). Speaking generally, a high degree of warmth and control in parents does appear to be associated with positive outcomes in children.

OTHER PARENTING RESEARCH

Other parenting research that aligns with that of Baumrind looks at parental control and discipline, and at how well integrated children are in the social milieu. In one study, more than 100 children, ages 6 to 11, were observed at home working with their parents on two different puzzles (Dekovic & Janssens, 1992). Parent nonverbal behaviors were coded for support (smiling, nodding) and negativity (physical takeover of the task, brief utterances of disapproval). Parents were also rated for warmth, responsiveness, power assertion, inductive reasoning, demandingness, and restrictiveness. A factor analysis on the various ratings resulted in two factors: authoritative/democratic (high or low on warmth, suggestions, induction, demanding of maturity) or authoritarian/restrictive (high or low in prohibitions, directiveness, and power assertion). Children's prosocial behavior was rated by their teachers and their peers, and sociometric status was gathered by asking peers to nominate the three people they liked most and least in their class.

Authoritative/democratic parenting was associated with children who were better liked by their peers and who were judged as more prosocial by their teachers. Children of authoritarian/restrictive parents, conversely, were least likely to be seen as helpful by their peers and teachers, and were more often disliked by their peers. Directions of effects cannot be determined from this data, but a directional interpretation is consistent with socialization theories.

In another study, preschoolers were observed on a playground, their peers gave sociometric ratings, and their parents were interviewed about their disciplinary styles (Hart, DeWolf, Wozniak, & Burts, 1992). The important disciplinary style for our purposes is inductive, a style consistent with authoritative parenting in which parents ask children to consider the consequences of their behavior, providing a reasoning rather than a power-assertive climate. In the study, an inductive disciplinary style on the part of the parent was associated with fewer disruptive playground behaviors by children, and with higher sociometric ratings by peers.

The prior two studies both concerned parenting styles and social development. Another study addressed cognitive development and parents' levels of directiveness during a free play situation and daily activities (Landry, Smith, Swank, & Miller-Loncar, 2000). These authors found interesting age-specific effects. For 2-year-olds, parents' directiveness was positively associated with cognitive measures. As children got older, however, parents' continued directiveness was associated with lower levels of cognitive functioning. Adult sensitivity to when a greater or lesser degree of scaffolding is needed is very important. All children benefit from some level of demandingness and control, but as children become more competent, adults' continued directiveness becomes negative.

Parents' level of autonomy support when children are young has also been related to executive function (Bernier, Carlson, & Whipple, 2010). Autonomy support during a problem-solving task was examined when children were 15 months old, and executive function was assessed at 18 and 26 months. Autonomy support was the strongest predictor of executive function, even when maternal education and children's level of cognitive functioning were controlled for.

A final study worthy of mention is a large-scale study asking adolescents about their parents' disciplinary practices and their own behaviors (Kindlon, 2001). Adolescents who claimed their parents were too lenient (as defined by the child) were at a higher risk for having an eating disorder, using steroids, being mean, underachieving, and having permissive attitudes toward early teen sex.

SUMMARY: RESEARCH ON PARENTING STYLES

Research on parenting styles and child outcomes suggests that children fare best when adults are high in warmth and control. Children thrive when given clear, solid structure, respectful communication, and emotional warmth. They fare best when parents set firm guidelines within which their children are allowed freedom. As children get older, they fare best when their parents gradually hand over more control. Overly permissive, lenient parenting and overly controlling, rigid parenting are both associated with poor child outcomes. These findings align with Dr. Montessori's recommendations for teachers.

Montessori's Call for Freedom Within Boundaries

Consistent with the work on authoritative parenting, Dr. Montessori advised teachers to give children freedom within clear boundaries. "Young people must have enough freedom to allow them to act on individual initiative. But in order that individual action should be free and useful at the same time it must be restricted within certain limits and rules that give the necessary guidance" (Montessori, 1948a/1976, p. 113).

Dr. Montessori also counseled that adults give reasons to children. This is particularly clear in *From Childhood to Adolescence,* where she discussed how to present material to children. "The mind of the child [particularly from 6 to 12 years old] is not satisfied with the mere collection of facts; he tries to discover their causes" (1948a/1976, p. 36). Children in the Elementary years, she wrote, need to understand why, not just what, and the research on parenting shows children fare better when parents do provide reasons.

Authoritative parents also have high expectations, and, relative to other school systems' expectations of children, those put forth in Montessori classrooms may well be considered high. In fact, Montessori's decline from an initial period of great popularity in the United States around 1920 is often attributed to the writing of education professor William Kilpatrick (1914), who opposed Montessori's introduction of reading and writing to children before they reach the age of 6 and is discussed further in chapter 12. Books at such an early age were deemed harmful by several of Montessori's contemporaries. Montessori clearly has high academic and behavioral expectations of children, which Dr. Montessori would say are the result of children themselves indicating what they were capable of and drawn to when free within a specially prepared environment.

As discussed in chapter 6, Dr. Montessori also wrote of people expecting too little of children by giving them many toys and fairy tales, but little of real life. If children can imagine fairy tales, she wrote, why not ask them to imagine parts of the real earth that they cannot see? Children apparently surprised her repeatedly by showing interest in real activities over play, and she responded by creating an educational system that expects maturity, as do authoritative parents. This can put people off, because they see Montessori education as not being sufficiently fun. Empirical research should more directly address this issue, but the Middle School study mentioned previously (Rathunde & Csikszentmihalyi, 2005a) and other research concerning children's motivation and affect when engaged in Montessori-like practices (collaborative learning, lack of extrinsic rewards, and so) in conventional settings suggest that it is probably not a concern. Children do appear to enjoy learning in the circumstances of Montessori classrooms.

As was discussed earlier, Dr. Montessori advised that adults show great emotional warmth when dealing with children. Children must have "a teacher who looks on them with love and hope" (Montessori, 1989, p. 79). Yet at the same time, the adult's ultimate control of the environment was clearly a high priority. The pitfalls of permissive adult attitudes were pointed out in her writing. "If freedom is understood as letting the children do as they like, using or more likely misusing, the things available, it is clear that only their 'deviations' are free to develop" (Montessori, 1967a/1995, p. 206). Permissive parents are often thought of as ones who want to be their children's friends; it is hard for them to exercise authority. Dr. Montessori saw the dangers in this: "The teacher must be superior and not just a friend. . . . [Children] need a dignified, mature person. . . . If they have no authority, they have no directive. Children need this support" (1989, p. 17). Some Montessori teachers, like some parents, err in this regard. They do not provide ultimate control over the environment, deal effectively with unproductive behaviors, or guide children's decisions in positive ways. Freedom can thus be taken to an extreme, and Dr. Montessori counseled against this repeatedly. "One time I saw an entire class of disorganized children who were using the materials completely wrongly. The teacher drifted about in the class, silent as the Sphinx. . . . This teacher was committing a grave error: She feared disturbing their disorder, instead of attempting to establish the order" (Montessori, 1956, p. 140).

Another not uncommon error in Montessori teaching is the opposite one: teachers being overly rigid about the method, in a manner reminiscent of authoritarian parents. Dr. Montessori also spoke against an authoritarian stance: "The teacher can address the pupil energetically and severely and thus jolt him out of his behavior, but those who know their jobs well have means more effective than coercion for recalling the pupil to order" (1956, p. 141). Authoritarian parents tell children to do things because the parent says so; they do not reason with the child, and they appear to take on a stance that they are infallible. Yet adults who work with children have to admit to being fallible (Montessori, 1967a/1995, p. 246). Education, she said, was traditionally "directed toward the suppression or bending of the child's will, and the substitution for it of the teacher's will, which demands from the child unquestioning obedience" (Montessori, 1967a/1995, p. 252). Against the behaviorist trend, she said, "We cannot directly mold ... individual forms of character, intelligence, and feeling" (1917/1965, p. 9).

The degree to which Montessori teachers take an authoritative stance, and whether their degree of authoritativeness is associated with more optimal academic, social, and personal outcomes, are important issues for empirical research. Dr. Montessori's ideas about how teachers should behave toward children were clearly in line with today's research on parenting styles. They should provide an appropriately structured environment in which children are free to make their own decisions and discoveries. They should intervene only when children's behavior is not constructive. They should have high expectations and give reasons, all with warm love.

Adult Behavior and Children's Self Theories

Whereas the attachment and parenting literatures concern how adults respond to children and child outcomes, the work on self theories concerns children's representations of the self and how malleable these are to adult feedback. As was mentioned in chapter 6, people's responses to challenges can be seen as fitting into two basic categories (Dweck, 1999; 2006). One is mastery oriented: People aim to overcome the challenges. Such people view mistakes as learning opportunities, and when they err, they continue to engage in the task with the aim of mastering it. The second is a helpless pattern, in which people back down from challenges, opting for easier tasks instead. They tend to view mistakes as reflections of some permanent defect of their character, and thus they seek to avoid tasks that will cast themselves in a negative light.

The two kinds of responses go along with two different theories of intelligence. The helpless pattern goes along with a theory of intelligence as a fixed entity, and the mastery pattern goes along with a theory of intelligence as malleable. Chapter 6 discussed studies indicating that grading appears to push people to adopt the performance goals that go with an entity theory of intelligence and choose activities that will indicate that they are highly intelligent. By contrast, mastery-oriented responses promote choosing of tasks that help one learn, which inspire one to master challenging tasks (Dweck, 1999; 2006). Longitudinal studies have shown that such self-theories predict achievement over time (Blackwell et al., 2007).

Dweck and her colleagues have shown that by implicitly endorsing one or the other theory, adults have a significant effect on children's learning and well-being. One study examined the influence of different types of adult feedback on fifth-graders' achievement goals, attributions, and performance (Mueller & Dweck, 1998). The researchers were particularly interested in how feedback about a child's success would affect a child's later response to failure, because of the common practice of praising children for their successes by telling them they are smart, good, and so on.

In the first experiment, children were given three sets of problems to solve. The first set was a moderately difficult one, so all the children did fairly well. At that point, all of the children were told, "Wow, you did very well on these problems." No matter how they had actually done, all the children were told they had gotten 80% right. "That's a really high score." (Children were "debriefed" about the experiment later.) Then, roughly a third of the children were told, "You must be smart at these problems," in effect giving them an entity or fixed-trait reason for their high score. A different third were told, "You must have worked hard at these problems," implying an incremental theory of intelligence. The remaining children received no additional feedback. Presumably these children retain their native theory of intelligence, which in the general population is about 43% incremental and about 43% entity. (The rest do not fit clearly into either pattern.)

Next, children were told they could do more problems, and were asked to choose what kind of problems they would like, as a measure of their achievement orientation. They were offered a choice of "Problems that aren't too hard, so I don't get many wrong," "Problems that are pretty easy, so I'll do well," or "Problems that I'm pretty good at, so I can show that I'm smart" (p. 35). These first three options endorse performance goals and go along with an entity theory, spawning a desire to perform well in order to look intelligent. A fourth option endorsed a learning goal and thus an incremental theory: "Problems that I'll learn a lot from even if I won't look so smart."

After stating their preferred choice, children went on to instead do a second, more difficult set of problems that they were told the experimenter had previously chosen. Their own choices would be granted, the experimenter told them, if there was extra time at the end of the session. After completing the second set of problems, they were told they had performed a lot worse on it than on the first set.

To check for the effect of the different feedback on their responses to this failure experience, children were next asked about their desire to take some more problems home with them, their enjoyment of the task, their perceptions about how they had done, and their attributions for how they had done. They were then given a third set of problems, which was moderately difficult, like the first set, to allow for an assessment of how the experimental intervention influenced performance. After this final task, all children were debriefed and told the second set of problems was much harder than the first, and was in fact designed for seventh-graders. The researchers ensured that all children felt proud of their performance before leaving the experiment.

The results of this study are extremely interesting in their implications for how rapidly children respond to feedback endorsing an entity or an incremental view. Regarding achievement motivation, 92% of the children who had received effort praise chose the learning goal after the first set of problems by asking to receive additional problems that they would learn from. By comparison, just 8% of the children who had received the intelligence praise chose this option. The other 92% of the children who had received intelligence praise opted for problems that would be easy so they could look smart or do well. Among the children who had gotten no feedback, about half chose performance and half chose learning goals, in keeping with the baseline representation of entity and mastery theorists in the general U.S. population.

Children's post-failure attributions after the second set of problems were also affected by the intervention. Those who had been praised for effort after the first problem set attributed their subsequent failure to diminished effort, whereas those who were praised for ability attributed their subsequent failure to lack of ability.

Task enjoyment was also very much affected, with children who were praised for intelligence reporting less enjoyment of the task than children who were praised for effort. In terms of persistence, children praised for effort were more likely to want to take some additional problems home.

Finally, performance on the third set of problems was also influenced by the intervention feedback after the first set. Children praised for effort did better on the third set of problems than they had on the first set, and children praised for intelligence performed worse. Children who had received no praise showed no change. Thus a single sentence of feedback attributing success to intelligence or effort was associated with a cascade of remarkably different reactions to a subsequent failure event.

In five subsequent experiments, the researchers replicated and extended these basic findings. When people with an entity view of intelligence (enduring or induced by feedback) face failure, they attribute the failure to a fixed quality of the self. In the context of such an attribution, people avoid further challenge, instead seeking evidence that they are indeed smart. If brief experimenter feedback can have such a large effect on children, parent and teacher feedback, which continues over time and comes from people who are very important to a child, would be expected to have even more. As was discussed in chapter 6, even when teachers simply told children a test would show "how good you are in relation to other children your age," children's performance declined (Graham & Golan, 1991). Indeed, Dweck finds that teachers who themselves have an entity theory of math intelligence comfort low-performing students, and such feedback lowers students' motivation and performance (Rattan, Good, & Dweck, 2012).

Many of Dweck's studies concern older children and adults, but the pattern holds even for preschoolers. Prior to elementary school, children do not seem to be concerned with their intelligence so much as with their goodness and badness, so their preschooler experiments ask about these characteristics as well. So as not to give such young children direct negative feedback, children in these experiments chose a doll to represent themselves (Kamins & Dweck, 1999). The experimenter then enacted a series of four events with the doll, in which the doll was successful (Experiment 1) or was not (Experiment 2). For example, one story was about the doll making a big tower, and then being asked by the teacher (another doll) to clean up the tower. The story went on,

> And so you start to put the blocks over where they are supposed to go, and you begin stacking them up. You really want to do a good job, but when you look down at what you did, you think to yourself, "Uh-oh, the blocks are all crooked and in a messy pile." But you worked hard to put them all away, and you say to the teacher, "Mrs. Billington, I put the blocks away." The teacher looks at the job you did and says, "The blocks are all crooked and in one big mess." (Kamins & Dweck, 1999, p. 838)

Then children heard different kinds of feedback. Children in the person feedback condition heard the teacher say to the doll, "I'm very disappointed in you." In the outcome criticism condition, the doll was told, "That's not the right way to do it, because the blocks are not straightened up and are still messy." This condition addresses the popular belief that one should focus on outcome rather than on person in giving feedback to children. For a third, strategy feedback condition, the doll was told, "Maybe you could think of another way to do it."

Following four such tasks, each with the same type of feedback, children were given a test scenario, in which the teacher asked the doll to make a beautiful LEGO house. The doll did so, then noticed she (or he) had forgotten to make windows, but gave it to the teacher anyway. The teacher looked at the house and commented, "That house has no windows." Children were then asked a number of questions, such as how nice they thought the house was, how the LEGO story made them and the doll feel about themselves, whether they would like to do the LEGO house story again, and what they would make happen next in the LEGO house story.

Children who had heard person-attribute feedback earlier thought the house was less nice, and rated it only 3 on a 6-point scale of beauty, as opposed to ratings of almost 5 from the strategy-feedback group. The outcome-criticism group had intermediate scores on this and all measures. Children in the person-feedback group had more negative feelings about themselves after hearing the story, and said that what had happened made the doll feel like she or he was not smart, not good, and not nice. Children in the strategy feedback group felt the opposite. Children in the person-feedback group were less apt to want to do the story again, and created less positive story endings. In contrast, children in the strategy-feedback group made up constructive endings in which they often found ways to get windows in the house, and said they would like to do the story again.

Even in Experiment 2, when the doll had succeeded rather than failed in the initial four stories, the same response pattern was obtained, showing that person-oriented success praise as "You are really good at that!" leads to a negative response following failure, with children going on to endorse fixed negative traits such as "badness." Recent research suggests that inflated praise ("That drawing is incredibly beautiful!") is particularly problematic for children with low-self-esteem—the very children to whom adults are most likely to give such praise (Brummelman, Thomaes, de Castro, Overbeek, & Bushman, 2014).

The studies just described show that a feedback event (or a short series of such events) can influence immediate reactions even in very young children. But mastery-oriented and helpless styles are not only temporary states of reaction to recent feedback. In the absence of particular feedback manipulations, children's responses to challenging situations has been shown to remain stable from kindergarten until fifth grade (Ziegert, Kistner, Castro, & Robertson, 2001), and there is no reason to believe they change thereafter. The research suggests that how adults talk to children about their accomplishments has a host of important consequences.

Dweck (1999; 2006) describes many other interesting outcomes and considerations regarding these two theories of self as malleable or fixed. That adult feedback appears to push children toward adopting one or the other such view is what is important to the ideas of this chapter. Adult feedback that endorses a malleable view of intelligence is clearly better for children.

Dr. Montessori and Incremental Versus Fixed Trait Feedback

Consistent with Dweck's findings, Dr. Montessori was against using any sort of entity evaluation of a child, positive or negative.

> To tell a person he is clever or clumsy, bright or stupid, good or bad, is a form of betrayal. The child must see for himself what he can do, and it is important to give him not only the means of education but also to supply him with indicators which tell him his mistakes.... The child's interest [is] in doing better. (1967a/1995, p. 250)

Condoning a mastery approach to one's mistakes, Dr. Montessori advised that "it is well to cultivate a friendly feeling towards error, to treat it as a companion inseparable from our lives, as something having a purpose, which it truly has" (1967a/1995, p. 246). Teachers were advised to have this sense about themselves and to pass this sense on to children. An attitude that mistakes are valuable because we can learn from them is consistent with a mastery approach to learning and with an incremental theory of intelligence.

Not correcting children's work was part of this incremental approach. Dr. Montessori held that children naturally correct their mistakes when they can perceive those mistakes, just as an infant corrects his or her own mistakes in learning to walk. A child learns through repetition of exercises where the mistakes are obvious, not from an adult's correcting his or her work. "What is meant by correcting exercise books? It means marking them from 0 to 10. How can a zero correct anyone's defects?" (1967a/1995, p. 245). Instead, Dr. Montessori counseled that correction comes from the child's own observation of his mistakes in the outcome, and that the materials the child works with should make it obvious to the child when he has erred (see the discussion in chapter 6 on the control of error). In this way the adult avoids passing judgment on the child and thus inadvertently promoting the performance goal of looking good for the adult.

Having children find their own errors through the materials, and work to master materials for their own sakes, would be expected to lead to (or preserve) a mastery orientation in Montessori-schooled children. Dr. Montessori clearly valued intrinsic over performance reasons for doing work: "If work comes from an inner source, it is much more intense and much more fruitful" (1989, p. 85). Whether Montessori children do have more of a mastery orientation toward schoolwork than do children in conventional schools is a question for empirical study. Children in other nonconventional school systems clearly do (e.g., Boaler, 1997; Boaler & Staples, 2008). Regardless, in counseling teachers never to give entity praise or criticism to children, Dr. Montessori's recommendations for teachers are consistent with what self-theories research suggests will produce the most optimal child outcomes.

Teacher Expectations and Control and Child Outcomes

Whereas the literature thus far has focused on parents and experimenters in home and laboratory situations, research on the same issues has also been done with teachers in schools. The basic thrust of the work presented here continues the theme from parenting, which is that children fare better when emotionally warm adults with high expectations give them more of a sense of control within a structured environment.

In one study, sixth-graders were asked about their perceptions of their teachers, and those perceptions were examined with respect to variables ranging from academic performance to social behavior and self-theories (Wentzel, 2002). These latter variables included prosocial behavior, social responsibility, sense of mastery, and locus of control (e.g., the extent to which the child or some external force controls events in their lives). The students were from two different populations: One school served an economically disadvantaged area, and the students were mostly African American, whereas the other served a middle socioeconomic status (SES) community. Here the students were mostly European American. An early important finding was that relationships across variables did not differ in the two schools. The same variables were related to positive outcomes in both the middle and the lower SES school.

The extent to which teachers were seen by the children as having high expectations for the children, a variable that is characteristic of authoritative parents, figured importantly for several outcomes. When teachers were perceived as having high expectations, children were more apt to pursue prosocial goals (such as sharing their learning with others), to be socially responsible, to be interested in class, and to have a strong mastery orientation: They wanted to learn, rather than simply get a good grade.

Another strongly related variable was teachers' negative feedback, a feature of authoritarian parenting. Teachers were rated high on negative feedback when students claimed that the teacher made them feel bad if they got the wrong answer, and that the teacher scolded them for not trying. When teachers were rated highly on such measures, students were less likely to engage in prosocial behavior, were more likely to behave irresponsibly, and were likely to get lower grades.

These data were collected in the spring, when children had been in the classroom with the teachers for about six months. The research suggests that teachers might influence how students fare in the classrooms, but the alternative interpretation, that the children led teachers to behave in certain ways, is also possible. The study described next, although concerned with control, to some extent addresses this "direction of effects" issue.

Control is an important recurrent issue in child–adult relations, both in the classroom and outside it. As was discussed in chapter 3, when children have more of a sense of control in the classroom, they fare better. Just how teachers strive to exert control appears to also have important influence on child outcomes. In one study showing this, teachers were shown a set of vignettes, such as the following, and asked to choose a response from among several options:

> Jim is an average student who has been working at grade level. During the past two weeks he has appeared listless and has not been participating during reading group. The work he does is accurate but he has not been completing assignments. A phone conversation with his mother revealed no useful information. The most appropriate thing for Jim's teacher to do is:
>
> 1. She should impress upon him the importance of finishing his assignments since he needs to learn this material for his own good.
> 2. Let him know that he doesn't have to finish all of his work now and see if she can help him work out the cause of the listlessness.
> 3. Make him stay after school until the day's assignments are done.
> 4. Let him see how he compares with the other children in terms of his assignments and encourage him to catch up with the others. (Deci, Schwartz, et al., 1981, p. 644)

Teachers' responses resulted in scores for the degree to which they promoted autonomy in the classroom (by choosing options such as 1). Autonomy scores were found to align significantly with their students' judgments of the atmosphere in the classroom, suggesting good correspondence between how students see the teacher and what the teacher thinks is appropriate to do. This data in hand, the authors went on to examine the level of intrinsic motivation and perceived competence of students in these teachers' classes, testing in both October and May of a regular academic year. Most of the children had been randomly assigned to classrooms, so one would not expect a priori differences in motivation across the classrooms.

In both October and May, levels of intrinsic motivation, specifically a preference for challenge, attempts at mastery, and curiosity, were significantly related to teacher's autonomy-endorsing responses on the questionnaire. Thus, just 2 months into the school year, children were more intrinsically motivated when they had teachers who promoted autonomy in the classroom. In addition, children whose teachers endorsed autonomy-encouraging approaches perceived themselves to be more cognitively competent and had a higher sense of self-worth. In contrast, when teachers endorsed more controlling (option 3) and social-comparison (option 4) strategies, children had less intrinsic motivation and a lower sense of competence in the classroom.

The fact that relations between teachers' autonomy orientations and child outcomes were found after just 2 months in the classroom and were the same the following spring might have some bearing on the "direction of effects" issue. Dweck's work suggests that adults can probably influence children quite rapidly to endorse different views of learning. The question one must ask regarding direction of effects is whether a teacher, faced with a new class of children who behave differently, would be influenced by a new class of children in how he or she answers such questions on a survey about hypothetical classroom situations 2 months into the school year.

In a study shedding light on this issue, 578 students in 34 high school classrooms reported on their level of engagement and their perceptions of autonomy at the very beginning of the school year—hence prior to when teachers would have gotten to know students well enough to adapt to a particular group (Hafen et al., 2012). The researchers examined how these initial perceptions, as well as the levels of student engagement researchers observed, related to how engaged students appeared to be and reported themselves to be at the end of the school year. Whereas students of these ages typically decline in engagement across the school year, students who perceived their classrooms as promoting autonomy in the first weeks of school increased their levels of engagement (both self-reported and as observed by researchers) across the school year.

In addition, other studies have shown that teachers who endorsed more autonomous classrooms prior to the school year in which they were studied had students who fared better than those whose teachers endorsed conventional practices. Using videotapes of mathematics classroom teaching to supplement teacher and student questionnaires and tests, researchers showed that "students in classrooms in which teachers emphasized effort, learning, and understanding rather than performance, and in which autonomy was encouraged ... reported experiencing relatively more positive emotions while doing fractions work and enjoying mathematics relatively more than other students" (Stipek et al. 1998, p. 483). Children in those classrooms also experienced greater learning gains, particularly in conceptual understanding. Positive emotion was related to achievement in the procedural domain.

The study of teacher responses and child outcomes mentioned earlier in this section was replicated in Russia and revealed the same basic pattern of results (Chirkov & Ryan, 2001), and more recent research from Austria is consistent (Bergsmann, Lüftenegger, Jöstl, Schober, & Spiel, 2013). Unfortunately, as children get older in conventional American schools, the schools increasingly take away, rather than increase, children's autonomy (Eccles, Midgley, et al., 1993); furthermore, recent standards-based large-scale school reforms also have the effect of making classrooms less autonomous (Olsen & Sexton, 2009; see also Deci, 2009). Research in psychology has shown that when teachers have independence goals for children, children tend to have more intrinsic motivation to learn and also to be higher in self-esteem (Deci, Nezlek, & Sheinman, 1981; Deci, Schwartz, et al., 1981). The current swing toward external testing standards promotes the opposite behaviors in teachers. In one study, when teachers were told their students would have to pass specific educational standards, teachers became more controlling, talked and commanded more, gave students less choice and autonomy, and expressed more criticism of students (Deci, Spiefel, Ryan, Koestner, & Kaufman, 1982). Both as children get older, and when standardized testing is emphasized, teachers in conventional schools become more prone to create classroom environments that are at odds with more optimal child outcomes.

In the context of conventional education, teachers can attempt to overcome the negative effects of grades and testing, and the inherently competitive, comparative system they create. The system, however, was designed for their use, and as the current enthusiasm for high-stakes testing shows, as a culture we keep returning to it. Teacher's expectations of children and how they communicate do impact learning and self theories in classrooms.

Teacher Expectations and Control in a Montessori Classroom

The literature on teachers and classrooms also mirrors Dr. Montessori's approach. First, as was discussed with reference to authoritative parenting, Montessori teachers' expectations are high. Children are expected to achieve a good deal both academically and socially in Montessori classrooms. Children achieve this in part by their own self-control, which is the Montessori's teacher's goal; the teacher's task is well done when the teacher is needed only to give additional lessons. "Any pedagogical action, if it is to be efficacious in the training of little children, must tend to help the children to advance upon this road of independence" (Montessori, 1912/1964, p. 97). Although the teacher oversees the Montessori classroom, it is truly the child's classroom, with everything scaled to and arranged for the children. The children have responsibility to care for the environment: to return objects to their places, to behave civilly, to water plants, to clean up their spills, and so on. In helping children toward independence, the adult simply provides whatever guidance is necessary to ensure that the children make good decisions and engage in productive behaviors. The expectations and attitudes toward control that Dr. Montessori endorsed in teachers are consistent with the literature on optimal classroom practices.

In the last sections of this chapter, I discuss three issues that are pertinent to adults in a Montessori environment: the role of the teacher in a Montessori classroom, the establishment of new classrooms, and how Montessori teachers are trained.

The Role of the Montessori Teacher

Established Montessori classrooms run quite differently from conventional ones, in that children arrive in the morning, choose their work, and go about their business. Once a classroom is established, the teacher's role is to actively observe the children and give new, appropriately timed lessons. Teachers intervene in children's activities only when they are disturbing or unproductive. Whereas conventional teachers have as a main role the imparting of knowledge, the Montessori teacher's main role is connecting the child to the environment. They intervene only when children need guidance or structure; otherwise they sit back and actively observe when they do not. Establishing a new classroom, however, requires a particular set of steps.

Establishing a New Montessori Classroom

During the early phase of establishing a classroom, Dr. Montessori rather colorfully maintained that the teacher "must be like the flame which heartens all by its warmth, enlivens and invites. There is no need to fear that she will interrupt some important psychic process, since these have not yet begun. Before concentration occurs, the directress may do more or less what she thinks best; she may interfere with the children's activities as much as she thinks necessary" (1967a/1995, p. 278). Dr. Montessori suggested that teachers begin with games, poetry, and singing, and activities to organize children's physical movements. Such activities might include arranging furniture or going outside to collect leaves. As described in chapter 2, the first specifically Montessori activities Primary teachers introduce to new children are the Exercises of Practical Life, such as polishing the classroom water pitcher and dusting the shelves. She wrote that experience had shown her that the Sensorial and Cultural activities should not be introduced before a child had shown concentrated work with Practical Life activities. Teachers are to watch for moments of concentration, this being the goal for every child, and when they occur, to protect the child from interruption.

If concentration leads to better self-regulation, as research presented in chapter 4 suggests it does, then teachers are probably most apt to see misbehavior in newly established Montessori classrooms, before children have begun to concentrate (although of course misbehavior might surface anytime). Dr. Montessori clearly noted that any disruptive or socially unacceptable behavior should always be checked, but by redirection rather than punishment: The teacher must give a disruptive child something else to do. "Interfere by all means to stop disturbances, but we need not punish or scold or admonish when we stop bad behavior; we can ask the child to come and pick flowers in the garden or offer a toy or any occupation that will appeal to [the child]" (Montessori, 1989, p. 16). She also recommended that misbehaving children be shown positive attention, such as being taken aside and shown something new as though they are very special. Thus at this stage, and indeed whenever a child is not productively engaged, misbehaving children should be redirected. In this manner Dr. Montessori echoes the characteristics of authoritative parenting: high warmth and high control. She believed there was no such thing as a bad child, only children with unfulfilled needs (Montessori, 1989, p. 78).

Eventually, as a new classroom settles, children will one by one begin to concentrate. Once children have begun to concentrate, the adult should step back. Dr. Montessori often described the adult's role at this point, once children have begun to concentrate, as passive, but she clearly meant a very attentive sort of passivity; "passive" apparently only referred to the idea that the adult not interfere with the child's concentration. She stated that adults often err by praising children who are concentrating, or by correcting their errors. Both, she said, lead children to abandon their work in moments of concentration. Praise and correction at the wrong time disrupt the very process that one was aiming for.

Dr. Montessori was not against all praise. She mentions that children, particularly early on, will bring the products of their work to adults and ask for praise, and at such times, she advised adults to give praise warmly and generously. The claim that calling a child "good" is a form of betrayal suggests she would not condone person praise, but leaves open whether she would condone product or process praise or both. When a child comes to an adult seeking praise, she said, then the child needs praise as assurance that he or she is on the right track (Montessori, 1946/1963, p. 88). But at the moment of concentration, when the child is not asking for anything from outside, then the child should be left alone.

The descriptions regarding new classrooms seem particularly geared to Primary, perhaps because that is where she saw teachers have the most difficulty. Children in Elementary Montessori classrooms have usually already had several years in Primary, and the teacher's task is to give lessons, facilitate the Going Out program, and oversee the environment in all its aspects, including social harmony.

This particular and different role for the teacher, Dr. Montessori maintained, required extensive training. The form of that training is the subject of the final section.

Montessori Teacher Training

Conventional teacher training in the United States generally involves a year of coursework covering classroom management, assessment, and such topics as how to teach reading, math, science, art, and/or social studies. Because the trainees will go on to use different curricula, the emphasis is on general principles and theories rather than specific lessons, which teachers later will need to create or might sometimes create as class assignments during graduate school.

In contrast, as has been mentioned, Montessori teacher training involves both how to teach specific lessons and learning Montessori theory. Dr. Montessori established training courses and the Association Montessori Internationale (AMI) to oversee training of future teachers and continuing evolution of the Montessori program. Although many other organizations now offer Montessori training, I will discuss the method that she devised, in keeping with the book's focus on Dr. Montessori's ideas. This training includes both personal preparation as well as education in the lessons and materials.

Before considering the training of teachers, I will describe the training of the people who train new Montessori teachers. AMI teacher trainers must have studied Montessori for at least 10 years before they begin to teach others to teach. This 10 years includes 1 year of their own training, a minimum of 5 years as a classroom teacher, and then at least 4 years working as an apprentice under other teacher trainers. AMI teacher trainers must also pass rigorous standards before taking on the training role. To show they meet these standards, they write a dozen essays on specific topics concerning Montessori education, which are reviewed by a committee. This level of rigor is unusual in Montessori training: In many Montessori teacher training programs, there are no specific standards for the people who train others to be Montessori teachers; they might simply have had a year (or even less) of teacher training and then taught in a Montessori classroom themselves for a few years.

PREPARATION OF THE MONTESSORI TEACHER

Future Montessori teachers are prepared for teaching in two ways: personally, and as practitioners versed in Montessori theory and knowledge. In terms of personal preparation, the capacity to observe is a main goal of training.

Personal Preparation: Training in Observation

An ability to observe children and detect their needs is fundamental to good Montessori teaching. Dr. Montessori maintained that the capacity to observe children has to be carefully developed through long practice (1917/1965, p. 130). In the AMI teacher training courses, scores of hours are spent with children, observing their actions, recording those observations, and crafting them into reports to be reviewed by the teacher trainer. In terms of a general undergraduate degree prior to the teacher training, Dr. Montessori advocated training in science, rather than in education, in part because of the emphasis on close observation (Montessori, 1917/1965, p. 138). She was also concerned that training in conventional education might make it more difficult to become a good Montessori teacher. "An ordinary teacher cannot be transformed into a Montessori teacher, but must be created anew, having rid herself of pedagogical prejudices" (Montessori, 1946/1963, p. 87). She was apparently concerned that years of learning the theories and techniques of conventional schooling would interfere with seeing education in the very different ways she had discovered.

In the service of excellent observation, Montessori teachers must also develop certain personal qualities. Excellent observation, Dr. Montessori wrote, requires a patient attitude and self-abnegation: "We must master and control our own wills, if we would bring ourselves into relation with the external world and appreciate its values. Without this preparation we cannot give due weight to the minute things from which science draws its conclusions" (1917/1965, p. 133). To observe clearly, Dr. Montessori held that teachers must first confront their own prejudices. "We insist on the fact that a teacher must prepare himself interiorly by systematically studying himself so that he can tear out his most deeply rooted defects, those in fact which impede his relations with children. . . . A good teacher does not have to be entirely free from faults and weaknesses [but should know what they are]" (Montessori, 1966, p. 149). To assist this, part of teacher training, she claimed, was for the trainers to point out to the trainees what they saw in the trainee's personalities, to urge honest personal assessment. Thus teacher trainers had to spend a sufficient amount of time with trainees to get to know them well. Teacher trainers also would be expected to have gone through such a process themselves.

Teachers had to rid themselves of pride and anger, to become humble and charitable, and to "check those inner attitudes characteristic of adults that can hinder our understanding of a child" (Montessori, 1966, p. 153). This is reminiscent of Ainsworth's discussion of sensitivity, in which the sensitive mother is free from distortions caused by her own needs and desires, a state that aids her in seeing the child's signals for what they are. This emphasis on one's personal preparation to be a teacher contrasts sharply with conventional teacher training, which focuses more on how one does things than on one's own psychology. In fact, the Montessori approach is more in keeping with training psychiatrists, as they must go through psychoanalysis themselves first.

The preparation of the Montessori teacher involves personal change, learning to be an astute observer, and learning to identify in oneself qualities that might be an impediment to fair observation and understanding of children.

Preparation of the Knowledge Base

A superficial judgment of the Montessori Method is too often
that it requires little of the teacher, who has to refrain from interference
and leave the children to their own activity. But when the
didactive material is considered, its quantity and the order and
details of its presentation, the task of the teacher becomes both
active and complex. . . . Her later "inactivity" is a sign of her success.

— Maria Montessori *(1946/1963, p. 86)*

In addition to personal preparation, the Montessori teacher is prepared by learning about the materials and their presentation. Learning about the Montessori materials for a Montessori Primary classroom is a considerable task, and learning the materials for the Elementary classroom may be twice as big a task.

To teach about the material and its presentation, AMI teacher training generally requires nine months of lectures and practicums intermingled with observations and internships in a variety of Montessori classrooms. The teacher trainer monitors the trainee's learning of lessons and supervises the internships and observations.

Lectures and practicums enable trainees to learn about the materials and the variety of ways in which they can be used to stimulate interest and use, as well as the interconnections between materials across the curriculum. Trainees learn to present the materials, with all the variations, to children (by practicing on the trainer and fellow trainees prior to internships). Trainees also make many of the classroom materials themselves, particularly the charts and diagrams used in the Elementary classroom. The deep level of familiarity with the material that results from creating it is considered to be important, just as it is considered to be important that the children make their own re-creations of maps and plant diagrams in the classroom. For this reason as well, as was described earlier, AMI training also involves making several "albums," normally three-ring binders of typed and illustrated pages describing everything one has been presented during the course. Effectively, the Montessori teacher-in-training writes his or her own textbook concerning Montessori materials and theory. The knowledge in these albums is of course not as deep and thorough as that of the teacher trainer, just as the notes of a student taking a college course would not reflect all the knowledge of the professor, but they are sufficiently thorough to allow the teacher to refer to them over the coming years, and to guide his or her lessons in the future. Some other Montessori teacher training courses routinely give teachers copies of the information rather than having them write and illustrate it themselves. This is not a good change: Research has shown that taking one's own notes leads to better learning than does reading prewritten ones (Annis, 1981; Kulhavy, Dyer, & Silver, 1975); indeed, even taking notes by hand rather than computers leads to deeper conceptual learning (Mueller & Oppenheimer, 2014).

At the end of the training year, trainees are tested by examiners from other AMI training centers, to ensure that the training upholds a standard of knowledge that is consistent across AMI training centers. An AMI standards board meets regularly to discuss these standards. High standards of training do not guarantee great Montessori teachers, any more than a medical degree from a top medical school guarantees a great doctor. They do, however, set a high standard of knowledge of Montessori principles and materials. As was stated, other Montessori training courses have other means by which they ensure standards in their Montessori training; I discuss those of the AMI because it is the organization that Dr. Montessori created to further the educational program she devised.

Chapter Summary

Dr. Montessori advocated particular ways of interacting with children that closely correspond to psychological research on more optimal child outcomes. Teachers were counseled to show warmth and sensitivity and to have high standards of behavior in the classroom. Within those standards, children are allowed considerable freedom to choose their activities and associates. Teachers were advised to sensitively observe children, and to ascertain that the environment is in order. For this, and for understanding the extensive Montessori materials, special training is required. The materials and their use, and indeed the entire Montessori environment, are very ordered. The next chapter concerns the issue of order in the Montessori environment, and how it is expected to promote the creation of order in the child's mind.

10 }

Order in Environment and Mind

The children in our schools are free, but that does not mean there is no organization. Organization, in fact, is necessary . . . if the children are to be free to work.

— Maria Montessori *(1967a/1995, p. 244)*

Pedagogically the work of the school is to organize the work of the child. . . . The organizing of the child's work and offering this work to the child is a very exact work for us. . . . It is the organization of the work which [leads to] . . . the establishment of mental order.

— Maria Montessori *(1997, pp. 31–33)*

When people enter a Montessori classroom, particularly for 3- to 6-year-olds, they are sometimes surprised, even disturbed, by how orderly the environment is, both spatially and auditorily. Spatially, the classrooms are ordered because everything is neat and in its place. Auditorily, Montessori classrooms feel ordered because they are so peaceful; the children are often rather quiet. Especially with young children, people expect a little mayhem.

Interestingly, the factory and behaviorist models both suggest that conventional schools should be very ordered. Factories are efficient. They are run on a strict schedule, everything is done in a set fashion, and things have their proper places. Behaviorism is also ordered—rigorous and scientific. However, the extent to which, and the areas in which, conventional schools are ordered varies by level.

Conventional schools typically have tightly ordered schedules at the elementary level, and some do in preschool. Within those schedules, elementary classes also tend to have set ways in which each portion of the schedule or class is carried out, whereas preschool activities are often more free to vary (e.g., there is no set script for playing dress-up).

As a rule, in terms of curriculum, conventional U.S. schools are not particularly well ordered. As has been discussed previously, curricula for individual subjects are usually developed without reference to other subjects. New textbooks and programs are adopted from one year to the next. This can create disorder in the curriculum overall.

315

And conventional classrooms vary widely, according to the teacher, in their physical order. Informal observation indicates that most conventional school classrooms are orderly in the center (desks in rows or clusters at elementary, and activity centers in preschool), but often disorderly on the periphery. The walls are often full of posters, drawings, and charts, which in many classrooms appear to be placed haphazardly wherever there was room. Extra materials and equipment are piled in corners or on shelves. Children's classrooms have been described as places of "visual bombardment" (Bullard, 2013, p. 110).

Montessori classrooms do not have tightly ordered daily schedules, but are very orderly in terms of how each task is enacted by the children. This will be discussed later in more depth. At the curricular level, Montessori education is extremely organized. Each lesson and material was designed with reference to the entire set across all topics, and across a wide age span. In terms of physical order, Montessori classrooms should be very organized, with no unnecessary items in view.

The organization of Montessori classrooms is no accident: Dr. Montessori believed that "the secret of free development of the child consists . . . in organizing for him the means necessary for his internal [development. . . . Within such an organized environment] the child's personality begins to organize itself and reveal its characteristics" (Montessori, 1917/1965, p. 70). She developed an organized system of education, and called on teachers to keep classrooms in good order.

Yet there is a sense in which Montessori is very disorderly, as compared to conventional schools: There is no set daily schedule. This allows for a degree of child choice and control. When one sees order in conventional schools, it is often implemented in ways that are at odds with choice and control. The research considered here speaks to what patterns of imposed order and freedom might be most positive for children's development.

Many of the studies presented here, especially the older ones, are not experimental. As has been discussed for other variables, when they are merely related, the possibility exists that other factors ("third variables") underlie the relation; the same problem exists for order and good outcomes (see Brody & Flor, 1997).[1] However, other studies statistically control for likely third variables, and experimental laboratory studies on order have also been conducted in recent years. Overall, there is strong evidence, including from

---

[1] Family stress, for example, is related to disruption in family routines (Steinglass, Bennett, Wolin, & Reiss, 1987), and would be expected to also directly impact children's development. The disrupted routines themselves might have no direct effect on child functioning. Another potential third variable is family income. Several studies have noted that a feature of low-income children's homes is the lack of order (Klaus & Gray, 1968; Pavenstedt, 1965), and low-income families are also often less educated and bear other features that could independently lead to poorer child outcomes. More recent studies, cited later in the chapter, address these issues.

many different populations, that order promotes more positive development in children (Evans & Wachs, 2010; MTA Cooperative Group, 1999; Seymour, Brock, During, & Poole, 1989).

In this chapter I consider order in four senses. One is temporal order: routines and rituals that occur in predictable linear sequence. The second is spatial order, involving organized physical layout. The third is noise and crowding, often anathema to an orderly environment. Finally, I consider research showing how brains "organize themselves" in response to sensory input, findings that bear on Montessori's orderly education of the senses. In each section, I discuss research on that type of order and its implementation in Montessori.

Temporal Order

Temporal order refers to the use of schedules and set routines. Temporal order is relevant at two levels: the macro level of the school day, and the micro level of tasks or routines within activities (such as the pattern of activity undertaken in math class). There is also a higher level of temporal order than the school day, namely the school year, but because Montessori and conventional schools are similar at this level, this will not be considered.

Conventional elementary school environments tend to be tightly organized at the macro level of daily schedules. For example, class might begin in the morning with the Pledge of Allegiance, then move into an hour of mathematics, a half hour of spelling, an hour of reading, then recess and snack, and so on for the remainder of the school day. There are time slots, and each is filled with a predetermined activity. At the micro level as well, conventional elementary school classes tend to be ordered. For example, most mathematics classes in the United States begin by reviewing homework, then show a new procedure, then practice that procedure in individual seat work (Hiebert, 1999; Stigler et al., 2000). Classes such as English and social studies are more likely to vary across teachers, but any given teacher probably follows a similar pattern on most days. Conventional elementary schooling seems to adhere to tight temporal order at both the macro and micro levels of temporal organization.

Conventional preschool, conversely, has historically tended to have little order on either level. Here I present that historical view, although there is evidence of at least kindergarten classrooms being more structured today (Bassok et al., 2016). By contrast, although some preschool classrooms do follow a macro-level schedule, many allow children to freely choose what they do, and when, throughout most of the day. Preschool children usually also freely choose at the micro level: how to do those activities (within reason). There is no one way to use a set of blocks or farm animals. Supporting these conjectures, in 2000, a study of 400 randomly selected child care centers across the United States reported that in most classrooms over the course of the preschool day "children have some opportunity for choices. For example, they may be assigned to activities, but are able to choose how they use the materials" (Peisner-Feinberg et al., 2000, p. 13).

Considering the temporal structure of both preschool and elementary programs, one sees that the child goes from a preschool system that might have little adult-imposed temporal order to a tightly ordered elementary school system. Tight structure and order are positive, as was seen in chapter 9, but this has to be viewed against the backdrop established in chapter 3: Children thrive when they have a sense of choice and control.

In a sense this chapter is a counterpart to chapter 3, because order is often imposed by adults on children and therefore reflects lack of child control. In Montessori and conventional classrooms alike, teachers and administrators are in the end responsible for whether there is order in the environment and for organizing how work is done. The resolution to the apparent contradiction with chapter 3 might be that children fare best when order and choice are imposed at different levels.

Montessori schooling varies in the level on which order is placed. At the macro, daily-schedule level, there is little adult-imposed structure. Children arrive and leave at a set time, and they might (or might not) have lunch at a set time. The teacher might also arrange to give a few lessons at fixed times during the day, which he or she might write on the board in the morning to help children know what to expect that day. Other than that, each child determines when he or she is ready to move on to the next activity (among the set of activities he or she knows how to do). Hence, at the macro level, there is little imposed order. At the micro level, however, Montessori education is very ordered. There is a specific set of steps one goes through to work with any Montessori material. Research suggests that this blend of order at the micro, routine level and freedom at the macro, daily-schedule level might be optimal for children's development.

The research on temporal order and child outcomes tends to concern order in the home, probably because temporal order varies from family to family whereas temporal order in conventional schools is ubiquitous at the elementary level. The home-based research has looked at microroutines, such as the set of activities one engages in to enact a bedtime ritual (e.g., brush teeth, put on pajamas, get parent[s], read story, and so on) and at macro-level scheduled events (a set bedtime). Importantly, families that engage in set times for such major events as dinnertime also tend to have orderly microroutines (Baxter & Clark, 1996). It is doubtful that having set times for major events at home translates into the degree of fixed schedule seen in conventional elementary schools, which would read something like "4–4:30, play with LEGO; 4:30–5, play ball with neighbor; 5–5:30, read books," and so on.

But set times for major events (dinner, bedtime) do appear to be associated with more orderly microroutines. Associations with such factors as set bedtimes, then, should probably be read as indicating tight micro-level routines, rather than a home life that is as scheduled to the same degree as the typical elementary school day.

COGNITIVE AND SOCIAL-PSYCHOLOGICAL OUTCOMES OF ROUTINES

Several studies have shown that children have better cognitive and psychosocial outcomes when their families engage in more regular routines. Next I begin with studies concerning elementary school children and adolescents, then turn to studies with younger children.

Elementary School Children

Temporal regularity and the implementation of family routines is related to positive outcomes in children in an array of family circumstances. One study asked parents of 4-year-olds to fill out an extensive questionnaire about their family rituals and routines across several settings, such as dinnertime, weekends, and cultural and religious traditions (Fiese & Kline, 1993). Two dimensions emerged from the responses: regularity and predictability of family routines, and the degree to which a routine has symbolic significance. Children's academic competence was also assessed 4 years later, at age 8. Results indicated that both the predictability and the symbolic meaning of routines at age 4 were significantly related to children's overall academic achievement at age 8. Predictability at 4 was also particularly related to math achievement at 8.

A study of first- through fifth-graders in divorced families showed that having set bedtimes at a first time point (on average, 4 years post-divorce) was related to several positive outcomes 2 years later (Guidubaldi, Cleminshaw, Perry, Nastasi, & Lightel, 1986). For boys and girls, having a set bedtime at time 1 was related to better physical health and fewer school absences 2 years later. Other findings varied by gender. For boys, having a regular bedtime at time 1 was associated with better academic performance at time 2. For girls, a regular bedtime at time 1 was associated with better psychosocial outcomes at time 2: Girls were happier, had more friends, and rated their relationships with their parents as more positive if they had regular time-1 bedtimes.

A similar array of outcomes was found in a study involving elementary school children with single mothers in the rural South (Brody & Flor, 1997). Routines were assessed using such items as "Working parent comes home from work at the same time each day" and "Family has a quiet time each evening." A videotape of mother–child interaction was rated for relationship quality, and children's self-regulation was measured on a scale with such items as "Plans before acting" and "Pays attention to what he or she is doing." Academic achievement was measured with standard cognitive tests, and children's teachers completed psychological inventories of the children. Results showed that engagement in family routines was significantly associated with children's academic achievement and self-regulation, and with higher mother–child relationship quality. It also predicted a child having fewer internalizing problems.

The positive impact of routines appears to continue into adolescence, although, as children get older, some measure of flexibility in family routines is most healthy (Henry & Lovelace, 1995; Baxter & Clark, 1996). This is probably because such flexibility shows the family is respecting the growing maturity of the adolescent.

THE EFFECT OF ORDERLY ROUTINES ON YOUNG CHILDREN

Order and routines are associated with better cognitive and psychosocial outcomes for young children as well. One study, for example, revealed that having regular times for bed and nap was significantly related to the cognitive measure of object permanence at 15 months, indicated by a child removing a cover to retrieve a just-hidden object (Wachs, 1976). Object permanence refers to a child's knowing that an object exists independently of the child's perceptual contact with it (Flavell, 1963). However, children's looking behavior shows that even rather young infants know the object is there; they simply don't know they can still get it (Baillargeon, 1987). Conventional object-permanence tasks are now thought to tap into a child's ability to coordinate actions with knowledge. As such, the conventional measure of object permanence—removing a cover to get a hidden object—may be related to a sense of "can-do" in children. Regularity and predictability in one's daily schedule might promote such a sense; habitual uncertainty about will happen next would lead to having a diminished sense of control (see chapter 3). In subsequent studies (Wachs & Gruen, 1982), the relationship between routines and object permanence appeared at somewhat different ages and sometimes only in males, but a general pattern of relationship is clear when considering the entire body of work. In families where there are set regular times and routines for major events, infants and toddlers are more cognitively advanced.

There is also research suggesting more positive developmental outcomes for preschoolers who have set bedtimes. A study of more than 200 children ages 4 and 5 showed that going to bed at a different time each night was associated with lower teacher ratings of positive adjustment and higher ratings of negative adjustment (Bates, Viken, Alexander, Beyers, & Stockton, 2002). This study also addressed the third variable problem by statistically controlling for two factors that could plausibly underpin both: family stress and parenting practices. Neither accounted for the relation between adjustment and having a set bedtime.

Another study examined the relation between having set times for both bed and meals and academic outcomes in Head Start children. Ninety-one low-income children were rated by their teachers on various social behaviors, and the children's parents responded to a set of questions about family routines (Keltner, 1990). Teacher-rated social behaviors were factor analyzed and fell along two dimensions: interest and participation in preschool, and cooperation and compliance. Children's scores on both of these dimensions were predicted by the extent to which the parents described the family as engaging in regular routines at bedtime and mealtimes. In addition, the more regular bed- and mealtimes were, the more cooperative, compliant, interested, and participatory teachers found children to be.

It bears repeating that having set times for major events has been related to having set ways of carrying out the microroutines associated with those events (Baxter & Clark, 1996). A family with a set dinnertime is probably also a family with a set dinner routine (set table, sit down, say prayer, serve food, discuss day, and so on). It does not likely mean the family schedules every moment of the day analogous to the typical school schedule.

Some studies of temporal order and young children involve the HOME inventory (Home Observation for Measurement of the Environment), a frequently used measure in child development research. The HOME organization subscale concerns physical as well as temporal organization, whereas research reports concerning the organization subscale do not consider physical and temporal items separately. The studies here thus also bear on physical order, the next major research topic in this chapter.

The HOME inventory was developed in the 1970s to measure the home environment of infants (Bradley & Caldwell, 1976b). Other research up to that time had used socioeconomic status (SES) as an indicator of infants' environments, but the HOME developers believed that such distal measures might not reflect what happens in the home on a proximal level, and indeed, the HOME has proven to be more predictive of child outcomes than has SES. To gather information for the HOME inventory, a researcher spends several hours observing in a child's home and interviewing the parents.

The 45 items on the infant HOME inventory are grouped into six clusters, with clusters relevant to such issues as emotional and verbal responsiveness of the mother and organization of the home. Importantly, the clusters were arrived at largely by statistical procedure (Bradley, personal communication, August 2003), so the groupings are meaningful about how homes are actually structured, not only in terms of researchers' ideas about those structures. On the organization subscale, three items seem related to temporal organization. These ask whether the child is taken to a doctor or clinic for medical care regularly, whether the child makes a trip to the grocery store at least weekly, and whether the child gets out of house at least four times a week. The latter item seems less obviously about temporal regularity—perhaps the child goes to the park at a different time each day—but it may often reflect whether the child has some set routine, such as regularly going to day care. At some level, one can see how these three items all tap into there being a regular schedule in the home. The two items that are more related to physical organization concern the child's having a special place to keep toys and whether the child's play space appears to be safe. The sixth item in the organization cluster asks whether, when the mother is away, the child has no more than three regular substitute caregivers, thus is about predictability of caregivers. Scores on these six items are reported in a total "organization score."

One set of longitudinal studies related scores on the HOME inventory at several points in infancy to child outcomes from 6 months through age 4½. Scores on the organization subscale of the HOME at 6 and 12 months were related to concurrent scores on the Mental Development Inventory of the Bayley Scales of Infant Development (Elardo, Bradley, & Caldwell, 1975), which includes tasks such as whether a child smiles at a mirror at 6 months or imitates the experimenter pushing a toy car at 12 months. Beginning around age 3, other measures, such as the Binet intelligence test, are more appropriate, and studies using this latter measure found that HOME organization scores at 24 months were significantly related to scores on the Binet intelligence test both at 36 months (Bradley & Caldwell, 1976a) and at 54 months (Bradley & Caldwell, 1976b).

The organization of the environment has also been shown to predict changes in intelligence scores. When the children in the longitudinal study just described were 3 years old, a subsample of children with scores on the middle range of the Bayley was selected and separated into three groups: those whose scores had decreased (relative to group norms) from 6 to 36 months, those whose scores had stayed the same, and those whose scores had increased (Bradley & Caldwell, 1976a). Statistically controlling for each child's initial scores, children whose scores increased over this time span were from homes that had been rated as more organized when the children were 6 months of age. Likewise, children whose scores decreased were from homes that were rated as less organized.

Further evidence of HOME organization scores being predictive of IQ scores was found in a study of Down syndrome children. Down syndrome children's scores on intelligence tests tend to decrease over time. In this study, the extent of decline in performance on an intelligence test could be predicted by scores on the organization factor of the HOME inventory 6 months earlier (Piper & Ramsay, 1980).

Some of the studies already mentioned control in various ways for other factors that might contribute to the relations, such as SES. Lower SES homes are often less organized (Klaus & Gray, 1968; Ramey, Mills, Campbell, &

O'Brien, 1975), and perhaps SES independently contributes to IQ, with organization simply being a by-product of SES. To address this, some researchers studied a sample consisting entirely of low SES children. Even within this group, and controlling for maternal IQ, the organization subscale of the HOME measured at 18 months was significantly related to Stanford-Binet performance, but only in a subset of the sample that spent 40 hours a week in the Frank Porter Graham day-care center, a highly successful intervention project (Ramey, Farran, & Campbell, 1979). Home organization was not predictive of IQ for children who were not in the center. The reasons for this are not clear. One possibility is that other variables have more influence in the absence of quality day care. For example, in this study, maternal IQ was very predictive of later IQ scores for the control children, but not for children in the day-care intervention. Perhaps providing the child with quality day care overcame the impact of a lower maternal IQ, making way for such other factors as home organization to have influence.

Of course, maternal IQ could be related to HOME organization scores, and thus in some studies could potentially explain the relation between the HOME and children's IQ. Perhaps parents who prefer more organized homes endow their children with genes that lead to higher scores on intelligence tests. Unfortunately, there is no study shedding light on this specifically for the organization subscale of the HOME, but there one study examined the overall preschool HOME. This study showed that while heredity plays some part in the equation, it does not explain it all. Researchers examined the relations between overall HOME scores, SES, and IQ in adoptive and nonadoptive families (Thompson, Fulker, DeFries, & Plomin, 1986). For both types of families, HOME scores had direct and independent effects on children's IQ scores.

Not every study with the HOME shows significant relations at every age between the organization subscale and cognitive measures (Gottfried, 1984), although the relations are usually in the expected direction (Field et al., 1978; Rice, Fulker, DeFries, & Plomin, 1988; Stevenson & Lamb, 1979; Thompson et al., 1986). Other aspects of the HOME, for example, the subscale indicating maternal involvement, are even more strongly and consistently related to child outcomes. But looking across studies, there is a general pattern of relation, the strength of which is greater when the administration of the HOME is closer in time to the cognitive test.

In sum, studies with the HOME, like studies of ritual and routine, suggest that order and predictability are associated with more positive outcomes for children. Research on the influence of an ordered versus chaotic home environment, especially on somewhat older children, expanded with the development of a parent scale, called CHAOS (for Confusion, Hubub, and Order Scale), which has been validated against objective observation (Matheny, Wachs, Ludwig, & Phillips, 1995). Studies using the CHAOS scale validate what has been shown using the HOME, linking household disorder to lower IQ and conduct problems, disruptive behavior, poor attention regulation, and a host of other negative outcomes, even when other variables that might induce the relation are statistically controlled (Deater-Deckard et al., 2009; Jaffee, Hanscombe, Haworth, Davis, & Plomin, 2012; Wang, Deater-Deckard, Petrill, & Thompson, 2012). The positive relation between environmental and temporal order and developmental outcomes continues in adolescence, although some flexibility in routines is also positive at that age. Having a few set events (such as bed- and/or dinnertime) is related to more organized microroutines in families (Baxter & Clark, 1996) and to better child outcomes.

One might interpret the work on temporal organization as suggesting that conventional elementary school environments, with tight schedules specifying what children do each hour, would be most optimal for children. However, this conclusion should be tempered by (1) the fact that home environments are rarely scheduled to the degree that conventional elementary schools are and (2) the research on choice and control and on parenting. The most optimal environment, it would seem, corresponds to the same pattern as was seen for authoritative parenting: a combination of firm limits, a tight structure, and freedom to make choices. One way of balancing the child's need for control with the child's need for structure is the way it is done in Montessori classrooms: little structure at the macro level, but tight organization at the level of tasks and routines.

Some readers may wonder about the alternative possibility to balance choice and control: order at the macro level with freedom of choice at the micro level. This would mean there is a set hour during which children must do math, but how they interact with the math materials is entirely up to them. Research on very unstructured discovery learning paradigms suggests this pattern would result in poor outcomes: Children apparently do not learn particular concepts from interacting with materials when there is very little structure at the microroutine level (Alfieri et al., 2011; Klahr & Nigam, 2004); in fact, preschool children make the smallest learning gains in classrooms characterized by free play (Chien et al., 2010). Children seem to benefit from structured steps to learn particular concepts from their interactions with the world. Montessori materials are designed to teach particular concepts when they are used in particular ways, and such micro-level structure is probably good for learning.

Before moving on to discuss temporal order in Montessori classrooms, a final topic concerns child outcomes based on temporal order in sleep routines. Although sleep might seem irrelevant to a school's imposition of order, this research is worth considering because it is experimental (rather than involving natural correlations) and shows another venue in which organized microroutines are beneficial for children's development.

Sleep Routines and Child Outcomes

Healthy sleep is very important to healthy development (El-Sheikh, & Sadeh, 2015). Research shows that learning depends on sleep (Maquet, 2001). If one learns a task and then sleeps normally, one shows improvement on the task 2 to 4 days later. However, if one is deprived of sleep for 30 hours after learning the new task, no improvement occurs (Stickgold, James, & Hobson, 2000). Sleep appears work its effects through the formation of dendritic spines (little protrusions on dendrites that increase neural communication); under sleep deprivation, the spines do not form, or do not last (Yang, Lai, Cichon, Ma, Li, & Gan, 2014). Even the smaller decrements in sleep that are routinely experienced by children in less organized homes may also be important. In a study of 9- to 12-year-old Israeli children, those who slept 1 more hour than usual for three nights running performed significantly better on cognitive tests than children who slept 1 hour less than usual (Sadeh, Gruber, & Raviv, 2003). Thus, gradual buildup of sleep had a positive impact, and accumulated loss a negative one, on children's performance on cognitive tests.

A second study looked at elementary school children's sleep patterns over a 1-week period and examined their performance on auditory and visual working memory tasks (the number of items one can hold in mind at once; Steenari et al., 2003). Children who experienced more night waking and children who took longer to fall asleep at night performed worse on these tasks. Sleep quality and working memory capacity appear to be related. A recent study of more than 10,000 seven-year-olds in the United Kingdom showed that those with more regular bedtimes earlier in their lives had significantly fewer behavioral problems, and that when regular bedtimes were implemented, behavioral problems decreased (Kelly, Kelly, & Sacker, 2013).

Some researchers have noted that many children with night waking problems have no orderly bedtime routine set by the parents. Instead, every night entails a different sequence of events (Seymour et al., 1989). To examine the effect of an organized routine on sleep, researchers randomly assigned 45 children, ranging in age from 9 months to 5 years, who were having trouble with regular night waking, to one of three groups. The first group was given a set of organized bedtime routines, including a regular procedure to follow if the child cried out in the night. A therapist was available to support the routines. The second group was given the same routine, but in written form without the therapist. The third control group was put on a waiting list.

Significant reduction in night waking occurred for the children whose parents began to follow a regular bedtime routine, regardless of whether there was therapist support for that routine. Those children also began to go to bed earlier when a routine was implemented, suggesting they may have also gotten more sleep. These positive effects were maintained at 1- and 3-month follow-ups. In contrast, no improvement was seen in the control group.

There is not complete consistency in the pediatric sleep literature such that any decrement in sleep always has negative effects on all kinds of performance. For example, 8- to 15-year-old children who were deprived of 4 hours' sleep for one night were sleepy, but showed no impairment on tests of sustained attention or response inhibition (Fallone, Acebo, Arnett, Seifer, & Carskadon, 2001). Further research is needed to tease apart what kinds of sleep deprivation are detrimental on what kinds of tasks at what ages. We do know that sleep deprivation is sometimes detrimental for some tasks, that established bedtimes and microroutines at bedtime are associated with children's sleeping better, and that regular bedtimes and healthy sleep are associated with important learning and adjustment measures.

Temporal Order in Montessori Classrooms

Montessori combines freedom of choice at the macro level with ordered routines at the micro level.

> We have already obtained a most interesting result, in that we have found it possible to present new means of enabling children to reach a higher level of calm and goodness, and we have been able to establish these means by experience. The whole foundation of our results rests upon these means which we have discovered, and which may be divided under two heads—the organization of work, and liberty. (Montessori, 1914/1965, p. 187)

As was described in chapter 3, Montessori classrooms impose little order at the level of the school day, having instead 3-hour uninterrupted periods during which children can focus on the tasks they choose. Yet within those times, the work children choose is very ordered.

Microroutines in Montessori education can be seen as analogous to specific dinnertime or bedtime rituals in a family: particular patterned sequences of activity. In giving children lessons, Montessori teachers demonstrate these activity sequences with few or no words, but with very precise movements. The Montessori teacher "teaches all the movements: how to sit, to rise from one's seat, to take up and lay down objects, and to offer them gracefully to others. In the same way she teaches the children to set the plates one upon the other and lay them on the table without making any noise" (Montessori, 1914/1965, p. 57). These movements are arranged into precise sequences that children learn via imitation. Such sequences are first introduced in Primary with the activities of Practical Life and the Sensory Materials.

Table Washing, introduced briefly in chapter 2, is a common Practical Life activity that illustrates the degree of precision and order involved in Montessori Practical Life work (Figure 10.1). To engage in Table Washing,

FIGURE 10.1 Table Washing. Photograph by An Vu.

children follow the routine shown earlier to them by the teacher and likely observed many times in the Table Washing of their classmates. The exact procedure might vary somewhat from classroom to classroom: The Practical Life activities are the ones to which Montessori teachers have the most individual input. Following is the description of one possible routine. For convenience, spatial order in the activity is also described; it will be pertinent later in the chapter.

First, the child selects a table to wash. To facilitate that selection, Dr. Montessori recommended that furniture be lightly colored so dirt can easily be noticed. From a shelf in the Practical Life area in the classroom, where the ensemble of matching Table Washing materials is kept, a plastic mat is carried over and laid on the floor beside the table. The child moves the chairs aside and then lifts the table (perhaps with help from a classmate) and places it on the mat. The child returns to the shelf, gets the empty pitcher, and fills it half full at the sink, with water. This is then brought to and placed in a particular spot on the mat—a spot carefully chosen by the teacher, when designing the activity, to facilitate the child's work. The child returns to the shelf for a basin to be filled with wash water from the pitcher and a bucket for wastewater, and then returns again for a tray carrying a neatly organized set of matching washing materials: soap in a soap dish, a sponge in a second soap dish, a soft scrub brush, and a towel. The child places these objects where they belong on the mat. The child fills the wash basin with about a half inch of water from the pitcher, then takes the sponge, wets it, squeezes it with both hands, then wets the table with a particular ordered motion, such as from left to right (allowing indirect preparation for the directionality of writing). The child checks the table for wetness, and continues if she or he sees dry spots. When the table is entirely wet, the child rinses the sponge with both hands, and gets the brush, which is wiped on the soap. Then the table is scrubbed, repeating the same activity sequence as was used with the sponge. And so on.

There is tremendous precision and order to Table Washing, as with all Practical Life and indeed all Montessori materials. Practical Life routines have many purposes relevant to order and development (Montessori, 1948a/1976, p. 17), several of which have already been alluded to but will be reiterated here. One point of these activities was to assist the child in independence, which Montessori saw as one of education's primary goals. A child's life, she believed, could be viewed as a journey toward increasing independence. By repeating simple routine acts, not only washing tables but also arranging flowers or polishing objects (Figure 10.2), children could acquire a sense of self as agent, able

FIGURE 10.2 Shoe Polishing. Photograph by An Vu.

to independently carry out useful, meaningful actions in the world. Repeating the ordered routines may be even more important to a sense of mastery than achieving the immediate goal of each routine. Dr. Montessori seems to say as much when she notes that children will repeat the act of polishing a silver pitcher even when they just did it, and the pitcher is already gleaming: Children seemed to derive benefit from merely engaging in the routine. Whether such repetition, as opposed to the result, better enhances a child's sense of mastery would be an interesting topic for further research.

A second purpose of Practical Life is the education of movement. By engaging in and repeating Practical Life activities, a child's actions become more orderly and precise. Dr. Montessori saw the precision of one's acts in Practical Life exercises as helpful and inspirational to young children:

> In fact, if we showed [children] exactly how to do something, this precision itself seemed to hold their interest. To have a real purpose to which the action was directed, this was the first condition [for interest, but the second condition was that] the exact way of doing it acted like a support which rendered the child stable in his efforts, and therefore brought progress in his development. Order and precision, we found, were the keys to spontaneous work in school. (Montessori, 1967a/1995, p. 186)

This is another topic that would be really interesting to examine in empirical research: Do children show more attraction to activities that are presented as an orderly routine, or are more random and disordered sequences as attractive to young children? The study of "overimitation" has recently blossomed in child development, with more attention to its role in the development of culture than in the development of the child.

Another purpose of Practical Life exercises is that the child is following a precise routine. Through this precision, Dr. Montessori believed children were developing a "mathematical mind" (a term borrowed from Pascal). Nature, she believed, does not give children articles of mathematical precision, and so for children to develop an appreciation of precision, such articles and routines need to be supplied in the artificial environment. The Sensorial Materials are another early avenue to such precision.

Besides assisting independence, educating movement, and promoting precision of thought, another important purpose of Practical Life routines was to exercise concentration. When the child is intensely concentrating, work and mind are ordered. The great advances of human civilization, Dr. Montessori noted, have come about not so much through knowledge as through concentrated thought (Montessori, 1956, p. 70)—often a wellspring of ideas. By giving very young children a goal that is easily visualized, then bringing them to work intensely toward it in an ordered sequence of steps, Practical Life activity was viewed as serving an important role in nurturing the child's ability to concentrate on a task.

Finally, Dr. Montessori saw an important role of Practical Life as being to restore the child's energy (Montessori, 1917/1965, p. 150). A child might choose Table Washing following intense concentration on math work, or following a difficult social encounter, and achieve renewed energy through the activity. In effect, such activity performs one of the important functions ascribed to recess in conventional schools, but the child chooses when to rest. This observation is also ripe for empirical research. There is an abundant literature showing the benefits of rest breaks and even 20-minute afternoon naps on adult performance (Hayashi, Watanabe, & Hori, 1999; Galinsky, Swanson, Sauter, Hurrell, & Schleifer, 2000); whether taking such breaks on one's own whim is even better than having them scheduled for one has not, to my knowledge, been studied.

Many of the skills honed through Practical Life exercises are applied to the other work children do in Montessori classrooms. Because the skills are achieved in Primary, there are no Practical Life exercises as such in Elementary: "The continuation of these exercises would be useless now that the child is independent; that is to say, he knows how to devote himself to an activity for which he will no longer need to ask help of the adult, and he has coordination of movement" (Montessori, 1948a/1976, p. 17). Children still care for themselves and their environment in Elementary, but it is in the context of other work.

In sum, Montessori classrooms have no daily schedule, except that 3 hours of uninterrupted work are respected, always in the morning, and in the afternoon as well for children who spend the full day in the classroom. Within those periods, children are free to choose constructive work. But microroutines are very important to Montessori work. Practical Life is only one example of this: Use of all the Montessori materials is governed by set routines. These particular routines differentiate Montessori from free and open-ended "discovery learning" paradigms. Children discover with Montessori materials by following an orderly set of steps.

Spatial Organization and Outcomes

Spatial organization is also related to important developmental outcomes. In this section, I consider research on the spatial organization of the elements of a task. Then I move to consider organization in the larger environment, such as the home and school, including research on crowding and noise.

TASK-LEVEL SPATIAL ORGANIZATION AND LEARNING

A first set of studies concerns spatial organization at what might be called the task level, in contrast to the level of the larger space of home or neighborhood.

Studies of human memory have shown that when information is presented in a conceptually organized way, as opposed to randomly, people learn it better. In one study, undergraduates were asked to memorize a list of words in a hierarchical tree structure (Bower, Clark, Lesgold, & Winzenz, 1969). For half of the undergraduates, the words were organized in the tree structure in a conceptually organized manner. For example, "Minerals" was listed at the top, and on the branches below "Metals" and "Stones" were listed, with stones divided into "Precious" and "Masonry," and so on. The other half of the subjects saw the same tree structure, but the items were inserted into the tree randomly, thus "Masonry" might have been at the top, with "Precious" and "Metals" on the branches below.

Memory was markedly influenced by the organization of the material during the learning phase. For example, on one trial, participants who had been shown an organized structure recalled an average of 73 of 112 words, whereas those presented with randomly arranged words recalled 21 of 112 words. Another experiment showed that the organization does not have to be categorical; associative organizational structures also result in better learning than random presentations. What is important is that the underlying structure is organized.

This same effect has been demonstrated for children remembering objects (Rogoff & Mistry, 1990). Unschooled children have more trouble recalling lists of items than do schooled children, a finding that could be taken as indicating that unschooled children are lacking in basic cognitive skills. The psychologist Barbara Rogoff and her colleagues reasoned that the finding might in fact be due to the children being asked to memorize lists of *unrelated* items. This is something children have to do in conventional schools, for example with lists of unrelated vocabulary or spelling words, but rarely outside of school. If the unschooled children were given a structural organization that made sense to them, their memory capacities might prove equivalent to those of schooled children. The structural organization involved was a diorama of a miniature town, into which 20 small items, including animals, cars, people, and so on, were logically placed while the children, Mayan and American 8- and 9-year-olds, looked on. The 20 objects were then replaced into the pool of 80 items from which they were drawn, and the children were asked to reconstruct the scene. Although the Mayan sample had shown much poorer memory previously on a standard list task, their performance was even slightly better than that of the American children in this organized task.

Another study showing the influence of task-level organization on cognitive function examined transitive inference in first graders (Schnall & Gattis, 1998). Transitive inference tasks are ones in which one learns that A > B and B > C, and one must infer that A > C. When the stimuli from which children made inferences were arranged in a physical order that mirrored their conceptual relations, children made correct inferences significantly more often than when the stimuli were arranged randomly. All of these studies suggest that organization at the task level assists cognitive processes.

PHYSICAL ORDER IN THE LARGER SPACE

Order in larger spaces has been shown to influence a range of developmental outcomes. The studies described earlier using the HOME inventory are one set showing this. Those studies showed that children performed better on cognitive tests to the extent that their homes were more ordered and predictable—for example, they had established places for their toys. One way that environments can be disorganized is "clutter"; the opposite of this is to be relatively sparse, or have fewer items.

Recent studies support more physically sparse learning environments for young children (Fisher, Godwin, & Seltman, 2014). In one experiment, kindergarten children were first familiarized for 5 hours with a new classroom, adjacent to their own, and were given science lessons and pretests on knowledge of such things as volcanos and bugs. Then the experiment began: In two groups of 12, over 2 weeks, children went six times to the classroom, and were read a different book about one of six science topics, for 5 to 7 minutes, then were given the paper and pencil test. Crucially, for three of the lessons, the room was decorated in a manner similar to most preschool classrooms. In the other three, the environment was sparse—more like a Montessori classroom—except for a few elements on the walls that were directly relevant to the day's lesson. Observers also coded children's attention from video: Were they looking at the teacher and the book, or were they off-task, looking at the walls or their peers?

The results were striking. Children were looking at the walls four times more when they were in the decorated classroom; they learned about half as much (their scores increased by 18%, versus 33% in the sparse classroom); and in individual children, the level of distraction and the level of learning were directly related. In a different study, Godwin and Fisher (2011) gave different children the same lessons in both types of environments, and results were similar. Finally, the results of this research dovetail with those of a large naturalistic U.K. study of 3,766 children ages 3 to 11, spread across 153 classrooms in 27 varied schools. In this study, across the school year, achievement gains were greatest in classrooms that had an intermediate level of stimulation: not too dull, and not too complex (Barrett, Davies, Zhang, & Barrett, 2015). Specifically, these researchers concluded that "the overall appearance, including the room layout and display on the wall has to be stimulating, but in balance with a degree of order, ideally without clutter. Similarly, colours with high intensity and brightness are better as accents or highlights instead of being the main colour theme of the classroom" (p. 129).

Other studies have also found that an orderly environment is associated with better functioning, and that less organized homes are linked to a range of negative outcomes, from poorer cognitive competence, to less adequate language, to more difficult temperaments, to lower mastery motivation, to more accidental injuries (see Wachs, 2000). One early study, for example, showed that when a child's neighborhood was rated as having "ordered, tended greenery," as well as when the child's home was rated as having "interior décor varied in an organized way," very young children showed a higher level of cognitive functioning (Wachs, Uzgiris, & Hunt, 1971).

A pertinent risk factor for physical disorganization is crowding. Crowding does not necessarily lead to physical disorderliness—airplanes can be very crowded but orderly. Yet research suggests that in homes, a higher density of people increases chaos (Wachs et al., 1971). Several studies have examined the effects of crowding, and they clearly indicate that it has a negative effect on human functioning. Living in more crowded environments is of course often related to lower SES and other risk factors for healthy development, but crowding appears to have negative effects even when these variables are controlled for.

People repeatedly exposed to crowded environments show higher levels of arousal, discomfort, and negative affect than people in uncrowded environments (Epstein, Woolfolk, & Lehrer, 1981). People also perform less well on complex cognitive tasks in crowded environments (Nagar & Pandey, 1987). A study of working-class middle school children in India showed a wide range of negative associations with chronic residential crowding, such as poor academic achievement, poor behavioral adjustment at school, learned helplessness, high blood pressure, and poorer parent-child relations (Evans, Lepore, Shejwal, & Palsane, 1998). All of the children were from the same middle-range SES band, suggesting an independent effect of crowding, or some other variable systematically related to crowding. A study of low-income children also showed that dense housing was associated with negative outcomes: Children in denser housing were less likely to persist in trying to solve difficult problems (Evans, Saegert, & Harrid, 2001).

These findings recall the effects of dense housing on helpless behaviors (Rodin, 1976). In one experiment, elementary school boys were given a task in which they were able to control the schedule on which they received candy rewards. Children from more densely populated residences were less likely to try to control the reward schedule. A second experiment found that junior high school students from higher-density homes were more affected by a helplessness-inducing procedure than ones from lower-density homes.

After working with an unsolvable puzzle, those from more densely populated homes were less likely to be successful with a solvable puzzle.

Another study found that even short-term crowding is associated with negative effects on children's psychological functioning (Aiello, Nicosia, & Thompson, 1979). Close to 200 fourth-, eighth-, and 11th-graders were placed in groups of four, in moderately or highly dense conditions. For those in densely crowded conditions, males in particular showed elevated stress during the crowding experience, and all children reported having felt tense and annoyed. After the crowding experience, those who had been in more densely crowded conditions were more competitive.

Thus crowded environments, which are often (but not necessarily) less organized, are associated with undesirable qualities such as learned helplessness, poorer physical and mental health, poorer academic achievement, and less task persistence. Why should crowded environments be associated with these qualities? One possibility that has been explored is that the negative impact of crowded, disorderly environments is not entirely caused by its direct effect on children (although experiments such as the last study described suggest that it is in part direct), but may be also mediated by the effect of those environments on how adults function in them.

For example, the homes of 1-year-olds from educated two-parent families were rated for such features as crowding, availability of objects, and chaos in the home, and their parents' behaviors were rated for degree of verbal and nonverbal responsiveness. "Structural and temporal disorganization together with a high crowding pattern at home related to parents being less responsive to child vocalizations, less likely to show or demonstrate an object to their child, and less vocally stimulating" (Corapci & Wachs, 2002). Thus for young children, crowded, disorganized, and noisy environments were related to less optimal child-directed adult behaviors, which would likely in turn impact development.

The findings regarding the benefits of a physically ordered space are qualified in one respect, at least in research with adults (such research with children has not yet been done): Adults created more novel uses for an object (a ping-pong ball) after being in a messy rather than an organized environment (Vohs, Redden, & Rahinel, 2013). Further study suggested the reason was because disorder favors novelty and order favors convention, at least among adults. On the positive side, adults were more likely to choose healthy food (an apple over a chocolate bar) and gave more money to a children's charity after being in an orderly environment. Other research shows that adults' self-regulation is higher in orderly environments (Chae & Zhu, 2014); the relation between creativity (of the sort tapped on the alternate uses task) and self-regulation is a complex one and further research is needed to elucidate it. Regardless, the findings for children are quite clear: A physically ordered space enhances positive developmental outcomes.

Spatial Order in Montessori Classrooms

The child, left at liberty to exercise his activities, ought to find in
his surroundings something organized in direct relation to his
internal organization which is developing itself by natural laws.

— Maria Montessori *(1917/1965, p. 70)*

Montessori is ordered not only in the sense of routines on objects, but also
in the sense of the physical space. Again, this sometimes puts people off;
they are used to children's environments being messy, and find the opposite
unsettling. Dr. Montessori observed that in her classrooms, children instead
seemed inclined toward order and precision.

> The children want the same things in the same place, they may move
> furniture and work in the garden, but they will return it to exactly the
> same spot. Once, I saw two children moving a table and continuing to
> adjust it for some time; I wondered at their action and asked what they
> were doing and they replied that the table had stood under the lamp and
> they were now trying to return it to its exact position. (1989, p. 67)

Certain material features of the environment, she noted, can facilitate the
manifestation of the child's sense of order, and the child's orderly actions:

> light furniture that [the child] can carry about; low dressers within reach
> of his arms; locks that he can easily manipulate; chests that run on cas-
> tors; light doors that he can open and shut readily; clothes-pegs fixed
> on the walls at a height convenient for him; brushes his little hand can
> grasp; pieces of soap that can lie in the hollow of such a hand; basins so
> small that the child is strong enough to empty them; brooms with short,
> smooth, light handles; clothes he can easily put on and take off himself;
> these are surroundings which invite activity, and among which the child
> will gradually perfect his movements without fatigue, acquiring human
> grace and dexterity. (1917/1965, p. 151)

In addition to carefully selecting objects and designing orderly routines,
Montessori teachers organize the physical classroom in a logical way. As discussed in chapter 1, each subject area is in a designated part of a Montessori
classroom. Thus, a Primary classroom will have areas for Practical Life,
Sensorial Materials, math, geography, language, and so on. Within that
order, each object has its place on a shelf. Teachers rotate what materials
are available, based on where children in the class are in the sequences of
materials, and what interests them. In fact, a brand-new classroom will typically have only 3-year-olds, and the teacher may have just a few Practical Life
activities and even some non-Montessori activities such as puzzles out. As
the teacher gives lessons, more Montessori materials will be added and the

non-Montessori ones removed. In any classroom, materials that the children do not use are put in storage for a time. In this way the room stays orderly, not becoming cluttered with materials the children do not use.

Paula Polk Lillard explained physical order as a key element in a Montessori environment:

> Order means that the child is assured the possibility of a completed cycle of activity in using the materials. He will find all the pieces needed for the exercise he chooses; nothing will be broken or missing. No one will be permitted to interrupt him or to interfere with his work. He will return the materials to the place—and in the condition—in which he found them. By returning the materials, the child not only participates in the full cycle of activity, but becomes an integral partner in maintaining the order of the classroom. (1972, pp. 56–57)

Putting things away is in part a social act. Yet Dr. Montessori also observed that children appeared to like to put things back in order even for order's sake, and that they appeared to want to maintain spatial order, just as they appeared to like to follow routines.

Thus, the classroom and the shelves are ordered in spatial layout. In addition, each kind of work has its own organization, reflecting the task level of organization. When the child goes to do silver polishing, he or she finds a tray with all objects in a logical place and ready to use. The sponge may well have been dampened by the teacher before children arrived, the polish container has sufficient polish in it, the dish in which the child will put silver polish is clean, as is the rag the child will polish with. The placement of each object on the tray might be from left to right in the order of use.

Aesthetics also recommends a degree of order: We tend to prefer patterns over random arrangements. A row of one type of tree or flower tends to be more pleasing than an assortment of them, and in choosing frames for pictures, we look for patterns that repeat or complement something in the picture. Dr. Montessori intended that the classroom be aesthetically pleasing. One way this manifests in Montessori classrooms is in repeating patterns of colors.

The colors of Montessori materials are carefully chosen. Indeed, many Montessori materials are the colors that experimental studies show both 4-month-old infants and adults find most pleasing and attractive: red and blue (Bornstein, 1975). The furniture and material casings are usually a blond wood such as maple that allows a child to easily see when they are dirty. Colors within Practical Life activities tend to match, so the materials on the Silver Polishing tray may all be blue, those comprising the Table Washing set all orange, and so on.

Beyond color, all the aesthetics of the material are intended to be such that they attract children to them, inviting activity. A broom might have tiny butterflies painted on its handle, and the Button Frame might have beautiful bone buttons. In addition to having aesthetically agreeable materials, the classroom was to have "pleasing, artistic pictures, which are changed from time to time as circumstances direct," showing "children, families, landscapes, flowers and fruit, and . . . historical incidents" (Montessori, 1914/1965, p. 40). Ornamental plants were also specified among the furnishings, including each child possibly having a plant to tend. These items were to be placed about in an orderly, uncluttered fashion.

There is also order across the materials in a curricular sequence. Examples already given include the colors of different decimal places in the math materials, colors of consonants and vowels in materials involving phonetic analysis (Sandpaper Letters, Movable Alphabet), and the different symbols for different parts of speech. The same materials repeat the same patterns at higher levels and even across classrooms, leading to a depth and extent of order that is truly remarkable. If order in the environment really does assist order in the mind—and the research suggests it does—then Montessori education should assist logical thinking via this element.

In addition to aesthetic and conceptual order, the work itself often is about putting things in order. The child takes the Wooden Cylinders from their base, mixes them up, and then puts them back in their proper order, from smallest to largest. The Pink Tower, the Brown Stair, the Red Rods, the Color Tablets, the Bells, the Sound Cylinders, and other objects all work in the same way. The child recreates order in the physical configuration of the materials, just as the larger room is kept in order.

Another feature of the Montessori space is that there is a good deal of open floor space in a Montessori classroom. Dr. Montessori suggested that about half the floor space be open for children to work on the floor and to allow free movement. She also suggested that Montessori classrooms need to be larger than conventional ones, to allow for this degree of movement. Increased size, of course, reduces crowding. Because Montessori schools do not need special rooms for art, music, and other extracurricular activities that normally have a special room in conventional schools, their overall size is not necessarily larger than that of schools serving comparable numbers of students. In addition, any school needs to work with local circumstances; I have seen very large numbers of children working beautifully in very small Montessori classrooms, for example, in densely-populated cities in India.

In sum, Montessori environments are very ordered in the physical–spatial sense as well as the temporal one. Objects have their place, in the classroom, on the shelf, and even on the tray. Sets of objects have their particular colors. Activities are often about putting things in order, making them clean, or getting them to their proper places.

Dr. Montessori's Claim of a Sensitive Period for Order

Dr. Montessori claimed that young children are actually in a sensitive period for order (see chapter 5 for a discussion of Dr. Montessori's use of the "Sensitive Period"). She noted, for example, that when soap is left out of the soap dish, 2-year-olds are quite likely to put it back, and that children of 3 and 4 years typically return Montessori materials to their exact places on the shelves without being asked.

She observed that when young children become upset, they are sometimes reacting to something being out of order. One anecdote concerned a child of about six months old who was very upset when an umbrella was sitting in the middle of a table but ceased crying when the umbrella was removed. A second concerned an older boy who wailed when his mother's coat was folded on her arm instead of being worn as normal; as soon as the mother put her coat back on, the child's crying ceased, as he muttered, "coat . . . shoulder" (Montessori, 1966, p. 51). Another concerned a boy who was very upset when a hat was on a table; he calmed down when it was put on a peg in the adjacent hallway, and said, "hall . . . peg" (Montessori, 1967a/1995, 134). Still another is of a child who was suddenly inexplicably unable to sleep and complained of an upset stomach. On learning that the family had recently moved him to a bed for sleeping, Dr. Montessori placed two pillows in a criblike formation on the bed, and the child crawled between them, muttering "bed" ("cama," in Italian), and slept (Montessori, 1966, p. 57). Children's distress, she suggested, is sometimes a manifestation of their need for order.

Dr. Montessori also made interesting order-relevant observations concerning how children play hiding games. She recounted a hiding game Piaget played with one of his children, hiding an object under a pillow, having his child leave the room, moving the object to another pillow, and then asking the child to find it. When the child did not see the object under the first pillow, the child gave up. Piaget then showed the child how he had moved the object, and repeated the procedure. The child behaved in exactly the same way, whereupon Piaget lifted the second pillow and asked, "Didn't you see I put it here?" (on the prior hiding trial). "Yes," his child replied, "but it should be there" (pointing to the first pillow) (Montessori, 1966, pp. 53–54). Although to Piaget this task was probably about inference, to Dr. Montessori the incident was about the child's need to find the object in its proper place. She also noted that children often play hide-and-seek by hiding in the same place over and over, or in the place where the last hider was just found. She saw this as also reflecting a need for order.

Having an ordered environment during this early period is important, she claimed, because the child is ordering his or her mind as a reflection of the environment. As discussed in chapter 4 with regard to human tendencies, having some order in the environment is a basic human need, as without it, we would have no means to orient and find what we need. Whereas for an adult, order can be a source of pleasure, she claimed that for children it is a true need.

Noisy Environs

Another feature of disordered, crowded environments is that they are often noisy, and noise (whether from crowded conditions or other external sources) is clearly related to decrements in cognitive functioning (Wohlwill & Heft, 1987). Montessori classrooms, particularly Primary ones, are often very quiet, because the children are concentrating on their activities. One study showing a strong effect of noise on development involved infants in five age groups ranging from 7 to 22 months old (Wachs et al., 1971). Half of the sample was from low-income homes, and half was from middle-income homes. The researchers examined cognitive development with such tasks as object permanence and means–ends understanding, and also examined features of the home environment. Across all ages, the variables most consistently and repeatedly related to cognitive development were those concerning noise. Children whose homes received affirmative responses for "high sound level in house," "child cannot escape noise in home," "house noisy and small," "television on most of the time," and "high activity level in home" had lower cognitive scores. Another study found that having a "stimulus shelter," a place in the home where the child could get away from noise, was positively related to several measures of cognitive development at multiple time points across the second year (Wachs, 1976).

A possible reason for the negative impact of noise on development is that in an effort to shut out the noise, children also shut out developmentally helpful stimuli (Wachs & Gruen, 1982). If children respond to noisy environments by shutting out stimuli, one might expect a particular pattern of results on tasks involving attention skills. One study investigated this by comparing the attention skills of preschoolers from quieter homes and noisier homes (Heft, 1979). Visual attention was examined by asking children to find a matching card in an array of 20 cards. This task was repeated 10 times, and the child's cumulative search time was recorded.

A second task measured the distribution of the child's attention during the first task, testing for incidental learning. To do this, the 10 "background" cards that were used in the first part of the task were shuffled with a new set of 10 cards, and children were asked to indicate which of the 20 cards they had seen previously. A third task examined how children fared under noisy and non-noisy conditions on a task requiring them to match familiar figures.

In the noisy condition, a list of common words was read at moderate volume while the child worked.

Children whose homes were described by their parents as noisier had longer overall search times on the first task than children from quieter homes. They also showed less incidental learning on the second task. These results held even when family income, the child's age, preschool experience, and other environmental measures, such as activity level of the home, were controlled for.

Another important finding in this study was that children from noisier homes were less negatively affected by extraneous noise when engaging in the matching figures task. This suggests that children from noisy homes adapt to some degree to working in noisy environments. In the noise condition, the children from the noisiest homes performed at about the same level as children from the quietest homes, whereas in the quiet condition, the children from quieter homes performed much better. This is consistent with the idea that children in noisy environments block out stimuli; under some circumstances that is adaptive, but it also hinders some developments.

Most obviously, blocking out stimuli in noisy environments would likely affect auditory discrimination skills. One study examined this hypothesis in elementary school children living in a high-rise building by a noisy expressway (Cohen, Glass, & Singer, 1973). Because the noise produced by the expressway would be attenuated as one moved up in the apartment building, one would expect noise effects would be reduced as one moved up as well. This is what was found. Even controlling for parent education, and with all apartment dwellers in a fairly narrow income band, children who lived in lower apartments had poorer auditory discrimination scores (discriminating word pairs such as "near" and "gear") than children on higher floors. In addition, the longer a child had lived in the building, the stronger was the relation between apartment noise level and auditory discrimination.

In addition to reporting a link between noise and auditory discrimination, this study also reported a link between auditory discrimination skills and reading scores. A different study reported the latter link as well, between auditory discrimination abilities and a host of reading skills, such as reading comprehension and vocabulary (Deutsch, 1964). For the auditory discrimination task, children were presented 40 pairs of words, 30 of which differed only in their initial or final sound, such as "tea" and "bee" and "root" and "room." For each pair, children were asked to say if the words were the same or different. Children who performed more poorly on this task were likely to be poor readers relative to others of the same SES cohort and age. Given that living in a noisy environment affects auditory discrimination, and auditory discrimination affects reading, the evidence strongly suggests that children chronically exposed to noisy environments will not read as well.

Another study directly examined the relation between home noise levels and language scores (Michelson, 1968, cited in Parke, 1978). This study compared 710 third graders within SES bands, mitigating the possibility that the extraneous factor of SES carried the result. Higher levels of noise in the home were related to lower spelling and language test scores within each SES band. Michelson also noted an important buffer against these effects: Children who had a quiet space in their homes—a stimulus shelter—to which they could retreat for scholarly work were insulated from the negative relation between noise and achievement.

These findings regarding noise in the home extend to the classroom as well. One study was conducted in a child-care center that originally had poor acoustical design, making the rooms quite noisy (Maxwell & Evans, 2000). Over one summer, sound-absorbing panels were installed in the classrooms, reducing noise markedly. Prereading skills, such as sound-letter correspondence and rhyming, of children in four classrooms in the center were examined in the spring, both in the year before and in the year after the installation. Although the mean ages and age ranges would be expected to be about the same across the years in each classroom, and teacher behaviors regarding language would not be expected to have changed, pre-reading skills in the second year were significantly better than in the first year. Unfortunately there was no control classroom in which sound panels were not installed, which would have helped toward ruling out other influences. Still, the results are suggestive and consistent with other research showing an effect of noise on auditory discrimination and language, and suggest that even in preschool classrooms, less noise is related to more optimal development.

Several studies have also shown an effect of chronic noise exposure on classroom functioning in older children. One group of studies examined airplane noise and its influence on cognitive functioning in the classroom. Third- and fourth-grade children attending schools in the flight pattern of the Los Angeles International Airport took longer to complete the puzzle, and were more likely to fail to complete it at all, than children in other schools (Cohen, Evans, Krantz, & Stokols, 1980; Cohen, Krantz, Evans, & Stokols, 1981). Furthermore, the effect increased as a function of the number of years the children had been at the school. Conversely, consistent with research presented earlier, on a test of auditory distractibility, children who had been at the school more than 2 years were less distracted by noise than children who had been there less time. Similar results were also demonstrated for children attending unsoundproofed schools in the flight path of the Paris Orly International Airport (Moch-Sibony, 1981). These children had poorer auditory discrimination skills and also lower frustration tolerance than children at soundproofed schools in the same areas of Paris. A more recent study of children attending elementary schools exposed to aircraft noise in London replicated the basic effects, measured against children in other schools matched for SES. Children in the noisier schools had impaired reading scores on more difficult tests (but not overall), and higher levels of annoyance, after controlling for age and household income. Other studies have shown similar patterns of results for children whose schools are near train tracks and freeways (see summary in Wohlwill & Heft, 1987).

Noise from pop music (with vocals) and television also negatively impacts cognitive functioning, with implications for the presence of television during homework and wearing music-playing devices during school study halls. For example, a study of infants showed that the emergent ability to learn action sequences from video was impaired when a bouncy soundtrack (used in television show *Curb your Enthusiasm*) played during the video (Barr, Shuck, Salerno, Atkinson, & Linebarger, 2010). An interesting set of studies suggests that the effects of television and music noise interact with personality among college students. Although all people appear to be negatively affected by background noise, introverts are affected even more strongly than extroverts (Furnham & Bradley, 1997; Furnham, Gunter, & Peterson, 1994; Furnham & Strbac, 2002).

In sum, high levels of noise in one's environment, whether home or school, chronic or temporary, have an array of negative effects on both children and adult's functioning; although some of the studies cited in this section are older classics, more recent findings are consistent and even extend to other health outcomes such as blood pressure (see Evans, 2006; Ferguson, Cassells, MacAllister, & Evans, 2013 for general reviews on environment and child development). Although noise can be regular and orderly, high noise levels probably often confer a sense of auditory confusion. The weight of the evidence suggests that quieter environments are associated with more positive developmental outcomes.

Montessori's Quiet Classrooms

Montessori environments are also orderly in the aural sense. Primary classrooms are particularly quiet, with perhaps some classical music playing and a little bit of quiet chatter. Dr. Montessori describes the classrooms as having an "atmosphere of quiet activity" and "peaceful surroundings" (1914/1965, p. 59). As was stated earlier, this can put people off; we are conditioned to think classrooms of 3- to 6-year-olds should be noisy and somewhat chaotic, but the evidence suggests the quiet order is advantageous. In addition to the Montessori classrooms being generally quiet, recall the exercise of Silence described in chapter 4.

The final research topic of this chapter considers order in a different sense. Recent research in neuroscience shows how the brain organizes itself in response to sensory input. Montessori education involves a very orderly education of the senses, and research on the self-organizing properties of the brain can be viewed as supportive of that process.

Order in the Education of the Senses

Sensory discrimination abilities are something we do not tend to think about much until we lose them. People often cease to enjoy food if they lose their sense of smell, socially withdraw as they lose their hearing, and become disconcerted when their eyesight begins to fade. Finely tuned sensory capacities are critical, and one can argue that the more finely tuned one's senses are (up to a point), the higher the level of human functioning. Supporting a hypothesis stemming from Galton (1883) and Spearman (1904), at least some sensory discrimination abilities are moderately associated with IQ. In one study of children (average age of 12 years), abilities to discriminate hues and sounds were significantly correlated with scores on several intelligence tests; weight discrimination was not. A second study with adults ranging from ages 18 to 62 confirmed this finding (this study, mentioned in chapter 2, also found that finger dexterity was importantly related to general intelligence; Dreary et al., 2004). The exact reasons for the underlying shared variance are not known, but the association was stronger in younger children, among whom the underlying latent factors showed a very strong association. Another study used different tasks with elementary school children and found that sensory discrimination (visual judgment of relative line length and haptic judgments regarding object weight) was strongly related ($r = .78$) to intelligence as derived from a standard set of tasks (Meyer Hagmann-von Arx, Lemola, & Grob, 2010). Interestingly, the relationship was stronger at ages 5 to 6 ($r = .81$) and 9 to 10 ($r = .95$) than 7 to 8 ($r = .61$), which they hypothesize is related to cognitive reorganization during elementary school.

One possibile reason for the relation is that sensory discrimination might feed into a multitude of higher-level abilities. For one, language is enabled by fine auditory discriminations between phonemes, and by making such discriminations very quickly. Language-processing difficulties are preceded in infancy by abnormally extended processing times for similar, rapidly presented streams of stimuli (Merzenich, 2001). The ability to make fine distinctions in a stream of input analogous to that used in language is impaired even prelinguistically in some children with language difficulties.

Advances in science are fueled by people's ability to carefully observe phenomena and make fine distinctions in what is perceived. Doctors presumably practice their art better when they can perceive finer differences in a patient's manifestations of a problem, say, a difference in tissue indicating melanoma. Appreciation and creation of music involves hearing fine distinctions between notes. For the visual arts as well, fine discrimination of colors and textures can enhance appreciation. Navigation through any space usually depends on fine visual and auditory discrimination, and performance under highly challenging situations, such as on the battlefield or in the sports arena, is enhanced by the speed and accuracy of such distinctions. One could go on. Sensory discrimination is an exceedingly important ability that we tend to take for granted.

Research suggests that the quality of one's sensory discrimination capacities is influenced by sensory experiences one has early in life. Those experiences serve to organize cognitive structures in a manner that optimizes discriminative capacities specific to the stimuli one experienced early in life. Furthermore, since higher cognitive processes arise out of lower ones, cognitive organization early in development could have an important impact at higher levels of processing.

A long-held view, shared by some ancient Greeks and the British empiricists alike, is that perception is the origin of all knowledge. The contrasting view, that knowledge is inborn, was held by Plato and later Rousseau. Exciting psychology research is exploring how far one can take the view that knowledge is inborn (Spelke & Newport, 1998). Yet, even if some knowledge is inborn, the importance of what we perceive for what we know is indisputable. And early environmental experiences clearly have a profound influence on discriminative capacities.

Particular input changes cortical structures in ways that optimize an organism's ability to discriminate that type of input. In one experiment, litters of rat pups and their mothers were placed for 10 to 16 hours each day in a sound chamber, where they were repeatedly exposed to a tone at a particular frequency—4 Hz for one group, and 19 Hz for another. This experience was carried out for 20 days, when the rat pups were 9 to 28 days old. For the remaining hours each day, the rats were in a normal laboratory sound environment. Over the course of treatment, recordings were made of neurons in the auditory cortex responding to tones at sound frequencies that spanned a range of 0.5 to 30 Hz. The recordings enabled the construction of a map showing the organization of cell assemblies in the auditory cortex responding to sounds of different frequencies.

Rat pups that were intensively exposed to the low tone showed neural responses specially tuned to low tones as early as 14 days old, 4 days earlier than rat pups without that exposure. Other differences were not simply a matter of precocity, but concerned sensitivity of response and structure that had a mark of more permanent difference. For example, the percentage of cortical area responding to low tones was greatly increased in low-tone exposed rats relative to those without such exposure. In addition, the receptive fields for those neurons were larger in the exposed rat pups; thus their overall responsiveness to tones of about 4 Hz was greater than it was in rats without the specific exposure. The rats exposed to repeated high-frequency tones showed the same effects for high-frequency signals. No such findings were obtained for adult rats (80 days old) that were given the same auditory experience, indicating that the postnatal period was a critical one for this sort of auditory cortex development in rats.

Summarizing findings from an extensive program of research of which this study is part, the neuroscientist Michael Merzenich noted:

> If an animal is trained to make progressively finer distinctions about specific sound stimuli, for example, then cortical neurons come to represent those stimuli in a progressively more specific and progressively amplified manner. In a learning phase of plasticity:
>
> 1. Cortical neuron populations that are directly excited by these behaviorally important stimuli grow progressively in number.
> 2. Growing neuronal populations respond with progressively greater specificity to the spectral (spatial) and temporal dimensions of the behaviorally important stimuli that are processed in the skill learning.
> 3. The growing numbers of selectively responding neurons discharge with progressively stronger temporal coordination (distributed synchronicity). (2001, p. 68)

In addition, by providing particular experiences as input, one can dramatically shorten or lengthen cortical processing times in a developing brain. In part because of this timing issue, and in part because of the changes made in numbers, sizes, and responsiveness of neurons geared to a particular stimulus, these changes have import that extends up the cognitive system. The strength of one's neural response to specific object features predicts the degree to which one's perceptual organization is determined by those features (Ward & Chun, 2016). The importance of this differentiation lies not only in its implications for the discrimination that was inherent in the input, but also for its impact on other processes. The course of development is one of refining lower-level skills and combining them into higher-level ones. As William James (1890) pointed out, development is composed in part of increasing automaticity. These lower-level discriminations feed into higher ones. The organization of the adult brain is very deeply affected by early experiences.

> It should be emphasized that in these processes, the brain is not simply changing to record and store content. It is not merely a plastic machine that is filling its dictionaries and constructing its address systems to facilitate its complex associations and operations. By adjusting its spectral/spatial and temporal filters, *the cerebral cortex is actually selectively refining its processing capacities to fit each task at hand*—and *in toto*, establishes its own general processing capabilities. At the same time,

this "learning how to learn" determines the fidelity and facility with which specific classes of information can be recorded, associated, and manipulated. (Merzenich, 2001, p. 68, italics in original)

In considering this research, the issue arises as to what kinds of experiences young children might have to optimize their later capacities for language, art, science, and all activities involving perceptual discrimination. The end of this chapter details how the Sensory Materials in Montessori environments serve such development. Before proceeding, it is important to consider the conditions under which reorganization of the brain can occur following an initial period of plasticity.

Conventionally, neuroscientists have held that plasticity, the term for the brain flexibly organizing itself in response to experience, was a feature of young brains. Recently, organizational change has also been found in adult brains (see Lillard & Erisir, 2011). This is not entirely surprising, as we continue to learn throughout life. But learning can simply be about neural connections; finding more fundamental changes, such as the size of neural assemblies changing in response to particular input (e.g., tactile pressure on a finger) would be more surprising. One crucial difference in what permits reorganization in adult versus in developing brains may concern the relevance of the stimuli to the organism. In the study just described, with rat pups and tones, the stimulus was passively received by the organism. The sound bore no particular relevance for the rats; it did not have a meaning such as, "Food is now available in the right-hand food bowl."

In contrast to the capacity for young organisms to neurologically reorganize even in response to passively received input, when reorganization happens in more mature (yet not even necessarily adult) brains, it may happen only in the context of the stimuli being actively received by the organism. It appears from current evidence that for reorganization to occur after an initial period of plasticity, it might be necessary that the stimuli be meaningful to the organism, that the organism pay particular attention to it, and perhaps even that the organism act in relation to it. Exactly when the change from a period when passive input is sufficient to when this "meaningful" criterion sets in is a topic for empirical research; surely it differs across organisms and across types of sensory input.

In one illustrative study, young adult monkeys were given the task of retrieving 100 banana-flavored food pellets that were randomly placed, one by one, into five different-sized containers (Xerri, Merzenich, Jenkins, & Santucci, 1999). The monkeys never had much trouble retrieving from the larger bowls. From the small containers, however, retrieval was difficult. It required the monkeys to change the typical initial strategy of using a single finger to eject the pellet (which often resulted in its remaining in the smaller bowls, or in some cases, flying out of the bowl and onto the floor, unavailable to the monkey) to using two fingers, grasping the pellet between them. The monkeys were given three sessions per week with the bowls for 8 to 14 weeks, and the researchers noted changes in neural organization along with changes in behaviors and success rates.

With experience, the monkeys were able to successfully retrieve the pellets from the small bowls with fewer attempts, and the strategies they used to do so stabilized. Neural reorganization occurred in response to this experience, and the form of each monkey's reorganization was specifically associated with the fingers that monkey used with the small bowls. The fingers that a given monkey had come to use to retrieve pellets from the smaller bowls were represented in cortical areas that were enlarged to twice that of the areas representing the other fingers of the same hand, and also twice that of the areas representing the same fingers of the other hand. That this change was limited to those fingers, in concert with other evidence, shows that the neural reorganization in these young adult animals was occurring in response to a difficult and meaningful task. In addition, the degree of change in neural organization corresponded with change in the proficiency with which the monkeys retrieved the pellets: the greater the degree of neural change, the more proficient the behavior.

To summarize, work in neuroscience suggests that the brain organizes itself in response to input received early in development. The period of maximal plasticity is probably very early in life, before initial cell assemblies and neural connections are created. Later in the juvenile, and possibly in the adult, period, meaningful stimuli on which the organism acts still create structural changes in the brain that correspond to the organism's degree of proficiency in interacting with the stimuli.

This work can be taken to suggest that to optimize children's perceptual capacities, they should be exposed to an orderly progression of sensory information in early childhood. At some point, in order for such stimulation to have effect, research suggests that the child would need to act on the information. Exactly when the changeover occurs from passive reception being sufficient to impact neural organization to active interaction being necessary surely differs across types of perceptual information and across organisms. Because higher cognitive skills are built on the foundation of simpler ones, such organization could have exponential effects on higher cognitive functions. Preliminary research on this issue suggests that it does.

Order in the Sensory Materials of the Primary

Montessori's Sensory Materials are derived from ones used first by Itard, who worked with the Wild Boy of Aveyron, and his follower Séguin, from then-current psychological tests, and from her own research (Montessori, 1967b, p. 99). Like all the Montessori materials, she claimed the Sensory Materials were developed in response to observations of how children reacted to them, and refinements were made until she believed she had hit upon an optimal material for the purpose.

The Sensorial Materials embody order in many senses. One way in which they are ordered is that each material isolates the feature(s) of interest—normally just one feature (color, taste, or sound). For example, the Color Tablets vary from each other only in color; their weight, size, dimension, and feel are constant. When a material's quality by its nature would present itself to two senses simultaneously—for example, different grades of sandpaper both feel and look different—Dr. Montessori had such materials used with blindfolds, isolating the tactile sense: She noted that the eye can interfere with what the hand knows (Montessori, 1914/1965, p. 105). As was discussed in chapter 2, people are more sensitive to difference when a single aspect, rather than multiple aspects, of something is changed (Treisman & Gelade, 1980).

A second way in which the Sensorial Materials are ordered is that many of them entail a similar sequence of use. Initially the teacher will point out a sharp contrast for children. For example, the tactile sense is educated through the Rough and Smooth Boards. These wooden boards (about 4-inches square) have strips of rough and smooth sandpaper glued on them. The initial board has a very rough and a very smooth strip, side by side, and the teacher demonstrates to the child how to wash and dry her hands, sit down with the board, and feel the difference, naming the qualities. The second step is to take a set of boards with pairs of each grade, and match the different Rough and Smooth boards while blindfolded. A next step is to arrange a set of boards in a linear sequence, for example, from roughest to smoothest. Finer and finer grades of sandpaper are introduced, as the child learns to feel finer and finer distinctions. As with most of the Sensorial Materials, the child learns to identify particular types of material and to match pairs, then learns to put materials in sequence. Eventually the gradations between the materials become finer, further educating the child's sensitivity. The third way in which the Sensorial Materials are ordered is that many of them involve putting objects in a particular order.

There are many other exercises to educate the senses. Exercises for the thermic sense consist of feeling metal bottles containing different temperatures of water, or using tablets of different materials (e.g., felt, glass, cork, wood, steel, and slate) that feel warmer or colder to the touch. To educate the boric sense (weight), children pick up tablets of different species of wood that naturally have different weights, and again, pair them, order them in sequence, and finally learn to discriminate finer gradations. To educate the perception of color, there are Color Tablets. Children are initially given only three pairs—red, blue, and yellow—and are shown how to pair them. When the child has mastered the three pairs, the number of pairs is increased to 11 (the primary, secondary, and black and white colors). Finally, children are introduced to the final set of Color Tablets, in which there are nine basic colors and seven shades of each. Children learn to order the shades of a single color, say, seven tablets each displaying a different shade of green. The teacher helps the children in this task by giving them an organized approach, such as always to begin with the darkest color.

There are even more Sensory Materials than these; for example, to educate the sense of smell, there is a set of Smell Cylinders, wooden cylinders with cloth ends containing material of various scents. There are Sound Cylinders, wooden cylinders containing various objects that make different sounds when shaken. There are even materials to educate the sense of taste. Order is inherent in all the Sensory Materials.

Research on neurological development shows that the brain organizes itself in response to input and that organisms that are asked to make particular sensory discriminations do so more rapidly because of the neurological reorganization that ensues. A pertinent question for research is whether working with the Sensorial Materials leads Montessori children to more quickly and accurately perceive the environment, and whether this confers any advantage outside the exercises themselves and later in life. Existing research on this question has been correlational; Montessori programs present an opportunity for quasi-experimental research that could suggest whether the relation might be causal. The Sensorial exercises have many other purposes as well, including ordered activity and concentration, but research on the potential outcomes for observational skills and responses to the perceived environment later in life would be particularly interesting.

Chapter Summary

In sum, Montessori is not ordered on a macro level of daily schedule because children need to be at liberty to choose work over 3-hour periods in the classroom so as to develop concentration and engage in what she called the Great Work: deep, sustained, focused interaction with Montessori materials or other work (see chapter 4). In other ways, however, Montessori education is very ordered. The classroom layout is logical and organized, as are the layouts of each activity within the classroom. There are set routines for using each Montessori material. The aural environment is ordered, and the curriculum follows a logical progression that is coherent and internally consistent. Finally, Montessori education systematically trains sensory discrimination, an activity that might be related to patterns of neural organization that speed environmental processing, freeing cognitive resources for other activities.

11 }

Recent Research on Montessori Education

The basis of the reform of education and society, which is a necessity
of our times, must be built upon . . . scientific study.
　—Maria Montessori *(1949/1974, p. 12, italics in original)*

Writing the original text of this book in 2004 steeped me in evidence about what works well for children's development and education, and I saw that it aligns very well with the Montessori program. Sadly, I also realized that what typically happens in conventional classrooms is actually misaligned with what the evidence suggests are best practices. That is, Montessori education, and not conventional education, had strong indirect evidential support.

But as a developmental psychologist, I also had a core belief, shared by many and stated explicitly to me by Elizabeth Spelke, a chaired Professor of Psychology at Harvard University. When I told her about my first Montessori study (reported later), she responded by declaring that I was challenging her belief that no school program can really make a difference to children's outcomes. Indeed, based on a wealth of data, many developmental psychologists believe that parents are the only truly meaningful influence on children's outcomes. Parents influence children in two ways: (1) They confer their genes, and genes explain (on average) about half of any given individual trait a person has. For some traits they explain more, and for others less, but on average, a person's outcomes are about half conferred by their genes. (2) Parents have a strong influence over the environment in which children grow up. They create the home environment, where children are subject to their parents' motivations, desires, fears, and aspirations. Parents also determine the neighborhood children grow up in, the day cares and schools they attend, who babysits them, and so on. New research in epigenetics suggests how the environmental influences also change gene expression (Moore, 2015).

Supporting the idea that the influence of parents trumps all was the National Study of Early Child Care. In the early 1990s, some developmental psychologists were concerned about attachment relationships being disrupted as mothers were increasingly employed outside the home. Some early research had suggested that this might cause a slight increase in insecure-avoidant attachments. This led to a large study of day care, in which children were tracked from prior to birth through age 15 (Vandell, Belsky, Burchinal, Steinberg, & Vandergrift, 2010). Overall, the effects of day care were very small once parent-related factors were accounted for. Children who had high-quality care had slightly higher achievement and fewer social problems, whereas very long hours in center-based care, particularly when combined with an insensitive mother, led to small increases in aggressive behavior. Overall, this study added to the sense that after parenting is accounted for, schooling would have little influence on child outcomes: Even spending 40 hours a week in day care for the first several years of one's life had little effect.

Consequently, when I finished the book, on the one hand, I thought that after the effects of parents, school would make little difference. On the other hand, I had reviewed a great deal of evidence suggesting that Montessori schooling would be better for children than conventional schooling. So I set out to see if Montessori education actually makes a difference to child outcomes.

The existing research on Montessori outcomes was unsatisfactory, largely because of two fundamental problems. The first is nonrandom assignment. A study illustrating this was published in 1976: White, Yussen, and Docherty's "Performance of Montessori and Traditionally Schooled Nursery Children on Tasks of Seriation, Classification, and Conservation." Seriation is lining up objects in a logical series, such as from shortest to tallest; classification is organizing objects by category; and conservation is the understanding that changing certain superficial properties of something will not change other fundamental properties—for example, the changing shape of a ball of clay does not change its volume. The researchers hypothesized that Montessori children would be advanced in these three cognitive skills, which were central in the cognitive development literature of the time. The reason for their centrality was because they were important to Piaget, and his theory was then the driving force in cognitive development research. (Piaget, in fact, turned away from Montessori education because he believed Montessori taught children these skills when children were biologically incapable of their acquisition.) White and his colleagues tested 80 four-year-olds, 40 of whom were enrolled in Montessori school and 40 of whom were enrolled in a conventional nursery school, and they found that Montessori children performed better on seriation and classification, but that the groups were equivalent on conservation (which they decided, in keeping with Piaget, was because the skill was too advanced for the age, despite the education).

The problem with this study is that there is no way of knowing from the study design whether Montessori children had learned these skills in Montessori, or whether the Montessori children were different at the outset in some way that led to better performance on the two tests, such that they would have done better on those tests regardless of what school they were in. This goes back to the issue of the parents. Montessori is a unique school system. It is likely that certain types of parents choose certain unique school systems. Those same parents influence their children. Who is to say that it is an influence of the school system, then, and not the parents, especially given that we know parents are the strongest influence on child outcomes?

This is the fundamental problem with citing that Sergey Brin and Larry Paige, who founded Google; Jimmy Wales, who founded Wikipedia; Jeff Bezos, who founded Amazon; Will Wright, who created the Sims computer game; and several other creative leaders in our time all went to Montessori schools (Gaylord, 2012) as evidence that the school program nourishes extraordinary invention. Perhaps the real source of their inventiveness is their parents, who also favored a different school system, and these people would have created extraordinary inventions even had they been in conventional schools. To get around this problem, one needs a better "control group"—for example, either children who were put in Montessori without their parents choosing it, or children whose parents chose Montessori but could not get in because of lack of space. The next best thing, if some level of random assignment is unavailable, is matching children on characteristics that hopefully take care of the preexisting differences that might stem from the parents; parent education and income levels (which tend to covary) are often used, and gender and ethnicity are often thrown in for good measure (although the latter usually adds no variance once parent education and income are accounted for).

A second problem in the study by White and colleagues and across much Montessori research is inattention to the quality of the Montessori program. The joke term "Montessomething" arose for a reason: Schools that use the Montessori moniker can vary the program in myriad ways and stray quite far from the program described in Dr. Montessori's books. A close reading of Dr. Montessori's books suggests it is very important that there be a 3-year age range in the classroom corresponding to Montessori's Planes of Development (Montessori, 1946/1963, pp. 14–15). A 3-hour uninterrupted morning work period, 5 days per week, and a second 2- to 3-hour uninterrupted afternoon work period, is also important, to allow concentration to develop. A full complement of Montessori materials, a large group of peers, free choice, a well-trained teacher (and only one teacher), and the other features discussed here are important as well. Most researchers, however, would not know to look for these features, and assume that if a school calls itself Montessori, then it practices authentic Montessori. A related problem is that in some studies, children have had very little exposure to Montessori, for example, they might have had just a few months in a Montessori program.

Finally, a third problem is that there were not a lot of children involved. Although it is more difficult to get statistical significance with a small sample, small samples also sometimes yield "fluke" results, making replication very important. Related to this, many Montessori studies involve children from one or two Montessori classrooms, comparing them to children in one or two conventional classrooms. Under these circumstances, one cannot know if any effects found are due to the teachers, or some other aspect of the classroom, or the methods.

Two other older studies will be discussed with reference to these problems. One of the rare studies of distal Montessori outcomes (high school) was conducted in the Milwaukee public schools around 2003 (published as Dohrmann, Nishida, Gartner, Lipsky, & Grimm, 2007). This study was free of several of the problems just mentioned. It involved many Montessori teachers (in different classrooms), used data from large numbers of children, and used schools that apparently offered reasonably good Montessori quality. Although subject to state requirements imposed on all public schools they had "associated" status with the Association Montessori Internationale (AMI), the accrediting organization that Dr. Montessori started to oversee quality in Montessori schools. In addition, the children had an extended Montessori treatment, from ages 3 to 11. On the negative side, the sample was not randomly assigned. Although the public Montessori school children were originally admitted by lottery, the lottery losers were not tracked and so were unavailable as a comparison group. This self-selection is problematic. In an attempt to redress this, the group of children with whom the Montessori children were compared was a particularly challenging one with which to find difference: Fellow students at their current high schools, who were matched for gender, ethnicity, and socioeconomic status (SES; operationalized here as free lunch status). More than half of the 201 Montessori students in the study (59% ethnic minority) were placed in Milwaukee's top four high schools (a International Baccalaureate school in the study was the top high school in the state). Because many factors might operate to bring children into such high schools, this makes up a very high standard of group for comparison. It would be more optimal if the comparison group were matched at the onset of treatment, rather than 4 or more years post-treatment.

Given the comparison group, the results of this study are remarkable. Children who were in the public Milwaukee Montessori schools from preschool to fifth grade, when tested 4 to 8 years later, scored significantly higher on a math/science factor derived from standardized tests (the ACT and the Wisconsin Knowledge and Concepts Examination [WKCE]) than did matched controls from their same high schools; on grade point average [GPA], the Montessori group's raw average score was higher than that of the non-Montessori children (2.72 vs. 2.59) but not significantly so.

Still, the results have to be interpreted cautiously. The Montessori group in this study is a self-selected sample, and parental influences may be at the root of the outcomes. That is, the matching process (gender, ethnicity, free lunch status, and current high school) might not have neutralized the effects of parents; perhaps the parents of the Montessori children all shared some factor that led them to choose Montessori in the first place and that also led to their children performing well in math and science.

As stated, a second type of problem in existing Montessori research is quality control. An example of this is the Head Start Montessori studies from the 1970s (Karnes, Shewedel, & Williams, 1983; Miller & Dyer, 1975). In these studies, to their credit, children were randomly assigned to Montessori or a variety of other preschool programs that were popular at the time. This takes care of the parent choice problem. However, the Montessori implementation was far from what I have described in this book: In one of the studies, children spent 20 minutes per day with the Montessori materials. There were only 4-year-olds in the classrooms, rather than a 3-year age grouping. The teacher training was very short, occurring over the summer prior, and the Montessori treatment lasted only 6 months. It is hard to claim then, that these studies were actually testing authentic Montessori education, although surely some elements were in place. Although findings were not all that impressive immediately after the 6-month program, years later there were benefits to the quasi-Montessori education, particularly for boys (Miller & Bizzell, 1984). However, the numbers were very small by then, hence it could be a "fluke" effect.

Thus when the first edition of this book went to press, the state of published peer-reviewed research on Montessori education was poor. There were dozens of studies of Montessori education, but almost all lacked random assignment, adequate numbers of participants, and attention to the quality of the Montessori program. There were also unpublished research reports and reports published without peer review, or at least without the peer review standards of academic journals. These are often difficult to access, and once access is gained, one sees the same problems: lack of random assignment and lack of attention to Montessori quality. To this day no published study has addressed all three issues, although one in-progress study (described later) does so fairly well. Several more studies have addressed one or two of the problems and I discuss these here, beginning with the study that I was inspired to do on completion of the first edition.

2006 *Science* Study

To test whether Montessori education actually makes a difference to children's outcomes, one needs to compare a group of children attending high-quality Montessori programs with a control group of children whose parents wanted them to attend, but who did not get in for completely random reasons. After one of my first talks about this book at a Montessori conference, I was approached by the principal of a public Montessori school in Milwaukee, Wisconsin, which had opened about 10 years earlier (a different one than the ones in the Dohrmann et al. study). The school had always admitted by lottery because it only had space for 54 new 3-year-olds each year, and yet each year, about 100 parents sought to have their 3-year-olds enroll. Many public Montessori schools are oversubscribed, but most discard the lists of children who do not get in through the lottery. This principal knew the value of random assignment from his days studying psychology at the university level, so each year he had tucked the names into a file drawer in case they would ever be useful. Furthermore, this school was recognized by the AMI-USA, which held it to a high standard regarding teacher training and classroom practices. The designation meant the teachers had a full 9-month training course in Montessori education, taught by teacher trainers who themselves had been carefully trained over many years and had passed arduous exams certifying them to teach such courses (see chapter 9). The arduous training of the teacher trainers is a real distinction of the AMI training programs; to my knowledge, the other programs do not ask that the teacher trainers have any particular credentials at all, much less the length and breadth of training required by AMI. In addition, prior to graduation the incipient teachers are tested by certified examiners who are not trainers in their course, so there is an externally imposed standard of knowledge that every AMI-certified teacher has met. To be certified by AMI, the classrooms also adhere (within reason) to an external standard: They have a 3-hour work period, a full set of Montessori materials (and lack non-Montessori materials), 3-year age groupings representing the Montessori planes of development, and a teacher-to-child ratio of 1:25 to 1:35 with a non-teaching assistant. In sum, this school had random assignment and quality Montessori.

There are higher standards of random assignment. In medicine, the gold standard is double-blind random assignment: A person who is sick takes a pill and neither the subject nor the medical staff collecting outcome data knows if that pill contains the real ingredients being evaluated or is a placebo. Clearly that is not possible in a school program. On the next tier down in random assignment, one would take all the children in a particular school and randomly assign them to Montessori or business-as-usual classrooms. Such a design would be more telling, and the only case I know of was the Head Start studies already described (that did not have quality Montessori). The next best design is the one used here, in which everyone in the study was entered into the Montessori lottery, and a randomly chosen subset enrolled, while the rest were wait-listed and enrolled in business-as-usual schools.

The school and school district agreed to be part of a study. Two private foundations provided funding. A PhD student at the University of Wisconsin, Nicole Else-Quest, agreed to help put the materials together and run the subjects in exchange for dissertation-year funding, and we were off.

A first step was to obtain a sample of children. I decided to test children who were at the end of Montessori Primary and Montessori Elementary, accordingly, at ages 5 to 6 and 11 to 12. These children had been entered in the lottery to go to the Montessori school 3 and 9 years earlier, respectively.

The district-wide school lottery was conducted each February, following a well-advertised 3-week application period. Milwaukee has a tremendous amount of school choice; the year of the study, the catalog of school options was about an inch thick and included school programs ranging from Waldorf to Spanish immersion to the arts to environmental science. Milwaukee families are given this catalog and have the option to submit applications naming their top three school choices. School principals notify the school district of the number of open slots in their school, and a computer assigns each child a rank and admits children randomly in order of rank to fill the slots. Children whose rank is lower than the number of slots are placed on a wait list in rank order.

All the parents who were contacted about the study had listed the Montessori school as their first choice. The Montessori school strictly adheres to children's rankings with this wait list with the exception of admitting siblings of children who have already been admitted by the random lottery. Typically the school leaves five to eight slots open (beyond the number designated as open for the lottery) for incoming siblings each year. Because the older siblings were themselves admitted by random selection, other characteristics of the families with siblings would still be expected to be roughly the same as that of control families, if Montessori school applicants change little from one year to the next.

Along with letters from the principal of the Montessori school and the Milwaukee Public School District, we sent out three rounds of recruitment letters, explaining to parents:

> We are embarking on a very important study to evaluate the possible influence of a public Montessori education. Your child's participation in this study would be very valuable to our understanding of the possible impact of attending Craig Montessori School, and I am writing to see if you would be willing to have your child participate in this research. Participation would require 1–2 hours of your child's time, at school and at a time convenient to your child and his or her teacher. Your child would be asked questions that would tell the researchers about his or her social reasoning, personal motivation in school, academic knowledge, and the like. The researchers aim to make participation in the study fun and interesting for the children, and children who do not enjoy participating do not have to continue. All procedures have been approved by the Milwaukee Public Schools and by the University of Virginia's committee responsible for ensuring the protection of children engaged in research, and have been commonly used in other research with children.

If you would be willing to have your child participate, please fill out the enclosed information form. The reason that we need the information in this form is that we are comparing Craig Montessori children with other children whose parents lost the randomized lottery for admission to Craig when their children were 2 or 3 years old. It is important that we know if there are differences in certain factors like income or education levels across these two groups. Therefore the form asks about such factors. This information will be kept strictly confidential, and will not be used in any way except to ensure that the Montessori and non-Montessori samples are similar.

These letters (with the described demographic information form) were sent to families who had entered their child in the lottery years earlier, and who still had an address in the Milwaukee Public Schools database—presumably because their child was still in the school system. The relative stability of the Milwaukee community was a great advantage, as I was to learn later when we started another (ongoing) study in Hartford, Connecticut, public Montessori schools. Still in the database were 90 children at age 5 and 86 children at age 12 who had applied to the school years earlier, which comprised the potential control group. In the Montessori school, there were 54 children at age 5 and 36 children at age 12. There were fewer 12-year-olds in the school because Montessori schools typically have a pyramid structure, with fewer classes at the older grades. This is because families inevitably leave—some need to move, others opt for conventional education at some point—but few new children are admitted. Entering Montessori after age 3 requires a cultural transformation. For example, children in conventional classrooms are enculturated into the extrinsic reward system. One of my daughters explained this to me at age 13, after her first 2 weeks in conventional school: Asked if she needed to read something she had brought home from school, she said, "No, it's not something we will be tested on." With no tests in Montessori, this enculturated attitude does not lead to constructive classrooms, and therefore few children are admitted to Montessori after age 3. (Having a few conventionally schooled children in a large Montessori classroom is not typically a problem, because they adapt to the mores of the peer group.)

In the ensuing weeks, 32 control 5-year-olds returned a letter, and 33 control 12-year-olds did so. Excluding those who had attended another Montessori or were homeschooled brought the final numbers to 25 control 5-year-olds (who were compared to 30 Montessori 5-year-olds) and 28 control 12-year-olds (who were compared to 29 Montessori 12-year-olds). As would be expected based on the random lottery admission to the Montessori, the samples were very similar. Children were of the same mean ages and age ranges, and the median income of participating families was $20,000 to $50,000 across both samples. Both groups reported having fewer than 100 books in the home, on average, and parent levels of education were similar. Although direct ethnicity information was not taken, because we did not want parents to feel that ethnicity was a main concern of the study, both the Montessori school and the Milwaukee school district were 60% African American and 18% white.

I also had selected an array of outcome tests to analyze the development of the whole person, rather than just academics. We know that success in life depends on many abilities—self-regulation, social skills, insight—and I wanted to tap into an array of relevant abilities. I chose tests that were well-known—many had been used in the large National Study of Early Child Care mentioned earlier and many other studies of child outcomes, and they were easily available. Description of the tests and their results follow.

I went to Milwaukee in October, met with the research assistant, and showed her how to conduct the tests. She then started testing the 59 Montessori children at Craig Montessori, and the 53 control children at the 39 different schools they attended, moving back and forth between control and Montessori children. Most of the control children were at public city schools, but twelve went to suburban public, charter, and private voucher schools. In February, it became clear that the research assistant would not be able to complete the job of testing all the children, and three very competent graduate students from the University of Virginia went to Milwaukee to help. Come June, we had a full data set—and then came the exciting part: What would it show? Does Montessori make a difference? The short answer is that it made a significant difference. In what ways?

I begin with the 5-year-olds. Some of their tests were the standard Woodcock–Johnson tests that are given to assess learning issues and also are often used to measure outcomes of school programs. Two tests assessed early reading abilities: Letter Word, which has children first recognize letters ("Point to the 'a'"), then recall letters ("Which letter is this?"), and then read words, from simpler to more complex. One problem with Letter Word is that one could do well from remembering how sounds and words look, rather than from truly reading. The second reading test I used, Word Attack, gets around this by using nonsense words no one has likely seen before ("zoop"). On both of these reading tests, the Montessori 5-year-olds scored significantly higher than the others, suggesting something about the Montessori program was advancing their early literacy skills.

Another basic skill children get in school concerns numeracy. For this I chose the Applied Problems subtest of the Woodcock–Johnson, again because it is widely known and used. This test starts with simple counting of items, then simple addition ("If you had 3 cars [shown in picture] and someone gave you one more, how many would you have?"), then proceeds to clock faces ("Show me the clock that says 9:00") and coins ("How much money is this?") and mathematical word problems. It is actually quite a quick jump from the simple addition and subtraction to the special knowledge (if no one has yet shown a child an analog clock, or coins, then of course he or she will not do well on those questions), but the test is a standard one. On this test as well, Montessori 5-year-olds performed significantly better than did the control children.

On three other Woodcock–Johnson tests—Picture Vocabulary, Spatial Relations, Understanding Directions, and Concept Formation—the Montessori 5-year-olds scored slightly better than the control group, but with such a small sample, the differences were not significant.

Another test we gave was the Dimensional Change Card Sort (DCCS), which is a test of executive function, the set of prefrontal abilities that guide problem solving and goal-directed behavior, as reviewed in chapter 4. For the DCCS, children are shown a series of cards showing two objects in two colors (e.g., red and blue boats and flowers). Children are asked to sort the cards by one rule ("Put the blue ones here, and the red ones there") and after six cards are correctly sorted, they are given a different rule by which to sort the next six cards ("Put the flowers here, and the boats there.") This is a test of executive function because the child has to keep the first rule in mind while initially sorting, and then inhibit that first rule and hold the second rule in mind while sorting by it. Many 3-year-olds sort the first few cards in the second batch correctly, then revert to the initial rule and sort by color (or by shape, if that was the first rule given). This is despite the fact that the rules are repeated for every card and that children can recite the right rule—yet persist in sorting by the other rule! However, by age 5, many children can handle the rule switch, and this was the case in this study. Anticipating this, we also used a third phase, which is difficult even for adults: "If the card has a black border, sort by color; if it does not, sort by shape." The score was the number of cards correctly sorted. On this test as well, Montessori 5-year-olds scored significantly higher than the control children.

Another test of executive function used here was the Delay of Gratification, the classic marshmallow test devised by Walter Mischel that was described in chapter 4. For this, many children did not wait at all, and many other children waited the full 15 minutes, across both samples, creating a "bimodal distribution." But on average, Montessori children waited almost 2 minutes longer than control children. This was not a statistically different result, but it seems worth noticing.

Children were also given a "false belief" test, which is a standard test of social understanding. You and I know that people act in the world based not on how it is, but how they think it is, how they "mentally represent" it. Accordingly, if I think a large black shadow in the woods is a bear, I will react like it is a bear, even if it is actually just a rock. This is a fundamental understanding. In children, we test for the understanding by presenting a situation in which someone has a false belief. In the classic test (Wimmer & Perner, 1983), a boy named Maxi has some chocolate, which he leaves in a drawer while he goes out to play. While he is out, his mother sees the choco-late in the drawer and moves it to the cupboard. The test question is "Where will Maxi look for his chocolate when he returns?" The discovery that young children typically answer incorrectly, by claiming that he will look into the cupboard, led to a cottage industry of studies of false belief in the 1990s. The upshot of all this is that the finding is solid, across many ways of asking the question, and many similar paradigms to test the concept (Wellman, Cross, & Watson, 2001). In addition it has what is called *predictive validity*: Children who pass the false belief test at younger ages also tend to have more friends and are rated higher by their teachers for social competence (Wellman, 2014). Therefore I gave children one standard false belief test. Because there are only two response options (the cupboard and the drawer), guessing would result in 50% correct. The control 5-year-olds were at chance in answering this question, whereas the Montessori 5-year-olds were significantly above chance.

Another way to look at social competence is with a test of social problem solving. A classic test was designed by Ken Rubin in the 1970s. In the part of most concern here, children were told three short vignettes about two other children of about their same age who were having a social problem: One was using an item that the second child really wanted. For example, in one story, a child (of the tested child's same gender and ethnicity) had been on a swing for a long, long time, and another child (also of child's same gender and eth-nicity) really wanted to the swing. Children were asked what the second child could do or say so she could have the swing; to obtain more answers for each story, they were asked, "What else?" and "What would you do?" Children's answers to these stories can be rather mundane (such as "Say, 'Please. Please can I have it.'"), but they are sometimes very creative ("I would see if there was something else she wanted to do and she could do that for 10 minutes while I had the swing.") We were especially interested in these very creative solutions because they seemed to show a more advanced level of social moral reasoning, by taking two perspectives into account and coming up with a solution that would work for both people; such children were aiming for a socially "just" solution. We coded all of children's responses for such "social justice" responses, and we found that the Montessori children were signifi-cantly more likely to come up with them than were the controls.

Our final measure of social skills was taken on the playground. We watched each child for 15 minutes during recess and coded during each minute what the child's predominant activity was, from several categories. We found that chil-dren in Montessori were significantly more likely to be engaged in "positive shared play," meaning they were engaged with one or more other children and appeared to be happily getting along. They were also significantly less likely to be involved in a category dubbed "Ambiguous rough and tumble play," which is coded when the play looks a bit rough, and the observer cannot tell if the children are playing or are genuinely being aggressive. Finally, against the concern many have that Montessori Primary children isolate themselves from the group and therefore do not learn social skills, the Montessori children were slightly less likely than control children to be coded as playing alone.

In addition to all these tested social skills, two other remarks arose during this research suggesting positive social skills in Montessori. First, the researchers commented on how easy it was to work with the children there—they were respectful and compliant. Second, the head of school mentioned to me that the city school bus drivers reported wanting the Montessori routes because the Montessori children were so much more pleasant to bus around.

Across many domains, Montessori 5-year-olds were doing significantly better than the children who by lottery were in other schools. What about the 12-year-olds? It is important to know that the 12-year-olds were pioneers of sorts. The school had started just 2 years before they entered the Primary classroom at age 3, and so they were the first class of 3-year-olds with 5-year-old classmates, and those 5-year-old classmates had never had older classmates themselves. In Montessori, it is sometimes said that schools do not start functioning really well until the sixth year because learning from one's older peers is so important. If a child's older peers, when they started Montessori at age 3, themselves had older peers who had been in Montessori, then the child would be learning from well-regulated older children. Consequently, the 12-year-olds were disadvantaged because they were an early class. A second caveat concerns testing. Children in conventional schools are tested repeatedly, and some Woodcock–Johnson tests are similar to some of those tests. Montessori children are rarely tested; in Milwaukee, testing would have been largely confined to the "No Child Left Behind" tests they had to take during certain school years. This could also put the 12-year-olds at a disadvantage.

In keeping with this, although the Montessori 12-year-olds scores were higher on the Woodcock–Johnson measures than the controls, they were not significantly so. However, on several other tests, the Montessori 12-year-olds did score higher. One such test was Narrative Completion. Children were given 5 minutes to complete a story with the stem "____ had the best/worst day at school." Blind coders rated the stories for several factors, including the number of technical errors (errors of spelling, grammar, and punctuation), overall creativity, sophistication of sentence structures, vocabulary level. As examples, here is a conventionally-schooled child's story about a worst day that was rated highly for creativity:

> One day, Sora had the worst day at school. He had all of these test and he knew nothing about any of them. He had a math, social studies, reading, and language arts test. He didn't study and he had 2 months worth of warnings about them when the test began (they were all 1 test)

he looked at the first question cluelessly. The teacher looked at him and he looked back. Sora was so confused that he actually screamed. Everyone looked at him and laughed furiously. Sora cowered and his head in his test. He had no idea on what he had planned to do. And at the end, he got a completely failing grade.

Here is a Montessori child's story about a worst day that was rated highly for creativity (interestingly, this child chose to take a teacher's perspective):

One day, Sova had the worst day at school. One of her students were talking back to her and she sent her to the office. Not knowing if her student went directly to the office, she called on her white telephone to see if she went there. When she heard that her student wasn't there, she got really worried. About 5 minutes later, her student came back. Sova was so mad, she called her student's mother & told her what had happened. Her mom was ferouise & ask to speak to Sova's student. After about 5 minutes, her student hung up the phone crying. Sova felt sorry for her, so for the rest of the day she had every body color and write a story about it.

Both groups had their share of technical errors (and there were no differences on those scores), but overall, the Montessori children's stories were rated more highly on creativity, sophistication of the sentence structures they employed, and level of vocabulary used. The two stories just shown also reveal another way in which Montessori and control children were different—a way that was brought out in some other tests: Namely, the children seemed to have different feelings about school as a friendly or unfriendly place to be.

The Activities and Feelings test had several subtests including Feelings About School and Classroom. On this latter scale, there was a significant difference. The items on this scale were as follows:

Students in my class really care about each other.

Students in my class are willing to go out of their way to help someone.

Students in my class treat each other with respect.

People care about each other in this school.

Students at this school work together to solve problems.

My class is like a family.

When I'm having a problem, another student will help.

Student in this class help each other learn.

Students rated each item as Not true at all, Sort of true, or Very true. Montessori children scored significantly higher on these items. This is also consistent with studies by Rathunde and Csikzentmihalyi, discussed later in this chapter, but in their research children had not been randomly assigned to Montessori or a control school. Many things about Montessori education likely contribute to the stronger sense of community, for example, spending 3 years with the same children (and teacher), having 3-year mixed-age groups, working on self-selected projects together as they wish, and not having grades or other extrinsic rewards that enhance feelings of competition among classmates. Certainly it is a nice way to feel about one's classmates in sixth grade, and the difference is also apparent in the preceding stories.

Another scale addressed social issues in another way: how the 12-year-olds would solve social problems. School Stories (Crick & Ladd, 1990) presents children with six stories such as the following Lunch Story:

> You are at lunch one day and looking for a place to sit. You see kids you know at a table across the room. The kids are laughing and talking to each other and they look like they are having a good time. You go over to their table, sit down, and say hi to everyone. The kids look right at you, roll their eyes, and don't say anything to you. After a few seconds, the kids start talking again to each other, but no one talks to you at all.

After reading the story, children are given this forced-choice question about how they would manage the conflict, representing overt aggression, relational aggression, assertive friendliness, and avoidance:

What would you do if this happened to you?

A. I would ask the kids a question to get into the conversation.

B. I would hit one of the kids at the table.

C. I would move to another table.

D. I would say mean things about the kids at the table to my friends.

Montessori children were significantly more likely than controls to choose the most positive responses (assertive friendliness, as in option A).

In sum, in my first study of Montessori outcomes (Lillard & Else-Quest, 2006), children who were randomly assigned by lottery to attend an authentic public Montessori school in a low-income city school district performed significantly better on many measures than did the children who lost the lottery and were at a great variety of other (mostly) public schools in the area. At age 5, this included almost all the measures; at age 12, it was limited to social measures and measures concerning writing. On the latter, it is not clear if some of the benefits of Montessori decline over time, or if this class of 12-year-olds was at a disadvantage because they were one of the early classes in the school. One study shedding some light on this is the one by Dohrmann and coworkers (2007) described earlier. Using different public Montessori schools in Milwaukee—ones that also had lotteries, but had not saved the names of the lottery losers and therefore were not useful for my study—found better outcomes on a math-science composite for Montessori graduates.

Variations in Montessori Implementation

In the years that followed publication of Else-Quest's and my study in *Science* and the Dohrmann et al. article, with the Montessori community celebrating 100 years since the opening of the first Montessori school and this book in its second edition, I had the opportunity to travel the world speaking about Montessori education and visiting classrooms in many schools. The variety of Montessori implementations I saw was striking.

I saw schools that seemed like the ones described by Dr. Montessori, where the children were happy and peaceful, deeply engaged in work; children interacted naturally and kindly; the classrooms were neat and organized, with a full complement of Montessori materials and virtually no extraneous objects; and each classroom's teacher was observing or giving a lesson to a child or a small group. At the other end of the spectrum, I saw classrooms that can best be described as mayhem, with children using the Red Rods as guns, not putting their work away, leaving chairs out, stuffing materials back on the shelves, and not seeming to concentrate or show kindness to others. In some, hordes of plastic toys were mixed in with Montessori materials; sometimes there were several adults hovering over children (and which was the teacher was unclear); and so on. All these schools were called Montessori schools, and those in charge believed they were implementing a Montessori program. And on a checklist based on the chapters of this book (Is there free choice? Is the learning situated in context?), they would likely all have done well except perhaps on Order; indeed, I experimented with this checklist and found no difference in scores of schools I would consider to be implementing Montessori well and ones that seemed to me to have gone astray.

During this period when I was observing at a great variety of Montessori schools, a study came out suggesting less positive outcomes for Montessori children (Lopata, Wallace, & Finn, 2005). This study had compared fourth and eighth graders in a public Montessori school, an open magnet, a "back-to-basics" structured magnet, and a non-magnet school on district-administered standardized tests of math and language arts. Although the district is only specified as a "large urban district in western New York" (p. 8), and I was unable to reach the authors for confirmation, at the time there were not many Montessori public schools that went through eighth grade and the authors were all based in Buffalo, so it was quite likely the only Buffalo public Montessori school running at the time. The four schools were demographically similar, but as an added precaution the researchers controlled for gender, ethnicity, and SES in their analyses.

In fourth grade, there were no differences among the four schools in language arts. In math, the Montessori children scored higher than children in the open magnet, but less well than children in the traditional school. In eighth grade, there were no differences in math performance, but in language arts, the Montessori students performed less well than children at the other schools.

What might explain these differences, such that Montessori children were actually performing worse here, given the equal and better performance of children on the other two studies just described? One possibility is developmental. Perhaps children in Montessori have a different developmental trajectory than children in other sorts of schools, such that they do better in the early years, then worse in junior high school, then begin to excel again in high school. This would be in keeping with Montessori's contention that the early adolescent years are an important time for other types of growth, and not a good time to stress intellectual endeavors. More longitudinal research on Montessori is needed to test this.

But another possibility is that variations in performance are caused by variations in implementation fidelity. Lopata and colleagues noted that their study did not address fidelity, as they were simply studying an existing program. I examined the public Buffalo Montessori school's website in 2007. The school was clearly working to implement Montessori philosophy, but revealed several key deviations: homework assignments, grades, and a profusion of "specials" where children have non-Montessori lessons with different teachers. Every homework assignment (by definition) interferes with the principle of free choice, a grade is typically an extrinsically sourced judgment, and specials are said to diminish in-class concentration, free choice, and time with the carefully chosen interrelated set of Montessori materials.

The Lopata study is not alone in presenting less good Montessori outcomes from apparently less authentic Montessori programs. Krafft and Berk (1998) had shown less private speech in a Montessori than traditional play-oriented preschool; private speech is developmentally positive in preschool, associated with better self-regulation. However, a description of the Montessori school used in that study showed marked deviations from the Montessori program described in Dr. Montessori's books, as it had "'work stations' arranged on tables and on the floor" (p. 644) and short work periods. Thinking about these results coupled with the earlier Head Start studies in which implementation was also poor, and the extent of variation I had seen in Montessori schools around the world, I wondered whether deviations from an authentic Montessori program could explain different outcomes in existing research. This was my next Montessori research question: Does fidelity of implementation matter to Montessori outcomes, or is even "Montessomething" implementation associated with better outcomes?

THE CLASSIC-SUPPLEMENTED STUDY

This study used a convenience sample of children in 12 Montessori classrooms at four different Montessori schools (Lillard, 2012). As a measure of implementation fidelity, I looked at how many children at any given moment were engaged with Montessori versus other materials. This is of course, just a proxy for fidelity, but I reasoned that teachers who keep non-Montessori materials out of the classroom are likely to also be concerned about keeping non-Montessori practices out. A challenge with using this proxy is that there is not necessarily perfect agreement on exactly what the Montessori materials are, as Dr. Montessori herself did not leave a list. To derive a list of Montessori Primary materials, I conducted a small study with people who train Montessori teachers (Lillard, 2011a). It led to a list of materials we could use in determining how many children in a class were engaged with Montessori materials at four set observation points across the school year. For this, a research assistant stood in each classroom for about five minutes with a checklist itemizing all the Montessori materials for the Primary classroom level; the only stipulation was that the observation occur during a work period, not circle time or a meal time. The observer scanned the classroom and noted what each child was doing, and we tabulated the percentage engaged with Montessori materials versus other activities, then averaged the four observations for each classroom to get a percentage engagement score.

Consistent with what I had observed in my travels, there was great variety among the 12 classrooms regarding the percentage of children engaged with Montessori materials in each classroom, ranging from 38–100% averaged across the four observations. In many ways, however, all 12 classrooms adhered to a basic Montessori program: All had the 3-year age grouping (3–6 years), teachers taught lessons individually or to small groups, many Montessori materials were present and available on low shelves for children to choose at will, there were no obvious extrinsic rewards, and so on. Although in a few classrooms the work period was not a full 3 hours, they all had at least 2 hours devoted to concentrated work. Despite being "Montessori" in all these ways, there were large differences in how much children were engaged with the Montessori materials.

On this, the 12 classrooms fell into two distinct clusters. In three classrooms, virtually all (98–100%) of children were engaged with Montessori materials across the observations. In the other nine, the percentages ranged from 38–56%; the rest of the time children were engaged with other activities, such as arts and crafts projects, commercial puzzles, and filling in workbooks. I dubbed the former classrooms "classic" and the latter "supplemented" ones.

I was also interested in comparing both forms of Montessori with conventional school programs, to see if perhaps the supplemented would outperform conventional schools. Because children were not admitted by lottery to the private Montessori programs used in this study, factors related to "parents who choose Montessori for their children" were an issue. To get around this, conventional schools were selected by asking the Montessori parents, "If Montessori were not available, what school would your child attend?" The top few choices were public schools, but two private schools in the communities also were often chosen. There were six preschool classrooms at these two schools, which agreed to serve as the conventional sites. These were what one might consider typical preschool classrooms at good private schools, with pretend play activities, curricula devoted to teaching reading, math, science, and history, time set aside for music, art, and Spanish, and so on. One major difference was that children were divided by age, with separate classrooms for 3-, 4-, and 5-year-old children. In addition, although average ages were similar across school types, the conventionally schooled children were a bit older on average than the Montessori children (just younger than 5 years versus 4½ years old). Parent education, ethnicity, and gender representation were all similar across the school types.

In the Milwaukee study, we tested all children just once in the school year, but we had a lottery design ensuring sample similarity. In this study, control was sought in two ways: both by controlling for parent variables (income, education) known to be associated with developmental differences, and by using a pre- and post-test design, in which we obtained children's scores early in the school year, and then again late in the school year. Thus the study measured growth, asking, "How much do children's scores change from fall to spring, given the school program?"

As in the Milwaukee study, I was interested in testing a wide range of developmental outcomes associated with life success. A first was executive function, tested here with the Head Toes Knees Shoulders (HTKS) task. (A second "delay" task was used but was later found to be problematic; interested readers are referred to the paper for discussion.) HTKS is an "opposites" task that bears similarity to Simon Says. The experimenter tells children, "When I say touch your head, I want you to touch your toes, and when I say touch your toes, I want you to touch your head." If children do well on 10 such commands, the second rule (knees/shoulders) is added, and if they do well on 10 commands with both sets of rules, the rules are switched (so head means knees, and so on) and 10 more commands are given. In the fall, there were no differences in performance on this task. However, spring tests revealed gains that were significantly different by classroom type. Specifically, the gain among children in classic Montessori was 13.72 points, whereas for supplemented Montessori, the gain was 7.22, and for conventional programs, it was 7.67 (Figure 11.1). The gain was particularly large among 3-year-olds in classic Montessori.

In this study, rather than relying on a single false belief task to test Theory of Mind as we had in Milwaukee, I used a series of tasks asking about different mental states of graduated levels of difficulty (Wellman & Liu, 2004).

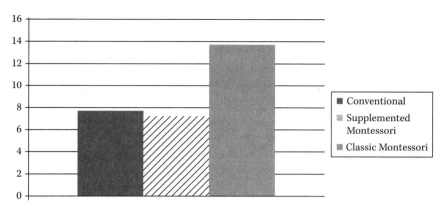

FIGURE 11.1 School year change on the Head Toes Knees Shoulders task (HTKS).

Test of statistical significance: $F(2, 170) = 11.09, p < .01$.

Children were first children given a false belief task. Instead of the vignette about Maxi and his chocolate, here children were shown a box of adhesive bandages and asked if they knew what was inside. Children almost always guessed the typical contents; if not, they were prompted ("What's usually in this box?"), and then guessed correctly. Then the box was opened, revealing the content, and the experimenter commented, "Ha! Look at that! There's actually a pencil in there!" The box was closed, and a doll was brought out. The experimenter explained that the doll (Peter) had never seen inside the box, and children were asked what he thought was in it, and what was actually in it. Children who answered both questions correctly were given two points and given a more difficult task assessing understanding that emotions can be hidden. Children who answered either question incorrectly received no points and were given an easier task assessing understanding perceptual access—namely, that one has to see something to know what it is.

For the Perceptual Access task, a nondescript wooden chest with a closed drawer containing a small shell was brought out, and children were asked, "What do you think is inside the drawer?" Regardless of what children guessed, the experimenter said, "Let's see," and opened the drawer. "There's really a shell inside!" The experimenter then explained that a doll named Polly had never seen inside this drawer, brought Polly out, and asked if Polly knew what was inside. For the more difficult Hidden Emotion task, children were told a story about Joey "who really wants a bicycle for his birthday, and he thinks his uncle is going to give him a bicycle." However, the uncle instead gave Joey a ball. Children were then asked how Joey "really feels when he gets the ball?" and "what Joey's *face* will look like when he gets the ball?" Answers could be provided verbally or by pointing to a face on a 5-face scale portraying expressions ranging from very sad to very happy.

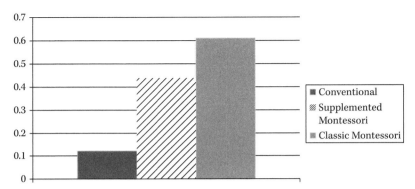

FIGURE 11.2 School year change in Theory of Mind.

Test of statistical significance: Kruskal-Wallis nonparametric test $p < .05$.

For theory of mind, a Pearson chi-squared test showed the groups were not significantly different in the fall, but they were in the spring (Figure 11.2). Specifically, although the conventional and the classic Montessori groups did not differ from each other, both scored more highly than the supplemented Montessori children. Recall that the conventional children were slightly older, which might explain why they did better than the supplemented Montessori children on some tasks.

On the next test of social understanding, the Social Problem Solving task used in the Milwaukee study, there was a significant difference between the conventional and the classic Montessori children. To conserve time in this study, we used just one of the stories, as children tended to respond in the same way on all stories. Children were shown a series of pictures of two children of their same gender and approximate age, one of whom had had a book for a really long time, which the other child really wanted to look at. On this task, differences were very striking, with classic Montessori children showing strong school-year growth in the tendency to use social strategies that took both children's perspectives into account, whereas children in the other groups showed no growth (supplemented Montessori) or even a loss in the ability from fall to spring (conventional) (Figure 11.3).

For all the academic tasks (Woodcock–Johnson tests of Letter Word, Applied [Math] Problems, and Picture Vocabulary; see Figures 11.4, 11.5, and 11.6, respectively,), there were significant differences favoring classic Montessori. Specifically, the growth in Letter Word scores for classic Montessori was more than 11 items (on average), whereas it was fewer than 6 items in both other types of program. For Applied Problems, gain was 3 and 3.5 for supplemented Montessori and conventional children, respectively, whereas it was 4.5 for classic Montessori children. For Picture Vocabulary, growth was close to 3 items for classic Montessori, whereas it was about 1 for both other groups.

In sum, this study found strong support for the idea that Montessori classrooms in which children exclusively use Montessori materials outperform

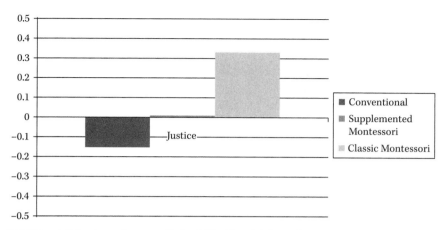

FIGURE 11.3 School year change on the Social Problem-Solving task.

Test of statistical significance: ANCOVA : $F(2, 170) = 2.30, p = .03$.
Simple Planned Contrasts Montessori vs. Conventional programs ($0.54, p = .04$).

both ones in which they spend quite a bit of time engaged in other activities, as well as highly regarded conventional programs. An interesting question is the degree to which the materials themselves were responsible for this.

A head of school approached me suggesting we examine this. Halfway through the school year, non-Montessori materials were removed from two of three primary level classrooms at a single school. Children were tested shortly after, and then again 4 months later. We found that children's executive function (HTKS) and Letter Word scores advanced significantly more in the two classrooms from which the supplementary materials were removed, and there was a trend toward those children also advancing more in math (Lillard & Heise, 2016). Although a small study, this suggests that children

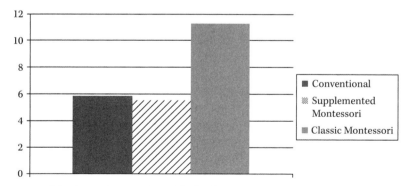

FIGURE 11.4 School year change in Letter Word task.

Test of statistical significance: $F(2, 169) = 4.17, p = .02$.

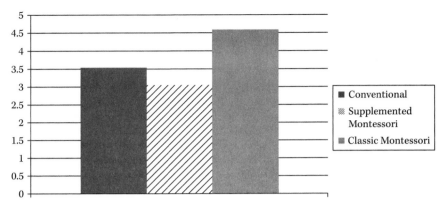

FIGURE 11.5 School year change in Applied Math Problems task.

Test of statistical significance: Kruskal-Wallis: 6.37, $p < .05$.

grow more in classrooms that only contain Montessori materials, and that something about only having Montessori materials is responsible.

The percentage of children using Montessori materials seems to be an important index of fidelity of implementation. Fidelity of implementation, then, does appear to matter for Montessori outcomes. Although there may be other outcomes on which children do well regardless of Montessori implementation—and perhaps other outcomes where they do better in supplemented Montessori or conventional programs—on the array tested for here (executive function, social knowledge and skills, and early academic skills), children in classic Montessori classrooms showed the strongest school-year gains.

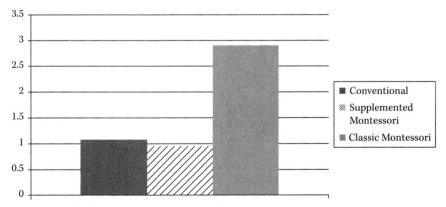

FIGURE 11.6 School year change in Picture Vocabulary task.

Test of statistical significance: $F(2, 168) = 4.08, p = .02$.

Other Recent Research on Montessori

Thus far I have reviewed five studies that were done since the publication of the first volume (Dohrmann et al., 2007; Lopata et al., 2005; and my own three studies). Although there continues to be little high-quality research on Montessori education (Walsh & Petty, 2007), a few other studies merit mention.

Rathunde and Csikszentmihalyi (2005a, 2005b) reported two studies on social climate and motivation with Montessori and conventional middle-school students. The samples were matched on many variables, including ethnic diversity, parent education, and parent employment rates. The five Montessori schools were carefully selected to be high-quality programs. Almost 300 students responded to the Experience Sampling Method, in which they were beeped at random points eight times a day for a week, and asked to fill out questionnaires about how they were feeling. The first study (2005a) addressed motivation and was referred to in chapter 5. Outside of academic contexts, the two groups were similar in terms of affect and motivation. Compared to controls, and controlling for a host of relevant variables, Montessori students reported more flow, energy, intrinsic motivation, and undivided interest, a variable combining high intrinsic motivation and importance while doing schoolwork. The conventional students reported higher salience while doing schoolwork, but this feeling was accompanied by low intrinsic motivation. The second study addressed feelings about school and the school context. Montessori students felt more teacher support, emotional safety, and classroom order. They engaged in more academic work and more chores at school, but they socialized less and spent less time in leisure activities, watching television or other media, and eating than students at conventional schools. In terms of classroom activities, the Montessori children spent much more time in collaborative work, more time working on individual projects, much less time in passive listening activities such as lectures, and much less time watching media. Although they claimed to spend the same amount of time with classmates, they also reported being with friends far more often, suggesting that they were more likely to consider their classmates their friends; this was particularly the case among eighth graders (less so at sixth grade). These two studies present a very different picture, then, of what life is like in high-quality Montessori middle schools compared to conventional middle schools serving the same demographic. Excepting the few questions pertinent to these issues in my Milwaukee study, these two studies are stand-alones in addressing Montessori school climate and motivation. Two recent studies addressed creativity.

Besançon and Lubart (2008) examined creativity in French elementary schools and found that children in Montessori, as opposed to those in traditional schools or a French alternative program called "Frienet," were most creative from first to fourth grade. Here there was no mention of the quality of Montessori implementation, and children were not matched or randomly assigned, so it is not clear what led to the results. Another recent study (Kirkham & Kidd, 2016) found Montessori primary children to be less creative in drawing (echoing an earlier Steiner–Montessori drawing comparison by Cox & Rowlands, 2000) and more apt to use a substitute object than an imagined object in pretense than children in Steiner classrooms. There are many issues with the research design in these studies, but it is certainly possible that Steiner children, being as they are in a curriculum that emphasizes free-flowing creativity and fantasy, do perform better on such measures. No other measures were taken.

Other recent studies have examined fine motor skills in Montessori children, as preschool fine motor skills have recently been shown to strongly predict academic success (Cameron et al., 2012; Grissmer et al., 2010). Bhatia, Davis, and Shamas-Brandt (2015) used a pretest and post-test design to compare 50 five-year-old children in Montessori with 50 children of the same age in a high-performing suburban elementary school. Controlling for pretest differences, the Montessori children showed significantly stronger fine motor skills near the end of the school year. Just as one might not be surprised to find Steiner-schooled children excel at tests of artistic creativity, it is not surprising that children who engage with Montessori materials excel at fine motor skills—but it is important information given its predictive value.

Ansari and Winsler (2014) examined the test scores of thousands of children in Miami's Title 1 public school prekindergarten (pre-K) programs from 2002 through 2007; 770 children were in Montessori, and almost 13,000 were in HighScope preschool programs. About a third of the Montessori children were Latino and most of these children spoke Spanish in the home, and two thirds of the Montessori were Black (as described in the article). Children were tested in fall and spring, with direct assessments of cognitive, language, and fine motor skills, and teacher and parent assessments of social skills and behavioral concerns. The overarching finding was that all children were helped by pre-K programs, yet Latino children in Montessori improved much more from fall to spring than children in any other group; change in the Black children was trivially different across school programs. Although I applaud the massive amount of data examined, I have two questions about this study. First, I question the Montessori implementation; the authors claim it to be a classic implementation but give no concrete supporting evidence. In fact, the only concrete information provided is that the classrooms were limited to 4-year-olds; because the 3-year age span is key to Montessori, this is an important deviation from a classic implementation. Second, they state that five Montessori schools were in predominantly Black neighborhoods and three were in primarily Hispanic neighborhoods. Without some assurance of fidelity of implementation, it is possible that the three Latino schools were better functioning, rather than that the Montessori curriculum particularly helps Latino children. Regarding ethnicity differences, my Milwaukee study and the Dohrmann study had positive results in Milwaukee city schools in which African Americans predominate. My ongoing longitudinal study in high-fidelity Hartford, Connecticut, public Montessori schools should shed more light on ethnicity and Montessori education outcomes.

Two recently published studies looked specifically at math and Montessori, on the grounds that the Montessori materials should support children in learning place value. The first study (which did not address Montessori program quality, nor give much information about any of the schools used) tested children longitudinally in kindergarten, first, second, and third grade (with somewhat different subsets of children at different time points). In kindergarten, Montessori children outperformed the others, but this advantage went away over time (Laski, Vasilyeva, & Shiffman, 2016). In stark contrast, a second study with the same aims found "sleeper effects," with Montessori children performing similarly to conventionally schooled children at the end of kindergarten, but significantly better on math at second grade (Mix, Smith, Stockton, Cheng, & Barterian, 2016). To address program quality, this study mentioned that all three Montessori schools involved had strong local reputations and had been in operation for more than 25 years: One was accredited by AMI, and all teachers in the other two schools were accredited by either AMI or AMS (American Montessori Society). Montessori children particularly excelled at more conceptual math problems. The inspiration for this study was finding that conventionally schooled children who engaged in training programs with Montessori-like materials also advanced more in math. Further research is needed to tease apart the reasons for the different patterns of results in these two recent studies of math performance. The differences might be caused by the actual math tests involved. As stated, the Mix et al. (2016) study found that Montessori children did particularly well on tests tapping deeper conceptual understanding. For example, on the School Sale problem, children had to understand hierarchical relations; they were asked to figure out how many bags they would need to pack 38 erasers, when 5 erasers could fit in each bag. The tests used in the Laski et al. (2016) study were more basic, for example, solving simple subtraction problems presented with no context.

Finally, one other new study bears mention. Pate et al. (2014) monitored physical activity using accelerometers on 301 preschool children attending nine Montessori and eight conventional preschools. Controlling for sex, race, parent education, neighborhood poverty, and body mass index, the Montessori children moved significantly more than the conventionally schooled children.

Montessori research is in its infancy, but there are signs that much more will come soon. I know of two groups examining neural function in Montessori children, and two journals devoted to Montessori research (in the United States, the *Journal of Montessori Research,* and in Europe, the *Journal of Montessori Research and Education*) were recently launched, along with an initiative to address the gap. Hopefully in the years to come we will have a much fuller understanding of the outcomes of Montessori education, including different variations on the program.

Chapter Summary

Although some research was done on Montessori education prior to 2005, significant methodological problems, including poor Montessori implementation, made it inconclusive. The picture is improving. I have done two studies involving high-fidelity Montessori programs, one using a lottery approach and the other a pre- and post-test approach, and found strong positive outcomes. A study currently underway combines these two approaches with a 3-year longitudinal design and reasonably large sample sizes. Others have contributed important studies as well, thus far with too little attention to Montessori quality, but nonetheless showing intriguing findings on which to base further exploration.

Education *for* Children

One of the most urgent endeavors to be undertaken on behalf of
the reconstruction of society is the reconstruction of education. It
must be brought about by giving . . . children the environment
that is adapted to their [nature].

— Maria Montessori *(1949/1974, p. 100)*

As has been too rarely noted in public discourse, the models that form the
backbone of our conventional educational system are not well adapted to
children. Although some children manage to excel in the system regardless,
the common cultural attitude is that school is painful and not particularly
fun. This should suggest to us that something is very wrong. Learning can be
an engaging, inspiring activity, so schooling could be looked on with joy. The
mismatch between the models underlying our conventional system of education and the nature of children is at the root of the problem.

How big is this problem? Certainly not every school has worked poorly for
every child. More progressive schools have adopted practices (no grades, frequent group work) that are better suited to how children learn. Some might
fear that children educated with such practices would not fare well in more
competitive cultures, but they apparently do. For children whose elementary education is more conventional, excellent teachers can still keep children inspired, although the research presented in this book suggests learning
outcomes would be even better in a different educational system. Among
children whose teachers are less than superb, those from families that instill
strong educational values and help their children learn the skills needed to
succeed in school still do reasonably well.

But things could be much better. When education reform is considered,
the emphasis tends to be on teacher and family factors or relatively minor
program issues instead of on the foundations of schooling. The No Child Left
Behind testing program was supposed to improve *teaching* by making schools
accountable, and numerous programs seek to improve schooling with little
fixes or by helping families. But such programs are fighting uphill battles,
because the root of the problem is deeper. Our cultural models of what a

school should be and how children learn have a poor fit. Children do not thrive in a factory, where they are all treated alike and ushered passively from one lesson to the next. Nor do they learn well when treated as empty vessels to be filled with knowledge. As progressive educators from Dewey on have realized, and as psychological research in the past half century has made abundantly clear, children actively construct their knowledge.

The right approach for designing a system of education that suits children's nature would be to study how they learn and develop, and change schools accordingly. This is exactly what Maria Montessori did a century ago. Her insights about children brilliantly forecast several main tenets of psychological research today. In fact many of them correspond to the top 20 teaching and learning principles recently published by a coalition of psychologists for the American Psychological Association (APA Coalition, 2015).

The mind and the hand are closely related, and we learn best when we can move our bodies in ways that align with our cognition. This is no wonder, since our minds evolved for action, for behaving in an environment. Conventional schooling takes no heed of this fact, but Dr. Montessori understood it long ago.

People also fare better when they can make choices about their lives and environments, not when others have all the control. Conventional schooling does not allow children this control, but in a Montessori classroom, the child decides what to do when, within the limits of what is constructive for the child and good for society. Allowing children this freedom gives them experience making choices, an important skill for life. It also sets up a situation in which children must learn to regulate themselves, rather than being regulated largely by external forces.

One of the most important predictors of success in life is executive function. By focusing so much on academic content, rather than the development of the personality, conventional schooling has misfired. Dr. Montessori saw that control of attention was fundamental to human development, and that many positive developments flow from there. As the Coalition for Psychology in Schools and Education expressed it, "Students' self-regulation assists learning, and self-regulatory skills can be taught" (APA Coalition, 2015, p. 6). In Montessori, self-regulation is more fundamental than this, and the self-regulatory skills manifest naturally in the prepared environment.

People learn best about the topics they are most interested in. Conventional schooling, which has all children proceed on a set schedule through a pre-established curriculum, is not equipped to respond well to individual interests. Montessori allows each child to choose what to work on, and when, with occasional limits if a child is not getting to parts of the curriculum. The Elementary child invests a great deal of time researching and writing about topics of personal interest. Children's studies radiate from a core of deep interests into all curricular areas, rather than having all curricular areas delivered in a predetermined array and schedule. In the APA Coalition's words, "Students tend to enjoy learning and perform better when they are more intrinsically than extrinsically motivated" (2015, p. 6). Interest is intrinsic motivation.

Very young children are motivated to learn, but that intrinsic motivation decreases each year in conventional schools. The provision of rewards, in the form of stars and grades, may be part of the reason. Substantial research has shown that when people expect to be and are rewarded for activities they were already motivated to perform in the absence of rewards, their motivation declines. The children in Dr. Montessori's first classroom showed her that intrinsic rewards were inspiration enough for engaging in the kind of learning they could do in her schools. Perhaps in part because Montessori work is very interesting, children do not need external motivators. Without extrinsic motivators, children also sustain mastery goals, rather than adopting performance goals. The APA Coalition stated that "Students persist in the face of challenging tasks and process information more deeply when they adopt mastery goals rather than performance goals" (2015, p. 6).

The APA Coalition also notes that "[l]earning is situated within multiple social contexts" and that interpersonal relationships are important to learning (p. 6). However, in conventional schooling, the preschool years are historically the only ones considered an important time for social learning; only then are children free to interact for most of the day. When children hit elementary school, social time is over: Children are usually moved to separate desks and must generally work and be tested alone. Yet this is opposite to what we know about children: Preschoolers often prefer parallel play because their social skills are often not well honed. In elementary school, children become intensely social and really want to interact with each other. Montessori works with children the way they are. It capitalizes on the fact that children can learn very well from peers and excellent materials, freeing the teacher to work with children individually and in small groups. Elementary school children usually love to work together, children learn well when they work together, and in Montessori classrooms, they can do so.

Conventional schooling often separates learning from the context of use. One result is that sometimes children learn information and procedures in school, but cannot see how they are relevant or can be applied outside the school context. In Montessori classrooms, the hands-on materials provide a context that can make application more obvious. As children get older, individual interests take them out into the community via the Going Out program, allowing learning to be directly connected to the contexts from which it arises and to which it applies: "Learning is based on context" (APA Coalition, 2015, p. 6).

Conventional schooling does not appear to mandate any one way that a teacher should teach, but psychological research clearly suggests more optimal ways for adults to interact with children. Children need firm structure and warm love, and to be treated in ways that recognize their need for freedom with guidance. They are harmed by evaluations that suggest static personal qualities, even positive ones. Dr. Montessori captured these optimal styles of interaction in her discussions of how a teacher should behave toward the children. She also incorporated control of error in the materials, which largely frees the teacher and child from an openly evaluative relationship. The APA Coalition principles also align with Montessori in their directives regarding good teaching.

Research suggests that children respond well to order and predictability in their lives. Conventional schooling is tightly ordered in elementary school, but usually not in preschool. Montessori is ordered spatially and temporally at the level of the microroutine. However, at the macro level, the daily schedule is open for the child to arrange as he or she goes. The child is at liberty to choose to work on what interests him or her. In this way Montessori education allows for a blend of order and free choice, giving the child structured routines but the freedom to decide what routine to enact when. The research suggests this combination may be most optimal. When the routines are not specified, children might well not learn much yet when the day's schedule is set, children's sense of control is compromised. The orderly education of the senses in Montessori is also notable, as it could conceivably have a significant effect on perceptual capacities; recent research supports Spearman's (1904) conjecture that sensory discrimination is fundamental to intelligence.

Montessori education, then, seems to be more in line than conventional schooling is with what we know about children's development, how they learn, and the conditions under which they thrive. Since 2005 several reports have been published in peer-reviewed journals regarding the outcomes of Montessori education. As discussed in chapter 11, those reports are mostly favorable, and especially when the Montessori was implemented in the ways Dr. Montessori describes in her books. Montessori children tend to do better academically, and, even more important, have more developed executive function. They also tend to be more creative and to feel strong social connections than their conventionally schooled peers.

Frequently Asked Questions and Concerns About Montessori

The remainder of this chapter addresses some common questions and concerns about Montessori education. They include questions about Montessori programs and implementation, the suitability of Montessori for particular children, how to learn more about Montessori, and issues concerning Montessori and society.

PROGRAM AND IMPLEMENTATION

Is Montessori a back-to-basics approach or a progressive one?

Montessori is both. This may be why people in both camps sometimes shun it, and why, if they understood it, they might actually esteem it. Montessori teaches children the basic facts of grammar, mathematics, biology, and so on. They learn a great deal of nomenclature, and their work is tightly structured. All this suggests "back to basics." However, Montessori children are also free to choose what they work on and when, they often work collaboratively, there are no grades, much work is project focused, and so on—all marks of progressive schools.

Although in a sense Montessori is a "discovery learning" approach, it is not the unguided sort that research shows does not work as well as direct teaching (Alfieri et al., 2011; Klahr & Nigam, 2004). Montessori education guides children closely in their discoveries, with the intention that with repeated use, they cannot fail to discover what the materials are explicitly designed to teach. Montessori incorporates the best of back-to-basics and progressive programs. Properly understood and implemented, Montessori could end "the wars" over school curricula.

You've said not all Montessori classrooms practice Montessori in the ways you describe here. Why is there variation?

For one, it is hard for people to abandon culturally transmitted ideas about children and schooling, and Montessori teachers often adopt conventional school practices because those practices feel familiar (to parents and to themselves) and on the surface, seem to work. For example, if a teacher offers a gold star to children when they engage in a Practical Life activity, they will begin to do so, and the teacher might think she or he has found a great new Montessori technique, not realizing that instead an important path in class development toward self-selected activity has been blocked. If a Montessori teacher has never been in a really good Montessori classroom, he or she might not even notice the contrary effects of using conventional practices. Furthermore, Montessori practices surely work synergistically. If one removes choice, for example, interest immediately suffers, which has an effect on intrinsic rewards. Therefore change in just one practice might really change the quality of the Montessori program.

Anticipating the problem of changing Montessori toward conventional methods, Dr. Montessori advised that Montessori teachers not take conventional education courses, because such courses would deepen their adherence to conventional methods and ideas (Montessori, 1946/1963, p. 86). Even when they reject conventional practices personally, teachers at public Montessori schools are often required to adopt such mainstream practices as using workbooks or testing children frequently.

Another problem for quality implementation is that a Montessori teacher might not be well trained, or even trained at all. Several factors can affect quality of teacher training. Many Montessori teacher training programs are very short, lasting only a few weeks or months. Some programs attempt to educate Montessori teachers largely through internships, yet they do not ensure that the supervising Montessori teachers meet any standard. Even if there were established standards, learning through classroom practice can leave out important information that would be provided in lectures and practicums with the materials. Good classroom teachers are usually too focused on the children during the school day to simultaneously explain to an intern the many variations and nuances of the materials (if they even learned about them in their own training) and at the end of the day, might be too tired to do so. Correspondence courses have also become common, with obvious potential problems.

Another problem is that in some training programs, the teacher trainers might not have received adequate training themselves, even if they had many years of classroom experience. Surprisingly, most Montessori training organizations have no or low standards for teacher trainers. An analogous case would be if a person with an undergraduate degree in English literature were to train others to become English teachers. We instead require that people in such a position get special training and obtain a doctorate before they teach others to become English teachers. Teaching Montessori involves knowing a tremendous number of procedures for working with the materials. In addition, the depth of the Montessori philosophy and the vast array of interconnections between the materials and the philosophy might well require in-depth study with well-trained teacher trainers, rather than with teacher trainers who mainly have field experience. One exception to this is the Association Montessori Internationale (AMI), which has an intensive preparation program for people interested in training future Montessori teachers.

In sum, not all Montessori classrooms implement the program in a way Dr. Montessori would endorse, judging from the descriptions in her books. Montessori is not a trademarked term, and a school may have the materials but lack the emphasis on free choice, the organization and order, the collaborative learning and interaction, and so on. Some schools do practice the Montessori method as she described it in her lectures, and researchers should use more authentic schools to test the Montessori approach fairly. In this book, I rely heavily on Dr. Montessori's own descriptions of what a Montessori class should be, and on descriptions from Montessori teachers who have taken the training courses she developed. Later in this chapter, I address how to locate a Montessori school that is likely to have excellent implementation.

It seems that no static system can be good and there is always room for improvement. What is Montessori's stance on innovation?

Dr. Montessori encouraged innovation, and many Montessorians have gone on to innovate (Chattin-McNichols, 1992; Wentworth, 1999). But although the practice of innovation and change sounds positive, especially to American ears, these innovations sometimes result in suboptimal Montessori classrooms. Dr. Montessori worked full time in Montessori schools around the world for almost 50 years to develop the Montessori school system and its materials. Few, if any, practitioners and professors working on new school programs today can claim such longevity of dedication and cultural scope in their implementations.

There are at least three potential problems with developing innovations on the basic Montessori system. First, an innovator might not have a deep grasp of what makes Montessori education work before he or she begins changing it. Some teachers are encouraged to begin changing Montessori's system while they are still in training, when they have not even observed in an excellent Montessori classroom, much less taught in one. As in most fields, one should master a method before attempting to change it.

Second, an innovator might not be a careful observer of children. In the training courses that Dr. Montessori designed, scores of hours of training are dedicated to observation: A trainee sits in a classroom, doing nothing but watching the children and taking notes, which are later transcribed and read by the teacher trainer. Not all training courses spend so many hours teaching the skill of observation to the future teachers, with a very carefully and extensively trained teacher trainer commenting on the observations. Innovations would best be created by superb observers of children, as, it seems, was Dr. Montessori.

Third, an innovator might never have had a good environment in which to observe children. Dr. Montessori claimed that children should be given freedom only in a properly prepared environment, and that only under such free conditions would they reveal their "true nature." We should not set elementary children free on the Internet or city streets, nor set toddlers free in unsafe homes, because these are not prepared environments. Unprepared environments could, in Dr. Montessori's view, bring out "deviations" rather than "normalized," healthy development. From a Montessori perspective, studying children in an environment that is not well prepared would be like trying to study normal cell growth in an infected petri dish. Changes to a Montessori program would probably best come from observing positive effects of those changes in a well-functioning Montessori program, not a Montessori program that was not well implemented to begin with.

For these reasons, classrooms that adhere more closely to Dr. Montessori's original methods and materials are more appropriate places to study the method and its outcomes than are classrooms that attempt to innovate. Dr. Montessori clearly endorsed innovation, but only from a position of mastery. People who make revisions based on a deep understanding of Montessori, with careful attention to the repercussions throughout the system of those innovations, surely could make positive and viable changes that could improve the system.

Montessori schools are too free; My children need more structure.

This common concern about Montessori might reflect parents' desire for a school that looks more rigid, like the school of their youth, but it is also true that some teachers take the "liberty" call so far that the classroom is mayhem (see chapter 9). This might be all right early in the year in a new Primary class: Dr. Montessori talked of the need for the teacher to wait patiently, connecting children with the environment and watching for the day when one by one, the children begin to concentrate. However, some classes never do get down to business. One problem could be that the teacher allows children to be free to disturb each other, to use the materials in ways they were not intended, and so on. Dr. Montessori was quite clear that this is not what she meant by liberty. Freedom comes with a responsibility to be constructive for oneself and society. AMI can send consultants to classrooms to observe teachers with AMI training in order to help diagnose such problems when they occur.

Montessori schools are too strict; children should be allowed more freedom.

Sometimes this concern also reflects more about the person who made it than the school. Some parents are disturbed by their child's not being allowed to build houses with the Pink Tower, or to carelessly and quickly draw dozens of pictures each morning. Children need freedom *and* limits. But like the opposite concern discussed in the previous paragraph about Montessori being too free, the concern that it is too rigid is valid for some teachers (see chapter 9). Some teachers are attracted to the orderly aspect of Montessori and take it too far, watching over children's every move and correcting it. This is also clearly not what Dr. Montessori meant by order, but striking the balance can be difficult for some teachers.

Montessori downplays language development.

This criticism even shows up in scholarly reports on Montessori (Stodolsky & Karlson, 1972), but it reveals ignorance of the curriculum. The Montessori math materials are often described in accounts of the system because they are so unusual and well thought out; the language materials are perhaps less unusual and seem simpler (e.g., acting out sentences), but the curriculum regarding language is actually very rich and well thought out too.

Dr. Montessori was intentionally capitalizing on early childhood's being a sensitive period for the acquisition of language (Montessori, 1967a/1995).

Consider some of the language curriculum. The Sensorial Materials (Sound Cylinders, Musical Bells) sharpen hearing and listening skills, on the reasoning that helping the child to focus on sound in general would assist in language development. Whether it does so should be tested empirically. The lesson of Silence also is intended to train attention to sound. Regarding semantics, the Sensorial Materials emphasize qualities that describe the world: large, larger, thin, thick, blue, green, rough, smooth, and so on. The child is thus learning about different qualities of objects and how to name those differences, with an emphasis on accurate use of words to describe the world. The materials work to develop language by refining the child's ability to judge and describe.

Montessori uses a wealth of materials for vocabulary development. In addition to simply labeling more common objects and actions as they learn to read and write, Montessori children learn the parts of the plant, the countries of the world, the variety of geological formations, and so on, even before age 6. The phonemic analysis involved in learning to read and write in Montessori also heightens awareness of the sounds used in language and might assist pronunciation—another interesting topic for research.

As in most preschools, in Montessori classrooms there is usually a well-stocked book corner. The difference in Montessori as compared to many preschool programs is that by age 5, most of the children in the room can read the books because of the work they did at ages 3 and 4 in the classroom. Older children might then read to younger children in the Primary classroom.

Conversation, which the teacher leads at circle time, is also considered part of the curriculum. The teacher was specifically advised to be careful in her pronunciation and to speak very clearly and articulately (Montessori, 1914/1965, p. 244). In fact, baby talk was discouraged because it was thought to interfere with language learning. This is a point on which research differs from Montessori, because baby talk actually appears to heighten a baby's attention to language and to assist language learning (Kemler Nelson, Hirsh-Pasek, Jusczyk, & Cassidy, 1989; Ma, Golinkoff, Houston, & Hirsh-Pasek, 2011). Singing songs is also part of the Montessori curriculum, and Dr. Montessori believed that singing also would aid language development.

In Montessori Elementary classrooms, children appear to engage in much more talk than they do in conventional ones. When children talk less in Primary, it is their choice. Meanwhile, as they work with materials, they do a good deal that develops language. Montessori classrooms appear to provide very well for language development.

There is no foreign-language learning in Montessori.

Dr. Montessori did not create a set of foreign-language materials. But she knew that learning language in one's earlier years was most optimal. In *Dr. Montessori's Own Handbook*, she says, "Early childhood is, in fact, the age in which language is formed, and in which the sounds of a foreign language can be perfectly learned" (1914/1965, p. 102). In *The Formation of Man*, she mentions and 8-year-old child in India taking on the learning of a foreign language in school, as an independent project. Today, some Montessori schools implement foreign-language training by having language tapes and other independent language work children can choose, others have a dual-language environment by having an assistant always speak a different language, and yet others offer language lessons at the end of the school day. Learning second languages at a young age is clearly positive for children, and an emergent body of research suggests that children who learn second languages are higher in executive control of attention (Bialystok, 1999, 2015). One theory is that children have to inhibit their primary language in order to use the second one, and that this develops self-regulation generally. Montessori schools can incorporate second-language learning.

There is too little parental involvement in Montessori.

A great deal of research shows that when parents are more involved in conventional school classrooms, children do better (Connors & Epstein, 1995). Indeed, "studies addressing methods of enabling and empowering parents to become involved in the school suggest that it is important to provide parents with choices regarding their participation, and a role in decision-making processes, creating an atmosphere in which parents feel like valued partners in their children's education" (Fantuzzo & Ginsburg-Block, 1998, pp. 135–36). Some Montessori schools may fall short in this regard, although Dr. Montessori's original writings about her San Lorenzo school stressed parental involvement. Parents who did not regularly confer with the teacher and extend Montessori practices to the home did not retain the privilege of having their children in the school. These parents were poor and uneducated, and one would assume that they did see it as a great privilege and convenience to have their children in school instead of at large in the tenement while they were at work.

The parents who seek to be involved in Montessori schools today are perhaps not like those parents. Some come to Montessori with a very superficial understanding of the program, possibly misinformed by poorly implemented programs, and some feel empowered to mandate that teachers change their practices. Because the method is so different, Montessori schools need to work hard on educating parents. Referring to a non-Montessori progressive alternative school in Utah, Rogoff and colleagues claimed a major ingredient to the school's success to be the continual restatement to the parents of the school's philosophy and of the underlying belief system that led to the practices they enacted (Rogoff, Turkanis, et al., 2001). It is the same for Montessori: The philosophy is very different, and the practices make good sense, but well-meaning, conventionally schooled parents often do not understand them. To help the children, schools must help the parents to understand the system, and parents must find time to become educated about it.

Parent participation *in the classroom*, however, is antithetical to Montessori, because a key ingredient is that the Montessori classroom is the children's place. Children may cease to help one another in the face of readily available adult assistance. Parents also may try to run the show and influence children's choices and interests. It thus may not work to put parents in Montessori classrooms. What parents can do, if properly trained not to interfere with children's independence, is serve as escorts for the Elementary Going-Out program, or as mentors for middle school internship programs. Parents might also serve as specialists who occasionally give short talks or demonstrations to children. But parents need to respect that their day-to-day involvement in a Montessori classroom, contrary to conventional systems, may not be positive, because Montessori is about helping children become independent, whereas conventional education has relatively more emphasis on adults transmitting knowledge to children and controlling their behavior, goals that are more readily achieved when more adults are present.

Montessori education seems out of date, particularly with computers.

Dr. Montessori recommended that an area of the Elementary school classroom have "technology of the times," so that children would learn to use it. This suggests that if she were to set up an Elementary classroom today, she would put a sample computer or two in Elementary. At issue here, as I see it, is not what *she* would do, but to what extent and under what circumstances computers can help children toward leading meaningful lives as useful, contributing members to society. These should be the criteria in making educational decisions.

Some adults think children must master computers as early as possible to succeed in today's world. But studies have not shown that, all things being equal, having computers in the classroom assists children. Sometimes computers are used well, but other times they seem to even distract from the educational mission, so the task becomes how to master the technicalities of PowerPoint rather than how to find, analyze, judge, integrate, and communicate information, which children can learn quite well from books with much less expense to the school (Oppenheimer, 2003). Computers not only incur expense at initial purchase, but are tremendously expensive to keep up to date. There is no evidence that the educational benefit they confer is commensurate with their expense.

I once heard someone observe that what young children need to learn about is the world of nature and the world of people. Computers are not the best medium for either, although properly programmed, they could help with both (and yet why bother, if one can present people and nature directly?). James O. Freedman, president emeritus of Dartmouth University, told graduates of the University of Rochester in May 2002:

> Telephones, televisions, VCRs, fax machines, computers, the Internet, e-mail, cell-phones, beepers, and all these forms of instant communication often create a bewildering barrage of noise and frenetic movement. It is almost as if we have surrounded ourselves with such technology in order to avoid suspended moments of silence and contemplation.
>
> If we are to succeed in preserving our individuality against such technological tyranny, we need to slow the tempo of our lives and extend the span of our attention. We need to emphasize a form of humane education that helps students to establish a rich interior life and an enduring openness of mind. A sturdy, private self where moral self-examination can occur. (Steinberg, 2002)

Montessori environments offer children that quiet; most computer software for children does not. As noted in chapter 4, computer software may often be problematic for the same reasons I suspect television is: Many computer programs regulate children's attention for them, rather than helping them learn to regulate their own attention. Certainly computers can be a wonderful resource when a person understands how to discriminate good from unreliable information and helpful from unhelpful programs, but they might not provide what young children really need.

Some studies show benefits of computer-aided instruction relative to conventional schooling. If one examines the methods in those studies, what is responsible for the benefits is probably not the computer itself, but the elements of choice, personalized instruction, and interest that are incorporated in the software. These are difficult to implement in conventional schools, and are achieved in other ways in Montessori. In some new research in my laboratory, we have found that children learn the states of Australia better from a Montessori puzzle map than from an app designed to mimic that material, and that over time, their learning from the physical map is more efficient (Eisen & Lillard, 2016-a).

Another consideration regarding the supposed need for children to use computers is the pace of technological change. If the QWERTY keyboard will not still be used 10 years from now, do children need to learn typing skills? The computer skills I learned as a child—BASIC programming and using the punch card—are useless to me today, when I need to use Microsoft Word commands, statistical software, and the Internet, all of which are easy enough not to require lifelong training. We do not know what technical skills will be useful to people in 20 or even 10 years. Exposure to the technology of one's age can be helpful, but one must approach it wisely, asking how much, and at what age, it can really assist development, and whether the cost is justified by the benefits.

Montessori feels like a cult.

Sometimes it does. This may happen particularly when a person is at the root of an approach: People who follow the approach keep going back to the person and idolize him or her, rather than scrutinizing the person's ideas. Freud and Piaget are sometimes subject to this as well. The goal of the Montessori approach is to help children. Clearly children are not best served by blind adherence to a particular view, but by careful evaluation of what helps them the most.

MONTESSORI'S SUITABILITY FOR PARTICULAR CHILDREN

Montessori is fine for preschoolers, but after that children should be in conventional schools. How else can they adjust to our culture?

The best answer for this will be from research on the outcomes of children who stayed in Montessori past preschool. Most of this evidence is anecdotal and suggests the transition is rarely problematic, but there is never a control condition: We do not know if any given child would have fared well or poorly had he or she been in conventional schools all along, either. The recent Milwaukee study of children who were in the Milwaukee public Montessori through fifth grade may be the most useful current data on this topic. As presented in chapter 11, this study showed that children who had been in Montessori fared as well or better than other children—who were mostly in programs for more gifted students—on standardized tests and also with such issues as school absence and delinquency. One would like to see much more thorough exploration of the lives of these graduates. Do they tend to have more productive and constructive careers? Are they more apt to aid humanity? Our standardized tests do not get at such issues. Even if they could, studies need the right control sample: Children in both the Montessori and the non-Montessori treatment groups have to be randomly assigned, or one must control for parent variables by using a group of lottery losers, people who wanted their children to get into Montessori schools but who were rejected based on random selection procedures. This kind of research can address the adjustment issue.

Montessori preschools are fine for girls, but my boy is rowdy and noisy. It is not right for him.

Along with academic skills and knowledge, children in Montessori learn to control their movements to an end, to make choices, to get along with others, to work as part of a community, to concentrate, and so on. Those skills are as relevant for boys as they are for girls. In fact, given the higher prevalence of attention and reading problems in boys generally, Montessori, with its special work on attention and on phonemic analysis at early ages, might be especially beneficial to boys. One of the two major Head Start studies using random assignment showed Montessori particularly benefits boys (Miller & Bizzell, 1984), something also hinted at in my study in *Science* (Lillard & Else-Quest, 2006): Although the sample was too small to report the finding, at age 12 we found school differences on the academic measures for the boys; girls fared about equally well in both types of school. Other research has not shown particular benefits for either gender.

Montessori is mainly for children with learning disabilities.

Children with learning disabilities can fare well in Montessori classrooms. For example, children with dyslexia might especially benefit from the phonic approach taken to reading, and children with attention deficit disorders might benefit particularly from the emphasis on focused concentration and routines. The origins of the method lie in the extraordinary successes of retarded children using early versions of the Sensorial Materials. However, Montessori is *not* mainly for children with learning disorders. Rather, it suggests it is a system of education that might be particularly well suited to all children.

LEARNING MORE ABOUT MONTESSORI

How does one find a good Montessori school to visit?

The quality of Montessori programs varies widely, sometimes even across classrooms within a single school. A wonderful web-based resource is Montessori Guide (montessoriguide.org). There one can see many good examples of Montessori classrooms, interspersed with Montessori teacher trainers discussing the method. But there is no substitute for a live viewing. One way to increase the chances of seeing good Montessori in action is to locate a school that is recognized (or certified) by AMI, a distinction available only to schools in the United States. There are certainly excellent schools that are not recognized by AMI, because they do not even seek that distinction, or because they do not fit every one of the requirements, but using AMI's recognized schools list is one way that newcomers to Montessori can be assured that they are seeing a school that complies closely with Dr. Montessori's methods. AMI-USA's website (http://amiusa.org) lists recognized schools (and the levels at which they are recognized), and those schools must be recertified every 3 years.

Visitor protocols vary by school. Some have visitors look through one-way glass into classrooms, accompanied by a staff member who explains what is happening, whereas others have visitors sit in classrooms on their own. If a school allows visitors into the classrooms alone, then one should aim to spend 1 to 2 hours in a classroom. The children will go about their work while the observer sits quietly, keeping interaction to a minimum so as not to disturb the children's concentration (Montessori, 1989, p. 8). Respect for the child's activity is very important not only for the child, but also so the observer can see the transformation that Montessori schooling produces in attention. Sometimes children will spontaneously greet visitors and proudly show their work, but not instigating or prolonging such interaction allows observers to get a clearer picture of Montessori in action.

The following questions reflect what one should look for when observing in a Montessori classroom:

Is the physical environment beautiful?

Is there a feeling of peace?

Is there a variety of different kinds of work being done?

Is there an absence of worksheets and workbooks?

Does the environment contain only Montessori materials and no commercial toys?

Do the children seem to be relaxed and happy?

Do the children seem to have a sense of purpose?

Are the children kind and courteous with each other?

Are the children concentrating very hard on their work in Primary?

Are the children in Elementary appearing to work seriously even while some are casually carrying on conversations with others?

Does the teacher appear to be constantly aware of the whole room, intervening only when children seem aimless or nonconstructive or are bothering others?

Is the teacher's love and respect for the children palpable?

In the very best Montessori classrooms, the answer to all these questions is yes.

How else can I learn more about Montessori?

Of Dr. Montessori's books, *The Absorbent Mind* is probably the most accessible introduction to Dr. Montessori's ideas. *The Child in the Family* and *The Creative Development of the Child* (two volumes) are also wonderful. Her other books are less accessible, for several reasons. Dr. Montessori did not actually write most of her books. Most of her books are transcriptions of her speeches, compiled to create book-length volumes. Her speeches were not organized and written down by her either. Dr. Montessori would arrive at a lecture hall, usually with no notes, and begin to speak (Montessori, 1989). This can work well in speeches, but less well in writing.

Second, Dr. Montessori was of her time and place: turn of the last century, Italy. Like that of her famous American contemporary G. Stanley

Hall, her language can seem odd today. Her speeches could be very grand, and her language at times "flowery." Although she was a scientist swept up in the wave of logical positivism, Dr. Montessori's writings in other places suggest she was a deeply religious Roman Catholic. One must pick among these features of her writing to find the straightforward details about the theory and method of education she developed. In addition, some of the information in the early books is out of date because she later changed an aspect of the method (or AMI's education board changed it more recently). Early on, for example, children built the Pink Tower, then knocked it down. Later, she changed the procedure to having them take it down block by block.

Further sources of information about Montessori, including books by other authors, are recommended on the websites of major Montessori organizations. Again, I also recommend the Montessori Guide website.

MONTESSORI AND SOCIETY

Many of the research-supported insights discussed are incorporated at our local elementary school. There are no grades until junior high, children often work collaboratively, and I see many hands-on activities. Clearly reform from within works better than radical change, so isn't the best approach to improving schools slow, gradual transformations of the system that we have?

It is true that conventional schools are gradually discovering and incorporating as best they can some of the same principles that Dr. Montessori arrived at. Some of the best conventional schools are looking a little like Montessori schools, minus the materials. Yet Barbara Rogoff's statement from chapter 1 bears repeating again: "Adding new 'techniques' to the classroom does not lead to the developmental of a coherent philosophy. For example, adding the technique of having children work in 'co-operative learning' teams is quite different than a system in which collaboration is inherent in the structure" (Rogoff, Turkanis, et al., 2001, p. 13). The models underpinning conventional schools are the factory and the empty vessel, and these models still peek out through the better practices that some teachers and administrators layer on top. Still, such changes should improve the fit of conventional schooling to children.

Unfortunately, the vast majority of children do not have the advantages of such innovation. For example, regarding math teaching in the United States, a prominent researcher recently wrote, "It may surprise some people to learn that we have a quite consistent, predictable way of teaching mathematics in the United States and that we have used the same basic methods for nearly a century" (Hiebert, 1999, p. 11). This method, described elsewhere in this book, would be familiar to anyone who went through conventional schools: Review the homework, show the new procedure on the board, have students practice it, then assign the next night's homework. Most children in this country do not have the benefit of progressive innovations in their schools.

Montessori programs are increasingly being implemented in public charter and magnet schools. Some, like the Milwaukee schools, are in their third decade. Time will tell whether they are able to successfully bring Montessori education to the mainstream, or whether incremental changes in existing systems obtain better outcomes.

Why is Montessori not more well known?

Given how ahead of her time Dr. Montessori was, it is interesting that she is close to ignored in psychology and education circles. One can only speculate as to why. One consideration is that she was a woman, working at a time when the only women who survived the passage of time in the behavioral sciences were the wives and daughters of famous men, such as Margaret Mead and Anna Freud.[1]

Another contributing factor is a publication by William Kilpatrick (1914), professor of education at Columbia Teachers College, titled *The Montessori System Examined*. It is clear on reading this book that Kilpatrick did not have a good grasp of what he was examining, and that in fact he was not a very deep thinker. But nonetheless, the book was influential with cadres of beginning teachers, in part because Kilpatrick was a popular teacher whose lectures were enticing and well attended (Zilversmit, 1993).

Kilpatrick's book on Montessori contained some praise, but in the end concluded her educational system would not be lasting or important because she had no new and correct ideas. Dr. Montessori's good ideas, such as the importance of liberty and learning skills of practical life, Kilpatrick said, were better stated and implemented by John Dewey, Kilpatrick's mentor. Perhaps to Kilpatrick, Dr. Montessori might have seemed a threat to Dewey (or perhaps even to plagiarize him). Dewey and Dr. Montessori shared insights, and he slightly preceded her: Dewey's first major publication came out in 1903, 4 years before the first Montessori school opened. However, it does not seem likely that she had read his work. The United States and Europe were a long ocean liner voyage apart, and although there was certainly some passage of ideas (Montessori was hailed in the United States and spent a year lecturing here in 1915), America and Europe were proceeding on different paths in the behavioral sciences, with experiment and behaviorism prominent in the United States, and Europe turning from the sorts of experiments conducted by Wundt and others and following the very different path laid by Freud and psychoanalysis. Although quite aware of Pestalozzi, Froebel, and her other

---

[1] Interestingly, male education writers of the time mention many women researchers and educators I have never heard of, as if they were well known in the early 1900s.

predecessors in Europe, Dr. Montessori seemed to know little about the state of American education. The second reason that I doubt she knew of Dewey's work is that Dr. Montessori's pattern is to generously cite others in her work. If she had known about his ideas when she wrote her first book, I think she would have cited him.

Besides claiming that Montessori had no new good ideas, Kilpatrick claimed she had several bad ones. One was that a child's personality was pre-formed, and that education was merely a process of helping that personality unfold. As behaviorism was taking a strong hold in the United States, such a criticism could have great impact. The criticism reflects a simplistic reading of Dr. Montessori, however. Although she did believe that development was biologically guided to a much greater extent than did her most prominent contemporaries, and that certain capacities, such as learning language, were innate, she also clearly believed in adaptation to an environment, which is exactly why she set about devising environments more conducive to healthy development than conventional schools.

Kilpatrick also criticized Montessori teaching children "the three Rs" in preschool, which he said was not a good use of their time. He advocated play-ing and learning social skills, along with such rudimentary skills as using paste and scissors, and a repertoire of songs and stories. Indeed, many great educators of the day believed that teaching children to read early was prob-lematic. Dewey wrote that learning to read before age 8 "cripples rather than furthers intellectual development" (J. Dewey, 1972, pp. 254–61, cited in Ravitch, 2001, p. 215), and G. Stanley Hall claimed empirical evidence that reading, writing, spelling, and math prior to age 8 were not positive for children's development (Hall, 1911). We now know this is not true, but here again, Dr. Montessori was swimming against the tide, ahead of her time. Even Piaget criticized Montessori for introducing concepts before children were ready for them (Piaget, 1970), yet most researchers today concur that Piaget underestimated children's capabilities.

Another of Kilpatrick's criticisms of Montessori was that it taught use-less skills, because he believed, in keeping with the then-influential work of Thorndike, his colleague at Columbia, that skills were not transferable. Thus children learning to distinguish different weights, for example, with Montessori materials would not transfer to the practical skill of knowing whether a letter needed another stamp. The view that skills generally do not transfer no longer holds sway. Sometimes people indeed do not see the appli-cability of abstract learning to real life, as discussed in chapter 8, but, *contra* Thorndike, many skills do transfer.

Kilpatrick's book is said to have been very influential in America's dis-missing Montessori in the early 1900s. Montessori was revived in the 1960s and has grown ever since. But Dr. Montessori's ideas have still not penetrated psychology and education circles. A possible reason is that Dr. Montessori did not document her experiments in a way that allows others to follow them. She repeatedly stated that the method was arrived at by experiment, and she provided an occasional anecdote, but readers are put in the position of having to trust her "experiments." Contrast Dr. Montessori with Piaget, who is very much alive in the academy today (contrary to a recent article titled "Piaget Is Dead, and I Don't Feel So Good Myself," Bjorklund, 1997) in this regard. Piaget gave detailed accounts of how he arrived at his ideas, so people could replicate his experiments. Of course, he was still virtually unknown in this country until a beautifully lucid writer named John Flavell (1963) rendered his ideas in plain English.

An even more important reason for Dr. Montessori's lack of presence in the field might be her lack of interest in theory. After all, Lev Vygotsky did not leave a legacy of carefully experimental work either, but he is today an important figure in the field. Piaget also left the legacy of a carefully crafted, detailed theory. Dr. Montessori clearly has many testable theoretical ideas, but the theory is harder to reach in her work. She was not really interested in coming up with a theory of how children learn and develop. She was a practitioner; she wanted to help children, not theorize about them. In this very regard she criticized Wundt and admired Itard: The former was only interested in cataloging the limits of human perception, whereas the latter was interested in extending those limits. Although some theory naturally comes from Dr. Montessori's work, it was not theory that she was focused on.

Dr. Montessori's legacy may also suffer because of her willingness to step from science to religion and back all in the same sentence. At times she speaks in passionate language that does not fit the language of science. But perhaps it is this very passion that enabled her to develop such interesting materials for learning. The Great Lessons are the work of a master storyteller. Dr. Montessori's well-roundedness and her combination of science and passion might be part of what makes the Montessori curriculum so rich.

One also wonders if things would have come out differently had Montessori not chosen to leave her position at the University of Rome to head her new educational movement, but instead had stayed in the academy, writing articles for scientific journals instead of newspapers, and giving lectures to psychologists and students instead of a mix of the general public. It is possible that she would have used language and developed theories that would have given her position in the academy today. She was no doubt brilliantly insightful and rightfully should inspire the study of child development today.

Given that psychological research so clearly shows that much of what we do in conventional schools is wrong, why do we still do it? Why is research not more influential?

Many educational theorists have written about this issue. Lauren Resnick, mentioned in chapter 1, pointed out several reasons why schools still use a

Lockean model of the child (in her terms, an "associationist theory of learning"; Resnick & Hall, 1998). For one, education reform in the United States has mainly been about changing institutional arrangements (grouping, accountability, and management) and not about patterns of teaching and methods of pedagogy. The latter is left to teachers and local decision-makers. Added to this are people's tendency to teach as they were taught, expectations of parents that schools will look and feel like their own childhood schools did, and a need to adopt particular textbooks and take standardized tests. The very structure of such tests, breaking learning into components that are tested in a disjointed manner, discourages integrated learning and reinforces the associationist view. Although teachers in training read constructivist accounts of learning, they are placed in a system that is designed for associative learning. Furthermore, many progressive schools were not successful owing to a lack of discipline, too extreme a follow-the-child approach, and a failure to teach basic facts and procedures. I think that Montessori does not come up short when it comes to learning facts, because the curriculum has a backbone of core materials that teach a core set of facts. But it is sometimes lumped together with other follow-the-child programs and assumed to be weak on teaching the basics.

Another source mentioned in chapter 1 on why the progressive schools engendered by Dewey did not succeed in supplanting conventional ones is Zilversmit (1993). In addition to some of the problems already mentioned, he cites the Great Depression, Sputnik, and McCarthyism as scaring the nation out of a great educational experiment in progressive education. He describes progressive school systems that appeared to work very well in the first half of this century, but still eventually retreated to conventional practices in the face of threats to society.

How could we give more children the benefit of Montessori education?

Bringing Montessori to more children has to be a slow process, because it entails two major steps. First, it involves a major commitment to training more Montessori teachers. Montessori teachers need to be trained well by people deeply versed in Montessori. Becoming a Montessori teacher trainer is a tremendous commitment, requiring perhaps a decade or more: a year of one's own training to teach children, several years as a teacher, and then several more years working as an apprentice to a teacher trainer. Many more people need to be inspired to make that commitment, so more trainers are available to train more Montessori teachers, and more Montessori teachers are available to teach more children.

A second major step is a national commitment to begin education at age 3, rather than 5 or 6. Montessori education was designed to begin then, and when one begins it later, one misses out on important fundamentals. As school systems start Primary classes, beginning with groups of 3-year-olds, they can begin to train a cadre of Elementary level teachers. Obviously this kind of change requires a long-range vision that is not characteristically American. We tend to want quick fixes. Furthermore, such a turnover from conventional to Montessori school programs does nothing for the millions of children already in the midst of conventional schools and past the point when they can thrive in Montessori.

These practical considerations mean that any transformation of schooling that occurs will be slow, one school system or even one class at a time. This may be to the good, as it allows time for experiments to be conducted to resolve some of the outstanding issues regarding Montessori education.

Dr. Montessori was a genius observer of children, who arrived at many of the same insights suggested by research that has come after her. Her ultimate goal of finding a better way to educate children became grander with each passing year, as she watched the world become torn apart by two world wars. Ultimately, her aim was to help humanity be its best self.

> Our principal concern must be to educate humanity—the human beings of all nations—in order to guide it toward seeking common goals. We must turn back and make the child our principal concern. The efforts of science must be concentrated on [the child], because he is the source of and the key to the riddles of humanity. The child is richly endowed with powers, sensitivities, and constructive instincts that as yet have neither been recognized nor put to use. In order to develop, he needs much broader opportunities than he has been offered thus far. Might not this goal be reached by changing the entire structure of education? (Montessori, 1972, p. 31)

WORKS CITED

Acredolo, L., Goodwyn, S., Abrams, D., & Hanson, R. (2002). *Baby signs* (2nd ed.). New York: McGraw-Hill.

Adam, E. K., Gunnar, M. R., & Tanaka, A. (2004). Adult attachment, parent emotion, and observed parenting behavior: Mediator and moderator models. *Child Development, 75*(1), 110–22.

Adolph, K. E., & Berger, S. E. (2006). Motor development. In D. Kuhn, R. S. Siegler & W. Damon (Eds.), *Handbook of child psychology: Cognition, perception, and language* (6th ed., Vol. 2, pp. 161–213). Hoboken, NJ, US: Wiley.

Adolph, K. E., & Robinson, S. (2015). Motor development. In L. S. Liben & U. Mueller (Eds.), *Handbook of child psychology and developmental science. Vol 2,* pp. 113-157. *Cognitive development.* New York: Wiley.

Aiello, J. R., Nicosia, G., & Thompson, D. E. (1979). Physiological, social, and behavioral consequences of crowding on children and adolescents. *Child Development, 50*(1), 195–202.

Ainley, M. (2012). Students' interest and engagement in classroom activities. In S. L. Christenson, A. L. Reschly, & C. Wylie (Eds.), *Handbook of research on student engagement* (pp. 283–302). New York: Springer.

Ainsworth, M. (1967). *Infancy in Uganda: Infant care and the growth of love.* Baltimore: Johns Hopkins University Press.

Ainsworth, M. D. S. (1969, March 10). *Maternal sensitivity scales.* Retrieved from: www.psychology.sunysb.edu/attachment/measures/content/ainsworth_scales.html

Ainsworth, M. D. S., Blehar, M. C., Waters, E., & Wall, S. (1978). *Patterns of attachment: A psychological study of the Strange Situation.* Hillsdale, NJ: Lawrence Erlbaum.

Alfieri, L., Brooks, P. J., Aldrich, N. J., & Tenenbaum, H. R. (2011). Does discovery-based instruction enhance learning? *Journal of Educational Psychology, 103,* 1–18. doi:10.1037/a0021017

Alibali, M. W., & Goldin-Meadow, S. (1993). Gesture-speech mismatch and mechanisms of learning: What the hands reveal about a child's state of mind. *Cognitive Psychology, 25*(4), 468–523.

Allan, B. M., & Fryer, R. G. (2011). The powers and pitfalls of education incentives. Washington, DC: The Hamilton Project.

Allen, C., & Allen, J. (2009). *Escaping the endless adolescence: How we can help our teenagers grow up before they grow old.* New York: Random House.

Alvarez, A. L., & Booth, A. E. (2014). Motivated by meaning: Testing the effect of knowledge-infused rewards on preschoolers' persistence. *Child Development, 85,* 783–91.

Amabile, T. M. (1979). Effects of external evaluation on artistic creativity. *Journal of Personality & Social Psychology, 37*(2), 221–33.

Amabile, T. M., DeJong, W., & Lepper, M. R. (1976). Effects of externally imposed deadlines on subsequent intrinsic motivation. *Journal of Personality & Social Psychology, 34*(1), 92–98.

Amabile, T. M., & Gitomer, J. (1984). Children's artistic creativity: Effects of choice in task materials. *Personality & Social Psychology Bulletin, 10*(2), 209–15.

Amabile, T. M., Hennessey, B. A., & Grossman, B. S. (1986). Social influences on creativity: The effects of contracted-for reward. *Journal of Personality & Social Psychology, 50*(1), 14–23.

American Psychological Association, Coalition for Psychology in Schools and Education (APA Coalition). (2015). *Top 20 principles from psychology for preK–12 teaching and learning.* Retrieved from www.apa.org/ed/schools/cpse/top-twenty-principles.pdf

Ames, C. (1992). Classrooms: Goals, structures, and student motivation. *Journal of Educational Psychology, 84*(3), 261–71.

Ames, C., & Archer, J. (1988). Achievement goals in the classroom: Students' learning strategies and motivation processes. *Journal of Educational Psychology, 80*(3), 260–67.

Anand, P. G., & Ross, S. M. (1987). Using computer-assisted instruction to personalize arithmetic materials for elementary school children. *Journal of Educational Psychology, 79*(1), 72–78.

Anderman, E. M., & Maehr, M. L. (1994). Motivation and schooling in the middle grades. *Review of Educational Research, 64*(2), 287–309.

Anderman, E. M., Maehr, M. L., & Midgley, C. (1999). Declining motivation after the transition to middle school: Schools can make a difference. *Journal of Research & Development in Education, 32*(3), 131–47.

Anderson, J. R. (1983). *The architecture of cognition.* Hillsdale, NJ: Lawrence Erlbaum.

Anderson, J. R. (1990). *Cognitive psychology and its implications* (3rd ed.). New York: W.H. Freeman.

Anderson, J. R., Reder, L. M., & Simon, H. A. (1996). Situated learning and education. *Educational Researcher, 25*, 5–11.

Anderson, R. C., Mason, J., & Shirey, L. (1984). The reading group: An experimental investigation of a labyrinth. *Reading Research Quarterly, 20*(1), 6–38.

Annis, L. F. (1981). Effect of preference for assigned lecture notes on student achievement. *Journal of Educational Research, 74*(3), 179–82.

Annis, L. F. (1983). The processes and effects of peer tutoring. *Human Learning: Journal of Practical Research & Applications, 2*(1), 39–47.

Ansari, A., & Winsler, A. (2014). Montessori public school pre-k programs and the school readiness of low-income black and latino children. *Journal of Educational Psychology, 106*, 1066-1079. doi: 10.1037/a0036799

Armstrong, T., & Detweiler-Bedell, B. (2008). Beauty as an emotion: The exhilarating prospect of mastering a challenging world. *Review of General Psychology, 12*(4), 305–29.

Aronson, E. (2002). Building empathy, compassion, and achievement in the jigsaw classroom. In J. Aronson (Ed.), *Improving academic achievement: Impact of psychological factors on education* (pp. 209–25). San Diego: Academic Press.

Aronson, E., & Patnoe, S. (1997). *The jigsaw classroom: Building cooperation in the classroom* (2nd ed.). New York: Longman.

Arrighi, R., Cartocci, G., & Burr, D. (2011). Reduced perceptual sensitivity for biological motion in paraplegia patients. *Current Biology, 21*, R910–11.

Asher, S. R. (1979). Influence of topic interest on black children's and white children's reading comprehension. *Child Development, 50*(3), 686–90.

Asher, S. R., Hymel, S., & Wigfield, A. (1978). Influence of topic interest on children's reading comprehension. *Journal of Reading Behavior, 10*(1), 35–47.

Asher, S. R., & Markell, R. A. (1974). Sex differences in comprehension of high- and low-interest reading material. *Journal of Educational Psychology, 66*(5), 680–87.

Aslin, R. N., Jusczyk, P. W., & Pisoni, D. B. (1998). Speech and auditory processing during infancy: Constraints on and precursors to language. In D. Kuhn & R. S. Siegler (Eds.), *Handbook of child psychology, Vol. 2: Cognition, perception, and language development* (5th ed., pp. 147–98). New York: Wiley.

Atkinson, J. W., & Litwin, G. H. (1960). Achievement motive and test anxiety conceived as motive to approach success and motive to avoid failure. *Journal of Abnormal & Social Psychology, 60*, 52–63.

Au, W. (2011). Teaching under the new Taylorism: High-stakes testing and the standardization of the 21st century curriculum. *Journal of Curriculum Studies, 43*, 25–45.

Ayers, L. (1909). *Laggards in our schools.* New York: Charities Publication Committee.

Azmitia, M. (1988). Peer interaction and problem solving: When are two heads better than one? *Child Development, 59*(1), 87–96.

Azmitia, M. (1996). Peer interactive minds: Developmental, theoretical, and methodological issues. In P. B. Baltes & U. M. Staudinger (Eds.), *Interactive minds: Lifespan perspectives on the social foundation of cognition* (pp. 133–62). New York: Cambridge University Press.

Azmitia, M., & Crowley, K. (2001). The rhythms of thinking: The study of collaboration in an earthquake microworld. In K. Crowley, C. D. Schunn, & T. Okada (Eds.), *Designing for science: Implications from everyday, classroom, and professional settings* (pp. 51–81). Mahwah, NJ: Lawrence Erlbaum.

Azmitia, M., & Hesser, J. (1993). Why siblings are important agents of cognitive development: A comparison of siblings and peers. *Child Development, 64*, 430–44.

Azmitia, M., & Montgomery, R. (1993). Friendship, transactive dialogues, and the development of scientific reasoning. *Social Development, 2*(3), 202–21.

Bagot, R., van Hasselt, F., Champagne, D., Meaney, M., Krugers, H., & Joëls, M. (2009). Maternal care determines rapid effects of stress mediators on synaptic plasticity in adult rat hippocampal dentate gyrus. *Neurobiology of Learning and Memory, 92*(3), 292–300.

Bahrick, H. P., Fitts, P. M., & Rankin, R. E. (1952). Effect of incentives upon reactions to peripheral stimuli. *Journal of Experimental Psychology, 44*, 400–406.

Bai, D. L., & Bertenthal, B. I. (1992). Locomotor status and the development of spatial search skills. *Child Development, 63*(1), 215–26.

Bailey, D. B., Burchinal, M. R., & McWilliam, R. A. (1993). Age of peers and early childhood development. *Child Development, 64*, 848–62.

Baillargeon, R. (1987). Object permanence in 3½- and 4½-month-old infants. *Developmental Psychology, 23*, 655–64.

Bakermans-Kranenburg, M. J., & van Ijzendoorn, M. H. (1993). A psychometric study of the Adult Attachment Interview: Reliability and discriminant validity. *Developmental Psychology, 29*(5), 870–79.

Bakermans-Kranenburg, M. J., van Ijzendoorn, M. H., & Juffer, F. (2003). Less is more: Meta-analyses of sensitivity and attachment interventions in early childhood. *Psychological Bulletin, 129*(2), 195–215.

Bandura, A., Ross, D., & Ross, S. A. (1963). Imitation of film-mediated aggressive models. *Journal of Abnormal & Social Psychology, 66*(1), 3–11.

Bara, F., Gentaz, E., & Cole, P. (2007). Haptics in learning to read with children from low socio-economic status families. *British Journal of Developmental Psychology, 25*(4), 643–63.

Bargh, J. A. (2001). The psychology of the mere. In J. A. Bargh & D. K. Apsley (Eds.), *Unraveling the complexities of social life: A festschrift in honor of Robert B. Zajonc* (pp. 25–37). Washington, DC: American Psychological Association.

Bargh, J. A., Chen, M., & Burrows, L. (1996). Automaticity of social behavior: Direct effects of trait construct and stereotype activation on action. *Journal of Personality & Social Psychology, 71*, 230–44.

Bargh, J. A., & Schul, Y. (1980). On the cognitive benefits of teaching. *Journal of Educational Psychology, 72*(5), 593–604.

Barnes, J. L., Bernstein, E., & Bloom, P. (2015). Fact or fiction? Children's preferences for real versus make-believe stories. *Imagination, Cognition and Personality, 34*, 243–58.

Barnett, W., Jung, K., Yarosz, D., Thomas, J., Hornbeck, A., Stechuk, R., & Burns, S. (2008). Educational effects of the Tools of the Mind curriculum: A randomized trial. *Early Childhood Research Quarterly, 23*, 299–313. doi:10.1016/j.ecresq.2008.03.001

Barr, R., Lauricella, A., Zack, E., & Calvert, S. L. (2010). Infant and early childhood exposure to adult-directed and child-directed television programming: Relations with cognitive skills at age four. *Merrill-Palmer Quarterly, 56*, 21–48.

Barr, R., Shuck, L., Salerno, K., Atkinson, E., & Linebarger, D. L. (2010). Music interferes with learning from television during infancy. *Infant and Child Development, 19*, 313–31.

Barrett, P., Davies, F., Zhang, Y., & Barrett, L. (2015). The impact of classroom design on pupils' learning: Final results of a holistic, multi-level analysis. *Building and Environment, 89*, 118–33.

Barsalou, L. (2002). Being there conceptually: Simulating categories in preparation for situated action. In N. L. Stein, P. J. Bauer, & M. Rabinowitz (Eds.), *Representation, memory, and development: Essays in honor of Jean Mandler* (pp. 1–16). Mahwah, NJ: Lawrence Erlbaum.

Barsalou, L. (2008). Grounded cognition. *Annual Review of Psychology, 59*, 617–45.

Bassok, D., Latham, S., & Rorem, A. (2016). Is kindergarten the new first grade? *AERA Open, 1*(4), 1–31. doi:10.1177/2332858415616358

Bates, J. E., Viken, R. J., Alexander, D. B., Beyers, J., & Stockton, L. (2002). Sleep and adjustment in preschool children: Sleep diary reports by mothers relate to behavior reports by teachers. *Child Development, 73*(1), 62–74.

Bauer, P. J. (1995). Recalling past events: From infancy to early childhood. *Annals of Child Development, 11*, 25–71.

Baumrind, D. (1989). Rearing competent children. In W. Damon (Ed.), *Child development today and tomorrow* (pp. 349–78). San Francisco: Jossey-Bass.

Baumrind, D. (1991). The influence of parenting style on adolescent competence and substance use. *Journal of Early Adolescence, 11*(1), 56–95.

Bavelas, J. B., Black, A., Chovil, N., Lemery, C. R., & Mullett, J. (1988). Form and function in motor mimicry: Topographic evidence that the primary function is communicative. *Human Communication Research, 14*(3), 275–99.

Bavelas, J. B., Black, A., Lemery, C. R., & Mullett, J. (1987). Motor mimicry as primitive empathy. In N. Eisenberg & J. Strayer (Eds.), *Empathy and its development. Cambridge studies in social and emotional development* (pp. 317–38). New York: Cambridge University Press.

Baxter, L. A., & Clark, C. L. (1996). Perceptions of family communication patterns and the enactment of family rituals. *Western Journal of Communication, 60*, 254–68.

Beach, K. (1995). Activity as a mediator of sociocultural change and individual development: The case of school-work transition in Nepal. *Mind, Culture, & Activity: An International Journal, 2*(4), 285–302.

Beck, I. L., McKeown, M. G., & Gromoll, E. W. (1989). Learning from social studies texts. *Cognition & Instruction, 6*(2), 99–158.

Beck, I. L., McKeown, M. G., Sinatra, G. M., & Loxterman, J. A. (1991). Revising social studies text from a text-processing perspective: Evidence of improved comprehensibility. *Reading Research Quarterly, 26*(3), 251–76.

Bennett, E. L., Rosenzweig, M. R., & Diamond, M. C. (1969). Rat brain: Effects of environmental enrichment on wet and dry weights. *Science, 163*(3869), 825–26.

Bennett, K. P., & LeCompte, M. D. (1990). *How schools work: A sociological analysis of education.* New York: Longman.

Benson, J. B., & Uzgiris, I. C. (1985). Effect of self-initiated locomotion on infant search activity. *Developmental Psychology, 21*(6), 923–31.

Benware, C. A., & Deci, E. L. (1984). Quality of learning with an active versus passive motivational set. *American Educational Research Journal, 21*(4), 755–65.

Bergsmann, E. M., Lüftenegger, M., Jöstl, G., Schober, B., & Spiel, C. (2013). The role of classroom structure in fostering students' school functioning: A comprehensive and application-oriented approach. *Learning and Individual Differences, 26*, 131–38.

Berlyne, D. (1960). *Conflict, arousal, and curiosity.* New York: McGraw-Hill.

Berndt, T. J. (1989). Friendships in childhood and adolescence. In W. Damon (Ed.), *Child development today and tomorrow. The Jossey-Bass Social and Behavioral Science Series* (pp. 332–48). San Francisco: Jossey-Bass.

Bernier, A., Carlson, S., & Whipple, N. (2010). From external regulation to self-regulation: Early parenting precursors of young children's executive functioning. *Child Development, 81*, 326–39.

Bernieri, F. J. (1988). Coordinated movement and rapport in teacher-student interactions. *Journal of Nonverbal Behavior, 12*(2), 120–38.

Besançon, M., & Lubart, T. (2008). Differences in the development of creative competencies in children schooled in diverse learning environments. *Learning and Individual Differences, 18*, 381–89. doi:10.1016/j.lindif.2007.11.009

Bhatia, P., Davis, A., & Shamas-Brandt, E. (2015). Educational gymnastics: The effectiveness of Montessori practical life activities in developing fine motor skills in kindergartners. *Early Education and Development, 26*(4), 594–607.

Bialystok, E. (1999). Cognitive complexity and attentional control in the bilingual mind. *Child Development, 70*(3), 636–44.

Bialystok, E. (2015). Bilingualism and the development of executive function: The role of attention. *Child Development Perspectives, 9*, 117–21.

Biederman, I., & Shiffrar, M. M. (1987). Sexing day-old chicks: A case study and expert systems analysis of a difficult perceptual-learning task. *Journal of Experimental Psychology: Learning, Memory, & Cognition, 13*(4), 640–45.

Bjorklund, D. F. (1997). In search of a metatheory for cognitive development (or, Piaget is dead and I don't feel so good myself). *Child Development, 68*(1), 144–48.

Bjorklund, D. F., & Thompson, B. E. (1983). Category typicality effects in children's memory performance: Qualitative and quantitative differences in the processing of category information. *Journal of Experimental Child Psychology, 35*(2), 329–44.

Blackwell, L. S., Trzesniewski, K. H., & Dweck, C. S. (2007). Implicit theories of intelligence predict achievement across an adolescent transition: A longitudinal study and an intervention. *Child Development, 78*, 246–63.

Blair, C., & Raver, C. C. (2012). Individual development and evolution: Experiential canalization of self-regulation. *Developmental Psychology, 48*, 647–57. doi:10.1037/a0026472

Blair, C., & Raver, C. C. (2014). Closing the achievement gap through modification of neurocognitive and neuroendocrine function: Results from a cluster randomized controlled trial of an innovative approach to the education of children in kindergarten. *PloS One, 9*(11), e112393. doi:10.1371/journal.pone.0112393

Blair, C., & Razza, R. P. (2007). Relating effortful control, executive function, and false belief understanding to emerging math and literacy ability in kindergarten. *Child Development, 78*, 647–63. doi:10.1111/j.1467-8624.2007.01019.x

Blake, W. (1794/1984). The schoolboy. In *Songs of experience*. New York: Dover.

Blumberg, M. S., Marques, H. G., & Iida, F. (2013). Twitching in sensorimotor development from sleeping rats to robots. *Current Biology, 23*, R532–37.

Boaler, J. (1997). *Experiencing school mathematics: Teaching styles, sex, and setting.* Buckingham, UK: Open University Press.

Boaler, J., & Staples, M. (2008). Creating mathematical futures through an equitable teaching approach: The case of railside school. *The Teachers College Record, 110*, 608–45.

Bodrova, E., & Leong, D. (2007). *Tools of the mind: The Vygotskian approach to early childhood education* (2nd ed.). Upper Saddle River, NJ: Pearson.

Boerger, E. A., Tullos, A., & Woolley, J. D. (2009). Return of the candy witch: Individual differences in acceptance and stability of belief in a novel fantastical being. *British Journal of Developmental Psychology, 27*, 953–70.

Borke, H. (1975). Piaget's mountains revisited: Changes in the egocentric landscape. *Developmental Psychology, 11*, 240–43.

Bornstein, M. H. (1975). Qualities of color vision in infancy. *Journal of Experimental Child Psychology, 19*, 401–19.

Bornstein, M. H. (1989). Sensitive periods in development: Structural characteristics and causal interpretations. *Psychological Bulletin, 105*(2), 179–97.

Bouffard, T., & Vezeau, C. (1998). The developing self-system and self-regulation of primary school children. In M. D. Ferrari & R. J. Sternberg (Eds.), *Self-awareness: Its nature and development* (pp. 246–72). New York: Guilford Press.

Bouffard, T., Vezeau, C., & Bordeleau, L. (1998). A developmental study of the relation between combined learning and performance goals and students' self-regulated learning. *British Journal of Educational Psychology, 68*(3), 309–19.

Bower, G. H., Clark, M. C., Lesgold, A. M., & Winzenz, D. (1969). Hierarchical retrieval schemes in recall of categorized word lists. *Journal of Verbal Learning & Verbal Behavior, 8*(3), 323–43.

Bowlby, J. (1969). *Attachment and loss, Vol. 1: Attachment.* New York: Basic Books.

Bowman-Perrott, L., Davis, H., Vannest, K., Williams, L., Greenwood, C., & Parker, R. (2013). Academic benefits of peer tutoring: A meta-analytic review of single-case research. *School Psychology Review, 42*, 39–55.

Bradley, R. H., & Caldwell, B. M. (1976a). Early home environment and changes in mental test performance in children from 6 to 36 months. *Developmental Psychology, 12*(2), 93–97.

Bradley, R. H., & Caldwell, B. M. (1976b). The relation of infants' home environments to mental test performance at fifty-four months: A follow-up study. *Child Development, 47*(4), 1172–74.

Bransford, J. D., Brown, A. L., & Cocking, R. R. (1999). *How people learn: Brain, mind, experience, and school.* Washington, DC: National Academy Press.

Bransford, J. D., & Johnson, M. K. (1972). Contextual prerequisites for understanding: Some investigations of comprehension and recall. *Journal of Verbal Learning & Verbal Behavior, 11*(6), 717–26.

Bridgeman, D. L. (1981). Enhanced role taking through cooperative interdependence: A field study. *Child Development, 52*(4), 1231–38.

Brody, G. H., & Flor, D. L. (1997). Maternal psychological functioning, family processes, and child adjustment in rural, single-parent, African American families. *Developmental Psychology, 33*(6), 1000–11.

Brody, G. H., Graziano, W. G., & Musser, L. M. (1983). Familiarity and children's behavior in same-age and mixed-age peer groups. *Developmental Psychology, 19*(4), 568–76.

Brown, A. L., & Campione, J. C. (1990). Communities of learning and thinking, or a context by any other name. In D. Kuhn (Ed.), *Developmental perspectives on teaching and learning thinking skills* (Vol. 21, pp. 108–26). Basel: Karger.

Brown, A. L., & Campione, J. C. (1994). Guided discovery in a community of learners. In K. McGilly (Ed.), *Classroom lessons: Integrating cognitive theory and classroom practice.* Cambridge, MA: MIT Press.

Brown, A. L., & Kane, M. J. (1988). Preschool children can learn to transfer: Learning to learn and learning from example. *Cognitive Psychology, 20,* 493–523.

Brown, J. S., Collins, A., & Dugid, P. (1989). Situated cognition and the culture of learning. *Educational Researcher, 18*(1), 32–42.

Brownell, C. A., Ramani, G. B., & Zerwas, S. (2006). Becoming a social partner with peers: Cooperation and social understanding in one-and two-year-olds. *Child development, 77,* 803–21.

Brummelman, E., Thomaes, S., de Castro, B. O., Overbeek, G., & Bushman, B. J. (2014). "That's not just beautiful—that's incredibly beautiful!" the adverse impact of inflated praise on children with low self-esteem. *Psychological Science, 25*(3), 728–35. doi:10.1177/0956797613514251

Bruner, J. (1975). The ontogenesis of speech acts. *Journal of Child Language, 2,* 1–19.

Bruner, J. (1991). The narrative construction of reality. *Critical Inquiry, 18,* 1–21.

Bull, R., Espy, K. A., & Wiebe, S. A. (2008). Short-term memory, working memory, and executive functioning in preschoolers: Longitudinal predictors of mathematical achievement at age 7 years. *Developmental Neuropsychology, 33,* 205–28.

Bullard, J. (2013). *Creating environments for learning: Birth to age eight.* Upper Saddle River, NJ: Prentice-Hall.

Butler, R. (1990). The effects of mastery and competitive conditions on self-assessment at different ages. *Child Development, 61*(1), 201–10.

Butler, R., & Nisan, M. (1986). Effects of no feedback, task-related comments, and grades on intrinsic motivation and performance. *Journal of Educational Psychology, 78*(3), 210–16.

Butler, R., & Ruzany, N. (1993). Age and socialization effects on the development of social comparison motives and normative ability assessment in kibbutz and urban children. *Child Development, 64*(2), 532–43.

Buyse, E., Verschueren, K., & Doumen, S. (2011). Preschoolers' attachment to mother and risk for adjustment problems in kindergarten: Can teachers make a difference? *Social Development, 20*, 33–50.

Byrne, B., & Fielding-Barnsley, R. (1995). Evaluation of a program to teach phonemic awareness to young children: A two- and three-year follow-up and a new preschool trial. *Journal of Educational Psychology, 87*(3), 488–503.

Byron, K., & Khazanchi, S. (2012). Rewards and creative performance: A meta-analytic test of theoretically derived hypotheses. *Psychological Bulletin, 138*, 809–30.

Cahn, B. R., & Polich, J. (2006). Meditation states and traits: EEG, ERP, and neuroimaging studies. *Psychological Bulletin, 132*(2), 180–211.

California State Department of Education. (1992). *Mathematics framework for California public schools: Kindergarten through grade twelve.* Sacramento: California State Department of Education.

Callahan, R. E. (1962). *Education and the cult of efficiency.* Chicago: University of Chicago Press.

Camera, L. (2016). Federal education funding: Where does the money go? *US News and World Report*, January 2016. Retrieved on line from http://www.usnews.com/news/blogs/data-mine/2016/01/14/federal-education-funding-where-does-the-money-go on 6 June 2016.

Cameron, C. E., Brock, L. L., Murrah, W. M., Bell, L. H., Worzalla, S. L., Grissmer, D., & Morrison, F. J. (2012). Fine motor skills and executive function both contribute to kindergarten achievement. *Child Development, 83*, 1229–44.

Cameron, J., Banko, K. M., & Pierce, W. D. (2001). Pervasive negative effects of rewards on intrinsic motivation: The myth continues. *Behavior Analyst, 24*(1), 1–44.

Campos, J. J., Anderson, D. I., Barbu-Roth, M. A., Hubbard, E. M., Hertenstein, M. J., & Witherington, D. (2000). Travel broadens the mind. Infancy, 1(2), 149–219.

Cannon, E. N., Woodward, A. L., Gredebäck, G., von Hofsten, C., & Turek, C. (2012). Action production influences 12-month-old infants' attention to others' actions. Developmental Science, 15, 35-42.

Carbonneau, K. J., Marley, S. C., & Selig, J. P. (2013). A meta-analysis of the efficacy of teaching mathematics with concrete manipulatives. *Journal of Educational Psychology, 105*, 380–98.

Carey, S., & Bartlett, E. (1978). Acquiring a single new word. *Papers and Reports on Child Language Development, 15*, 17–29.

Carlson, S. M., Moses, L. J., & Hix, H. R. (1998). The role of inhibitory processes in young children's difficulties with deception and false belief. *Child Development, 69*, 672–91.

Carlson, S. M., Taylor, M., & Levin, G. (1998). The influence of culture on pretend play: The case of Mennonite children. *Merrill-Palmer Quarterly, 44*, 538–65.

Carlson, S. M., Zelazo, P. D., & Faja, S. (2012). Executive function. In P. D. Zelazo (Ed.), *Oxford handbook of developmental psychology* (Vol. 1, pp. 706–43). New York: Oxford University Press.

Carpenter, M., Akhtar, N., & Tomasello, M. (1998). Fourteen- through 18-month-old infants differentially imitate intentional and accidental actions. *Infant Behavior and Development, 21*, 315–30.

Carraher, T. N., Carraher, D. W., & Schliemann, A. D. (1985). Mathematics in the streets and in schools. *British Journal of Developmental Psychology, 3*(1), 21–29.

Casey, B. (2015). Beyond simple models of self-control to circuit-based accounts of adolescent behavior. *Annual review of psychology, 66*, 295–319.

Ceci, S. J., & Liker, J. K. (1986). A day at the races: A study of IQ, expertise, and cognitive complexity. *Journal of Experimental Psychology: General, 115*(3), 255–66.

Cerasoli, C. P., Nicklin, J. M., & Ford, M. T. (2014). Intrinsic motivation and extrinsic incentives jointly predict performance: A 40-year meta-analysis. *Psychological Bulletin, 140*, 980–1008. doi:10.1037/a0035661

Cesario, J. (2014). Priming, replication, and the hardest science. *Perspectives on Psychological Science, 9*, 40–48.

Chae, B., & Zhu, R. (2014). Environmental disorder leads to self-regulatory failure. *Journal of Consumer Research, 40*, 1203–18.

Chartrand, T. L., & Bargh, J. A. (1999). The chameleon effect: The perception-behavior link and social interaction. *Journal of Personality & Social Psychology, 76*, 893–910.

Chase, W. G., & Simon, H. A. (1988). The mind's eye in chess. In A. M. Collins & E. E. Smith (Eds.), *Readings in cognitive science: A perspective from psychology and artificial intelligence* (pp. 461–94). San Mateo, CA: Morgan Kaufmann.

Chattin-McNichols, J. (1992). *The Montessori controversy.* New York: Delmar.

Chi, M. T. H., & Bassok, M. (1989). Learning from examples via self-explanations. In L. B. Resnick (Ed.), *Knowing, learning, and instruction: Essays in honor of Robert Glaser* (pp. 251–82). Hillsdale, NJ: Lawrence Erlbaum.

Chi, M. T. H., & Ceci, S. J. (1987). Content knowledge: Its role, representation, and restructuring in memory development. In H. W. Reese (Ed.), *Advances in child development and behavior* (Vol. 20, pp. 91–142). San Diego: Academic Press.

Chi, M. T. H., Feltovich, P. J., & Glaser, R. (1981). Categorization and representation of physics problems by experts and novices. *Cognitive Science, 5*, 121–52.

Chien, N., Howes, C., Burchinal, M., Pianta, R., Ritchie, S., Bryant, . . . Barbarin, O. (2010). Children's classroom engagement and school readiness gains in pre-kindergarten. *Child Development, 81*, 1534–49. doi:10.1111/j.1467-8624.2010.01490.x

Chiong, C. & DeLoache, J. S. (2013). Learning the ABC's: What kinds of picture books facilitate young children's learning? *Journal of Early Childhood Literacy, 13*(13), 225–41.

Chirkov, V. I., & Ryan, R. M. (2001). Parent and teacher autonomy-support in Russian and US adolescents: Common effects on well-being and academic motivation. *Journal of Cross-Cultural Psychology, 32*(5), 618–35.

Chomsky, N. (1959). A review of B.F. Skinner's *Verbal Behavior. Language, 35*, 26–58.

Christakis, D. A., Ramirez, J., & Ramirez, J. (2012). Overstimulation of newborn mice leads to behavioral differences and deficits in cognitive performance. *Scientific Reports, 2*, 1–6.

Church, R. B., & Goldin-Meadow, S. (1986). The mismatch between gesture and speech as an index of transitional knowledge. *Cognition, 23*(1), 43–71.

Clark, C. D. (1995). *Flights of fancy, leaps of faith.* Chicago: University of Chicago Press.

Clearfield, M. W. (2011). Learning to walk changes infants' social interactions. *Infant Behavior and Development, 34*, 15–25.

Clements, D. H., Sarama, J., Unlu, F., & Layzer, C. (2012, March). *The efficacy of an intervention synthesizing scaffolding designed to promote self-regulation with an early mathematics curriculum: Effects on executive function.* Paper presented at the Society for Research on Educational Effectiveness, Washington DC.

Cognition and Technology Group at Vanderbilt. (2012). *The Jasper project: Lessons in curriculum, instruction, assessment, and professional development.* New York: Routledge.

Cohen, D. K., Raudenbush, S. W., & Ball, D. L. (2002). Resources, instruction, and research. In F. Mosteller & R. Boruch (Eds.), *Evidence matters: Randomized trials in education research* (pp. 80–119). Washington, DC: Brookings Institute.

Cohen, P. A., Kulik, J. A., & Kulik, C. C. (1982). Education outcomes of tutoring: A meta-analysis of findings. *American Educational Research Journal, 19*(2), 237–48.

Cohen, R. L. (1989). Memory for action events: The power of enactment. *Educational Psychology Review, 1*(1), 57–80.

Cohen, S., Evans, G. W., Krantz, D. S., & Stokols, D. (1980). Physiological, motivational, and cognitive effects of aircraft noise on children: Moving from the laboratory to the field. *American Psychologist, 35*(3), 231–43.

Cohen, S., Glass, D. C., & Singer, J. E. (1973). Apartment noise, auditory discrimination, and reading ability in children. *Journal of Experimental Social Psychology, 9*(5), 407–22.

Cohen, S., Krantz, D. S., Evans, G. W., & Stokols, D. (1981). Cardiovascular and behavioral effects of community noise. *American Scientist, 69*(5), 528–35.

Conley, D. (2015). A new era for educational assessment. *Education Policy Analysis Archives, 23*, 1–37.

Connors, L. J., & Epstein, J. L. (1995). Parents and school partnerships. In M. H. Bornstein (Ed.), *Handbook of parenting, Vol. 4: Applied and practical parenting* (pp. 437–58). Hillsdale, NJ: Lawrence Erlbaum.

Cook, L. S., Smagorinsky, P., Fry, P. G., Konopak, B., & Moore, C. (2002). Problems developing a constructivist approach to teaching: One teacher's transition from teacher preparation to teaching. *Elementary School Journal, 102*, 389–413.

Cook, S., Mitchell, Z., & Goldin-Meadow, S. (2008). Gesturing makes learning last. *Cognition, 106*, 1047–58.

Cooper, H., Robinson, J. C., & Patall, E. A. (2006). Does homework improve academic achievement? A synthesis of research, 1987–2003. *Review of Educational Research, 76*, 1–62.

Corapci, F., & Wachs, T. D. (2002). Does parental mood or efficacy mediate the influence of environmental chaos upon parenting behavior? *Merrill-Palmer Quarterly, 48*(2), 182–201.

Cordova, D. I., & Lepper, M. R. (1996). Intrinsic motivation and the process of learning: Beneficial effects of contextualization, personalization, and choice. *Journal of Educational Psychology, 88*(4), 715–30.

Corpus, J. H., McClintic-Gilbert, M. S., & Hayenga, A. O. (2009). Within-year changes in children's intrinsic and extrinsic motivational orientations: Contextual predictors and academic outcomes. *Contemporary Educational Psychology, 34*, 154–66.

Corpus, J. H., & Wormington, S. V. (2014). Profiles of intrinsic and extrinsic motivations in elementary school: A longitudinal analysis. *The Journal of Experimental Education, 82*, 480–501.

Cotton, J. L., & Cook, M. S. (1982). Meta-analyses and the effects of various reward systems: Some different conclusions from Johnson et al., *Psychological Bulletin, 92*, 176–83.

Covington, M. V. (2000). Goal theory, motivation, and school achievement: An integrative review. *Annual Review of Psychology, 51*, 171–200.

Cox, M. V., & Rowlands, A. (2000). The effect of three different educational approaches on children's drawing ability: Steiner, Montessori and traditional. *British Journal of Educational Psychology, 70,* 485–503.

Crandall, V. C., & Lacey, B. W. (1972). Children's perceptions of internal-external control in intellectual-academic situations and their Embedded Figures Test performance. *Child Development, 43*(4), 1123–34.

Crick, N. R., & Ladd, G. W. (1990). Children's perceptions of the outcomes of social strategies: Do the ends justify being mean? *Developmental Psychology, 26,* 612–20.

Crockenberg, S. B., & Bryant, B. K. (1978). Socialization: The implicit curriculum of learning environments. *Journal of Research & Development in Education, 12*(1), 69–78.

Csikszentmihalyi, M. (1997). *Finding flow: The psychology of engagement with everyday life.* New York: Basic Books.

Csikszentmihalyi, M., & Sawyer, K. (1995). Creative insight: The social dimension of a solitary moment. In R. J. Sternberg & J. E. Davidson (Eds.), *The nature of insight* (pp. 329–63). Cambridge, MA: MIT Press.

Cubberly, E. P. (1916/1929). *Public school administration* (3rd ed.). Boston: Houghton Mifflin/Riverside.

Cumberland-Li, A., Eisenberg, N., & Rieser, M. (2004). Relations of young children's agreeableness and resiliency to effortful control and impulsivity. *Social Development, 13*(2), 193–212.

Cunningham, A. E., & Stanovich, K. E. (1997). Early reading acquisition and its relation to reading experience and ability 10 years later. *Developmental Psychology, 33*(6), 934–45.

Damon, W. (1990). Social relations and children's thinking skills. In D. Kuhn (Ed.), *Developmental perspectives on teaching and learning thinking skills* (Vol. 21, pp. 95–107). Basel: Karger.

Damon, W., & Killen, M. (1982). Peer interaction and the process of change in children's moral reasoning. *Merrill-Palmer Quarterly, 28*(3), 347–67.

Davidson, R. J., Kabat-Zinn, J., Schumacher, J., Rosenkranz, M., Muller, D., Santorelli, S. F., ... Sheridan, J. F. (2003). Alterations in brain and immune function produced by mindfulness meditation. *Psychosomatic Medicine, 65*(4), 564–70.

Davis, B. E., Moon, R. Y., Sachs, H. C., & Ottolini, M. C. (1998). Effects of sleep position on infant motor development. *Pediatrics, 102*(5), 1135–40.

De Charms, R. (1976). *Enhancing motivation: A change in the classroom.* New York: Irvington.

De Lisi, R., & Golbeck, S. L. (1999). Implications of Piagetian theory for peer learning. In A. M. O'Donnell & A. King (Eds.), *Cognitive perspectives on peer learning. The Rutgers Invitational Symposium on Education Series* (pp. 3–37). Mahwah, NJ: Lawrence Erlbaum.

De Wolff, M., & van Ijzendoorn, M. H. (1997). Sensitivity and attachment: A meta-analysis on parental antecedents of infant attachment. *Child Development, 68*(4), 571–91.

Deater-Deckard, K., Lansford, J. E., Malone, P. S., Alampay, L. P., Sorbring, E., Bacchini, D., ... Di Giunta, L. (2011). The association between parental warmth and control in thirteen cultural groups. *Journal of Family Psychology, 25,* 790–94.

Deater-Deckard, K., Mullineaux, P. Y., Beekman, C., Petrill, S. A., Schatschneider, C., & Thompson, L. A. (2009). Conduct problems, IQ, and household chaos: A longitudinal multi-informant study. *Journal of Child Psychology and Psychiatry, 50,* 1301–308.

DeCasper, A. J., & Fifer, W. P. (1980). Of human bonding: Newborns prefer their mothers' voices. *Science, 208,* 1174–76.

Deci, E. L. (1971). Effects of externally mediated rewards on intrinsic motivation. *Journal of Personality & Social Psychology, 18*(1), 105–15.

Deci, E. L. (2009). Large-scale school reform as viewed from the self-determination theory perspective. *Theory and Research in Education, 7,* 244–52.

Deci, E. L., Koestner, R., & Ryan, R. M. (1999). A meta-analytic review of experiments examining the effects of extrinsic rewards on intrinsic motivation. *Psychological Bulletin, 125,* 627–68.

Deci, E. L., Nezlek, J., & Sheinman, L. (1981). Characteristics of the rewarder and intrinsic motivation of the rewardee. *Journal of Personality & Social Psychology, 40*(1), 1–10.

Deci, E. L., & Porac, J. (1978). Cognitive evaluation and human motivation. In M. R. Lepper & D. Greene (Eds.), *The hidden costs of reward: New perspectives on the psychology of human motivation* (pp. 149–76). Potomac, MD: Lawrence Erlbaum.

Deci, E. L., & Ryan, R. M. (1985). *Intrinsic motivation and self-determination in human behavior.* New York: Plenum.

Deci, E. L., & Ryan, R. M. (2011). Self-determination theory. In P. A. M. V. Lange, A. W. Kruglanski, & E. T. Higgins (Eds.), *Handbook of theories of social psychology* (Vol. 1, pp. 416–33). London: Sage.

Deci, E. L., Schwartz, A. J., Sheinman, L., & Ryan, R. M. (1981). An instrument to assess adults' orientations toward control versus autonomy with children: Reflections on intrinsic motivation and perceived competence. *Journal of Educational Psychology, 73*(5), 642–50.

Deci, E. L., Spiefel, N. H., Ryan, R. M., Koestner, R., & Kaufman, K. (1982). Effects of performance standards on teaching styles: Behavior of controlling teachers. *Journal of Educational Psychology, 74,* 852–59.

Dee, T. S., & Jacob, B. (2011). The impact of no child left behind on student achievement. *Journal of Policy Analysis and Management, 30,* 418–46.

Dekovic, M., & Janssens, J. M. (1992). Parents' child-rearing style and child's sociometric status. *Developmental Psychology, 28*(5), 925–32.

DeLoache, J. (2000). Dual representation and young children's use of scale models. *Child Development, 71,* 329–38.

DeLoache, J. S., Kolstad, V., & Anderson, K. N. (1991). Perceptual similarity and young children's understanding of scale models. *Child Development, 62,* 111–26.

DeLoache, J. S., Simcock, G., & Macari, S. (2007). Planes, trains, automobiles—and tea sets: Extremely intense interests in very young children. *Developmental Psychology, 43,* 1579–86.

DeLoache, J. S., Uttal, D. H., & Pierroutsakos, S. L. (1998). The development of early symbolization: Educational implications. *Learning & Instruction, 8,* 325–39.

Deutsch, C. P. (1964). Auditory discrimination and learning: Social factors. *Merrill-Palmer Quarterly, 10,* 277–96.

Devine, R. T., & Hughes, C. (2014). Relations between false belief understanding and executive function in early childhood: A meta-analysis. *Child Development, 85,* 1777–1794.

Dewey, C., Fleming, P., & Golding, J. (1998). Does the supine sleeping position have any adverse effects on the child? II. Development in the first 18 months. *Pediatrics, 101*(1), 1–5.

Dewey, J. (1913). *Interest and effort in education.* New York: Houghton Mifflin.

Diamond, A., Barnett, W., Thomas, J., & Munro, S. (2007). Preschool program improves cognitive control. *Science, 318,* 1387–88. doi:10.1126/science.1151148

Diamond, A., & Doar, B. (1989). The performance of human infants on a measure of frontal cortex function, the delayed response task. *Developmental Psychobiology, 22,* 271–94.

Diamond, A., & Lee, K. (2011). How can we help children succeed in the 21st century? What the scientific evidence shows aids executive function development in children 4–12 years of age. *Science, 333,* 959–64. doi:10.1126/science.1204529

Dohrmann, K. R., Nishida, T. K., Gartner, A., Lipsky, D. K., & Grimm, K. J. (2007). High school outcomes for students in a public Montessori program. *Journal of Research in Childhood Education, 22,* 205–17.

Doidge, N. (2015). *The brain's way of healing.* New York: Viking.

Dollaghan, C. (1985). Child meets word: "Fast mapping" in preschool children. *Journal of Speech & Hearing Research, 28*(3), 449–54.

Dore, R. A., Smith, E. D., & Lillard, A. S. (2015). *You are what you read (or whom you take the perspective of): Children adopt the traits of characters in fictional narratives.* Manuscript submitted for publication.

Doyle, A.-B., Connolly, J., & Rivest, L.-P. (1980). The effect of playmate familiarity on the social interactions of young children. *Child Development, 51*(1), 217–23.

Doymus, K. (2008). Teaching chemical bonding through jigsaw cooperative learning. *Research in Science & Technological Education, 26,* 47–57.

Dreary, I. J., Bell, P. J., Bell, A. J., Campbell, M. L., & Fazal, N. D. (2004). Sensory discrimination and intelligence: Testing spearman's other hypothesis. *The American Journal of Psychology, 117,* 1–18.

Duncan, G., Dowsett, C., Claessens, A., Magnuson, K., Huston, A., Klebanov, P., . . . Japel, C. (2007). School readiness and later achievement. *Developmental Psychology, 43,* 1428–46.

Duran, R. T., & Gauvain, M. (1993). The role of age versus expertise in peer collaboration during joint planning. *Journal of Experimental Child Psychology, 55,* 227–42.

Dweck, C. S. (1999). *Self-theories: Their role in motivation, personality, and development.* Philadelphia: Psychology Press/Taylor & Francis.

Dweck, C. S. (2006). *Mindset: The new psychology of success.* New York: Random House.

Dworkin, M. S. (1959). *Dewey on education: Selections with an introduction and notes by Martin S. Dworkin.* New York: Teachers College Press.

Early, D. M., Maxwell, K. L., Burchinal, M., Bender, R. H., Ebanks, C., Henry, G. T., . . . Zill, N. (2007). Teachers' education, classroom quality, and young children's academic skills: Results from seven studies of preschool programs. *Child Development, 78,* 558–80.

Eccles, J. S., Midgley, C., Wigfield, A., Buchanan, C. M., Reuman, D., Flanagan, C., & Iver, D. M. (1993). Development during adolescence: The impact of stage-environment fit on young adolescents' experiences in schools and in families. *American Psychologist, 48*(2), 90–101.

Eccles, J. S., Wigfield, A., Midgley, C., Reuman, D., MacIver, D., & Feldlaufer, H. (1993). Negative effects of traditional middle schools on students' motivation. *Elementary School Journal, 93*(5), 553–74.

Egan, K. (2002). *Getting it wrong from the beginning: Our progressivist inheritance from Herbert Spencer, John Dewey, and Jean Piaget.* New Haven: Yale University Press.

Egeland, B., Pianta, R., & O'Brien, M. A. (1993). Maternal intrusiveness in infancy and child maladaptation in early school years. *Development & Psychopathology, 5*(3), 359–70.

Ehrenberg, R. G., Brewer, D. J., Gamoran, A., & Willms, J. D. (2001). Class size and student achievement. *Psychological Science in the Public Interest, 2*(1), 1–30.

Eisen, S. L., & Lillard, A. S. (2016-a). As good as the real thing? A comparison of learning from hands-on materials versus apps. University of Virginia.

Eisen, S. L., & Lillard, A. S. (2016-b). Young children's thinking about touchscreens versus other media devices. University of Virginia.

Eisenberg, N., Cumberland, A., Spinrad, T. L., Fabes, R. A., Shepard, S. A., Reiser, M., Murphy, B. C., Losoya, S. H., & Guthrie, I. K. (2001). The relations of regulation and emotionality to children's externalizing and internalizing problem behavior. *Child Development, 72*(4), 1112–34.

Eisenberg, N., Fabes, R. A., Karbon, M., Murphy, B. C., Wosinski, M., Polazzi, L., Carlo, G., & Juhnke, C. (1996). The relations of children's dispositional prosocial behavior to emotionality, regulation, and social functioning. *Child Development, 67*(3), 974–92.

Eisenberg, N., Fabes, R. A., Murphy, B., Maszk, P., Smith, M., & Karbon, M. (1995). The role of emotionality and regulation in children's social functioning: A longitudinal study. *Child Development, 66*(5), 1360–84.

Eisenberg, N., Guthrie, I. K., Fabes, R. A., Reiser, M., Murphy, B. C., Holgren, R., Maszk, P., & Losoya, S. (1997). The relations of regulation and emotionality to resiliency and competent social functioning in elementary school children. *Child Development, 68*(2), 295–311.

Eisenberg, N., Smith, C. L., & Spinrad, T. I. (2011). Effortful control: Relations with emotion regulation, adjustment, and socialization in childhood. In K. D. Vohs & R. F. Baumeister (Eds.), *Handbook of self-regulation: Research, theory, and applications* (pp. 263–83). New York: Guilford.

Eisenberg, N., Spinrad, T. L., Fabes, R. A., Reiser, M., Cumberland, A., Shepard, S. A., Valiente, C., Losoya, S. H., Guthrie, I. K., & Thompson, M. (2004). The relations of effortful control and impulsivity to children's resiliency and adjustment. *Child Development, 75*(1), 25–46.

Eisenberger, R., & Cameron, J. (1996). Detrimental effects of reward: Reality or myth? *American Psychologist, 51*(11), 1153–66.

Eisenberger, R., & Shanock, L. (2003). Rewards, intrinsic motivation, and creativity: A case study of conceptual and methodological isolation. *Creativity Research Journal, 15*, 121–30.

El-Sheikh, M., & Sadeh, A. (2015). Sleep and development: Advancing theory and research. *Monographs of the Society for Research in Child Development, 80*, 1–215. doi: 10.1111/mono.12141

Elardo, R., Bradley, R., & Caldwell, B. M. (1975). The relation of infants' home environments to mental test performance from six to thirty-six months: A longitudinal analysis. *Child Development, 46*(1), 71–76.

Elkind, D. (1967). Piaget and Montessori. *Harvard Educational Review, 37*(4), 535–45.

Elkind, D. (1976). *Child development and education.* New York: Oxford University Press.

Elkind, D. (2007). *The power of play*. Cambridge MA: Da Capo Lifelong Books.

Engelhardt, L. E., Briley, D. A., Mann, F. D., Harden, K. P., & Tucker-Drob, E. M. (2015). Genes unite executive functions in childhood. *Psychological Science, 26*, 1151–63. doi:10.1177/0956797615577209

Engelkamp, J., Zimmer, H. D., Mohr, G., & Sellen, O. (1994). Memory of self-performed tasks: Self-performing during recognition. *Memory & Cognition, 22*(1), 34–39.

Epstein, Y. M., Woolfolk, R. L., & Lehrer, P. M. (1981). Physiological, cognitive, and nonverbal responses to repeated exposure to crowding. *Journal of Applied Social Psychology, 11*(1), 1–13.

Estes, T. H., & Vaughan, J. L. (1973). Reading interest and comprehension: Implications. *The Reading Teacher, 27*, 149–53.

Evans, G. W. (2006). Child development and the physical environment. *Annual Review of Psychology, 57*, 423–51.

Evans, G. W., Lepore, S. J., Shejwal, B. R., & Palsane, M. N. (1998). Chronic residential crowding and children's well-being: An ecological perspective. *Child Development, 69*(6), 1514–23.

Evans, G. W., Saegert, S., & Harrid, R. (2001). Residential density and psychological health among children in low-income families. *Environment & Behavior, 33*(2), 165–80.

Evans, G. W., & Wachs, T. D. (Eds.) (2010). *Chaos and its influence on children's development*. Washington, DC: American Psychological Association.

Fabes, R. A., Fultz, J., Eisenberg, N., May-Plumlee, T., & Christopher, F. S. (1989). Effects of rewards on children's prosocial motivation: A socialization study. *Developmental Psychology, 25*(4), 509–15.

Fagot, B. I., Gauvain, M., & Kavanagh, K. (1996). Infant attachment and mother-child problem-solving: A replication. *Journal of Social & Personal Relationships, 13*(2), 295–302.

Fallone, G., Acebo, C., Arnedt, J. T., Seifer, R., & Carskadon, M. A. (2001). Effects of acute sleep restriction on behavior, sustained attention, and response inhibition in children. *Perceptual & Motor Skills, 93*(1), 213–29.

Falvey, M. A., & Grenot-Scheyer, M. (1995). Instructional strategies. In M. A. Falvey (Ed.), *Inclusive and heterogeneous schooling: Assessment, curriculum, and instruction* (pp. 131–58). Baltimore, MD: Brookes.

Fantuzzo, J., & Ginsburg-Block, M. (1998). Reciprocal peer tutoring: Developing and testing effective peer collaborations for elementary school students. In K. Topping & S. Ehly (Eds.), *Peer-assisted learning* (pp. 121–44). Mahwah, NJ: Lawrence Erlbaum.

Fantuzzo, J. W., King, J. A., & Heller, L. R. (1992). Effects of reciprocal peer tutoring on mathematics and school adjustment: A component analysis. *Journal of Educational Psychology, 84*(3), 331–39.

Fantuzzo, J. W., Riggio, R. E., Connelly, S., & Dimeff, L. A. (1989). Effects of reciprocal peer tutoring on academic achievement and psychological adjustment: A component analysis. *Journal of Educational Psychology, 81*(2), 173–77.

Fantz, R. (1961). The origin of form perception. *Scientific American, 204*, 72.

Farran, D., Wilson, S. J., Lipsey, M. W., & Turner, K. (2012, June). *The effect of tools of the mind curriculum on children's achievement and self-regulation*. Paper presented at the Head Start Research Conference, Washington DC.

Ferguson, K. T., Cassells, R. C., MacAllister, J. W., & Evans, G. W. (2013). The physical environment and child development: An international review. *International Journal of Psychology, 48*, 437–68

Fernald, A. (1984). The perceptual and affective salience of mothers' speech to infants. In L. Feagans, C. Garvey, R. Golinkoff, M. T. Greenberg, C. Harding, & J. N. Bohannon (Eds.), *The origins and growth of communication* (pp. 7–29). Norwood, NJ: Ablex.

Fiedler, K. (2001). Affective states trigger processes of assimilation and accommodation. In L. L. Martin & G. L. Clore (Eds.), *Theories of mood and cognition: A user's guidebook* (pp. 85–98). Mahwah, NJ: Lawrence Erlbaum.

Field, T., Hallock, N., Ting, G., Dempsey, J., Dabira, C., & Shuman, H. (1978). A first-year follow-up of high-risk infants: Formulating a cumulative risk index. *Child Development, 49*(1), 119–31.

Fiese, B. H., & Kline, C. A. (1993). Development of the Family Ritual Questionnaire: Initial reliability and validation studies. *Journal of Family Psychology, 6*(3), 290–99.

Fisher, A. V., Godwin, K. E., & Seltman, H. (2014). Visual environment, attention allocation, and learning in young children when too much of a good thing may be bad. *Psychological Science, 25,* 1362–70. doi:10.1177/0956797614533801

Fisher, K. R., Hirsh-Pasek, K., Newcombe, N., & Golinkoff, R. M. (2013). Taking shape: Supporting preschoolers' acquisition of geometric knowledge through guided play. *Child Development, 84,* 1872–78.

Fitzpatrick, C., McKinnon, R. D., Blair, C. B., & Willoughby, M. T. (2014). Do preschool executive function skills explain the school readiness gap between advantaged and disadvantaged children? *Learning and Instruction, 30,* 25–31.

Flanagan, R. (2013). Effects of learning from interaction with physical or mediated devices. *Cognitive Processing, 14,* 213–15.

Flavell, J. H. (1963). *The developmental psychology of Jean Piaget.* New York: D. Van Nostrand.

Flavell, J. H. (1999). Cognitive development: Children's knowledge about the mind. *Annual Review of Psychology, 50,* 21–45.

Flynn, E., & Whiten, A. (2012). Experimental "microcultures" in young children: Identifying biographic, cognitive, and social predictors of information transmission. *Child Development, 83,* 911–25.

Fodor, J. A. (1983). *The modularity of mind.* Cambridge, MA: Bradford Books/MIT Press.

Fogel, A., Dedo, J. Y., & McEwen, I. (1992). Effect of postural position and reaching on gaze during mother-infant face-to-face interaction. *Infant Behavior & Development, 15*(2), 231–44.

Fox, K. C., Nijeboer, S., Dixon, M. L., Floman, J. L., Ellamil, M., Rumak, S. P., ... Christoff, K. (2014). Is meditation associated with altered brain structure? A systematic review and meta-analysis of morphometric neuroimaging in meditation practitioners. *Neuroscience & Biobehavioral Reviews, 43,* 48–73.

Frankel, K. A., & Bates, J. E. (1990). Mother-toddler problem solving: Antecedents in attachment, home behavior, and temperament. *Child Development, 61*(3), 810–19.

Frankel, L. A., Hughes, S. O., O'Connor, T. M., Power, T. G., Fisher, J. O., & Hazen, N. L. (2012). Parental influences on children's self-regulation of energy intake: Insights from developmental literature on emotion regulation. *Journal of Obesity, 2012,* article ID 327259. doi:10.1155/2012/327259

Fredrickson, B. L. (2001). The role of positive emotions in positive psychology: The broaden-and-build theory of positive emotions. *American Psychologist, 56*(3), 218–26.

Frijters, J. C., Barron, R. W., & Brunello, M. (2000). Direct and mediated influences of home literacy and literacy interest on prereaders' oral vocabulary and early written language skill. *Journal of Educational Psychology, 92*(3), 466–77.

Furnham, A., & Bradley, A. (1997). Music while you work: The differential distraction of background music on the cognitive test performance of introverts and extraverts. *Applied Cognitive Psychology, 11*(5), 445–55.

Furnham, A., Gunter, B., & Peterson, E. (1994). Television distraction and the performance of introverts and extraverts. *Applied Cognitive Psychology, 8*(7), 705–11.

Furnham, A., & Strbac, L. (2002). Music is as distracting as noise: The differential distraction of background music and noise on the cognitive test performance of introverts and extraverts. *Ergonomics, 45*(3), 203–17.

Galanter, E. (Ed.). (1968). *Automatic teaching: The state of the art.* New York: Wiley.

Galinsky, A. D., Wang, C. S., & Ku, G. (2008). Perspective-takers behave more stereotypically. *Journal of Personality and Social Psychology, 95*, 404–19.

Galinsky, T. L., Swanson, N. G., Sauter, S. L., Hurrell, J. J., & Schleifer, L. M. (2000). A field study of supplementary rest breaks for data-entry operators. *Ergonomics, 43*(5), 622–38.

Galton, F. (1883). Inquiries into the human faculty & its development. London: JM Dent.

Garon, N., Bryson, S. E., & Smith, I. M. (2008). Executive function in preschoolers: A review using an integrative framework. *Psychological Bulletin, 134*, 31–60.

Gasper, K., & Clore, G. L. (2002). Attending to the big picture: Mood and global versus local processing of visual information. *Psychological Science, 13*, 34–40.

Gauvain, M. (2001). *The social context of cognitive development.* London: Guilford.

Gauvain, M., & Rogoff, B. (1989). Collaborative problem solving and children's planning skills. *Developmental Psychology, 25*(1), 139–51.

Gaylord, C. (2012, August 31). Maria Montessori and 10 famous graduates from her schools. *The Christian Science Monitor.* Retrieved from www.csmonitor.com/Technology/Tech-Culture/2012/0831/Maria-Montessori-and-10-famous-graduates-from-her-schools/Google-founders-Larry-Page-and-Sergey-Brin

Gentner, D., & Toupin, C. (1986). Systematicity and surface similarity in the development of analogy. *Cognitive Science, 10*(3), 277–300.

Gergely, G., Bekkering, H., & Kiraly, I. (2002). Rational imitation in preverbal infants. *Nature, 415*(6873), 755.

Gerken, L., Balcomb, F. K., & Minton, J. L. (2011). Infants avoid 'labouring in vain' by attending more to learnable than unlearnable linguistic patterns. *Developmental Science, 14*(5), 972–79.

Gerson, S. A., Schiavio, A., Timmers, R., & Hunnius, S. (2015). Active drumming experience increases infants' sensitivity to audiovisual synchrony during observed drumming actions. *PloS One, 10*(6), e0130960.

Gick, M. L., & Holyoak, K. J. (1980). Analogical problem solving. *Cognitive Psychology, 12*(3), 306–55.

Ginsburg, H., & Oper, S. (1979). *Piaget's theory of intellectual development.* Englewood Cliffs, NJ: Prentice-Hall.

Ginsburg-Block, M. D., Rohrbeck, C. A., & Fantuzzo, J. W. (2006). A meta-analytic review of social, self-concept, and behavioral outcomes of peer-assisted learning. *Journal of Educational Psychology, 98*, 732–49.

Glachen, M., & Light, P. (1982). Peer interaction and learning: Can two wrongs make a right? In G. Butterworth & P. Light (Eds.), *Social cognition: Studies of the development of understanding* (pp. 238–62). Brighton, England: Harvester Press.

Glass, D. C., & Singer, J. E. (1972). Behavioral aftereffects of unpredictable and uncontrollable aversive events. *American Scientist, 60*, 457–65.

Glenberg, A., & Kaschak, M. P. (2002). Grounding language in action. *Psychonomic Bulletin & Review, 9*(3), 558–65.

Glenberg, A. M., Witt, J. K., & Metcalfe, J. (2013). From the revolution to embodiment 25 years of cognitive psychology. *Perspectives on Psychological Science, 8*, 573–85.

Glucksberg, S. (1962). The influence of strength of drive on functional fixedness and perceptual recognition. *Journal of Experimental Psychology, 63*(1), 36–41.

Godden, D. R., & Baddeley, A. D. (1975). Context-dependent memory in two natural environments: On land and underwater. *British Journal of Psychology, 66*(3), 325–31.

Godwin, K. E., & Fisher, A. V. (2011). *Allocation of attention in classroom environments: Consequences for learning.* Paper presented at the Proceedings of the 33rd Annual Conference of the Cognitive Science Society.

Gogtay, N., Giedd, J. N., Lusk, L., Hayashi, K. M., Greenstein, D., Vaituzis, A. C., . . . Thompson, P. M. (2004). Dynamic mapping of human cortical development during childhood through early adulthood. *Proceedings of the National Academy of Science, USA, 101*(21), 8174–79.

Goldin-Meadow, S. (2002). From thought to hand: Structured and unstructured communication outside of conventional language. In E. Amsel & J. P. Byrnes (Eds.), *Language, literacy, and cognitive development: The development and consequences of symbolic communication* (pp. 121–50). Mahwah, NJ: Lawrence Erlbaum.

Goldin-Meadow, S., & Alibali, M. W. (2013). Gesture's role in speaking, learning, and creating language. *Annual Review of Psychology, 64*, 257–83.

Goldin-Meadow, S., & Butcher, C. (2003). Pointing toward two-word speech in young children. In S. Kita (Ed.), *Pointing: Where language, culture, and cognition meet* (pp. 85– 107). Mahwah, NJ: Lawrence Erlbaum.

Goldin-Meadow, S., Cook, S. W., & Mitchell, Z. A. (2009). Gesturing gives children new ideas about math. *Psychological Science, 20*, 267–72.

Goldin-Meadow, S., Goodrich, W., Sauer, E., & Iverson, J. (2007). Young children use their hands to tell their mothers what to say. *Developmental Science, 10*, 778–85.

Goldin-Meadow, S., & Singer, M. A. (2003). From children's hands to adults' ears: Gesture's role in the learning process. *Developmental Psychology, 39*(3), 509–20.

Goldstein, T. R., & Bloom, P. (2015). Characterizing characters: How children make sense of realistic acting. *Cognitive Development, 34*, 39–50.

Goldstein, T. R., & Woolley, J. D. (2016). Ho! Ho! Who? Parent's promotion of belief in and live encounters with Santa. *Cognitive Development, 39*, 113–27. doi:10.1016/j.cogdev.2016.04.002

Goodman, R. (1997). Strengths and difficulties questionnaire. *Journal of Child Psychology and Psychiatry, 38*, 581–86.

Goodwyn, S. W., & Acredolo, L. P. (1993). Symbolic gesture versus word: Is there a modality advantage for onset of symbol use? *Child Development, 64*(3), 688–701.

Goodwyn, S. W., Acredolo, L. P., & Brown, C. A. (2000). Impact of symbolic gesturing on early language development. *Journal of Nonverbal Behavior, 24*(2), 81–103.

Gottfried, A. W. (Ed.). (1984). *Home environment and early cognitive development: Longitudinal research.* Orlando, FL: Academic Press.

Graef, R., Csikszentmihalyi, M., & Gianinno, S. M. (1983). Measuring intrinsic motivation in everyday life. *Leisure Studies, 2*(2), 155–68.

Graesser, A. C., & Person, N. K. (1994). Question asking during tutoring. *American Educational Research Journal, 31*(1), 104–37.

Graham, S., & Golan, S. (1991). Motivational influences on cognition: Task involvement, ego involvement, and depth of information processing. *Journal of Educational Psychology, 83*(2), 187–94.

Grazzini, C. (2004a). Maria Montessori and algebra: The binomial theorem. *NAMTA Journal, 29*, 79–104.

Grazzini, C. (2004). The four planes of development. *NAMTA Journal, 29*, 27–62.

Greenfield, P. M., & Childs, C. P. (1977). Weaving, color terms, and pattern representation: Cultural influences and cognitive development among the Zinacantecos of southern Mexico. *Interamerican Journal of Psychology, 11*, 23–48.

Greeno, J. G. (1998). The situativity of knowing, learning, and research. *American Psychologist, 53*(1), 5–26.

Greenwood, C. R., Delquadri, J. C., & Hall, R. V. (1989). Longitudinal effects of class-wide peer tutoring. *Journal of Educational Psychology, 81*(3), 371–83.

Greenwood, C. R., Dinwiddie, G., Bailey, V., Carta, J. J., Dorsey, D., Kohler, F. W., . . . Schulte, D. (1987). Field replication of classwide peer tutoring. *Journal of Applied Behavior Analysis, 20*(2), 151–60.

Greenwood, C. R., Terry, B., Utley, C. A., Montagna, D., & Walker, D. (1993). Achievement, placement, and services: Middle school benefits of classwide peer tutoring used at the elementary school. *School Psychology Review, 22*(3), 497–516.

Greer, R. D., & Polirstok, S. R. (1982). Collateral gains and short-term maintenance in reading and on-task responses by inner-city adolescents as a function of their use of social reinforcement while tutoring. *Journal of Applied Behavior Analysis, 15*(1), 123–39.

Griffin, M. M. (1995). You can't get there from here: Situated learning, transfer, and map skills. *Contemporary Educational Psychology, 20*(1), 65–87.

Grissmer, D., Grimm, K. J., Aiyer, S. M., Murrah, W. M., & Steele, J. S. (2010). Fine motor skills and early comprehension of the world: Two new school readiness indicators. *Developmental Psychology, 46*, 1008–17.

Grolnick, W. S., & Ryan, R. M. (1987). Autonomy in children's learning: An experimental and individual difference investigation. *Journal of Personality & Social Psychology, 52*(5), 890–98.

Grossmann, K., Grossmann, K. E., Fremmer-Bombik, E., Kindler, H., Scheuerer-Englisch, H., & Zimmermann, P. (2002). The uniqueness of the child-father attachment relationship: Fathers' sensitive and challenging play as a pivotal variable in a 16-year longitudinal study. *Social Development, 11*(3), 307–31.

Grusec, J. E. (1991). Socializing concern for others in the home. *Developmental Psychology, 27*, 338–42.

Guidubaldi, J., Cleminshaw, H. K., Perry, J. D., Nastasi, B. K., & Lightel, J. (1986). The role of selected family environment factors in children's post-divorce adjustment. *Family Relations: Journal of Applied Family & Child Studies, 35*(1), 141–51.

Hafen, C. A., Allen, J. P., Mikami, A. Y., Gregory, A., Hamre, B., & Pianta, R. C. (2012). The pivotal role of adolescent autonomy in secondary school classrooms. *Journal of Youth and Adolescence, 41*, 245–55.

Hall, G. S. (1911). *Educational problems* (Vol. 1). New York: Appleton.

Hamre, B. K., & Pianta, R. C. (2001). Early teacher-child relationships and the trajectory of children's school outcomes through eighth grade. *Child Development, 72*(2), 625–38.

Hamre, B. K., & Pianta, R. C. (2007). Learning opportunities in preschool and early elementary classrooms. In R. C. Pianta, M. J. Cox, & K. L. Snow (Eds.), *School readiness and the transition to kindergarten* (pp. 49–84). Baltimore: Paul H. Brookes.

Hanh, T. (2001/2009). *You are here: The power of the present moment* (S. C. Kohn, Trans.). Boston: Shambhala.

Hanna, E., & Meltzoff, A. N. (1993). Peer imitation by toddlers in laboratory, home, and day-care contexts: Implications for social learning and memory. *Developmental Psychology, 29*(4), 701–10.

Harackiewicz, J. M., Manderlink, G., & Sansone, C. (1984). Rewarding pinball wizardry: Effects of evaluation and cue value on intrinsic interest. *Journal of Personality & Social Psychology, 47*(2), 287–300.

Harris, P. L. (2012). *Trusting what you're told: How children learn from others.* Cambridge, MA: Harvard University Press.

Hart, C. H., DeWolf, D. M., Wozniak, P., & Burts, D. C. (1992). Maternal and paternal disciplinary styles: Relations with preschoolers' playground behavioral orientations and peer status. *Child Development, 63*(4), 879–92.

Harter, S. (1978). Pleasure derived from challenge and the effects of receiving grades on children's difficulty level choices. *Child Development, 49*(3), 788–99.

Harter, S. (1981). A new self-report scale of intrinsic versus extrinsic orientation in the classroom: Motivational and informational components. *Developmental Psychology, 17*(3), 300–312.

Hartup, W. W. (1983). Peer relations. In E. M. Hetherington (Ed.), *Handbook of child psychology: Socialization, personality, and social development* (4th ed.) (Vol. 4, pp. 103–96). New York: Wiley. (P. H. Mussen, General Ed.).

Havas, D., Glenberg, A., & Rinck, M. (2007). Emotion simulation during language comprehension. *Psychonomic Bulletin & Review, 14*, 436–41.

Havas, D. A., Glenberg, A. M., Gutowski, K. A., Lucarelli, M. J., & Davidson, R. J. (2010). Cosmetic use of botulinum toxin-a affects processing of emotional language. *Psychological Science, 21*(7), 895–900.

Hayashi, M., Watanabe, M., & Hori, T. (1999). The effects of a 20 min nap in the midafternoon on mood, performance and EEG activity. *Clinical Neurophysiology, 110*(2), 272–79.

Heathcock, J. C., Lobo, M., & Galloway, J. C. (2008). Movement training advances the emergence of reaching in infants born at less than 33 weeks of gestational age: A randomized clinical trial. *Physical Therapy, 88*, 310–322.

Hebb, D. (1949). *The organization of behavior: A neuropsychological theory.* New York: Wiley.

Heckman, J. J., & Kautz, T. (2012). Hard evidence on soft skills. *Labour Economics, 19*, 451–64.

Heft, H. (1979). Background and focal environmental conditions of the home and attention in young children. *Journal of Applied Social Psychology, 9*, 47–69.

Held, R., & Hein, A. (1963). Movement-produced stimulation in the development of visually guided behavior. *Journal of Comparative & Physiological Psychology, 56*(5), 872–76.

Hendrickson, G., & Schroeder, W. H. (1941). Transfer of training in learning to hit a submerged target. *Journal of Educational Psychology, 32*, 205–13.

Hennessey, B. A. (2000). Rewards and creativity. In C. Sansone & J. M. Harackiewicz (Eds.), *Intrinsic and extrinsic motivation: The search for optimal motivation and performance* (pp. 55–78). San Diego: Academic Press.

Henry, C. S., & Lovelace, S. G. (1995). Family resources and adolescent family life satisfaction in remarried family households. *Journal of Family Issues, 16*(6), 765–86.

Herricks, T. (2004). For these educations, the diet of worms isn't just history, *The Wall Street Journal.* Published 15 June 2004. Retrieved from http://www.wsj.com/articles/SB108725077538636819 on 6 June 2016.

Hesse, E. (1999). The adult attachment interview: Historical and current perspectives. In J. Cassidy & P. R. Shaver (Eds.), *Handbook of attachment: Theory, research, and clinical applications* (pp. 395–433). New York: Guilford.

Hidi, S. (1990). Interest and its contribution as a mental resource for learning. *Review of Educational Research, 60*(4), 549–71.

Hidi, S. (2000). An interest researcher's perspective: The effects of extrinsic and intrinsic factors on motivation. In C. Sansone & J. M. Harackiewicz (Eds.), *Intrinsic and extrinsic motivation: The search for optimal motivation and performance* (pp. 309–39). San Diego: Academic Press.

Hidi, S., & McLaren, J. (1990). The effect of topic and theme interestingness on the production of school expositions. In H. Mandl, E. deCorte, N. Bennett, & H. F. Friedrich (Eds.), *Learning and instruction* (Vol. 2.2, pp. 295–308). Oxford: Pergamon.

Hidi, S., & Renninger, K. A. (2006). The four-phase model of interest development. *Educational Psychologist, 41*, 111–27.

Hiebert, J. (1999). Relationships between research and the NCTM Standards. *Journal for Research in Mathematics Education, 30*(1), 3–19.

Hilgard, E. R. (1987). *Psychology in America: A historical survey.* San Diego: Harcourt Brace Jovanovich.

Hiroto, D. S., & Seligman, M. E. (1975). Generality of learned helplessness in man. *Journal of Personality & Social Psychology, 31*(2), 311–27.

Hirsh-Pasek, K., Golinkoff, R., Berk, L., & Singer, D. (2009). *A mandate for playful learning in preschool: Presenting the evidence.* New York: Oxford University Press.

Hogan, D. M., & Tudge, J. R. H. (1999). Implications of Vygotsky's theory for peer learning. In A. M. O'Donnell & A. King (Eds.), *Cognitive perspectives on peer learning. The Rutgers Invitational Symposium on Education Series* (pp. 39–65). Mahwah, NJ: Lawrence Erlbaum.

Hölzel, B. K., Lazar, S. W., Gard, T., Schuman-Olivier, Z., Vago, D. R., & Ott, U. (2011). How does mindfulness meditation work? Proposing mechanisms of action from a conceptual and neural perspective. *Perspectives on Psychological Science, 6*(6), 537–59.

Hopkins, E. J., & Lillard, A. S. (submitted). The effect of specific fantasy elements on children's learning from storybooks.

Hostetter, A. B. (2011). When do gestures communicate? A meta-analysis. *Psychological Bulletin, 137*(2), 297–315.

Huntsinger, J. R., Isbell, L. M., & Clore, G. L. (2014). The affective control of thought: Malleable, not fixed. *Psychological Review, 121*, 600–18.

Iqbal, S. T., & Horvitz, E. (2007). *Disruption and recovery of computing tasks: Field study, analysis, and directions.* Paper presented at the Proceedings of the SIGCHI Conference on Human Factors in Computing Systems, San Jose, CA.

Iriki, A., Tanaka, M., & Iwamura, Y. (1996). Coding of body schema during tool use by macaque postcentral neurons. *NeuroReport, 7,* 2325–30.

Isen, A. M. (2000). Positive affect and decision making. In M. Lewis & J. M. Haviland-Jones (Eds.), *Handbook of emotions* (2nd ed., pp. 417–35). New York: Guilford.

Istomina, J. M. (1975). The development of voluntary memory in preschool age children. *Soviet Psychology, 13,* 5–64.

Iyengar, S. S., & Lepper, M. R. (1999). Rethinking the value of choice: A cultural perspective on intrinsic motivation. *Journal of Personality & Social Psychology, 76,* 349–66.

Iyengar, S. S., & Lepper, M. R. (2000). When choice is demotivating: Can one desire too much of a good thing? *Journal of Personality & Social Psychology, 79*(6), 995–1006.

Jaffee, S. R., Hanscombe, K. B., Haworth, C. M., Davis, O. S., & Plomin, R. (2012). Chaotic homes and children's disruptive behavior a longitudinal cross-lagged twin study. *Psychological Science, 23*(6), 643–50. doi:10.1177/0956797611431693

Jain, S., Shapiro, S. L., Swanick, S., Roesch, S. C., Mills, P. J., Bell, I., & Schwartz, G. E. (2007). A randomized controlled trial of mindfulness meditation versus relaxation training: Effects on distress, positive states of mind, rumination, and distraction. *Annals of Behavioral Medicine, 33*(1), 11–21.

James, W. (1890). *The principles of psychology* (Vol. 1). New York: Henry Holt.

Jennings, J. L., & Bearak, J. M. (2014). "Teaching to the test" in the NCLB era: How test predictability affects our understanding of student performance. *Educational Researcher, 43,* 381–89. doi:10.3102/0013189X14554449

Jha, A. P., Krompinger, J., & Baime, M. J. (2007). Mindfulness training modifies subsystems of attention. *Cognitive, Affective & Behavioral Neuroscience, 7,* 109–19.

Johnson, D. W., & Johnson, R. T. (1979). Conflict in the classroom: Controversy and learning. *Review of Educational Research, 49*(1), 51–69.

Johnson, D. W., & Johnson, R. T. (2009). An educational psychology success story: Social interdependence theory and cooperative learning. *Educational researcher, 38,* 365-379.

Johnson, D. W., Maruyama, G., Johnson, R. T., Nelson, D., & Skon, L. (1981). Effects of cooperative, competitive, and individualistic goal structures on achievement: A meta-analysis. *Psychological Bulletin, 89*(1), 47–62.

Johnson, R. T., & Johnson, D. W. (1983). Effects of cooperative, competitive, and individualistic learning experiences on social development. *Exceptional Children, 49*(4), 323–29.

Johnson, S. L., McPhee, L., & Birch, L. L. (1991). Conditioned preferences: Young children prefer flavors associated with high dietary fat. *Physiology & Behavior, 50*(6), 1245–51.

Jolin, E. M., & Weller, R. A. (2011). Television viewing and its impact on childhood behaviors. *Current Psychiatry Reports, 13,* 122–28.

Jonich, G. M. (Ed.). (1962). *Psychology and the science of education: Selected writings of Edward L. Thorndike.* New York: Teachers College Press.

Kabat-Zinn, J. (1990). *Full catastrophe living.* New York: Delta.

Kabat-Zinn, J. (1994). *Wherever you go, there you are: Mindfulness meditation in everyday life.* New York: Hyperion Books.

Kaderavek, J. N., & Justice, L. M. (2005). The effect of book genre in the repeated readings of mothers and their children with language impairment: A pilot investigation. *Child Language Teaching and Therapy, 21,* 75–92.

Kamins, M. L., & Dweck, C. S. (1999). Person versus process praise and criticism: Implications for contingent self-worth and coping. *Developmental Psychology, 35*(3), 835–47.

Kang, M. J., Hsu, M., Krajbich, I. M., Loewenstein, G., McClure, S. M., Wang, J. T.-y., & Camerer, C. F. (2009). The wick in the candle of learning: Epistemic curiosity activates reward circuitry and enhances memory. *Psychological Science, 20*, 963–73.

Karnes, M., Shewedel, A., & Williams, M. (1983). A comparison of five approaches for educating young children from low-income homes. In the Consortium for Longitudinal Studies (Ed.), *As the twig is bent: Lasting effects of preschool programs* (pp. 133–71). Hillsdale, NJ: Lawrence Erlbaum.

Kawakubo, Y., Kono, T., Takizawa, R., Kuwabara, H., Ishii-Takahashi, A., & Kasai, K. (2011). Developmental changes of prefrontal activation in humans: A near-infrared spectroscopy study of preschool children and adults. *PloS One, 6*(10), e25944.

Kelly, Y., Kelly, J., & Sacker, A. (2013). Changes in bedtime schedules and behavioral difficulties in 7 year old children. *Pediatrics, 132*, 1184–90.

Keltner, B. (1990). Family characteristics of preschool social competence among black children in a Head Start program. *Child Psychiatry & Human Development, 21*(2), 95–108.

Kemler Nelson, D. G., Hirsh-Pasek, K., Jusczyk, P. W., & Cassidy, K. W. (1989). How the prosodic cues in motherese might assist language learning. *Journal of Child Language, 16*(1), 55–68.

Kerr, C. E., Sacchet, M. D., Lazar, S. W., Moore, C. I., & Jones, S. R. (2013). Mindfulness starts with the body: Somatosensory attention and top-down modulation of cortical alpha rhythms in mindfulness meditation. *Frontiers in Human Neuroscience, 7*, 12.

Keupp, S., Behne, T., & Rakoczy, H. (2013). Why do children overimitate? Normativity is crucial. *Journal of Experimental Child Psychology, 116*, 392–406.

Kidd, C., Piantadosi, S. T., & Aslin, R. N. (2012). The Goldilocks effect: Human infants allocate attention to visual sequences that are neither too simple nor too complex. *PLoS One, 7*(5), e36399. doi:10.1371/journal.pone.0036399

Kidd, C., Piantadosi, S. T., & Aslin, R. N. (2014). The Goldilocks effect in infant auditory attention. *Child Development, 85*, 1795–1804.

Killingsworth, M. A., & Gilbert, D. T. (2010). A wandering mind is an unhappy mind. *Science, 330*, 932.

Kilpatrick, W. H. (1914). *The Montessori system examined.* Boston: Houghton Mifflin.

Kim, S., Nordling, J. K., Yoon, J. E., Boldt, L. J., & Kochanska, G. (2013). Effortful control in hot and cool tasks differentially predicts children's behavior problems and academic performance. *Journal of Abnormal Child Psychology, 41*, 43–56.

Kindlon, D. (2001). *Too much of a good thing.* New York: Hyperion.

King, R. B., McInerney, D. M., Ganotice, F. A., & Villarosa, J. B. (2015). Positive affect catalyzes academic engagement: Cross-sectional, longitudinal, and experimental evidence. *Learning and Individual Differences, 39*, 64–72.

Kirkham, J. A., & Kidd, E. (2016). The effect of Steiner, Montessori, and national curriculum education upon children's pretence and creativity. *The Journal of Creative Behavior.* Advance online publication. doi:10.1002/jocb.83

Kitayama, S., & Uskul, A. K. (2011). Culture, mind, and the brain: Current evidence and future directions. *Annual Review of Psychology, 62*, 419–49.

Klahr, D., & Nigam, M. (2004). The equivalence of learning paths in early science instruction: Effects of direct instruction and discovery learning. *Psychological Science, 15*(10), 661–67.

Klaus, R. A., & Gray, S. W. (1968). The early training project for disadvantaged children: A report after five years. *Monographs of the Society for Research in Child Development, 33*(4), 1–66.

Kleim, J. A., Swain, R. A., Armstrong, K. A., Napper, R. M. A., Jones, T. A., & Greenough, W. T. (1998). Selective synaptic plasticity within the cerebellar cortex following complex motor skill learning. *Neurobiology of Learning & Memory, 69*(3), 274–89.

Klingberg, T. (2014). Childhood cognitive development as a skill. *Trends in Cognitive Sciences, 18*, 573–79.

Klingberg, T., Forssberg, H., & Westerberg, H. (2002). Training of working memory in children with ADHD. *Journal of Clinical & Experimental Neuropsychology, 24*(6), 781–91.

Koenig, M. A., Clément, F., & Harris, P. L. (2004). Trust in testimony: Children's use of true and false statements. *Psychological Science, 15*, 694–98.

Kohn, A. (1993). *Punished by rewards.* New York: Houghton Mifflin.

Kohn, A. (2007). *The homework myth: Why our kids get too much of a bad thing.* Boston: Da Capo Press.

Krafft, K. C., & Berk, L. E. (1998). Private speech in two preschools: Significance of open-ended activities and make-believe play for verbal self-regulation. *Early Childhood Research Quarterly, 13*, 637–58.

Kramer, R. (1976). *Maria Montessori: A biography.* New York: Putnam.

Krauss, R. M., & Hadar, U. (1999). The role of speech-related arm/hand gestures in word retrieval. In L. S. Messing & R. Campbell (Eds.), *Gesture, speech, and sign* (pp. 93–116). New York: Oxford University Press.

Kruger, A. C. (1992). The effect of peer and adult-child transductive discussions on moral reasoning. *Merrill-Palmer Quarterly, 38*(2), 191–211.

Kruglanski, A. (1978). Issues in cognitive social psychology. In M. R. Lepper & D. Greene (Eds.), *The hidden costs of reward: New perspectives on the psychology of human motivation* (pp. 19–30). Potomac, MD: Lawrence Erlbaum.

Kruglanski, A. W., Friedman, I., & Zeevi, G. (1971). The effects of extrinsic incentive on some qualitative aspects of task performance. *Journal of Personality, 39*(4), 606–17.

Kubovy, M. (1999). Pleasures of the mind. In D. Kahneman, E. Diener, & N. Schwartz (Eds.), *Well-being: The foundations of hedonic psychology* (pp. 134–54). New York: Russell Sage.

Kuhn, D. (1972). Mechanisms of change in the development of cognitive structures. *Child Development, 43*(3), 833–44.

Kuhn, D. (2001). Why development does (and does not) occur: Evidence from the domain of inductive reasoning. In J. L. McClelland & R. S. Siegler (Eds.), *Mechanisms of cognitive development: Behavioral and neural perspectives. Carnegie Symposia on Cognition* (pp. 221–49). Mahwah, NJ: Lawrence Erlbaum.

Kulhavy, R. W., Dyer, J. W., & Silver, L. (1975). The effects of notetaking and test expectancy on the learning of text material. *Journal of Educational Research, 68*(10), 363–65.

Kurosawa, K., & Harackiewicz, J. M. (1995). Test anxiety, self-awareness, and cognitive interference: A process analysis. *Journal of Personality, 63*(4), 931–51.

Kusché, C. A., & Greenberg, M. T. (1994). *The paths curriculum.* Seattle, WA: Developmental Research and Programs.

Kyndt, E., Raes, E., Lismont, B., Timmers, F., Cascallar, E., & Dochy, F. (2013). A meta-analysis of the effects of face-to-face cooperative learning. Do recent studies falsify or verify earlier findings? *Educational Research Review, 10,* 133–49.

Laird, J. D., Wagener, J. J., Halal, M., & Szegda, M. (1982). Remembering what you feel: Effects of emotion on memory. *Journal of Personality & Social Psychology, 42*(4), 646–57.

Lakoff, G., & Johnson, M. (1999). *Philosophy in the flesh: The embodied mind and its challenge to Western thought.* New York: Basic Books.

Lamborn, S. D., Mounts, N. S., Steinberg, L., & Dornbusch, S. M. (1991). Patterns of competence and adjustment among adolescents from authoritative, authoritarian, indulgent, and neglectful families. *Child Development, 62*(5), 1049–65.

Lancy, D. F. (1996). *Playing on the mother ground.* New York: Guilford.

Lancy, D. F., & Strathern, A. J. (1981). "Making twos": Pairing as an alternative to the taxonomic mode of representation. *American Anthropologist, 8,* 773–95.

Landry, S. H., Smith, K. E., Swank, P. R., & Miller-Loncar, C. L. (2000). Early maternal and child influences on children's later independent cognitive and social functioning. *Child Development, 71*(2), 358–75.

Langer, E. J., & Rodin, J. (1976). The effects of choice and enhanced personal responsibility for the aged: A field experiment in an institutional setting. *Journal of Personality & Social Psychology, 34*(2), 191–98.

Langlois, J. H., Roggman, L. A., Casey, R. J., Ritter, J. M., Rieser-Danner, L. A., & Jenkins, V. Y. (1987). Infant preferences for attractive faces: Rudiments of a stereotype? *Developmental Psychology, 23*(3), 363–69.

Larkin, J. H., McDermott, J., Simon, D. P., & Simon, H. A. (1980). Expert and novice performance in solving physics problems. *Science, 208,* 1335–42.

Laski, E. V., Vasilyeva, M., & Shiffman, J. (2016). Longitudinal comparison of place-value and arithmetic knowledge in Montessori and non-Montessori-students. *Journal of Montessori Research, 2,* 1–15.

Lave, J. (1988). *Cognition in practice: Mind, mathematics, and culture in everyday life.* New York: Cambridge University Press.

Lave, J., & Wenger, E. (1991). *Situated learning: Legitimate peripheral participation.* New York: Cambridge University Press.

Lazar, S. W., Kerr, C. E., Wasserman, R. H., Gray, J. R., Greve, D. N., Treadway, M. T., . . . Fischl, B. (2005). Meditation experience is associated with increased cortical thickness. *Neuroreport: For Rapid Communication of Neuroscience Research, 16,* 1893–97.

Lazarowitz, R., Hertz-Lazarowitz, R., & Baird, J. H. (1994). Learning science in a cooperative setting: Academic achievement and affective outcomes. *Journal of Research in Science Teaching, 31*(10), 1121–31.

LeBarton, E. S., Goldin-Meadow, S., & Raudenbush, S. (2015). Experimentally induced increases in early gesture lead to increases in spoken vocabulary. *Journal of Cognition and Development, 16,* 199–220.

Lebel, C., & Beaulieu, C. (2011). Longitudinal development of human brain wiring continues from childhood into adulthood. *The Journal of Neuroscience, 31,* 10937–47.

Lepper, M. R., Corpus, J. H., & Iyengar, S. S. (2005). Intrinsic and extrinsic motivational orientations in the classroom: Age differences and academic correlates. *Journal of Educational Psychology, 97*, 184–96.

Lepper, M. R., & Greene, D. (1975). Turning play into work: Effects of adult surveillance and extrinsic rewards on children's intrinsic motivation. *Journal of Personality & Social Psychology, 31*(3), 479–86.

Lepper, M. R., Greene, D., & Nisbett, R. E. (1973). Undermining children's intrinsic interest with extrinsic reward: A test of the "overjustification" hypothesis. *Journal of Personality & Social Psychology, 28*(1), 129–37.

Lepper, M. R., & Henderlong, J. (2000). Turning "play" into "work" and "work" into "play": Twenty-five years of research on intrinsic versus extrinsic motivation. In C. Sansone & J. M. Harackiewicz (Eds.), *Intrinsic and extrinsic motivation: The search for optimal motivation and performance* (pp. 257–307). San Diego: Academic Press.

Lepper, M. R., Sagotsky, G., Dafoe, J. L., & Greene, D. (1982). Consequences of superfluous social constraints: Effects on young children's social inferences and subsequent intrinsic interest. *Journal of Personality & Social Psychology, 42*(1), 51–65.

Lepper, M. R., Sethi, S., Dialdin, D., & Drake, M. (1997). Intrinsic and extrinsic motivation: A developmental perspective. In S. S. Luthar (Ed.), *Developmental psychopathology: Perspectives on adjustment, risk, and disorder* (pp. 23–50). New York: Cambridge University Press.

Levin, I., Siegler, R. S., & Druyan, S. (1990). Misconceptions about motion: Development and training effects. *Child Development, 61*(5), 1544–57.

Lewis, M., Alessandri, S. M., & Sullivan, M. W. (1990). Violation of expectancy, loss of control, and anger expressions in young infants. *Developmental Psychology, 26*(5), 745–51.

Lewkowicz, D. J., & Hansen-Tift, A. M. (2012). Infants deploy selective attention to the mouth of a talking face when learning speech. *Proceedings of the National Academy of Sciences, 109*, 1431–36.

Li, H., Boguszewski, K., & Lillard, A. S. (submitted). Can children acquire anthropomorphic information from media? Lessons from "Thomas the Tank Engine".

Li, D., Sham, P. C., Owen, M. J., & He, L. (2006). Meta-analysis shows significant association between dopamine system genes and attention deficit hyperactivity disorder (ADHD). *Human Molecular Genetics, 15*, 2276–84.

Lillard, A. S. (2011a). *Materials: What belongs in a Montessori primary classroom? Results from a survey of AMI and AMS teacher trainers.* Rochester, NY: Association Montessori Internationale USA. (Also published as Lillard, A. S. (2011). Materials: What belongs in a Montessori primary classroom? Results from a survey of AMI and AMS teacher trainers. *Montessori Life, 22*, 18–32).

Lillard, A. S. (2011b). Mindfulness practices in education: Montessori's approach. *Mindfulness, 2*, 78–85. doi:10.1007/s12671-011-0045-6

Lillard, A. S. (2012). Preschool children's development in classic Montessori, supplemented Montessori, and conventional programs. *Journal of School Psychology, 50*, 379–401. doi:10.1016/j.jsp.2012.01.001

Lillard, A. S. (2013). Playful learning and Montessori education. *American Journal of Play, 5*, 157–86.

Lillard, A. S. (2015). The development of play. In L. S. Liben & U. Mueller (Eds.), *Handbook of child psychology and developmental science: Cognitive processes* (7th ed., Vol. 2, pp. 425–68). New York: Wiley-Blackwell.

Lillard, A. S., Drell, M., Richey, E., Boguszewski, K., & Smith, E. D. (2015). Further examination of the immediate impact of television on children's executive function. *Developmental Psychology, 51,* 792–805. doi:10.1037/a0039097

Lillard, A. S., & Else-Quest, N. (2006). Evaluating Montessori education. *Science, 313,* 1893–1894. doi: 10.1126/science.1132362

Lillard, A. S., & Erisir, A. (2011). Old dogs learning new tricks: Neuroplasticity before and after critical periods. *Developmental Review, 31,* 207–39. doi:10.1016/j.dr.2011.07.008

Lillard, A. S., & Heise, M. J. (2016). Removing supplementary materials from Montessori classrooms changed child outcomes. *Journal of Montessori Research, 2,* 17–27.

Lillard, A. S., Lerner, M. D., Hopkins, E. J., Dore, R. A., Smith, E. D., & Palmquist, C. M. (2013). The impact of pretend play on children's development: A review of the evidence. *Psychological Bulletin, 139,* 1–34. doi:10.1037/a0029321

Lillard, A. S., & Peterson, J. (2011). The immediate impact of different types of television on young children's executive function. *Pediatrics, 128,* 644–49. doi:10.1542/peds.2010-1919

Lillard, A. S., Pinkham, A., & Smith, E. D. (2011). Pretend play and cognitive development. In U. Goswami (Ed.), *Handbook of cognitive development* (2nd ed., pp. 285–311). London: Blackwell.

Lillard, A. S., Smith, E. D., & Richey, E. M. (2015). *Checking on Bobo.* Paper presented at the LIFE Academy, Konstanz, Germany.

Lillard, A. S., & Woolley, J. D. (2015). Grounded in reality: How children make sense of the unreal. *Cognitive Development, 34,* 111–14. doi:10.1016/j.cogdev.2014.12.007

Lillard, P. P. (1996). *Montessori today.* New York: Schocken.

Lillard, P. P., & Jessen, H. L. (2003). *Montessori from the start.* New York: Schocken.

Linkenauger, S. A., Witt, J. K., Stefanucci, J. K., Bakdash, J. Z., & Proffitt, D. R. (2009). The effects of handedness and reachability on perceived distance. *Journal of Experimental Psychology: Human Perception and Performance, 35,* 1649–60. doi:10.1037/a0016875

Llinas, R. R. (2001). *I of the vortex: From neurons to self.* Cambridge, MA: MIT Press.

Lonigan, C. J., & B. M. Phillips. (2012, March). *Comparing skills-focused and self-regulation focused preschool curricula: Impacts on academic and self-regulatory skills.* Paper presented at the Society for Research on Educational Effectiveness, Washington, DC.

Lopata, C., Wallace, N. V., & Finn, K. V. (2005). Comparison of academic achievement between Montessori and traditional education programs. *Journal of Research in Childhood Education, 20,* 5–13.

Loveless, T. (Ed.). (2001). *The great curriculum debate.* Washington, DC: Brookings Institute.

Lucker, W., Rosenfield, D., Sikes, J., & Aronson, E. (1977). Performance in the interdependent classroom: A field study. *American Educational Research Journal, 13,* 115–23.

Luetkenhaus, P., Grossmann, K. E., & Grossmann, K. (1985). Infant-mother attachment at twelve months and style of interaction with a stranger at the age of three years. *Child Development, 56*(6), 1538–42.

Luna, B., Paulsen, D. J., Padmanabhan, A., & Geier, C. (2013). The teenage brain cognitive control and motivation. *Current Directions in Psychological Science, 22,* 94–100.

Lyubomirsky, S., King, L., & Diener, E. (2005). The benefits of frequent positive affect: Does happiness lead to success? *Psychological Bulletin, 131,* 803–55.

Ma, W., Golinkoff, R. M., Houston, D. M., & Hirsh-Pasek, K. (2011). Word learning in infant-and adult-directed speech. *Language Learning and Development, 7,* 185–201.

Maccoby, E. E., & Martin, J. A. (1983). Socialization in the context of the family: Parent-child interaction. In E. M. Hetherington (Ed.), *Handbook of child psychology* (Vol. 4, pp. 1–101). New York: Wiley.

Macmillan, M. (2000). An odd kind of fame: Stories of Phineas Gage. Cambridge, MA: MIT Press.

Maheady, L. (1998). Advantages and disadvantages of peer-assisted learning strategies. In K. Topping & S. Ehly (Eds.), *Peer-assisted learning* (pp. 45–65). Mahwah, NJ: Lawrence Erlbaum.

Maheady, L., & Sainato, D. M. (1985). The effects of peer tutoring upon the social status and social interaction patterns of high and low status elementary school students. *Education & Treatment of Children, 8*(1), 51–65.

Manches, A., & O'Malley, C. (2012). Tangibles for learning: A representational analysis of physical manipulation. *Personal and Ubiquitous Computing, 16*, 405–19.

Manches, A., O'Malley, C., & Benford, S. (2010). The role of physical representations in solving number problems: A comparison of young children's use of physical and virtual materials. *Computers & Education, 54*, 622–40.

Maquet, P. (2001). The role of sleep in learning and memory. *Science, 294*(5544), 1048–52.

Mark, G., Gonzalez, V. M., & Harris, J. (2005). *No task left behind?: Examining the nature of fragmented work.* Paper presented at the Proceedings of the SIGCHI Conference on Human Factors in Computing Systems, Portland, OR.

Mark, G., Iqbal, S. T., Czerwinski, M., & Johns, P. (2014). *Bored Mondays and focused afternoons: The rhythm of attention and online activity in the workplace.* Paper presented at the Proceedings of the 32nd Annual ACM Conference on Human Factors in Computing Systems, Toronto, ON.

Markman, E. M. (1977). Realizing that you don't understand: A preliminary investigation. *Child Development, 48*(3), 986–92.

Markson, L., & Bloom, P. (1997). Evidence against a dedicated system for word learning in children. *Nature, 385*(6619), 813–15.

Markus, H. R., & Kitayama, S. (1991). Culture and the self: Implications for cognition, emotion, and motivation. *Psychological Review, 98*, 224–53.

Matheny, A. P., Wachs, T. D., Ludwig, J. L., & Phillips, K. (1995). Bringing order out of chaos: Psychometric characteristics of the confusion, hubbub, and order scale. *Journal of Applied Developmental Psychology, 16*, 429–44.

Maxwell, L. E., & Evans, G. W. (2000). The effects of noise on pre-school children's pre-reading skills. *Journal of Environmental Psychology, 20*(1), 91–97.

Mayer, R. E. (2004). Should there be a three-strikes rule against pure discovery learning? *American Psychologist, 59*(1), 14–19.

McCall, R. B., Kennedy, C. B., & Appelbaum, M. I. (1977). Magnitude of discrepancy and the distribution of attention in infants. *Child Development, 48*(3), 772–85.

McCaslin, M., Good, T. L., Nichols, S., Zhang, J., Wiley, C. R., Bozack, A. R., . . . Cuizon-Garcia, R. (2006). Comprehensive school reform: An observational study of teaching in grades 3 through 5. *The Elementary School Journal, 106*, 313–331.

McClary, A. (1997). *Toys with nine lives.* North Haven, CT: Linnett.

McDonald, A. S. (2001). The prevalence and effects of test anxiety in school children. *Educational Psychology, 21*(1), 89–101.

McGhee, P. E., & Crandall, V. C. (1968). Beliefs in internal-external control of reinforcements and academic performance. *Child Development, 39*(1), 91–102.

McGraw, K. (1978). The detrimental effects of reward on performance: A literature review and a prediction model. In M. R. Lepper & D. Greene (Eds.), *The hidden costs of reward: New perspectives on the psychology of human motivation* (pp. 33–60). Potomac, MD: Lawrence Erlbaum.

McGraw, K. O., & Fiala, J. (1982). Undermining the Zeigarnik effect: Another hidden cost of reward. *Journal of Personality, 50*(1), 58–66.

McGraw, K. O., & McCullers, J. C. (1979). Evidence of a detrimental effect of extrinsic incentives on breaking a mental set. *Journal of Experimental Social Psychology, 15*(3), 285–94.

McNeil, N. M., Uttal, D. H., Jarvin, L., & Sternberg, R. J. (2009). Should you show me the money? Concrete objects both hurt and help performance on mathematics problems. *Learning and Instruction, 19*, 171–84.

McNeill, D. (1992). *Hand and mind.* Chicago: University of Chicago Press.

Meaney, M. (2010). Epigenetics and the biological definition of gene-environment interactions. *Child Development, 81*, 41–79.

Meltzoff, A. N. (1988a). Infant imitation after a 1-week delay: Long-term memory for novel acts and multiple stimuli. *Developmental Psychology, 24*, 470–76.

Meltzoff, A. N. (1988b). Infant imitation and memory: Nine-month-olds in immediate and deferred tests. *Child Development, 59*(1), 217–25.

Meltzoff, A. N., & Moore, M. K. (1983). Newborn infants imitate adult facial gestures. *Child Development, 54*, 702–09.

Mervis, J. (2004). Meager evaluations make it hard to find out what works. *Science, 304*, 1583.

Merzenich, M. M. (2001). Cortical plasticity contributing to child development. In J. L. McClelland & R. S. Siegler (Eds.), *Mechanisms of cognitive development: Behavioral and neural perspectives. Carnegie Symposia on Cognition* (pp. 67–95). Mahwah, NJ: Lawrence Erlbaum.

Meyer, C. S., Hagmann-von Arx, P., Lemola, S., & Grob, A. (2010). Correspondence between the general ability to discriminate sensory stimuli and general intelligence. *Journal of Individual Differences, 31*, 46–56.

Miller, L. B., & Bizzell, R. P. (1983). The Louisville experiment: A comparison of four programs. In the Consortium for Longitudinal Studies (Ed.), *As the twig is bent: Lasting effects of preschool programs* (pp. 171–99). Hillsdale, NJ: Lawrence Erlbaum.

Miller, L. B., & Bizzell, R. P. (1984). Long-term effects of four preschool programs: Ninth- and tenth-grade results. *Child Development, 55*(4), 1570–87.

Miller, L. B., & Dyer, J. L. (1975). Four preschool programs: Their dimensions and effects. *Monographs of the Society for Research in Child Development, 40*(5–6, serial no. 162).

Miller, L. B., & Estes, B. W. (1961). Monetary reward and motivation in discrimination learning. *Journal of Experimental Psychology, 61*, 501–04.

Mischel, W. (2014). *The marshmallow test: Mastering self-control.* New York: Little, Brown & Co.

Mischel, W., Shoda, Y., & Peake, P. K. (1988). The nature of adolescent competencies predicted by preschool delay of gratification. *Journal of Personality and Social Psychology, 54*, 687–96.

Mischel, W., Shoda, Y., & Rodriguez, M. L. (1989). Delay of gratification in children. *Science, 244*, 933–38. doi:10.1126/science.2658056

Mix, K. S., & Cheng, Y.-L. (2012). The relation between space and math: Developmental and educational implications. In J. B. Benson (Ed.), *Advances in child development and behavior* (Vol. 42, pp. 197–243). New York: Elsevier.,

Mix, K. S., Smith, L. B., Stockton, J. D. S., Cheng, Y.-L., & Barterian, J. A. (2016). Grounding the symbols for place value: Evidence from training and long term exposure to base-10 models. *Journal of Cognition and Development.* doi: 10.1080/15248372.2016.1180296

Miyake, A., & Friedman, N. P. (2012). The nature and organization of individual differences in executive functions: Four general conclusions. *Current Directions in Psychological Science, 21*, 8–14.

Miyake, A., Friedman, N. P., Emerson, M. J., Witzki, A. H., & Howerter, A. (2000). The unity and diversity of executive functions and their contributions to complex 'frontal lobe' tasks: A latent variable analysis. *Cognitive Psychology, 41*(1), 49–100. doi:10.1006/cogp.1999.0734

Moch-Sibony, A. (1981). The effects of prolonged exposure to noise on certain psychomotor, intellectual and personality aspects of children: The comparison between a sound-proofed and a nonsound-proofed school. *Travail Humain, 44*(1), 169–78.

Moffitt, T. E., Arseneault, L., Belsky, D., Dickson, N., Hancox, R. J., Harrington, H. L., … Ross, S. (2011). A gradient of childhood self-control predicts health, wealth, and public safety. *Proceedings of the National Academy of Sciences, 108*, 2693–2698.

Mol, S. E., & Bus, A. G. (2011). To read or not to read: A meta-analysis of print exposure from infancy to early adulthood. *Psychological Bulletin, 137*, 267–96.

Montessori, M. (1912/1964). *The Montessori method.* New York: Schocken.

Montessori, M. (1914/1965). *Dr. Montessori's own handbook.* New York: Schocken.

Montessori, M. (1916). *The advanced Montessori method—II* (A. Livingston, Trans.). Oxford: Clio.

Montessori, M. (1917/1965). *Spontaneous activity in education: The advanced Montessori method* (F. Simmonds, Trans.). New York: Schocken.

Montessori, M. (1939). *The secret of childhood* (B. B. Carter, Trans.). New York: Frederick A. Stokes.

Montessori, M. (1946/1963). *Education for a new world.* Madras, India: Kalakshetra.

Montessori, M. (1948a/1976). *From childhood to adolescence.* New York: Schocken.

Montessori, M. (1948b/1967). *To educate the human potential.* Madras, India: Kalakshetra.

Montessori, M. (1949/1974). *Childhood education.* Chicago: Henry Regnery.

Montessori, M. (1956). *The child in the family* (N. R. Cirillo, Trans.). New York: Avon.

Montessori, M. (1966). *The secret of childhood* (M. J. Costello, Trans.). New York: Ballantine.

Montessori, M. (1967a/1995). *The absorbent mind* (C. A. Claremont, Trans.). New York: Henry Holt.

Montessori, M. (1967b). *The discovery of the child.* New York: Ballantine.

Montessori, M. (1972). *Education and peace* (H. R. Lane, Trans.). Washington, DC: Henry Regnery.

Montessori, M. (1989). *The child, society, and the world: Unpublished speeches and writings* (Vol. 7). Oxford: Clio.

Montessori, M. (1994a). *Creative development in the child I* (R. Ramachandran, Trans.). Madras, India: Kalakshetra Press.

Montessori, M. (1994b). *Creative development in the child II* (R. Ramachandran, Trans.). Madras, India: Kalakshetra Press.

Montessori, M. (1997). *The California lectures of Maria Montessori, 1915.* Oxford: Clio.

Montessori, M. M. (1966). *The human tendencies and Montessori education.* Amsterdam: Association Montessori Internationale.

Montessori, M. M. (1976). *Education for human development.* New York: Schocken.

Montie, J. E., Xiang, Z., & Schweinhart, L. J. (2006). Preschool experience in 10 countries: Cognitive and language performance at age 7. *Early Childhood Research Quarterly, 21*, 313–31.

Moore, A., Gruber, T., Derose, J., & Malinowski, P. (2012). Regular, brief mindfulness meditation practice improves electrophysiological markers of attentional control. *Frontiers in Human Neuroscience, 6*(18). doi:10.3389/fnhum.2012.00018

Moore, D. S. (2015). The developing genome: An introduction to behavioral epigenetics: Oxford University Press.

Moss, E. (1992). The socioaffective context of joint cognitive activity. In L. T. Winegar & J. Valsiner (Eds.), *Children's development within social context* (Vol. 2, pp. 117–54). Hillsdale, NJ: Lawrence Erlbaum.

MTA Cooperative Group. (1999). A 14-month randomized clinical trial of treatment strategies for attention-deficit/hyperactivity disorder: Multimodal treatment study of children with ADHD. *Archives of General Psychiatry, 56*(12), 1073–86.

Mueller, C. M., & Dweck, C. S. (1998). Praise for intelligence can undermine children's motivation and performance. *Journal of Personality & Social Psychology, 75*(1), 33–52.

Mueller, P. A., & Oppenheimer, D. M. (2014). The pen is mightier than the keyboard: Advantages of longhand over laptop note taking. *Psychological Science, 25*, 1159–68. doi:10.1177/0956797614524581

Müller, U., & Kerns, K. (2015). The development of executive function. In L. S. Liben & U. Mueller (Eds.), *Handbook of child psychology and developmental science: Cognitive processes* (7th ed., Vol. 2, pp. 571–623). New York: Wiley-Blackwell. (R. Lerner, Series Ed.).

Murray, K. T., & Kochanska, G. (2002). Effortful control: Factor structure and relation to externalizing and internalizing behaviors. *Journal of Abnormal Child Psychology, 30*, 503–14.

Nadler, A., Romek, E., & Shapira-Friedman, A. (1979). Giving in the kibbutz: Pro-social behavior of city and kibbutz children as affected by social responsibility and social pressure. *Journal of Cross-Cultural Psychology, 10*(1), 57–72.

Nagar, D., & Pandey, J. (1987). Affect and performance on cognitive task as a function of crowding and noise. *Journal of Applied Social Psychology, 17*(2), 147–57.

Nathanson, A. I., Alade, F., Sharp, M. L., Rasmussen, E. E., & Christy, K. (2014). The relation between television exposure and executive function among preschoolers. *Developmental Psychology, 50*, 1497–1506. doi:10.1037/a0035714

National Assessment of Educational Progress (NAEP). (2012). The nation's report card: Summary of major findings. Retrieved from: www.nationsreportcard.gov/ltt_2012/summary.aspx

National Association for the Education of Young Children (2009). Developmentally appropriate practice in early childhood programs serving children from birth through age 8. Washington D.C. NAEYC.

National Center for Education Statistics (2016). Retrieved on line from https://nces.ed.gov/fastfacts/display.asp?id=66 on 6 June 2016.

National Council of Teachers of Mathematics. (1989). *Curriculum and evaluation standards for school mathematics*. Reston, VA: NCTM.

Needham, A. (2000). Improvements in object exploration skills may facilitate the development of object segregation in early infancy. *Journal of Cognition & Development, 1*(2), 131–56.

Needham, A., Barrett, T., & Peterman, K. (2002). A pick me up for infants' exploratory skills: Early simulated experiences reaching for objects using "sticky" mittens enhances young infants' object exploration skills. *Infant Behavior & Development, 25*(3), 279–95.

Nelson, J. L. (2002). School. In *The World Book Encyclopedia* (Vol. 17, pp. 180–85). Chicago: World Book.

Nestojko, J. F., Bui, D. C., Kornell, N., & Bjork, E. L. (2014). Expecting to teach enhances learning and organization of knowledge in free recall of text passages. *Memory & Cognition, 42*, 1038–48.

Neumann, R., & Strack, F. (2000). "Mood contagion": The automatic transfer of mood between persons. *Journal of Personality & Social Psychology, 79*(2), 211–23.

NICHD Early Child Care Research Network. (1997). The effects of infant child care on infant-mother attachment security: Results of the NICHD study of early child care. *Child Development, 68*(5), 860–79.

NICHD Early Child Care Research Network. (2005). A day in third grade: A large-scale study of classroom quality and teacher and student behavior. *The Elementary School Journal, 105*, 305–23.

Niedenthal, P., Winkielman, P., Mondillon, L., & Vermeulen, N. (2009). Embodiment of emotion concepts. *Journal of Personality and Social Psychology, 95*, 1120–36.

Niedenthal, P. M. (2007). Embodying emotion. *Science, 316*, 1002–1005.

Nielsen, M. (2006). Copying actions and copying outcomes: Social learning through the second year. *Developmental Psychology, 42*, 555–65.

Nikkelen, S. W., Valkenburg, P. M., Huizinga, M., & Bushman, B. J. (2014). Media use and ADHD-related behaviors in children and adolescents: A meta-analysis. *Developmental Psychology, 50*, 2228–41.

Nisbett, R. E. (2003). *The geography of thought: How Westerners and Asians think differently . . . and why*. New York: Free Press.

Nisbett, R. E. (2009). *Intelligence and how to get it: Why schools and cultures count*. New York: Norton.

Noice, H., & Noice, T. (2006). What studies of actors and acting can tell us about memory and cognitive functioning. *Current Directions in Psychological Science, 15*, 14–18.

Noice, H., Noice, T., & Kennedy, C. (2000). Effects of enactment by professional actors at encoding and retrieval. *Memory, 8*(6), 353–63.

O'Conaill, B., & Frohlich, D. (1995). *Timespace in the workplace: Dealing with interruptions*. Paper presented at the Proceedings of the SIGCHI Conference on Human Factors in Computing Systems, Denver, CO.

O'Donnell, A. M., & King, A. (Eds.). (1999). *Cognitive perspectives on peer learning*. Mahwah, NJ: Lawrence Erlbaum.

O'Donnell, M. (2007). *Maria Montessori* (Vol. 7). London: Continuum.

Ochs, E., Gonzales, P., & Jacoby, S. (1996). "When I come down I'm in the domain state": Grammar and graphic representation in the interpretive activity of physicists. In E. Ochs, E. A. Schegloff, & S. A. Thompson (Eds.), *Interaction and grammar* (pp. 328–69). New York: Cambridge University Press.

Okada, T., & Simon, H. A. (1997). Collaborative discovery in a scientific domain. *Cognitive Science, 21*(2), 109–46.

Olsen, B., & Sexton, D. (2009). Threat rigidity, school reform, and how teachers view their work inside current education policy contexts. *American Educational Research Journal, 46*, 9–44.

Oppenheim, D., Sagi, A., & Lamb, M. E. (1988). Infant-adult attachments on the kibbutz and their relation to socioemotional development four years later. *Developmental Psychology, 24*, 427–33.

Oppenheimer, T. (2003). *Flickering minds*. New York: Random House.

Orr, J. (1987). *Talking about machines*. Palo Alto: Xerox PARC.

Pagani, L. S., Fitzpatrick, C., & Barnett, T. A. (2013). Early childhood television viewing and kindergarten entry readiness. *Pediatric Research, 74*, 350–55.

Palincsar, S., & Herrenkohl, R. (1999). Designing collaborative contexts. In A. M. O'Donnell & A. King (Eds.), *Cognitive perspectives on peer learning. The Rutgers Invitational Symposium on Education Series* (pp. 151–77). Mahwah, NJ: Lawrence Erlbaum.

Papert, W. (1980). *Mindstorms: Children, computers, and powerful ideas*. New York: Basic.

Parke, R. D. (1978). Children's home environments: Social and cognitive effects. In I. Altman & J. F. Wohlwill (Eds.), *Children and the environment*. New York: Plenum.

Parker, L. E., & Lepper, M. R. (1992). Effects of fantasy contexts on children's learning and motivation: Making learning more fun. *Journal of Personality & Social Psychology, 62*(4), 625–33.

Parish-Morris, J., Mahajan, N., Hirsh-Pasek, K., Golinkoff, R. M., & Collins, M. F. (2013). Once upon a time: Parent–child dialogue and storybook reading in the electronic era. *Mind, Brain, and Education, 7*, 200–11.

Patall, E. A. (2013). Constructing motivation through choice, interest, and interestingness. *Journal of Educational Psychology, 105*, 522–34.

Patall, E. A., Cooper, H., & Robinson, J. C. (2008). The effects of choice on intrinsic motivation and related outcomes: A meta-analysis of research findings. *Psychological Bulletin, 134*, 270–300.

Patall, E. A., Cooper, H., & Wynn, S. R. (2010). The effectiveness and relative importance of choice in the classroom. *Journal of Educational Psychology, 102*, 896–915.

Pate, R. R., O'Neill, J. R., Byun, W., McIver, K. L., Dowda, M., & Brown, W. H. (2014). Physical activity in preschool children: Comparison between Montessori and traditional preschools. *Journal of School Health, 84*, 716–21.

Pavenstedt, E. (1965). A comparison of the child-rearing environment of upper-lower and very low–lower class families. *American Journal of Orthopsychiatry, 35*(1), 89–98.

Peisner-Feinberg, E. S., Burchinal, M. R., Clifford, R. M., Culkin, M. L., Howes, C., Kagan, S. L., . . . Zelazo, J. (2000). *The children of the cost, quality, and outcomes study go to school: Technical report*. Chapel Hill: University of North Carolina at Chapel Hill, Frank Porter Graham Child Development Center.

Pellegrini, A., & Bohn, C. (2005). The role of recess in children's cognitive performance and school adjustment. *Educational Researcher, 34*, 13–19. doi:10.3102/0013189X034001013

Pellis, S. M., & Pellis, V. C. (2009). *The playful brain: Venturing to the limits of neuroscience.* Oxford: Oneworld.

Perlmuter, L. C., & Monty, R. A. (1977). The importance of perceived control: Fact or fantasy? *American Scientist, 65*(6), 759–65.

Perry, M., Church, R. B., & Goldin-Meadow, S. (1988). Transitional knowledge in the acquisition of concepts. *Cognitive Development, 3*(4), 359–400.

Perry, M., & Elder, A. D. (1997). Knowledge in transition: Adults' developing understanding of a principle of physical causality. *Cognitive Development, 12*(1), 131–57.

Petersen, S. E., & Posner, M. I. (2012). The attention system of the human brain: 20 years after. *Annual Review of Neuroscience, 35*, 73–89.

Peterson, P. L., Fenneman, E., Carpenter, T. P., & Loef, M. (1989). Teachers' pedagogical content beliefs in mathematics. *Cognition and Instruction, 6*, 1–40.

Petitto, L. A., Katerelos, M., Levy, B. G., Gauna, K., Tetreault, K., & Ferraro, V. (2001). Bilingual signed and spoken language acquisition from birth: Implications for the mechanisms underlying early bilingual language acquisition. *Journal of Child Language, 28*(2), 453–96.

Phelps, E., & Damon, W. (1989). Problem solving with equals: Peer collaboration as a context for learning mathematics and spatial concepts. *Journal of Educational Psychology, 81*(4), 639–46.

Piaget, J. (1926). *The language and thought of the child.* London: Routledge & Kegan Paul.

Piaget, J. (1970). *Science of education and the psychology of the child* (D. Coltman, Trans.). New York: Orion Press.

Piaget, J. (1981). *Intelligence and affectivity: Their relationship during child development.* (T. A. Brown & C. E. Kaegi, Trans.). Palo Alto, CA: Annual Reviews.

Pianta, R. C., Hamre, B. K., & Allen, J. P. (2012). Teacher-student relationships and engagement: Conceptualizing, measuring, and improving the capacity of classroom interactions. In C. M. Christensen (Ed.), *Handbook of research on student engagement* (pp. 365–86). New York: Springer.

Pianta, R. C., Mashburn, A. J., Downer, J. T., Hamre, B. K., & Justice, L. (2008). Effects of web-mediated professional development resources on teacher–child interactions in pre-kindergarten classrooms. *Early Childhood Research Quarterly, 23*, 431–51.

Piantadosi, S. T., Kidd, C., & Aslin, R. (2014). Rich analysis and rational models: Inferring individual behavior from infant looking data. *Developmental Science, 17*, 321–37.

Pine, K. J., & Messer, D. J. (1998). Group collaboration effects and the explicitness of children's knowledge. *Cognitive Development, 13*(1), 109–26.

Piper, M. C., & Ramsay, M. K. (1980). Effects of early home environment on the mental development of Down syndrome infants. *American Journal of Mental Deficiency, 85*(1), 39–44.

Plötner, M., Over, H., Carpenter, M., & Tomasello, M. (2015). The effects of collaboration and minimal-group membership on children's prosocial behavior, liking, affiliation, and trust. *Journal of Experimental Child Psychology, 139*, 161–73.

Polirstok, S. R., & Greer, R. D. (1986). A replication of collateral effects and a component analysis of a successful tutoring package for inner-city adolescents. *Education & Treatment of Children, 9*(2), 101–21.

Poulin-Dubois, D., Brooker, I., & Polonia, A. (2011). Infants prefer to imitate a reliable person. *Infant Behavior and Development, 34,* 303–309.

Pouw, W. T., Van Gog, T., & Paas, F. (2014). An embedded and embodied cognition review of instructional manipulatives. *Educational Psychology Review, 26,* 51–72.

Povell, P. (2009). *Montessori comes to America.* Lanham, MD: University Press of America.

Qin, Y., & Simon, H. A. (1990). Laboratory replication of scientific discovery processes. *Cognitive Science, 14*(2), 281–312.

Qin, Z., Johnson, D. W., & Johnson, R. T. (1995). Cooperative versus competitive efforts and problem solving. *Review of Educational Research, 65*(2), 129–43.

Quinn, H., Schweingruber, H., & Keller, T. (Eds.). (2012). *A framework for k-12 science education: Practices, crosscutting concepts, and core ideas.* Washington, DC: National Academies Press.

Ramey, C. T., Farran, D. C., & Campbell, F. A. (1979). Predicting IQ from mother-infant interactions. *Child Development, 50*(3), 804–14.

Ramey, C. T., Mills, P., Campbell, F. A., & O'Brien, C. (1975). Infants' home environments: A comparison of high-risk families and families from the general population. *American Journal of Mental Deficiency, 80*(1), 40–42.

Rathunde, K. R., & Csikszentmihalyi, M. (1993). Undivided interest and the growth of talent: A longitudinal study of adolescents. *Journal of Youth & Adolescence, 22*(4), 385–405.

Rathunde, K. R., & Csikszentmihalyi, M. (2005a). Middle school students' motivation and quality of experience: A comparison of Montessori and traditional school environments. *American Journal of Education, 111*(3), 341–71.

Rathunde, K. R., & Csikszentmihalyi, M. (2005b). The social context of middle school: Teachers, friends, and activities in Montessori and traditional school environments. *Elementary School Journal, 106,* 59–79.

Rattan, A., Good, C., & Dweck, C. S. (2012). "It's ok—not everyone can be good at math": Instructors with an entity theory comfort (and demotivate) students. *Journal of Experimental Social Psychology, 48,* 731–37.

Raver, C. C., Jones, S. M., Li-Grining, C., Zhai, F., Bub, K., & Pressler, E. (2011). CSRP's impact on low-income preschoolers' preacademic skills: Self-regulation as a mediating mechanism. *Child Development, 82,* 362–78.

Ravitch, D. (2001). It is time to stop the war. In T. Loveless (Ed.), *The great curriculum debate* (pp. 210–28). Washington, DC: Brookings Institute.

Rayner, K., Foorman, B. R., Perfetti, C. A., Pesetsky, D., & Seidenberg, M. S. (2001). How psychological science informs the teaching of reading. *Psychological Science in the Public Interest, 2*(2), 31–74.

Reader, M. J., & Dollinger, S. J. (1982). Deadlines, self-perceptions, and intrinsic motivation. *Personality & Social Psychology Bulletin, 8*(4), 742–47.

Renninger, K. A. (1990). Children's play interests, representation, and activity. In R. Fivush & J. A. Hudson (Eds.), *Knowing and remembering in young children* (pp. 127–65). New York: Cambridge University Press.

Renninger, K. A. (1992). Individual interest and development: Implications for theory and practice. In K. A. Renninger, S. Hidi, & A. Krapp (Eds.), *The role of interest in learning and development* (pp. 361–95). Hillsdale, NJ: Lawrence Erlbaum.

Renninger, K. A. (1998). Developmental psychology and instruction: Issues from and for practice. In I. E. Siegel & K. A. Renninger (Eds.), *Handbook of child psychology, Vol. 4: Child psychology in practice* (pp. 211–74). New York: Wiley.

Renninger, K. A., & Bachrach, J. E. (2015). Studying triggers for interest and engagement using observational methods. *Educational Psychologist, 50*, 58–69.

Renninger, K. A., & Hidi, S. (2011). Revisiting the conceptualization, measurement, and generation of interest. *Educational Psychologist, 46*, 168–84.

Renninger, K. A., Hidi, S., & Krapp, A. (Eds.). (1992). *The role of interest in learning and development.* Hillsdale, NJ: Lawrence Erlbaum.

Renninger, K. A., & Wozniak, R. H. (1985). Effect of interest on attentional shift, recognition, and recall in young children. *Developmental Psychology, 21*(4), 624–32.

Resnick, L. B., Bill, V. I., Lesgold, S. B., & Leer, M. N. (1991). Thinking in arithmetic class. In B. Means, C. Chelemer, & M. S. Knapp (Eds.), *Teaching advanced skills to at-risk students* (pp. 27–53). San Francisco: Jossey-Bass.

Resnick, L. B., & Hall, M. W. (1998). Learning organizations for sustainable education reform. *Daedalus, 27*, 89–118.

Rhodes, G., Geddes, K., Jeffery, L., Dziurawiec, S., & Clark, A. (2002). Are average and symmetric faces attractive to infants? Discrimination and looking preferences. *Perception, 31*(3), 315–21.

Rice, T., Fulker, D. W., DeFries, J. C., & Plomin, R. (1988). Path analysis of IQ during infancy and early childhood and an index of the home environment in the Colorado Adoption Project. *Intelligence, 12*(1), 27–45.

Richert, R. A., & Smith, E. I. (2011). Preschoolers' quarantining of fantasy stories. *Child Development, 82*, 1106–19.

Rieser, J. J., Garing, A. E., & Young, M. F. (1994). Imagery, action, and young children's spatial orientation: It's not being there that counts, it's what one has in mind. *Child Development, 65*(5), 1262–78.

Riggs, N. R., Greenberg, M. T., Kusché, C. A., & Pentz, M. A. (2006). The mediational role of neurocognition in the behavioral outcomes of a social-emotional prevention program in elementary school students: Effects of the PATHS curriculum. *Prevention Science, 7*, 91–102.

Riggs, N. R., Jahromi, L. B., Razza, R. P., Dillworth-Bart, J. E., & Müeller, U. (2006). Executive function and the promotion of social-emotional competence. *Journal of Applied Developmental Psychology, 27*, 300–309.

Roberts, M. S., Fulton, M., & Semb, G. (1988). Self-pacing in a personalized psychology course: Letting students set the deadlines. *Teaching of Psychology, 15*(2), 89–92.

Robinson, S. R., Kleven, G. A., & Brumley, M. R. (2008). Prenatal development of inter-limb motor learning in the rat fetus. *Infancy, 13*, 204–28.

Rodin, J. (1976). Density, perceived choice, and response to controllable and uncontrollable outcomes. *Journal of Experimental Social Psychology, 12*(6), 564–78.

Rogoff, B. (1981). Schooling and the development of cognitive skills. In H. C. Triandis & A. Heron (Eds.), *Handbook of cross-cultural psychology* (Vol. 4, pp. 233–94). Boston: Allyn & Bacon.

Rogoff, B., Bartlett, L., & Turkanis, C. G. (2001). Lessons about learning as a community. In B. Rogoff, C. G. Turkanis & L. Bartlett (Eds.), *Learning together: Children and adults in a school community* (pp. 3–17). New York: Oxford University Press.

Rogoff, B., & Mistry, J. (1990). The social and functional context of children's remembering. In R. Fivush & J. A. Hudson (Eds.), *Knowing and remembering in young children* (pp. 197–222). Cambridge: Cambridge University Press.

Rogoff, B., Turkanis, C. G., & Bartlett, L. (Eds.). (2001). *Learning together: Children and adults in a school community.* New York: Oxford University Press.

Roisman, G. I., Booth-LaForce, C., Cauffman, E., Spieker, S., & NICHD Early Child Care Research Network (2009). The developmental significance of adolescent romantic relationships: Parent and peer predictors of engagement and quality at age 15. *Journal of Youth and Adolescence, 38*(10), 1294–303.

Ross, S. M. (1983). Increasing the meaningfulness of quantitative material by adapting context to student background. *Journal of Educational Psychology, 75*(4), 519–29.

Rotgans, J. I., & Schmidt, H. G. (2014). Situational interest and learning: Thirst for knowledge. *Learning and Instruction, 32*, 37–50.

Rothbart, M. K., Ahadi, S. A., & Hershey, K. L. (1994). Temperament and social behavior in childhood. *Merrill-Palmer Quarterly, 40*(1), 21–39.

Röthlisberger, M., Neuenschwander, R., Cimeli, P., & Roebers, C. M. (2013). Executive functions in 5-to 8-year olds: Developmental changes and relationship to academic achievement. *Journal of Educational and Developmental Psychology, 3*, 153–67.

Rovee-Collier, C., & Hayne, H. (2000). Memory in infancy and early childhood. In E. Tulving & F. I. M. Craik (Eds.), *The Oxford handbook of memory* (pp. 267–82). London: Oxford University Press.

Rovee-Collier, C., Hayne, H., Collier, G., Griesler, P. C., & Rovee, G. B. (1996). Diet selection by chicks. *Developmental Psychobiology, 29*(3), 241–72.

Rowe, M. L., & Goldin-Meadow, S. (2009). Early gesture selectively predicts later language learning. *Developmental Science, 12*, 182–87.

Rueda, M. R., Rothbart, M. K., McCandliss, B. D., Saccomanno, L., & Posner, M. I. (2005). Training, maturation, and genetic influences on the development of executive attention. *Proceedings of the National Academy of Science, 102*, 14931–936.

Ruff, H. A., & Rothbart, M. K. (1996). *Attention in early development: Themes and variations.* New York: Oxford University Press.

Rumbaugh, D. M., & Washburn, D. A. (1996). Attention and memory in relation to learning: A comparative adaptation perspective. In G. R. Lyon & N. A. Krasnegor (Eds.), *Attention, memory, and executive function* (pp. 199–220). Baltimore: Brookes.

Russell, J. E. (1926). Thorndike and Teachers College. *Teachers College Record, 27.*

Ryalls, B. O., Gul, R. E., & Ryalls, K. R. (2000). Infant imitation of peer and adult models: Evidence for a peer model advantage. *Merrill-Palmer Quarterly, 46*(1), 188–202.

Ryan, R. M., & Deci, E. L. (2000). Self-determination theory and the facilitation of intrinsic motivation, social development, and well-being. *American Psychologist, 55*(1), 68–78.

Ryan, R. M., & Grolnick, W. S. (1986). Origins and pawns in the classroom: Self-report and projective assessments of individual differences in children's perceptions. *Journal of Personality & Social Psychology, 50*(3), 550–58.

Ryan, R. M., & Laguardia, J. G. (1999). Achievement motivation within a pressured society. *Advances in motivation and achievement, 11*, 45–85.

Sackett, G. (2015). The human tendencies. Notes from Teacher Training Course 38. Portland OR: Montessori Institute Northwest. Downloaded from *static.squarespace. com/static/.../t/.../1383937521585/**Human+Tendencies**+C38.pdf on 6 June 2016.*

Sadeh, A., Gruber, R., & Raviv, A. (2003). The effects of sleep restriction and extension on school-age children: What a difference an hour makes. *Child Development, 74*(2), 444–55.

Sansone, C., & Harackiewicz, J. M. (Eds.). (2000). *Intrinsic and extrinsic motivation: The search for optimal motivation and performance.* San Diego: Academic Press.

Santangelo, T., & Tomlinson, C. A. (2012). Teacher educators' perceptions and use of differentiated instruction practices: An exploratory investigation. *Action in Teacher Education, 34*, 309–27.

Sayeki, Y., Ueno, N., & Nagasaka, T. (1991). Mediation as a generative model for obtaining an area. *Learning & Instruction, 1*, 229–42.

Schiefele, U., & Csikszentmihalyi, M. (1994). Interest and the quality of experience in classrooms. *European Journal of Psychology of Education, 9*(3), 251–70.

Schiefele, U., & Csikszentmihalyi, M. (1995). Motivation and ability as factors in mathematics experience and achievement. *Journal for Research in Mathematics Education, 26*(2), 163–81.

Schiefele, U., Krapp, A., & Winteler, A. (1992). Interest as a predictor of academic achievement: A meta-analysis of research. In K. A. Renninger, S. Hidi, & A. Krapp (Eds.), *The role of interest in learning and development* (pp. 183–212). Hillsdale, NJ: Lawrence Erlbaum.

Schlam, T. R., Wilson, N. L., Shoda, Y., Mischel, W., & Ayduk, O. (2013). Preschoolers' delay of gratification predicts their body mass 30 years later. *The Journal of Pediatrics, 162*, 90–93.

Schlip, P. (1949). *Albert Einstein: Philosopher-scientist.* Evanston, IL: Library of Living Philosophers.

Schnall, S., & Gattis, M. (1998). Transitive inference by visual reasoning. In M. A. Gernshbacher & S. J. Derry (Eds.), *Proceedings of the 20th annual conference of the Cognitive Science Society* (pp. 929–34). Mahwah, NJ: Lawrence Erlbaum.

Schoenfeld, A. H. (1988). When good teaching leads to bad results: The disasters of "well-taught" mathematics courses. *Educational Psychologist, 23*(2), 145–66.

Schunk, D. H. (1996). Goal and self-evaluative influences during children's cognitive skill learning. *American Educational Research Journal, 33*(2), 359–82.

Schwartz, B. (2000). Self-determination: The tyranny of freedom. *American Psychologist, 55*(1), 79–88.

Schwartz, B. (2004). *The paradox of choice.* New York: HarperCollins.

Schwartz, D. L., & Black, T. (1999). Inferences through imagined actions: Knowing by simulated doing. *Journal of Experimental Psychology: Learning, Memory, & Cognition, 25*(1), 116–36.

Scott, C. L., Harris, R. J., & Rothe, A. R. (2001). Embodied cognition through improvisation improves memory for a dramatic monologue. *Discourse Processes, 31*(3), 293–305.

Sedlmeier, P., Eberth, J., Schwarz, M., Zimmermann, D., Haarig, F., Jaeger, S., & Kunze, S. (2012). The psychological effects of meditation: A meta-analysis. *Psychological Bulletin, 138*, 1139–71. doi:10.1037/a0028168

Seiler, B. (1989). How the West Was One + Three × Four. New York: Sunburst Communications.

Seligman, M. E. (1975). *Helplessness: On depression, development, and death.* San Francisco: W. H. Freeman.

Seymour, F. W., Brock, P., During, M., & Poole, G. (1989). Reducing sleep disruptions in young children: Evaluation of therapist-guided and written information approaches: A brief report. *Journal of Child Psychology & Psychiatry & Allied Disciplines, 30*(6), 913–18.

Shaefer Zener, R. (2006). The secret of childhood: Normalization and deviations Lecture given in the AMI 3-6 course. Nakhon Pathon, Thailand. Retrieved 16 May, 2016, from www.michaelolaf.net/lecture_secret.html

Shamay-Tsoory, S. G. (2011). The neural bases for empathy. *The Neuroscientist, 17*, 18–24.

Shapira, Z. (1976). Expectancy determinants of intrinsically motivated behavior. *Journal of Personality & Social Psychology, 34*(6), 1235–44.

Shapiro, L. A. (2011). *Embodied cognition*. London: Routledge.

Sherman, L. J., Rice, K., & Cassidy, J. (2015). Infant capacities related to building internal working models of attachment figures: A theoretical and empirical review. *Developmental Review*. Advance online publication. doi:10.1016/j.dr.2015.06.001

Shoda, Y., Mischel, W., & Peake, P. K. (1990). Predicting adolescent cognitive and self-regulatory competencies from preschool delay of gratification: Identifying diagnostic conditions. *Developmental Psychology, 26*, 978–86.

Shouse, R. (2001). The impact of traditional and reform-style practices on student mathematics achievement. In T. Loveless (Ed.), *The great curriculum debate* (pp. 108–33). Washington, DC: Brookings Institute.

Shutts, K., Banaji, M. R., & Spelke, E. S. (2010). Social categories guide young children's preferences for novel objects. *Developmental Science, 13*, 599–610.

Shutts, K., Kinzler, K. D., McKee, C. B., & Spelke, E. S. (2009). Social information guides infants' selection of foods. *Journal of Cognition and Development, 10*, 1–17.

Siegler, R. S. (1994). Cognitive variability: A key to understanding cognitive development. *Current Directions in Psychological Science, 3*(1), 1–5.

Siegler, R. S. (1998). *Children's thinking* (2nd ed.). Upper Saddle River, NJ: Prentice-Hall.

Simon, H. A. (2001a). Learning to research about learning. In S. M. Carver & D. Klahr (Eds.), *Cognition and instruction: Twenty-five years of progress* (pp. 205–26). Mahwah, NJ: Lawrence Erlbaum.

Simon, H. A. (2001b). "Seek and ye shall find": How curiosity engenders discovery. In K. Crowley, C. D. Schunn, & T. Okada (Eds.), *Designing for science: Implications from everyday, classroom, and professional settings*. Mahwah, NJ: Lawrence Erlbaum.

Simpson, M. L., & Randall, S. N. (2000). Vocabulary development at the college level. In R. F. Flippo & D. C. Caverly (Eds.), *Handbook of college reading and study strategy research* (pp. 43–73). Mahwah, NJ: Lawrence Erlbaum.

Singley, M. K., & Anderson, J. R. (1987). A keystroke analysis of learning and transfer in text editing. *Human-Computer Interaction, 3*(3), 223–74.

Slavin, R. E. (1980). Cooperative learning. *Review of Educational Research, 50*(2), 315–42.

Slavin, R. E. (1983). When does cooperative learning increase student achievement? *Psychological Bulletin, 94*(3), 429–45.

Slavin, R. E. (1996). Research on cooperative learning and achievement: What we know, what we need to know. *Contemporary Educational Psychology, 21*(1), 43–69.

Smith, C. L., Gelfand, D. M., Hartmann, D. P., & Partlow, M. E. (1979). Children's causal attributions regarding help giving. *Child Development, 50*(1), 203–10.

Smith, S. M., & Manzano, I. (2010). Video context-dependent recall. *Behavior Research Methods, 42*, 292–301.

Snow, C. E. (1990). Building memories: The ontogeny of autobiography. In D. Cicchetti & M. Beeghly (Eds.), *The self in transition: Infancy to childhood* (pp. 213–42). Chicago: University of Chicago Press.

Söderqvist, S., Matsson, H., Peyrard-Janvid, M., Kere, J., & Klingberg, T. (2014). Polymorphisms in the dopamine receptor 2 gene region influence improvements during working memory training in children and adolescents. *Journal of Cognitive Neuroscience, 26*, 54–62.

Solomon, J., & George, C. (2015). The measurement of attachment security and related constructs in infancy and early childhood. In P. Shaver & J. Cassidy (Eds.), *Handbook of attachment: Theory, research, and clinical applications* (3 ed.). New York: Guilford.

Sommerville, J. A., Hildebrand, E. A., & Crane, C. C. (2008). Experience matters: The impact of doing versus watching on infants' subsequent perception of tool-use events. *Developmental Psychology, 44*, 1249–56.

Sommerville, J. A., & Woodward, A. L. (2005). The relationship between action processing and action production in infancy. *Cognition, 95*(1), 1–30.

Sommerville, J. A., Woodward, A. L., & Needham, A. (2005). Action experience alters 3-month-old infants' perception of others' actions. *Cognition, 96*(1), B1–11.

Soundy, C. (2009). Young children's imaginative play: Is it valued in Montessori classrooms. *Early Childhood Education Journal, 36*, 381–83.

Sowell, E. R., Thompson, P. M., Holmes, C. J., Jernigan, T. L., & Toga, A. W. (1999). In vivo evidence for post-adolescent brain maturation in frontal and striatal regions. *Nature Neuroscience, 2*, 859–61.

Spearman, C. (1904). "General intelligence," objectively determined and measured. *The American Journal of Psychology, 15*, 201–92.

Spelke, E. S., & Newport, E. L. (1998). Nativism, empiricism, and the development of knowledge. In R. Lerner (Ed.), *Handbook of child psychology, Vol. 1: Theoretical models of human development* (pp. 275–340). New York: Wiley.

Stallings, J. A., & Stipek, D. (1986). Research on early childhood and elementary school teaching programs. In M. C. Wittrock (Ed.), *Handbook of research on teaching* (3rd ed., pp. 727–53). New York: Macmillan.

Standing, E. M. (1957). *Maria Montessori: Her life and work*. London.

Stanovich, K. E., & Cunningham, A. E. (1993). Where does knowledge come from? Specific associations between print exposure and information acquisition. *Journal of Educational Psychology, 85*(2), 211–29.

Steenari, M.-R., Vuontela, V., Paavonen, E. J., Carlson, S., Fjaellberg, M., & Aronen, E. T. (2003). Working memory and sleep in 6- to 13-year-old schoolchildren. *Journal of the American Academy of Child & Adolescent Psychiatry, 42*(1), 85–92.

Steinberg, J. (2002, June 2). In commencement speeches, 9/11s a familiar theme. *The New York Times*. Retrieved from www.nytimes.com/200206/02/education

Steinglass, P., Bennett, L. A., Wolin, S. J., & Reiss, D. (1987). *The alcoholic family*. New York: Basic Books.

Stephenson, M. E. (2000). The human tendencies. *NAMTA Journal, 25*, 5–22.

Stevenson, H. W., Lee, S.-y., Chen, C., Stigler, J. W., Hsu, C. C., & Kitamura, S. (1990). Contexts of achievement: A study of American, Chinese, and Japanese children. *Monographs of the Society for Research in Child Development, 55*(1–2 serial no. 221), pp. 1-119.

Stevenson, M. B., & Lamb, M. E. (1979). Effects of infant sociability and the caretaking environment on infant cognitive performance. *Child Development, 50*(2), 340–49.

Stickgold, R., James, L., & Hobson, J. A. (2000). Visual discrimination learning requires sleep after training. *Nature Neuroscience, 3*(12), 1237–38.

Stigler, J. W. (1984). "Mental abacus": The effect of abacus training on Chinese children's mental calculation. *Cognitive Psychology, 16*(2), 145–76.

Stigler, J. W., Gallimore, R., & Hiebert, J. (2000). Using video surveys to compare classrooms and teaching across cultures: Examples and lessons from the TIMSS video studies. *Educational Psychologist, 35*(2), 87–100.

Stigler, J. W., Lee, S.-y., & Stevenson, H. W. (1987). Mathematics classrooms in Japan, Taiwan, and the United States. *Child Development, 58*(5), 1272–85.

Stipek, D., Salmon, J. M., Givvin, K. B., Kazemi, E., Saxe, G., & MacGyvers, V. L. (1998). The value (and convergence) of practices suggested by motivation research and promoted by mathematics education reformers. *Journal for Research in Mathematics Education, 29*(4), 465–88.

Stodolsky, S. S., & Karlson, A. L. (1972). Differential outcomes of a Montessori curriculum. *Elementary School Journal, 72*(8), 419–33.

Sullivan, P., Jorgensen, R., Boaler, J., & Lerman, S. (2013). Transposing reform pedagogy into new contexts: Complex instruction in remote Australia. *Mathematics Education Research Journal, 25*, 173–84.

Swann, W. B., & Pittman, T. S. (1977). Initiating play activity of children: The moderating influence of verbal cues on intrinsic motivation. *Child Development, 48*(3), 1128–32.

Swing, E. L., Gentile, D. A., Anderson, C. A., & Walsh, D. A. (2010). Television and video game exposure and the development of attention problems. *Pediatrics, 126*, 214–21.

Tandon, P. S., Zhou, C., Lozano, P., & Christakis, D. A. (2011). Preschoolers' total daily screen time at home and by type of child care. *The Journal of Pediatrics, 158*, 297–300.

Tang, Y.-Y., Hölzel, B. K., & Posner, M. I. (2015). The neuroscience of mindfulness meditation. *Nature Reviews Neuroscience, 16*, 213–25.

Tang, Y.Y., Ma, Y., Wang, J., Fan, Y., Feng, S., Lu, Q., . . . Posner, M. I. (2007). Short-term meditation training improves attention and self-regulation. *Proceedings of the National Academy of Sciences, 104*(43), 17152–56.

Tao, S., & Dong, Q. (1997). *Referential gestural communication and locomotor experience in urban Chinese infants.* Beijing: Normal University.

Tare, M., Chiong, C., Ganea, P., & DeLoache, J. (2010). Less is more: How manipulative features affect children's learning from picture books. *Journal of Applied Developmental Psychology, 31*(5): 395–400.

Taylor, C., Clifford, A., & Franklin, A. (2013). Color preferences are not universal. *Journal of Experimental Psychology: General, 142*, 1015–27. doi:10.1037/a0030273

Taylor, E. V. (2009). The purchasing practice of low-income students: The relationship to mathematical development. *The Journal of the Learning Sciences, 18*, 370–415.

Teasley, S. D. (1995). The role of talk in children's peer collaborations. *Developmental Psychology, 31*(2), 207–20.

Teper, R., Segal, Z. V., & Inzlicht, M. (2013). Inside the mindful mind: How mindfulness enhances emotion regulation through improvements in executive control. *Current Directions in Psychological Science, 22*, 449–54. doi:10.1177/0963721413495869

Thelen, E. (2001). Dynamic mechanisms of change in early perceptual-motor development. In J. L. McClelland & R. S. Siegler (Eds.), *Mechanisms of cognitive development: Behavioral and neural perspectives. Carnegie Symposia on Cognition* (pp. 161–84). Mahwah, NJ: Lawrence Erlbaum.

Thoermer, C., Woodward, A., Sodian, B., Perst, H., & Kristen, S. (2013). To get the grasp: Seven-month-olds encode and selectively reproduce goal-directed grasping. *Journal of Experimental Child Psychology, 116*, 499–509.

Thoman, D. B., Sansone, C., Fraughton, T., & Pasupathi, M. (2012). How students socially evaluate interest: Peer responsiveness influences evaluation and maintenance of interest. *Contemporary Educational Psychology, 37*, 254–65.

Thomas, E. L., & Robinson, H. A. (1972). *Improving reading in every class: A sourcebook for teachers.* Boston: Allyn & Bacon.

Thompson, L. A., Fulker, D. W., DeFries, J. C., & Plomin, R. (1986). Multivariate genetic analysis of "environmental" influences on infant cognitive development. *British Journal of Developmental Psychology, 4*(4), 347–53.

Thompson, R. A. (1999). Early attachment and later development. In J. Cassidy & P. R. Shaver (Eds.), *Handbook of attachment: Theory, research, and clinical applications* (pp. 265–86). New York: Guilford.

Thorell, L., Lindqvist, S., Nutley, S., Bohlin, G., & Klingberg, T. (2009). Training and transfer effects of executive functions in preschool children. *Developmental Science, 12*, 106–13.

Thorndike, E. L. (1906/1962). The principles of teaching. In G. M. Jonich (Ed.), *Psychology and the science of education: Selected writings of Edward L. Thorndike* (pp. 55–69). New York: Teachers College Press.

Thorndike, E. L. (1917). *The Thorndike arithmetic, Book 1.* Chicago: Rand McNally.

Thorndike, E. L. (1921a). *The new methods in arithmetic.* New York: Rand McNally.

Thorndike, E. L. (1921b). *The teacher's word book.* New York: Columbia Teachers College.

Thorndike, E. L., & Woodworth, R. S. (1962). The influence of improvement in one mental function on the efficiency of other functions. In G. M. Jonich (Ed.), *Psychology and the science of education: Selected writings of Edward L. Thorndike* (pp. 48–55). New York: Teachers College Press. (Original work published in 1906.)

Tobias, S. (1994). Interest, prior knowledge, and learning. *Review of Educational Research, 64*(1), 37–54.

Tomasello, M., Kruger, A. C., & Ratner, H. H. (1993). Cultural learning. *Behavioral and Brain Sciences, 16*, 495–552.

Tomasello, M., Melis, A. P., Tennie, C., Wyman, E., & Herrmann, E. (2012). Two key steps in the evolution of human cooperation. *Current Anthropology, 53*, 673–92.

Tomasello, M., Striano, T., & Rochat, P. (1999). Do young children use objects as symbols? *British Journal of Developmental Psychology, 17*, 563–84.

Tomlinson, C. A. (2014). *Differentiated classroom: Responding to the needs of all learners* (2nd ed.). Alexandria, VA: ASCD.

Topping, K., & Ehly, S. (Eds.). (1998). *Peer-assisted learning.* Mahwah, NJ: Lawrence Erlbaum.

Treboux, D., Crowell, J. A., & Waters, E. (2004). When "new" meets "old": Configurations of adult attachment representations and their implications for marital functioning. *Developmental Psychology, 40*(2), 295–314.

Treisman, A. M., & Gelade, G. (1980). A feature-integration theory of attention. *Cognitive Psychology, 12*(1), 97–136.

Tucker, M., & Ellis, R. (2001). The potentiation of grasp types during visual object catego-rization. *Visual Cognition, 8*, 769–800.

Turiel, E., & Rothman, G. R. (1972). The influence of reasoning on behavioral choices at different stages of moral development. *Child Development, 43*(3), 741–56.

Urban, J., Carlson, E., Egeland, B., & Sroufe, L. A. (1991). Patterns of individual adapta-tion across childhood. *Development & Psychopathology, 3*(4), 445–60.

Urry, H. L., Nitschke, J. B., Dolski, I., Jackson, D. C., Dalton, K. M., Mueller, C. J., . . . Davidson, R. J. (2004). Making a life worth living: Neural correlates of well-being. *Psychological Science, 15*(6), 367–72.

Uttal, D. H., O'Doherty, K., Newland, R., Hand, L. L., & Deloache, J. S. (2009). Dual representation and the linking of concrete and symbolic representations. *Child Development Perspectives, 3*, 156–59.

Vandell, D. L., Belsky, J., Burchinal, M., Steinberg, L., & Vandergrift, N. (2010). Do effects of early child care extend to age 15 years? Results from the NICHD study of early child care and youth development. *Child Development, 81*, 737–56.

Van Driel, J. H., & Berry, A. (2012). Teacher professional development focusing on peda-gogical content knowledge. *Educational Researcher, 41*, 26–28.

Vasta, R., Haith, M. M., & Miller, S. M. (1999). *Child Psychology: The modern science.* New York: Wiley.

Vaughn, B. E., & Bost, K. K. (1999). Attachment and temperament: Redundant, indepen-dent, or interacting influences on interpersonal adaptation and personality develop-ment? In J. Cassidy & P. R. Shaver (Eds.), *Handbook of attachment: Theory, research, and clinical applications.* New York: Guilford Press.

Verdine, B. N., Golinkoff, R. M., Hirsh-Pasek, K., & Newcombe, N. S. (in press). Links between spatial and mathematical skills across the preschool years. *Monographs of the Society for Research in Child Development.*

Vohs, K. D., Redden, J. P., & Rahinel, R. (2013). Physical order produces healthy choices, generosity, and conventionality, whereas disorder produces creativity. *Psychological Science, 24*(9), 1860–67. doi:10.1177/0956797613480186

Vygotsky, L. S. (1978). *Mind in society.* Cambridge, MA: Harvard University Press.

Wachs, T. D. (1976). Utilization of a Piagetian approach in the investigation of early expe-rience effects: A research strategy and some illustrative data. *Merrill-Palmer Quarterly, 22*(1), 11–30.

Wachs, T. D. (2000). *Necessary but not sufficient: The respective roles of single and mul-tiple influences on individual development.* Washington, DC: American Psychological Association.

Wachs, T. D., & Gruen, G. E. (1982). *Early experience and human development.* New York: Plenum.

Wachs, T. D., Uzgiris, I. C., & Hunt, J. M. (1971). Cognitive development in infants of different age levels and from different environmental backgrounds: An explanatory investigation. *Merrill-Palmer Quarterly, 17*(4), 283–317.

Wallbott, H. G. (1991). Recognition of emotion from facial expression via imitation? Some indirect evidence for an old theory. *British Journal of Social Psychology, 30*(3), 207–19.

Walsh, B. A., & Petty, K. (2007). Frequency of six early childhood education approaches: A 10-year content analysis of early childhood education journal. *Early Childhood Education Journal, 34*, 301–305.

Wang, M. C., Haertel, G. D., & Walberg, H. J. (1993). Toward a knowledge base for school learning. *Review of Educational Research, 63*(3), 249–94.

Wang, M.-T., & Eccles, J. S. (2012). Social support matters: Longitudinal effects of social support on three dimensions of school engagement from middle to high school. *Child Development, 83*, 877–95.

Wang, M.-T., & Eccles, J. S. (2013). School context, achievement motivation, and academic engagement: A longitudinal study of school engagement using a multidimensional perspective. *Learning and Instruction, 28*, 12–23.

Wang, Y., & Su, Y. (2009). False belief understanding: Children catch it from classmates of different ages. *International Journal of Behavioral Development, 33*, 331–37. doi:10.1177/0165025409104525

Wang, Z., Deater-Deckard, K., Petrill, S. A., & Thompson, L. A. (2012). Externalizing problems, attention regulation, and household chaos: A longitudinal behavioral genetic study. *Development and Psychopathology, 24*, 755–69.

Want, S. C., & Harris, P. L. (2001). Learning from other people's mistakes: Causal understanding in learning to use a tool. *Child Development, 72*(2), 431–43.

Ward, E. J., & Chun, M. W. (2016). Neural discriminability of object features predicts perceptual organization. *Psychological Science, 27*, 3–11

Warneken, F., Chen, F., & Tomasello, M. (2006). Cooperative activities in young children and chimpanzees. *Child Development, 77*, 640–63.

Warneken, F., & Tomasello, M. (2007). Helping and cooperation at 14 months of age. *Infancy, 11*, 271–94.

Warneken, F., & Tomasello, M. (2008). Extrinsic rewards undermine altruistic tendencies in 20-month-olds. *Developmental Psychology, 44*, 1785–88.

Waters, E., & Deane, K. (1985). Defining and assessing individual differences in attachment relationships: Q-methodology and the organization of behavior in infancy and early childhood. *Growing points of attachment theory and research. Monographs of the society for research in child development, 50*, 41–65.

Waters, E., Merrick, S., Treboux, D., Crowell, J., & Albersheim, L. (2000). Attachment security in infancy and early adulthood: A 20-year longitudinal study. *Child Development, 71*(3), 684–89.

Watson, J. S. (1971). Cognitive-perceptual development in infancy: Setting for the seventies. *Merrill-Palmer Quarterly, 17*(2), 139–52.

Watson, J. S., & Ramey, C. T. (1972). Reactions to response-contingent stimulation in early infancy. *Merrill-Palmer Quarterly, 18*(3), 219–27.

Wegner, D. M. (1989). *White bears and other unwanted thoughts: Suppression, obsession, and the psychology of mental control.* New York: Elsevier.

Weinfield, N. S., Sroufe, L. A., Egeland, B., & Carlson, E. A. (2008). The nature of individual differences in infant-caregiver attachment. In J. Cassidy & P. R. Shaver (Eds.), *Handbook of attachment: Theory, research, and clinical applications* (2nd ed., pp. 78–101). New York, NY: Guilford

Weisberg, D., Sobel, D., Goodstein, J., & Bloom, P. (2013). Young children are reality-prone when thinking about stories. *Journal of Cognition and Culture, 13*, 282–407.

Weiss, I. R. (1995, April). *Mathematics teachers' response to the reform agenda.* Paper presented at the American Educational Research Association, San Francisco.

Weiss, I. R., Pasley, J. D., Smith, P. S., Banilower, E. R., & Heck, D. J. (2003). *Looking inside the classroom: A study of K–12 mathematics and science education in the United States*. Chapel Hill, NC: Horizon Research.

Wellman, H. M. (2011). Reinvigorating explanations for the study of early cognitive development. *Child Development Perspectives, 5*, 33–38.

Wellman, H. M. (2014). *Making minds: How theory of mind develops*. New York: Oxford.

Wellman, H. M., Cross, D., & Watson, J. (2001). Meta-analysis of theory of mind development: The truth about false belief. *Child Development, 72*, 655–84.

Wellman, H. M., & Liu, D. (2004). Scaling of theory-of-mind tasks. *Child Development, 75*, 523–541.

Wells, G. L., & Petty, R. E. (1980). The effects of overt head movements on persuasion: Compatibility and incompatibility of responses. *Basic & Applied Social Psychology, 1*(3), 219–30.

Wentworth, R. A. L. (1999). *Montessori for the new millennium: Practical guidance on the teaching and education of children of all ages, based on a rediscovery of the true principles and vision of Maria Montessori*. Mahwah, NJ: Lawrence Erlbaum.

Wentzel, K. R. (2002). Are effective teachers like good parents? Teaching styles and student adjustment in early adolescence. *Child Development, 73*(1), 287–301.

Wertheimer, M. (1959). *Productive thinking*. New York: Harper & Row.

White, J. M., Yussen, S. R., & Docherty, E. M. (1976). Performance of Montessori and traditionally schooled nursery children on tasks of seriation, classification, and conservation. *Contemporary Educational Psychology, 1*, 356–68.

White, K., & Owen, D. (1970). Locus of evaluation for classroom work and the development of creative potential. *Psychology in the Schools, 7*(3), 292–95.

Whitehurst, G. J., & Lonigan, C. J. (1998). Child development and emergent literacy. *Child Development, 69*(3), 848–72.

Whitson, J., & Galinsky, A. (2008). Lacking control increases illusory pattern perception. *Science, 322*, 115–17.

Wigfield, A., & Eccles, J. S. (1989). Test anxiety in elementary and secondary school students. *Educational Psychologist, 24*(2), 159–83.

Williams, L. R., Degnan, K. A., Perez-Edgar, K. E., Henderson, H. A., Rubin, K. H., Pine, D. S., … Fox, N. A. (2009). Impact of behavioral inhibition and parenting style on internalizing and externalizing problems from early childhood through adolescence. *Journal of Abnormal Child Psychology, 37*, 1063–75.

Willingham, D. B. (2001). *Cognition: The thinking animal*. Upper Saddle River, NJ: Prentice-Hall.

Willingham, D. T. (2006). How knowledge helps. *American Educator, 30*, 31–37.

Wimmer, H., & Perner, J. (1983). Beliefs about beliefs: Representation and constraining function of wrong beliefs in young children's understanding of deception. *Cognition, 13*, 103–28. doi:10.1016/0010-0277(83)90004-5

Wineburg, S., & Grossman, P. (2001). Affect and effect in cognitive approaches to instruction. In S. M. Carver & D. Klahr (Eds.), *Cognition and instruction: Twenty-five years of progress* (pp. 479–92). Mahwah, NJ: Lawrence Erlbaum.

Winning, A. P., & Boag, S. (2015). Does brief mindfulness training increase empathy? The role of personality. *Personality and Individual Differences, 86*, 492–98.

Witt, J. K., Proffitt, D. R., & Epstein, W. (2004). *Remapping near space influences perceived distance.* Unpublished manuscript, University of Virginia.

Wohlwill, J. F., & Heft, H. (1987). The physical environment and the development of the child. In D. Stokols & I. Altman (Eds.), *Handbook of environmental psychology* (Vol. 2, pp. 281–328). New York: John Wiley.

Wompack, J. (1996). *Lean thinking.* New York: Simon and Schuster.

Wood, L. A., Kendal, R. L., & Flynn, E. G. (2012). Context-dependent model-based biases in cultural transmission: Children's imitation is affected by model age over model knowledge state. *Evolution and Human Behavior, 33*, 387–94.

Wood, L. A., Kendal, R. L., & Flynn, E. G. (2013). Whom do children copy? Model-based biases in social learning. *Developmental Review, 33*, 341–56.

Woodward, A. L. (1998). Infants selectively encode the goal object of an actor's reach. *Cognition, 69*, 1–34.

Woodward, A. L., & Guajardo, J. J. (2002). Infants' understanding of the point gesture as an object-directed action. *Cognitive Development, 17*(1), 1061–84.

Woolley, J. D., Boerger, E. A., & Markman, A. B. (2004). A visit from the candy witch: Factors influencing young children's belief in a novel fantastical being. *Developmental Science, 7*, 456–68. doi:10.1111/j.1467-7687.2004.00366.x

Wright, S., & Cowen, E. L. (1985). The effects of peer-teaching on student perceptions of class environment, adjustment, and academic performance. *American Journal of Community Psychology, 13*(4), 417–31.

Wright, W. (2007). *Spore: Birth of a game.* TED talk. Retrieved from: www.ted.com/talks/will_wright_makes_toys_that_make_worlds?language=en#t-42206

Xerri, C., Merzenich, M. M., Jenkins, W., & Santucci, S. (1999). Representational plasticity in cortical area 3b paralleling tactual-motor skill acquisition in adult monkeys. *Cerebral Cortex, 9*(3), 264–76.

Xiao, Y., Ma, F., Lv, Y., Cai, G., Teng, P., Xu, F., & Chen, S. (2015). Sustained attention is associated with error processing impairment: Evidence from mental fatigue study in four-choice reaction time task. *PLoS one, 10*, e0117837–e0117837.

Yang, G., Lai, C. S. W., Cichon, J., Ma, L., Li, W., & Gan, W.-B. (2014). Sleep promotes branch-specific formation of dendritic spines after learning. *Science, 344*, 1173–78.

Yeager, D. S., & Dweck, C. S. (2012). Mindsets that promote resilience: When students believe that personal characteristics can be developed. *Educational Psychologist, 47*, 302–14.

Zajonc, R. B. (1960). The process of cognitive tuning in communication. *Journal of Abnormal & Social Psychology, 61*, 159–67.

Zajonc, R. B. (1965). Social facilitation. *Science, 149*(3681), 269–74.

Zajonc, R. B., Alderman, K. A., Murphy, S. T., & Niedenthal, P. M. (1987). Convergence in the physical appearance of spouses. *Motivation and Emotion, 11*, 335–46.

Zajonc, R. B., Pietromonaco, P., & Bargh, J. A. (1982). Independence and interaction of affect and cognition. In M. S. Clark & S. T. Fiske (Eds.), *Affect and cognition: The 17th Annual Carnegie Symposium on Cognition.* Hillsdale, NJ: Lawrence Erlbaum.

Zelazo, P. D., & Lyons, K. E. (2012). The potential benefits of mindfulness training in early childhood: A developmental social cognitive neuroscience perspective. *Child Development Perspectives, 6*, 154–60.

Zhang, T., & Meaney, M. (2010). Epigenetics and the environmental regulation of the genome and its function. *Annual Review of Psychology, 61*, 439–66.

Ziegert, D. I., Kistner, J. A., Castro, R., & Robertson, B. (2001). Longitudinal study of young children's responses to challenging achievement situations. *Child Development, 72*(2), 609–24.

Zigler, E., & Bishop-Josef, S. (2004). Play under siege: A historical overview. In E. F. Zigler, D. G. Singer, & S. J. Bishop-Josef (Eds.), *Children's play: The roots of reading* (pp. 1–14). Washington, DC: Zero to Three.

Zilversmit, A. (1993). *Changing schools: Progressive education theory and practice, 1930–1960.* Chicago: University of Chicago Press.

Zimmerman, F. J., & Christakis, D. A. (2007). Associations between content types of early media exposure and subsequent attentional problems. *Pediatrics, 120*, 986-92.

Zmyj, N., & Seehagen, S. (2013). The role of a model's age for young children's imitation: A research review. *Infant and Child Development, 22*, 622–41.

AUTHOR INDEX

Abrams, D., 67
Acebo, C., 326
Acredolo, L. P., 67
Adam, E. K., 288
Adolph, K. E., 39, 42–43
Ahadi, S. A., 111
Aiello, J. R., 334
Ainley, M., 139, 160
Ainsworth, M. D. S., 285, 288–90, 292, 311
Aiyer, S. M., 41
Akhtar, N., 223
Alade, F., 114
Albersheim, L., 288
Alderman, K. A., 56
Aldrich, N. J., 3, 210
Alessandri, S. M., 87
Alexander, D. B., 320
Alfieri, L., 3, 210, 324, 381
Alibali, M. W., 67, 76–77
Allan, B. M., 178
Allen, C., 137, 252
Allen, J., 137, 252
Allen, J. P., 34
Alvarez, A. L., 182, 265
Amabile, T. M., 86, 100, 188
Ames, C., 173, 194–96
Anand, P. G., 141
Anderman, E. M., 2, 195
Anderson, C. A., 114
Anderson, J. R., 167, 252, 260, 271
Anderson, K. N., 271
Anderson, R. C., 144
Annis, L. F., 235, 312
Ansari, A., 374
Appelbaum, M. I., 151
Archer, J., 195
Arend, R. A., 286
Armstrong, T., 161
Arnedt, J. T., 326
Aronson, E., 237–38
Arrighi, R., 51
Asher, S. R., 142
Aslin, R. N., 117, 151
Atkinson, E., 342
Atkinson, J. W., 196
Au, W., 7

Ayduk, O., 109
Ayers, L., 5
Azmitia, M., 237, 240–42, 248

Bachrach, J. E., 137
Baddeley, A. D., 272
Bahrick, H. P., 187
Bai, D. L., 42
Bailey, D. B., 228
Baime, M. J., 130
Baird, J. H., 238
Bakdash, J. Z., 40
Bakermans-Kranenburg, M. J., 287, 290
Balcomb, F. K., 117
Ball, D. L., 11
Banaji, M. R., 227
Bandura, A., 222
Banilower, E. R., 14
Banko, K. M., 182
Bara, F., 26
Bargh, J. A., 55–56, 223, 235–36
Barnes, J. L., 211
Barnett, T. A., 114
Barnett, W., 210
Barr, R., 114, 342
Barrett, L., 332
Barrett, P., 332
Barrett, T., 40
Barron, R. W., 143
Barsalou, L., 38, 54
Barterian, J. A., 375
Bartlett, E., 169
Bartlett, L., 13, 250
Bassok, D., 7, 317
Bassok, M., 249
Bates, J. E., 290, 320
Bauer, P. J., 223
Baumrind, D., 293–94
Bavelas, J. B., 56
Baxter, L. A., 318, 320–21, 324
Beach, K., 270, 272
Bearak, J. M., 3
Beaulieu, C., 32
Beck, I. L., 171
Behne, T., 124
Bekkering, H., 223

Bell, A. J., 41
Bell, P. J., 41
Belsky, J., 352
Benford, S., 63
Bennett, E. L., 189
Bennett, K. P., 5–7
Bennett, L. A., 316
Benson, J. B., 51
Benware, C. A., 235
Berger, S. E., 42
Bergsmann, E. M., 306
Berk, L., 210, 215
Berk, L. E., 366
Berlyne, D., 151, 167
Berndt, T. J., 241
Bernier, A., 296
Bernieri, F. J., 227
Bernstein, E., 211
Berry, A., 171
Bertenthal, B. I., 42
Besançon, M., 373
Beyers, J., 320
Bezos, J., 4, 353
Bhatia, P., 374
Bialystok, E., 386
Biederman, I., 272
Bill, V. I., 142
Birch, L. L., 118
Bishop-Josef, S., 7, 219
Bizzell, R. P., 33–34, 355, 390
Bjork, E. L., 235
Bjorklund, D. F., 258, 395
Black, A., 56
Black, T., 52
Blackwell, L. S., 192, 299
Blair, C., 106, 109, 113, 211
Blair, C. B., 109
Blake, William, 1
Blehar, M. C., 288
Bloom, P., 169, 211, 212
Blumberg, M. S., 43
Boag, S., 131
Boaler, J., 274, 277, 303
Bobbitt, J. F., 6
Bodrova, E., 113, 210
Boerger, E. A., 209
Boguszewski, K., 115, 164
Bohlin, G., 112
Bohn, C., 73
Boldt, L. J., 109
Booth, A. E., 182, 265
Booth-LaForce, C., 286
Bordeleau, L., 195
Borke, H., 257
Bornstein, M. H., 32, 336

Bost, K. K., 290
Bouffard, T., 195
Bower, G. H., 331
Bowlby, J., 284, 285, 288
Bowman-Perrott, L., 231
Bradley, A., 342
Bradley, R. H., 321–22
Bransford, J. D., 2, 10, 32, 167, 170–71, 173,
  253–54, 261, 268
Brewer, D. J., 229
Bridgeman, D. L., 238
Briley, D. A., 112
Brin, S., 4, 353
Brock, P., 317
Brody, G. H., 242, 316, 319
Brooker, I., 227
Brooks, P. J., 3, 210
Brown, A. L., 2, 235, 238, 248–49
Brown, C. A., 67
Brown, J. S., 234
Brownell, C. A., 239
Brumley, M. R., 43
Brummelman, E., 302
Brunello, M., 144
Bruner, J., 10, 210, 267, 290
Bryant, B. K., 191
Bryson, S. E., 107
Bub, K., 109
Bui, D. C., 235
Bull, R., 109
Bullard, J., 316
Burchinal, M., 352
Burchinal, M. R., 228
Burr, D., 51
Burrows, L., 223
Burts, D. C., 295
Bus, A. G., 26
Bushman, B. J., 114, 302
Butcher, C., 67
Butler, R., 189, 191, 193–94
Buyse, E., 288
Byrne, B., 26
Byron, K., 189

Cahn, B. R., 132
Cai, G., 118
Caldwell, B. M., 321–22
Callahan, R. E., 5, 6, 7
Calvert, K., 44
Calvert, S. L., 114
Camera, L., 7
Cameron, C. E., 41, 109, 374
Cameron, J., 182, 184
Campbell, F. A., 322–23
Campbell, M. L., 41

Campione, J. C., 238, 249
Campos, J. J., 42–43
Cannon, E. N., 41
Carbonneau, K. J., 70
Carey, S., 169
Carlson, E. A., 285–86
Carlson, S. M., 108, 111, 214, 296
Carpenter, M., 223, 239
Carpenter, T. P., 10
Carraher, D. W., 270
Carraher, T. N., 270
Carskadon, M. A., 326
Cartocci, G., 51
Casey, B., 106, 108
Cassells, R. C., 342
Cassidy, J., 286
Cassidy, K. W., 385
Castro, R., 302
Cauffman, E., 286
Ceci, S. J., 258–59
Cerasoli, C. P., 183–84, 195
Cesario, J., 224
Chae, B., 334
Chartrand, T. L., 223
Chase, W. G., 258
Chattin-McNichols, J., 383
Chen, F., 239
Chen, M., 223
Chen, S., 118
Cheng, Y.-L., 59, 375
Chi, M. T. H., 171, 249, 258
Chien, N., 210, 324
Childs, C. P., 270
Chiong, C., 26, 144
Chirkov, V. I., 306
Chomsky, N., 32, 148
Chovil, N., 56
Christakis, D. A., 113–14
Christopher, F. S., 190
Christy, K., 114
Chun, M. W., 345
Church, R. B., 75–76
Cichon, J., 325
Cimeli, P., 109
Clark, A., 163
Clark, C. D., 216
Clark, C. L., 318, 320–21, 324
Clark, M. C., 331
Clearfield, M. W., 43
Clément, F., 227
Clements, D. H., 210
Cleminshaw, H. K., 319
Clifford, A., 163
Clore, G. L., 2
Cocking, R. R., 2

Cognition and Technology Group at
    Vanderbilt, 256
Cohen, D. K., 11
Cohen, P. A., 237
Cohen, R. L., 54
Cohen, S., 340–41
Cole, P., 26
Collier, G., 118
Collins, A., 234
Collins, M. F., 144
Conley, D., 251–52
Connelly, S., 231
Connolly, J., 242
Connors, L. J., 386
Cook, L. S., 12
Cook, M. S., 247
Cook, S. W., 76
Cooper, H., 81, 83, 91
Corapci, F., 334
Cordova, D. I., 255
Corpus, J. H., 179, 195
Cotton, J. L., 247
Covington, M. V., 195
Cowen, E. L., 237
Cox, M. V., 374
Crandall, V. C., 85–86
Crane, C. C., 41
Crick, N. R., 364
Crockenberg, S. B., 191
Cross, D., 361
Crowell, J., 288
Crowell, J. A., 287
Crowley, K., 237
Csikszentmihalyi, M., 122, 142, 195, 214, 217,
    239, 247, 297, 363, 373
Cubberly, E. P., 5
Cumberland-Li, A., 110
Cunningham, A. E., 26
Czerwinski, M., 112

Dafoe, J. L., 102, 183
Daildin, D., 179
Damon, W., 234, 237–38
Davidson, R. J., 56, 131
Davies, F., 332
Davis, A., 374
Davis, B. E., 45–46
Davis, O. S., 324
Deane, K., 287
Deater-Deckard, K., 294, 324
DeCasper, A. J., 152
de Castro, B. O., 302
De Charms, R., 88–90
Deci, E. L., 82, 89, 101, 180–84, 196, 235, 305–7
Dedo, J. Y., 40

Dee, T. S., 4
DeFries, J. C., 323
DeJong, W., 100
Dekovic, M., 295
De Lisi, R., 220
DeLoache, J. S., 26, 64, 69–70, 143–44, 216, 271
Delquadri, J. C., 219
Derose, J., 130
Detweiler-Bedell, B., 161
Deutsch, C. P., 340
Devine, R. T., 111
de Vries, H., 32
Dewey, C., 46
Dewey, J., 10–11, 139, 378, 393–94, 396
DeWolf, D. M., 295
De Wolff, M., 288, 290
Diamond, A., 108, 112–13, 210
Diamond, M. C., 189
Diener, E., 2
Dillworth-Bart, J. E., 111
Dimeff, L. A., 231
Doar, B., 108
Docherty, E. M., 352
Dohrmann, K. R., 138, 354, 356, 364–65,
    373, 375
Doidge, N., 39
Dollaghan, C., 169
Dollinger, S. J., 101
Dong, Q., 42
Dore, R. S., 224
Dornbusch, S. M., 293
Doumen, S., 288
Downer, J. T., 290
Doyle, A.-B., 242
Doymus, K., 238
Drake, M., 179
Dreary, I. J., 41, 343
Drell, M., 115, 164
Druyan, S., 52
Dugid, P., 234
Duncan, G., 109
Duran, R. T., 234
During, M., 317
Dweck, C. S., 86, 173, 192, 195, 298–99, 301–2
Dworkin, M. S., 10
Dyer, J. L., 33, 34, 355
Dyer, J. W., 312
Dziurawiec, S., 163

Early, D. M., 34
Eberth, J., 130
Eccles, J. S., 2, 137, 179, 182, 196, 252, 306
Egan, K., 3, 16
Egeland, B., 285–86, 290
Ehly, S., 222

Ehrenberg, R. G., 230
Einstein, A., 2
Eisen, S. L., 55, 164, 388
Eisenberg, N., 110–11, 190
Eisenberger, R., 182, 184, 189
Elardo, R., 322
Elder, A. D., 76, 78
Elkind, D., 18, 27, 94, 210
Ellis, R., 54
Else-Quest, N., 364–65, 390
El-Sheikh, M., 325
Emerson, M. J., 107
Engelhardt, L. E., 112
Engelkamp, J., 54
Epstein, J. L., 386
Epstein, W., 40
Epstein, Y. M., 333
Erisir, A., 33, 43, 260, 346
Espy, K. A., 109
Estes, B. W., 187
Estes, T. H., 140, 175
Evans, G. W., 317, 333, 341–42

Fabes, R. A., 190
Fagot, B. I., 290
Faja, S., 108
Fallone, G., 326
Falvey, M. A., 230
Fantuzzo, J. W., 231, 247, 386
Fantz, R., 151
Farran, D. C., 210, 323
Fazal, N. D., 41
Feltovich, P. J., 171
Fenneman, E., 10
Ferguson, K. T., 342
Fernald, A., 152
Fiala, J., 183
Fiedler, K., 2
Field, T., 323
Fielding-Barnsley, R., 26
Fiese, B. H., 319
Fifer, W. P., 152
Finn, K. V., 365
Fisher, A. V., 332
Fisher, J. O., 118
Fisher, K. R., 143
Fitts, P. M., 187
Fitzpatrick, C., 109, 114
Flanagan, R., 53
Flavell, J. H., 240, 259, 320
Fleming, P., 46
Flor, D. L., 316, 319
Flynn, E. G., 227
Fodor, J. A., 147
Fogel, A., 40

Foorman, B. R., 26
Ford, M. T., 183
Forssberg, H., 164
Fox, K. C., 131–32, 285, 293
Frankel, K. A., 290
Frankel, L. A., 118
Franklin, A., 163
Fraughton, T., 139
Fredrickson, B. L., 2, 145
Freedman, J. O., 388
Freud, A., 393
Friedman, I., 181
Friedman, N. P., 107
Frijters, J. C., 143
Frolich, D., 126
Fry, P. G., 12
Fryer, R. G., 178
Fulker, D. W., 323
Fulton, M., 101
Fultz, J., 190
Furnham, A., 342

Galanter, E., 230
Galinsky, A. D., 82, 224
Galinsky, T. L., 330
Gallimore, R., 14
Galloway, J. C., 43
Galton, F., 343
Gamoran, A., 230
Gan, W.-B., 325
Ganea, P., 144
Ganotice, F. A., 2
Gard, T., 130
Garing, A. E., 52
Garon, N., 107
Gartner, A., 138, 354
Gasper, K., 2
Gauvain, M., 233–34, 237, 290–91
Geddes, K., 163
Geier, C., 108
Gelade, G., 58, 348
Gelfand, D. M., 191
Gentaz, E., 26
Gentile, D. A., 114
Gentner, D., 271
George, C., 285
Gergely, G., 223
Gerken, L., 117
Gerson, S. A., 41
Gianinno, S. M., 217
Gick, M. L., 273
Gilbert, D. T., 111
Ginsburg, H., 28
Ginsburg-Block, M. D., 231–32, 386
Gitomer, J., 86

Glachen, M., 237
Glaser, R., 171
Glass, D. C., 83, 340
Glenberg, A. M., 51, 53, 56
Glucksberg, S., 187
Godden, D. R., 272
Godwin, K. E., 332
Gogtay, N., 33
Golan, S., 186, 301
Golbeck, S. L., 220
Golding, J., 46
Goldin-Meadow, S., 66–67, 75–78, 241
Goldstein, T. R., 209, 212
Golinkoff, R. M., 59, 143–44, 210, 215, 385
Gonzales, P., 54
Gonzalez, V. M., 126
Good, C., 301
Goodman, R., 108
Goodrich, W., 67
Goodstein, J., 211
Goodwyn, S. W., 67
Gottfried, A. W., 323
Graef, R., 217
Graesser, A. C., 249
Graham, S., 186, 301
Gray, S. W., 316, 322
Graziano, W. G., 242
Grazzini, C., 106
Gredebäck, G., 41
Greenberg, M. T., 113
Greene, D., 102, 180, 183, 205
Greenfield, P. M., 270
Greenwood, C. R., 219, 231–32
Greer, R. D., 235
Grenot-Scheyer, M., 230
Griesler, P. C., 118
Griffin, M. M., 52
Grimm, K. J., 41, 138, 354
Grissmer, D., 41, 374
Grob, A., 343
Grolnick, W. S., 89, 185
Grommoll, E. W., 171
Grossman, B. S., 188
Grossman, P., 272
Grossmann, K., 286, 288
Grossmann, K. E., 286
Gruber, R., 325
Gruber, T., 130
Gruen, G. E., 320, 339
Grusec, J. E., 190
Guajardo, J. J., 41
Guidubaldi, J., 319
Gul, R. E., 118, 227
Gunnar, M. R., 288

Gunter, B., 342
Gutowski, K. A., 56

Haarig, F., 130
Hadar, U., 54
Haertel, G. D., 3
Hafen, C. A., 306
Hagmann-von Arx, P., 343
Halal, M., 55
Hall, G. S., 16, 45, 391–92, 394
Hall, M. W., 8, 396
Hall, R. V., 219
Hamre, B. K., 7, 34, 219, 288, 290
Hand, L. L., 70
Hanna, E., 118
Hanscombe, K. B., 324
Hansen-Tift, A. M., 148
Hanson, R., 67
Harackiewicz, J. M., 183, 196
Harden, K. P., 112
Harrid, R., 333
Harris, J., 126
Harris, P. L., 223, 225, 227
Harris, R. J., 55
Hart, C. H., 295
Harter, S., 2, 179, 182, 184, 217, 247
Hartmann, D. P., 191
Hartup, W. W., 221, 250
Havas, D. A., 56
Haworth, C. M., 324
Hayashi, M., 330
Hayenga, A. O., 195
Hayne, H., 43, 87, 118
Hazen, N. L., 118
He, L., 113
Heathcock, J. C., 43
Hebb, D., 260
Heck, D. J., 14
Heckman, J. J., 109
Heft, H., 339, 342
Hein, A., 39, 42, 46
Heise, M. J., 371
Held, R., 39, 42, 46
Heller, L. R., 232
Henderlong, J., 181, 281
Hendrickson, G., 273
Hennessey, B. A., 188
Henry, C. S., 320
Herrenkohl, R., 238
Herricks, T., 253
Herrmann, E., 239
Hershey, K. L., 111
Hertz-Lazarowitz, R., 238
Hesse, E., 287
Hesser, J., 242

Hidi, S., 138–40, 143, 163
Hiebert, J., 13, 14, 219, 317, 392
Hildebrand, E. A., 41
Hilgard, E. R., 9, 11
Hiroto, D. S., 83
Hirsh-Pasek, K., 59, 143–44, 210, 215, 385
Hix, H. R., 111
Hobson, J. A., 325
Hogan, D. M., 220
Holmes, C. J., 106
Holyoak, K. J., 273
Hölzel, B. K., 130
Hopkins, E. J., 212
Hori, T., 330
Hostetter, A. B., 54
Houston, D. M., 385
Howerter, A., 107
Hughes, C., 111
Hughes, S. O., 118
Huizinga, M., 114
Hunnius, S., 41
Hunt, J. M., 333
Huntsinger, J. R., 2
Hurrell, J. J., 330
Hymel, S., 142

Iida, F., 43
Inzlicht, M., 131
Iqbal, S. T., 112
Iriki, A., 40
Isbell, L. M., 2
Isen, A. M., 2
Istomina, J. M., 257
Itard, J.-M., 15
Iverson, J., 67
Iwamura, Y., 40
Iyengar, S. S., 82, 84, 95, 128, 179

Jacob, B., 4
Jacoby, S., 54
Jaeger, S., 130
Jaffee, S. R., 324
Jahromi, L. B., 111
Jain, S., 131
James, L., 325
James, W., 345
Janssens, J. M., 295
Jarvin, L., 70
Jeffery, L., 163
Jenkins, W., 346
Jennings, J. L., 3
Jernigan, T. L., 106
Jessen, H. L., 45
Jha, A. P., 130
Johns, P., 112

Johnson, D. W., 220, 237, 245, 247
Johnson, M., 38
Johnson, M. K., 167, 254
Johnson, R. T., 220, 237, 245, 247
Johnson, S. L., 118
Jolin, E. M., 114
Jones, S. M., 109
Jones, S. R., 132
Jonich, G. M., 8, 9, 178
Jorgensen, R., 274
Jöstl, G., 306
Juffer, F., 290
Jusczyk, P. W., 151, 385
Justice, L. M., 144, 290

Kabat-Zinn, J., 130, 132–33
Kaderavek, J. N., 144
Kahn, D., 280
Kamins, M. L., 301
Kane, M. J., 235
Kang, M. J., 117, 140, 161
Karlson, A. L., 24, 384
Karnes, M., 33–34, 355
Kaschak, M. P., 53
Kaufman, K., 307
Kautz, T., 109
Kavanagh, K., 290
Kawakubo, Y., 106
Keller, T., 170
Kelly, J., 325
Kelly, Y., 325
Keltner, B., 321
Kemler Nelson, D. G., 385
Kendal, R. L., 226
Kennedy, C., 55
Kennedy, C. B., 151
Kere, J., 113
Kerns, K., 106–8, 111
Kerr, C. E., 132
Keupp, S., 124
Khazanchi, S., 189
Kidd, C., 117
Kidd, E., 374
Killen, M., 234
Killingsworth, M. A., 111
Kilpatrick, W. H., 297, 393–94
Kim, S., 109
Kindlon, D., 296
King, A., 220
King, J. A., 232
King, L., 2
King, R. B., 2
Kinzler, K. D., 227
Kiraly, I., 223
Kirkham, J. A., 374

Kistner, J. A., 302
Kitayama, S., 82
Klahr, D., 324, 381
Klaus, R. A., 316, 322
Kleim, J. A., 43
Kleven, G. A., 43
Kline, C. A., 319
Klingberg, T., 112–13, 164
Kochanska, G., 108–9
Koenig, M. A., 227
Koestner, R., 182, 307
Kohn, A., 81, 178
Kolstad, V., 271
Konopak, B., 12
Kornell, N., 235
Krafft, K. C., 366
Kramer, R., 14, 16, 27
Krantz, D. S., 341
Krapp, A., 139–40
Krauss, R. M., 54
Kristen, S., 41
Krompinger, J., 130
Kruger, A. C., 222, 249
Kruglanski, A. W., 181, 185
Ku, G., 224
Kubovy, M., 121, 203
Kuhn, D., 10, 117, 234, 248
Kulhavy, R. W., 312
Kulik, C. C., 237
Kulik, J. A., 237
Kunze, S., 130
Kurosawa, K., 196
Kusché, C. A., 113

Lacey, B. W., 85
Ladd, G. W., 364
Laguardia, J. G., 182
Lai, C. S. W., 325
Laird, J. D., 55
Lakoff, G., 38
Lamb, M. E., 288, 323
Lamborn, S. D., 293
Lancy, D. F., 124, 160, 258
Landry, S. H., 295
Langer, E. J., 87
Langlois, J. H., 163
Larkin, J. H., 171
Laski, E. V., 375
Latham, S., 7
Lauricella, A., 114
Lave, J., 252, 270
Layzer, C., 210
Lazar, S. W., 130, 131, 132
Lazarowitz, R., 238
LeBarton, E. S., 66

Lebel, C., 32
LeCompte, M. D., 5, 7
Lee, K., 112, 113, 210
Lee, S.-Y., 220
Leer, M. N., 142
Lehrer, P. M., 333
Lemery, C. R., 56
Lemola, S., 343
Leong, D., 113, 210
Lepore, S. J., 333
Lepper, M. R., 82, 84, 95, 100, 102, 128, 179–81, 183, 197, 205, 247, 255, 281
Lerman, S., 274
Lesgold, A. M., 331
Lesgold, S. B., 142
Levin, G., 214
Levin, I., 52
Lewis, M., 87
Lewkowicz, D. J., 148
Li, D., 113
Li, W., 325
Light, P., 237
Lightel, J., 319
Li-Grining, C., 109
Liker, J. K., 259
Lillard, A. S., 33, 43, 47, 113, 115, 124, 132, 160, 164, 210–12, 214, 222, 224, 260, 346, 364, 367, 371, 388, 390
Lillard, P. P., 45, 208, 336
Lindqvist, S., 112
Linebarger, D. L., 342
Linkenauger, S. A., 40
Lipsey, M. W., 210
Lipsky, D. K., 138, 354
Litwin, G. H., 196
Liu, D., 368
Llinas, R. R., 39
Lobo, M., 43
Locke, J., 8
Loef, M., 10
Logan, G. D., 107
Lonigan, C. J., 144, 211
Lopata, C., 365, 373
Lorenz, K., 32
Lovelace, S. G., 320
Loveless, T., 3
Loxterman, J. A., 171
Lozano, P., 113
Lubart, T., 373
Lucarelli, M. J., 56
Lucker, W., 238
Ludwig, J. L., 323
Luetkenhaus, P., 286
Lüftenegger, M., 306
Luna, B., 108

Lv, Y., 118
Lyons, K. E., 132
Lyubomirsky, S., 2

Ma, F., 118
Ma, L., 325
Ma, W., 385
MacAllister, J. W., 342
Macari, S., 143
McCall, R. B., 151
McCandliss, B. D., 112
McCaslin, M., 13
McClary, A., 44
McClintic-Gilbert, M. S., 195
Maccoby, E. E., 293
McCullers, J. C., 187
McDermott, J., 171
McDonald, A. S., 196
McEwen, I., 40
McGhee, P. E., 86
McGraw, K. O., 183, 187
McInerney, D. M., 2
McKee, C. B., 227
McKeown, M. G., 171
McKinnon, R. D., 109
McLaren, J., 163
MacMillan, M., 106
McNeil, N. M., 70
McNeill, D., 54
McPhee, L., 118
McWilliam, R. A., 228
Maehr, M. L., 2, 195
Mahajan, N., 144
Maheady, L., 231, 237
Malinowski, P., 130
Manches, A., 53, 63
Manderlink, G., 183
Mann, F. D., 112
Manzano, I., 272
Maquet, P., 325
Mark, G., 112, 126
Markell, R. A., 142
Markman, A. B., 209
Markman, E. M., 225
Markson, L., 169
Markus, H. R., 82
Marley, S. C., 70
Marques, H. G., 43
Martin, J. A., 293
Maruyama, G., 237
Mashburn, A. J., 290
Mason, J., 144
Matas, L., 286, 290
Matheny, A. P., 323
Matsson, H., 113

Maxwell, L. E., 341
Mayer, R. E., 3
May-Plumlee, T., 190
Mead, M., 393
Meaney, M., 220, 286, 287
Melis, A. P., 239
Meltzhoff, A. N., 118, 223
Merrick, S., 288
Mertheimer, M., 270
Mervis, J., 33
Merzenich, M. M., 343, 345–46
Messer, D. J., 241
Metcalfe, J., 51
Meyer, C. S., 343
Midgley, C., 195–96, 306
Miller, L. B., 33, 34, 187, 355, 390
Miller-Loncar, C. L., 295
Mills, P., 322
Minton, J. L., 117
Mischel, W., 108–9, 360
Mistry, J., 331
Mitchell, Z. A., 76
Mix, K. S., 59, 375
Miyake, A., 107
Moch-Sibony, A., 341
Moffitt, T. E., 109–10
Mohr, G., 54
Mol, S. E., 26
Mondillon, L., 56
Montagna, D., 232
Montessori, M., *See* Subject Index
Montgomery, R., 241
Montie, J. E., 44
Monty, R. A., 83
Moon, R. Y., 45
Moore, A., 130, 131
Moore, C., 12
Moore, C. I., 132
Moore, D. S., 287, 351
Moore, M. K., 223
Moses, L. J., 111
Moss, E., 290
Mounts, N. S., 293
Mueller, C. M., 299
Mueller, P. A., 312
Müeller, U., 106–8, 111
Mullett, J., 56
Munro, S., 210
Murphy, S. T., 56
Murrah, W. M., 41
Murray, K. T., 108
Musser, L. M., 242

Nadler, A., 191
Nagar, D., 333

Nagasaka, T., 70
Nastasi, B. K., 319
Nathanson, A. I., 114
National Association for the Education of
    Young Children, 220
National Council of Teachers of Mathematics, 281
National Research Council, 170–72
National Study of Early Child Care, 288, 351, 359
Needham, A., 40, 41
Nelson, D., 237
Nelson, J. L., 6
Nestojko, J. F., 235
Neuenschwander, R., 109
Neumann, R., 223
Newcombe, N. S., 59, 143
Newland, R., 70
Newport, E. L., 344
Nezlek, J., 306
Nicklin, J. M., 183
Nicosia, G., 334
Niedenthal, P. M., 55–56
Nielsen, M., 227
Nigam, M., 324, 381
Nikkelen, S. W., 114
Nisan, M., 193
Nisbett, R. E., 47, 180, 220
Nishida, T. K., 138, 354
Noice, H., 55
Noice, T., 55
Nordling, J. K., 109
Nutley, S., 112

Obama, B., 3
O'Brien, C., 323
O'Brien, M. A., 290
Ochs, E., 54
O'Conaill, B., 126
O'Connor, T. M., 118
O'Doherty, K., 70
O'Donnell, A. M., 220
O'Donnell, M., 14
Okada, T., 237
Olsen, B., 306
O'Malley, C., 53, 63
Oper, S., 28
Oppenheim, D., 288
Oppenheimer, D. M., 312, 387
Ott, U., 130
Ottolini, M. C., 45
Over, H., 239
Overbeek, G., 302
Owen, M. J., 113

Paas, F., 53, 70
Padmanabhan, A., 108

Pagani, L. S., 114
Paige, L., 4, 353
Palincsar, S., 238
Palsane, M. N., 333
Pandey, J., 333
Papert, W., 255
Parish-Morris, J., 144, 161
Parke, R. D., 341
Parker, L. E., 255
Partlow, M. E., 191
Pasley, J. D., 14
Pasupathi, M., 139
Patall, E. A., 81, 83, 91, 95
Pate, R. R., 74, 375
Patnoe, S., 237
Paulsen, D. J., 108
Pavenstedt, E., 316
Peake, P. K., 109
Peisner-Feinberg, E. S., 318
Pellegrini, A., 73
Pellis, S. M., 220
Pellis, V. C., 220
Pentz, M. A., 113
Perfetti, C. A., 26
Perlmuter, L. C., 83
Perner, J., 360
Perry, J. D., 319
Perry, M., 76, 77, 78
Person, N. K., 249
Perst, H., 41
Pesetsky, D., 26
Peterman, K., 40
Petersen, S. E., 107
Peterson, E., 342
Peterson, J., 114–15, 164
Peterson, P. L., 10, 12
Petitto, L. A., 67
Petrill, S. A., 324
Petty, K., 373
Petty, R. E., 53
Peyrard-Janvid, M., 113
Phelps, E., 237, 238
Phillips, B. M., 211
Phillips, K., 323
Piaget, J., 10, 15, 27–28, 66, 75, 139, 220, 234,
    238, 248, 257, 338, 352, 394–95
Pianta, R. C., 7, 34, 219, 288, 290
Piantadosi, S. T., 117
Pierce, W. D., 182
Pierroutsakos, S. L., 69
Pietromonaco, P., 55
Pine, K. J., 241
Pinkham, A., 210
Piper, M. C., 322
Pisoni, D. B., 151

Pittman, T. S., 85
Plato, 344
Plomin, R., 323–24
Plötner, M., 239
Polich, J., 132
Polirstok, S. R., 235
Polonia, A., 227
Poole, G., 317
Porac, J., 181
Posner, M. I., 107, 112, 130
Pottish-Lewis, P., 154
Poulin-Dubois, D., 227
Pouw, W. T., 53, 70
Povell, P., 14
Power, T. G., 118
Pressler, E., 109
Proffitt, D. R., 40

Qin, Y., 175, 237
Quinn, H., 170

Rahinel, R., 334
Rakoczy, H., 124
Ramani, G. B., 239
Ramey, C. T., 86, 322–23
Ramirez, J., 114
Ramsay, M. K., 322
Randall, S. N., 142
Rankin, R. E., 187
Rasmussen, E. E., 114
Rathunde, K. R., 142, 195, 214, 247, 297, 363, 373
Ratner, H. H., 222
Rattan, A., 301
Raudenbush, S. W., 11, 66
Raver, C. C., 109, 113, 211
Ravitch, D., 394
Raviv, A., 325
Rayner, K., 26
Razza, R. P., 106, 109, 111
Reader, M. J., 101
Redden, J. P., 334
Reder, L. M., 252
Reiss, D., 316
Renninger, K. A., 11, 137, 139–41, 143–45, 215
Resnick, L. B., 8, 142, 395–96
Rhodes, G., 163
Rice, K., 286
Rice, T., 323
Richert, R. A., 212
Richey, E., 115, 164, 222
Rieser, J. J., 52
Rieser, M., 110
Riggio, R. E., 231
Riggs, N. R., 111
Rinck, M., 56

Rivest, L.-P., 242
Roberts, M. S., 101
Robertson, B., 302
Robinson, H. A., 260
Robinson, J. C., 81, 83
Robinson, S., 39, 42, 43
Robinson, S. R., 43
Rochat, P., 68
Rodin, J., 87, 333
Rodriquez, M. L., 109
Roebers, C. M., 109
Rogoff, B., 13, 233–34, 237–38, 250, 331,
   386–87, 392
Rohrbeck, C. A., 231
Roisman, G. I., 286
Romek, E., 191
Rorem, A., 7
Rosenfield, D., 238
Rosenzweig, M. R., 189
Ross, D., 222
Ross, S. A., 222
Ross, S. M., 141–42, 254
Rotgans, J. I., 143, 161
Rothbart, M. K., 111, 112
Rothe, A. R., 55
Röthlisberger, M., 109
Rothman, G. R., 117, 234
Rousseau, J.-J., 344
Rovee, G. B., 118
Rovee-Collier, C., 43, 87, 118
Rowe, M. L., 66
Rowlands, A., 374
Rubin, K., 361
Rueda, M. R., 112–13
Ruff, H. A., 111
Rumbaugh, D. M., 112
Russell, J. E., 8
Ruzany, N., 191, 194
Ryalls, B. O., 118, 227
Ryalls, K. R., 118, 227
Ryan, R. M., 82, 89, 101, 182, 185, 196, 306–7

Sacchet, M. D., 132
Saccomanno, L., 112
Sachs, H. C., 45
Sacker, A., 325
Sackett, G., 119
Sadeh, A., 325
Saegert, S., 333
Sagi, A., 288
Sagotsky, G., 102, 183
Sainato, D. M., 231
Salerno, K., 342
Sansone, C., 139, 183
Santucci, S., 346

Sarama, J., 210
Sauer, E., 67
Sauter, S. L., 330
Sawyer, K., 239
Sayeki, Y., 70
Schiavio, A., 41
Schiefele, U., 140, 142
Schlam, T. R., 109
Schleifer, L. M., 330
Schliemann, A. D., 270
Schlip, P., 2
Schmidt, H. G., 143, 161
Schober, B., 306
Schroeder, W. H., 273
Schul, Y., 235, 236
Schuman-Olivier, Z., 130
Schunk, D. H., 195
Schwartz, A. J., 89, 305–6
Schwartz, B., 82, 95, 97
Schwartz, D. L., 52
Schwarz, M., 130
Schweingruber, H., 170
Schweinhart, L. J., 44
Scott, C. L., 55
Sedlmeier, P., 130–31
Seehagen, S., 227
Segal, Z. V., 131
Seguin, E., 15
Seidenberg, M. S., 26
Seifer, R., 326
Selig, J. P., 70
Seligman, M. E., 83, 88
Sellen, O., 54
Seltman, H., 332
Semb, G., 101
Sethi, S., 179
Sexton, D., 306
Seymour, F. W., 317
Shaefer Zemer, R., 116
Sham, P. C., 113
Shamas-Brandt, E., 374
Shamay-Tsoory, S. G., 132
Shanock, L., 189
Shapira, Z., 184
Shapira-Friedman, A., 191
Shapiro, L. A., 38
Sharp, M. L., 114
Sheinman, L., 89, 306
Shejwal, B. R., 333
Sherman, L. J., 286
Shewedel, A., 33, 355
Shiffman, J., 375
Shiffrar, M. M., 272
Shirey, L., 144
Shoda, Y., 109

Shouse, R., 253, 281
Shuck, L., 342
Shutts, K., 227
Siegler, R. S., 52, 78, 221
Sikes, J., 238
Silver, L., 312
Simcock, G., 143
Simmonds, F., 123
Simon, D. P., 171
Simon, H. A., 139, 171, 175, 237, 252, 258
Simpson, M. L., 142
Sinatra, G. M., 171
Singer, D., 210, 215
Singer, J. E., 83, 340
Singer, M. A., 77
Singley, M. K., 271
Skon, L., 237
Slavin, R. E., 237–38, 247
Smagorinsky, P., 12
Smith, C. L., 191
Smith, E. D., 115, 164, 210, 222, 224
Smith, E. I., 212
Smith, I. M., 107
Smith, K. E., 295
Smith, L. B., 375
Smith, P. S., 14
Smith, S. M., 272
Sobel, D., 211
Söderqvist, S., 113
Sodian, B., 41
Solomon, J., 285
Sommerville, J. A., 41
Soundy, C., 212
Sowell, E. R., 106
Spearman, C., 343, 380
Spelke, E. S., 227, 344, 351
Spiefel, N. H., 307
Spieker, S., 286
Spiel, C., 306
Sroufe, L. A., 285–86
Stallings, J. A., 217
Standing, E. M., 14, 94
Stanovich, K. E., 26
Staples, M., 277, 303
Steele, J. S., 41
Steenari, M.-R., 325
Stefanucci, J. K., 40
Steinberg, J., 388
Steinberg, L., 293, 352
Steinglass, P., 316
Stephenson, M. E., 119
Sternberg, R. J., 70
Stevenson, H. W., 220
Stevenson, M. B., 323
Stickgold, R., 325

Stigler, J. W., 14, 53, 194, 220, 275, 317
Stipek, D., 2, 217, 281, 306
Stockton, J. D. S., 375
Stockton, L., 320
Stodolsky, S. S., 24, 384
Stokols, D., 341
Strack, F., 223
Strathern, A. J., 258
Strbac, L., 342
Striano, T., 68
Su, Y., 228
Sullivan, M. W., 87
Sullivan, P., 274
Swank, P. R., 295
Swann, W. B., 85
Swanson, N. G., 330
Swing, E. L., 114
Szegda, M., 55

Tanaka, A., 288
Tanaka, M., 40
Tandon, P. S., 113
Tang, Y. Y., 130–31
Tao, S., 42
Tare, M., 144
Taylor, C., 163
Taylor, E. V., 271
Taylor, M., 214
Teasley, S. D., 237
Tenenbaum, H. R., 3, 210
Teng, P., 118
Tennie, C., 239
Teper, R., 131
Terry, B., 232
Thelen, E., 38
Thich Nacht Hanh, 132, 135
Thoermer, C., 41
Thomaes, S., 302
Thoman, D. B., 139, 160
Thomas, E. L., 260
Thomas, J., 210
Thompson, B. E., 258
Thompson, D. E., 334
Thompson, L. A., 323–24
Thompson, P. M., 106
Thompson, R. A., 286
Thorell, L., 112
Thorndike, E. L., 8–11, 139, 153, 254, 283
Timmers, R., 41
Tobias, S., 139, 167
Toga, A. W., 106
Tomasello, M., 68, 190, 222–23, 237, 239–40
Tomlinson, C. A., 12
Topping, K., 222
Toupin, C., 271

Treboux, D., 287–88
Treisman, A. M., 58, 348
Trzesniewski, K. H., 192
Tucker, M., 54
Tucker-Drob, E. M., 112
Tudge, J. R. H., 220
Tullos, A., 209
Turek, C., 41
Turiel, E., 117, 234
Turkanis, C. G., 13, 238, 250, 387, 392
Turner, K., 211

Ueno, N., 70
Unlu, F., 210
Urban, J., 286
Urry, H. L., 132
Uskul, A. K., 82
Utley, C. A., 232
Uttal, D. H., 69–70
Uzgiris, I. C., 51, 333

Vago, D. R., 130
Valkenburg, P. M., 114
Vandell, D. L., 352
Vandergrift, N., 352
Van Driel, J. H., 171
Van Gog, T., 53, 70
van Ijzendoorn, M. H., 287–88, 290
Van Zandt, T., 107
Vasilyeva, M., 375
Vaughan, J. L., 140, 175
Vaughn, B. E., 290
Verbruggen, F., 107
Verdine, B. N., 59
Vermeulen, N., 56
Verschueren, K., 288
Vezeau, C., 195
Viken, R. J., 320
Villarosa, J. B., 2
Vohs, K. D., 334
von Hofsten, C., 41
Vygotsky, L. S., 78, 220, 238, 248, 290, 395

Wachs, T. D., 317, 320, 323, 333–34, 339
Wagener, J. J., 55
Wagenmakers, E.-J., 107
Walberg, H. J., 3
Wales, J., 4, 353
Walker, D., 232
Wall, S., 288
Wallace, N. V., 365
Wallbott, H. G., 56
Walsh, B. A., 373
Walsh, D. A., 114
Wang, C. S., 224

Wang, M. C., 3
Wang, M.-T., 2, 137, 252
Wang, Y., 228
Wang, Z., 324
Want, S. C., 223
Ward, E. J., 345
Warneken, F., 190, 239
Washburn, D. A., 112
Watanabe, M., 330
Waters, E., 287, 288
Watson, J., 361
Watson, J. S., 86
Wegner, D. M., 107
Weinfield, N. S., 285–86
Weisberg, D., 211
Weiss, I. R., 14, 154
Weller, R. A., 114
Wellman, H. M., 111, 265, 361, 368
Wells, G. L., 53
Wenger, E., 252
Wentworth, R. A. L., 383
Wentzel, K. R., 304
Westerberg, H., 164
Whipple, N., 296
White, J. M., 352
Whitehurst, G. J., 144
Whiten, A., 227
Whitson, J., 82
Wiebe, S. A., 109
Wigfield, A., 142, 179, 182, 196
Williams, L. R., 293
Williams, M., 33, 355
Willingham, D. B., 270, 272
Willms, J. D., 230
Willoughby, M. T., 109
Wilson, N. L., 109
Wilson, S. J., 210
Wimmer, H., 360
Wineburg, S., 272
Winkielman, P., 56
Winning, A. P., 131
Winsler, A., 374
Winteler, A., 140
Winzenz, D., 331
Witt, J. K., 40, 51
Witzki, A. H., 107
Wohlwill, J. F., 339, 342
Wolin, S. J., 316
Wompack, J., 13
Wood, L. A., 226–27
Woodward, A. L., 41
Woodworth, R. S., 153
Woolfolk, R. L., 333
Woolley, J. D., 209, 211
Wormington, S. V., 179

Wozniak, P., 295
Wozniak, R. H., 144
Wright, S., 237
Wright, W., 4, 353
Wyman, E., 239
Wynn, S. R., 91

Xerri, C., 346
Xiang, Z., 44
Xiao, Y., 118
Xu, F., 118

Yang, G., 325
Yeager, D. S., 195
Yoon, J. E., 109
Young, M. F., 52
Yussen, S. R., 352

Zack, E., 114
Zajonc, R. B., 55–56, 205, 236
Zeevi, G., 181
Zelazo, P. D., 108, 132
Zerwas, S., 239
Zhai, F., 109
Zhang, T., 220, 287
Zhang, Y., 332
Zhou, C., 113
Zhu, R., 334
Ziegert, D. I., 302
Zigler, E., 7, 219
Zilversmit, A., 10–11, 393, 396
Zimmer, H. D., 54
Zimmerman, F. J., 114
Zimmermann, D., 130
Zmyj, N., 227

SUBJECT INDEX

References to figures are denoted by an italicized *f*

ability grouping, 18, 196, 228–29
The Absorbent Mind (Montessori), 148, 391
abstraction, human tendency, 120
active learning, peers, 249
Activities and Feelings, 363
AdLib game, 100–101
adolescents, 133, 137
    Erdkinder program, 279–81
    growth in, 366
    impact of routines, 319–20
    parenting of, 294, 296
    risk-taking by, 108
Adult Attachment Interview, 287
adult-child interaction, 28, 31–32
    attachment, 284–91
    child's self theories and, 298–302
    conventional teachers, 283
    Going Out trips, 72–73
    guidelines for Montessori, 283–84
    Montessori call for freedom within
        boundaries, 296–98
    Montessori teachers, 291–93
    parenting styles, 293–96
    teacher and child, 303–7
The Advanced Montessori Method II
    (Montessori), 160
aesthetics, 161, 163, 336–37
aggression, 90, 109, 112, 364
altruism, 191
Amber Hill school, 275–77
American Montessori Society (AMS), 375
American Psychological Association
    (APA), 378–80
Applied Problems, Woodcock-Johnson test,
    359, 370, 372*f*
Aronson, Elliot, 327
artistic competence, creativity and,
    188–89
assimilation, 259–60
associationist theory of learning, 396
Association Montessori Internationale (AMI),
    16, 34, 138, 262, 310, 312–13, 354, 356, 382,
    390, 392
associative learning, 331, 396

attachment, 284–91
    antecedents of secure, 288–91
    beyond infancy, 287–88
    epigenetic mechanisms, 286–87
    insecure, 285–86, 288, 292
    outcomes by style, 285–86
    secure, 284–88, 291
    sensitivity and, 290
    Strange Situation paradigm, 285, 287–88, 290
attention, 19
    adult-child interactions, 289, 294, 308
    choice, 99, 102
    control of, 378
    executive function, 107–13, 115–19,
        121–26, 386
    focused, 139–40
    interest and, 161–65, 167
    lesson of Silence for, 385
    meaningful contexts, 275
    memory and, 144–45
    mindfulness, 132–33
    Montessori education, 28, 29, 386,
        388, 390–91
    motivation and, 250
    movement and cognition, 60, 72–73
    noisy environs, 339–40
    order and, 324, 326, 329, 332
    rewards and, 187, 191, 200, 207, 210
    selective shifts, 148
    training, 130–31
    Walking on the Line, 134–36
attention deficit hyperactivity disorder
    (ADHD), 110, 112–14
auditory discrimination skills, noisy
    environment, 340
authoritarian parents, 31–32, 89
    feedback, 304
    research on, 295, 298
    style, 293*f*, 293–94
authoritative parents, 32, 89, 284
    Montessori and, 296–98, 304, 307, 309
    order, 324
    research on, 295
    warmth and control, 293*f*, 294

autonomy, 82
  children, 89–90
  classroom, 305–7
  parental support, 296

babies. *See* infants
baby talk, 151–52
back-to-basics program, 365, 381–82
Bank Game, 174, 244
Bead Bars, 64
Bead Chains, 64, 65*f*, 66*f*
beauty, inspiring interest, 161
bedtime routine, 318–21, 325–26
behavioral management, 105
behaviorism, 4, 8–10
  constructivism over, 10
  Montessori education, 393–94
  observation and imitation, 222
  order, 315
  reward/punishment, 139, 178, 180
Big Bang, 156
Binomial Cube, 68–69, 69*f*, 169, 278
Birth of the Universe, 155–56
blank-slate model, 1, 8, 38
Boaler's case studies, 274–77
Bobbitt, John Franklin, 6
botany, movement in, 70–71
Botany Cabinet, 21, 22*f*
brain, 235, 292
  executive function, 106, 108
  learning language, 148
  memory and, 161
  movement and cognition, 28, 32, 39, 51
  neural changes, 131–32
  order in, 317, 342–43, 345–47, 349
  Sensorial Materials and, 57
  visual areas of, 151
Brown Stair, 57, 60, 61*f*, 64, 125, 129, 337
buddy reading, 113
bullying, 74
Button Frame, 146, 337
buyer's regret, 97

Caillou (television series), 114
Candy Witch, 209
Casa dei Bambini, 16, 17*f*
CHAOS (Confusion, Hubub, and Order
  Scale), 323
The Child in the Family (Montessori), 391
children
  attachment, 284–91
  choice and task performance, 83–87
  gesture and symbolic understanding, 66–68
  learning and noisy environment, 339–42
  Montessori and structure, 384

Montessori's suitability, 389–90
  observations of, 213
  orderly routines for young, 320–26
  play of elementary, 212–13
  prosocial behavior, 189–92
  reactions to Montessori, 214
  research on play and fantasy in young, 209–17
  self-control of, 109–11
  self theories, 298–302
  sleep routines, 325–26
  teacher expectations and control, 303–7
  teacher ways and ways of, 31–32
  television and executive function of, 113–15
  temporal order and elementary
    school, 319–20
choice
  balancing control and, 324
  benefits of limited, 95
  self-development, 99–100
  societal limitations, 98–99
  see also free choice
Christmas myths, 209, 212
classic-supplemented study, Montessori, 367–72
classroom, Montessori
  activity cycle, 123*f*
  classroom autonomy, 305–7
  computer-aided instruction, 387–88
  environment facilitating
    concentration, 122–24
  establishing a new, 308–9
  choices, 81, 95–97
  functioning without rewards and evaluation,
    199–207
  furniture, 94
  limiting choice in, 95–100
  movement in primary and elementary, 56–66
  number of choices, 95–97
  observation questions, 391
  order of, 9, 32, 93–94, 326–30, 335–37
  parental involvement, 386–87
  quiet in, 19, 128, 133–34, 198, 315, 339, 342–43
  role of Montessori teacher, 307–8
  Sensorial Materials in primary, 57–61
  societal limitations, 98–99
  spatial order in, 335–37
  specification of completion times, 101–3
  teacher expectation and control, 307
  temporal order in, 318, 326–30
classroom visitors, concentration and
    choice, 128–29
class size, 229–30
Coalition for Psychology in Schools and
    Education, 378–80
cognition, 28–29
  distributed, 248–49

gesture leading, 75–76
  movement and, 28–29
  research on, 51–56
cognitive function
  noisy environment, 341–42
  rewards, 185–88
  spatial organization, 331–32
collaborative learning, 237–45
  limiting conditions for beneficial, 240–41
  Montessori education, 242–45
  optimal collaborators, 241–42
  use of rewards in, 245, 246*f*, 247
college, influence of interest, 140–43
Color Tablets, 57, 164, 165*f*, 200, 337, 348–49
Columbia Teachers College, 8, 393–94
Coming of Humans, 156–57
Coming of Life on Earth, 156
Command Cards, 71–72
Common Core standards, 3
Communicating in Signs, 157–58
communication, human tendency, 121
Community of Learners program, 238, 249
competence, 19, 78, 271
  choice and, 89
  elementary children, 319, 333
  executive function, 109, 111, 117
  parenting styles and, 294, 305
  rewards and, 188–89, 217
  social, 109, 111, 361
  well-being, 217, 288
competition, 191
computer-aided instruction
  collaborative learning, 240
  conventional schooling, 164
  Montessori classroom, 387–88
  orienting learners, 255
computer math game
  choice, 84–85, 255–56
  motivation, 261
concentration
  3-hour work cycle, 126–28
  classroom visitors and children's, 128–29
  Montessori education, 115–24
  Montessori environments, 122–24
  Practical Life routines, 329
Concept Formation, Woodcock-Johnson
    test, 360
conceptual learning, 186
conservation tasks, 5, 75–76, 260, 352
constructivism, 10–11
control
  balancing choice and, 324
  locus of, 85–86
  Montessori classroom, 307
  Montessori education, 91–94

parenting, 293*f*
  teacher, and child outcomes, 303–7
  see also autonomy; free choice
control error, human tendency, 121
Control Map, 201
Control of Error, 59, 122, 129, 199, 200–201, 206,
    303, 380
correspondence courses, 382
Cosmic Education, 154
Craig Montessori School, 357–59
crawling, impact of, 39, 42–43, 45, 47–49, 51
The Creative Development of the Child
    (Montessori), 391
creativity
  research, 373–74
  rewards and, 188–89
crisis in education
  dissatisfaction with, 1–2
  pendulum response, 2–4
  poor models, 4–12
crowded environment, 333–34, 339
cubes/cubing, 37, 57–60, 64, 68–70, 162–63, 169,
    190, 243–44, 263, 278
cult, 5, 389
curiosity, 29, 161, 175, 179, 213, 281, 305
curriculum, Montessori
  choice, 100, 102–3
  error control, 59, 200–201
  executive function, 113
  expertise, 170, 171
  field-tested, 16
  generalist *vs.* specialist teachers, 172–73
  integration, 170
  interest, 137–38, 152–54, 158–59, 167–69
  movement, 44, 70–71
  music in, 24
  Sensorial Material, 60
  social behavior, 225–26
  structure, 20, 26–27, 30, 34
curriculum, traditional
  choice, 81–82, 103, 128
  innovations, 13–14
  transfer learning, 272

daily life
  Erdkinder program and, 279–81
  knowledge transfer and, 252–53, 269–77
  as meaningful contexts, 278–79
  play imitation, 326
  see also Practical Life activities
day care, 37, 227, 288, 322–23, 351–52
deadlines, performance and motivation,
    100–101
Delay of Gratification, 360
depression, children, 110, 131, 286, 294

developmental psychology, 32–35, 147
diagramming sentences, 202*f*
Dimensional Change Card Sort (DCCS), 360
direction of effects, 284, 290, 304–6
discovery learning, 3, 9, 324, 330, 381
discrimination learning, 187
distributed cognition, 248–49
Divergent and Convergent Lines, 268, 269*f*
Down Syndrome, 322
drawing game, choice, 85
Dressing Frames, 49–50, 50*f*
Dr. Montessori's Own Handbook, 386
dyslexia, 390

Easter Bunny, 216
education
    balancing expertise and integration, 170–73
    class size, 229–30
    conventional *vs.* Montessori, 377–80
    dissatisfaction with schooling, 1–2
    frequently asked questions about
        Montessori, 380–97
    natural school settings, 88–91
    reform, 377–80
    reward/punishment system and, 177–207
    traditional schools, 10–12, 128, 366, 373
    see also crisis in education; Montessori
        education
Education and the Cult of Efficiency
    (Callahan), 5
Education for Human Development (Mario
    Montessori), 213
education research, executive function, 107
Einstein, Albert, 2
electroencephalography (EEG), 131
elementary school, influence of interest, 140–43
emotion regulation, 106, 111, 130–32, 210
empathy, 31, 111, 131–32, 289
empty-vessel model
    interests and learning, 139
    rewards and punishments, 177–78
    schooling, 8–10, 12–14
entity theory of intelligence, 192–94, 196–97,
    299, 301
environments
    classroom, and learning goals, 194–96
    facilitating concentration, 122–24
    learning and noisy, 339–42
    order in, 32
epigenetic mechanisms, attachment, 286–87
Erdkinder program, 279–81
executive function, 29, 105–7, 109–15
    development of, 108–12
    emotion regulation and empathy, 131–32
    human tendencies, 119–22

neural changes, 131–32
prefrontal processes, 106–7
pretend play, 210–11
psychology and education research, 107
Sensorial Materials, 125–29
television and children's, 113–15
term, 107
what it predicts, 109–12
what predicts, 112–15
Exercises of Practical Life. *See* Practical Life
    activities
Experience Sampling Method, 373
expertise, 171, 258–59
exploration, 119
extensions, 60
extrinsic rewards, 177–79
    artistic competence and creativity, 188–89
    avoiding, 30
    cognitive functioning, 185–88
    collaborative learning programs, 245,
        246*f*, 247
    creativity, 188–89
    enhancing performance, 182–83
    goals, 192–94
    grades, 192–94
    Montessori classroom functioning without,
        199–207
    negative effects of, 181–82
    peer tutoring, 232–33, 245, 246*f*, 247
    prosocial behavior, 189–92
    research on, 179–85, 196–97
    self theories, 192–94

faces, 55–56, 96, 143, 151, 163
factory model, 219, 392
    choice in conventional classroom, 82
    external controls in, 82
    failures in, 315, 378
    failures of, 38, 102, 138, 174, 241
    interests and learning, 138
    meaningful contexts and, 251–52, 266, 275
    rewards/punishment in, 177–78
    school as, 4, 5–7, 12–14, 27, 35
    teaching expectations in, 283–84
fairy tales, 208, 213, 217, 297
false belief test, 228, 360–61, 368–69
familiarity effect, 11, 97, 169, 257–58, 260,
    271–72, 312
fantasy
    play and, 207–9, 211–12
    problem of life without, 216
field trips, 73, 93, 128, 279
fine motor skills, 374–75
fixed entity intelligence theory, 192, 299
Flanker tasks, 113, 131

follow-the-child programs, 396
foreign language learning, 386
The Formation of Man (Montessori), 386
Fraction Insets, 264*f*
free choice, 29, 81–82
  benefits of, 82–88
  classroom visitors and children's, 128–29
  completion times in Montessori classroom, 101–3
  deadline effect on performance and motivation, 100–101
  locus of control, 85–86
  memory and, 83–84
  Montessori education, 91–94
  natural school settings, 88–91
  nutrition, 118
  principle of, 92
  task performance, 83–87
  well-being and, 87–88
Freedman, James O., 388
Freud, Anna, 393
Freud, Sigmund, 389
Froebel, Friedrich, 393
From Childhood to Adolescence (Montessori), 159, 296
Function of Words, 148, 263
furniture, Montessori classroom, 94

Gage, Phineas, 106
gender, 197, 361, 365
  bedtime routines, 319
  imitation, 227
  locus of control, 86
  Montessori education, 353–54, 390
  Montessori's suitability, 389–90
  parenting style, 368, 370
generalist teachers, 172–73
geography, 70–71, 201
Geometric Solids, 162*f*, 162–63
geometry, 96, 158–59, 255, 264, 268
Geometry Cabinet, 21, 22*f*, 23, 263
gesture/gesture-speech mismatches
  instruction and, 76–77
  leading cognition, 75–76
  learning environment through, 75–78
  symbolic understanding and, 66–68
  teachers and, 77–78
Glass Beads, 263
glass materials, 52, 64, 161, 348
goals, 192–94
  classroom environments and learning, 194–96
  movement with, 43
  rewards and motivations, 192–94
"God with No Hands," 155

Going Out trips, 72–73, 146
  knowledge transfer and, 278–79
  meaningful context, 253
  Montessori classroom, 309, 379, 387
  parent participation, 387
Golden Beads, 64, 243*f*, 243–44
Golden Bead Thousand Cube, 163
Goldilocks effects, 117, 126, 147, 150
Good Player Award, 180, 188
Grace and Courtesy, 225–26
grade point average (GPA), 354
grades, rewards and motivations, 192–94
grammar, 16, 71, 81, 148, 160, 263–64, 362, 381
Grammar Box, 102, 201, 245
grasping, 40–41, 44–45
Great Depression, 11, 396
Great Lessons (Great Stories), 154–58, 173, 212, 245, 267
Great Work, 122, 349
guided play, 210, 291

Hall, G. Stanley, 394
Head Start program, 33–34, 103, 321, 355–56, 366, 390
Head Toes Knees Shoulders (HTKS) task, 368, 369*f*, 371
Hershey Montessori Farm School (Cleveland, Ohio), 280–81
HOME (Home Observation for Measurement of the Environment) order, 321–24, 332
Honor Roll Board, 180
Horse report, 174
How Geometry Got Its Name, 158–59
human psychology, mindfulness and, 130–32
human tendencies, 119–22

imagination, 137, 159
  child's, 30, 52, 152–53, 244, 267
  elementary child, 212–13
  human tendency, 120
  life without fantasy, 216
  Montessori education, 152–53
  play and fantasy, 208–9
imitation, 55
  best models for, 226–28
  learning from peers, 222
  Montessori education, 224–25, 230
  observational learning, 223–24, 248, 326
  tasks, 41
implementation
  Montessori program and, 381–89
  variations in Montessori, 365–72, 381–82
incremental theory of intelligence, 192–94, 299, 303
individualized instruction, 5, 12, 191, 230
Industrial Revolution, 5

infants
  attachments beyond infancy, 287–88
  gesture and symbolic understanding, 66–68
  impact of crawling, 42–43
  impact of grasping objects, 40–41
  listening to baby talk, 151–52
  maternal sensitivity beyond infancy, 290–91
  noise effects on, 339, 342
  observational learning, 223
innovation
  children, 392–93
  Montessori system, 383–84
insecure attachment, 285–86, 288, 292
integrative mind-body training (IBMT), 130–31
intelligence
  entity theory of, 192–94, 196–97, 299, 301
  fixed entity theory, 192, 299
  incremental theory of, 192–94, 299, 303
  theories of, 298–99
interest, 29–30
  balancing expertise and integration in
    education, 170–73
  beauty inspiring, 161
  as biologically motivated and
    adaptive, 150–52
  concerns with, driving learning, 173–74
  expertise and teaching, 171
  influence from elementary through
    college, 140–43
  influence on preschoolers, 143–46
  material inspiring, 161–65
  Montessori education, 137–39, 159–60
  Montessori environment and
    materials, 160–65
  Montessori teacher, 165–67
  prior knowledge, 167–69
  reading comprehension, 175
  studies of learning and, 139–46
  see also personal interest; topic interests
intrinsic rewards, 215, 379, 381
IQ (intelligence quotient), 86, 109–10, 259,
  322–24, 343

Jasper project (Vanderbilt University),
  256–57, 268
Jigsaw model, 237–38, 245
Journal, 174, 375–76
judgment, 53–54, 57, 59

Karnes Montessori program, 34
kindergarten, 7, 146, 189, 219, 240, 258, 288, 302,
  317, 322, 375
knowledge
  Erdkinder adolescence program, 279–81
  failure to transfer, 269–71
  orienting learners with old, 254–59
  source and target similarity, 271–74
  successful transfer of, 271–77
  teacher preparation, 311–13
  transfer, 252–53, 269–77
  see also meaningful context

Labyrinth, 101
The Language and Thought of the Child
  (Piaget), 27
language development, Montessori and, 384–85
language learning
  gestures and, 75–78
  home noise and, 341–43
  as innate, 32, 394
  Montessori critics on, 384–85, 386
  movement in, 53–54, 67–68
  nomenclature, 168, 203–4
  phoneme-based, 26, 343, 385, 390
  sensitive period, 147–48
  sensory discrimination, 343
  spelling and, 129, 266–67
learning
  concerns with letting interest drive, 173–74
  in context, 31
  impact of grasping objects, 40–41
  with and from peers, 30–31
  through gesture, 75–78
  see also collaborative learning; meaningful
    context; peer learning
Learning Center, 177
learning disabilities, 7, 390
learning goals, classroom environments
  and, 194–96
lessons
  activity sequence in, 326–28
  extensions of, 60
  five Great Stories as basis of, 154–58,
    171, 267
  Function of Words, 148
  inspiring interest in, 153–59
  integration of, 79, 153–54, 170–73, 237
  observational learning and, 224–25
  teacher's scripts for, 77, 137–38, 145
Letter Word, Woodcock-Johnson test, 359,
  370–71, 371*f*
listening, baby talk, 151–52
Locke, John, 8
Lockean model, schooling, 8–10, 12–14, 396
locomotor experience, 42, 47
locus of control, 85–86
LOGO graphics program, 255
Lorenz, Konrad, 32
low-income children, 109, 231, 270, 274, 316*n*1,
  321, 333, 339, 364

McCarthyism, 11
marshmallow task, 108, 109, 360
Master Mind, 177
mastery orientation
  children beginning school with, 198
  interest, 173
  Montessori education, 303
  response to challenges, 298–99
  teacher expectation and control, 304
materials, Montessori, 23, 30, 34, 356, 394
  abstract concepts, 68–70
  choices, 93–94, 97–98
  clarifying meaning, 265–67
  classic-supplemented study, 367–72
  control of error in, 199, 200–201, 203
  Elementary child, 212–13
  engaging children, 123
  fine motor skills, 374
  generalist *vs.* specialist teachers, 172–73
  gestures, 79
  implementation of, 365–66
  imposed structures, 216, 233
  interest, 136, 137–38, 161–65
  math, 61–66, 375
  movement, 51–53, 56–60
  observational learning, 224–25
  order in Sensory Materials, 347–48
  orderly routines, 318, 320–24
  peer tutoring, 236–37
  play and fantasy, 209–12
  Practical Life routines, 328, 330
  Primary classroom, 312–13
  quality, 353, 355
  sensitive period for order, 338–39
  similarities in play and work, 214–15
  spatial order, 335–37
  surface similarity in, 278
mathematical mind, 329
mathematics
  classroom autonomy, 306
  collaborative learning, 243–45
  enhancing learners, 256–57
  failure to transfer knowledge, 270
  interest and performance, 141–42
  meaningful context of learning, 274–77
  Montessori children, 366, 375
  order in materials, 337
  orienting learners with old knowledge, 254–55
  rendering the symbolic concrete, 68–70
  research, 375
  space, objects and, 51–53
  teaching Pythagorean theorem, 265–66
Math Game, 256
Math Material, 61–66, 169, 172, 203, 256, 324,
    337, 384

mealtime routines, 321, 367
meaning
  clarity of, 265–68
  familiarity on thinking, 257–58
  giving knowledge, 253–61
meaningful context
  assimilation, 259–60
  assisting learning, 259–61
  case studies of learning, 274–77
  conventional schooling, 251–53
  fitting new knowledge with old, 262–65
  influence of expertise, 258–59
  knowledge transfer, 269–77
  Montessori education and, 253, 261–69
  motivation, 261
  orienting learners with old knowledge, 254–59
  processing, 260
  stories for learning, 267–68
mechanisms, peer learning, 247–50
meditation, 130
memory
  children's attention and, 144–45
  choice and, 83–84
  movement and cognition, 54–55
  spatial organization, 331
mental organs, 147
Metal Insets, 19–20, 20*f*, 23–24, 24*f*, 44, 97, 129,
    225, 229, 264
Miller (Louisville) study, 33–34
Milwaukee Montessori outcomes study, 103,
    197, 354–59, 362, 364, 368–70, 373, 375,
    389, 393
mind, order in, 32
mindfulness, 112
  human psychology and, 130–32
  Montessori education, 132–36
  training attention, 130–31
mind modularity theory, 147
misbehavior, 199
  children, 206–7, 308
  choice and control, 98–99
  concentration and, 122
models, best, for imitation, 226–28
moderate discrepancy hypothesis, 117, 147, 151
Montessomething, 353, 366
Montessori, Maria, 1, 11, 13, 35
  adult-child interaction, 283
  attention, 136
  children, 377, 397
  developmental psychology, 32–35
  education, 14–17, 105, 351
  freedom, 81, 98, 103–4
  Going Out trips, 278–79
  incentives, 177
  incremental *vs.* fixed trait feedback, 302–3

Montessori, Maria (*Cont.*)
  interest, 137, 153
  Kilpatrick dismissing, 394–95
  meaningful context, 251, 261
  mental organs, 147
  movement, 37, 39, 56, 78–79
  order, 315, 335
  peer learning, 219–21, 228
  peer tutoring, 230, 236
  perceiving rewards negatively, 198–99
  recess and physical education, 73–75
  teacher characteristics, 291
  teacher preparation, 311
Montessori, Mario, 118, 213
Montessori education
  activities eliciting interest, 159–60
  awakening interests, 137–39
  awareness of, 393–95
  basic development, 46–48
  bringing more children into, 396–97
  Casa dei Bambini, 16, 17*f*
  children misbehaving, 206–7
  children's reaction to, 214
  choice in, 91–94
  collaborative learning, 242–45
  concentration in, 115–24
  control in, 91–94
  control of error, 200–201
  exercises of practical life, 48–51
  freedom within boundaries, 296–98
  frequently asked questions, 380–97
  generalist *vs.* specialist teacher, 172–73
  going out of classroom, 72–73
  historical overview, 14–16
  individual personal interests, 152–53
  innovation, 383–84
  interest in, 152–69
  language development, 384–85
  learning in, 20–27
  learning more about, 390–92
  meaningful contexts in learning, 253, 261–69
  mindfulness, 132–36
  models of child and school, 27–28
  movement in infant-toddler and primary
    programs, 44–48
  movement in other domains, 70–73
  observational learning in, 224–25
  parental involvement, 386–87
  peer learning, 220–22
  peers for feedback and inspiration, 205–6
  peer tutoring in, 236–37
  personal interests in, 146–53
  play and fantasy, 208–9
  portrait of classroom, 18*f*, 18–20
  prepared environment of, 93–94
  principles of, 28–32
  rendering the symbolic concrete, 68–70
  repetition, 203
  Science study (2006), 355–65
  Silence, 133–34
  similarities between play and, 214–16
  social behavior learning, 225–26
  standardized tests, 206
  standard materials, 201–3
  teachers and interest, 165–67
  teacher's ongoing evaluation, 204–5
  technology in classroom, 387–89
  theory, 116–22
  three period lesson, 203–4
  three-year age grouping, 228–29
  topic interest, 153–69
  transfer in, 278–81
  variations in implementation, 365–72
  Walking on the Line, 134–36, 135*f*
  writing and reading, 20–27
Montessori High School (Cleveland), 280
Montessori Middle School study, 214, 247,
    297, 373
The Montessori System Examined
    (Kilpatrick), 393
Montessori teacher
  expectation and control, 303–7
  preparation of, 310–13
  role of, 307–8
  training, 309–12
  warmth and sensitivity of, 291–93
Montessori theory
  normalization, 116–19
  research, 351–55
mother
  education, 296
  habitual use of rewards, 190–91
  infant's sleep position, 46
  interaction with children, 43
  IQ, 323
  language development in children, 67
  routine regularity and, 319–22, 338, 344
  secure attachment, 288–91
  sensitivity, 288, 290–91
motivation
  education reform, 379
  effect of deadlines, 100–101
  extrinsic rewards and, 177–79
  peer learning, 249–50
  research on, 179–85
  social climate and, 373
  studies on, 183–85
motivational deficit, 179
Movable Alphabet, 25–26, 99–100, 169, 170*f*,
    229, 337

movement, 28–29
    basic developmental processes, 38–43
    cognition and, 28–29
    conventional classrooms, 37–38
    crawling, 42–43, 44–45
    education of, 329
    with goals, 43
    grasping, 40–41, 44–45
    infant-toddler and primary programs, 44–48
    judgment and, 53–54
    other domains in Montessori
        education, 70–73
    research on, 51–56
    self-locomotion, 42–43, 45–46
    spatial order of classroom, 337
Multiplication Board, 201, 202*f*
Multiplication Rule, 255
Multiplication Table, 201–2
music, 16, 18–20, 24, 25*f*, 37, 71, 92, 96, 128, 142,
    161, 225, 337, 342–43, 368
Musical Bells, 37, 92, 92*f*, 127, 337, 385

Narrative Completion, 362
National Assessment of Educational Progress
    (NAEP), 3–4
natural school settings, choice, 88–91
neglecting parents, 293*f*, 294
neural function, 375–76
No Child Left Behind, 3, 362, 377
noisy environment, 339–42
normalization, Montessori theory, 116–19
Number Rods, 61–64, 62*f*

obesity, childhood, 74–75
object manipulation, 28
object permanence, 320, 339
observational learning
    class size, 229–30
    experimental findings, 223–24
    imitation and, 222–30
    Montessori education, 224–25
    Montessori's 3-year age grouping, 228–29
    social behavior in Montessori, 225–26
Ohio Hershey Montessori Farm School, 280
open-ended solutions, 182, 193
order
    aesthetics, 336–37
    conventional classrooms, 315–16
    crowded environments, 333–34, 339
    education of senses, 343–47
    environment and mind, 32
    human tendency, 119–20
    Montessori classroom, 93–94, 326–30
    Montessori's claim of sensitive period
        for, 338–39

noisy environs lacking, 339–42
    physical, in larger space, 332–34
    Sensory Materials of the primary, 347–49
    spatial, in Montessori classroom, 335–37
    spatial organization and outcomes, 330–34
    temporal, 317–26
orientation, 88–90, 119
origin orientation, classrooms, 88–90
overimitation, 124, 329

parents/parenting
    attachment beyond infancy, 287–88
    fantasy perpetuation by, 209, 216
    Going Out trip, 279
    healthy diet/exercise as responsibility
        of, 74–75
    involvement in Montessori, 386–87
    noisy environment and, 339–42
    praise from, 128–29, 191
    research, 295–96
    school choice by, 274
    styles, 284, 291, 293–94, 296, 298
    warmth and control of, 293*f*
Pascal, Blaise, 329
PATHS (Promoting Alternative Thinking
    Strategies), 113
pawn orientations, classrooms, 88–90
peer learning, 30–31, 219–22
    class size, 229–30
    imitation models, 226–28
    language lesson, 221, 221*f*
    mechanisms of, 247–50
    Montessori education, 205–6
    observation and imitation, 222–30
    social behavior, 225–26
    three-year age grouping, 228–29
    see also collaborative learning
peer tutoring, 230–37
    adults *vs.* peers, 233
    benefits of being a tutor, 234–36
    conventional school programs, 231–32
    Montessori education, 236–37
    optimum level of peer tutee, 233–34
    structure and rewards in, 232–33
    use of rewards in, 245, 246*f*, 247
Peg Board, 245
perception, 344, 395
    adult interactions, 304–6
    choice and control, 82, 89–90
    color, 348
    interest and, 142, 163
    moderate discrepancy hypothesis and, 117,
        147, 151
    noisy environ and, 344–46
    reality, 209, 211, 300

perception (*Cont.*)
  rewards and performance, 177–78, 191, 194
  self-generated locomotion and, 40, 42
  sensitive period and, 149
  Sensorial Materials and, 57–61, 164–66
Perceptual Access task, 369
perfection, 121
performance
  ability-oriented self theory and, 194–96
  adult feedback and, 298–99, 298–301, 302
  deadlines and, 100–101
  executive function predicting, 109
  extrinsic rewards and, 181–83
  fixed entity intelligence theory and, 192, 299
  free choice and, 83–87
  interest and, 141–42, 173–74
  mastery orientation *vs.*, 173, 178, 195–96,
    298–99, 302–4
permissive parenting
  Montessori and, 296–97
  style, 293*f*, 293–94, 296
Perry Preschool Project, 108
personal interests, 137–39
  biologically guided, 146–50
  Montessori education, 146–53
  sensitive periods, 146–50
Pestalozzi, Johann, 393
Phoenix Park school, 275–77
physical education, 73–75, 375
Picture Vocabulary, Woodcock-Johnson test,
    360, 370, 372*f*
Pink Tower, 57–60, 68, 97, 120, 146, 216, 225,
    337, 392
Planes of Development, 208, 234, 280, 353, 356
plants, 5, 22*f*, 39, 47–49, 88, 156, 160, 168, 241,
    307, 337, 362, 366
play
  executive function and pretend, 210–11
  fantasy and, 207–9
  similarities between Montessori education
    and, 214–16
Pledge of Allegiance, 317
points of sensitivity, 147
polishing activity, 124, 125*f*
positive shared play, 361–62
Pottish-Lewis, Phyllis, 154
Practical Life activities, 48–51, 393
  beyond infancy, 48–51
  clear meaning, 265
  executive function, 119, 120–24, 136
  interest, 150, 160
  mindfulness, 133
  Montessori classroom, 308, 326–30,
    335–36, 381
  movement, 39, 329
  routine, 329

Sensorial Materials, 125–26
praise, 128–29, 184, 190–92, 198, 204–5, 217, 300,
    302–3, 309, 393
precision, 37, 124–25, 326, 328–29, 335
  attention and, 125, 135
  child's inclination toward, 48, 120
  human tendency, 120
  sensitive period for, 149–50
predictive validity, 361
prefrontal processes, 106–7
preschoolers
  adult feedback and, 301–2
  attachment style, 286, 287–88
  extrinsic rewards and, 180–83
  familiarity effects on cognition of, 257–58
  interest and, 143–46, 161, 163
  language and, 147–48
  learning three R's, 394
  maternal sensitivity beyond infancy, 290–91
  Montessori's suitability for, 389–90
  reading/writing learning by, 15, 20–27
  sensitive periods and, 146–49
  tutoring by, 228
pretend play, 113, 178, 209–12, 214–15, 217, 368
principles, Montessori education, 28–32
prior knowledge, interest building on, 167–69
problem solving, rewards and, 187
Program for International Student Assessment
    (PISA), 3–4
progressive schools, 377, 381, 396
  critics of, 3, 31–32, 396
prosocial behavior
  executive function, 111
  learning from peers, 239–40
  parenting style and, 295–96, 304
  rewards and, 178, 183, 185, 189–92
  teachers and, 304
  see also misbehavior
psychological deviations, 130
psychology
  executive function, 107
  misbehavior of children, 206–7
puzzles, 55, 69, 71, 83, 100, 143, 161, 180–81, 239,
    240, 278, 295, 334–35, 341, 367, 388
Pythagoras, 158–59, 267
Pythagorean theorem, 265

Q-sort, attachment, 287
quality control, Montessori research, 355
quiet, Montessori classrooms, 19, 128, 133–34,
    198, 315, 339, 342–43

Raven's Progressive Matrices, 131
reading, 3, 13, 15
  auditory discrimination and, 340–42
  buddy, 113

cognitive functioning and, 185–86
comprehension, 175
early introduction, 297, 353, 359, 368
executive function, 108
gender, 390
instruction through writing, 59, 71
interest and, 140–43, 155, 167, 175
learning in Montessori, 20–27
meaningful contexts, 254, 260, 273–74
Montessori teacher, 309
movement in, 37, 44, 51, 56, 71–72
order and, 317
peer tutoring, 231, 235, 245, 249
preschoolers and interest, 143–44
rewards for, 28, 177, 190, 198, 213
real life. *See* daily life; Practical Life activities
recess, 73–75, 78, 82, 128, 177, 215, 250, 268, 317, 330, 361
reciprocal peer tutoring (RPT), 232
recruitment letters, research, 357–59
Red Rods, 57, 60–61, 64, 115, 125, 204, 337, 365
repetition, 9, 60, 121–22, 199, 203, 303, 329
report writing, 205–6, 266, 268, 310
research
    12-year-olds, 362–65
    2006 *Science* study, 355–65
    5-year-olds, 359–62
    benefits of choice, 82–88
    biologically motivated and adaptive interest, 150–52
    choice and well-being, 87–88
    classic-supplemented study, 367–72
    control group, 353
    executive function, 107
    gesture and symbolic understanding, 66–68
    impact of rewards and evaluation, 196–97
    interest and learning, 139–46
    Montessori outcomes, 33–35
    Montessori theory, 351–55
    motivation and rewards, 179–85
    movement and cognition, 51–56
    parenting, 295–96
    play and fantasy, 209–17
    recent, on Montessori, 373–76
    recruitment letters, 357–59
    sample of children, 356–57
rewards. *See* extrinsic rewards
Rope Stretchers, 158, 267
rote learning, 184, 186, 235, 238
Rough and Smooth Boards, 57, 204, 348
Rousseau, Jean-Jacques, 344
Rubin, Ken, 361

Sandman, 209, 212
Sandpaper Letters, 24–25, 25*f*, 37, 63, 96, 146, 337

Sandpaper Numbers, 63
Santa Claus, 209, 212, 216
The Schoolboy (Blake), 1–2
schooling
    choice in conventional classroom, 81–82
    classroom environments and goals, 194–96
    class size, 229–30
    dissatisfaction with, 1–2
    factory model, 4, 5–7
    implications of models for, 12–14
    innovations, 13
    Lockean child, 8–10
    Montessori children in conventional, 103
    motivation, 183–85
    peer learning, 249–50
    peer tutoring, 231–32
    why poor models stick, 10–12
Science study (2006), 355–65
second-language learning, 386
secure attachment, 284–88, 291
Seguin, Eduard, 15, 204, 347
self-control, 105–6
    childhood, 109–11
    social behavior and, 111–12
self-determination theory, 101
self-development, 103, 125–26, 160, 292
    limited choices, 99–100
self-esteem, 142, 286, 302, 306
self-imposed deadlines, 101
self-locomotion, 42–43, 45–46
self-preservation, 121
self-regulation, 104, 106, 292, 359, 366
    children's skills, 207
    concentration and, 116, 308
    executive function, 109–12, 115
    foreign-language learning, 386
    learning, 195, 378
    order and, 319–20, 334
self theories
    adult-child interactions, 298–302
    rewards and motivations, 192–94
senses, order in education of, 343–47
sensitive periods
    language learning, 147–48
    Montessori's claim of, 338–39
    perception of tiny objects, 149
    precision or exactness, 149–50
    walking, 148–49
sensitivity, 288–89
    Ainsworth's concept, 288–89
    attachment and, 290, 311
    maternal, 288
    maternal, beyond infancy, 290–91
    Montessori teachers, 291–93

Sensorial Materials, 120, 123, 165, 169, 200
  concentration, 122, 125–29
  early math, 61–66
  Montessori classroom, 57–61, 123
  movement, 56
sensory discrimination, order, 343–47
Sensory Materials, 326, 346, 347–49
sentences, diagramming, 202*f*
Sesame Street, 87, 257
Shoe Polishing, 328*f*
Siblings, learning from, 242
Silence Game, 133–34, 198, 385
Silver Polishing, 336
Simon, Herbert, 175
Simon Says, 108
Simple Planned Contrasts, 371*f*
sleep, 37
  children and routines, 325–26
  infant position and, 43, 45–47
Smell Cylinders, 349
Smooth Boards, 57, 204, 348
Snake Game, 263, 263*f*
Soccer, 174
social behavior
  learning in Montessori education,
    225–26, 379
  self-regulation and, 111–12
social cognitive processing, 55–56
social interaction, 43, 359
  attachment style and, 284–87, 290
  friendship/learning factor and,
    241–42, 286
  Grace and Courtesy lessons and, 225–26
  large class size and, 229–30
  Montessori *vs.* traditional school, 74, 191
  as motivation, 249–50
  peer tutoring, 242, 248
  playground and, 361–62
Social Problem Solving task, 361, 370, 371*f*
social sharing of knowledge, 268–69
society
  limiting choices, 98–99
  Montessori and, 392–97
sound, 4, 120, 383, 385
  foreign language, 386
  interest in, 138
  for language, 148, 157
  of letters, 24–26
  Montessori teacher, 165–66
  movement, 41, 57
  noisy environs, 339–42
  observational learning, 223
  order, 344–46
  quiet classrooms, 342–43
  Silence Game, 133–34

Sound Cylinders, 57, 81, 165, 166, 200, 337,
    349, 385
Space Quest, 256
spatial organization
  outcomes, 330–34
  physical order in larger space, 332–34
  task-specific, 330–32
Spatial Relations, Woodcock-Johnson test, 360
spatial representation, 42, 51–53
specialist teachers, 172–73
spelling, 129, 266–67
Spindle Box, 63*f*, 63–64
SpongeBob SquarePants (television
    series), 114–15
standardized tests, 3, 11, 34, 179, 199, 206, 307,
    354, 365, 389, 396
Steiner (Waldorf) program, 93
Story of Numerals, 158
Strange Situation paradigm, 285, 287–88, 290
Stroop task, 108
sudden infant death syndrome, 45
Swiss Montessori Society, 27
symbolic understanding, gesture and, 66–68

Table Washing, 48–49, 81, 225, 326–28, 327*f*, 336
task performance, effect of choice, 83–87
teachers
  child outcomes, 303–7
  child ways and teacher ways, 31–32
  class size and, 229–30
  conventional training, 309
  expertise, 171, 258–59
  generalist *vs.* specialist, 172–73
  Montessori classroom, 307
  Montessori training, 309–13, 382
  noticing gesture, 77–78
  ongoing evaluation, 204–5
  praise from, 204–5
  warmth and sensitivity of Montessori, 291–93
Teachers College, Columbia University, 8, 393
The Teacher's Word Book (Thorndike), 9
technology, Montessori education, 387–89
television, children's executive function, 113–15
temporal order, 317–26
  conventional schools, 317–18
  elementary school children, 319–20
  Montessori classroom, 318, 326–30
  orderly routines and young children, 320–26
test anxiety, 196
tests, 3, 11, 15, 19
  creativity, 100
  executive function, 114
  intelligence, 322–23, 343
  learning with and from peers, 30, 31
  locus of control, 86

memorizing for, 71
Montessori absence of, 173, 176, 358
Montessori education, 28
No Child Left Behind, 362
performance on, 270–71, 275–76, 325, 352
pre- and post-, 85, 142, 368, 376
reading comprehension, 26
self-control, 110
standardized, 11, 206, 220, 251, 258, 275–76, 354, 389, 396
teacher approach to, 306, 320
Woodcock-Johnson, 359–60, 362, 370
Test Tubes, 245
Thematic Apperception Task, 89
theory of mind, 111, 209, 368, 369*f*, 370
three-hour work cycle, 122, 123*f*, 126–28
three-mountain task, 257
Three Period Lesson, 62, 203–4
three-year age grouping, Montessori education, 228–29
Timeline of Life, 146, 156, 157*f*
toddlers, 39
    maternal sensitivity, 290
    movement in, 44, 48–51
    order and routines, 320
    peer learning, 223, 227
    rewards and, 178, 190
Tone Bars, 24, 25*f*
Tools of the Mind, 113, 210–11
topic interest
    inspiring through Montessori lessons, 153–59
    Montessori education, 153–69
topic interests, 137–39
toys, 271, 285, 297, 322, 365
    Montessori classroom lack of, 198–99, 212–14, 216–17
    new Montessori classroom, 308–10
    play and fantasy, 207–9
    preschooler interest studies and, 143–45
    as reward, 178
    see also 40, 44–45, 58, 64
tracing, 21, 26, 44, 71
training
    knowledge base preparation, 311–13
    Montessori teacher, 309–13, 382
    personal preparation of teacher, 310–11
transactive dialogue, 240, 242, 248–49
transfer of knowledge, 12–13, 272, 273
    case studies of, 274–78
    failure in, 269–71
    Montessori education and, 278–81
    in Montessori system, 252–53, 269–77
    success in, 271–77
transitive inference tasks, 331
Triangle Tray, 22*f*

Trinomial Cube, 68–69, 70*f*, 169, 278
tutoring
    adults *vs.* peers, 233
    benefits of being a tutor, 234–36
    optimal level of peer tutee, 233–34
    see also peer tutoring

Understanding Directions, Woodcock-Johnson test, 360
United Kingdom, 110, 274, 325
University of Chicago, 6
University of Rome, 16, 17*f*, 395
university research, 27

Vanderbilt University, 256
visual perception, 40, 41, 57, 82, 348
vocabulary, 9, 385
    early reading, 26
    elementary children, 158
    interest, 140, 142
    materials for development, 385
    meaningful contexts, 253, 266
    memory, 331
    movement in, 71–72
    peer tutoring, 231
    preschool years, 148
    Primary classroom, 30, 51
    reading comprehension and, 340
    research, 362–63, 370, 372
    sensitive periods for acquisition, 169, 204
Vries, Hugo de, 32

walking, 51–52, 72, 121, 127, 268
    sensitive periods, 148–49
Walking on the Line, 134–36, 135*f*
warmth, 120, 283, 291–93
    parenting, 293*f*, 294–97, 309, 313
Washing Clothes, 254
well-being, free choice and, 87–88
whole-class teaching, 6, 11, 250
    adults *vs.* peers, 233
    collaborative learning, 247
    tutoring and, 237
whole-language reading approach, 26
Wild Boy of Aveyron, 15, 347
Wisconsin Knowledge and Concepts Examination (WKCE), 354
Woodcock-Johnson tests, 359–60, 362, 370
    Applied Problems, 359, 370, 372*f*
    Letter Word, 359, 370–71, 371*f*
wooden blocks ("prisms"), 60
Wooden Cylinders, 20, 21*f*, 23, 29, 30, 57, 146, 161, 200, 225
Wooden Maps, 156, 201
work cycle, 3-hour, 126–28

Work Journal, 101, 102, 174, 205, 207
writing, 7, 15, 127, 328
    knowledge sharing, 268
    learning in context, 31
    learning in Montessori, 20–27
    movement and, 37–38, 44, 51, 54, 59, 71–72
    peer feedback, 205–6

    personal interests, 152
    rewards for, 181, 188–89
    techniques of, 174
    vocabulary acquisition, 266
Wundt, William, 393, 395

zone of proximal development, 78, 220, 234